T0343429

E–Strategies for Technological Diffusion and Adoption:
National ICT Approaches for Socioeconomic Development

Sherif Kamel
The American University in Cairo, Egypt

INFORMATION SCIENCE REFERENCE

Hershey · New York

Director of Editorial Content:	Kristin Klinger
Director of Book Publications:	Julia Mosemann
Acquisitions Editor:	Lindsay Johnston
Development Editor:	Julia Mosemann
Publishing Assistant:	Keith Glazewski
Typesetter:	Michael Brehm
Production Editor:	Jamie Snavely
Cover Design:	Lisa Tosheff
Printed at:	Yurchak Printing Inc.

Published in the United States of America by
Information Science Reference (an imprint of IGI Global)
701 E. Chocolate Avenue
Hershey PA 17033
Tel: 717-533-8845
Fax: 717-533-8661
E-mail: cust@igi-global.com
Web site: http://www.igi-global.com/reference

Library of Congress Cataloging-in-Publication Data

E-strategies for technological diffusion and adoption : national ICT approaches for socioeconomic development / Sherif Kamel, editor.
      p. cm.
   Includes bibliographical references and index.
   Summary: "This book covers a variety of issues and concepts that relate to the changing nature of doing ICT strategy formulation, development and deployment, with the main focus on ICT eStrategy design and delivery and the related implications, challenges and opportunities"--Provided by publisher.
   ISBN 978-1-60566-388-3 (hbk.) -- ISBN 978-1-60566-389-0 (ebook) 1. Information technology--Economic aspects. 2. Technological innovations--Economic aspects. 3. Diffusion of innovations--Economic aspects. I. Kamel, Sherif.
   HC79.I55E195 2010
   338.9'26--dc22
                                        2010017382

British Cataloguing in Publication Data
A Cataloguing in Publication record for this book is available from the British Library.

All work contributed to this book is new, previously-unpublished material. The views expressed in this book are those of the authors, but not necessarily of the publisher.

List of Reviewers

Anil Aggarwal, *University of Baltimore, USA*
Nahed Amin, *The American University in Cairo, Egypt*
Zacharoula S. Andreopoulou, *University of Thessaloniki, Greece*
Todd A. Boyle, *St. Francis Xavier University, Canada*
Stephen Burgess, *Victorial University, Australia*
Stephen A. Clarke, *University of Hull, UK*
Khaled Dahawy, *The American University in Cairo, Egypt*
Geoffrey Elliot, *London South Bank University, UK*
Gerald Goh Guan Gan, *Multimedia University, Malaysia*
Arunabha Ghosh, *Seoul National University, South Korea*
Michael Gurstein, *Centre for Community Informatics Research, Training and Development, Canada*
Hameed Tahir, *Korea Advanced Institute of Science and Technology, South Korea*
Laura Hosman, *University of California Berkeley, USA*
Kas Kalba, *Kalba International, Inc, USA*
Sherif Kamel, *The American University in Cairo, Egypt*
Melih Kirlidog, *Marmara University, Istanbul*
Stephen E. Little, *Open University Business School, UK*
Nick Maynard, *RAND Corporation, USA*
Marco Platania, *University of Catania, Italy*
Andreja Pucihar, *University of Maribor, Slovenia*
Khaled Samaha, *The American University in Cairo, Egypt*
Carmine Sellitto, *Victoria University, Australia*
Bory Seng, *Council of Ministers, Cambodia*
Magdy Serour, *University of Technology, Australia*
Jawed Siddiqi, *Sheffield Hallam University, UK*
John Sullivan, *Charleston Southern University, USA*
Manthou Vicky, *University of Macedonia, Greece*

Table of Contents

Detailed Table of Contents

Chapter 1
    Laura Hosman, Illinois Institute of Technology, USA

This chapter presents a unique national initiative in Macedonia reflecting a multi-partner, scaled ICT for education project where every school across Macedonia was equipped with computing and wireless Internet connections leading the Internet to reach all citizens across the nation. The chapter demonstrates some best practices including pre-deployment training of teachers in IT adoption, equality of provision to promote positive inter-ethnic relations, and the long-term focus on all stakeholders in terms of outcomes. The ultimate goals of the project relate to educational and socioeconomic development issues.

Chapter 2
    Gerald Goh Guan Gan, Multimedia University, Malaysia
    Khor Yoke Lim, Universiti Sains Malaysia, Malaysia

The chapter presents the case of Malaysians aspiring to leapfrog from the developing nations rank to one that hopes to be fully developed by 2020 based on their vision that was formulated in the 1990s. One of the building blocks of such vision is the provision of world-class information and communication technology infrastructure and the creation of competitive human capacities that are skilled and electronically ready. Therefore, the Malaysian government embarked on the Smart School Initiative, a flagship application that aims to transform the way students are being taught. With an implementation plan in 88 different schools across Malaysia, a growing and completed ICT infrastructure is shaping up coupled with educational courseware and a clear transformation in various learning practices. The chapter includes lessons learned from the initiative that could be replicated representing an invaluable resource to education policy makers, administrators and the school community in other countries with similar ecosystem and environmental settings.

Chapter 3

Andreja Pucihar, University of Maribor, Slovenia
Gregor Lenart, University of Maribor, Slovenia

The authors present the e-Strategies, initiatives and action planes in the European Union intended for the successful implementation of the Lisbon Strategy which should see Europe become the most competitive and dynamic society based on knowledge by 2010. The chapter focuses on the policies, legislative setting and initiatives adopted in Slovenia with an emphasis on e-Business development. The chapter demonstrates the lagging experience and stature of SMEs with respect to the adoption and utilization of e-Commerce leading to the formulation of the eSMEs Slovenia initiative and action plan aiming at accelerating e-Business introduction and adoption in SMEs.

Chapter 4

Melih Kirlidog, Marmara University, Turkey
Stephen E. Little, The Open University Business School, UK

The chapter addresses the growing fact that an overwhelming majority of developing and developed nations are formulating national information and communication technology strategies with an objective to realize socioeconomic growth and competitiveness status. The chapter demonstrates the differences between developed and developing nations in formulating and realizing these strategies with nations such as Japan that is increasingly outward oriented to sub-Saharan African nations that are developing their strategies with the support of international agencies and non-government organizations. The chapter provides an exploratory analysis of the internationalization of national ICT strategies.

Chapter 5

Khaled Samaha, The American University in Cairo, Egypt
Khaled Dahawy, The American University in Cairo, Egypt

This chapter addresses Egypt's diversified economy which has historically performed below its potential; however with growing interest by the government of Egypt recognizing the importance of SMEs. The chapter provides an investigation into the information system strategy of SMEs in Egypt and its importance in organizational success. The chapter enforces the importance of IS and business strategy alignment coupled with top management support and engagement in the different stages of the decision making process amongst other lessons learned.

Chapter 6

Peter Trkman, University of Ljubljana, Slovenia
Tomaž Turk, University of Ljubljana, Slovenia

The chapter analyses the use of broadband in EU countries to identify the differences across the continent with an emphasis on enablers and means, the utilization of different services and the overall ICT sector development. The chapter focuses on the development of a two-dimensional framework that enables the classification of policy actions depending on the influencing factor and type of influence.

This chapter addresses the evolution of Electronic Government in Egypt. The chapter addresses the role of e-Government in reshaping the public sector and remake the relationship between citizens and government. The objective of the chapter is to present a framework that assesses e-Government readiness in Egypt, focusing on public administration while addressing internal factors affecting e-Government readiness including strategy, processes, people, and technology through studying two public sector organizations in Egypt.

This chapter brings a much-needed focus in the literature on the factors affecting SME ICT adoption decision with emphasis on e-Business adoption models. Therefore, the objective of the chapter is to review the literature on the factors affecting SMEs adoption decision, propose a theoretical framework of e-Business adoption for SMEs and to provide insightful discussions on the driving factors and barriers of the SMEs e-Business adoption decision.

This chapter addresses the notion that information and communication technology leads to socioeconomic development in developing nations pushing many nations to implement ICT for development projects in rural areas in collaboration with international organizations and donor agencies. This chapter focuses on identifying the actual impact at the micro, community, level while identifying the key challenges, which influence the success of ICT4D projects through proposing a conceptual framework aimed to improve the situation at the micro level.

Chapter 10

Nicholas C. Maynard, RAND Corporation, USA

The author addresses the path that both Thailand and Malaysia have gone through with respect to the transformation of their ICT sector including their telecommunications networks, national policies, institutions, and regulatory regimes. The chapter demonstrates the importance of competitive markets and government regulators. The objective of the chapter is to provide a set of tools for local and international policy makers and technology providers to help assess the benefits of technology initiatives while tying them to the larger issue of economic development.

Chapter 11

Sajda Qureshi, University of Nebraska at Omaha, USA
Peter Keen, Keen Innovations, USA
Mehruz Kamal, University of Nebraska at Omaha, USA

This chapter discusses the efforts of organizations through interconnectivity to source talent, goods and services from other organizations in different locations around the world and supporting socioeconomic development. The chapter considers the fundamental tenets of business models and ways in which value can be created for development effort with an emphasis on the application of global capability sourcing model to enable businesses to compete globally with insights into the sustainability of business models for development.

Chapter 12

Hany Abdelghaffar, Middlesex University, UK

The author discusses the fact that many developing nations face difficulties in applying successful electronic government projects based on the lack of use by citizens due to the lack of appropriate ICT infrastructure that support e-Government services. The chapter introduces an empirical research that investigates various e-Government weaknesses in developing nations while focusing on e-Readiness and trust. The chapter proposes a model based on e-Readiness assessments and relevant literature that investigates the impact of citizens' readiness for e-Government on e-Government success within developing nations.

Chapter 13

Jawed Siddiqi, Sheffield Hallam University, UK
Ja'far Alqatawna, Sheffield Hallam University, UK
Mohammad Hjouj Btoush, Sheffield Hallam University, UK

This chapter addresses the issues related to the digital divide facing developing nations. The chapter focuses on asserting that insecurity and the digital divide are highly dependent on each other. The chapter proposes to extend the concept of the digital divide to include information security features by putting forward a new model of security that is multi-faceted and that is able to assist in bridging the digital divide.

Chapter 14

D. Puthira Prathap, Sugarcane Breeding Institute (Indian Council of Agricultural Research), India

This chapter highlights the importance of knowledge and information in agricultural development. The chapter focuses on how traditional mass media channels have been instrumental in India's agricultural technology transfer. The chapter also addresses the role of emerging media and the associated challenges as well as provides a comparative study on the effectiveness of traditional versus emerging media in communicating farm technologies.

Chapter 15

Khaled Dahawy, The American University in Cairo, Egypt

The author addresses the role of information in today's marketplace and its interrelation to management information systems in rationalizing the decision making process to managers and decision makers. The focus of the chapter is a case study addressing the issues related to the deployment of accounting information system. The case indicates the importance of the integration of accounting and technology coupled with strong management support and commitment to insure successful implementation.

Chapter 16

Melih Kirlidog, Marmara University, Turkey

This chapter addresses the fact that all developing and industrialized nations strive to get benefits of information society and to this end almost all of them have developed strategies for effective utilization and development of information and communication technology. These strategies usually require substantial funds from domestic and international sources. This chapter analyzes the types of these sources.

Chapter 17

Sherif Kamel, The American University in Cairo, Egypt
Dina Rateb, The American University in Cairo, Egypt

The final chapter demonstrates how emerging information and communication technology is setting the pace for a changing, competitive and dynamic global marketplace and representing an enabling platform for business and socioeconomic development in the 21st century. The chapter shows that building the ICT infrastructure and infostructure will not realize quantum leaps in the development process unless it is coupled with concrete projects and initiatives that engage the society at large with its multiple stake-holders from public, private, government and civil society organizations irrespective of their locations whether urban or remote, gender or background. The chapter describes the evolution of the ICT sector in Egypt over the last decade with an emphasis on national ICT strategy development and deployment as an integral element of Egypt's overall development process within the context of an emerging economy and the various growing potentials ICT offers for its socioeconomic development.

Preface

Information and communication technology (ICT) innovations are increasingly having important implications on business and socioeconomic development due to their role in introducing and diffusing the concepts of knowledge sharing, community development and equality. Moreover, the impact of the advances in information, knowledge, production, exchange and processing may exceed the one brought about by the industrial revolution. Such implications can be felt at the individual, organizational and societal levels. While the basic needs of humankind have long been food, clothing and shelter, the time has come to add information and knowledge to a growing list of requirements that are becoming invaluable on a daily-basis. The implications on developing nations could be remarkably effective if these technology innovations are properly introduced, implemented and institutionalized. However, if the design and delivery process is not well supported and controlled, the result could be an increasing digital divide between the developed and developing worlds, such divide also exists within nations, especially among developing nations, in other words both inter and intra digital divides. It is important to avoid the fact that ICT could be marginalized in the development process. Therefore, there is an urgent need to show that ICT generates the wealth of the enterprise, which in turn pays for socioeconomic development at large. It also helps expose communities to repositories of knowledge across different cultures supporting the exchange of information in terms of acquisition and dissemination. In a globally digitally-driven marketplace, it is important to note that it is emerging ICT that is delivering the productivity gains enabling lives of material comfort for many around the world that would have been unthinkable some two centuries ago.

ICT should be looked at as a platform for development within a macro perspective that addresses different individual, organizational and developmental needs. Therefore, over the past three decades, numerous research studies have underlined the importance of collaboration for the formulation of national ICT strategies with the emergence of eStrategies that cater for the changing market needs in a growing setting dominated by information networks, virtual settings and the emergence of outsourcing. These elements availed a platform for the development of a successful partnership model bringing government, the private sector and the civil society to work together for the development of society and benefiting from emerging ICT tools and applications. The need for resources mobilization, proper environment, legislations and regulations, amongst other elements is important for building and sustaining an outcome-driven ICT infrastructure that could support the development process. For different societies to develop, grow, and benefit from the ICT evolution, nationwide introduction, adoption, diffusion and adaptation of technology should take place, something that is hardly seen in developing nations where most of the technology implementations and infrastructure are focused in the capital and the major cities. However, it is important to note that this has been gradually changing in the early years of the 21st century due to the remote outreach created and availed by wireless technologies. In that respect, for ICT to be rationally deployed, there needs to be comprehensive national ICT strategies that address different societal requirements.

There are a number of challenges that face the development plans of the developing world when it comes to ICT, including electronic readiness, policies and regulations, infrastructure development and deployment, legal framework, universal access, illiteracy, language, culture readiness, appropriate business models for public-private partnership, transparency and governance, intellectual property rights, privacy, and security amongst others. It is important to address the issues faced by developing nations in striving to develop and grow while capitalizing on the opportunities enabled by emerging ICT. This book addresses the issue of the development of national ICT strategies as one of the recommendations of the "Plan of Action" of the World Summit on the Information Society. The book addresses the importance of such strategies in setting the national agendas to complement the efforts and resources allocated, enabling the optimization of benefits and the returns on the local communities in specific and on the society at large. The book includes a number of model strategies, implications and case studies from the developing world to work as models for future implementations in similar environments as well as to share the accumulated knowledge in terms of lessons learnt.

It is important to note that developing national ICT strategies in recent years has been the culmination of efforts undertaken by many countries since the 1980s. Strategies during that time were focusing on computerization of the government administrative and operational procedures, coordination of computer education and training as well as the development and promotion of a computer services industry. Highly articulated ICT policies were developed in the 1990s, inspired by the Unites States announcement of the development of a national information infrastructure (NII) plan that focuses on private investment, competition, access and universal services (Economic Commission for Africa (2003a). Developing nations followed two different approaches in defining their national ICT strategies. Some focused on developing ICT as an economic sector either to boost exports as in the case of Costa Rica and Taiwan or to build domestic capacity as in the case of Brazil, India and Korea (World Bank, 2006). These nations strengthened the market orientation of their economic policies and institutions, have gradually dismantled barriers to trade and investment, and facilitated rapid changes in production and telecommunications technologies. These nations made combined efforts to educate their people to keep them on track of global developments, promoted ICT as an enabler of a wider socioeconomic development, and worked on repositioning their economy to secure competitive advantage in the global economy.

In the context of Egypt, as an African nation and part of the framework of the African Information Society Initiative that emerged from recommendations of the conference of African ministers of economic development and planning in 1996, strived to develop its national information and communication infrastructure plans strategies and policies that articulate long-term policy, infrastructure, content and application as an integral part of overall national development (Economic Commission for Africa, 2003b). Egypt is considered among the nations that have advanced their national strategies from conceptualization to implementation. This was translated in the deployment of a two-tier approach, developing national strategies and harnessing ICT applications in key sectors such as education and commerce with an emphasis on promoting electronic commerce, attracting foreign direct investment to stimulate the knowledge-based economy and to create jobs for the youth and to harness the potential of ICT.

Egypt ICT strategy goes beyond telecom reaching a cross-sectoral approach to creating an enabling environment and mainstreaming ICT into national development policies by addressing all sectors such as trade, finance, investment, education, government, health and media amongst others. The target is to transform Egypt into becoming a vibrant and dynamic ICT hub in the Middle East with a thriving digital economy and IT-empowered citizens (MCIT, 2007a). The national ICT strategy is a product of the collaboration of many stakeholders including the community, the government, private and public sector organizations as well as the civil society.

Egypt national ICT strategy objectives were mainly formulated to promote the information society and to build an export oriented ICT industry. The national ICT strategy was formulated to encourage social inclusion in the information age. Locally, the commitment to maximum social inclusion of its population required considerable pro-active support including financial investment to ensure that the nation at large is given universal access. Moreover, the strategy addressed issues such as human resources capacity development and upgrading the physical infrastructure to be able to compete in global deregulated markets. Globally, access became invaluable in shaping the role Egypt plays in global trade and markets. Respectively, convergence became vital. The emerging role of ICT and its integration in major sectors such as education, entertainment, health, and financial services also became a prerequisite for developing nations to be able to integrate in the global information economy and Egypt factored that element in its national ICT strategy. The government of Egypt has made a strong commitment to advance the cause of human development in the context of an open economy. The structural adjustment program that began in the early 1990s has caused positive and profound changes in the competitiveness of the country. Three main elements could characterize the economy being more open and that includes strengthening of market mechanisms, privatization of government enterprises and an increasing role for the private sector and the civil society (Kamel, 2006).

The role of MCIT required the provision of a policy framework for the ICT sector to grow and become competitive both locally and globally. The majority of the projects were implemented by the private sector with financial and technical support and guidance from MCIT (MCIT, 2007b). Since 2002 there has been continuous development in the ICT sector in Egypt requiring multiple revisits to the strategy with the most recent covering the period 2007-2010. The new strategy has been formulated to cater for three main components, ICT sector restructuring, ICT for reform and development and ICT industry development.

In terms of using ICT for reform and development, the strategy intends to follow three main paths including deploying ICT tools through increasing the penetration rates to mobiles, PCs, Internet usage, broadband services and ICT clubs; developing the postal services with its over 4000 branches representing the largest network in the nation; and completing the technology infrastructure in different institutions. Moreover, the strategy will focus on using ICT as a catalyst in reforming a number of sectors including education, health, and government institutions (ministries) amongst others.

In terms of industry development, the strategy intends to focus on innovation, research, and development in ICT through the formulation of partnership agreements with multinational companies in the ICT sector. This will also include the development of technology incubators for SMEs in the ICT sector, investing in human capital, media convergence, development of electronic content, promoting ICT exports to increase from 250 million US dollars to 1.1 billion US dollars by 2010 through outsourcing. The strategy intends to look at ICT as a platform for empowering the community as a key element for socioeconomic development (Kamel, 2009).

To conclude, successful ICT strategies need a number of elements in order to be effective and to realize its targeted objectives. This includes leadership from top executives and policy makers, involving all stakeholders in implementation, deploying a holistic approach covering all sectors, enabling a liberalized economy, monitoring ICT developments, tailoring towards the nation's requirements and mainstreaming ICT into national socioeconomic development plans. There is a need to emphasize the role of the government in creating the right atmosphere that encourages private sector investment in ICT related businesses. The liberalization of the telecom sector is important to encourage competition and promote FDI. The creation of a universal access policy through broadband is invaluable to induce mass-market deployment of ICT leading to improving the service quality and speed. Moreover, instituting the necessary foreign investment laws and enforcing software piracy and copyright infringement laws, which encourage ICT multinationals to establish regional operations, thus providing work opportunities for skilled individuals and limiting the brain drain effect. Many developing nations have already shown over the last decade some headway on the ICT development path. However, they need to strengthen their commitment and speed the process for a long-term sector development and growth. Such a strategy would invariably drive faster growth across all economic sectors, which will lead to a sustainable socioeconomic development that can be reflected at the individual and societal level. The strategy should also factor the role of the different constituencies including the private sector and the civil society with an eye on realizing the Millennium Development goals (MDGs).

The E-Strategies for Technological Diffusion and Adoption: National ICT Approaches for Socioeconomic Development is part of the Advances in Global Information Management Book Series. The book is beneficial as it provides comprehensive coverage and definitions of the most important issues, concepts, trends and technologies and cases related with the introduction, adoption, diffusion and adaptation of national electronic strategies for ICT for the purpose of socioeconomic development. The roster of chapters include cases and lessons learnt from Egypt, European Union, India, Japan, Kenya, Korea, Macedonia, Malaysia, Slovenia, Sub Saharan Africa and Thailand. This vital new publication will be distributed worldwide among academic and professional institutions and will be instrumental in providing researchers, scholars, students and professionals access to the latest knowledge related to the adoption and usage of ICTs and other related issues to ICT strategy formulation, development and implementation.

ORGANIZATION OF THE BOOK

The book covers through its 17 different chapters a variety of issues and concepts that relate to the changing nature of doing ICT strategy formulation, development and deployment. The focus is on ICT eStrategy design and delivery and the related implications, challenges and opportunities. Following is a brief description of each of the chapters included in the book.

Chapter 1 titled "A National ICT in Education Initiative: Macedonia Connects" by Laura Hosman presents a unique national initiative in Macedonia reflecting a multi-partner, scaled ICT for education project where every school across Macedonia was equipped with computing and wireless Internet connections leading the Internet to reach all citizens across the nation. The chapter demonstrates some best practices including pre-deployment training of teachers in IT adoption, equality of provision to promote positive inter-ethnic relations, and the long-term focus on all stakeholders in terms of outcomes. The ultimate goals of the project relate to educational and socioeconomic development issues.

Chapter 2 titled "Developing Human Capital for National Development: Lessons from the Malaysian Smart School Initiative" by Gerald Goh Guan Gan and Khor Yoke Lim presents the case of Malaysians aspiring to leapfrog from the developing nations rank to one that hopes to be fully developed by 2020 based on their vision that was formulated in the 1990s. One of the building blocks of such vision is the provision of worldclass information and communication technology infrastructure and the creation of competitive human capacities that are skilled and electronically ready. Therefore, the Malaysian government embarked on the Smart School Initiative, a flagship application that aims to transform the way students are being taught. With an implementation plan in 88 different schools across Malaysia, a growing and completed ICT infrastructure is shaping up coupled with educational courseware and a clear transformation in various learning practices. The chapter includes lessons learned from the initiative that could be replicated representing an invaluable resource to education policy makers, administrators and the school community in other countries with similar ecosystem and environmental settings.

Chapter 3 titled "eSME Slovenia: Initiative and Action Plan for the Accelerated Introduction of eBusiness in SMEs" by Andreja Pucihar and Gregor Lenart presents the e-Strategies, initiatives and action planes in the European Union intended for the successful implementation of the Lisbon Strategy which should see Europe become the most competitive and dynamic society based on knowledge by 2010. The chapter focuses on the policies, legislative setting and initiatives adopted in Slovenia with an emphasis on e-Business development. The chapter demonstrates the lagging experience and stature of SMEs with respect to the adoption and utilization of e-Commerce leading to the formulation of the eSMEs Slovenia initiative and action plan aiming at accelerating eBusiness introduction and adoption in SMEs.

Chapter 4 titled "Regional-National ICT Strategies" by Melih Kirlidog and Stephen E. Little addresses the growing fact that an overwhelming majority of developing and developed nations are formulating national information and communication technology strategies with an objective to realize socioeconomic growth and competitiveness status. The chapter demonstrates the differences between developed and developing nations in formulating and realizing these strategies with nations such as Japan that is increasingly outward oriented to sub-Saharan African nations that are developing their strategies with the support of international agencies and non-government organizations. The chapter provides an exploratory analysis of the internationalization of national ICT strategies.

Chapter 5 titled "Information System Strategy Development and Implementation in the Egyptian Small and Medium Construction Enterprises" by Khaled Samaha and Khaled Dahawy addresses Egypt's diversified economy which has historically performed below its potential; however with growing interest by the government of Egypt recognizing the importance of SMEs. The chapter provides an investigation into the information system strategy of SMEs in Egypt and its importance in organizational success. The chapter enforces the importance of IS and business strategy alignment coupled with top management support and engagement in the different stages of the decision making process amongst other lessons learned.

Chapter 6 titled "Broadband Development Challenges and Measures: The Analysis of EU Countries" by Peter Trkman and Tomaz Turk analyses the use of broadband in EU countries to identify the differences across the continent with an emphasis on enablers and means, the utilization of different services and the overall ICT sector development. The chapter focuses on the development of a two-dimensional framework that enables the classification of policy actions depending on the influencing factor and type of influence.

Chapter 7 titled "Assessing Electronic Government Readiness in Egypt: Comparison between Two Public Organizations" by Nahed Amin addresses the evolution of Electronic Government in Egypt. The chapter addresses the role of e-Government in reshaping the public sector and remake the relationship between citizens and government. The objective of the chapter is to present a framework that assesses e-Government readiness in Egypt, focusing on public administration while addressing internal factors affecting e-Government readiness including strategy, processes, people, and technology through studying two public sector organizations in Egypt.

Chapter 8 titled "An Information Communication Technology Adoption Model for Small and Medium Sized Enterprises" by Dan J. Kim addresses the much-needed focus in the literature on the factors affecting SME ICT adoption decision with emphasis on eBusiness adoption models. Therefore, the objective of the chapter is to review the literature on the factors affecting SMEs adoption decision, propose a theoretical framework of eBusiness adoption for SMEs and to provide insightful discussions on the driving factors and barriers of the SMEs eBusiness adoption decision.

Chapter 9 titled "ICT for Development (ICT4D) Projects in Developing Countries: A Proposed Conceptual Framework" by Mahfuz Ashraf and Bushra Malik addresses the notion that information and communication technology leads to socioeconomic development in developing nations pushing many nations to implement ICT for development projects in rural areas in collaboration with international organizations and donor agencies. This chapter focuses on identifying the actual impact at the micro, community, level while identifying the key challenges, which influence the success of ICT4D projects through proposing a conceptual framework aimed to improve the situation at the micro level.

Chapter 10 titled "The Challenges of the National ICT Policy Implementation Process: A Comparative Study of Malaysia and Thailand" by Nicholas Maynard addresses the path that both Thailand and Malaysia have gone through with respect to the transformation of their ICT sector including their telecommunications networks, national policies, institutions, and regulatory regimes. The chapter demonstrates the importance of competitive markets and government regulators. The objective of the chapter is to provide a set of tools for local and international policy makers and technology providers to help assess the benefits of technology initiatives while tying them to the larger issue of economic development.

Chapter 11 titled "Business Models for Development: The Global Capability Sourcing Model" by Peter Keen, Sajda Qureshi and Mehruz Kamal discusses the efforts of organizations through interconnectivity to source talent, goods and services from other organizations in different locations around the world and supporting socioeconomic development. The chapter considers the fundamental tenets of business models and ways in which value can be created for development effort with an emphasis on the application of global capability sourcing model to enable businesses to compete globally with insights into the sustainability of business models for development.

Chapter 12 titled "Citizens' Readiness for E-Government in Developing Countries (CREG)" by Hany Abdel Ghaffar discusses the fact that many developing nations face difficulties in applying successful electronic government projects based on the lack of use by citizens due to the lack of appropriate ICT infrastructure that support e-Government services. The chapter introduces an empirical research that investigates various e-Government weaknesses in developing nations while focusing on e-Readiness and trust. The chapter proposes a model based on e-Readiness assessments and relevant literature that investigates the impact of citizens' readiness for e-Government on e-Government success within developing nations.

Chapter 13 titled "Do Insecure Systems Increase Global Digital Divide?" by Jawed Siddiqi, Ja'far Alqatawna and Mohammad Hjouj Btoush addresses the issues related to the digital divide facing developing nations. The chapter focuses on asserting that insecurity and the digital divide are highly dependent on each other. The chapter proposes to extend the concept of the digital divide to include information security features by putting forward a new model of security that is multi-faceted and that is able to assist in bridging the digital divide.

Chapter 14 titled "Communicating Farm Technologies through Traditional and New Media Channels: Lessons from India" by D. Puthira Prathap highlights the importance of knowledge and information in agricultural development. The chapter focuses on how traditional mass media channels have been instrumental in India's agricultural technology transfer. The chapter also addresses the role of emerging media and the associated challenges as well as provides a comparative study on the effectiveness of traditional versus emerging media in communicating farm technologies.

Chapter 15 titled "Strategy of Accounting Automation: The Case of the Egyptian International Motors Company (EIM)" by Khaled Dahawy addresses the role of information in today's marketplace and its interrelation to management information systems in rationalizing the decision making process to managers and decision makers. The focus of the chapter is a case study addressing the issues related to the deployment of accounting information system. The case indicates the importance of the integration of accounting and technology coupled with strong management support and commitment to insure successful implementation.

Chapter 16 titled "Financial Aspects of National ICT Strategies" by Melih Kirlidog addresses the fact that all developing and industrialized nations strive to get benefits of information society and to this end almost all of them have developed strategies for effective utilization and development of information and communication technology. These strategies usually require substantial funds from domestic and international sources. This chapter analyzes the types of these sources.

Chapter 17 titled "ICT Strategy for Development Lessons Learnt from the Egyptian Experience in Developing Public-Private Partnerships" by Sherif Kamel and Dina Rateb demonstrates how emerging information and communication technology is setting the pace for a changing, competitive and dynamic global marketplace and representing an enabling platform for business and socioeconomic development in the 21ˢᵗ century. The chapter shows that building the ICT infrastructure and infostructure will not realize quantum leaps in the development process unless it is coupled with concrete projects and initiatives that engage the society at large with its multiple stakeholders from public, private, government and civil society organizations irrespective of their locations whether urban or remote, gender or background. The chapter describes the evolution of the ICT sector in Egypt over the last decade with an emphasis on national ICT strategy development and deployment as an integral element of Egypt's overall development process within the context of an emerging economy and the various growing potentials ICT offers for its socioeconomic development.

REFERENCES

Economic Commission for Africa. (2003a). *Policies and Plans on the Information Society: Status and Impact.*

Economic Commission for Africa. (2003b). *E-Strategies, National, Sectoral and Regional ICT Policies: Plans and Strategies.*

Ministry of Communications and Information Technology. (2007a). Retrieved February 10, 2009, from http://www.mcit.gov.eg

Ministry of Communications and Information Technology. (2007b). *Egypt's ICT Golden Book.*

Kamel, S. (2009). The Evolution of the ICT Sector in Egypt – Partnership4Development. In *Proceedings of the 11ᵗʰ International Business Information Management Association (IBIMA) Conference on Innovation and Knowledge Management in Twin Track Economies: Challenges and Opportunities,* Cairo, Egypt, 4-6 January (pp. 841-851).

Kamel, T. (2006). *Egypt Reforms: An update from the ICT Sector.*

World Bank. (2006). *Information and Communication Technology for Development: Global Trends and Policies.*

Acknowledgment

This book titled "E-Strategies for Technological Diffusion and Adoption: National ICT Approaches for Socioeconomic Development" is the compilation of different invaluable efforts of so many parties including but not limited to the authors, the reviewers, the editor and the publisher. The importance of the book stems from the importance and timeliness of the issues addressed which are of high priority to many nations both developed and developing in their quest to continuous improvement, development and growth while deploying state-of-the art e-Strategies. I would like to seize this opportunity and acknowledge the help of all those who were involved in the different stages of the production of this book, without whose support and assistance this important product could not have been satisfactorily completed with such high quality.

The different stages and preparation elements a book of such magnitude goes through require a tremendous and continuous cooperation and assistance by everyone involved for a long duration of time that extends over a long period, in this project it was almost three years. Therefore, I would like to express my sincere gratitude to all the contributors of this book who, with a collaborative team spirit, provided through their submitted chapters a comprehensive overview of national ICT e-Strategies, cases and applications from different parts of the world coupled with an in-depth analysis of the important elements for the implementation and institutionalization of ICT strategies. The importance of the book relates to the fact that it addresses the research interest of researchers, academic scholars as well as industry professionals engaging in ICT strategy development and deployment.

I would like to acknowledge the authors of the different chapters for sharing their invaluable experiences and accumulated knowledge. Moreover, I would like to acknowledge those selected authors who in addition to contributing to chapters to the book have contributed as reviewers of manuscripts and played an important role in a rigorous double-blind review process. Thanks go to all those who provided constructive and comprehensive reviews and invaluable inputs throughout the different stages of the review process. This includes my assistants at the American University in Cairo, Lina Nada, Radwa Morsy and Maha Ismail who provided administrative support throughout the different phases of the project. This project would not have been completed without the continuous timely and efficient support of the IGI Global team including Julia Mosemann, Rebecca Beistline, Heather Probst, Megan Childs, Kristin Roth and Jan Travers under the leadership of Mehdi Khosrow-Pour. In closing, I would like to thank my family Paquinam, Nehad and Hussein for their love, support, and encouragement throughout the different stages of producing this book.

Sherif Kamel, PhD
Cairo, Egypt
March 2010

Chapter 1
A National ICT–in–Education Initiative:
Macedonia Connects

Laura Hosman
Illinois Institute of Technology, USA

ABSTRACT

This chapter presents a unique national initiative: Macedonia Connects, a multi-partner, scaled ICT-for-education project wherein every school across Macedonia was equipped with both computers and wireless Internet connections and through which the Internet was made available to citizens across the entire country. A number of best practices may be identified, including the pre-deployment training of teachers in IT adoption, the equality of provision to promote positive inter-ethnic relations, and the long-term focus on the part of all stakeholders in terms of outcomes. The goals of this project target both educational and socio-economic development. There are many aspects of this case that may be applicable to future ICT-for-development endeavors, and some of Macedonia's neighboring states have already indicated interest in following this model.

INTRODUCTION

Growth in the number of projects that bring information and communications technology (ICT) to the developing world has been remarkable in recent years, reflecting the high and ever-increasing expectations placed on ICT in terms of quality of life improvement, empowerment, and economic development for the technology users. Despite the soundness of theory and the promise that today's new technologies hold, it is vital to recognize that they are not diffused and absorbed automatically. Capacity-building, through education, is absolutely necessary to build the human capital required to take advantage of advancing technologies (Lee, 2001).

Thus schools have been a target of numerous ICT-related development projects, with the rationale that education is a powerful tool that contributes seminally to economic growth through the development of a skilled workforce and in-

DOI: 10.4018/978-1-60566-388-3.ch001

creased productivity. It is equally vital to social development, as it empowers people to improve their health, environment, and governance.

Still, it is just as important to recognize that the introduction of ICT-related projects has the propensity either to intensify inequality and social exclusion, or to promote equality and social inclusion, and this applies in particular when ICT is introduced into educational contexts. Technology is always and everywhere introduced into a society that is far from neutral; the individual characteristics of each society greatly affect fundamental issues such as whether and how technology will be adopted and used, and who will benefit from it. If social inclusion is to be promoted by ICTs, there must be a specific provision or plan for this in technology-related development projects.

Most ICT-related interventions in developing countries take the form of pilot projects, at least at the outset. From a financial point of view, this is sound reasoning: the proof-of-concept demonstrated by an effective, successful pilot project is often what convinces stakeholders to invest in larger projects. Even so, while this strategy seems rational, problems may assert themselves through the perceived privileging of any given region, city, or school over another in terms of pilot location, particularly in societies divided by ethnic, religious, or any other differences.

One technique that would avoid locational objections entirely would be to undertake an inclusive, macro-level, state-wide technology deployment. However, risk is extremely high with this strategy: projects deemed unsuccessful mean a squandering of scarce development resources on a nationwide level, and bring about unfulfilled aspirations for the participants. This chapter gives an overview and discussion of potential lessons to learn from just such a national-level case: a national ICT-in-education initiative—*Macedonia Connects*. The fact that so few projects have been undertaken at this level means that an in-depth

analysis of such endeavors offers the potential to contribute a great deal to the literature and body of knowledge on the subject.

In September, 2005, Macedonia announced that it had become world's first "all-wireless nation." This was seen as quite an achievement for a country that just four years earlier was faced with the very real possibility of ethnic civil war. This ambitious project, *Macedonia Connects* was centered on education, and was the result of a public-private partnership initiative. Through a single technology deployment, *Macedonia Connects* provided the entire country with a broadband wireless network by connecting all 460 of the nation's schools (as well as 70 other sites, including dormitories, hospitals, and NGOs) to the Internet and using these sites as hubs for commercial and residential Internet connectivity nationwide.

One of the long term goals for the *Macedonia Connects* project is to train a new generation of ICT-literate students with skills that will ultimately create a workforce that can participate in the knowledge economy, allowing Macedonia to become a regional technology hub. Additionally, there are hopes that the uniform deployment across all schools will lead to increased levels of peace and understanding among the ethnic groups within the state; not just through school-led projects that promote inter-ethnic communication and cooperation, but in the longer term as well. Abundant potential exists for economic growth and technology adoption to be realized in the shorter term too, because the same initial deployment that connected all of the schools simultaneously provided high-speed Internet connectivity to the entire country at affordable subscription rates.

This project is unparalleled for a number of reasons. To our knowledge, this is the first nationwide ICT-in-education deployment that simultaneously provided Internet connectivity to the entire nation. The government views this project as a long-term investment in its youth, in terms of human-capacity building, and appears committed to long term support, and even expansion of, the project. Teacher training was recognized to be a requisite element for the technology to be incorporated into curriculum and was provided prior to the technological deployment. Additionally, the government realizes the duration of time and level of financial commitment necessary for project goals and outcomes to be realized.

The rare occurrence of near ideal conditions in terms of funding, technical know-how, receptiveness of government institutions, and regulatory and policy support all contributed to successful project deployment. In addition, many elements that often impede results and lead to short term failure of development projects were not issues in this case: project management and technical assistance were of a high level, resources were sufficient, and it was based on a viable business model. As such, it is possible to identify best practices that can inform future similar endeavors. In addition, the scale of the Macedonia Connects project provides a unique opportunity to learn how education, as well as social and economic change, may be furthered through broadband access and as such it is an exemplar for other nations looking to undertake similar ICT-related education and development projects.

This chapter proceeds as follows: The next section presents an overview of the literature on the effects of ICT investment and of the role of educational inputs on economic growth, as well as a presentation of the methodology used in this chapter. Following this is a discussion of public-private partnerships in ICT-related development projects. Next, a contextual overview of Macedonia and its educational system is presented, followed by the Macedonia Connects case study. This is followed by a discussion of best practices and lessons learned that can inform future ICT-related development projects and a conclusion.

BACKGROUND

Information Communications Technology and Economic Growth

Promoting economic growth is among the main motivations driving development-oriented ICT deployments. Similarly, ICT-in-education projects are frequently touted for the economic effects they will bring about for the economy as a whole. Both of these factors were cited as goals for *Macedonia Connects* project outcomes, and as such, this section gives an overview of academic research undertaken on these topics.

Numerous scholarly studies have focused the role that ICT can play to promote worker productivity and economic growth. Several macro-level economic studies put forth have demonstrated the positive impact that ICT inputs can have on economic growth and development (See, e.g., Roller and Waverman, 2001; Cronin et al., 1993; Norton, 1992). However, the majority of these analyses to date have focused on the developed world, utilizing data where it was available. Only recently has more reliable data from developing countries become available. As a result, there are fewer studies that address the same issues as they apply to the developing world, and until recently, most of the findings have been mixed.

Dewan and Kraemer's (2000) study indicates both positive and statistically significant returns to ICT capital investments for developed countries, but non-significant results for developing countries. The authors posit that developing countries may lack a substantive base of capital stock and the infrastructure necessary for ICT investment to bring about the positive returns seen in developed countries. Similarly, Pohjola's (2001) cross-sectional study across 39 countries from 1980-1995, reveals no significant impact on economic growth due to ICT investment when all countries in his sample are included. However, he finds a strong influence on growth from ICT investment in the developed countries, once the developing countries are removed from the sample, Seo and Lee (2006) present mixed findings as well in their analysis that specifically addresses the digital divide and the growth gap between developed and developing countries, On the one hand, they find that global digitalization has a negative impact as it widens the existing digital divide, but on the other, positive economic impact may be realized indirectly, through knowledge spillovers from the developed to the developing countries.

Papaioannou and Dimelis' (2007) contribution marks an important turn in the literature. Their findings indicate that ICT exhibits a positive and significant impact on productivity worlwide. Their study is the first to give evidence that ICT's positive returns to productivity, long a reality for the developed world, have begun to evidence themselves in the developing world as well. Hosman et al.'s (2008) findings are along the same lines: they demonstrate positive GDP per capita returns to ICT investment across 42 developing world countries from the period of 2000-2006. Since these findings were more robust than when the same regression was run earlier using data from 2000-2004, their conclusion is in line with Papaioannou and Dimelis' assertion that developing countries have started to benefit from ICT investment(2007, p.180).

Regarding new telecommunications technology that is increasingly available in the developing world, Waverman, Meschi, and Fuss (2005) have found that mobile phones are having a positive and significant effect on economic growth in developing countries. In fact, they find that because mobile phones provide the primary method of communications in developing countries with no or few fixed lines, the growth impact for developing countries may be twice as great as for developed countries, in which attributable growth would be split between fixed-line and mobile-phone use.

Even though a greater number of scholars have begun reporting positive returns to ICT invest-

ments in developing countries, such investment is only half of the story, for ICT's impact on growth depends not only on its own level, but also on the level of other complementary factors (Edwards, 2002). Infrastructural concerns, such as affordable and reliable sources of power, figure prominently for developing countries. Even so, perhaps the most important requisite for ICT adoption is the level of human skills and capabilities required to make use of new technologies. The most effective method for states to develop such capacities is through education (Lee, 2001, Jamali, Wandschneider, & Wunnava, 2007).

A rather limited number of scholars have focused on the interrelatedness of education and ICT, among other inputs, in affecting economic growth. Driouchi, Azelmad, and Anders (2006) find that a country's economic performance is closely linked to investments in knowledge-related inputs (p.241) and in fact, for developing countries, they found increasing returns to scale for such investments (p.248). Their results lead them to recommend developing countries focus their policy efforts on, among other things, expanding education and making future investments in the information infrastructure (p.249).

Jamali et al. (2007) assert that government type matters a great deal when it comes to ICT's effect on economic growth. In their study examining the effect of both political regimes and technology on economic outcomes, democracies were found to significantly outperform autocracies. Their findings also revealed two other major determinants of economic growth: human capital and technology. Countries can increase their level of economic growth by increasing levels of education and technology in the economy (p.1425).

Simply increasing the levels of education is a necessary but insufficient condition for promoting economic growth, however. With education, it may be the case that quality matters a great deal more than quantity, and Nomura (2007) cautions against oversimplifying measures of educational inputs, pointing out that the majority of empirical studies regarding education and economic growth fail to account for the quality of education, and rather, simply measure the quantity. Yet. if the desired educational outcome is a technologically literate populace and there is no technology in the schools, then increasing the amount of education will not help to meet this goal.

Nomura makes an additional salient point: not only does a relationship exist between levels of both quality and equality in education, but that those countries that focused on improving educational *equality* saw more robust and significant economic returns to education, while countries that increased only the levels of education without improving educational equality saw negligible economic growth as a result (2007:629, emphasis added).

Despite this section's emphasis on ICT's relationship to economic growth, we recognize that it represents but one area of human development. However, measuring the effect of increased investment in ICT and educational inputs on human development (including social, political, and quality of life outcomes) is not a straightforward task. We are not aware of any scholarly studies that have specifically or successfully done so. However, this subject is neither trivial nor frivolous and will be an important area for future research.

Though certain of the scholars cited above do make general policy recommendations, it is one thing to advocate for increased investment in education, and another thing entirely to put such a policy into place. The issues and actors involved are manifold and comprise infrastructural and regulatory issues, political and institutional considerations, and pedagogical and software concerns—and this is by no means a complete listTo understand the complicated nature of effectively designing and carrying out an educational project designed to increase technological capabilities on behalf of all students in a country requires an in-depth examination, and this is where case-level analysis becomes a necessary complement to macro-level studies.

Public Private Partnerships

Over the past few years, growth in the number of public-private partnerships with development aims has been remarkable. Such partnerships are becoming increasingly important in the ICT and development context, and the case at hand employs such a partnership. As such, this section gives an overview of public-private partnerships (PPPs), specifically in the field of ICT and development.

Public-private partnerships (PPPs)—which we define as agreements between private-sector, for-profit businesses and developing country public sector actors—are currently being promoted by governments, international organizations, non-governmental organizations (NGOs), and private firms alike. In fact, the United Nations Millennium Declaration specifically recommends the creation of public private partnerships to "ensure that the benefits of new technologies, especially information and communications technologies... are available to all," (Weigel & Waldburger 2004:XV).

Although no comprehensive theoretical framework yet exists that focuses specifically on public-private or international partnerships of this nature (Stewart and Gray, 2006), this chapter asserts that the subject of public-private partnerships is worthy of academic analysis because the phenomenon is *already taking place*: numerous Western-based technology multinationals have already formed public-private partnerships to bring telecommunications-based projects to the developing world. And it is a cause for concern that, to date, there has been a lack of systematic, unbiased research guiding and/or assessing the significant and growing amount of activity in this area.

Still, not a great deal is known about the PPP model and a theoretical framework for understanding how they work or what a partnership business model should look like has not yet been developed; this may help to explain the large number of unsuccessful initiatives (Angerer & Hammerschmid 2005). The fact that many failed cases go unreported does not help the learning process, either.

The concept of partnership has its origins—and finds its widest usage—among environmental and development scholars. For these scholars, the notion of *sustainability* has been a key concept since the 1970s (Stewart & Gray, 2006), while other fields of study have rather recently adopted the notion.

Ideally, public-private partnerships are thought to create synergistic results by combining the expertise and resources of the private partner with the administrative and political power of the governmental partner. They can take several forms, but are usually viewed as a business relationship, or agreement, between two or more parties that combine private sector capital (and sometimes public sector capital) to improve public services and the management of public sector assets (Gerrard 2001).

For the public partner, PPPs offer attractive advantages, such as increased private finance and investment, technological experience and expertise, risk-sharing, the public legitimacy that results from being associated with a successful private sector actor, and a potential downsizing of the public sector or a decrease in governmentally subsidized programs. A further argument for PPPs on economic grounds concerns the benefits associated with a liberalizing of regulations and markets (at least in the telecom sector), increased exposure to technology and more efficient ways of doing business, and a stronger incentive to adhere to the policies of fiscal discipline required to do business with global companies. An additional motivation for governments, and certainly for the recipients of the technology, is the value-adding potential of ICT, not just in terms of economic growth, but also through improvement of social and political capital.

Possible negative outcomes for governments include asymmetries of power and information, and political and financial risks in the event of failed projects. Even so, citizens' increase in demands for governmental services, paired with stagnant government revenues, points to the likelihood of more PPPs being created in the future, particularly in developing countries.

For the private partner, advantages may include access to new markets, risk-sharing and uncertainty-reduction, and an improved image as a result of their 'philanthropic' work. Public funds—particularly at the outset—may also make a project more financially attractive to the private partner, as its own up-front investment outlays are lessened. As stated above, ICT firms are looking to the developing world for new markets.

One major concern regarding PPPs in the developing world is that they will not address the larger issues of socio-economic development and poverty eradication if they are not sustainable or relevant in the daily lives of their intended beneficiaries. Kanungo (2004) reports that private sector participation in such projects has not demonstrated better results than previous public sector-only initiatives. Yet, this paper will assert that when public-private initiatives are well thought out, technologically appropriate, and designed with long term sustainability and the empowerment of the localities in mind, they have the potential to enable real socio-economic benefit.

Academic research on the subject of Public Private Partnerships has revealed cause for cautioned optimism: There are numerous cases of failed PPPs. Despite being touted as a promising solution, PPPs are often misunderstood and work well only under certain conditions. Because of this, a good deal of organizational and instructional literature has appeared with the goal of enumerating and promoting best practices involving PPPs, to ensure successful joint ventures (See, e.g. United Nations Foundation 2003, Weigel & Waldburger 2004, World Bank 2003, 2006). Most of the recommendations put forth in this literature are based upon case study. There is value in such an approach. However, a deeper theoretical understanding of the nature of PPPs is necessary, as this may lead to greater insight and more successful projects.

METHODOLOGY

This paper employs a qualitative, case study methodology, which is particularly relevant for researchers examining development strategies in emerging economies. In addition, the case study is the most appropriate method for studying the 'many variables-small *N*' type of subject presented herein (Lijphart 1971). The case study is best employed when there are a limited number of cases for analysis, as it allows the researcher to examine the study intensively. An additional strength of the case study methodology is the contribution it can make to theory building, and to best practices identification. We adopt Gerring's definition of a case study as "an intensive study of a single unit for the purpose of understanding a larger class of similar units" (2004:342).

In an interview in which Waverman expounded upon his macro-level study cited above, he asserted that more detailed analyses are important for increasing our understanding of cause and effect in such studies (Economist, 2007). Yet, research at both the theoretical and micro level is still notably lacking in this area (London & Hart, 2004; de Silva & Zainudeen, 2007). This chapter thus contributes to the case-study/empirical evidence body of literature.

The research informing this chapter comprises a combination of secondary literature review and a series of firsthand interviews with key project managers responsible for deployment of the project under examination. These interviews took place between October, 2007 and May, 2010. The case was chosen on the basis of its uniqueness, in terms of the project's scope, stated goals, and business model. These will be elaborated upon in the case study.

History has demonstrated that development is a multifaceted, complex process rooted in the socio-cultural, political, economic and historic reality, and what has been successful in one geographical location or society may be completely inappropriate for another. Any attempt at policy prescription must be preceded and informed by a sincere effort to understand the particular situation at that point in time, and of how it got there, on both a recent and historical time scale. We are mindful of this limitation.

Additionally, to increase the usefulness of case studies, it is important to be able test the applicability of findings across similar cases. Such testing will remain a challenge for future research, yet it is the author's intention to apply these findings across future cases to test their applicability. Given that both USAID and a number of Macedonia's neighboring states have already expressed interest in following the model of this project (Strachan, 2008), we are confident that the number of such cases will grow.

PRESENTATION OF THE CASE STUDY

Macedonia: Contextual Overview

The Former Yugoslav Republic of Macedonia gained its independence peacefully in 1991, during the breakup of Yugoslavia. It is a landlocked, mountainous country located in Southeastern Europe, with over 2 million inhabitants occupying approximately 25,000 square kilometers. The country has been a democracy since its independence, yet it faced severe economic hardship stemming from the collapse of the Yugoslav internal market and the discontinuation of subsidies from the former central government. The Republic still has one of the lowest per capita Gross National Incomes in Europe, at $3460 in current US Dollars and is considered a lower-middle income country (World Bank, 2008).

Macedonia has undergone considerable economic reform since independence, and since about 1996, has witnessed steady, though slow, economic growth. The country has developed an open economy, with trade accounting for upwards of 80 percent of GDP in recent years. Despite the progress it has made however, Macedonia still faces a high unemployment rate, at 36 percent (CIA factbook, 2006), while 22 percent of the population live below the poverty line (World Bank, 2008). Corruption and a legal system that is constrained in its effectiveness also act as significant restraints on economic development.

In addition to economic challenges, Macedonia has faced many of the same social problems faced by other former socialist East European countries during the transition to both a market economy and democracy. Under centralized Yugoslavian rule, ethnic groups were generally obliged to tolerate one another and the expression of cultural differences was suppressed. Since Yugoslavia's dissolution, however, these groups have asserted their independence to a far greater degree. According to a 2002 census, Macedonia's population comprises approximately 64 percent ethnic Macedonians, 25 percent ethnic Albanians, 4 percent Turkish, 3 percent Roma (Gypsy), 2 percent Serb, and 2 percent other (State Statistical Office, 2005).

Since Macedonia's independence in 1991, relations between ethnic communities—in particular interactions between majority ethnic Macedonians and minority ethnic Albanians—have been a defining feature of the state's politics. This has, in turn, had significant implications for its educational system.

In the year of independence, the 1991 Constitution of the Macedonian State was adopted. It denied non-majority communities equal status both on paper and in reality (Reka, 2008). Thus Albanian suppression and discrimination continued under the new government. The gradual accumulation of resentment, due to a mix of domestic and external factors, led to the Albanian uprising of 2001, which brought Macedonia to the brink of civil war (Reka, 2008:55).

As a result of both pressure and assistance from the International community, Albanian and Macedonian representatives met and eventually signed the *General Framework Agreement* of August,

2001 (commonly known as the *Ohrid Agreement*). This pact ended the armed conflict and addressed the demands of the Albanian minority, effectively guaranteeing reform of the Constitution, greater representation of Albanians in the civil service sector, and the provision of university education in the Albanian language (Reka 2008:59).

Language plays an important role in the abilities of ethnic cultures to assert their identities—this is no different in Macedonia's case. The Ohrid Agreement also recognized the Albanian language as an official language at the national level. Other minorities were guaranteed constitutional status in this document as well, and have seen their languages (Turkish, Serbian, and Roma) recognized as official in certain municipalities in which they are significantly represented (Reka, 2008).

In Macedonia, children of different ethnicities still attend separate schools, or, in some cases, go to the same school but in different shifts. Thus, in present form, the education system contributes directly to promoting social segregation within the country. Instruction takes place in the students' mother tongues: Macedonian, Albanian, Turkish, and Serbian. Most high schools offer bilingual education, Macedonian/Albanian, Macedonian/Turkish, or Albanian/Turkish, depending on the region (Dimova, 2003). Even so, in recent years English has become the most popular foreign language in schools, while the number of private institutions offering English as a foreign language continues to rise due to high demand (Dimova, 2003:20).

One important facet of having separate schools is that different versions of history and culture are taught, and interaction is minimized, reinforcing an "us-versus-them" mentality. There are, and have been, efforts to counter this unproductive trend and promote interethnic communication and collaboration. Yet, halfhearted or inauthentic efforts are rejected and will not generate positive results. As in 2004, Petroska-Beska and Najcevska found that in Macedonia's education system:

Children are surrounded by negative stereotypes and prejudices, whose authenticity they cannot challenge. If left unchanged, Macedonia's ethnically segregated educational system is likely to reinforce these conflicting understandings. The high level of tension within the education system is visible also outside the schools. It is becoming common for ethnic Albanian and ethnic Macedonian high school students to fight at bus stops and in the streets before and after school. (2004, pp. 3-4)

The stakes are high, and ethnicity-related issues are not about to disappear. Up to today, ethnic violence continues. The Parliamentary elections of June 1, 2008, saw violence, injury, and death in ethnic Albanian areas (Reuters, 2008), and this will certainly hurt the country's efforts to convince the European Union that it is democratic and peaceful enough to progress towards membership.

Yet, the educational system offers the potential to introduce the kind of social change that will be necessary, in the long run, to bring about peaceful co-existence. The ethnic tensions facing Macedonia have been cultivated through decades and even centuries of history: change will not take place overnight. Accordingly, educational solutions will not bring about quick-fix results either, but they must be promoted, supported, and encouraged if change is to come about.

Case Study: Macedonia Connects

The conception of Macedonias computers-in-schools program occurred in May, 2002; it was prompted by then-President Boris Trajkovski's official visit to the People's Republic of China. A strong believer in the need for Macedonian children to learn modern IT skills, Trajkovski returned to his country from the PRC with the promise of a donation of nearly 6,000 computers. In addition, Microsoft later donated over 6,000 licenses for software (Nairn, 2006).

The president, understanding that with no Internet connection, these computers—and the project's potential—would remain severely limited, approached USAID for assistance. USAID, which had been funding projects in the country for over a decade, in turn approached Washington D.C. based non-profit *Academy for Educational Development* (AED) to manage the project deployment. (Other stakeholders included: Macedonia's Ministry of Education and Science, and On.Net.)

Macedonia Connects' primary focus—from the outset—was connecting the nation's schools to the Internet. As the schools are distributed across the country, it became apparent that nationwide connectivity could also be provided through the same deployment. A small group of the project leaders suggested that the schools be leveraged as anchor tenants of a nationwide network; capital financing could be made doubly effective by being used both to build out the school network and to provide connectivity to all other potential constituent markets (Bilbilov, 2009, Strachan, 2007).

The project could not proceed, however, until the high prices and limited availability of telecom services within the country were addressed. This situation was due to the monopoly presence of MakTel, a Hungarian-owned subsidiary of Deutsche Telecom, in Macedonia's telecom sector. Without competition, there was simply no incentive for the monopoly to expand services or offer affordable telecom rates; MakTel charged as much as $150 per month for dial-up Internet services—a truly prohibitive fee where monthly salaries averaged around $200—and little more than half the country had telecom coverage in any case (Hunsberger, 2006, Kampschror, 2006).

In December, 2004, USAID put project implementation out for bids. MakTel was not allowed to bid because it was a monopoly; in response it attempted to derail the project and block pending anti-monopoly legislation. Its sent employees—posing as *Macedonia Connects* staff—to schools to attempt to sign them up for MakTel service, initiated a publicity campaign claiming that it was already providing free Internet service to all of the schools (which it was not), and made large contributions to politicians while threatening the government with loss of $51 million in annual dividends (Strahan, 2007).

The ultimate failure of the strong-arm tactics was likely assisted by Macedonia's mandate from the European Union to abolish the telecom's monopoly status and establish a regulator and regulatory laws as a precondition to EU membership. The government retained, Booz Allen Hamilton—an American consulting firm—to advise them on regulatory aspects of the newly-proposed laws. In the end, legislation establishing competition, regulation, and the freeing up of high-speed bandwidth from monopoly control passed through the legislature with a vote of 82-0 (Strachan, 2007).

USAID selected On.Net, a local start-up Internet Service Provider (ISP), to carry out the nation-wide broadband installation. As winning bidder, it was mandated not only to provide Internet to schools, but also to develop and market the same services to businesses and individual customers nationwide (Shamblin, 2005). This dual focus was necessary for the project's long-term sustainability. USAID subsidized school connectivity fees for only the first three years. At the end of this time period, the ISP had to become a profitable, sustainable business; it could only do so through the collection of individual and business subscription fees.

On.Net elected to provide wireless connectivity through the use of Motorola *Canopy* technology, which, by siting connection points on mountaintops across the country, took advantage of Macedonia's mountainous terrain. With topology so well suited to the physical infrastructure, the entire project's deployment was able to be completed within four months, in time for the start of the 2005 school year. Of course, infrastructure rollout and regulation are just the beginning of the story.

In order to integrate ICT into schools curriculua, USAID ultimately sponsored the training of

14,000 teachers both prior to and following the project's deployment (Nikolovska, 2009). This initiative—*eSchools*, part of the Macedonia National Education Development Strategy to implement modern education technology—employed the principles of interactive teaching to focus on creative learning, critical thinking, and problem-solving (Education Development Center, 2006). The training was broken into three components designed to promote project-based learning, ICT integration into curriculum, and community linkages.

Among the Participants' activities were blog writing, web publishing, learning how to use specific software, creating group projects and presentations, and re-writing their curriculum plans for the following academic year to emphasize ICT integration, problem-based learning, and community-building (Education Development Center, 2006). The project's ultimate goal is to bring Macedonia's educational standards into line with accepted European practice in technology supported learning; as has been seen before, European Union standards here again provide the impetus for moving forward. As the project is to be maintained by the four Pedagogical and Teacher Training Faculties from three Universities in Macedonia, it is fair to assume that student-teachers will undergo similar training in the future.

Though IT training was a crucial first step, promoting communication and collaboration across ethnicities will be a vitally important task for Macedonia, and indeed, across most of the 'emerging democracies' of Eastern Europe, where different ethnicities were forced to tolerate one another under communist rule, but have proven to be much less tolerant since the breakup of Yugoslavia and of the Soviet Union. Providing connectivity and training on an equitable basis were extremely important, but the project must take a pro-active stance if social inclusion and ethnic cooperation are to be promoted.

Early reports about the project seemed promising. In the spring of the program's first academic year, a new web portal was launched, which was to make communication among teachers, students, and parents from every school across the country possible. In addition, the site provided a space for each school to create its own website, and an email address, linked to the portal, was to be provided to each teacher and student (USAID, 2006).

Taking the Project to the Next Level

In December of 2006, the Macedonian government announced an ambitious new initiative: to provide a computer to every student in primary and secondary schools across the country, called the *Computer for Every Child* Initiative. The government's decision to expand the technology in schools was based at least in part on the success witnessed in the *Macedonia Connects* project, and this new project was projected to decrease the student-to-computer ratio from 1:56, to 1:1 or 1:2, and would require the purchase of between 150,000-180,000 new machines.

By late spring of 2007, the government had put forth an open bid process, and the tender for the project was ultimately awarded to another public-private partnership, this time formed between N-Computing (a Silicon-Valley, California based virtualization software and hardware company), Haier, (a Chinese PC Manufacturer) and Accent (A Macedonian integration and support firm). This group was to work directly with the Ministry of Education and the Minister of the Information Society to deploy the new technology.

NComputing's technological solution allows seven students to share one PC hard-drive simultaneously. Each user station consists of a monitor, mouse, keyboard, and speakers that are connected to the hard-drive device (the actual device is a box that attaches to the back of one of the terminals, to which six other user stations are connected). Because these devices require less maintenance and replacement of equipment and use 95 percent less energy than traditional PCs or individual lap-

tops, this solution offers significant cost savings. Each NComputing device uses one watt of power, versus 85 watts for a regular PC (Marshall, 2008). Thus, not only is this solution extremely environmentally friendly, it also addresses real concerns about high and increasing energy costs around the world. In fact, Macedonia initiated its technology search for the *Computer for Every Child* program by pricing individual laptops for students, and even at $175 per laptop, the price estimate came in at US $63 million. This is not including the additional costs of setup, deployment, maintenance, repair, or electricity. The NComputing technology offered an estimated cost of $70 per user station, and with the additional long-term cost savings in all of the areas mentioned above, the government decided to adopt this solution. As of May, 2008, 23 high schools had been equipped with the new computers (Macedonian Information Agency, 2008). The partners plan to finish equipping all of the secondary schools by the end of August, in time for the start of the new school year, while installation at the primary schools should be completed by the end of the year (Platt, 2008). Rollout of this project was ongoing at the time of field research, and remains for future evaluation.

In two signs of the public's support for the project, the government in power ran—at least partially—on the platform of the computers-in-schools projects, and the June 2008 reelection of the government in power is seen as a reaffirmation of public support for these ICT-in-the-schools initiatives. Additionally, on July 9, 2008, the newly-sitting Macedonian Parliament passed a bill creating a new Information Technology Ministry.

One additional proposed facet of the new plan is for the government to give full scholarships to 5,000 Macedonian students who are interested in majoring in information technology, to study at the University level in Macedonia. This plan is also to be implemented across the entire country, on an equal basis.

Internet Use Beyond the Schools

As stated above, one of the longer term goals of this project is to develop Macedonia's economy into a regional technology hub, which necessarily means promoting Internet use among the wider population. Additionally, the *Macedonia Connects* deployment provided wireless connectivity to 95 percent of Macedonia's population, with the intention that the start-up Internet Service Provider, On.Net, could offer lower priced subscription-based services in its attempt to become a profitable company.

In 2005, monthly dial-up Internet services from the monopoly provider cost (US)$150 and reached only half the population. Once high-speed Internet service became available across the country, subscription rates for households and local businesses immediately dropped to around 30 Euro per month, and were available for as low as 20 Euro per month for the most basic monthly subscription rates at the time that field research was carried out in May, 2009.

On.Net's revolutionary new offerings were showing early signs of success, taking on new clients at a rate of 1500-2000 new clients per month in the years following deployment (Strachan, 2007). On.Net has since been bought by Telecom Slovenia, which has resulted in a competitive duopoly in Macedonia's telecom market. The start-up's purchase by an established regional telecom leader is, in fact, a strong indicator that the project will be profitable.

In the most recent figures available, the numbers of internet subscribers and users in Macedonia have increased markedly in the brief period of time since this project was deployed in 2005. According to the International Telecommunications Union (2008), the number of Internet subscribers in Macedonia rose from 5.3 to 16.3 percent between 2005 and 2007, while the number of Internet users rose from 7.8 to 33.6 percent over the same period, as illustrated in Figure 1.

DISCUSSION

Macedonia Connects—a project completed and handed over to the Macedonian Ministry of Education in 2007—has of yet had no long-term evaluation or in-depth assessment. Still, it does offer valuable opportunities for measurement and evaluation of outcomes in the future in a number of areas, including ICT adoption and uptake in both the schools and communities. Even now, much information is available to inform projects of a similar nature.

Macedonia Connects, in fact, meets or exceeds the policy recommendations made in the literature review above. For example, Nomura (2007) emphasizes the importance of states focusing on both the quality of education and the equality of its provision. The *Macedonia Connects* project addressed these needs by deploying computers and simultaneously providing ICT training on an equitable basis across the country. Lee recommends that "to eliminate the digital divide, we need to not only make computers accessible but also secondary education available" (2001:148); *Macedonia Connects* has made computers accessible within a system of universally provided primary and secondary education. In addition, Macedonia benefits from a democratically elected government, and technology and education are precisely the focus of the *Macedonia Connects* project. This is in line with Jamali et al.'s (2007) findings that democracy, technology and education are all important determinants of economic growth.

Legislating for competition in—and regulation of—the telecom sector was crucial to the realization of *Macedonia Connects*. However, the benefits of a liberalized telecom sector are multitudinous and far-reaching. For instance, the growth, output, and technological adoption enabled through a well-functioning ICT sector enables nearly all other sectors of the economy to perform more efficiently promoting general growth and productivity. This effect is enhanced through increased competition, which drives

Figure 1. Internet use in Macedonia 2000-2007 (source: International Telecommunications Union (ITU) 2008)

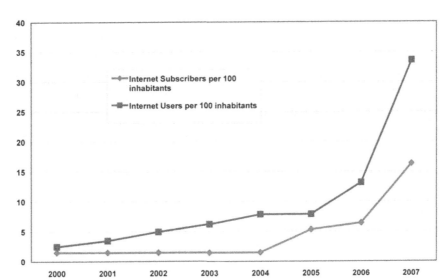

innovation up and costs down, causing positive repercussions across the economy and society.

A show of governmental support is an important factor in the long term success or failure of a project. In the case of *Macedonia Connects*, the current government's support is so strong that it based part of its reelection platform on the computer in schools initiatives, and has begun the process of expanding the project to one computer per child. The nation's newly-created Ministry of Information Technology should add even greater support to its regional technology hub aspirations.

Project stakeholders recognize the importance of pedagogical and technological synergy, and that success depends on the long-term commitment to technology incorporation and adoption necessary to develop the human capital and capacity-building important for sustainable economic growth. The training of teachers and development of curriculua prior to implementation was perhaps the most important human capacity building aspect of the project; it will, in many ways, determine whether computers will be meaningfully adopted in the schools.

Macedonia Connects' business model and its sustanibility-promoting incentive system deserve mentioning; the intersection of common interests of the parties involved was leveraged to the project's fullest advantage. Allowing each party to bring its unique expertise to the project offered the potential for pedagogy and technology to meet. A clear enumeration of goals—and their long term nature—from the outset was another important contributing factor. Stakeholders still involved appear to be committed to this project as the human capacity building effort that it is. USAID and AED's involvement in the project had an exit date built in to the project's plan—it is now under local control.

One critical factor frequently identified in ICT-related development projects is to involve local stakeholders and promote bottom-up input to ensure that locals feel that the project is "theirs," and to establish feedback loops. Although this initiative may be considered top-down in nature, with USAID funding the project, AED responsible for its management and implementation, and the Ministry of Education now running the project, it is important to note that the majority of project team leaders and members were Macedonians, all of the planning and design phases were carried out by or in consultation with Macedonians, and allowed for local involvement and input from the very beginning. School principals, teachers, and even students were encouraged to make suggestions (Hunsberger, 2006:50). Also, since education is a public good, governmental initiative and involvement are in line with the project's national policy objectives.

Another factor identified in the ICT for development literature is that for a project to be successful, locally appropriate technology must be deployed. 'Locally appropriate' in this case refers both to the stated wants and needs of the technology recipients as well as to what is possible given the physical, geographical, and/or infrastructural reality on the ground. In the case of *Macedonia Connects*, the technology may be considered locally appropriate in that there is already a strong emphasis on universal education within the state, a high literacy rate (at 96 percent), and the infrastructure necessary to support the project is already in place, in terms of sufficient school buildings, classrooms, teachers, electricity, and roads—all of which facilitate deployment.

An additional line of argument in the ICT-and-development literature emphasizes the inclusion of rural areas in development-oriented projects. This project included all schools across the country, providing the highest level of inclusion possible, ensuring that even remote areas are now connected to the Internet and service is available to these residents at uniform rates and speeds no matter where they live.

Yet there will be numerous challenges ahead as the project expands, for the process of scaling to accommodate a computer for every child will present new and different issues. The responsibilities for all aspects of the new Computer-for-Every-Child initiative—including planning, deployment, funding, maintenance, and the measurement of outcomes—rest with the Macedonian Ministry for Education and the newly-created Ministry

for Information Technology. Time will tell how this new, expanded project will be managed in the future, after the government has taken full control of it.

As stated above, the outcomes of this project have not yet been subject to systematic evaluation or measurement. It therefore presents a unique opportunity for further research, in order to measure outcomes and gauge progress towards goals.

CONCLUSION

This chapter presented a case study of a unique nation-wide education-focused ICT deployment that provided Internet connectivity to the entire country of Macedonia by connecting all of the schools within its borders. Both equipment and training were provided on an equitable basis to all schools, teachers, and students. This is an important consideration in a country where ethnic tensions remain high. The equality of provisioning, and of deploying the project on a macro-level was an important start in addressing these tensions, but the project must also follow through on its commitments to promote programs that encourage inter-ethnic communication and cooperation in the schools.

At the same time, even while the main focus was on education, the project leveraged the same deployment to provide affordable high-speed Internet to all citizens across the country: a resourceful use of development funds and an efficient method for providing broadband on a nation-wide basis. Even so, as noted in the literature review above, human capacity-building, particularly through education, is a necessary complement to ICT provision, in order to enable technology uptake and use. Since it focuses on training the entire generation of youth with ICT skills through the education system, this project bodes well for such uptake.

The project provides ICT as an enabling tool to contribute to the national economy, in the shorter term by the provision of ICT to both the public and to businesses that did not have access previously, and in the longer term, through the education of the youth in how to take advantage of it. Indeed, Macedonia's Internet use and subscription levels since the project's inception have increased significantly.

The project made use of an innovative business model in the form of a public-private partnership that was designed to become profitable by the end date for the international partners--the project is now locally-run. It is recognized that results from the project will not manifest themselves overnight, and all of the stakeholders appear committed to the long-term realization of the project. For these reasons, the case may be considered a promising one. It also holds best practices for future, similar endeavors, both regionally and around the globe.

Recognizing the potential that this project represents, neighboring countries, such as Albania and Bosnia-Herzegovina, have expressed interest to the partners involved with these projects, for replication within their borders, while USAID is investigating the possibility for replication of certain aspects of the project in African countries. Thus, numerous questions and lines of inquiry, including an analysis of the outcomes of this project, remain, with important and rather urgent implications both regionally and globally.

REFERENCES

Angerer, D. J., & Hammerschmid, G. (2005). Public private partnership between euphoria and disillusionment. Recent experiences from Austria and implications for countries in transformation. *Romanian Journal of Political Science*, *5*(1), 129–159.

Bilbilov, A. (2009). Technology Transfer Program Manager, Macedonia Connects. Interviews with the author, April 29, May 13, 2009.

Cronin, F. J., Colleran, E. K., Parker, E. B., & Dollery, B. (1993). Telecommunications infrastructure investment and economic development. *Telecommunications Policy*, *17*(6), 415–430. doi:10.1016/0308-5961(93)90013-S

De Silva, H., & Zainudeen, A. (2007 March). Teleuse on a Shoestring: Poverty reduction through telecom access at the bottom of the pyramid. *LIRNEasia*. Retrieved August 9, 2007, from http://www.lirneasia.net

Dewan, S., & Kraemer, K. L. (2000). Information technology and productivity: Preliminary evidence from country-level data. *Management Science*, *46*, 548–562. doi:10.1287/mnsc.46.4.548.12057

Dimova, S. (2003). Teaching and learning English in Macedonia. *English Today*, *19*(4), 16–22. doi:10.1017/S0266078403004036

Driouchi, A., Azelmad, E. M., & Anders, G. C. (2006). An econometric analysis of the role of knowledge in economic performance. *The Journal of Technology Transfer*, *31*, 241–255. doi:10.1007/s10961-005-6109-9

Economist. (2007, May 10). To do with the price of fish. *The Economist*. Retrieved October 16, 2007, from http://www.economist.com/finance/displaystory.cfm?story_id=9149142

Education Development Center. (2006). *Technology Implementation in Macedonia*. Retrieved June 3, 2008, from http://main.edc.org/newsroom/features/macedonia_technology.asp

Edwards, S. (2002). Information technology and economic growth in developing countries. *Challenge*, *45*(3), 19–43.

Gerrard, M. (2001, September). Public-Private Partnerships. *Finance & Development*, 48–51.

Gerring, J. (2004). What is a case study and what is it good for? *The American Political Science Review*, *98*(2), 341–354. doi:10.1017/S0003055404001182

Hosman, L., Fife, E., & Armey, E. (2008). The case for a multi-methodological, cross-disciplinary approach to the analysis of ICT investment in the developing world. *Information Technology for Development*, *14*(4), 308–327. doi:10.1002/itdj.20109

Hunsberger, K. (2006 June). A country connects. *PM Network*, 46-54.

ITU. (2008). *ICT Statistics Database. International Telecommunication Union*. Retrieved July 9, 2008 from http://www.itu.int/ITU-D/icteye/Indicators/Indicators.aspx#

Jamali, K., Wandschneider, K., & Wunnava, P. V. (2007). The effect of political regimes and technology on economic growth. *Applied Economics, 39*, 1425–1432. doi:10.1080/00036840500447906

Kampschror, B. (2006, March 28). From warfare to wireless in Macedonia. *The Christian Science Monitor.*

Kanungo, S. (2004). On the emancipatory role of rural information systems. *Information Technology & People*, *17*(4), 407–422. doi:10.1108/09593840410570267

Kara, J., & Quarless, D. (2002). *Guiding Principles for Partnerships for Sustainable Development ('type 2 outcomes') to be Elaborated by Interested Parties in the Context of the World Summit on Sustainable Development (WSSD)*. Johannesburg Summit, 7 June 2002.

Lee, J. W. (2001). Education for technology readiness: Prospects for developing countries. *Journal of Human Development*, *2*(1), 115–148. doi:10.1080/14649880120050

Lijphart, A. (1971). Comparative politics and the comparative method. *The American Political Science Review*, *65*, 682–693. doi:10.2307/1955513

London, T., & Hart, S. L. (2004). Reinventing strategies for emerging markets: beyond the transnational model. *Journal of International Business Studies*, *35*, 350–370. doi:10.1057/palgrave.jibs.8400099

Macedonian Information Agency. (2008, May 26). *Gostivar high school obtains 800 PCs within project 'Computer for Every Child.'* Retrieved June 4, 2008, from http://www.mia.com.mk/portal/page?_pageid=113,166290&_dad=portal&_schema=PORTAL&VestID=46388856&prikaz=24&cat=6

Marshall, M. (2008). NComputing raises $28M to spread cheap computers to poor. *VentureBeat.com*. Retrieved June 29, 2008, from http://venturebeat.com/2008/01/13/ncomputing-raises-28m-to-spread-cheap-computers-to-poor/

Nairn, G. (2006, March 28). Broadband network is the envy of the West. *Financial Times London.*

Nikolovska, Z. (2009). Chief of Party, eSchools Macedonia. Interview with the author, May 16.

Nomura, T. (2007). Contribution of education and educational equality to economic growth. *Applied Economics Letters*, *14*, 627–630. doi:10.1080/13504850500425857

Norton, S. (1992). Transaction costs, telecommunications, and the microeconomics of macroeconomic growth. *Economic Development and Cultural Change*, *41*(1), 175–196. doi:10.1086/452002

Papaioannou, S., & Dimelis, S. (2007). Information technology as a factor of economic development: Evidence from developed and developing countries. *Economics of Innovation and New Technology*, *16*(3), 179–194. doi:10.1080/10438590600661889

Petroska-Beska, V., & Najcevska, M. (2004). Macedonia: Understanding history, preventing future conflict. *United States Institute of Peace*, Special Report No. 115.

Platt, W. (2008). Senior Vice President of Engineering and Support, *NComputing*. Interviews with the author, June 17 & 30, July 23.

Pohjola, M. (2001). Information technology and economic growth: A cross country analysis. In Pohjola, M. (Ed.), *Information Technology and Economic Development*. Oxford, UK: Oxford University Press.

Reka, A. (2008). The Ohrid Agreement: The travails of inter-ethnic relations in Macedonia. *Human Rights Review*, *9*, 55–69. doi:10.1007/s12142-007-0029-z

Republic of Macedonia. (2005). *National Strategy for Information Society Development Action Plan*. Skopje, Macedonia: Author.

Reuters. (2008, June 1). *Macedonia election tainted by violence and fraud.*

Roller, L., & Waverman, L. (2001). Telecommunications Infrastructure and Economic Development: a simultaneous approach. *The American Economic Review*, *91*(4), 909–923.

Seo, H. J., & Lee, Y. S. (2005). Contribution of information and communication technology to total factor productivity and externalities effects. *Information Technology for Development*, *12*(2), 159–173. doi:10.1002/itdj.20021

Shamblin, L. (2005). Giving every Macedonian student a gateway to the world. In Bracey, B., & Culver, T. (Eds.), *Harnessing the Potential of ICT for Education: A Multistakeholder Approach*. New York: United Nations ICT Task Force.

State Statistical Office. Republic of Macedonia. (2005). Census of Population, Households, and Dwellings in the Republic of Macedonia, 2002, Final Data. Skopje, Macedonia: Author.

Stewart, A., & Gray, T. (2006). The authenticity of 'Type Two' multistakeholder partnerships for water and sanitation in Africa: When is a stakeholder a partner? *Environmental Politics*, *15*(3), 362–378. doi:10.1080/09644010600627592

Strachan, G. (2007, 2008). Project Director, *Macedonia Connects*. Interviews with the author, October 1, 23, 2007 & June 17, 2008.

United Nations Foundation & World Economic Forum. (2003). *Public Private Partnerships: Meeting in the middle*. Retrieved February 18, 2007, from https://www.weforum.org/pdf/Initiatives/GHI_2003_Meeting_in_the_middle.pdf

USAID. (2006, May 12). *Macedonia's first education web portal launched*. Retrieved June 3, 2008, from http://www.metamorphosis.org.mk/index.php?option=com_content&task=view&id=689&Itemid=26&lang=en

Waverman, L. Meschi, M., & Fuss, M. (2005). *The impact of telecoms on economic growth in developing countries*. Paper presented at 2005 TPRC conference. Retrieved November 6, 2007, from http://web.si.umich.edu/tprc/papers/2005/450/L%20Waverman-%20Telecoms%20Growth%20in%20Dev.%20Countries.pdf

Weigel, G., & Waldburger, D. (Eds.). (2004). ICT4D: Connecting People for a Better World. Lessons, Innovations and Perpsectives of Information and Communication Technologies in Development. Berne, Switzerland: Swiss Agency for Development and Cooperation (SDC) and Global Knowledge Partnership (GKP).

World Bank. (2003). *ICT for Development Contributing to the Millennium Development Goals: Lessons Learned from Seventeen InfoDev Projects*. Washington, DC: The World Bank.

World Bank. (2006). *Information and Communications for Development (IC4D)—Global Trends and Policies*. Washington, DC: The World Bank.

World Bank. (2008). *Europe and Central Asia. Selected World Development Indicators*. Retrieved November 15, 2008, from http://ddp-ext. worldbank.org

World Factbook, C. I. A. (2008). *Macedonia*. Retrieved November 15, 2008, from https://www. cia.gov/library/publications/the-world-factbook/ geos/mk.html

Chapter 2
Developing Human Capital for National Development:
Lessons from the Malaysian Smart School Initiative

Gerald Goh Guan Gan
Multimedia University, Malaysia

Khor Yoke Lim
Universiti Sains Malaysia, Malaysia

ABSTRACT

Leapfrogging from a developing nation status to one that is fully developed by 2020 is the 'futural role imagery' of most Malaysians ever since the Malaysian government laid out its bold Vision 2020 national development blueprint in the 1990s. Central to the attainment of this vision is the provision of world-class information and communication technology (ICT) infrastructure and the creation of an excellent human capital base that is skilled, knowledgeable, flexible and mobile. To this end, the Malaysian government embarked on the Smart School Initiative, a flagship application of the MSC Malaysia project that aims to transform the way students are being schooled. The smart school pilot project was implemented in 88 schools across the country which saw these schools being fitted and equipped with ICT infrastructure, educational courseware and radical changes in its teaching-learning practices. This chapter provides an overview of the smart school project and highlights some of the issues encountered in the pilot phase. The lessons learned from the smart school pilot project is an invaluable resource to education policy makers, administrators and the school community in other countries intending to introduce an ICT-infused curriculum in schools. It is discovered that a balanced development of all smart school components - ICT infrastructure deployment and maintenance, connectivity, school management system, educational courseware development, teacher development and continuous training is needed to create a smarter learning environment for effective human capital development.

DOI: 10.4018/978-1-60566-388-3.ch002

INTRODUCTION

In pursuit of Malaysia's national development goals, it is exigent that the country invests and develops its human capital to ensure that a trained, skilled and well-educated workforce is created (Azizah Ya'akob, Nor Fariza Mohd Nor, & Hazita Azman, 2005). From a resource-based perspective, human capital can be effectively leveraged as a source of competitive advantage to boost the country's productivity, economic performance and sustain its competiveness as it makes the shift from a manufacturing-driven economy into one that is ICT-driven and knowledge-based (Azizah Ya'akob, Nor Fariza Mohd Nor, & Hazita Azman, 2005; MDeC, 2007b). This is evident from the emphasis on ICT and human capital development through education and training in Malaysia's national development plans. As part of its national development aspirations, the Malaysian government established the Multimedia Super Corridor and came up with the National Information Technology Agenda to act as catalysts in the country's move and participation in the emerging digital economy (Azizah Ya'akob, Nor Fariza Mohd Nor, & Hazita Azman, 2005).

The key task in moving towards a developed nation status lies in Malaysia's ability to develop its human and intellectual capital to produce adequate supply of knowledge workers who are flexible, agile and mobile with relevant knowledge and skills required by the industry (Azizah Ya'akob, Nor Fariza Mohd Nor, & Hazita Azman, 2005; *Bank Negara Malaysia*, 2008). Statistics on Malaysia's expenditure on human capital development-related activities indicate that national budget spending on this sector has been on the rise in the past few decades (*Bank Negara Malaysia*, 2008). This has resulted in positive outcomes for Malaysia as the indicators for the country's human capital have improved over the years based on government expenditure on education and training, years of schooling, student enrolment (Azizah Ya'akob, Nor Fariza Mohd Nor, & Hazita Azman, 2005).

Therefore, the main objective of this chapter is to demonstrate the importance and role of education in developing human capital for national development. In line with this, we examine how and why Malaysia reformed its national education system to be student-centred and ICT-based in line with the human capital requirements of the economy and the benefits sought from such a bold move. In addition, it presents the Malaysian experience in transforming its education system through the bold Smart School Initiative.

This chapter is divided into five key parts. The first part of the chapter provides a brief overview of the importance of education for national development. The second part then presents Malaysia's national development aspirations that resulted in the creation of the Multimedia Super Corridor (MSC Malaysia) that is meant to leapfrog the nation into developed nation status by 2020. Due to the importance and emphasis on human capital development, the Smart School Initiative was developed as one of the MSC Malaysia's flagship applications with radical changes in terms of ICT infrastructure and the teaching-learning approaches adopted in these smart schools. Part four of this chapter provides a brief account of the teaching-learning components as well as ICT infrastructure models deployed. The fifth and final part of this chapter provides a critique of the smart school pilot project in terms of the learned lessons in the key components of the project. With an appreciation of the strengths and weaknesses of the pilot project, this chapter also outlines the lessons learned from this initiative and acts as a reference for other developing countries that are keen to develop their human capital based on the Malaysian smart school model.

EDUCATION FOR NATIONAL DEVELOPMENT

National development has been the key focus across the globe with countries formulating policies and frameworks on addressing key development issues such as education, healthcare, economic and technological development. The Asian Development Bank (2001) which plays an important role in promoting social and economic development activities in the region recognizes that a healthy, nourished and well-educated population is the key to realizing economic and social development. Education and the effective dissemination of knowledge play a central role in the development of societies and economies as an educated population is more productive and more receptive to the introduction of innovations and technologies (El-Halawany & Huwail, 2008). In addition to that, educated people tend to lead healthier lives with better medical care and take on a greater participation in civic activities (Asian Development Bank, 2001).

It is observed that countries that have achieved high levels of economic growth in recent decades have done so in part because of the efforts they have made in developing and strengthening its human capital trough their national education systems (Asian Development Bank, 2001). As such, the effective creation, dissemination and accumulation of knowledge and human capital development through effective education systems are key drivers in technological progress, innovation and economic growth (El-Halawany & Huwail, 2008). The newly industrialized economies (NIEs) of East Asia recognizes the importance of education and therefore place a strong priority on human capital development in addition to its clear and gender-neutral approach to its education and training initiatives (Fukasaku, Kawai, Plummer, & Trzeciak-Duval, 2005).

The emphasis on the importance on education has been acknowledged by the Malaysian Government ever since it gained independence from the British in 1957 and this is evident in its budget allocation and spending for education and training for the past half a century (Hussein Ahmad, 2008). Since the inception of the First Malaysia Plan (1MP) in 1966, education has been

the main vehicle employed by the government to implement its two-pronged strategy of poverty eradication and the elimination of the identification of race with a particular economic function (Hussein Ahmad, 2008, pp. 73-74). In view of the emphasis on education and training for Malaysia's social and economic development, the government has spent a total of RM42,372.9 million for education and training in the Eighth Malaysia Plan (8MP) from 2000 to 2005 (Economic Planning Unit, 2001). In the Ninth Malaysia Plan (9MP), an even larger sum of RM45,149.1 million was allocated for education and training (Economic Planning Unit, 2001).

MALAYSIA'S VISION 2020 AND THE MULTIMEDIA SUPER CORRIDOR

Even before the United Nations formulated the Millennium Development Goals as the development guide for all countries in the world, Malaysia displayed its far-sightedness and pragmatism with the creation of its own national vision for development (Ibrahim Ahmad Bajunid, 2008). The national vision or 'Vision 2020' as it is called was mooted by Tun Dr Mahathir Mohamed, the former Prime Minister of Malaysia and contains many profound ideas drawn from the various fields (Ibrahim Ahmad Bajunid, 2008; Mahathir Mohamed, 1998). The vision emphasizes the need for Malaysia to develop in a Malaysian-centric manner and balanced manner (Mahathir Mohamed, 1998). Not only should the country be developed economically, Vision 2020 aims for a more holistic development goal that includes balancing Malaysia's economic and technological growth with political, spiritual, psychological and cultural development (Mahathir Mohamed, 1998).

Vision 2020 has inspired the nation and has become the basis for all programmes, projects and activities in Malaysia. Among the main projects conceived from this vision is the Multimedia Super Corridor (MSC Malaysia) project that was launched in 1996 to promote both the national information and communication technology (ICT) industry and to provide a test-bed for the global ICT industry with the primary aim of leapfrogging Malaysia to a developed nation status by the year 2020 (Ibrahim Ahmad Bajunid, 2008). MSC Malaysia is modelled after the Silicon Valley in California in addition to ideas drawn from various science and innovation parks worldwide (Bala Ramasamy, Anita Chakrabarty, & Cheah, 2002). Like MSC Malaysia, the development of techno poles such as the Singapore Science Park and the Kanagawa Science Park in Japan have been made in line with the respective government's plan to spur knowledge-intensive activities in the economy (Bala Ramasamy, Anita Chakrabarty, & Cheah, 2002).

MSC Malaysia provides a conducive enabling environment designed to facilitate companies in harnessing the full potential of ICT and multimedia technologies. By providing the infrastructure and necessary environment that encourages innovation and creativity, Malaysia is paving the way to be a platform for growth and advancement as well as a leader in ICT (MDeC, 2007a). MSC Malaysia is developed specifically to explore the frontiers of information and multimedia technologies, revealing its full potential through the creation and implementation of cyberlaws, cutting-edge technologies and excellent infrastructure (MDeC, 2007a).

Ibrahim Ahmad Bajunid (2008) stresses that Vision 2020 plays an important role in the lives of all Malaysians since its inception as it is the 'futural role imagery' of the nation. Singer's (1974) notion of 'futural role imagery' is particularly important when it comes to formulating strategic plans in education as the students who are in school in 1990s when Vision 2020 was formulated will be the ones who will be leading and managing the country in 2020.

This futures perspective in education policy and planning raises several key issues for educational administrators and planners. These include the adequacy of the curriculum, knowledge, learning processes and life experiences gone through by these students in preparing them for their future roles in the country (Ibrahim Ahmad Bajunid, 2008). More importantly, the education system needs to be structured in a way so that it prepares students for the challenges that the future holds by providing them with the tools for learning, relearning and unlearning (Halimah Awang, 2004; Ibrahim Ahmad Bajunid, 2008). Learning will take place in both formal and informal educational settings and the resulting capability and resourcefulness of the workforce will be a key determinant to the degree to which Malaysia is successful in achieving Vision 2020 (Leong, 1997).

THE MALAYSIAN SMART SCHOOL INITIATIVE

In cognisance of the need for effective human capital development via a dynamic and holistic education system to ensure that Malaysians are well-prepared to brace themselves in the competitive knowledge-based economy, the Malaysian government has embarked on a move to redesign the primary and secondary education system by making them 'smart' by equipping schools with computers and multimedia courseware to enhance the teaching-learning process (MDeC, 2007b). The goal of the Malaysian smart school initiative is to transform all schools in the country to become smart schools by 2010 (MDeC, 2007b).

In essence, the Malaysian smart school is defined as "… a learning institution that has been systematically reinvented in terms of teaching-learning practices and school management in order to prepare children for the Information Age" (Smart School Task Force, 1997, p. 10). In addition to that, the smart school will continue to evolve over time, thereby developing its professional staff, its educational resources, and its administrative capabilities to allow the school to adapt to changing conditions, while continuing to prepare students for life in the information age (Smart School Task Force, 1997).

Among the key benefits of an ICT-infused curriculum such as the smart schools is that it transforms the learning environment so that it increases student-centred learning to enhance basic skills, increases the likelihood of inter-disciplinary and authentic learning experiences, encourages collaborative learning and increases global awareness among students (Ang, 2002; Cox, 1997). In other words, ICT would allow schools to create learning environments that will improve student achievement and equip them with skills for the information age (Ang, 2002; MDec, 2005). Positive effects on the behaviour, communication and process skills were observed by teachers amongst students as a result of the use of an ICT-infused curriculum and learning environment (Comber, Watling, Lawson, Cavendish, Mceune, & Paterson, 2002). More importantly, Cox (1997) notes that ICT leads to higher levels of motivation amongst students.

From a school management point of view, research in the UK have shown that the use of ICT particularly the use of electronic mail and virtual message boards leads to more efficient communication, both within and between schools (Flecknoe, 2001). Schools in the past were constrained by the physical resources due to budgetary limitations are now able to access and exploit the wide range of teaching-learning resources that are available on the Internet (Harrison, Comber, Fisher, Haw, Lewin, Lunzer, McFarlane, Mavers, Scrimshaw, Somekh, & Watling, 2002; Telem, 2001). Greene, Lee, Springall and Bemrose (2002) found in their study that teachers and administrative support staff are able to complete administrative and planning tasks in a more efficient manner.

The implementation of the smart school project is based on four 'waves' projected over two decades from 1999 to 2020. The first wave witnessed the launching of the pilot project in which the the smart school model was trialed in 88 schools[1] (MDeC, 2007b). The second wave involved the post-pilot examination and analysis of the project in preparation for the nationwide roll-out of the smart school project where all schools will be made smart schools in the third wave from 2005 to 2010 (Smart School Task Force, 1997, p. 11). The final and fourth wave involves consolidating and stabilising all the smart school project components to achieve a higher level of smart school attainment in Malaysian schools from 2010 to 2020 (Smart School Task Force, 1997, p. 11).

The smart school initiative aims to contribute to Malaysia's Vision 2020 by being a catalyst to the growth of the ICT industry and creating a well-qualified pool of professionals in addition to preparing Malaysians for the information age through an innovative education delivery process (MDeC, 2007a; Smart School Task Force, 1997). Regarded as one of the most forward-looking ICT-mediated learning initiatives in the world, the Smart School Initiative attempts to reinvent the teaching-learning processes (MDeC, 2007a; Smart School Task Force, 1997). The smart school initiative is premised on the belief that ICT is a key enabler in imparting the desire for learning to every Malaysian (MDeC, 2007a; Smart School Task Force, 1997). Capitalizing on leading-edge technologies and the rapid deployment MSC Malaysia's technological infrastructure to jump-start the deployment of enabling technologies in schools, the smart school project aims to facilitate the changing role of teachers in the electronic classroom from that of mere information providers to facilitators whose main role is to assist students in developing their know-how and judgement to select information that they need to accomplish their tasks (Azizah Ya'akob, Nor Fariza Mohd Nor, & Hazita Azman, 2005).

The ability to exercise correct judgement when selecting information from a wide array of choices in the information age and the acquisition of the necessary skills for lifelong learning are critical factors in ensuring the creation a talented workforce that is abreast with developments in their respective vocations (Halimah Awang, 2004;

MDeC, 2007b). While the smart school initiative encompasses six major components i.e. teaching and learning; management and administration; people, skills and responsibilities; technology; processes and policies, the two key components that have received much attention by the government are the student-centred teaching and learning concepts and the ICT enabling technologies (Ibrahim Ahmad Bajunid, 2008; Smart School Task Force, 1997).

TEACHING AND LEARNING CONCEPTS

The smart school initiative has profound implications to the way students are educated at the primary and secondary schools in Malaysia (Halimah Awang, 2004). Ong (2006) explains that the most distinctive feature of smart schools is its teaching and learning practices that is drawn from the best practices from around the world. This is attributed to the mutually-reinforcing and coherent alignment of the key teaching and learning components *vis-à-vis* its curriculum, pedagogy, assessment and teaching-learning materials (Cloke, Sabariah Sharif, & Abdul Said Ambotang, 2006; Ong, 2006).

The curriculum for the smart schools is designed to ensure that it remains meaningful, socially-responsible, multicultural, reflective, holistic, global, open-ended, goal-based and technologically-focused (Smart School Task Force, 1997). It is envisaged that the curriculum will promote holistic learning for students thereby allowing them to progress and develop at their own pace whilst catering to their different capabilities, interests and needs (Ong, 2006; Smart School Task Force, 1997). In addition to that, the curriculum places adequate emphasis on the development of critical and creative thinking skills. To develop civic-consciousness amongst students, the smart school curriculum is infused with sixteen values which include compassion, self-reliance, coopera-

tion, diligence, love, courage and honesty (Smart School Task Force, 1997).

Ong (2006) points out that although the curricula for the smart school and mainstream education system do not differ much in terms of their content coverage, the former adopts a different format in that its intended learning outcomes are explicitly stated at the different levels. As such, this ensures that students are able to pace their learning across the different school grades without having to compromise on the quality of their learning process (Ong, 2006). In an effort to encourage the development of instructional techniques that will help students develop a deep understanding of content and thinking skills, the smart school curriculum incorporates Perkins and Simmons'(1998) integrative model that consists of four mutually interactive frames of knowledge which are the content knowledge, problem solving knowledge, epistemic knowledge and inquiry knowledge (Smart School Task Force, 1997). As recommended by Perkins and Simmons (1998), instruction in smart schools should include all four frames with the substance of these frames and their inter-relationships being explicitly articulated by both teachers and students.

Pedagogically, the smart schools represent a paradigm shift from the traditional objectivist approach to one that is based on a constructivist approach (Muhammad Z.M. Zain, Hanafi Atan, & Rozhan M. Idrus, 2004). This is because the mainstream education system which has been traditionally-focused on rote or memory-based learning well-suited to students of average-level ability and aptitude will be replaced with a system that is learner-based, one that stimulates thinking, creativity and caring (Smart School Task Force, 1997). With the introduction of ICT in the classroom, teachers need to ensure that their pedagogic practice is relevant and meaningful to students.

As such, these smart schools will focus on constructivist teaching-learning activities that are self-directed, collaborative, learner-paced, continuous and reflective utilising teaching a variety of teaching materials such as printed books, multimedia, software, interactive courseware, the Internet and databases (El-Halawany & Huwail, 2008; Smart School Task Force, 1997). By virtue of its student-centred focus, smart schools therefore cater to individual student differences and their varied learning styles (Halimah Awang, 2004; Ong, 2006). In this manner, an appropriate mixture of different learning strategies could be effectively employed by teachers to cater for student diversity in terms of their abilities and learning styles to achieve basic competencies and ensure that learners develop in a holistic manner (El-Halawany & Huwail, 2008; Ong, 2006).

In addition to that, teachers need to re-orientate themselves from being a 'sage on the stage' to a 'guide on the side' (Smart School Task Force, 1997, p. 131). This is because teachers will now identify goals, provide direction to their students, guide their students' progress towards these goals and then step back to allow the students to learn at their own pace (Smart School Task Force, 1997). Throughout the entire process, teachers will play a supporting role to the students by providing them with psychological support and encouragement. They will periodically step in to check on student progress, recognize and compliment their strengths and efforts, identify weaknesses and decide on the practices their students will need to improve their understanding on the particular topic (Azizah Ya'akob, Nor Fariza Mohd Nor, & Hazita Azman, 2005; Smart School Task Force, 1997).

Central to the student-centred learning approach is the need for reflection and reflexivity by both students and the teachers. Teachers need to constantly reflect on their teaching practices and classroom strategies to continuously improve student learning and therefore their achievement in the new student-centred approach (MDeC, 2007b). In short, teachers will be instrumental in creating learning conditions that will promote self-directed learning. They need to teach students strategies to competently and selectively navigate

for information. In addition, team effort, group collaboration, flexibility, far-sightedness and language competency need to be mastered by the students (Azizah Ya'akob, Nor Fariza Mohd Nor, & Hazita Azman, 2005).

The *Smart School Conceptual Blueprint* states that the assessment system adopted by smart schools '… will involve a significant departure from traditional assessment systems' as it shall involve continuous criterion-referenced, learner-centred, online assessments that are conducted at various levels i.e. classroom-based, school-based and national so as to allow students to demonstrate their strengths, abilities and knowledge (Smart School Task Force, 1997, p. 48). In addition, it shall also employ multiple approaches and instruments to perform authentic, alternative and performance assessments for students (Ong, 2006). Ong (2006, p. 4) stresses that while the proposed assessment system has its merits and is indeed a bold move for Malaysia, '… these aspirations are far from reality … [as] students from the smart schools are taking similar school-based and centralised assessments as their counterparts in the mainstream schools'.

Teaching-learning materials designed to support the teaching-learning strategies of the Smart Schools to meet curricular and instructional needs are cost effective, as well as aesthetically and technically adequate (Ong, 2006). As most learning courseware available when the smart school initiative was launched was proprietary and developed for a generic market, the Malaysian government had to develop its own courseware for the smart schools based on the specified curriculum (MDec, 2005). A total of 1,494 multimedia courseware titles on Malay Language, English Language, Science and Mathematics have been specifically developed for use in smart schools (MDec, 2005, p. 18). These materials are designed to be cognitively challenging and attractive to motivate students to learn and actively participate in learning activities (Cloke, Sabariah Sharif, & Abdul Said Ambotang, 2006; Ong, 2006).

Table 1. Smart school ICT configuration levels

Level	Level A (Full Classroom Model)	Level B+ (Limited Classroom Model)	Level B (Laboratory Model)
Number of schools	4 schools	4 schools	79 schools
Personal computers	520 computers	81 computers	37 computers
Notebooks	5 notebooks	2 notebooks	2 notebooks
Servers	6 servers (communications, databases, applications)	3 servers (communications, databases, applications)	3 servers (communications, databases, applications)
Networking	Fast Ethernet backbone (100 baseT) with 512/256 kbps leased line	Fast Ethernet backbone (100 baseT) with 128/64 kbps leased line	Fast Ethernet backbone (100 baseT) with 128/64 kbps leased line

(Adapted from: MDeC, 2007b; Smart School Task Force, 1997)

ICT INFRASTRUCTURE IN SCHOOLS

The ICT infrastructure in the schools that were selected by the Ministry of Education to pilot the smart school initiative involved the installation of computers, software and networking depending on their model or level. The most advanced level is the full classroom model (Level A) with computers installed in classrooms and laboratories for teaching and learning purposes (Smart School Task Force, 1997). In the four Level A schools, the ratio of students to computers is 5 to 1. Meanwhile, the Level B+ or limited classroom model was piloted in four schools, each equipped with computers in selected classrooms and science laboratories (Smart School Task Force, 1997). The other 79 schools are classified as Model B schools that are equipped with a single computer laboratory (Bismillah Khatoon bt Abdul Kader, 2008). Table 1 provides outlines the ICT configuration of the smart schools.

To effectively manage these smart schools, the Smart School Management System (SMSS) which is an integrated information system that assists in the management and administration of the school, student affairs, educational resources, finances, human resources, external resources, facilities, technology and hostel facilities was developed and deployed in all smart schools (Smart School Task Force, 1997). The SMSS also allows the school to stay connected with local and national

educational authorities and has a function that lets the students' parents to monitor their children's progress and to stay in touch with the school (MDec, 2005).

In short, the smart school initiative is a comprehensive education initiative spearheaded by the Malaysian government that encompasses all the key aspects of educational planning, instructional design, technological deployment and human capital development. However, as with any major innovation, issues and problems are bound to emerge. The following section provides an overview of the key issues that were identified and what was learned in the first wave of the Malaysian smart school initiative.

LESSONS LEARNED FROM THE PILOT PHASE

At the end of the pilot phase, several studies were conducted to gauge the impacts of the smart school project with the aim of improving the deficiencies that existed before the national roll-out of the project. In general, it is acknowledged that the smart school initiative is a 'one of a kind' project embarked by a developing country that sets out to automate and reinvent the national school system (MDec, 2005, p. 18). The smart school initiative also resulted in the training and development of a large pool of ICT-skilled teachers, students and administrators. More importantly, the stakeholders of the smart school project are able to manage and implement technological change in schools, plan and manage ICT-enabled learning environments apart from managing the broader societal, ethical and human-related issues that comes with the use of technology in schools (MDec, 2005).

A study by Ministry of Education and MDeC involving 33 of the 88 smart schools to identify the changes brought about by smart schools and its impact on teachers, students and school administrators found that 90 per cent of students in smart schools were ICT literate and were able to use of ICT for their learning (Bismillah Khatoon bt Abdul Kader, 2008, p. 20). The teachers however did not fare as well as their students with only 83 per cent of them being ICT literate. This raises a key question on the effectiveness of the entire smart school initiative as 17 per cent of the teachers in the study were not able to use computers at all. In order for the full benefit of the smart school to be realized, it is important the teachers understand the relevance, usefulness and applicability of ICT in enhancing the teaching learning process and how it facilitates the school's transition to a student-centred learning environment (Bismillah Khatoon bt Abdul Kader, 2008). Ideally, teachers need to be comfortable with ICT and competent in using these tools to enhance their own professional development and to enrich the learning experiences of their students (Bismillah Khatoon bt Abdul Kader, 2008; MDec, 2005).

SMART SCHOOL TEACHERS AND STUDENT-ORIENTED LEARNING

To prepare teachers for their new roles in smart schools, the Teacher Education Division of the Ministry of Education organised a series of workshops and training sessions on the use of ICT in education and computer applications. Among the computer applications that were included in the training are Microsoft Power Point

and website development (Azizah Ya'akob, Nor Fariza Mohd Nor, & Hazita Azman, 2005). Most of the teachers found these training sessions useful in preparing them to use ICT in their classes. As such, a majority of the teachers in the smart schools reported that they have since used ICT to prepare their lessons and to develop teaching materials. Teachers are also using the computer laboratory for their classes with 73 per cent of them experiencing improved productivity with the use of ICT facilities (Bismillah Khatoon bt Abdul Kader, 2008, p. 20; MDec, 2005).

Nevertheless, it was found that too few teachers were trained in the field of courseware development. Furthermore, many teachers were of the opinion that the courseware supplied to them by the Ministry of Education were not sufficient for their teaching thereby requiring them to come up with their own customized courseware which many of them are not trained to do (Azizah Ya'akob, Nor Fariza Mohd Nor, & Hazita Azman, 2005). As such, while teachers are well-trained in terms of subject content, the student-centred pedagogy adopted in smart schools and technology use, they are not well-trained in terms of technological pedagogical content knowledge (Azizah Ya'akob, Nor Fariza Mohd Nor, & Hazita Azman, 2005; Koehler & Mishra, 2005).

According to Zhao (2003), for teachers to be conversant and fluent in the use of educational technology, it requires them to go beyond mere competence with the latest tools, applications and technologies. They need to develop an understanding of the complex web of relationships that exist between the various users, practices, technologies and tools (Zhao, 2003). Technology as it is applied in the smart school context therefore represents a knowledge system (Hickman, 1990) that has its own affordances and biases that makes some technologies more applicable in certain situations and contexts than others (Bromley, 1998; Bruce, 1993). Koehler and Mishra (2005) explain that for true technology integration, teachers need to possess technological pedagogical content knowledge

(TPACK) to fully understand and negotiate the relationships between the pedagogical, technological and content components of knowledge. They further assert 'good teaching is not simply adding technology to the existing teaching and content domain' but involves 'developing a sensitivity to the dynamic, transactional relationship between' the three components of knowledge (Koehler & Mishra, 2005, p. 134). Hence, teachers need to be trained to possess TPACK to enable them to teach more effectively in the smart schools.

Another issue identified is the lack of training for new teachers in smart schools (Bismillah Khatoon bt Abdul Kader, 2008). Teachers who were newly transferred to these schools were not given specific smart school teaching training and had difficulties fitting into their new roles as teachers in a student-oriented system which requires teachers to reposition themselves from instructors to facilitators in the learning process of their students.

In a study conducted on the teaching of the English language in smart schools, it was found that 76.5 per cent of teachers were comfortable with the new roles of facilitating their students' learning (Azizah Ya'akob, Nor Fariza Mohd Nor, & Hazita Azman, 2005, p. 22). Although this figure is encouraging, 70.6 per cent of the teachers found that they were still playing the traditional role of 'information providers' to students with 64.7 per cent of them reporting that students still required a significant amount of instruction and assistance to accomplish their work in class (Azizah Ya'akob, Nor Fariza Mohd Nor, & Hazita Azman, 2005; Bismillah Khatoon bt Abdul Kader, 2008, p. 22).

Therefore, there is a pressing need for the Ministry of Education to look into the ICT competency of teachers in smart schools to ensure that all teachers attain a prescribed minimum ICT competency level which encompasses the areas of knowledge of key ICT applications, Internet literacy, Web technologies and digital media. This would ensure that smart school teachers are able to integrate these ICT applications in their classes

apart from developing teaching materials and performing administrative functions. Among the key ICT applications that they need to be able to use include word processors, spreadsheets, database management systems, presentation systems, and the ability to search and integrate materials available on the Internet.

The paradigm shift towards a student-centred learning environment poses some difficulties for students as 83.3 per cent of the students reported that they are not comfortable with this student-centred learning approach and it is difficult to change their role as passive knowledge receivers to self-directed learners in smart schools (Azizah Ya'akob, Nor Fariza Mohd Nor, & Hazita Azman, 2005, p. 22). Sinacore, Blaisure, Justin, Healy and Braver (1999, p. 267) suggest that students would only be able to 'learn to observe and locate themselves as knowers within certain cultural and sophisticated contexts' when students and teachers practice reflexivity in the classroom.

Teachers in smart schools need to engage in reflexive practice to attain self-awareness, scholarly accountability and recognition of a range of human truths that will further prepare both students and teacher to attain better learning outcomes in smart schools (Sinacore *et al.*, 1999). Reflexive teaching allows teachers to be able to evaluate the effectiveness of ICT on their teaching and on their students' learning from an outcomes-based perspective (Bismillah Khatoon bt Abdul Kader, 2008).

Apart from technological knowledge and skills, teachers should also be given adequate training and grounding in pedagogy and subject content as well as TPACK (Koehler & Mishra, 2005). This is necessary so as to ensure that teachers are able to effectively deploy their technological skills in the classroom and to nurture an effective student-centred learning environment in smart schools (Bismillah Khatoon bt Abdul Kader, 2008; Koehler & Mishra, 2005).

As such, professional development activities conducted by the Ministry of Education needs to ensure that teachers possess adequate knowledge and are able to exercise judgement in evaluating ICT resources to be used for their teaching and decide on which resources best fit the lesson purpose, teaching strategies, student abilities and a host contextual factors (Bismillah Khatoon bt Abdul Kader, 2008). Once they have selected the ICT tools and material to be used in their classes, they would need to then decide on how these could be effectively integrated into their lessons (Bismillah Khatoon bt Abdul Kader, 2008; MDeC, 2007b). Bismillah Khatoon (2008, p. 18) explains that while 'many aspects of education can be enriched with the judicial use of technology .... some topics and aspects cannot'.

USE OF COURSEWARE IN SMART SCHOOLS

The main impact of the smart school initiative in terms of courseware development is the creation of a good collection of teaching-learning materials for smart schools that were developed based on the Malaysian national school curriculum. Apart from that, it has contributed to the healthy growth of the educational technology sector especially in terms of courseware development and web-based learning (MDeC, 2007b). Over one hundred local and foreign companies worked together to develop the courseware used in the pilot phase, creating over 5000 jobs in this relatively new industry in Malaysia (MDec, 2005, pp. 14-15).

In a study by local academics in 2003, they found that while the educational courseware developed for smart schools were well-received by both students and teachers, its use in the smart schools was somewhat limited because teachers do not use these materials as the main teaching resource (MDec, 2005). Furthermore, their report claims that '...the frequency of their usage was limited as some of the lessons could not adequately cater to the students' needs and did not reflect the complete curriculum' (MDec, 2005, p. 16).

Furthermore, it was also revealed that teachers only used the computer labs on an average of four times per month, citing reasons such as the limitations of courseware and the need to focus on the printed study materials to ensure that students get good grades in public examinations (MDec, 2005). This is because if teachers used materials that were directly related in preparing students for examinations, it saved them a great deal of time and effort in terms of teaching, delivering and preparation (Bismillah Khatoon bt Abdul Kader, 2008).

A *laissez faire* approach to the use of smart school courseware also led to issues of its infrequent use. Due to the lack of monitoring and support in the use of these smart school courseware, teachers seem to be less inclined in utilizing them fully in their teaching (MDec, 2005). Proper monitoring, adequate training and proper provision of support are necessary in ensuring that teachers fully utilize these customized teaching-learning resources in smart schools.

ICT INFRASTRUCTURAL ISSUES AND INTERNET CONNECTIVITY

The smart school ICT deployment model that is categorized into three levels i.e. A, B+ and B is an issue that needs to be seriously considered before the national rollout of the smart school project. The Level A full-classroom model where schools are equipped with 520 computers is the ideal model that should be the entry-level smart school model adopted by the Ministry of Education. This is because the B+ model (81 computers per school) and B model (37 computers per school) are not effective in terms due to the limited accessibility of computers to student and teacher access who need access to these resources for regular ICT-integrated teaching-learning activities (Smart School Task Force, 1997). Instead of relying on absolute numbers of computers in schools as practiced in the A, B+ and B models, a student-to-computer ratio-based model should be developed to ensure that issues of limited of computer access and availability do not become a problem in the smart schools of the future.

A common complaint by teachers and students of level B and B+ schools is that they face a shortage of computers and that the number of computer labs is not sufficient for effective implementation of the smart school learning environment (Bismillah Khatoon bt Abdul Kader, 2008; MDec, 2005). In addition to that, a major concern is with the issue of technical problems faced with the local area network, computers and servers in smart schools (MDec, 2005). The Ministry of Education needs to seriously investigate the issue of ICT maintenance and support in schools as it is crucial for smart schools to have good technical support to ensure that the computers remain accessible for use by the school community.

The development and management of the smart school help desk was outsourced to Telekom Smart School in the pilot phase had satisfactory performance evaluations by its users (MDC, 2004). However when the operations of the help desk was handed over to the Ministry at the end of the pilot phase, performance issues began to surface which resulted in the help desk being handed over to Telekom Smart School who has since managed to provide a better level service than the Ministry of Education who had no specialist personnel for this task (MDC, 2004). Problems were encountered when the help desk was managed by the Ministry of Education as it did not have dedicated personnel tor experience in handling such support systems (MDeC, 2007b). This serves as an important lesson for policy makers to pay adequate attention on critical support services such as help desks. These services need to be managed by professionals and long-term plans need to be in place to ensure that performance and quality lapses such as those experienced by the smart school help desk when it was handed back to its owners i.e. the Ministry of Education do not recur.

Attaining a consistent level of ICT fit-out and capacity in schools is a major challenge due to the disparity in ICT infrastructure in schools located in the urban and rural areas (Bismillah Khatoon bt Abdul Kader, 2008). Due to the nature of the courseware and systems used in smart schools, Internet connectivity is an important enabler of these schools' effectively (Berends, 2005). However, in many rural areas the connectivity is limited and even if there is Internet access, the quality in terms of bandwidth, stability and speed leaves much to be desired (Bismillah Khatoon bt Abdul Kader, 2008). If the connectivity issue is not resolved, it is feared that the smart school initiative may end up widening the digital divide between rural and urban areas as the students in rural locations will be trailing even farther behind their urban counterparts in terms of ICT literacy and learning experience.

In cognisance of the critical nature this issue, the Ministry of Education has embarked on an intervention programme to provide schools in rural areas with special training programmes to come up with alternative teaching strategies and to equip these teachers with notebook computers (Berends, 2005). Teaching-learning materials are also supplied to these teachers in the form of CD-ROMs to overcome the current limitations in terms of connectivity in rural areas faced in Malaysia (Berends, 2005; Bismillah Khatoon bt Abdul Kader, 2008).

Management of Smart Schools

The smart school management system (SMSS) which assists school administrators in routine school operations received positive feedback from the school principals surveyed (MDec, 2005). Closer examination however revealed that principals were only familiar and had utilized only 16 of the 31 components in the SMSS (MDec, 2005, p. 17). On-site inspections by the Ministry of Education found that the actual use of the SMSS was fair but more benefits could have been realized if principals were using all the components in the system instead of a selected few (MDec, 2005).

Of the 31 components, the financial management, personnel management and facilities management components were the ones that most principals had problems and issues with (MDec, 2005, p. 17). As the SMSS had many different components and modules, many principals and administrators were overwhelmed by this sudden change and complained of having to implement too many components at once (MDec, 2005).

It is also surprising when studies revealed that many students were not aware of the SMSS that was being used in their respective schools (MDec, 2005). Similarly, parents and guardians of students studying in smart schools are not fully aware of the exact nature of the 'smart' approaches and applications in their children's school (MDec, 2005). They are only aware that their children are in a smart school and are unaware of its implications and benefits (MDec, 2005).

Despite these setbacks, school administrators reported that they were able to manage their schools better and that they were more efficient in doing their work (MDec, 2005). Initiatives are currently being undertaken by the Ministry of Education to enhance the user-friendliness of the SMSS apart from integrating it with the Teaching of Science and Mathematics in English Initiative (PPSMI), the school computerization programme and the SchoolNet project (MDec, 2005). The issues and lessons learned in the pilot phase by the 88 smart schools in terms of teaching-learning practices, courseware development, ICT infrastructure and the smart school management system are invaluable lessons for education policymakers and administrators from Malaysia and abroad in improving their national school systems for national development.

CONCLUSION

The first wave of the smart school initiative from 1999 to 2002 was a challenging phase for the project as it involved piloting the entire blueprint in 88 schools across the nation (MDec, 2005). When the project took off in 1999, no one had any experience in such a bold move before and the only reference the Ministry of Education that spearheaded this entire initiative had was the smart school blueprint that served as the definitive guide for this mammoth task as well as examples of best practices in other countries that were selected to fit the Malaysian smart school context akin to the pieces of a jigsaw puzzle. In actual sense, the pilot phase was actually work-in-progress as from 1999 to 2002, involving a wide range of development activities which included development, testing, refining and implementation of all aspects of the project. As such, the full deployment and use of the completed smart school solution was only realized in early 2003. Based on the initial development of the smart school initiative and the experiences gained, it must be noted that a range of issues ranging from educational change management, ICT infrastructure deployment and maintenance, connectivity, school management system, educational courseware development and continuous training warrant the attention of the Ministry of Education.

In the post-pilot phase from 2004-2005, strategies were being undertaken to address these issues and deficiencies. However, it is important to note that the most crucial elements of the smart school initiative that function as the key pillars of the project are its teachers and ICT infrastructure. As discussed in this chapter, teachers play an integral role in this educational paradigm shift in Malaysia as they are the agents of change whereby they will the ones who will have to change their teaching approaches to ensure that an effective learning environment for their students is nurtured. Apart from that, they need to be competent and skilled in their craft.

To be skilled in the craft of teaching, teachers need to possess adequate knowledge and skills in the areas of technology, pedagogy, subject content and its overlapping domains such as pedagogical content knowledge and TPACK. Only when teachers have mastered these skills and knowledge, they would then be able to come up with innovative interventions that are ICT-infused to maximize their students' learning outcomes. In addition, regular and continuous professional development for teachers is important for their ongoing development and to ensure that they are abreast with the latest developments in teaching practice and ICT applications.

ICT infrastructure is one of the key enablers of smart schools. Adequate ICT provision is necessary to ensure that all students and teachers in smart schools have access to computers for their teaching-learning activities. More importantly, proper infrastructural support and maintenance is necessary to ensure that the 'return-on-investment' on ICT infrastructure is realized. While the smart school initiative is neither complete nor perfect, the lessons learned from the pilot phase serves as a potent lesson and reminder to educationists in Malaysia and other developing countries. While the use of ICT in education presents many benefits and opportunities for developing human capital and accelerating national development, embarking on such a move does not only involve investments in ICT infrastructure alone. Instead, a balanced development of all components - ICT infrastructure deployment and maintenance, connectivity, school management system, educational courseware development, teacher development and continuous training is needed to create a smarter learning environment.

REFERENCES

Ahmad, H. (2008). History, policy and reform in Malaysian education. In Bajunid, I. A. (Ed.), *Malaysia - From Traditional to Smart Schools: The Malaysian Educational Odyssey* (pp. 35–83). Kuala Lumpur, Malaysia: Oxford-Fajar.

Ang, J. E. (2002). *Malay and English Language Achievement in Technologically Rich and Non-Technologically Rich Malaysian Schools*. USA: Unpublished EdD, University of Houston.

Asian Development Bank. (2001). *Education and National Development in Asia: Trends, issues, policies and strategies*. Manila, Philippines: Asian Development Bank.

Awang, H. (2004). Human Capital and Technology Development in Malaysia. *International Education Journal*, 5(2), 239–246.

Bajunid, I. A. (2008). Towards a grand narrative of Malaysian education. In Bajunid, I. A. (Ed.), *Malaysia - From Traditional to Smart Schools: The Malaysian Educational Odyssey* (pp. 1–34). Kuala Lumpur, Malaysia: Oxford Fajar.

Bank Negara Malaysia. (2008). *Bank Negara Malaysia*. Retrieved 10 October, 2008, from http://www.bnm.gov.my

Berends, H. (2005). Exploring knowledge sharing: moves, problem solving and justification. *Knowledge Management Research & Practice*, 3(2), 93–105. doi:10.1057/palgrave.kmrp.8500056

Bismillah Khatoon bt Abdul Kader. (2008). Malaysia's Experience in Training Teachers to Use ICT. In E. Meleisea (Ed.), *ICT in Teacher Education: Case Studies from the Asia-Pacific Region* (pp. 10-22). Bangkok: UNESCO.

Bromley, H. (1998). Introduction: Data-driven democracy? Social assessment of educational computing. In Bromley, H., & Apple, M. (Eds.), *Education, technology, power* (pp. 1–28). Albany, NY: SUNY Press.

Bruce, B. C. (1993). Innovation and social change. In Bruce, B. C., Peyton, J. K., & Batson, T. (Eds.), *Network-based classrooms* (pp. 9–32). Cambridge, UK: Cambridge University Press.

Cloke, C., Sabariah Sharif, & Ambotang, A. S. (2006). A qualitative study of pedagogical issues arising from the introduction of the Malaysian Smart School initiative. *Jurnal Pendidik dan Pendidikan, 21*, 129-147.

Comber, C., Watling, R., Lawson, T., Cavendish, S., Mceune, R., & Paterson, F. (2002). *ImpaCT2: Learning at Home and School: Case Studies*. Coventry, UK: BECTA.

Cox, M. J. (1997). *Effects of information technology on students' motivation: final report*. Coventry, UK: NCET.

Economic Planning Unit. (2001). *Third Outline Perspective Plan, 2001-2010*. Kuala Lumpur, Malaysia: Economic Planning Unit, Government of Malaysia.

El-Halawany, H., & Huwail, E. I. (2008). Malaysian Smart Schools: A Fruitful Case Study for Analysis to Synopsize Lessons Applicable to the Egyptian Context. *International Journal of Education and Development using ICT, 4*(2).

Flecknoe, M. (2001). *The use of virtual classrooms for school improvement*. Paper presented at the BELMAS Annual Conference.

Fukasaku, K., Kawai, M., Plummer, M. G., & Trzeciak-Duval, A. (2005). *Policy Coherence Towards East Asia*. Tokyo, Japan: OECD.

Greene, K., Lee, B., Springall, E., & Bemrose, R. (2002). Administrative support staff in schools: ways forward. London: DfES.

Harrison, C., Comber, C., Fisher, T., Haw, K., Lewin, C., Lunzer, E., et al. (2002). ImpaCT2: The impact of information and communication technologies on pupil attainment. London: DfES/Becta.

Hickman, L. (1990). *John Dewey's pragmatic technology*. Bloomington, IN: Indiana University Press.

Koehler, M. J., & Mishra, P. (2005). What happens when teachers design educational technology? The development of technological pedagogical content knowledge. *Journal of Educational Computing Research, 32*(2), 131–152. doi:10.2190/0EW7-01WB-BKHL-QDYV

Leong, Y. K. (1997). Lifelong Learning and Vision 2020 in Malaysia. In Hatton, M. J. (Ed.), *Lifelong Learning: Policies, Practices, and Programs* (pp. 129–139). Ontario, Canada: Canadian International Development Agency.

MDC. (2004). *Multimedia Super Corridor Impact Survey 2004 - Performance of MSC-status companies in phase I (2003) (Report)*. Malaysia: Cyberjaya.

MDec. (2005). The Smart School Roadmap 2005-2020: An Educational Odyssey - A consultative paper on the expansion of the Smart School initiative to all schools in Malaysia. Kuala Lumpur, Malaysia: MDec.

MDeC. (2007a). *Malaysian Smart Schools*. Retrieved 15 August, 2007, from http://www.msc.com.my/smartschool/

MDeC. (2007b). *Multimedia Development Corporation of Malaysia*. Retrieved January 10, 2007, from http://www.mdc.com.my

Mohamed, M. (1998). *The Way Forward*. London: Weidenfeld & Nicolson.

Ong, E.-T. (2006, December). *The Malaysian Smart Schools Project: An Innovation to Address Sustainability*. Paper presented at the 10th UNESCO-APEID International Conference on Education Learning Together for Tomorrow: Education for Sustainable Development, Bangkok, Thailand.

Perkins, D. N., & Simmons, R. (1998). Patterns of misunderstanding: An integrative model for science, math and programming. *Review of Educational Research, 5*(3), 303–326.

Ramasamy, B., Chakrabarty, A., & Cheah, M. (2002). *Malaysia's leap into the future: an evaluation of the Multimedia Super Corridor* (Research Paper Series No. 08/2002). Nottingham, UK: Centre in Europe Asia Business Research, Nottingham University Business School.

Sinacore, A. L., Blaisure, K. R., Justin, M., Healy, P., & Brawer, S. (1999). Promoting Reflexivity in the Classroom. *Teaching of Psychology*, *26*(4), 267–270. doi:10.1207/S15328023TOP260405

Singer, B. B. (1974). The future-focussed role-image. In Toffler, A. (Ed.), *Learning for Tomorrow* (pp. 19–32). New York: Vintage Books.

Smart School Task Force. (1997). *The Malaysian Smart School - An MSC Flagship Application: A conceptual blueprint*. Kuala Lumpur, Malaysia: Author.

Telem, M. (2001). Computerization of school administration: impact on the principal's role – a case study. *Computers & Education*, *37*, 345–362. doi:10.1016/S0360-1315(01)00058-6

Ya'akob, A., Mohd Nor, N. F., & Azman, H. (2005). Implementation of the Malaysian Smart School: an investigation of teaching-learning practices and teacher-student readiness. *Internet Journal of e-Language Learning and Teaching, 2*(2).

Zain, M. Z. M., Atan, H., & Idrus, R. M. (2004). The impact of information and communication technology (ICT) on the management practices of Malaysian Smart Schools. *International Journal of Educational Development*, *24*(2), 201–211. doi:10.1016/j.ijedudev.2003.10.010

Zhao, Y. (Ed.). (2003). *What teachers should know about technology: Perspectives and practices*. Greenwich, CT: Information Age Publishing.

ENDNOTE

[1] The smart school pilot project was initially implemented in 82 schools in 1999. Since then, a total of 6 newly constructed schools in the Klang valley were included in the pilot project. These 6 schools are SMK Putrajaya 1, Sekolah Alam Shah, Sekolah Seri Puteri, SK Putrajaya 1, SK Putrajaya 2 and SMK Bintang Selatan. SMK Sungai Pusu was formerly known as SMK Ulu Yam during its construction phase. SMK (P) Bukit Bintang was renamed SMK Seri Bintang Utara in 2000.

Chapter 3
eSME Slovenia:
Initiative and Action Plan for the Accelerated Introduction of E-Business in SMEs

Andreja Pucihar
University of Maribor, Slovenia

Gregor Lenart
University of Maribor, Slovenia

ABSTRACT

This chapter introduces e-strategies, initiatives and action planes in the European Union intended for the successful implementation of the Lisbon Strategy, according to which Europe should become the most competitive and dynamic society based on knowledge by 2010. These strategies are the baseline for the national policies, strategies and initiatives in every European Union country. The chapter presents policies, legislation environment and initiatives being adopted in Slovenia. Moreover, data about e-business development in Slovenia is also presented. As in other EU countries, it is evident that SMEs are generally lagging behind large organizations as far as the adoption and usage of e-commerce is concerned. The situation was a background for the preparation of the eSMEs Slovenia initiative and action plan to accelerate e-business introduction and adoption in SMEs. The initiative and action plan consist of 12 actions, which are elaborated in this chapter. The initiative was supported by the ministers of the Ministry of Higher Education and Technology, the Ministry of Public Administration, the Ministry of Economy, the Ministry of Finance, the Ministry of Economic Growth and Development and other involved institutions. Thus, the initiative presents an important framework for the further uptake of e-business adoption by SMEs. The chapter is concluded by a summary of the chapter's main contributions.

INTRODUCTION

Presently, companies are faced with a rapidly changing business environment with raised customer expectations in expanded markets with increased competition. This increases the pressure on companies to change their existing business practices and procedures to achieve lower total costs of operation in the entire supply chain (Umble

DOI: 10.4018/978-1-60566-388-3.ch003

et al., 2003; Jafari et al., 2006) and efficiently coordinate business operations in global markets.

Successful adoption and implementation of information and communication technologies (ICT) enables companies to actively and efficiently participate in local, regional and global markets. E-commerce, defined as the buying and selling of information, products, and services via computer networks, including servicing customers, collaboration with business partners and conducting of electronic transactions (Turban et al., 2008; Kartiwi and MacGregor, 2007; Kalakota and Whinston, 1997) is radically changing the dynamics of the business environment and the way in which people and organizations are conducting business with one another. For SMEs, e-commerce has the potential to become a source of competitive advantage. E-commerce is a cost effective way of accessing customers globally and competing equally with large businesses (Kartiwi and MacGregor, 2007).

Although SMEs are generally considered to be flexible, adaptive and innovative (Rao, et al., 2003) and thus have more ability to respond to the new opportunities and innovations than larger enterprises (Lomerson et al., 2004), various studies have reported that SMEs are generally lagging behind large organizations as far as the adoption and usage of e-commerce is concerned (Eleftheriadou, 2008; Kartiwi and MacGregor, 2007; Levy et. al., 2005; Levenburg, 2005; Chitura, 2008; Riquelme, 2002). This is becoming a serious issue since SMEs make up the backbone of the European economy. Across the EU, there are around 23 million SMEs; i.e. 99% of all enterprises (Eleftheriadou, 2008; European Commission, 2008; European Commission, 2002). SMEs account for about 75 million jobs. Moreover, in some key industries, such as textiles, construction and furniture-making, they account for as much as 80% of all jobs. They are, therefore, the generators of dynamic and economic growth (Eleftheriadou, 2008; European Commission, 2008).

SMEs are not simply scaled-down large businesses. They have special characteristics that distinguish them from large businesses. Although size is a major distinguishing factor, SMEs also differ from large companies in important ways affecting their ICT adoption (Bouanno et al., 2005, Ramdani and Kawalek, 2009). Many SMEs report practical difficulties in adoption of e-business. SMEs often lack of inadequate levels of technical expertise, a lack of managerial resources, a lack of financial resources for ICT investments and a lack of awareness about possible benefits of ICT usage (Pucihar et al., 2009, Kartiwi and MacGregor, 2007, MacGregor and Vrazalic, 2005, Cragg and King, 1993). Many SMEs also consider a lack of trust and confidence as barriers to their engagement in B2B e-business (European Commission, DG Enterprise and Industry, 2008a). In contrast, the perceived benefits, organisational readiness, and external pressure seem to be major drivers for ICT adoption (Mehrtens et al., 2001). Past experience has indicated that currently obstacles or incentives for a broader use of e-business are especially dependent on the standard commercial practices, business environment as well as the state examples and incentives.

In this challenging race of competitiveness and excellence, where new technologies and innovation play a central role, SMEs cannot afford to be left behind. For this reason, more and more governments around the world have been seeking opportunities to promote ICT and e-business models as a way of enhancing the competitiveness of their SMEs (Eleftheriadou, 2008). Governments in many countries have established intervention projects and offer financial incentives to encourage SMEs to adopt the internet and subsequently to develop e-commerce systems that will enable them to trade more effectively with business partners (Levy et al 2005, Zhu et al. 2003; Stansfield and Grant, 2003; Chitura, 2008).

EU efforts for the implementation of the Lisbon Strategy, according to which Europe should become the most competitive and dynamic society based on knowledge by 2010, are largely also based on building an environment that will stimulate growth and performance of SMEs. In this direction the EU has identified numerous challenges that SMEs encounter and made numerous guidelines and action plans. Several strategic documents have been launched in this direction: Lisbon Strategy 2000, eEurope 2002, eEurope 2005, i2010 and Helsinki Manifest 2006 - "The Helsinki Manifesto - We have to move fast before it is too late".

Each European country strives to achieve the Lisbon strategy goals and tries to provide the supporting environment that will help to achieve these goals. The Government of the Republic of Slovenia has launched the strategic document "si2010" with an action plan for the faster and better development of Information Society in Slovenia. The document provides technological, societal and regulative frameworks for the full development of Information Society. Faster e-business implementation in SME sector is one of the strategic goals of this strategic document (Government of the Republic of Slovenia, 2007).

In Slovenia, a country with no more than two million citizens, 96.2% of enterprises are micro or small enterprises in which 45.0% of employees are employed. In the less than 1% of Slovenian enterprises that are ranked among large enterprises, one third of employees are employed (SURS – Statistični urad Republike Slovenije, 2007).

In spite of this, many SMEs still operate mostly on local markets based on traditional paper-based commerce. All of these companies need support, education and training to better understand and adopt e-business advantages. With broader adoption of e-business, SMEs would be able to simplify their business processes, lower operational costs, accelerate productivity and achieve equal position on national, European and global markets.

Slovenia has implemented legislation on e-business, e-signatures and the protection of documentary and archive materials and archives, has achieved a 91% rate of electronic payment

transactions and established national standards for electronic document exchange (e-Slog). This is the groundwork for the broader uptake of e-business in companies that need incentives from the environment and the state.

The situation shows several opportunities for accelerated introduction and implementation of e-business for SMEs. For these purposes, appropriate IT solutions, awareness creating, advanced training and consulting is needed.

Considering the situation, the "eSMEs Initiative and Action plan" for the broader adoption of e-business to SMEs has been prepared by representatives from IT industry, government institutions and universities in Slovenia. It represents the initiative to all actors in Slovenia that could contribute to the faster introduction, training and adoption of new ICT solutions and e-business in SMEs. The "eSMEs Initiative" proposes an action plan for ICT and e-solutions providers, larger organizations, universities, chambers of commerce and industry, chambers of crafts, technological platforms, supporting SMEs environment (such as regional development agencies) and government institutions.

The section further presents e-strategies, initiatives and action plans in EU and Slovenian e-strategies, initiatives and implementation related to policy making and umbrella e-strategies, e-business legislation environment and infrastructure and usage. Further on, developing e-strategies for SMEs are presented with adoption of national standards for e-commerce, eSME initiative and activities and status of e-SMEs initiatives.

E-STRATEGIES, INITIATIVES AND ACTIONS PLANS IN EU

In March 2000, the Lisbon European Council summit issued a new strategic goal for the Europe for the next decade: to become the most competitive and dynamic knowledge-based economy in the world, capable of sustainable economic growth with more and better jobs and greater social cohesion. The target date for achieving these goals was set at 2010. Achieving this goal requires an overall strategy aimed at (European Parliament, 2000):

- preparing the transition to a knowledge-based economy and society with better policies for the information society and R&D, as well as by stepping up the process of structural reform for competitiveness and innovation and by completing the internal market;
- modernizing the European social model, investing in people and combating social exclusion;
- sustaining a healthy economic outlook and favourable growth prospects by applying an appropriate macro-economic policy mix.

Implementing this strategy will be achieved by improving the existing processes, introducing a new open method of coordination at all levels, coupled with a stronger guiding and coordinating role for the European Council to ensure more coherent strategic direction and effective monitoring of progress.

The Lisbon Council agreed that progress should be evaluated at the spring meetings of the European Council of Heads of State or Government. Since then, every spring the European Council has discussed matters associated with the Lisbon process, evaluated the progress made by the European Union and the Member States and decided on further measures to be taken. European Commission reports form the basis for the analysis and for setting priorities (European Council, 2008).

For example, during the Finnish presidency of EU in the second half of 2006, the Helsinki Manifesto was launched. The manifesto emphasized that new, concrete measures are needed for turning the Lisbon Strategy into a living reality and making Europe more competitive and innovative in a human-centred way. The following initiatives were launched: opening EU-wide procurement of R&D for innovation within public services, opening EU-wide procurement of R&D for innovation within public services, the European Network of Living Labs as a way to enhance European innovativeness, increasing interoperability and creating EU-wide standards and eServices, setting up a Strategic Task Force over the Presidencies in 2007-2008, the horizontal programme within the 7th Framework programme for EU-wide knowledge-intensive service society development and enabling working environments (Finland EU presidency, 2006).

During Slovenia's EU presidency in first half of 2008, in respect of the four pillars or main strands of the Lisbon Strategy, the emphases were as follows (Slovenia EU presidency, 2008):

- Member States should strive to adopt measures to promote creativity and enterprise with a view to making Europe the most creative environment in the world;
- Europe's economic and social development should centre upon its cultural heritage and richness;
- investment in human resources and framing measures to ensure flexicurity are of crucial importance for Europe;
- environmental policy should be highlighted as a key force driving innovation and economic growth.

The i2010 strategy, launched on 1 June 2005, was the first coherent policy framework for the era of convergent telecommunication and media services. The i2010 strategy brings together all European Union policies, initiatives and actions that aim to boost the development and the use of digital technologies in everyday working and private life. These technologies – also known as information and communication technologies (ICT) – make a positive contribution to economic growth, job creation and the enhancement of the quality of life. i2010 is part of the Lisbon strategy to make Europe a more competitive and dynamic knowledge-driven economy (European Commission, DG Information Society and Media, 2008).

i2010 aims to establish a European information space, i.e. a true single market for the digital economy so as to exploit fully the economies of scale offered by Europe's 500 million strong consumer market; reinforce innovation and investment in ICT research, given that ICTs are a principle driver of the economy; and promote inclusion, public services and quality of life, i.e. extending the European values of inclusion and quality of life to the information society (European Commission, DG Information Society and Media, 2008).

Another accelerator of Lisbon strategy adoption was the eEurope 2005 Action Plan that was launched at the Seville European Council in June 2002 and endorsed by the Council of Ministers in the eEurope Resolution of January 2003. It aimed to develop modern public services and a dynamic environment for e-business through the widespread availability of broadband access at competitive prices and a secure information infrastructure (European Commission, DG Information Society, 2005).

In 1998, the European Commission has launched the 5th Framework program to strengthen the European Union's research, technological development and demonstration; this framework lasted to 2002. From 2002 to 2006, the 6th Framework program was launched and in 2007 the 7th Framework program was launched for the 2007-2013 period. The Seventh Framework Programme (FP7) bundles all research-related EU initiatives together, playing a crucial role in reaching the goals of growth, competitiveness and employment; along with a new Competitiveness and Innovation Framework Programme (CIP), Education and Training programmes, and Structural and Cohesion Funds for regional convergence and competitiveness. It is also a key pillar for the European Research Area (ERA) (Information So-

ciety Technologies, 2008; Cordis, 2007). The ICT Work Programme under FP7 is divided into seven 'Challenges' of strategic interest to European society, plus research into 'Future and Emerging Technologies' and support for horizontal actions, such as international cooperation (Cordis, 2007):

- **Challenge 1:** Pervasive and trusted network and service infrastructures
- **Challenge 2:** Cognitive systems, interaction and robotics
- **Challenge 3:** Components, systems and engineering
- **Challenge 4:** Digital libraries and content
- **Challenge 5:** Sustainable and personalized healthcare
- **Challenge 6:** Mobility, environmental sustainability and energy efficiency
- **Challenge 7:** Independent living and inclusion

The current achievements of European policies implementation in the field of e-business adoption are annually measured by the e-Business W@tch initiative, which studies the impact of ICT and e-business on enterprises, industries and the economy in general. It highlights barriers to a wider or faster uptake of ICT and identifies public policy challenges arising from these developments. In this way, it supports the work of the European Commission's Enterprise and Industry Directorate General to enhance the competitiveness of the ICT sector, and to facilitate the efficient uptake of ICT for European enterprises in general (European Commission, DG Enterprise and Industry, 2008b). The latest research results shows evidence that SMEs are generally lagging behind large organizations as far as the adoption and usage of e-commerce is concerned.

In the past few years many successful policy initiatives have been developed at national, regional or local levels to promote the innovative use of ICTs by SMEs. These policies could be further enhanced by networking, learning from each other, sharing good practice and ultimately coordinating actions to achieve broader EU-wide impact. This is why, in 2003, the Commission established the eBSN (European e-Business Support Network for SMEs), a virtual network of decision-makers and public policy experts, a tool to make existing e-Business policies more interconnected (eBSN, 2008).

The eBSN builds upon the results of the "Go Digital" initiative (2001-2003), an umbrella policy covering many activities to support SMEs in using ICT for doing business (Information Society 2001). In 2002, the benchmarking study on "national and regional policies in support of e-business for SMEs" found many successful policy initiatives in Europe, but pointed out that their efficiency could be further enhanced by learning from each other and sharing best practices and information material.

The eBSN was founded to address this goal, by improving co-operation and using synergies within the European e-business policy community. The activities of the eBSN focus on networking and the exchange of good policy practice. More specifically, the objectives are (eBSN, 2008):

• To bring together decision makers in the fields of e-business, with a view to sharing information and discussing strategic policy orientation;

• To provide a platform for policy coordination among Member States;

• To provide a "one-stop shop" for information about regional, national and European initiatives and funding possibilities for SMEs;

• To organize special meetings of governmental e-business experts as a platform for sharing practical experience and identifying future challenges.

The eBSN is open to all relevant policy initiatives in support of e-business for SMEs in the Member States, the Candidate Countries and the EEA EFTA States which are willing to share experience and information, as well as to e-business experts and representatives of the business community.

More recently, eBSN confirmed a new policy trend: the sectoral policy approach for e-business i.e. supporting SMEs to develop their e-business strategy in full cooperation with their business partners, i.e. their suppliers, customers, or knowledge providers. Emphasis is given to the productive use of ICT by an entire group of enterprises that are interacting in daily business transactions, either within the same sector or between interacting sectors.

Moreover, eBSN provides opportunities for international collaboration, among the eBSN members. A good example is to be found in the eInvoicing field: promoting "eInvoicing by SMEs," a very practical e-business initiative running under Finnish regional policy in South Karelia, was successfully transferred to Slovenia, thus demonstrating that the transferability of best practices in e-business is feasible. This in turn quickly triggered a new series of cross-border joint policy initiatives, between Slovenia, Italy, Croatia, Hungary and Austria. In parallel, the Finnish regional eInvoicing initiative expanded into cross-border exchanges with Sweden and Denmark.

With its activities, the eBSN is an important pillar of the ICT and e-business-related policies of DG Enterprise and Industry, in combination with other policy pillars (for example the Sectoral e-Business Watch Function, the European e-Skills Forum, ICT standardisation and interoperability and policies in support of a favourable legal environment for e-business).

Since 2005/06, eBSN has focused on the following thematic priorities (eBSN, 2008):

• Sector-specific approaches: identify which sectors are most promising for e-business support measures, and whether sectoral policy initiatives are more efficient than others;

- e-Business for micro-enterprises: discuss policies in this field and what should be the way forward;
- Improving e-business solutions for SMEs: review the specific needs of SMEs and identify good policy practices in helping SMEs to find appropriate solutions;
- e-Invoicing and e-procurement: identify public policies and public-private partnerships that aim at further promoting the efficient usage of e-procurement and e-invoicing in SMEs.

Much progress has been made in recent years. A few examples suffice to show the breadth of achievements: a new regulatory framework for audiovisual media services is in place; proposals to reform the regulation of electronic communications have been launched; regulation to create a single market for mobile phone use across borders is in operation; initiatives to boost online content in Europe are under discussion; major new R&D and innovation funding initiatives are up and running (the Seventh Research Framework and the ICT Policy Support Programme under the Competitiveness and Innovation Programme – CIP); ground-breaking public private partnerships (Joint Technology Initiatives) have just been launched; and new eInclusion initiatives are on track (European Commission, DG Information Society and Media, 2008).

Meanwhile, Europe is among the world leaders in the development of the digital economy. The European broadband market, with 90 million lines, has more subscribers than any other economic region, and half of European citizens use the internet on a regular basis. Some Member States top the world league in broadband take-up, mobile penetration, data traffic. But gaps between Member States are significant and Europe is under-investing when compared to other industrialized regions, as well as facing growing competition

from China and India. That is why the policy framework provided by i2010 is needed more than ever today (European Commission Information Society and Media, 2008b).

SLOVENIAN E-STRATEGIES, INITIATIVES AND IMPLEMENTATION

Policy Making and Umbrella E-Strategies

Each European country strives to efficiently adopt the European policies in its national environment. European countries therefore try to speed up the adoption of above mentioned policies by various national strategies.

In June 2007, the Slovenian government adopted the si2010 strategy with the main purpose of defining a national framework for promoting the development of the information society in Slovenia by 2010 and thereby setting development guidelines that take into consideration the technological, social and legal frameworks (Government of the Republic of Slovenia, 2007).

For the 2006-2013 period, further development of the information society is dictated by the Slovenian National Strategy for 2006-2013 (SRS), adopted in 2005, which specifies an "increase in global competitiveness through promoting innovation and entrepreneurship, spreading the use of information & communications technologies, and through efficient modernization and investments in training, education, learning and R&D" as one of the national development goals for this period. At the same time, the topic of the information society implicitly relates to all key priority development tasks and reform actions based thereupon, as defined in the Framework of Economic and Social Reforms for Increasing Welfare in Slovenia.

Based on these policies, individual bodies have already prepared plans for the future development of individual sectors, which also include individual fields of the information society. These are (Government of the Republic of Slovenia, 2007):

- e-Health 2010 – Strategy of computerizing the Slovenian healthcare system 2005-2010 (Government of the Republic of Slovenia, Ministry for Health, 2005);
- Strategy of transition to digital broadcasting (Government of the Republic of Slovenia, Ministry of the Economy, 2006);
- Strategy of the Republic of Slovenia for introducing fixed wireless systems on the territory of the Republic of Slovenia (Government of the Republic of Slovenia, Ministry of the Economy, 2006);
- Strategy of developing broadband data networks in the Republic of Slovenia (Government of the Republic of Slovenia, Ministry of the Economy, 2006);
- Strategy of e-government for the 2006-2010 period (SEP-2010) (Government of the Republic of Slovenia, Ministry of Public Administration, 2006);
- National strategy of e-learning 2006-2010 (Government of the Republic of Slovenia, Ministry of Higher Education, Science and Technology).

At the same time on the national level, the points of origin of the National Development Programme for 2007-2013 and the National Strategic Reference Framework for 2007-2013 were being prepared in order to take advantage of funding through structural funds. Here, areas relating to the information society represent priority development tasks in operative programmes for obtaining funding from the European Regional Development Fund and the European Social Fund.

This strategy will connect and harmonize the priority tasks and activities on the national level allowing pursuit of the adopted goals of the European and national development strategies (Government of the Republic of Slovenia, 2007).

The implications of si2010 towards the wider e-business implementation in Slovenian organizations lay in the following strategic goals (Government of the Republic of Slovenia, 2007):

- establishing a national infrastructure for broad-scale application of e-business systems (e-invoicing, e-payments, e-contracting) in SMEs;
- establishing a national interoperability framework to define integration schemes, and establishing principles to ensure interoperability between individual systems. This will create conditions that enable easier development of new application systems and their interoperability. The greatest advantage of the publicized integration schemes and the principles that these schemes were based on is their ease of reapplication.
- Promoting the reuse of thus established schemes would allow for the simplification of business operations, and the reduction of operating costs and costs of developing electronic services. It is imperative that a national portal be set up, whose purpose will be to create, publish and maintain the national interoperability framework. The national interoperability network will determine the minimum set of technical guidelines and specifications for managing information flows between the public sector, economic subjects and other segments of society. It will define all three aspects of interconnectivity of information systems: the organizational, semantic and technical aspects;
- establishing an environment to develop national open standards for electronic data interchange;
- establishing a single electronic register that will allow for collecting basic data on e-business.

To ensure the results in this field, Government of Republic of Slovenia intends to provide the following scope of activities (Government of the Republic of Slovenia, 2007):

- support for ensuring an efficient environment for encouraging the implementation of e-business in the B2B, B2C and B2G segments;
- encouraging, educating and exchanging best practices from the area of e-business (introduction to e-business, technology, legislation, advantages and threats, etc.);
- support for enterprises, especially SMEs, in their implementation of e-business in everyday operations;
- government incentives and facilities to introduce e-business to companies.

E-Business Legislation

Since the year 2000, e-Business in Slovenia has been regulated with the following legislation:

- Electronic Commerce and Electronic Signature Act (adopted in 2000 and has several amendments),
- Decree on Conditions for Electronic Commerce and Electronic Signatures (adopted in 2000)

Besides the fact that the Electronic Commerce and Electronic Signature Act implements Directive 1999/93/EC, it is also entirely in accordance with the provisions of the United Nations' Commission or the International Trade Law's (UNCITRAL) Model Law of electronic commerce.

Besides other regulations, the Electronic Commerce and Electronic Signature Act defines that electronic signatures are legally equivalent to a written signature and are admissible as evidences in legal proceedings.

The Decree on conditions for electronic commerce and electronic signature defines the requirements and conditions for certification-service providers.

The following act and decree regulate the archiving of electronic documents:

- Protection of Documents and Archives and Archival Institutions Act
- Decree on Protection of Documents and Archives

Both acts define methodological and organizational definitions of electronic archiving. The Decree further defines software and hardware conditions for e-archiving. The Value Added Tax Act defines which data is obligatory for invoices, also the time framework and special conditions regarding archiving invoices.

All these acts and decrees present the framework for the possible full deployment of e-business in Slovenia.

Infrastructure and Usage

Based on data of the Statistical Office of Republic in Slovenia (Zupan, 2007), in the first quarter of 2008, 97% of enterprises with 10 or more persons employed had internet access. 88% of enterprises used e-Government services.

The usage of intranets in enterprises depends on the activity and the size of the enterprise (number of persons employed). Intranet usage was highest in large enterprises (250 and more persons employed) with 74%, followed by medium-sized enterprises (50-249 persons employed) with 40% and small enterprises (10-49 persons employed) with 26%.

Fifteen percent of enterprises used third party free or open source operating systems that enable insight into the source code and the possibility of modifying it. The share increased by two percentage points in comparison with the same period of 2007. The usage is the highest in large enterprises with 51% (growth by 14 percentage points), while the share in small enterprises remained with 11%

unchanged in comparison with the same period of 2007.

In the first quarter of 2008, 97% of enterprises with 10 or more persons employed had internet access, which represents a one percentage point increase after the stagnation in the last three years. Ninety-two percent of enterprises with 10 or more persons employed used the internet for conducting banking and financial services and 41% for training and education of their employees. The share of enterprises that use e-Government services is increasing. In comparison with 2006, the share increased by 5 percentage points to 88% in 2007. The biggest increase of the usage of eGovernment services was perceived in small enterprises; by six percentage points to 86%.

In the first quarter of 2008, 71% of enterprises with 10 or more persons employed had a website, four percentage points more than in the same period of 2007. Regarding the size of the enterprise (number of persons employed), the share of enterprises increased the most in small enterprises; by six percentage points to 67% in comparison with the same period of 2007. The content and the presentation of the enterprises on the websites are also changing. A total of 42% of enterprises provided visitors access to product catalogues or price lists, 18% of enterprises published open job positions on their websites, 9% of enterprises enabled online ordering on their website and 2% of enterprises also online payment. The content of the website also depends on the size of the enterprise. Of large enterprises, 18% enabled online ordering, as did 9% of medium-sized and small enterprises. The percentage of enterprises that made online payment possible is also the highest in the large enterprises with 5%, in comparison to a 2% share in small and medium-sized enterprises.

In 2007, 11% of enterprises received orders via computer networks (via websites and EDI-Electronic Data Interchange). The value of orders received via computer networks represented 8% of total turnover of the enterprises (excluding VAT) with 10 or more persons employed. Six percent of enterprises sold their products and/or services via websites, one percentage point less than in 2006. Twenty-six percent of enterprises ordered goods and/or services via websites in 2007, three percentage points more than in 2006.

Automated data exchange was used by 40% of enterprises in the first quarter of 2008. The highest percentage of usage was with 72% between large enterprises. Twenty-one percent of enterprises received orders via automated data exchange, and 18% sent orders to their suppliers. For sending e-invoices, 4% of enterprises used automated data exchange (the same as in the same period of 2007); 7% of enterprises received e-invoices (increase by one percentage point in comparison with the same period of 2007). Eighteen percent of enterprises sent payment instructions to financial institutions via automated data exchange and 29% sent/received data to/from public authorities.

With their customers, 13% of enterprises shared information electronically on inventory levels, production plans or demand forecasts and 16% of enterprises on progress of deliveries. Nineteen percent of enterprises used websites and 8% automated data exchange to electronically share information. Twenty-seven percent of enterprises used electronic sharing of information on supply chain management, while 17% of enterprises electronically shared with their suppliers information on inventory levels, productions plans or demand forecast and 19% of enterprises on the progress of deliveries.

The reasons why enterprises do not use the automated data exchange: 20% lack of interest; 18% lack of appropriate software and 14% of enterprises do not use automated data exchange because the return of the investment is to low or the lack of in-house expertise. The problem of lack of in-house expertise (15%) and lack of appropriate software (19%) is the highest in small enterprises.

Although some results have shown progress in some areas of e-business adoption, it is obvious that

SMEs still lag behind large organizations, being less competitive in operation of their business.

DEVELOPING E-STRATEGIES FOR SMES

eSLOG Project; Standardization for E-Commerce

A good example of a national initiative for the fostering of e-business implementation in national environment was e-SLOG initiative. In 2001, the Chamber of Commerce and Industry of Slovenia in cooperation with large agriculture, manufacturing, electricity, wholesale, retail, transport and financial companies, and representatives from the public administration launched the e-SLOG project, which was aimed at developing simpler standards for electronic business messages and at promoting e-business among SMEs.

The primary purpose of the project was (Zupančič, 2004):

- The implementation of standardized electronic business documents for business operations between enterprises, financial institutions and public administration,
- The preparation and implementation of solutions for secure e-business by using e-signature technology,
- The implementation of open technological solutions for small, medium-sized and large enterprises as well as the promotion of e-business in the Slovenian enterprise sector.

The project was led by a Project Council, which directed and controlled the activities of the project, while the work was carried out by four working groups (Working Group for Business Content Standards, Working Group for Technological Solutions, Working Group for Electronic Signatures, Working Group for Payment Standards).

The project resulted in e-SLOG standards, a simplification of GS1 EANCOM. The standards have been integrated into pre-written business operating systems/enterprise resource planning solutions that automate all aspects of company management (accounting, finances, tracking materials, issuing orders etc.). As a result, every document that can be used in e-commerce is automatically composed according to e-SLOG standards by those systems. It has been estimated that investments in these applications have been paid off after an average six months. Smaller companies can also use computer-based services offered over a network by applications service providers (European Commission, 2007).

Companies mostly use e-SLOG schemes for invoicing, ordering and order confirmation, whereas schemes for control order and dispatch advice are only rarely used. While the standards have mainly positively affected the connections between large companies and their smaller partners, and between cluster companies, many small companies are still unaware of their existence or the benefits of e-commerce in general.

The project is unique in two aspects. The first is in the special approach of e-SLOG, where large companies were used as pioneers in using the standards, while market pressures than ensured that SMEs were quick to follow. The standards are now used by approximately 3,000 companies of all sizes in Slovenia.

In 2007, the project was presented as a national best practice approach for wider e-business implementation in European Commission report "Sectoral e-Business Policies in Support of SMEs. Innovative approaches, good practices and lessons to be learned".

eSMEs Initiative

Slovenia has legislation on e-business, e-signature and the protection of documentary and archive materials and archives, a 91% rate of electronic payment transactions and established national standards for document exchange (e-SLOG). Together with the si2010 strategy, this is the groundwork for the broader uptake of e-business in companies that need incentives from the environment and the state.

In December 2007, representatives of Faculty of Organizational Sciences at the University of Maribor, the company Datalab and the Public Agency for Entrepreneurship and Foreign Investments presented the eSMEs Initiative and Action plan for wider acceleration and implementation of e-business, especially in SMEs.

The action plan lays out proposed measures and activities to be carried out by the state in order to boost e-business between companies and the public administration. The document is limited to a comprehensive package of actions, incentives and small steps that are quickly actionable and yield immediate results. This would not require changing the existing legislation, but merely expanding its implementation in practice. The proposed measures follow the objectives of the European Commission and complement or carry on initiatives, projects and programmes already carried out in Slovenia.

The goals involve improving the competitiveness of the Slovenian economy by:

- Reducing the operating costs of companies and the public administration;
- Improving the phasing of European funds;
- Establishing registries in support of e-business;
- Raising the awareness of the benefits of ICT and the use thereof, not only in large but in particular in SMEs.

The action plan involves two levels – state and business. At the state level, it proposes incentives and measures that could benefit the target groups of the initiatives, whilst at the same time presenting additional proposals which could be introduced at the state level in order to help achieve the set objectives.

At the business level the introduction – and possible implementation – of the actions can further be divided between providers and users of solutions. The providers will play an instrumental role in arousing the users' interest for the introduction of new solutions in their business processes, taking part in the promotion of new solutions, and ensuring the inter-operability of the solutions and the carrying out of accompanying activities.

The action plan involves 12 actions that are described in more details further in this section.

Action No. 1: Programme Promoting the Introduction of Information and Communication Know-How in SMEs

The Introduction of Information and Communication Technologies in SMEs Training Companies programme is intended for improving the skills of employees in the support environment (employees of local entrepreneurial centres and specialist consultants), the promotion of use of new solutions in e-business and the promotion of application of these solutions at the level of SMEs and other target groups.

Goals or this action are the following:

- Supply of skilled consultants for the introduction of new technologies in business environments,
- Activation of the support network of local entrepreneurial centres and participation of faculties and other institutions in the introduction of new e-business solutions in SMEs,
- Participation of international experts in the promotion of use of e-business.

Implementation plan:

- Preparation of expert papers and the development of a methodology for the implementation of selected e-business segments in SMEs,

- Training of employees in support institutions for the promotion of introduction of new e-business and ICT technologies and solutions in SMEs,
- Training of independent providers of consultancy services (consultants) for the introduction of new e-business and ICT technologies and solutions in SMEs,
- Transfer of know-how from international experts as part of technical assistance,
- Design of promotional materials and activities.

Action No. 2: Voucher Consultancy Programme for the Introduction of E-Business in Micro Companies and SMEs

The purpose of the voucher consultancy programme is to motivate entrepreneurs to consult experts and attend training programmes in order to obtain additional knowledge and skills to equip themselves for independent resolution of problems and seizing of business opportunities. As a result, the programme increases the number of dynamic, fast-growing SMEs, preserves old and creates new jobs, and encourages self-employment. The programme also includes consulting on e-business.

The goals of this action are the following:

- Provide appropriate expert support for the introduction of e-business in business systems,
- Increase the use of ICT solutions,
- Improve the efficiency of investment in ICT,
- Give employees appropriate skills.

Implementation plan:

The programme pools the resources of various providers to offer different target groups subsidised consultancy and training services. Access to services is guaranteed through local providers who represent access points where potential users of services can enrol in a programme and use its services. The beneficiaries of the programme can get subsidised consultancy and training services from selected consultants registered in a catalogue of entrepreneurship consultants published on the web page www.japti.si.

Action No. 3: Mandatory Sending of Invoices to the Public Administration in Electronic Form

Advanced countries have introduced electronic invoices in their public finances and thus significantly simplified and sped up transactions, reduced processing and archiving costs and brought in additional services for public sector suppliers and customers.

The current state of readiness in Slovenia is very high at the declarative level but very low at the operational level. 2006 was a year of preparation for the adoption of the euro, which meant all initiatives for the introduction of cutting-edge solutions were postponed. Nevertheless, it is only a question of time before the public administration is forced to streamline its operations through electronic services.

The initiative includes a proposal for an approach to the introduction of electronic invoices in the public sector which is based on existing best practices of the single state accounting system and envisages the formation of a Processing Centre for Electronic Invoices at the same level as the state accounting system, i.e. at the Ministry of Finance.

The public administration adopts the decision (like the US[1] before it with the Clinton memorandum of 1993 and Denmark with the decree on the issuance and reception of e-invoices in 2005[2]) that it wishes to receive invoices for delivered goods and services electronically. Sending is carried out on the basis of e-SLOG (business documents electronic schemes) or the BMS standard (GS1 standard).

In the event that the supplier is not capable of electronic invoicing, it is charged the cost of manual processing after the expiry of a six-month transitional period. To mitigate technological conditions and requirements for SMEs, their accounting firms or other authorised companies may e-invoice on their behalf.

The goals of this action are the following:

- Considerable reduction of the workload in the entry and archiving of received invoices in public administration and the reduction of associated costs[3].
- Creating a critical mass of e-business users.

The result:

- The introduction of uniform standards of communication between suppliers and the state, which will also be used for mutual e-invoicing,
- Due to e-business with the state, companies, suppliers and public sector customers will use e-business for mutual transactions,
- Transactions between companies and with the state will effect a simplification of single standards and solutions, which will gradually be more broadly adopted by SMEs as well as in transactions with physical persons,
- The introduction of new solutions and greater use of e-business will encourage the development of new services and lead to new providers on the market; for example, providers of e-invoice management who will offer go-between and archiving services as well as gross settlement, direct debit and others.

Implementation plan:

E-invoicing will require new ways of checking and confirming the payment of invoices. The existing processing methods for hardcopy invoices will remain intact, but it is expected that the volume of e-invoicing is going to increase, which will make it possible to streamline processing. In any case, both pathways will run simultaneously in the first phase.

Unlike paper invoices made out directly to the contracting party, e-invoices for the whole state will be collected at a single entry point. Access to e-invoices will be granted to employees depending on their clearance. The authorising body confirms payment (unless the authority is transferred).

Accordingly, the management of received invoices requires the following basic processes:

- Tight integration with the MFERAC system which contains data on bodies (items, projects, contracts/orders, depositaries of contracts and items),
- Record of received e-invoices in which checking and confirmation or rejection of e-invoice are administered,
- Direct transfer of data on approved e-invoices to the MFERAC,
- Storage of e-invoices.

The number of participants in the process will be high, which requires appropriate customer support processes as well as reports and statistics.

The MFERAC application needs to be adapted to support e-invoices in e-SLOG and BMS formats, which is feasible over a three to six month period. In the first phase, only incoming e-invoices would be implemented (which represents the biggest cost saving for the state), whereupon e-invoice issuance and e-order reception and issuance would be phased in.

Most of the infrastructure is in place or at least designed. It is possible to use the main building blocks of the e-taxes system; the legislative framework is in place, as is the design concept for the required technological platform.

The introduction of the solution was managed by the Ministry of Finance, which manages state accounting and is overwhelmed by huge quantities of hardcopy documents (invoices and annexes).

Implementation of the Processing Centre for Electronic Invoices would proceed through several phases and involve the provision of the following services:

- E-invoicing by large suppliers (package),
- E-invoicing by random suppliers and interactive invoice creation,
- Reception of scanned paper invoices and processing thereof by the public administration,
- Issuance of e-invoices by the public administration (e.g. schools, kindergartens).

Accordingly, new legal frameworks need to be put in place (executive regulations issued by the Finance Ministry), new processes implemented and the organisation of transactions changed.

As the workload associated with the processing and control of received invoices is reduced, this will free up human resources in financial departments. This staff can then be assigned to other departments or tasked with performing higher-value-added services.

E-business reduces the need for the physical archiving of hardcopy documents, but it increases the need for optimal and safe management of electronic archives. We propose that a part of the savings over the coming years be channelled into the creation of additional e-services which will improve the user experience of citizens.

Action No. 4: Investment in E-Business Eligible for Development Relief

Tax policy is a key instrument of the state for directing the investment activities of companies. This measure is central to, and vital for, the broad uptake of e-business.

The Finance Ministry adopted a supplement to the Rules on Exercising the Rights to Relief concerning investments in research and development[4] making investment in e-business a tax deductible development relief in 2007 and 2008.

The investment is deducted as lump sum depending on the type of electronic exchange. The

lump sum is taken in order to simplify accounting and checking.

Two types of development investments are deductible: exchange of data with the public administration, inter-company e-invoicing, electronic archiving and electronic inspection.

The goal of this action is the following:

- Raising awareness of the importance of corporate investment in e-business and a broad of technology facilitating e-business across all segments of the economy.

Implementation plan:

- **Exchange of data with the public administration.** If a company submits in 2007 at least 6 VAT return forms electronically and commits to submitting all VAT return forms electronically in the next two years, it is eligible for a EUR 4,200 lump sum tax deduction[5]. The measure is associated with the Tax Procedure Act (ZdavP-2) in which electronic submittal of VAT return forms is already mandatory for large enterprises and becoming mandatory for all taxpayers as of 1.1.2009. The same tax relief is available for companies filing forms on behalf of other companies (e.g. accounting firms). Companies whose forms are filed by proxies (accounting firms) are not eligible.
- **Inter-company e-invoicing.** Upon the introduction of electronic data exchange (either e-SLOG, EDIFACT or BMS), a company registers at the Agency for Public and Legal Records and Services (AJPES) as ready for e-business. Once it has exchanged at least 100 documents electronically, it becomes eligible for the EUR 4,200 tax deduction.
- **E-archiving.** Upon the introduction of electronic archiving of data and the obtaining of the appropriate permits, a com-

pany is eligible for a tax deduction of EUR 2,100.

- **E-inspection.** Upon introduction of electronic data exchange for e-inspection in accordance with the format prescribed by the Tax Administration,[6] a company is eligible for a tax deduction of EUR 420.

Action No. 5: Co-Financing of E-Business in the National Development Programme 2007-2013

The Government Office of Local Self-Government and Regional Policy (Office) has prepared the second draft of the National Development Programme 2007-2013 (NDP)[7] for public debate. The second draft, which has been published online, is still missing several sections, in particular those conditional on the national budgets for 2007 and 2008. The NDP deals with content that will be co-funded from the EU budget in the 2007-2013 financial perspective, so the drafting process involves informal communication with the European Commission. The Office is completing the Operational Programmes which – after they have been coordinated with all stakeholders and confirmed by the European Commission – will represent the basis for the phasing of European funds in the 2007-2013 financial perspective.

The Ministry of Higher Education, Science and Technology has participated in the design of operational programmes of EU funding priorities as the competent ministry. The NDP envisages EUR 20m for the development of e-content and e-services in the 2007-2013 period.

Financial assistance will be given to providers of e-business services for faster development and design of software or services for e-business of third companies. Only companies whose products or services are based on open standards (domestic or international) and which support interoperability are eligible for the funds.

Co-funding priority is given to projects involving products and services whose introduction or use makes companies eligible for tax relief specified in Action No. 4.

The goals of this action are the following:

- Advanced, simple and cost-efficient software for e-business.
- Operational e-business services (e.g. document exchange, e-archives).

Implementation plan:
Funding is available for companies developing:

- Systems or services for submittal of e-forms and other data to the state,
- Systems or services for electronic exchange of business documents,
- E-archiving systems,
- Business support systems,
- Support systems for the above mentioned systems.

The disbursement of Slovenian as well as mixed (Slovenian-European) funds will be carried out through established channels. Since availability depends on negotiations, certain activities and funds need to be planned as soon as the funds are available. Co-funding priority is given to projects that can be quickly implemented and projects with great impact (many potential users).

Action No. 6: Portals Offering Information on Best E-Business Practice

The key to the general adoption of best practices of cooperation in e-business lies in the appropriate dissemination of knowledge. This calls for the creation and popularisation of web portals, libraries of knowledge about solutions, services and best practices in e-business. Additionally, dissemination of knowledge may usefully involve providers of business software who can prepare documentation for e-business in their solutions and publish it on their web pages, which are frequently visited by their existing users. Communication between portals would be desirable, while the creation of a joint search engine would be ambitious.

The goals of this action are the following:

- Portal with information structured depending on skill level, existing use of e-business and the absorption capacity of e-business users.
- E-business content on portals intended for users of business software (instructions for fast and cost-effective implementation).

Implementation plan:

The preparation of project proposals for obtaining funds for e-business portals is needed. Public-private partnerships with educational institutions are desired. This portal will present examples of best practices related to Action No. 8 (e-business in supply chains) and No. 9 (best e-company). For that purpose organization of public tender for co-financing of preparation of best practices portal is needed.

Action No. 7: Opening and Adaptation of State Registries to E-Services

Presently companies must enter by hand and correct basic information on companies, which represents a significant administrative burden considering the demand for absolute correctness. At the same time, serious use of e-business requires a registry of e-business-enabled companies. The registry of legal entities operated by AJPES must be opened to public use[8] and upgraded with e-business attributes. Alternatively, the existing tax registry which already contains this data could be used. This proposal implements the Decree on Digital Certificate record system (Official Gazette RS, no. 128/2006).

The goals of this action are the following:

- Up-to-date information on companies and sole traders,
- Drastic drop in operating errors,
- Full automation and reliability of delivery of electronic messages.

Implementation plan:

The AJPES creates a web service with automatic search and acquisition of company data (name, tax file number, company ID number, address, contact information, status, bank account numbers, etc.). In addition, AJPES makes a registry of e-business data in which a company applying for e-business enters which standards it uses and which documents it can send and receive. The minimum that a company must meet is the reception and issuance of e-invoices. At registration, the company pays AJPES a one-time registration fee of EUR 16. Correction of entered data is electronic and free of charge.

The AJPES creates a public web service based on the eBXML (ISO 15000) standard, which makes it possible for every computer to establish which data can be sent electronically by using a company's tax file number. This service has been provided by AJPES for at least 10 years.

Action No. 8: Introduction of a Single System for Calculation and Payment of Fees

The existing tax regulations and regulations governing individual forms of social insurance (pension, disability, health, and unemployment insurance) provide for different methods of administering registries of taxpayers and insurants. In practice, the same records are kept in different ways by different authorities, while some records are not kept by any authority. Similarly, existing records on the calculation and payment of taxes and contributions, especially contributions from salaries, are incomplete and turn out to be a limiting factor in the exercise of pension and health insurance rights and in the settlement of tax obligations.

On the basis of the recently completed reform of the tax system, some adopted but not yet fully realised provisions of tax regulations (Tax Procedure Act – ZdavP-2) and pension and disability insurance (Pension and Disability Insurance Act – ZPIZ-1), we propose a single system of registration, reporting on levied taxes and contributions and the payment thereof.

The goals of this action are the following:

The following goals could be achieved with the implementation of this concept:

- Better framework for the observance of tax and other regulations and more efficient collection of taxes and contributions,
- Reorganisation and modernisation of participant institutions (in particular, the Tax Administration and the Pension and Disability Insurance Institute),
- Removal of unnecessary burdens of complex reporting and payment for taxable persons,
- Transparent work of state institutions.

Implementation plan:

The creation of a single registry of all persons liable for taxes/contributions and all insurants (pension, disability, health and unemployment insurance), forms a new system of reporting on levied and paid taxes and contributions, which will be available to all state institutions for the performance of their basic tasks. This concept is based on best practices in other countries as well as recommendations by international financial institutions.

The management of the central registry and the collection and keeping of data should be carried out by the Tax Administration, which already operates the tax registry that contains most of the data for the future central registry that is acquired either from other institutions or directly from taxable persons. The initial central registry would be based on the tax registry as well as the registries of other state authorities (Pension and Disability Insurance Institute, Health Insurance Institute, Employment Service and over 20 registers of independent activities). As the operator of the registry, the Tax Administration would give institutes and, in certain cases, companies' permanent access to the central registry so that they can use the data as per their jurisdiction.

The second part consists of an altered method for the collection and processing of data on levied taxes and contributions. Employees would submit to the Tax Administration (before or at payment of personal income) a single calculation of taxes and contributions (as already defined in existing legislation due to take effect on 1.7.2008). Real time delivery of these calculations would eliminate the need for ex post (for the previous year) delivery of control data by employers and render income tax statements obsolete. This would reduce the costs of administration and improve the transparency of the tax system.

The Tax Administration would check whether the data is correct, on time and complete in single calculations immediately upon reception of the data. Considering the quantity of data and forms (approx. one million forms per month), persons liable would be requested to submit the forms electronically. Insurants would carry out all the correspondence uniformly through a single access point, while tax officials would deal mostly with supervisory procedures.

The third part of the concept entails a change in the system for payment of taxes and contributions. Instead of the current multitude of accounts and payment orders, the proponent of the single tax and contributions account would settle the obligation with a single payment on one order to the account of the Tax Administration. Only the taxable person's tax number would be used as the reference for payment.

The existing solution in which payment of taxes and contributions is carried out for each tax type and each recipient separately, with the Tax

Administration managing over 3,000 tax accounts and persons liable completing payments through a complex multitude of payment orders separately for each account, would be replaced with a system where all taxes and contributions are payable to a single account at the Tax Administration. The Tax Administration would transfer the funds from this single account to the state's central account on a daily basis, specifying the recipients (national budget, institutes, municipalities, other recipients). The Treasury would disburse the funds to the appropriate recipients on the same day.

The Tax Administration provides all users of the central registry with real time data on all levied taxes and contributions through a new information system[9]. Under appropriate conditions, all data could be used for other purposes (e.g. statistical monitoring and analysis, social and other transfers).

Action No. 9: Introduction of Electronic Certificates

Despite the provisions of Article 139 of the Administrative Procedure Act (ZUP), the public administration requests from companies and individuals certain proofs in processes that it carries out itself and which it could obtain itself. One such example is the demand stemming from the Public Procurement Act (ZJN) for the submittal of proof of paid taxes with every bid. The same is true for the exercise of social rights, where individual state bodies demand that citizens submit the decision on the assessment of personal income tax as proof of income. These proofs are a result of computerised records in public administration systems and therefore easily electronically accessible to all appropriate authorities.

Goal of this action is the following:

The introduction of electronic checking/acquisition of proofs in tax records eliminates the unnecessary burden of cumbersome acquisition of paper proofs for companies and individuals.

Implementation plan:

Through e-taxes, the Tax Administration provides the option of electronic orders (for companies and citizens) and electronic automated checking (for other state authorities) of data from tax records.

Action No. 10: Initiative "I Don't Spend, I Invest"

An SME initiative in which companies urge their suppliers to send documents electronically and express their intention to migrate to full electronic business in the shortest possible period with the purpose of reducing costs. The initiative is open for all companies and does not require membership.

The goal of this action is the following:

In the first phase, SMEs receive e-invoices from major suppliers (e.g. telecoms, post, energy), whereupon they involve all other suppliers until a critical mass is achieved and e-business becomes the dominant form.

Implementation plan:

A template letter is prepared, which companies (in particular SMEs) send out to their suppliers. The letter states that they want to become an even better and more stable customer, which however requires modernisation and a reduction of costs of cooperation. The letter defines a transitional period of at least six months in which the supplier must send invoices (and other documents) electronically. If after the expiry of the transitional period the supplier does not regularly send e-invoices, the buyer may reduce the payment due to the supplier by for example EUR 4.20 per invoice.

Suppliers are divided to multiple groups depending on the number and complexity of received invoices, and gradually signed up for the programme.

A special logo is designed, which is consistently used in promotional activities, letters and other materials in order to raise awareness of the initiative.

The initiative is promoted by chambers, business support organisations and the companies themselves.

Action No. 11: Initiative "E-Business in Supply Chains"

This incentive is intended for larger and large enterprises which have clout with suppliers. It is designed to cut the costs of supply and introduce appropriate infrastructure for just-in-time delivery in order to improve competitiveness.

Whereas Action No. 10 deals with the basic use of e-business, this initiative goes one step further technologically in that it supports the tighter integration of systems. In addition to e-invoices, these supply chains use a wider range of electronic messages on, for example, inventories and orders.

The goals of this action are the following:

- Boost the competitiveness of large enterprises,
- Improve the competitiveness of Slovenian suppliers,
- Establishing best practices for future cross-border cooperation,
- Establishing best practices for broader use of advanced integration.

Implementation plan:

Companies identify their main suppliers and agree with them to introduce the electronic exchange of at least e-invoices if not other documents. Larger enterprises organise internal seminars to which suppliers are invited. If possible, the IT staff of larger enterprises should help the suppliers.

It would be very useful to have a public recognition for companies that provide suppliers with the best assistance in this joint improvement of competitiveness.

Action No. 12: Recognition for Best E-Company in Slovenia

Affirmation and awareness of the role of e-business is a vital component. Accordingly, we propose a competition for the best Slovenian e-company carried out by the Public Agency of the Republic of Slovenia for Entrepreneurship and Foreign Investments (JAPTI) with the sponsorship of the Ministry of Higher Education, Science and Technology. It would be ideal if the award was conferred personally by the minister, as this would give the competition appropriate media attention. The competition was started in 2007 and became an annual practice in 2008.

The goals of this action are the following:

- Media recognition for companies investing in e-business.
- Promotion of best practice.
- Implementation of examples of best practice.

Implementation plan:

Establishment of an annual award for the best e-company. The winner is the company with the most successful e-business implementation (e-invoices, web orders, e-archives, e-supply-chains etc.). Every applicant describes the applied solution and makes an economic assessment of it. There are multiple categories determined by a jury. In each category, the jury shortlists three finalists and selects the winners who are given commendations at the final ceremony.

Proposed categories:

- SMEs,
- Large enterprises,
- Best e-solution provider.

Descriptions of the e-business solutions of the finalists are published as examples of best practices by Slovenian enterprises on appropriate websites. The selection procedure is carried out by JAPTI and Chamber of Commerce and Industry of Republic of Slovenia, which organise the competition and the selection in conjunction with organisers of similar events and interested experts, and the award ceremony.

Activities and Status of e-SME

The eSMEs Action Plan and Initiative was supported by ministers of the Ministry of Higher Education and Technology, the Ministry of Public Administration, the Ministry of Economy, the Ministry of Finance, the Ministry of Economic Growth and Development and by the presidents of Chamber of Commerce and Industry of Slovenia, Chamber of Commerce of Slovenia, JAPTI (Public Agency for Entrepreneurship and Foreign Investments), the company Datalab and the Slovenian Business Software Developers KODA.SI, and representatives from the Faculty of Organisational Sciences of the University of Maribor.

However for further successful implementation of the action plan and initiative, all parties in the business environment must contribute: service providers, users of services, public administration and universities.

Most service providers already offer e-business services and solutions for SMEs. To support the action plan, the providers will have to design solutions for broader uptake of e-business and help train consultants. Successful introduction of e-business solutions in SMEs will give the providers the opportunity to transfer know-how and solutions to foreign markets.

Larger enterprises must improve competitiveness. In 2006, their resources were mainly focused on the adoption of the euro, which means that e-business was sidelined. The enterprises feel that and fear lagging behind so most have already announced "increased investment in e-business immediately after the introduction of the euro."[10]

SMEs are well integrated in the supply chains of larger enterprises, forming a tightly-knit ecosystem. Given proper incentive by larger enterprises and other measures, their cooperation is very likely.

Public administration must focus on companies and sole traders more than ever. It has to create conditions for simpler transactions with companies by:

- Simplifying procedures, which become faster and cheaper with the increasing use of ICT, as well as more accessible and transparent,
- Adopting appropriate regulations that facilitate the collection and use of data and information, reducing the burden of unnecessary double reporting,
- Introducing separate information sources and reusing collected data, disburdening data providers, accelerating procedures for the acquisition and checking of proofs, and avoiding unnecessarily disturbing companies, which allows them to focus on their core competences.

Specifically, this means:

- Formation of a single system for the collection of various (all) types of information from companies and sole traders for all public administration bodies,
- Introduction of mandatory sending and receiving of e-invoices,
- Introduction of mandatory reporting to the public administration in electronic format for all entities above a certain threshold, and the establishment of service centres for all below the threshold for the duration of the transitional period,
- Electronic fact checking is introduced for all proofs kept in databases in the public administration, starting with:
  ◦ Upgrade of the E-Taxes Portal with option of checking the statement of

paid tax obligations in public procurement procedures, which would reduce the number of documents by 100,000 and eliminate an unnecessary burden for bidders,

  ◦ Upgrade of the E-Taxes Portal with access to decision on assessment of income tax, for the purposes of checking statements about personal income,

• Introduction of mandatory e-invoicing by large and medium-sized enterprises within six months and for all others within one year,

• Providing access to the registry of taxable persons for the purposes of e-business.

Universities also have an important role, especially in education, training and ICT knowledge and ICT best practice implementation transfer to SMEs. In cooperation with regional development agencies for SMEs, Chambers of Commerce and Industry and Chambers of Crafts, universities create an important know-how environment for SMEs.

For example, the Faculty of Organizational Sciences of the University of Maribor has established the "Slovenia eLivingLab" focusing to the following areas of e-commerce: e-collaboration, e-invoicing, e-markets, RFID supply chain, e-government and eSMEs. The living lab is a new concept for R&D and innovation to boost the Lisbon strategy for jobs and growth in Europe. Living labs can be defined in several ways because of the major differences between operating living labs. However, one thing is common for all: the human-centred involvement and its potential for development of new ICT-based services and products. It is all done by bringing different stakeholders together in a co-creative way (European Network of Living Labs, 2006).

"Slovenia eLivingLab" has been a member of European Network of Living Labs since 2006 (European Network of Living Labs, 2006). The idea of living labs was launched during the Finnish presidency in 2006, aimed at bringing new concepts for research & development and innovation to boost the Lisbon strategy for jobs and growth in Europe. The European Commission has supported the idea under the common umbrella European Network of Living Labs, which is now a mature initiative sponsored by the European Community through various programmes and coordinating actions.

As living labs are bringing together all parties that need to be involved for innovative human-centred product or service development, including users, ICT providers, government and universities), this is a promising approach to bring eSMEs initiative and action plan into the life.

SUMMARY

SMEs are a key part of European industry. There are some 23 million of them in the European Union (EU), providing around 75 million jobs and accounting for 99 percent of all enterprises (Eleftheriadou, 2008).

Nonetheless, SMEs are the firms that suffer the most from their limited possibilities to fully exploit the ICT potential. SMEs often lack the managerial understanding, the knowledge, and the skills required to fully grasp the potential of ICT as a major enabler of organizational innovation and structural reforms. In today's challenging race of competitiveness and excellence, where new technologies and innovation play a central role, European SMEs cannot be left behind (Eleftheriadou, 2008).

The 2008 e-Business W@tch report presents strong evidence that large companies are significantly more likely to use ICT than SMEs are. Surveys indicate that their uptake of ICT remains too low. Given the other key findings, this also implies that large companies are more likely to introduce ICT-enabled innovations more often than their smaller competitors. It seems that the gap in

ICT use between SMEs and large companies (the so-called digital divide) is expected to increase rather than narrow (European Commission, 2008).

For this reason, not just European Commission but also more and more governments around the world have been seeking opportunities and means to promote ICT and e-business models as a way of enhancing the competitiveness of SMEs.

Supporting the European Commission's strategic goals and documents (e.g. Lisbon Agenda, i2010, and others), Slovenia has also launched several strategic documents, including si2010, e-Health 2010 – Strategy of computerizing the Slovenian healthcare system 2005-2010 (Ministry of Health), Strategy of transition to digital broadcasting (Ministry of the Economy), Strategy of the Republic of Slovenia for introducing fixed wireless systems on the territory of the Republic of Slovenia (Ministry of the Economy), Strategy of developing broadband data networks in the Republic of Slovenia (Ministry of the Economy), Strategy of e-government for the period 2006-2010 (SEP-2010) (Ministry of Public Administration) and National strategy of e-learning 2006-2010 (Ministry of Higher Education, Science and Technology).

Slovenia also has legislation on e-business, e-signature (in 2009 and the protection of documents and archives, it has achieved a 91% rate of electronic payment transactions and established national standards for document exchange (e-SLOG), providing schemes for basic business documents (order, order confirmation, despatch advice and invoice). Together with the support of strategic documents, this is the foundation for the broader uptake of e-business in companies that need incentives from the environment and the state.

Based on results of 2008 i2010 Mid-Term Review (European Commission, 2008) Slovenia is well advanced in the information society: many benchmarking indicators are significantly above the EU average, with a leading position for eGovernment services and significant increases in the last three years in ICT investment by firms.

The situation of broadband penetration stands at 17.3% (January 2008), which is below the EU27 average of 20%. Growth in uptake is very much at the level of the EU average both among households and enterprises. The same can be said about the growth in the usage of online services. Slovenia has a very good position in the field of online availability of basis public services, as 90% of them are fully available online. Availability of services to citizens is the 2nd highest in Europe and for services to enterprises it is the 5th highest. Online sophistication is now close to 100%. Remarkably Slovene citizens are currently better served than businesses. Slovenia is generally above average in use of e-business applications and is in the top ten countries for e-commerce turnover. Broadband connectivity among enterprises is slightly better than the EU average. Skill levels both in the general population and the workforce are close to the EU average (European Commission, 2008).

All this presents a very good environment for even higher ICT uptake. However the situation in the field of SMEs is still below the expectations.

Data from Statistical Office of Republic of Slovenia (Zupan, 2008) show that the internet is highly available to all companies. For example, in the first quarter of 2008, 97% of enterprises with 10 or more persons employed had internet access. The same situation is for websites. Seventy-one percent of enterprises with 10 or more persons employed had a website, four percentage points more than in the same period of 2007. Regarding the size of the enterprise (number of persons employed), the share of enterprises increased the most in small enterprises; by six percentage points to 67% in comparison with the same period of 2007.

The results for automated data exchange are worse. Automated data exchange was used by less than half of companies: 40% of enterprises in the first quarter of 2008. It is evidenced that the highest percentage of usage was with 72% between large enterprises. The reasons companies do not use the automated data exchange are the following: 20%

lack of interest; 18% lack of appropriate software and 14% of enterprises do not use automated data exchange because the return of the investment is to low and the lack of in-house expertise. The problem of lack of in-house expertise (15%) and lack of appropriate software (19%) is the highest in small enterprises.

This situation requires measures to achieve higher adoption of e-business, especially in the field of SMEs. Some of the actions were presented in the "eSMEs Initiative and Action plan" for wider acceleration and implementation of e-business specifically in SMEs in December 2007. The initiative consists of 12 actions, each introduced with the introduction, goal and implementation plan (for detail description see section 4.2 eSMEs Initiative 2007):

- **Action No. 1:** Programme promoting the introduction of information and communication know-how in SMEs
- **Action No. 2:** Voucher consultancy programme for the introduction of e-business in micro companies and SMEs
- **Action No. 3:** Mandatory sending of invoices to the public administration in electronic form
- **Action No. 4:** Investment in e-business eligible for development relief
- **Action No. 5:** Co-financing of e-business in the National Development Programme 2007-2013
- **Action No. 6:** Portals offering information on best e-business practices
- **Action No. 7:** Opening and adaptation of state registries to e-services
- **Action No. 8:** Introduction of a single system for calculation and payment of fees
- **Action No. 9:** Introduction of electronic certificates
- **Action No. 10:** Initiative "I don't spend, I invest"
- **Action No. 11:** Initiative "E-business in Supply Chains"
- **Action No. 12:** Recognition for Best E-company in Slovenia

The key point of the initiative is that all the actions can be undertaken based on the full exploitation of possibilities and opportunities within current legal framework and does not require major financial investments. The initiative is build upon existing policies, legislation and ICT environment. It includes e-business best practice transfer from other European countries e.g. the Danish case of e-invoicing decree in 2005 (initiated by government of Denmark). The initiative refers to the actions needed from all involved: SMEs, large companies, government, Chamber of Commerce and Industry, Chamber of Craft and Small Business, national and regional agencies for small business development, large companies, ICT providers, universities and SMEs.

Some actions were already undertaken e.g. promotion and introduction of information and communication know-how in SMEs, voucher consultancy programme for the introduction of e-business in micro companies and SMEs and recognition/yearly award for best e-company in Slovenia. Other actions are in progress. Some of them will need governmental incentives; some will appear from market maturity.

The initiative was supported by the heads of all crucial ministries: the Ministry of Higher Education and Technology, the Ministry of Public Administration, the Ministry of Economy, the Ministry of Finance, the Ministry of Economic Growth and Development and by the presidents of the Chamber of Commerce and Industry of Slovenia, the Chamber of Commerce of Slovenia, JAPTI (Public Agency for Entrepreneurship and Foreign Investments), the Slovenian Business Software Developers KODA.SI, and representatives from universities. This represents the framework for the wider successful adoption of e-business to the all parties involved, and especially to SMEs.

REFERENCES

Buonanno, G., Faverio, P., Pigni, F., & Ravarini, A. (2005). Factors affecting ERP system adoption: A comparative analysis between SMEs and large companies. *Journal of Enterprise Information Management*, *18*(4), 384–426. doi:10.1108/17410390510609572

Chitura, T., Mupemhi, S., Dube, T., & Bolongkikit, J. (2008). Barriers to Electronic Commerce Adoption in Small and Medium Enterprises: A Critical Literature Review. *Journal of Internet Banking and Commerce*, *13*(2), 1–13.

Cordis. (2007). *Information & Communication Technologies. Introduction.* Retrieved March 18, 2009, from http://cordis.europa.eu/fp7/ict/programme/home_en.html

Cragg, P. B., & King, M. (1993). Small-firm computing: Motivators and inhibitors. *Management Information Systems Quarterly*, *17*(1), 47. doi:10.2307/249509

eBSN. (2008). *The European e-Business Support Network: What is eBSN?* Retrieved March 18, 2009, from http://ec.europa.eu/enterprise/e-bsn/about/ebsn/index_en.html

Eleftheriadou, D. (2008). Small - and Medium-Sized Enterprises Hold the Key to European Competitiveness: How to Help Them Innovate through ICT and E-business. *The Global Information Technology Report 2007-2008.* World Economic Forum.

European Commission. (2002). Benchmarking National and Regional E-business Policies for SMEs. Final report of the E-business Policy Group of the European Union, Brussels.

European Commission. DG Information Society and Media (2005). eEurope 2005. *Europe's Information Society Thematic Portal.* Retrieved March 18th 2009 from http://ec.europa.eu/information_society/eeurope/2005/index_en.htm

European Commission. (2007). *Sectoral e-Business Policies in Support of SMEs: Innovative approaches, good practices and lessons to be learned.*

European Commission. (2008). *The European e-Business Report 2008.* The impact of ICT and e-business on firms, sectors and the economy. 6th Synthesis Report of the Sectoral e-Business Watch.

European Commission. DG Information Society and Media. (2008). *Strategy for an innovative and inclusive European Information Society.* Retrieved April 18, 2009, from http://ec.europa.eu/information_society/doc/factsheets/035-i2010-en.pdf

European Commission. DG Enterprise and Industry. (2008a). *A comprehensive policy to support SMEs.* Retrieved from http://ec.europa.eu/enterprise/entrepreneurship/sme_policy.htm

European Commission. DG Enterprise and Industry. (2008b). *Sectoral e-Business Watch.* Retrieved July 19, 2008, from http://www.ebusiness-watch.org/about/sectoral_ebiz.htm

European Council. (2008). Lisbon Strategy. Slovenian Presidency of the EU. Retrieved April 18th 2009 from http://www.eu2008.si/en/Policy_Areas/European_Council/Lissabon.html

European Network of Living Labs. (2006). *eLivingLab Kranj.* Retrieved April 18, 2009, from http://www.openlivinglabs.eu/slovenia-elivinglab.html

European Parliament. (2000). *Lisbon European Council 23 And 24 March 2000 - Presidency Conclusions.* Retrieved July 19, 2009, from http://www.europarl.europa.eu/summits/lis1_en.htm

Finland, E. U. Presidency. Helsinki manifesto Launching Event - European Network of Living Labs: A Step Towards a European Innovation System. Retrieved April 18th 2009 from http://www.tietoyhteiskuntaohjelma.fi/ajankohtaista/events/en_GB/1147340579176

Government of the Republic of Slovenia. Ministry of Public administration. (2006). *Strategy of e-government for the period 2006–2010 (SEP-2010)*. Retrieved March 18, 2009, from http://www.mju.gov.si/fileadmin/mju.gov.si/pageuploads/mju_dokumenti/pdf/SEP- 2010.pdf

Government of the Republic of Slovenia. (2007). *Development Strategy for the Information Society in the Republic of Slovenija – si2010*. Retrieved July 19th 2009 from: http://www.mvzt.gov.si/fileadmin/mvzt.gov.si/pageuploads/pdf/informacijska_druzba/61405-EN_Strategija_razvoja_informacijske_druzbe_v_RS_si2010.pdf

Government of the Republic of Slovenia, Ministry for Health. (2005). *eHealth 2010 – Strategy of computerising the Slovenian healthcare system 2005–2010*. Retrieved March 18, 2009, from http://www.ris.org/uploadi/editor/1130935067OsnutekeZdravje2010-01.pdf

Government of the Republic of Slovenia, Ministry of Higher Education, Science and Technology. National strategy of e-learning 2006–2010.

Government of the Republic of Slovenia, Ministry of the Economy. (2006a). *Strategy of transition to digital broadcasting*.

Government of the Republic of Slovenia, Ministry of the Economy. (2006b). *Strategy of developing broadband networks in the Republic of Slovenia*. Retrieved March 18, 2009, from http://www.mg.gov.si/fileadmin/mg.gov.si/pageuploads/EKP/Predlogi/V_medresorskem/ Z.Unijat_-_Strategija_BB_Rev3_medresorsko.pdf

Information Society. (2001). *eEurope Go Digital. Getting Europe on-line and doing e-business*. Retrieved March 18, 2009, from http://ec.europa.eu/information_society/topics/ebusiness/godigital/index_en.htm

Information Society Technologies. (2008). *About IST The overall vision*. Retrieved March 18, 2009, from http://cordis.europa.eu/ist/about/vision.htm

Jafari, S. M., Osman, M. R., Yusuff, R. M., & Tang, S. H. (2006). ERP Systems Implementation In Malaysia: The Importance Of Critical Success Factors. *International Journal of Engineering and Technology, 3*(1), 125–131.

Kalakota, R., & Whinston, A. B. (1997). *Electronic commerce: A manager's guide*. Reading, MA: Addison-Wesley.

Kartiwi, M., & MacGregor, R. C. (2007). Electronic Commerce Adoption Barriers in Small to Medium-Sized Enterprises (SMEs) in Developed and Developing Countries: A Cross-Country Comparison. *Journal of Electronic Commerce in Organizations, 5*(3), 35–51.

Levenburg, N. M., Schwarz, T. V., & Motwani, J. (2005). Understanding adoption of internet technologies among SMEs. *Journal of Small Business Strategy, 16*(1), 51–69.

Levy, M., Powell, P., & Worrall, L. (2005). Strategic Intent and E-Business in SMEs: Enablers and Inhibitors. *Information Resources Management Journal, 18*(4), 1–20.

Lomerson, W. L., McGrath, L. C., & Schwager, P. H. (2004). An examination of the benefits of e-business to small and medium size businesses. In *Proceedings of the 7th Annual conference of the Southern Association for Information System*. Southern Association for Information System.

Mac Gregor, R., & Vrazalic, L. (2005). The Role of Small Bsuiness Clusters in Prioritising Barriers to E-commerce Adoption: A Study of Swedish Regional SMEs. In CRIC Cluster conference: Beyond Cluster-Current Practicies & Future Strategies, Ballarat, June 30 – July 1, 2005.

Mehrtens, J., Cragg, P. B., & Mills, A. M. (2001). A model of Internet adoption by SMEs. *Information & Management, 39*(3), 165–176. doi:10.1016/S0378-7206(01)00086-6

Pucihar, A., Bogataj, K., & Lenart, G. (2009). Increasing SMEs' efficiency through the single European electronic market as a new business model. In Paape, B., & Vuk, D. (Eds.), *Synthesized organization* (pp. 347–368). Frankfurt am Main, Deutschland: P. Lang.

Ramdani, B., & Kawalek, P. (2009). Predicting SMEs' adoption of enterprise systems. *Journal of Enterprise Information Management, 22*(1/2), 10–24. doi:10.1108/17410390910922796

Rao, S. S., Metts, G., & Monge, C. A. M. (2003). Electronic commerce development in small and medium-sized enterprises: a stage model and its implications. *Business Process Management Journal, 9*(1), 11–32. doi:10.1108/14637150310461378

Riquelme, H. (2002). Commercial Internet adoption in China: Comparing the experiences of small, medium and large businesses. *Internet Research: Electronic Networking Applications and Policy, 12*(3), 276–286. doi:10.1108/10662240210430946

Slovenia, E. U. *Presidency*. (2008). Retrieved March 18, 2009, from http://www.eu2008.si/en/

Stansfield, M., & Grant, K. (2003). An investigation into issues influencing the use of the Internet and electronic commerce among small-medium-sized enterprises. *Journal of electronic commerce research, 4*(1), 15-33.

SURS – Statistični urad RS. (2007). *Uporaba informacijsko-komunikacijske tehnologije v podjetjih z 10 in več zaposlenimi osebami. 1 Četrtletje 2007*. Retrieved March 18, 2009, from http://www.stat.si/novica_prikazi.aspx?id=1284

Turban, E., Lee, J. K., King, D., & McKay, J. (2008). *Electronic Commerce 2008: A Managerial Perspective* (International Ed.). Upper Saddle River, NJ: Prentice Hall.

Umble, E. J., Haft, R. R., & Umble, M. M. (2003). Enterprise resource planning: implementation procedures and critical success factors. *European Journal of Operational Research, 146*(2), 241–257. doi:10.1016/S0377-2217(02)00547-7

Zhu, K., Kramer, K., & Xu, S. (2003). Electronic business adoption by European firms. *European Journal of Information Systems, 12*, 251–268. doi:10.1057/palgrave.ejis.3000475

Zupan, G. (2008). Internet usage in enterprises with 10 or more persons employed, Slovenia 1s quarter 2008. Statistical Office of the Republic of Slovenia.

Zupančič, D. (2004). *Cross-border eInvoicing in eRegion – Companies & Chambers of Commerce Perspective*. Merkur day 2004 & 8th Executive Business, Government, and University Meeting On Cross-border eInvoicing in eRegion, Slovenia.

ENDNOTES

[1] Clinton memorandum: http://govinfo. library.unt.edu/npr/library/direct/memos/ eleccom.htm.l.

[2] eInvoicing Denmark: http://europa.eu.int/ idabc/en/document/4215/194.

[3] Phasing out of certain tasks is projected to free up the available resources. These resources can later be reduced (reduction of labour costs and labour-associated costs such as offices) or used for other tasks in public administration, for example EU presidency.

[4] Article 6 of the Rules should be amended with the item: "f. costs associated with the introduction of e-business, whereby a company may deduct these costs as stated: f.1 – for introduction of exchange of forms with the public administration up to EUR 4,200 f.2 – for introduction of inter-company e-invoicing up to EUR 4,200 f.3. – for introduction of an e-archiving system

up to EUR 2,100 f.4. – for introduction of e-inspection up to EUR 410." and the *Methodology for the filling out of forms for relief for investment in research and development* appropriately amended.

5 Actual relief is 25% on 20% of the investment = EUR 210 per company.

6 Meeting of the DURS working group of 15.11.2006 at which standards for the exchange of data for e-inspection were agreed with larger business software providers. The OECD uses the SAF-T format and the instructions *Guidance on Tax Compliance for Business and Accounting SW* published at http://www.oecd.org/searchResult/0,266 5,en_2649_201185_1_1_1_1_1,00.html.

7 Second draft NDP 2007-2013, http://www.svlr.gov.si/si/delovna_podrocja/drzavni_razvojni_program/predstavitev_drp_2007_2013/.

8 Similarly, Great Britain solved this through the Prime Minister's Cabinet Office with the E-Government Office, http://www.cabinet-office.gov.uk/e-government/.

9 This is already requested by adopted regulations, for example the ZdavP-2.

10 From *Initiative for e-invoice project in e-region*, FOV2005, in which support for the project is expressed by Merkur d.d., SRC d.d., NLB d.d., Abanka Vipa d.d., Banka Koper d.d., Directorate of Public Accounting, Customs Administration and the General Tax Office.

Chapter 4
Regional–National ICT Strategies

Melih Kirlidog
Marmara University, Turkey

Stephen E. Little
The Open University Business School, UK

ABSTRACT

An overwhelming majority of developing and industrialized countries have developed national Information and Communication Technology (ICT) strategies. Developing countries hope to leapfrog towards social and economic progress, modernization, and wealth, and industrialized countries do not want to be left behind in the race for ICT capabilities. While industrialized countries have distinct advantages in formulating and realizing these strategies, some developing countries' objectives are too ambitious, seeking to achieve an information society by these strategies alone. An important reflection of today's globalization on this issue is the cross-country aspect of "national" ICT strategies. Japan's ICT strategy is increasingly outward oriented, sub-Saharan African countries are developing their strategies with the support of international agencies and non-government organizations, and Caribbean countries have established a common regulatory framework for the telecommunications sector. The aim of all these efforts is to develop a regional synergy for fostering ICT. This chapter is an exploratory analysis of the internationalization of national ICT strategies.

INTRODUCTION

The effectiveness of national and regional policies depends on the freedom of action and the effectiveness of governance enjoyed by the policy makers. Camilleri and Falk (1992) analyze national sovereignty in the context of the mesh of

intentional undertakings restrictions and commitments which have developed from international conflict and cooperation. Page (1999) argues that regional economic alignments such as NAFTA and Mercosur are either short-lived or become a means to ultimately closer integration. In Europe, Delamaide (1994) has identified what he describes as "super-regions" with, for example a re-emergence of the characteristics of the Han-

DOI: 10.4018/978-1-60566-388-3.ch004

seatic League in developments around the Baltic since the end of the cold War and the expansion of regional associations such as NATO and the European Union.

Post-colonial Africa is faced with regional realignments of even greater complexity. The Cold War concept of "Third World" identified the bulk of humanity through its exclusion from either superpower camp. The end of the Cold War has meant reduced attention from the former blocs. In some respects this has been beneficial, as major power confrontations are less frequently played out with third party proxies. However, there was also a reduction in the flow of resources and technology, albeit often related to militarization and its requirements; in many areas attention has returned to post-colonial infrastructures whose orientation may owe little to regional needs or potential synergies.

Many African countries face a task made even harder by a colonial past as contributors of raw materials, whether from primary and extractive industry, or through migration of labor. Infrastructure, both for physical transport (Headrick, 1981) and for science and technology, has been developed around the needs of the external consumers of locally produced resources, rather than for coherent and balanced internal development. Such legacies limit the capacity to absorb or develop the capabilities necessary to negotiate a national space within an emerging global order. With the rise of China and India and the subsequent resources boom, a renewal of interest has brought the same concerns of distorted development (Shaxson, 2007) and an argument that the emergence of new manufacturing super-powers constrains prospects of an industrial development pathway for African and other less developed economies (Kaplinsky & Morris, 2007).

This international order is increasingly dependent upon information and communication technologies (ICTs) and the term "digital divide" has come to encapsulate the imbalance of infrastructure and capability between the developed and less developed regions. However, the divide is equally one of knowledge and power. Science and technological capabilities lie at the centre of the knowledge divide described by Chataway *et al.* (2003).

Despite the diverse problems of the mid 1990s, the East Asian development model retains its allure for much of the world (Thorpe & Little, 2001). The fact remains that in 1960 Ghana had a higher per capita Gross Domestic Product than South Korea but that by 1997 Korea had broken the US$10,000 barrier and the country had embraced manufacturing successfully and moved into key fields of high technology and innovation. There are, however, both internal and external dimensions to the development trajectory pursued by the nations of East Asia.

This example shows that some countries can perform better than the others in the race for development. Further, given that not only Korea, but many of the countries in Southern and Eastern Asia have been in fast-track development over the last few decades, it can be argued that the economic and social development of an entire region has an important effect on the development of individual countries within that region. The perceived importance of ICT on development and on the formulation of national ICT strategies has become closely intertwined with regional development goals. This chapter is an exploratory analysis of the extension of individual national ICT strategies to the regions surrounding the countries.

Perhaps the most notable regional ICT strategy is the "Lisbon strategy" of the European Union (EU) that was launched in 2000 "to make EU the world's most dynamic and competitive economy by 2010." Given the current economic climate, the achievement to this target seems doubtful. Excluding this example due to that fact that it involves mainly industrialized countries, three cases are used in this chapter as examples of cooperation in formulating and implementing national ICT strategies for development. Thus, this chapter employs a case study approach to gain an insight to the topic. Document analysis was the main data collection method. The cases are used not for comparison with each other, but for highlighting different dimensions of regional cooperation in the sphere of the ICT strategy. The first case is that of Japan's ICT strategy and its enlargement over time with the intention to create a spillover effect to other Asian countries. The second case concerns the development of national ICT strategies by sub-Saharan countries where strategy formulation can make use of similarities between these countries and thus create a synergy in formulation and implementation. The first case is different from the second from two points of view: Firstly, the entity in the first case is a country whereas it is a group of countries in the second. Secondly, the first case illustrates an industrialized country that actively pursues a spillover effect to its region and the second case is on the other side of the spectrum with poor countries seeking ICT support for development. However, such support sometimes requires the aid of non-locals in strategy formulation. The third case illustrates a model that has the potential to become common in the future: five Eastern Caribbean states established a common regulatory framework which later evolved into a regulatory body for telecommunications. Given the interconnectedness of ICT strategies in the first two cases, it doesn't seem unreasonable to expect that the synergy sought in a region via ICT may lead countries to develop similar common regulatory or executive bodies in future. It is argued that such an exploratory analysis of several dimensions of regional cooperation in ICT strategy formulation and implementation is beneficial for understanding the big picture of emerging trends that aim to develop regional synergy in this area.

The chapter is organized as follows: The next section contains a literature review about the effect of ICTs on development. Contrary to the hype and exaggeration commonly found in ICT vendors' documents and trade journals, academic literature has a much more sober tone about the catalyst role of ICTs on development. This tone draws several caveats and the section highlights them. The following section deals with the recent calls for developing national ICT strategies and the positive response they receive from almost all countries in the world. This section also draws attention to the requirements of benchmarking, monitoring, and evaluation of the strategies and their impacts. The subsequent section investigates the tangible and intangible difficulties of ICT diffusion in developing countries and it is followed by a section that underlines the regional dimensions of national ICT strategies. The chapter concludes after the three cases of regional ICT strategies.

PREVIOUS LITERATURE ABOUT ICT AND DEVELOPMENT

By "development" two interrelated concepts are meant: economic development and social development which includes human development. Although it is relatively easy to gauge economic development in terms of widely-accepted parameters such as income per capita, social and human development is more problematic. Nevertheless, the level of social and human development can also be assessed through life quality parameters such as life expectancy, access to schooling and health services, level of achievement in science and technology, and the existence of participative democracy. The UNDP's (United Nations Development Program) annual Human Development Index (see www.undp.org) is a commonly referenced source that compares countries by their economic and social development levels. The comparative development status of societies is subject to change in the course of history. For example, China is accepted to have been more developed prior to the enlightenment than Western Europe, then had a backward status for more than half a millennium, and is currently developing fast in such a way that it will be more developed than Western Europe in about half a century, provided that the current development rates are maintained.

Likewise, some countries in South East Asia region made successful development efforts over the last three decades. This has encouraged several developing countries to believe in the possibility of leapfrog development in today's world. The perceived contribution of ICT in the development efforts of countries like Ireland and India led several countries to concentrate on ICT as a possible catalyst for development.

There is a wide and growing literature about the contribution of ICT to both economic and social development. This literature is centered on the ICT's role as catalyst for this development. Since, by definition, the concept of development is mainly a preoccupation for developing countries, ICT for development literature is primarily pertinent for these countries.

Can ICT act as a catalyst for social and economic development? Today's academic literature usually responds positively to this question. Walsham and Sahay (2006) contend that the debate in this area has been resolved with a clear yes and the debate is currently centered on not whether, but how ICTs can be beneficial for development. The authors, however, warn about lingering difficulties with ICTs. Although currently the bulk of the literature has a positive connotation of ICT's effect on development some authors like Avgerou (2002) strike a more cautious note about ICTs in institutions by suggesting that their value has become a "rational myth." These caveats are important to balance the hype that tends to exaggerate the effects of technology that is seen as an *independent* agent that has the power of automatically leading to development. Such a techno-deterministic view (MacKenzie & Wajcman, 1999) implicitly regards the technology as a *necessary and adequate* agent that has a decisive influence in human history. This view is usually associated with a positivist mindset (Giddens, 1974) where social events are seen as following laws of nature and the "scientific method" is the sole technique that paves the way to development. Positivism is a common philosophy among the technocrats who believe that social progress is strongly associated with scientific progress (Schunk, 2003) and the technology has a supreme importance in this process. On the other hand, a more sober view tends to see the technology as a *necessary but inadequate* factor on the winding road to economic and social development. Since the word development is particularly pertinent for developing countries that strive toward a fast pace of progress in order to match the industrialized world, their leaders should have a wise approach to reaping the benefits offered by technology and should have internalized the fact that buying hardware alone would never be adequate for transforming into an information society. Beyond wasting hard-earned or hard-borrowed currency, such an approach would harm the hopes for technology itself due to possible failures resulting from technology-led development. Moodley (2005) criticizes the South African Government's approach that views ICTs as an external and autonomous agent. Technology in general and ICTs specifically should be viewed only as supporting tools that act as catalysts for all-encompassing development efforts. In other words, the national ICT strategy of a country should be part of and dependent on the overall development strategy of that country.

The "productivity paradox" is another caveat for developing countries. Landauer (1995) provides an explanation and justification of the so-called "productivity paradox" through a comprehensive review of the literature addressing the evident gap between investment of time and money in computer systems and any corresponding improvement in organizational performance. The concept was introduced by Solow (1987) who expressed his doubts about the contribution of ICT to productivity but in many respects began with Attewell and Rule's (1984) attempt to discover some empirical evidence of the benefits of computers to organizations. Landauer points out that much of the literature extolling such benefits turns out on closer examination to be describing anticipated rather than documented gains. Landauer argues that those gains that can be demonstrated are associated with increased volumes of work handled, particularly in the service sector, rather than any identifiable productivity improvement.

Twenty years after Solow's statement it is generally agreed that ICTs do indeed contribute to productivity increase in industrialized countries, but their contribution is still regarded as doubtful in developing countries (Lucas, 1999; Brynjolfsson & Hitt, 1996; Souter, 2004; Bollou & Ngwenyama, 2008). However, most researchers agree that reasonable ICT spending is important for developing countries for the reason that a time-dependent learning curve is important for the productive use of ICTs and even if developing countries get little productivity increase by using the ICTs now, they can be regarded as following the industrialized countries' pattern in that they have invested for their longer term future. The key to ICT-based productivity lies therefore in its intelligent application to specific contexts, rather than its technical sophistication, a point demonstrated by Vodafone (2005) in a collection of case studies of the economic benefits of cellular telephony in sub-Saharan Africa.

Butt *et al.* (2008) criticize the ICT for development literature for sharing uncomfortable similarities with the issues in industrialized economies such as a focus on new technologies disregarding their economic and social costs; limited discussion of risks or unintended consequences associated with ICT; and "an abstract theoretical model for economic development through technology that downplays cultural and social issues." In other words, the authors maintain that ICT for development literature has taken the easier path of following industrialized economies' issues and concerns and disregarded the particular needs of developing countries.

Heeks (2002) maintains that ICT replaces the handling of information that has the potential to be used for development into digital format only; therefore the role of information in development

should be understood first. This role has two main aspects, namely processes and outcomes. The most important processes are changing data with potential value into actual value and communication. The outcomes that actually contribute to development are learning where information is transformed into knowledge and better decision making. Heeks also argues that in order for ICT to be useful for development in the "South" ICT-based systems should be designed by people who are knowledgeable about the problems and they should focus on information rather than technology; the systems they design must be integral to their environments and they should be integrated with development objectives.

In a recent article Heeks (2008) argues that ICT4D 1.0 has already paved the way into 2.0 which presents opportunities for professionals and vendors in new kinds of ICT implementations in developing countries. ICT4D 1.0 lasted for about a decade beginning around the mid-1990s and it had sought quick, off-the-shelf solutions for the rural poor in the form of telecenters or telecottages. These pro-poor efforts occurred on behalf of poor communities but were outside them. Perhaps because of this, these efforts had large "design versus reality gaps" and as a result they had little success in terms of providing any intended benefit to the disadvantaged. Heeks maintains that ICT4D 2.0 will involve para-poor efforts where innovation is done working alongside poor communities and per-poor efforts where innovation occurs within and by poor communities.

BACKGROUND: STRIVING FOR A STRATEGY

The second half of the 20th Century witnessed a major scientific development in the industrialized parts of the world that resulted in major transformations in the lives of people not only in economic but also in social terms. With their ever-increasing capacities ICTs were in the forefront of this transformation. The transformation had such far-reaching effects that according to many it was comparable to the two major revolutions in human history, namely the agricultural and industrial revolutions (Toffler, 1980). Theorists like Machlup (1962) and Bell (1999) popularized the concepts of information society and post-industrialized society where knowledge becomes a very important asset along with the technologies that enable its efficient storage, process, and dissemination.

These transformations in the industrialized regions of the world diffused to the developing world in varying degrees of intensity which resembles the pattern of diffusion of the industrial revolution in the 19th and 20th Centuries. This is quite plausible, because the new transformation builds on the industrial revolution and the regions that have made continuing progress since the industrial revolution have natural advantages in transforming themselves into the information society. The slower progress of some regions of the world in reaping the benefits offered by ICTs is known as the digital divide and it operates not only between regions and countries, but also within individual countries. The digital divide within a country may be based on different regions in that country or on specific characteristics the population such as gender, age, and educational status.

ICTs are regarded as very important component of development, modernization, and wealth creation both in developing and industrialized countries. At the end of the First World Summit on the Information Society (WSIS) in Geneva in 2003 political leaders of the participating countries committed themselves to developing their national ICT strategies by the next summit in 2005 in Tunis. The Geneva summit also adopted a Plan of Action to achieve ten targets by 2015 (WSIS, 2003). These targets are mainly connectivity-based and are beyond traditional measures of telecommunications development:

1. To connect villages ICTs and establish community access points

2. To connect universities and primary and secondary schools with ICTs

3. To connect scientific and research centers with ICTs

4. To connect public libraries, cultural centers, museums, post offices, and archives with ICTs

5. To connect health centers and hospitals with ICTs

6. To connect all local and central government departments and establish web sites and e-mail addresses

7. To adapt all primary and secondary school curricula to meet the challenges of the Information Society, taking into account national circumstances

8. To ensure that all of the world's population has access to television and radio services

9. To encourage the development of content and put in place technical conditions in order to facilitate the presence and use of all world languages on the Internet

10. To ensure that more than half of the world's inhabitants have access to ICTs within their reach.

Partly to achieve these targets and partly due to the strategy commitment almost all countries have developed or are in the process of developing ICT strategies that aim to foster the diffusion of these technologies in their societies. Ulrich and Chacko (2005) compare these strategies to a road map that guides countries to becoming information societies and knowledge economies. The authors, however, warn that policies and e-strategies alone cannot guarantee the desired outcome, because development implies action, not just abstract policy or strategy documents. Like national development strategies, national ICT strategies are formed by choosing from alternatives in a wide range of issues such as the importance attributed to the public sector as opposed to the private sector. Thus, these choices are affected by the *weltanschauung* of policy makers. Ikiara *et al.* (2004)

define policy as "specific statements, guidelines and pronouncements" and policy making as "the process by which such government statements are arrived." With the inclusion of the *regions*, Lanvin (2005) describes an e-strategy as

a set of coordinated actions and policies that seek to accelerate the social, economic, and political development of a given country (or region) through the use of telecommunications, information networks, and the technologies associated with them (p. 48).

Developing an ICT strategy requires not only an excellent comprehension of the strengths and weaknesses of a myriad of domestic factors, but also a thorough knowledge of experiences in other countries. Although all countries' conditions are different, "best practices" and the knowledge of what works in other countries and what doesn't may prove to be extremely valuable in formulating and implementing the strategy. Such a learning process might be even more important among the neighboring countries in a region where ICT strategies have the potential to develop synergy. The strategies should incorporate action plans and indicators to measure success in implementation. Such indicators are also useful for benchmarking the quality of strategy formulation and implementation.

Adamali *et al.* (2006) argue that national ICT strategies have three broad steps. The first two are the steps of strategy formulation and implementation. The third step, namely monitoring and evaluating the results is usually overlooked. The authors analyzed the national ICT strategy documents of 40 developing and industrialized countries and scored them according to four aspects, namely their links to the overall development strategy, use of indicators, implementation mechanisms, and monitoring and evaluation. They found that monitoring and evaluation aspect of the strategy documents were much weaker than the other two steps. One can expect that this will be projected

to the actual implementation where there will be flaws in understanding the real benefits incurred by the strategy.

Benchmarking the strategy documents and implementations are becoming widespread in the literature due to the general increase in ICT strategy research. For example, Aligula (2005) compares the ICT strategy of Kenya with that of four other countries, namely South Africa, Egypt, Malaysia, and Singapore with the objective of "highlighting Kenya's relatively poor performance in applying ICTs to achieve its development goals" (p.258). The author draws some lessons for Kenya from the experiences of others.

DIFFICULTIES OF ICT DIFFUSION IN DEVELOPING COUNTRIES

Since currently 5 billion people have no access to the Internet (Heeks, 2008) and an overwhelming majority of these people live in developing countries, the most severe aspect of today's digital divide is that between countries. Understandably, formulating ICT strategy development is as difficult as diffusing ICT into the broader society for developing countries, since the barriers for diffusion in these countries are much higher than those in industrialized countries. There are several obstacles to ICT diffusion for human populations that are on the disadvantaged side of the divide and ICT policy makers in developing countries should be knowledgeable about these obstacles. These barriers can be categorized in two major groups, namely tangible and intangible barriers.

The most important tangible barrier for ICT diffusion is the lack of funds. A country's national income seems to be the most important predictor of the level of its ICT diffusion (Baliamoune-Lutz, 2003; Neto *et al.*, 2005), and all low-income countries are on the disadvantaged side of the digital divide. They are also accompanied by several middle-income countries. If ICTs really contribute to development then developing countries face with a dilemma: they do not have the funds necessary for ICTs, and they do have the necessary ICT diffusion required for development and the accumulation of funds. Scarce funds in these countries have to be spent on more acute needs such as feeding the people living in poverty. However, expectations for ICTs are so high that some countries make very high ICT expenditures perhaps to the cost of those more acute needs. For example, Cross (2005) reports that although Ethiopia is one of Africa's poorest countries it is spending one tenth of its GDP every year on IT.

Since the adoption of ICTs is strongly correlated with the level of education (Lee, 2001; Caselli & Coleman, 2001), another tangible barrier for developing countries is the level of education in the society. Barro and Lee (2000) estimate that average schooling year is 4.89 years in developing countries as of 2000. This figure is 9.80 for industrialized countries. It must also be kept in mind that the quality of education differ significantly in developing and industrialized countries mainly due to the fact that the latter have much more resources to spend for education. The net result of this is that education systems in developing countries are mainly based on rote learning which is cheap; because usually a book and a teacher is adequate for this type of learning. It is natural that a lower education level in a society should have implications in the effective production and implementation of ICTs. Lower levels of education have far-reaching effects which are pertinent for ICT diffusion in a country such as managerial quality and skill availability. It is also a prohibiting factor for effective usage of the Internet where more than half of the content is in English language.

The intangible group of barriers is constituted by the cultural constraints. These constraints do not imply inferiority for the cultures prevalent in developing countries. On the contrary, an aspect of traditional cultures such as collectivism can be regarded as more human due to its proximity with solidarity. This trait contradicts the excessive

individualism that comes with "development" which Putnam (2000) bemoans for being an important reason for the declining social capital in the US. Policy makers and researchers in developing countries should have a sober approach to the underlying psyche of their communities. As a prerequisite, such an approach should regard no culture or cultural trait as superior or inferior to others. Cultural traits should be regarded as "given" and they should be investigated from the point of view of their suitability or unsuitability to ICT. Since it is very difficult to change cultural traits that have been formed over centuries or ICTs that have been shaped as a result of prevalent Western cultural assumptions, strategy formulations should be creative in finding ways to "gather around" cultural obstacles and give emphasis to any cultural attributes that might be useful for ICT diffusion in the society.

In analyzing the difficulty of ICT diffusion in China Mansell and Wehn (1998) argue that the problem is related by three facts one of which is culture (the other two are technical skills and the management structure). According to these authors Hofstede's (2001) "power distance dimension" which is the measure of the fact that power in the society is distributed unequally is associated with the cultural difficulty of ICT diffusion in China. The authors contend that "Chinese organizations are modeled on the family and are operated under a highly unequal distribution of power" (p.61). Quoting Zhao and Grimshaw (1991), the authors further argue that this contradicts with the increased transparency and information sharing across the organization that comes with the ICT and ICT's marginalizing effect for the older, more senior people in the organization. Power distance is high in most developing countries (Hofstede, 2001) and it must have implications for ICT diffusion in these countries.

As with societies, cultural values change in the course of the history. Quoting the medieval historian Clancy, Zuboff (1988) argues that written documents did not inspire trust in the early English history and the procedures used to legitimate legal transactions required witnesses. In case of a dispute, the accounts of those witnesses provided the required evidence. Zuboff further argues that "to the modern mind, the evanescence of the spoken word seems more plastic, quixotic, and undependable than the printed word." Such a transformation where emphasis shifts from oral to written is common not only in England where the industrial revolution started but all over the industrialized world and there is no reverse trend in the course of human development. These cultural changes have implications for the interaction of societies with ICTs as much as the presumed catalyst role of the ICTs in development and some broad patterns of cultural transformation in the long run of development need attention when analyzing the association of ICT and development.

The overwhelming mode of communication is oral (as opposed to written) in most of the developing countries. Menou (1993) argues that oral tradition continues to be a vital component of many cultures. Although communication technologies which are based on oral communication such as television and telephones have a reasonably high level of diffusion in these countries[1], information technologies which are based on written communication such as the Internet are comparably scarce. This situation is also reflected in economic terms. For example, being a member of the OECD, Turkey's telecommunication sector's proportion of GDP (3.3%) is close to the OECD average (3.2%), yet this ratio is far behind the OECD average for information technologies (0.8% to 2.9%) (see http://www.bilgitoplumu. gov.tr/yayin/Information%20Society%20Strategy_Turkey.pdf). These figures clearly indicate that the C of ICT has an overwhelming emphasis compared to the I in Turkey and this stems from the obvious inclination to oral rather than written communication in the country. However, advanced information technologies which are regarded as crucial to development mainly make use of written rather than oral communication. Although exceptions are possible, human-computer interaction is overwhelmingly performed through keyboard, screen, and paper all of which are based on written communication. This is clearly a barrier not only for illiterate people that might form an important percentage in developing countries, but also for some part of the population that can read and write at a basic level, but not very comfortable in written communication.

Tacit and codified knowledge constitute the opposite ends of a spectrum. While it is difficult to extract tacit knowledge or make it independent of the person who developed it (Walsham, 2001), codified knowledge can be more easily transferred to other parties. Since ICTs provide an excellent medium for that transformation as well as the further processing and storage of codified knowledge, they are strongly associated with economic and societal development. Thus, it can be argued that economic and social development leads to the increase of the share of codified knowledge in the society to the cost of tacit knowledge and ICT use is one of the prime factors in this transformation. Modern ICT-assisted education is an important enabler of this fact. However, this is not to say that tacit knowledge will disappear at some future fictional level of development. On the contrary, there will always be some knowledge in the minds of people that cannot be codified. Although information technologies excel in storing, processing, and disseminating codified knowledge (Roberts, 2000), they have limited capacities for performing these tasks for tacit knowledge.

As a concept, codified knowledge has a close association to written communication as much as tacit knowledge is close to oral communication. Although the deep psyche of the societies in developing countries are inclined to oral communication and tacit knowledge rather than written communication and codified knowledge, ICTs are more efficient on the other ends of these two spectrums. This poses a dilemma for developing countries in their quest for using ICT for development: their societies are on the "wrong" side of these two spectrums for getting real benefit from ICT. The passing of a certain threshold in these two dimensions seems to be pertinent for developing countries to achieve the necessary cultural transformation in order to gain real benefits from ICT.

Another cultural difficulty for the efficient use of ICTs is the level of abstraction in the traditional and developing societies. Traditional communities tend to have limited level of abstraction and perceive the world "as is." However, abstraction can be regarded as formed through a "process" that is related to the individual and societal development of the human species and is specific to humans among all living creatures. Abstraction is a prerequisite for developing and implementing sophisticated systems like computers. Brookshear (2003) argues that abstraction in computer science "refers to the distinction between the external properties of an entity and the details of the entity's internal composition" (p.10). Hence, abstraction allows us to ignore the internal details of an entity at various levels and concentrate on the level that interests us. With the exception of a few cases such as numerically controlled machine tools or embedded software in mechanical devices, computers overwhelmingly have abstract inputs and outputs. For example, inventory management systems show an abstract figure for the quantity available for a part. The concrete information can only be achieved after a manual inventory count. In developing countries, the comparatively lower level of abstraction has important implications for the tendency to computer usage where abstraction is of primary importance.

These cultural constraints pose difficulties for obtaining higher order, economically viable benefits from ICT. Using a telephone only for ordinary conversation among friends does not add any value in terms of economic and social development. In such a case oral communication that is conducted face-to-face is simply replaced by the same type of communication through an electronic device. This can be extended to chatting through the computer for the same purpose. Al-

though oral communication is replaced by written communication in this case, it also provides little benefit as such. In order to obtain economically viable benefit from ICT such as reducing transaction costs (Ciborra, 1993; Wigand *et al.*, 1997) the above-mentioned cultural constraints need to be overcome.

It must also be stated that these constraints do not constitute absolute obstacles for attempts to close the digital divide; they only imply an environment where more effort and time is required for reaping the benefits offered by computers. In analyzing Geographical Information System (GIS) technology in India, Sahay (1998) argues that the space is conceptualized in Indian culture subjectively "in-here" and this contradicts with comprehending the output of the GIS as an objective reality that has been formed as a result of technological process. Likewise, in an article about the software industry in India Krishna *et al.* (2000) contend that

the concept of producing a product or service for an unknown customer in exchange for monetary returns (...) is alien to the Indian traditions, as it would have been to crafts-people in the West before industrialization (p. 193).

However,

software professionals are able to convert traditional sense of duty to working for a person in the community to a sense of duty to a client because s/he is identifiable (p. 194).

This is a striking example where cultural constraints did not prevent India from developing a world-class software industry. Likewise, China is developing at a fast pace and ICTs have some effect on this development in spite of high power distance in that country.

As a result of these problems an overwhelming majority of humanity is on the disadvantaged side of the digital divide and this is identified by Barrantes (2007) as "digital poverty." This concept "seeks to grasp the multiple dimensions of inadequate levels of access to ICT services by people and organizations, as well as the barriers to their productive use." Barrantes argues that there are three major causes for digital poverty: lack of supply which manifests itself as nonexistent connectivity access; lack of demand which is associated with inadequate income; and lack of need or capacity to use ICT which is the problem of non-poor people with no access or use due to age or inadequate literacy. In terms of national ICT strategies Barrantes argues that each of these three kinds of digital poverties will require a different public policy.

REGIONAL DIMENSIONS OF ICT STRATEGIES

Geographical regions may impose some common characteristics on the countries that are located in them. Beyond similarities in demographical attributes such as race, religion, and sometimes language, countries in a region may share common traits such as economic backwardness or a successful leap forward. Western enlightenment started in Western Europe and almost all countries in that region benefited from it. Likewise, the four "Asian Tigers" (Singapore, South Korea, Hong Kong, and Taiwan) in East and South Asia had high rate economic development rates after the 1970s. Currently, the world witnesses the rise of two populous countries of the region, namely China and India. On the opposite end of the development spectrum all sub-Saharan African countries, with the exception of South Africa, can be found. Likewise, countries in Northern America are approximately at the same level of development. This is also true for Latin American and Mid-Asian countries. These examples lead one to think that there might indeed be a relationship between development levels of countries within a region which might benefit from some mechanism

that allows the diffusion of "development" to the neighbors. In development literature this spatial effect is called "regional knowledge spillovers" (Rodriguez-Pose & Crescenzi 2008; Doring & Schnellenbach, 2006) where it is assumed that the dissemination of knowledge among the neighbors in a region create a synergy that leads to benefit for all.

With a caveat against a "one size fits all" approach, countries might formulate their national ICT strategies with the hope of benefiting from the development of such a regional synergy. Butt *et al.* (2008) urge countries to have a holistic view and consider not only the national, but also the regional landscape when they develop their strategies. The authors suggest a three-phase plan for this purpose:

Forming a regional position also involves determining all of the governmental and non-governmental agencies that need to be co-opted to work together to bring high-level ICT policy to practical fruition. First, the practical goals of the policy must be worked out. Second, who is empowered to do what is necessary to bring it to fruition should be identified. And third, the responsibilities towards achieving the policy goals should be delegated and a clear review process and schedule to monitor progress should be agreed upon. In short, political will is necessary to achieve ICT growth (ibid.).

JAPAN'S NATIONAL ICT STRATEGY

Japan is the first Eastern society that managed to develop a formidable industrial base after its counterparts in Western Europe and North America. This industrial base includes the production of state-of-the-art ICT hardware which encouraged the country to start its Fifth Generation Computer Project (FGCP) in 1982 (Nakamura & Shibuya, 1996; Feigenbaum & McCorduck, 1983). The FGCP involved developing very fast and "intelligent" computers with massive parallelism, i.e., with an extensive number of processors. Although this project never achieved commercial success and was abandoned in 1993, it gives a rich insight of Japan's capabilities in hardware and software production where the project's main problems were related to the latter (the computer language used by the system, system software, etc.) rather than former (Chiang, 2000). Japan also used to have some deficiencies in ICT implementation in transforming itself into an information society.

Possibly in an attempt to address these deficiencies in ICT, "Strategic Headquarters for the Promotion of an Advanced Information and Telecommunications Network Society" (IT Strategic Headquarters) was established in January 2001 under the provisions of the Basic Law on the Formation of an Advanced Information and Telecommunications Network Society (IT Basic Law). According to the Law, the Director-General of the Headquarters is the Prime Minister and the members are some of the Cabinet members and high-level bureaucrats.

The same year IT Strategy Headquarters acknowledged the backwardness of the country in ICT compared to its Western European and North American rivals:

Japan falls far behind other nations in embracing the IT revolution. The Internet usage in Japan is at the lowest level among major industrial nations and is by no means high even compared with other nations in the Asia-Pacific region. Japan lags behind others even in terms of how widely information technology is used in businesses and public administration. In an environment of rapid change, we must recognize that Japan's current tardiness in embracing the IT revolution may result in an irreparable gap in competitive advantages in the future (E-Japan, 2001a, p.2).

This recognition, which has been stated in the strategy document dated 22 January 2001, led to the objective of making Japan "the world's most advanced IT nation within five years" (*ibid.*). The

E-Japan strategy should have a "concrete vision and steps for socio-economic structural reform and ensure its common and shared understanding among the nation's citizens" and formulated four priority policy areas for the development of a new national ICT infrastructure: 1) establishment of an ultra high-speed network infrastructure and competition policies, 2) facilitation of electronic commerce, 3) realization of an electronic government, and 4) nurturing high-quality human resources.

On 19 January 2006 at the end of the five-year period that encompassed the E-Japan strategy, a new strategy document was issued. This formulated the ICT policies for the next five years (E-Japan, 2006). Having a much more confident tone, the new strategy announces that most of the objectives of the first E-Japan Strategy have been realized and Japan has already become the world's most advanced IT nation.

In a retrospect, the document argues that there have been remarkable achievements including the development and utilization of one of the world's most advanced broadband infrastructures; the world's leading usage of sophisticated mobile phones; and the development of an environment for e-commerce and its expansion into one of the world's largest e-commerce markets. In other words, the first two priority policy areas of the first strategy have been fully realized.

Possibly encouraged by these achievements, the strategy document has almost a techno-deterministic (MacKenzie & Wajcman, 1999) tone:

(...) Japan, with the aim of developing an IT infrastructure that will serve as a base for the revolution of our society, has enacted the IT Basic Law and policies such as the e-Japan Strategy" (E-Japan, 2006, p.3).

This technology is so great that it has the potential of serving as a springboard for the reformation of our existing social structures (ibid., p.4).

However, it is also acknowledged that further efforts are needed and will become the components of the E-Japan Strategy 2006. These efforts will concentrate around fuller and more effective ICT-based government services, wider ICT implementation in services like health care, education, disaster preparedness, and corporate management. Further, the report acknowledges the digital divide between regions and generations in the country and calls for further strengthening international competitiveness of Japan. One of the most important tenets of the new strategy is that it has

(...) been formulated in order to help contribute to the creation of a borderless co-existence and co-prosperity society with Asia as its center (ibid., p.4).

By definition, national ICT strategies are formulated for individual countries and such an emphasis on regional cooperation in ICT is not common in national ICT strategies.

On 26 June 2001, five months after the first ICT strategy document was released, "IT Strategy Headquarters" added the fifth priority area of "Reinforcement of International Activities" to the E-Japan strategy in the E-Japan 2002 program (E-Japan 2001b). In the program, it is stated that Japan will play a central role in Asia as an Internet hub, engage in international cooperation concerning IT-related rules and regulations, and it will contribute to the expansion of the global IT revolution mainly in Asia and the development of human resources.

This position was further reinforced by the decision of the IT Strategic Headquarters on 10 September 2004 (E-Japan, 2004) and by the first E-Japan Strategy evaluation document that was issued on 24 February 2005, the last year of the strategy (E-Japan, 2005). The document officially formulated Japan's interest and desire for cooperation in the region in terms of ICT as well as

targets, policy measures to achieve these targets, and key evaluation points.

Japan's interest in the region in ICT issues is self-justified from several aspects. Firstly, South-East Asia is the fastest growing region in the world and an important part of this growth is attributable to high value-added ICT products. Secondly, the region hosts the two most populous countries in the world, India and China that are on their way to establishing sophisticated software and hardware production bases, respectively. Thirdly, although currently the overwhelming majority of the populations in these two countries do not have the economic means to access ICT goods and services, the immense size of these populations will be attractive markets for Japanese ICT products in future due to the growing middle classes and the wealth that is expected to come to some segments of the population through high growth rates. Fourthly, currently the second largest economy in the world and wanting to keep this position, Japan is seeking alliances in its competition in the "triad", i.e., against the US and the EU (Ohmae, 1985). As the above mentioned Japanese ICT strategy documents suggest, such an alliance would cover wide areas such as technical cooperation in developing and promoting ICT standards, an important aspect of competition in ICT goods and services (Hawkins, 1996). And finally, although not explicitly stated in the strategy documents, Japan is striving to sell its products to the world markets like all ICT-producing countries. Developing ICT-based close relations in a supra-region where about half of humanity lives has some natural implications for opening up new markets and further developing existing ones for its products. As a matter of fact, according to "Special Terms for Economic Partnership", goods procured from Japan should be no less than 30% of the total amount of ICT contracts (E-Japan, 2004). These objectives are abstracted in the official E-Japan Strategy 2006 document with high self-esteem and with a barely diplomatic tone:

Solving important social problems that face all humankind by making use of the unique characteristics of our nation. (...) We will be in a position to provide various solutions to world problems. (...) It is particularly in Japan's own interest to actively make such global contributions in the IT area focusing on the Asia region (E-Japan, 2006, p.8).

An important aspect of Japan's regional ICT strategy is the development of different modes of relationships with the Asian countries depending on their advancements in ICT. To this end, Japan categorizes the countries in three major groups (E-Japan, 2005). The first group contains the countries which have comparatively advanced ICT infrastructures, utilization, and human resources. Japan's strategy envisages high-level cooperation with the countries in this group, such as the promotion of various ICT standards, cooperation in research and development efforts, and joint development of ICT applications.

The second group of countries is those that have a stark domestic digital divide. These countries actively promote ICT infrastructure in urban regions but their wider rural regions have deficiencies in ICT infrastructure. Japan will support these countries to bridge their domestic divides by its hardware products and to develop public service systems such as e-government, disaster prevention, and distance education.

The third group includes the countries that lag in developing ICT infrastructure such as a domestic backbone network or ICT utilization in general terms. Japan will seek cooperation with these countries in closing their deficiencies in ICT. The efforts will include assisting these countries developing their national ICT strategies and developing a domestic human-resource base with ICT skills.

There is a long list of activities in Japan's ICT strategies aiming Asia. The strategy contains a set of activities targeting most of the Asian countries. These activities can be categorized in three main groups, namely joint R&D and standardization efforts; collaboration among governments, ministries, and organizations to foster ICT deployment and utilization in Asian countries; and assistance to countries in ICT-related "soft" issues such as developing human resources with necessary skills and strategy formulation. As can be expected, the first group of activities targets the countries that are relatively advanced in ICT deployment and utilization, the third group is for the countries that lag in ICT, and the second group is for the ones that are somewhere in between. Table 1 shows some of the Asian countries targeted by the Japan's Asia ICT strategy with the some areas of cooperation, assistance, and ICT sales (E-Japan, 2005).

Overall, one can trace the *zeitgeist* in Japan's ICT strategy aiming the region. The strategy *per se* is to establish and further develop ICT-based networks in a world where networks constitute the dominant mode of production (Castells, 2000).

NATIONAL AND REGIONAL ICT STRATEGIES IN AFRICA

Africa's development problem manifests itself in all aspects of ICT. Sub-Saharan Africa is the least developed region of the world. Increasing prices of import goods and decreasing prices of exports (mainly agricultural) are reducing living conditions in many parts of the region. The region's development problem is exacerbated by mismanagement and corruption as well as tribal and national conflicts and wars. Like almost all development indicators, the region's ICT indicators demonstrate very low levels of ICT utilization and almost nonexistent hardware and software production.

However, the explosive increase of mobile phones all over the world in the last decade spread to Africa where there was a five-fold increase in the 1990s. Between 2000-2005 Africa had a fast growth rate of Internet usage—186.6 percent as compared to the world average of 126.4 percent

Table 1. Some of the Asian countries targeted by the Japan's Asia ICT strategy and the areas of cooperation

	China	S. Korea	Singapore	India	Malaysia	Indonesia, Philippines, Thailand	Cambodia, Laos, Myanmar, Vietnam	Pakistan, Bangladesh, Mongolia
R&D and standardization in new technologies	√	√	√	√	√			
Copyright and pirated s/w issues	√	√						
Distance education			√			√		
E-commerce			√					
HR – skills development, education					√	√	√	√
E-government						√		
IC cards & cross-border issues			√			√		
Providing h/w & s/w'						√	√	√

and the number of mobile phone users increased from 4.2 million in 1998 to 82 million in 2005. Yet, Africa is still the least connected continent having only 1.6 percent of world's Internet users and 3.6 percent of mobile phone users and there are large disparities among the countries where Internet users in South Africa and Egypt comprise about half of the entire continent (Zeleza, 2005). Another problem is the slower growth rate of advanced information systems compared to personal communication devices.

Recently, there have been several attempts for developing an ICT base in the region. These include developing regional and national ICT strategies. Most of these attempts were either originated or supported by United Nations agencies such as UNECA (Economic Commission for Africa). UNECA's AISI (African Information Society Initiative) is an endeavor that aims to address the challenges and opportunities of the information age in the African context. The AISI framework was developed by eleven ICT experts appointed by UNECA who coordinates its activities and it was endorsed by the Organization of African Unity (OAU) summit in July 1996. AISI aims to realize the very difficult task of establishing sustainable information societies in Africa by 2010.

Along with other activities, AISI aims to support the development of a National Information and Communication Infrastructure (NICI) plan in every country of Africa. Etta (2005) argues that AISI has been successful not only in creating national ICT strategies in a continent where none existed prior to 1996, but also in articulating national e-government strategies. Rather than regarding ICT as an aim *per se,* the ICT strategies fostered by AISI emphasize the supporting role of ICT for broader and more urgent development objectives such as poverty eradication, industrialization, and debt management. Further, since many of the problems are common to the countries of the region, individual countries' experiences and best practices are to be taken into account in the strategy development process.

In the context of the AISI, governments are encouraged to join in the "African Information Society" that are to be realized by national ICT strategies. Like several of the national ICT strategies (Turkey (2006-2010) and Japan (2001-2005)), AISI envisages the development of five year plans starting in the years 1997, 2002, and 2007. Mainly as a result of these efforts, several African countries either have currently national

ICT strategies or are in the process of developing them (see http://www.uneca.org/aisi/nici/).

Lance and Bassole (2006) describe the NICI approach as consensus-based and consisting of well-established steps and corresponding outputs. This approach allows for the monitoring of progress and assessment of achievements. The authors argue that the NICIs are also comprehensive and address e-strategy at four levels: national, sectoral, village, and regional. The national e-strategy provides the common process for turning strategies from each level into operational actions and the commitment of the Office of President, Prime Minister, Cabinet, or equivalent office is sought as a first step. Then, a policy framework that involves the following is developed: (a) the undertaking of surveys and need analysis, (b) the identification of priorities and opportunities for NICI with respect to the economy, (c) and the assessment of current strategic information systems projects in the country. The next step is the formulation of strategic goals and targets which is followed by identification of decision making processes for oversight of the NICI strategy and resource mobilization. As implementation progresses, the NICI framework, policy, and plan are iteratively reexamined.

There are two important and interrelated facts that justify the development of African national ICT policies with a regional flavor. Firstly, sub-Saharan Africa that constitutes the bulk of the continent is the most under-developed region in the world and secondly, partly due to this underdevelopment, sub-Saharan countries have economic and social similarities in several aspects. Without disregarding the differences among individual countries, efforts for developing national ICT strategies can create a synergy not only for formulating but also implementing the strategies. The countries may learn from other countries' experiences what works and what doesn't and best practices may be disseminated easily.

These two basic facts also lead to some secondary conditions that justify the regional flavor.

Technological limitation is one of them and it results from various reasons all of which are related to the underdevelopment of the region. For example, lack of investment, lack of qualified personnel, and lack of technological supply and demand are all results of underdevelopment and all are pertinent to the region. These similarities result in similar usage patterns which in turn can be the basis for some aspects of the ICT strategies. For example, Longwe and Rulinda (2005) report on the lack of efficient paths to carry the data traffic between Internet Service Providers (ISPs) in Africa which occurs both on a national as well as on a regional or inter-country scale. As a result, an African Internet user's message travels to Europe or the US first before ending up in the mailbox of the recipient who lives in a neighboring city or country. It is estimated that this use of international bandwidth for national or regional data costs African Internet users about US$400 million each year. Such a transfer of funds from the poor to the rich is unacceptable since the investment needed to solve the problem is unlikely to exceed a few years' money that has been lost this way. This situation also applies to telephony where it may be easier to route a call from say Nairobi via Europe or the US to a neighboring country than to do so directly. Only 11 out of 53 African countries have Internet Exchange Points (IEP) which results in an inefficient exchange of African inter-country traffic through hubs located overseas mainly in the US and Europe. Since direct Internet communication among two countries requires both countries to have their IEPs, a regional ICT strategy that address similar problems would be beneficial not only for increasing the buyer's power through bulk purchases, but also for several other reasons such as developing best practices in hardware implementation.

Drawing attention to the widespread state failures of the 1980s and 1990s in Africa and calling for responsible policy making, Etta (2005) argues that the ICT policy making process in Rwanda is among the best in the continent due to three reasons. Firstly, it had a clear and simple vision which was constructed around the realistic aspirations of the people. That was confirmed by the interviews conducted by the author in Rwanda. Secondly, the mission for ICTs was solidly based on the country's main development strategy, the National 2020 Vision. Etta argues that this linkage is a little harder to see in other African countries. Thirdly, the President of Rwanda personally invested in the process by laboriously sitting through the initial policy consultations and asking questions as part of the listening audience. It is yet to be seen whether this success in strategy formulation will be replicated in the strategy implementation.

There is a fair chance that the geographical proximity of countries leads to cultural proximity. Neighboring countries may share a common language perhaps with some dialectical differences and this language can be a common platform for developing information systems through which the region benefits. Butt *et al.* (2008) argue that the regional angle can also come into play in formulating ICT strategies with components such as open source software development. The Kiswahili language is commonly used in East Africa and countries in the region may join their efforts in open source software development for various areas of application such as health and education. Quoting Moshi (2005), Zeleza (2005) argues that Kiswahili is a regional language that has the capacity to become a global language but East Africans should be the architects of Kiswahili's globalization rather than leave it to Western corporations like Microsoft which has announced in April 2004 that it would launch Microsoft Windows and Office programs in the Kiswahili language. Otherwise, control and ownership over the language might be lost as software and hardware designers in far away places set new protocols of linguistic standardization. Such a situation would lead to "foreign indigenous languages" as happened during the colonial period with European Christian missionaries.

Table 2 shows the countries in varying degrees of strategy development. Currently, 33 countries have already developed their policies. The process continues in 12 countries the process continues and 7 countries do not have any activity yet.

There are also attempts for developing strategies for particular ICT applications in some regions of Africa. For example, ECOWAS (Economic Community of West African States) sought the assistance of ECA to develop a regional legal framework for e-commerce. The framework should be consistent with the member states' strategic plan for the years 2004-2007. There is also an attempt to develop a broader ICT legal framework for the member states.

Some regions in the continent have attempted to formulate strategies for their own needs. For example, CEMAC (Economic and Monetary Community of Central Africa) is currently developing the regional ICT strategy called e-CEMAC. The strategy is envisaged to cover the countries in Central African region. International organizations like DISD (Development Information Services Division), SRO-CA (ECA Sub-Regional Office for Central Africa), and SRO-EA (ECA Sub-Regional Office for Eastern Africa) provide assistance to formulate the strategy.

There are also some non-government organizations that have activities in Africa to help governments to develop their ICT strategies. The Association for Progressive Communications (APC) is one of them. Established in 1990, APC is a network of civil society organizations that aim to support civil society through the use of ICT. Besides issues such as advocating freedom of expression on the Internet, communication rights and open source software, APC focuses on developing national ICT strategies in Africa. In doing so, its main approach is to assist governments developing their own strategies, rather than to develop strategies for them. In realizing its objective, APC's method resembles the "gift culture" that is the main motivation in developing open source software (Castells, 2001).

Table 2. African countries in varying degrees of strategy development

Countries with an ICT policy	Countries in the process of developing an ICT policy	Countries where the ICT policy development process is not launched
Algeria	Angola	Equatorial Guinea
Benin	Botswana	Eritrea
Burkino Faso	Chad	Guinea-Bissau
Burundi	Cameroon	Liberia
Cape Verde	Central African Republic	Libyan Arab Jamahiriya
Comoros	Dem. Republic of the Congo	Sao Tome and Principe
Congo	Gabon	Somalia
Cote d'Ivoire	Lesotho	
Djibouti	Sierra Leone	
Egypt	Togo	
Ethiopia	Zambia	
Gambia	Zimbabwe	
Ghana		
Guinea		
Kenya		
Madagascar		
Malawi		
Mali		
Mauritania		
Mauritius		
Morocco		
Mozambique		
Namibia		
Niger		
Nigeria		
Rwanda		
Senegal		
Seychelles		
South Africa		
Sudan		
Swaziland		
Tanzania		
Tunisia		
Uganda		

An important aspect of ICT strategy formulation through AISI seems to be the lack or inadequacy of domestic dynamics. As an "outsider",

UNECA has the definitive roles of not only strategy formulation and monitoring its implementation in national and regional levels through AISI, but it is also in charge of handling fund-raising activities for various AISI activities (AISI, 2003). There are 33 activities that have been organized through partnership between over seventy international organizations and non-African governments, but the involvement of local resources seems minimal. Only two African governments have been mentioned as partners in two of these activities; "African member states" in three activities; "Schoolnet Africa" in one activity; and Francophonie (an international organization of French-speaking countries and governments) in two activities.

Recently, van Grop (2008) investigated the influence of the region on national ICT policy and regulation making focusing on regional regulators' association. Using the case of the Southern African Development Community's (SADC) Communications Regulators' Association of Southern Africa (CRASA) she found that the association "has two primary mechanisms of influence on national ICT policy and regulation making in its member states, namely through capacity building and policy lobbying."

Another example for regional regulatory body for ICT, the first in the world, is the topic of the final case.

COMMON REGULATORY POLICY FRAMEWORK IN THE CARIBBEAN

Regional cooperation over ICTs may take even closer forms among smaller sovereign countries. Five Eastern Caribbean states, namely Dominica, St. Kitts & Nevis, Grenada, St. Lucia, and St. Vincent established a common regulatory framework for the telecommunications sector in 1998 (Kenny *et al.*, 2007). This framework led to the establishment of Eastern Caribbean Telecommunications Authority (ECTEL) in 2000. This is the first regional telecommunications regulatory authority in the world. The purpose of ECTEL is to facilitate the harmonization of the regulatory regime in

the region and to "design a transparent, objective, competitive, and investor-friendly licensing and regulatory regime to be implemented at the national level" (p.411). The member countries retain their sovereign power over licensing and regulation, ECTEL only provides technical expertise, advice, and support for national regulations.

Kenny *et al.* (2007) argue that ECTEL has provided several benefits for the region such as the increase of mobile telephone penetration from 2.3% in 2000 to 63% in 2004. Additionally, ECTEL's establishment resulted in the increase of network capacity and competition among operators which led to price reduction for most services and in the increase of direct investments and employment.

According to Hoekman and Mattoo (2007) regional cooperation organizations like ECTEL can potentially lower costs and realize economies of scale by spreading the fixed costs over a larger area and regional regulatory cooperation may allow the fixed costs of regulatory bodies to be shared. Additionally, cooperation through ECTEL has the potential for development of harmonized and transparent regulation in the region, allows a greater degree of independence and credibility in regulatory advice, and enhances bargaining power in negotiations with incumbents and potential entrants.

CONCLUSION

Social and economic development is a very complicated process which is affected by a myriad of factors. Development in these areas determines the level of production and utilization of ICTs. Regarded as the main tools of the information society which is associated with welfare, modernization, and wealth, ICTs are widely thought to have a special and very important role in all countries striving to transform themselves into an "information society." Thus, the cross-cutting and ubiquitous presence of ICT hardware and software in all facets of life distinguish them from other technologies and tools. Partly affected by the call of the World Summit on the Information Society for developing national ICT strategies, this race led to the formulation of national ICT strategies in an overwhelming majority of countries.

The unequal development levels in "core" and "periphery" regions and countries, however, are reflected not only in ICT utilization and production, but also in related strategy formulation and the realization capacity of the strategy. Although several developing country strategies target the information society, this is a very difficult target for them to achieve in the short term. Information society has some quantifiable universal attributes such as a low percentage of the population working in agriculture (Bell, 1973), and none of the national ICT strategies have such broad objectives. Transformation of the "periphery" into an information society involves very broad social and economic developments, and national ICT strategies must be regarded as *necessary but insufficient* steps on this long journey.

Partly due to the extent to which they are already realizing an information society and partly due to their accumulated social and economic capacity, the national ICT strategies of "core" countries usually have more realizable objectives. Japan, for example, has declared that it has achieved most of its targets after implementing its five-year strategy. Further, as the example of the Japanese ICT strategy towards Asia shows, some parts of the "core" eagerly pursues the development of the "periphery" in ICT terms, and taking an optimistic view, it can be suggested that this interest is not only in selling goods, but in achieving a win-win relationship. Perhaps the most meaningful relationship between "core" and "periphery" in this aspect is based on the "gift culture" aiming the development of ICT strategies in the least developed countries. Time will show the level of effectiveness of these efforts.

REFERENCES

Adamali, A., Coffey, J. O., & Safdar, Z. (2006). Trends in national e-strategies: A review of 40 countries. In *Information and communications for development: Global trends and policies* (pp. 3–14). Washington, DC: World Bank Publications.

AISI. (2003). *AISI: An action framework to build Africa's information and telecommunication infrastructure*. Retrieved January 19, 2007, from http://www.uneca.org/aisi/

Aligula, E. M. (2005). Benchmarking information & communication technology (ICT) performance: Lessons for Kenya. In Etta, F. E., & Elder, L. (Eds.), *At the crossroads: ICT policy making in East Africa* (pp. 257–271). Nairobi, Kenya: East African Educational Publishers Ltd., & IDRC.

Attewell, P., & Rule, J. (1984). Computing and organizations: What we know and what we don't know. *Communications of the ACM, 27*(12), 1184–1191. doi:10.1145/2135.2136

Avgerou, C. (2002). *Information systems and global diversity*. Oxford, UK: Oxford University Press.

Baliamoune-Lutz, M. (2003). An analysis of the determinants and effects of ICT diffusion in developing countries. *Information Technology for Development, 10*(3), 151–169. doi:10.1002/itdj.1590100303

Barrantes, R. (2007). Analysis of ICT demand: What is digital poverty and how to measure it? In *Digital poverty: Latin American and Caribbean perspectives* (pp. 29–54). Warwickshire, UK: Practical Action Publishing.

Barro, R. J., & Lee, J. (2000). *International data on educational attainment: Updates and implications*. CID (Center for International Development Working Paper at Harvard University) Working Paper No. 42. Retrieved December 6, 2006, from http://www2.cid.harvard.edu/cidwp/042.pdf

Bell, D. (1973). *The Coming of the post-industrial society*. New York: Basic Books.

Bollou, F., & Ngwenyama, O. (2008). Are ICT investments paying off in Africa? An analysis of total factor productivity in six West African countries from 1995 to 2002. *Information Technology for Development, 14*(4), 294–307. doi:10.1002/itdj.20089

Brookshear, J. G. (2003). *Computer science: An overview* (7th ed.). Boston: Addison Wesley.

Brynjolfsson, E., & Hitt, L. (1996). Paradox lost? Firm-level evidence on the returns to information systems spending. *Management Science, 42*(4), 541–558. doi:10.1287/mnsc.42.4.541

Butt, D., Sreenivasan, R., & Singh, A. (2008). ICT4D in Asia Pacific—An overview of emerging issues. In F. Librero (Ed.), Digital review of Asia Pacific 2007-2008 (3-18). New Delhi, India: Sage Publications and IDRC.

Camilleri, J. A., & Falk, J. (1992). *The end of sovereignty? The politics of a shrinking and fragmented world*. Aldershot, UK: Edward Elgar.

Caselli, F., & Coleman, W. J. (2001). Cross-country technology diffusion: The case of computers. *The American Economic Review, 91*(2), 328–335.

Castells, M. (2001). *The Internet galaxy: Reflections on the Internet, business and society*. Oxford, UK: Oxford University Press.

Chataway, J. C., Gault, F., Quintas, P., & Wield, D. V. (2003). *Dealing with the knowledge divide*. Geneva: World Summit on the Information Society, United Nations and the International Telecommunications Union.

Chiang, J. T. (2000). Institutional frameworks and technological paradigms in Japan: Targeting computers, semiconductors, and software. *Technology in Society, 22*(2), 151–174. doi:10.1016/S0160-791X(00)00002-6

Ciborra, C. U. (1993). *Teams markets and systems*. Cambridge, UK: Cambridge University Press.

Cross, M. (2005, August 4). Ethiopia's digital dream. *Guardian Unlimited*. Retrieved November 20, 2008, from http://technology.guardian.co.uk/online/story/0,3605,1541785,00.html

Delamaide, D. (1994). *The new super-regions of Europe*. New York: Penguin.

Doring, T., & Schnellenbach, J. (2006). What do we know about geographical knowledge spillovers and regional growth? A survey of the literature. *Regional Studies, 40*(3), 375–395. doi:10.1080/00343400600632739

E-Japan. (2001a). *E-Japan strategy*. Retrieved January 12, 2007, from http://www.kantei.go.jp/foreign/it/network/0122full_e.html

E-Japan. (2001b). *E-Japan 2002 program*. Retrieved January 16, 2007, from http://www.kantei.go.jp/foreign/it/network/0626_e.html

E-Japan. (2004). *Basic concept on IT international policy centered on Asia (provisional translation)*. Retrieved January 13, 2007, from http://www.kantei.go.jp/foreign/policy/it/040910concept_e.pdf

E-Japan. (2005). *IT policy package - 2005 - Towards the realization of the world's most advanced IT nation – (provisional translation)*. Retrieved January 3, 2007, from http://www.kantei.go.jp/foreign/policy/it/itpackage2005.pdf

E-Japan. (2006). *New IT reform strategy - Realizing ubiquitous and universal network society where everyone can enjoy the benefits of IT*. Retrieved January 18, 2007, from http://www.kantei.go.jp/foreign/policy/it/ITstrategy2006.pdf

Etta, F. (2005). Policy matters: The new development El Dorado. In Etta, F. E., & Elder, L. (Eds.), *At the crossroads: ICT policy making in East Africa* (pp. 3–15). Nairobi, Kenya: East African Educational Publishers Ltd., & IDRC.

Etta, F. (2005). Policy matters: Recommendations for responsible policy making. In Etta, F. E., & Elder, L. (Eds.), *At the crossroads: ICT policy making in East Africa* (pp. 295–297). Nairobi, Kenya: East African Educational Publishers Ltd., & IDRC.

Feigenbaum, E. A., & McCorduck, P. (1983). *The fifth generation: Artificial intelligence and Japan's computer challenge to the world.* Boston, MA: Addison Wesley.

Giddens, A. (Ed.). (1974). *Positivism and sociology.* London: Heinemann.

Hawkins, R. (1996). Standards for communication technologies: Negotiating institutional biases in network design. In Mansell, R., & Silverstone, R. (Eds.), *Communication by design: The politics of information and communication technologies* (pp. 157–186). New York: Oxford University Press.

Headrick, D. R. (1981). *The tools of empire: Technology and European imperialism in the nineteenth century.* Oxford: Oxford University Press.

Heeks, R. (2002). i-development not e-development: Special issue on ICTs and development. *Journal of International Development, 14*(1), 1–11. doi:10.1002/jid.861

Heeks, R. (2008). ICT4D 2.0: The Next Phase of Applying ICT for International Development. *Computer, 41*(6), 26–33. doi:10.1109/MC.2008.192

Hoekman, B., & Mattoo, A. (2007). Regulatory cooperation, aid for trade And the GATS. *Pacific Economic Review, 12*(4), 399–418. doi:10.1111/j.1468-0106.2007.00366.x

Hofstede, G. (2001). *Culture's consequences: Comparing values, behaviors, institutions, and organizations across nations* (2nd ed.). London: Sage Publications.

Ikiara, G. K., Olewe-Nyunya, J., & Odhiambo, W. (2004). Kenya: Formulation and implementation of strategic trade and industrial policies. In Soludo, C., Ogbu, O., & Chang, H. (Eds.), *The politics of trade and industrial policy in Africa* (pp. 205–224). Ottawa, Canada: IDRC and Africa World Press, Inc.

ITU. (1984). *The missing link: Report of the independent commission for worldwide telecommunications development.* Retrieved November 5, 2008, from http://www.itu.int/osg/spu/sfo/missinglink/index.html

Kaplinsky, R., & Morris, M. (2007). Do Asian drivers undermine export-oriented industrialization in SSA? *World Development, 36*(2), 254–273. doi:10.1016/j.worlddev.2007.06.007

Kenny, C., Schware, R., & Williams, E. (2007). The impact of reform on telecommunications prices and services in the countries of the OECS. *Information Technology for Development, 13*(4), 411–415. doi:10.1002/itdj.20069

Krishna, S., Ojha, A. K., & Barrett, M. (2000). Competitive advantage in the software industry: An analysis of the Indian experience. In Avgerou, C., & Walsham, G. (Eds.), *Information technology in context: Studies from the perspective of developing countries* (pp. 182–197). Aldershot, UK: Ashgate.

Lance, K., & Bassole, A. (2006). SDI and National Information and Communication Infrastructure (NICI) Integration in Africa. *Information Technology for Development, 12*(4), 333–338. doi:10.1002/itdj.20051

Landauer, T. K. (1995). *The trouble with computers: Usefulness, usability, and productivity.* Cambridge, MA: MIT Press.

Lanvin, B. (2005). E-strategies for development: Efficient e-strategies require strong monitoring and evaluation. In Schware, R. (Ed.), *E-development: From excitement to effectiveness* (pp. 47–63). Washington, DC: The World Bank Group.

Lee, J. W. (2001). Education for technology readiness: Prospects for developing countries. *Journal of Human Development, 2*(1), 115–151. doi:10.1080/14649880120050

Longwe, B., & Rulinda, C. (2005). Of gateways and gatekeepers: The history of Internet exchange points in Kenya and Rwanda. In Etta, F. E., & Elder, L. (Eds.), *At the crossroads: ICT policy making in East Africa* (pp. 199–212). Nairobi, Kenya: East African Educational Publishers Ltd., & IDRC.

Lucas, H. C. (1999). *Information technology and the productivity paradox*. New York: Oxford University Press.

Machlup, F. (1962). *The production and distribution of knowledge in the United States*. Princeton, NJ: Princeton University Press.

MacKenzie, D., & Wajcman, J. (1999). *The social shaping of technology* (2nd ed.). Buckingham, UK: Open University Press.

Mansell, R., & When, U. (1998). *Knowledge societies: Information technology for sustainable development*. New York: Oxford University Press.

Menou, M. J. (1993). *Measuring the impact of information on development*. Ottawa, Canada: IDRC.

Moodley, S. (2005). A critical assessment of the state ICT for poverty reduction discourse in South Africa. *Perspectives on Global Development and Technology, 4*(1), 1–26. doi:10.1163/1569150053888254

Moshi, L. (2005, March-April). *African languages in a global age: The case of Kiswahili*. Paper presented at the 36th Conference on African Linguistics, Savannah, GA.

Nakamura, Y., & Shibuya, M. (1996). Japan's technology policy - A case study of the R&D of the fifth generation computer systems. *International Journal of Technology Management, 12*(5-6), 509–533.

Neto, I., Kenny, C., Janakiram, S., & Watt, C. (2005). Look before you leap: The bumpy road to e-development. In Schware, R. (Ed.), *E-development: From excitement to effectiveness* (pp. 1–22). Washington, D.C.: The World Bank Group.

Ohmae, K. (1985). *Triad power*. New York: The Free Press.

Page, S. (1999). *Regionalism among developing countries*. Basingstoke, UK: Macmillan. doi:10.1057/9780333982686

Putnam, R. D. (2000). *Bowling alone*. New York: Simon & Schuster.

Roberts, J. (2000). From know-how to show-how? Questioning the role of information and communication technologies in knowledge transfer. *Technology Analysis and Strategic Management, 12*(4), 429–443. doi:10.1080/713698499

Rodriguez-Pose, A., & Crescenzi, R. (2008). Research and development, spillovers, innovation systems, and the genesis of regional growth in Europe. *Regional Studies, 42*(1), 51–67. doi:10.1080/00343400701654186

Sahay, S. (1998). Implementing GIS technology in India: Issues of time and space. *Accounting. Management and Information Technologies, 8*(2-3), 147–188. doi:10.1016/S0959-8022(98)00002-2

Schunk, D. H. (2003). *Learning theories: An educational perspective* (4th ed.). Upper Saddle River, NJ: Prentice-Hall.

Shaxson, N. (2007). *Poisoned wells: the dirty politics of oil in Africa*. London: Palgrave.

Solow, R. (1987, July 12). We'd better watch out. *Book Review No. 36, The New York Times*.

Souter, D. (2004). ICTs and economic growth in developing countries. *The DAC Journal*, *5*(4), 7–40.

Thorpe, R., & Little, S. E. (Eds.). (2001). *Global change: The impact of Asia in the 21ˢᵗ Century*. London: Palgrave.

Toffler, A. (1980). *The third wave*. New York: Bantam Books.

Ulrich, P., & Chacko, J. G. (2005). Overview of ICT policies and e-strategies: An assessment on the role of governments. *Information Technology for Development*, *11*(2), 195–197. doi:10.1002/itdj.20011

Van Grop, A. (2008). *Increasing regulatory capacity: The role of the region in shaping national ICT policy in southern Africa.* Unpublished doctoral dissertation, The Pennsylvania State University.

Vodaphone. (2005). Africa: the impact of mobile phones. *Vodafone Policy Paper Series No. 2*. Retrieved January 13, 2008, from http://www.vodafone.com/assets/files/en/GPP%20SIM%20paper.pdf

Walsham, G. (2001). *Making a world of difference: IT in global context*. New York: John Wiley & Sons, Ltd.

Walsham, G., & Sahay, S. (2006). Research on information systems in developing countries: Current landscape and future prospects. *Information Technology for Development*, *12*(1), 7–24. doi:10.1002/itdj.20020

Wigand, R. T., Picot, A., & Reichwald, R. (1997). *Information, organisation, and management: Expanding markets and corporate boundaries*. New York: Wiley.

World Bank. (2005). *Financing information and communication infrastructure needs in the developing world: Public and private roles – Draft for discussion*. Retrieved January 18, 2007, from http://lnweb18.worldbank.org/ict/resources.nsf/a693f575e01ba5f385256b500062af05/04c3ce1b933921a585256fb60051b8f5/$FILE/financingICT_Draft.pdf

WSIS. (2003). *Plan of action*. Retrieved October 15, 2008, from http://www.itu.int/wsis/docs/geneva/official/poa.html

Zeleza, P. T. (2005). Postscript: Challenges of the ICT revolution in East Africa. In Etta, F. E., & Elder, L. (Eds.), *At the crossroads: ICT policy making in East Africa* (pp. 283–294). Nairobi, Kenya: East African Educational Publishers Ltd., & IDRC.

Zhao, P., & Grimshaw, D. J. (1991). *A comparative study of the application of IT in China and the West: Culture and stages of growth model (Warwick Business School Research Papers, No. 32)*. Coventry, UK: Warwick Business School Research Bureau.

Zuboff, S. (1988). *In the age of the smart machine: The future of work and power*. New York: Basic Books.

ENDNOTE

[1] In 1984 the International Telecommunication Union (ITU, 1984) issued the well-known "Missing Link" report. The report observed that "neither in the name of common humanity nor on grounds of common interest is such a disparity (in telephone penetration) acceptable." However, the previous decades' often-quoted phrase of the "Manhattan having more telephones than entire Africa" does not hold true any more. By 2002, there were 22 million fixed and 37 million mobile lines

in Africa. The situation is the same or better in other parts of the developing world. This is partly attributable to the massive rollout of mobile phones in the 1990s and beyond (World Bank, 2005). The diffusion of mobile phones is so fast that by 2002 the number of mobile phones had exceeded fixed-line phones in the world. The takeover was realized in only one decade after the introduction of mobile phones. Comparing this to the lifetime of fixed telephone lines which is more than one century gives an idea about the diffusion speed of new technologies.

Chapter 5
Information System Strategy Development and Implementation in the Egyptian Small and Medium Construction Enterprises

Khaled Samaha
The American University in Cairo, Egypt

Khaled Dahawy
The American University in Cairo, Egypt

ABSTRACT

Egypt's diversified economy has historically performed below its potential; however the Egyptian government is recognizing the importance of small to medium enterprises (SMEs). SMEs face many constraints including weak supply of skilled labor, limited access to capital and poor access to IT. This chapter provides an investigation into the Information System (IS) strategy of SMEs in Egypt using questionnaires and case studies to explore whether SMEs in Egypt follow a comprehensive IS strategy or whether IS is not viewed as an important factor in organisational success. It was evidenced that most Egyptian SMEs lack the structure needed to successfully plan an IS strategy. However it was discovered from three case studies that organisations operating with a structured hierarchy proved to be far more advanced with regard to IS strategy planning. In addition, communication between levels was more efficient; therefore alignment of IS strategy with business strategy was inevitable. It was also evidenced that top management involvement is present at the decision making stages and through implementation, and IS planning is undertaken in some way by Egyptian SMEs. However they face many problems with lack of resources and lack of expertise. This is mainly due to management not understanding the need to recruit experienced individuals.

DOI: 10.4018/978-1-60566-388-3.ch005

INTRODUCTION

Small and medium-sized enterprises (SMEs) are a vital part of any national economy. Nowadays, to survive in the global knowledge-based economy, SMEs have to improve their products, services and processes, exploiting their intellectual capital in a dynamic network of knowledge-intensive relations inside and outside their borders (Levy and Powell, 2005). The managerial challenge, then, consists of creating new knowledge management (KM) configurations – in term of technological and organisational tools – leading to organisational models sustainable from the competitive point of view (Metaxiotis, 2009). On the other hand, it is nowadays clear that advanced decision support systems (DSS) as well as business information systems (BIS) assist enterprises in automating and integrating corporate cross-functions and provide the basis for business process management integration in order to minimise costs and increase efficiency and effectiveness of enterprises (Kirytopoulos et al.., 2009)

In the European Union, there is currently a debate concerning the necessity to support SMEs and enhance their competitiveness through tools fostering technological and strategic-organisational innovation. Janez Potočnik, the European Commissioner for Science and Research, stressed in Paris (15 September 2008) that SMEs are the DNA of the European economy (Metaxiotis, 2009). The figures prove this statement:

- There are 23 million SMEs in Europe… some 99% of all businesses
- They employ 100 million people… some 70% of the workforce.

However, it is agreed that many SMEs do not invest in ICTs. The 2005 e-business report shows that while many medium-sized SMEs are now catching up, small firms (up to 49 employees) remain behind. Some remain sceptical about ICT and e-business, finding many IT solutions still too expensive or untrustworthy. In general, SMEs hesitate to implement IT methodologies, mainly due to the following factors (Ergazakis et al., 2009):

- KM is being considered as an unaffordable luxury
- SMEs consider that KM cannot offer them strong advantages
- They doubt whether they can apply KM into their processes.

It have been noted that in most developing countries, SMEs have low interest in obtaining foreign technologies and are even less able to absorb and adapt these technologies to their own use (Levy and Powell, 2005). This research gives a chance to identify whether SMEs in Egypt follow a comprehensive IS strategy (ISS) or whether IS is not viewed as an important factor in organisational success. Strategic IS planning was ranked on the top of the listings of critical issues in IS management (Niederman et al., 1991). Earl (1989) stated that the planning approach should not differ too much from the organisation's general planning style and control structure and it should also reflect the complexity and significance of the organisation's IS and the consensus about the mission of the organisation's IS department. Formulating an ISS is now seen as a fundamental necessity in the modern organisation, where business tasks are linked both internally and via networks (Bentley, 1998).

In this manuscript, we present an investigation whose objective is to achieve an investigation into the IS strategy of SMEs in Egypt, by exploring whether Egyptian SMEs follow the traditional IS models that are used by organisations in the Western5 civilisation or do they have an equally effective procedure. In Egypt, the business environment is characterised by certain organizational practices and management style deficiencies (such as authoritarian management style) and limitations of financial resources (Lynch, 2006). Therefore, investigating the ISS of SMEs in Egypt could open the door to improved procedures and practices. While SMEs constitute more than 99% (MOEFT, 2004) of all non-agricultural private enterprises in Egypt and account for nearly three-quarters of new employment generation, the sector suffers from inadequate resources and inefficient labour utilisation. This necessitates the adoption of development strategies and policies that make the economic environment conductive to its growth and integration in the mainstream economy. The Egyptian SMEs sector have been dramatically shaped and reshaped by major shifts in the national political economy (MOEFT, 2005). The Egyptian Government are now recognising the importance of SMEs and have joined together with the Canadian International Development Agency (CIDA) and the International Development Research Centre (IDRC) to aid SMEs, giving them a chance to blossom in a dynamic global environment (MOEFT, 2006). SMEs stimulate private ownership and entrepreneurial skills; they are flexible and can adapt quickly to changing market demand and supply conditions; they generate employment, help diversify economic activities and make significant contribution to export and trade (Levy et al., 2003). SME contributions to employment creation, productivity improvement and income generation are under-utilised in Egypt at a time when economic transformation is shifting the onus for productivity from the public sector to the private sector (MOEFT, 2006). In this context, this study aims at discovering if a trans-national global IS can be applied to SMEs in Egypt. A trans-national global IS can be described as an accumulation of different 'best-practices' from around the world regarding IS, including frameworks and models from different theorists (Palvia et al., 2006).

In this emerging new economy, information technology (IT) is expected to significantly contribute to the managerial modernisation of Egyptian companies, which are under increasing pressure from global economic competitiveness

and face problems of low productivity (Salmela and Spil, 2002; and Wynn, 2009). By improving the complex relations between the IS function and other business functions in a firm, IS is becoming a unique capability and a source of sustainable competitive advantage (Mata et al., 1995; and Levy and Powell, 2005). Delone and Mclean (2003) recommended that the relevance of the variables to be included in a model depends on the objective of the study, the organisational context and the aspect of IS addressed by the study.

BACKGROUND

For understanding the information in this chapter it is necessary to define information system strategy and SME policy in an Egyptian context. This section is divided into two subsections. Section 2.1 provides an overview of information system strategy development and implementation. Section 2.2 provides a brief description and analysis of SMEs in Egypt, and the Egyptian Governments attempts to support them. The factors outlined in this section will be used in the manuscript later to draw relevant conclusions.

Information System Strategy: An Overview

Defining Strategy

Strategies help to explain the things that managers and organisations do. *"Strategy is a broad based formula for how business is going to compete, what its goals should be, and what policies will be needed to carry out those goals. The essence of formulating competitive strategy is relating a company to its environment"* (Porter, 1980). These actions or activities are designed and carried out in order to fulfill certain designated purposes, some of them short term in nature, others long term. Specific milestones and targets (objectives) can help to guide specific actions and measure

Figure 1. IS strategic planning process (Adapted from Boar, 2001)

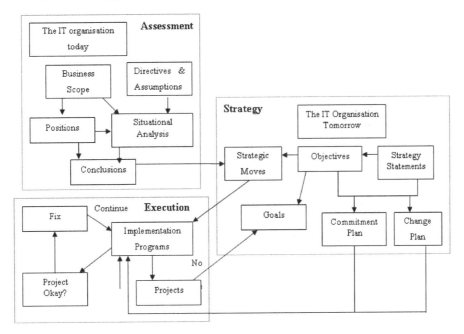

progress. Strategies therefore, are means to ends (Levy and Powell, 2005). They are relevant for the organisation as a whole, and for the individual businesses and/or functions that comprise the organisation. They are created and changed in a variety of ways. They have, however, one common feature: they all have lifecycles and need changing, either marginally or dramatically, at certain times (Thompson, 2001).

An information system links together data inputs, processes and information outputs in a coherent, structured way. Information Technology in this project is used to mean the physical hardware involved in computers and communications networks as well as any software that runs on the hardware (Ward, 1995). IS adopted by SMEs tend to be simple (Duhan et al., 2001) as most SMEs view IS as a cost and are reluctant to invest after start-up. However, some SMEs recognise the potential of IS to change their business, primarily those seeking growth (Levy et al., 2003; and Wynn, 2009).

Strategic Thinking and Planning

ISS is no longer an option in the rapid changing business environment of today (Boar, 2001). The IS strategic planning process (Figure 1) provides an ordered set of steps designed to culminate in the development and execution of a comprehensive IS strategic business plan.

Each section of the process is a separate activity that must be joined together to ensure that the whole process is executed efficiently, each function is described:

• **Assessment** is the activity of developing a clear and through understanding of the business situation from both an internal and external perspective. It identifies 'conclusions' that pinpoints critical issues requiring strategic attention. Positioning provides a graphical way to understand the 'position' or state of IS in all relevant strategic areas. Situational analysis is the use of various analytical methods to inter-

Table 1. Barriers to success in IS/IT strategic planning (Adapted from Ward, 1995)

Barrier	Importance ranking	
	Development	Implementation
Measuring benefits of the plan	1	3
Nature of the business-rate of change	2	2
Difficulty in recruiting IT staff	3	1
Political conflicts in the organisation	4	6
Existing IT investments-constraining effect	5	5
Lack of resources to educate users	6	4
Doubts about application benefits	7	10
Telecommunications problems	8	9
Middle management attitudes to change	9	7
Senior management attitudes	10	8

pret the data about the organisation and its environment.

- **Strategy** consists of identifying strategy statements for the business. Objectives are descriptive of what we wish to achieve, and strategic moves are prescriptive, identifying the actions to be undertaken.
- **Execution** is the action of putting the plan into motion. It is the translation of intent to reality. Strategies are made operational through implementation programs that are partitioned into multiple projects.

For more empowered organisations, emphasis can be put on the definition of the strategy statements for the organisation and the specifics of how it can be left to the entrepreneurial talents of the management team (Boar, 2001). This will apply to innovative style SMEs who encourage employee's participation. Strategic IS planning is described as the process of formulating IS objectives, defining strategies and policies to achieve them and developing detailed plans to achieve the objectives (Earl, 1989). The strategic IS planning process also involves a long-range planning horizon for funds, human services, technical expertise and hardware and software capabilities needed

to take advantage of any opportunities that may arise (Teo et al., 1997).

There are many issues when considering IS strategic planning, and many obstacles that can hinder the success. Ward (1995) identified a number of barriers that prevent an effective strategic plan being developed and then implemented. Table 1 lists the issues in descending order of priority regarding the developing the strategy, and implementing it.

A key outcome of IS strategy planning (ISSP) is a portfolio of IS that will assist an organisation in executing its business plans and realising its business goals (Lederer and Sethi, 1988). ISSP within the organisational environment to date in SMEs is surprisingly sparse and underdeveloped (Levy et al., 1999; and Levy and Powell, 2005). Hagmann and McCahon (1993) found that less than 50% of the SMEs that owned or planned to purchase a specific IS devoted any specific planning effort of IS but associated issues such as management of the systems, organisational changes and integration with current technology architectures. Galliers (1991) recommends that the organisation's information requirement should be the key driver for IS.

The lack of strategic planning, both business and IS/IT, which takes place in SMEs, has implica-

Figure 2. Four cycle's method (adapted from Salmela et al., 2000)

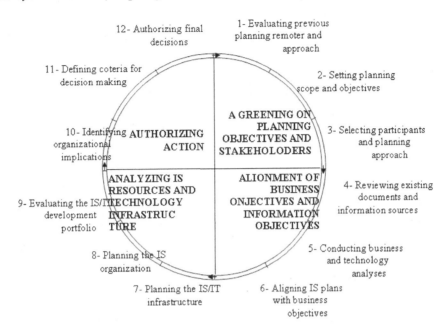

tions for IS/IT evaluation. One major implication is the lack of clear yardsticks or objectives against which to measure the feasibility of potential IS and guides the decision process (Ballantine et al., 1998). However, the experience of strategic IS planning that some SMEs have, is usually focused on improving operational processes rather than achieving strategic objectives (Hagmann and McCahon, 1993). Another important objective in ISSP is to ensure senior management commitment for implementing the selected projects and to create a partnership between IS and user groups for successful implementation efforts (Teo and Ang, 2001).

The research paper by Salmela et al. (2000) state that early strategic IS planning methods are too static for formulating IS strategies in the new age. The objective of the four cycles method (Figure 2) is to promote continuous planning that involves sufficient degree of formalism to ensure that all critical areas of IS planning are addressed periodically. It provides a periodic planning schedule and identifies issues (Each period had a constant focus on external developments and the

fit with internal possibilities) that should be addressed periodically (Salmela et al., 2000). Hence, the method should be useful in organisations that prefer to have some degree of formalism in their IS planning process.

The four cycles method divides a chosen period of time into four different planning cycles: (1) agreeing on planning objectives, (2) aligning business objectives and information objectives, (3) analysing IS resources and IT infrastructure, and (4) authorizing actions. The four cycles method is a combined method (Salmela et al., 2000), and incorporates both comprehensive and incremental planning.

Opponents of comprehensive IS planning have suggested that the need to reply on formal planning methodologies and predefined criteria can trivialise planning so much that it becomes merely a simple top-down exercise (Galliers, 1991). In addition, formal planning has also been shown to replace, rather than support informal communication (Salmela et al., 2000). On the other hand, given the complexity of issues in the planning agenda and the broad (inter) organisational implications that the new web-based systems often have, relying on a totally informal and incremental planning process involves risks as well (Henderson and Sifonis, 1988).

In the incremental approach, explicit planning methods are seen as having only a minor role. While methods can be used, they are seen more as process enablers to be used in an ad hoc manner (Earl, 1993). The incremental approach does not provide similar explicit step-by-step methods for IS planning, as was the case with comprehensive approaches. The process is informal and rests very much on the ability of key managers to include the right people and conduct the right analyses. Incremental planning is based in the theory that organisations learn and benefit by adapting based on their learning (Salmela et al., 2000). A mixture of incremental approach and comprehensive planning would be ideal allowing managers to make decisions but keeping to a structure to ensure a methodological approach. This will include empowering employees that will ultimately improve motivation. A combined method would be needed to support the synthesising of qualitative and quantitative data into visions of the appropriate direction to pursue (Levy and Powell, 2005).

Top Management Involvement

The actions of others may well affect what the firm has to do or can do (Ward and Peppard 2002). A previous survey had shown that obtaining top management commitment to the process was a prerequisite for success, but that it was often difficult to obtain (Ward, 1995). The survey identified the following reasons:

- Top management lack awareness of the impact IS/IT is having generally and did not understand how IS/IT offered strategic advantages.
- They perceive a credibility gap between the 'hype' of the IT industry as to what IT can do and how easy it is to do it, and the difficulties their organisation has had in delivering the claimed benefits.
- Top managers do not view information as a business resource to be managed for long-term benefit.
- In spite of the difficulty in expressing all IS benefits in economic terms, top management demand to see financial justification for investments.

Abdul-Gader (1999) stresses the lack of top management awareness of systems impact on organisational processes as a barrier to systems diffusion in developing countries. In addition, the empirical evidence from Arab countries, suggests that systems effectiveness is likely to depend on top management support (Abdul-Gader, 1990).

There is a general agreement in IS literature that greater top management support for a system will lead to greater system effectiveness (Bentley, 1998). Top management support includes adoption of a broad IS vision and leadership, alignment of IS strategies with business strategies, allocation of organisational resources to support its IS vision and communication to all members of the organisation. Cultural acceptance of systems in an organisation cannot be attained without top management's political clout (Abul-Gader 1990). IS researchers have shown for a long time without ever really formalising it, that '*whether or not an asset can be considered a resource depends as much on the organisational context as on the properties of the asset itself*' (Duhan et al., 2001). This reinforces the IS view that it is the use and management of IS that confer advantage, not their mere existence.

Alignment

Much of the literature on alignment states that the IS planning process is the crucial time during which alignment is forged. Partial support for this hypothesis was reported in a study showing that IT executives who participate more in business planning believe they have a better understanding of top management's objectives than those who participate less (Lederer and Salmela, 1996).

A common theme running through the ISSP literature is the connection of IS/IT strategy with business strategy, and so frameworks from strategic planning are adapted and utilised with an IS perspective. IS plans and strategies should be linked directly to the objectives and strategies of the business unit and be considered as part of the overall business planning process (Duhan et al., 2001). One process that may be considered close to an incremental method is the Continuous Strategic Alignment method described by researchers from the MIT-school in the early 1990's (Ward, 1995). In essence, the method identifies alignment mechanisms.

- Technological capability process, which specifies and modifies the IT products and services needed to support and shape business strategy.
- Human capability process, which specifies and modifies the various human skills to support and shape business strategy.
- Value management process, which allocates the required resources and ensures maximal benefits from IT investment.
- Strategic control, which attempts to maintain internal consistency among the four mechanisms.

The method acknowledges the need for a dynamic administrative process to ensure continuous strategic alignment between the business and IT fields.

Cultural Differences

Cultural factors are likely to be powerful explanations for why those from technically advanced societies who attempt to implement technology are often challenged in terms of their own ideas, beliefs, and values about how technology "should be" utilised in developing countries (Seliem et al., 2003). Cultural factors also explain why individuals, situated in the upper strata of the society who either work for international companies or who have spent some time in industrialised countries (such as U.S., Western Europe, or Japan), bring with them from abroad significant cultural biases when implementing systems at home. At home they experience cultural conflicts with mid-level managers and workers who, unlike the owners, directors, and top administrators in instructions and businesses, are not widely traveled and ultimately have the responsibility for daily use of technology (Straub et al., 2001).

Compared to Westerners, Arabs, including Egyptians, demonstrate more power distance (reflected in high centralization and autocratic leadership) and more uncertainty avoidance (manifested in high formalisation and low tolerance to ambiguity) (Abdul-Gader, 1990). Most Arab organisations (public or private) ate highly centralized and adopt an authoritative structure, regardless of corporate strategy or technology (De Boer and Walbeek, 1999).

Outsourcing and IS Investment

Outsourcing is the contracting of various systems sub-functions, such as data entry, programming, facilities management, systems integration, support operations of maintenance, service and disaster recovery, managing of data centers, and telecommunications by user firms to vendors (Grover et al., 1996). This trend towards outsourcing has currently become a major information systems phenomenon.

Companies are increasingly outsourcing the development and management of IS and IT for reasons that include access to specialised skills, cost, staff utilisation, reduced recruitment and training, high standards of control and security, and proliferation of information services (Udo, 2000). One source predicted the growth in such IT professional services to more than double between

1998 and 2004 and there has been a near consensus that IT outsourcing contracts will dramatically increase in number in the coming years (Hogbin and Thomas, 1994).

However, many reasons remain for developing IS/IT applications internally. These reasons include the need to accommodate customised products or services, confidentiality of business data, the desire to reduce vendor risk, ease of development, ease of internal adaptation of software, and the desire to develop leading-edge competence (Downing et al., 2003). Additionally, companies are increasingly using software purchased off-the-shelf to assist with their processes.

Investment in IS/IT is estimated to be on a par with spending on research and development (Willcocks and Lester, 1991). IS/IT evaluation is problematic, principally as a result of the difficulties inherent in measuring the benefits and costs associated with such investments (Ballantine et al., 1998). Investing in IT can be an extremely expensive and time-consuming exercise and its justification is difficult to quantify because of ineffective Information Management Systems (Gunasekaran et al., 2001). IS is an ever increasing problem to managers, as they constantly have to invest and justify their decisions to update software and hardware to keep abreast of their competitors. Essentially, the purpose of IT investment is to improve operational efficiency of an organisation so as to reduce costs and improve profit levels.

In stating a case for the justification of IS, managers must embrace various appraisal techniques such as IT budgeting, IT investment management, IT project planning, investment budgeting, payback period performance metrics and return on investment (ROI) (Hochstrasser and Griffiths, 1991). However, the justification of IT is a complex issue due to many intangibles and non-financial benefits. According to Parker and Benson (1989), most chief executive officers (CEOs) are not comfortable with the current tools and techniques used to justify their investments in

IT, because they lack the preciseness of definition in the financial methods used.

Well-managed IT investments that are carefully selected and focused on meeting business needs can have a positive impact on an organisation's performance. Likewise, poor investments, those that are inadequately justified or whose costs, risks, and benefits are poorly managed can hinder and even restrict an organisation's performance (Gunasekaran et al., 2001). Hochstrasser and Griffiths (1991) argues that the high rate of failure in IT projects is partly attributed to a lack of solid but easy to use management tools, for evaluating, prioritising, monitoring and controlling investments in IT. Many traditional appraisal techniques are used to evaluate tangible benefits, which are based on direct project costs. Willcocks and Lester (1991) concluded that many industry sectors when looking to introduce IT still use the cost benefit and competitive advantage as their primary evaluation criteria.

Owing to the dynamic factors inherent in IT investments, evaluation must be regarded as a continuous process that needs to be constantly reviewed (Ward and Peppard 2002). It cannot be acceptable to justify a policy proclaiming a single one-off evaluation procedure. Without regular re-evaluation, additional potential benefits may be missed for the following reasons (Mata et al., 1995):

- Technology may develop to a stage where cheaper technical solutions become viable.
- Users may outgrow the current system.
- The demands of the market environment in which a company operates may change so older systems no longer address current needs.

SME Policy: The Egyptian Experience

The Egyptian economy and it's small to medium sector have been dramatically shaped and reshaped by major shifts in the national political economy (MOEFT, 2006). This section provides a brief description and analysis of SMEs in Egypt, and the Egyptian Governments attempts to support them. The factors outlined in this section will be used in the manuscript later to draw relevant conclusions. The section has emphasised many constraints that SMEs face, the governments role in the development of SMEs and provided a definition of SMEs for the purpose of this study.

In developing a definition for Egyptina SMEs, several considerations should be noted. Firstly, there is no such thing as a correct definition. A definition's adequacy however is a result of several factors, including the availability and reliability of data, the size structure of enterprises in the country (or within business sectors), and the government's purpose (access to certain services or privileges), among others. Second, while more complex definitions that use several variables may seem to be more accurate, some experts warn us against using certain variables (Levy and Powell, 2005). According to the Ministry of Economy and Foreign Trade (2002) 'because assets and receipts are measured in currency, and the value of almost all currencies changes from time to time, employment is the preferred measurement dimension.' In fact, the poor quality of data in Egypt, especially that relating to annual receipts and capital investments poses an additional problem when it comes to utilizing these indicators. For the purpose of this report the definition that is to be used is based on number of employees, as the research is focusing on organisational size and not turnover. For an organisation to be defined as a SME they must employ between 1-1000 employees (Seliem et al., 2003).

Constraints for Egyptian SMEs

Non-Financial Constraints

SMEs face many non-financial constraints including weak supply of skilled labour, poor access to information and technology, limited access to production inputs, and inadequate physical facilities and bad locations (Ministry of Economy and Foreign Trade 2000). Furthermore, when recruited, the retention of trained workers is a general problem. As skills level increase, they tend to leave the enterprise to start their own or to work in large firms that provide more benefits. In most developing countries, SMEs have low interest in obtaining foreign technologies and are even less able to absorb and adapt these technologies to their own use (Straub et al., 2001). This is a disadvantage to Egyptian SMEs and can hinder the enterprise growing, as technology is the key in today's business environment.

The lack of adequate physical locations also affects the entry of new SMEs as well as the growth of current enterprises. The locations of SMEs in new and relatively under-serviced industrial towns keep them away from their markets and hence raise the costs of buying inputs and selling products. As 84% of SMEs occupy rented workspace, (more than 61% acquire their working space through inheritance), the new non-residential rent law may have several adverse impacts on the future development of the SMEs sector (MOEFT, 2002).

Financial Constraints

The main constraint faced by virtually all SMEs is their limited access to capital and financial services that can meet their working and fixed capital needs on a sustainable basis. The formal financial structure (banks, capital markets... etc.) is generally alien to SMEs (MOEFT, 2004). Due to the lack of adequate institutional and financial resources, the SME sector faces significant barriers to the entry of new enterprises as well as the growth of existing ones. Accordingly, financial services came to constitute the major component in SME development efforts for the Egyptian Government (MOEFT, 2002).

SMEs in Egypt are usually perceived as unreliable customers to banks. They generally do not have the capacity to provide adequate feasibility studies and business plans that larger clients can present (MOEFT, 2002). Furthermore, SMEs lack the collateral that can guarantee the recovery of loans by the banks. Moreover, even if collateral does exist in a limited number of cases, the slow, costly and uncertain court proceedings disproportionately hamper lending to small firms, as the involved overhead costs make collateral recovery prohibitively expensive (MOEFT, 2002).

Recent studies conclude that the share of small and medium enterprises of the collective loan portfolio of the banking sector in Egypt does not exceed 6%. It is thus not surprising to find that 92% of small enterprises never obtain a loan from any of the banks operating in Egypt. Seventy eight percent of the small enterprises in Egypt did not even attempt to obtain a bank loan (MOEFT, 2006). Research of SMEs in Egypt has shown that the vast majority of SMEs in Egypt rely on their personal savings (or loans from family members) in establishing their enterprises. Similarly, in expanding their enterprises they rely predominantly on their savings or the profits, which their enterprises have generated. The sources are insufficient to spur growth in a highly dynamic and competitive environment (MOEFT, 2006). Banks also refrain from providing savings services to SMEs because their accounts are often too small to be profitable and can be administratively burdensome.

Employment Constraints

SME operations in Egypt also suffer from regulatory constraints. Local level regulations (especially on health safety and workplace conditions) prescribe in great detail procedures, operational standards, and administrative set-ups (committees, staffing, and periodicity of meetings…. etc.) that businesses must adhere to (MOEFT, 2002). Changes in production techniques or the introduction of new products require a re-approval of the establishment and operations (E&O) license (MOEFT, 2006). SMEs face management constraints because they often lack the basic skills in management, accounting, information technology,

and cannot access consulting and support services (MOEFT, 2002).

For Egyptian SME sector, full formality is an expensive undertaking. As a recent research study shows, only 54% of enterprises comprising 1-10 workers can be considered fully formalised, with 14% considered semi-formal, and 32% classified as informal. This also points to the massive size of the informal sector, which provides employment for approximately 21% of the labour force in Egypt (per 1995 estimates) and, according to conservative estimates, contributes 30% of the GDP (MOEFT, 2002). Informality, however, has its price. An informal enterprise will have to keep a low profile to avoid detection by the authorities. In addition, in most cases it cannot expand and has to remain relatively invisible (MOEFT, 2002).

Lack of Access to Information Technology

SMEs competitiveness is reduced by their inability to upgrade the utilized technology, as well as tap on the courses of information on market trends, consumer preferences, and product specifications (MOEFT, 2006). Like elsewhere in the developing world, SMEs in Egypt have low interest in obtaining foreign technologies and pertinent information, and are even less able to absorb and adapt these technologies and information to their own use. In addition to regulatory constraints, the underdevelopment of linkages and subcontracting with larger and more sophisticated local and international partners further contributes to the underdevelopment of the technological base of SMEs (MOEFT, 2002).

Lack of Market Information

Nearly two-thirds of small businesses consider the lack of market information to be a very severe constraint (MOEFT, 2002). SMEs lack the mass, and their owners lack the education (only 9% are believed to have attained a university degree) to tap sources of relevant information (new products, consumer trends, technological developments…

etc). Moreover, given their weak resource base, SMEs are unlikely to invest in market research or employ the marketing talent that larger firms can easily recruit (MOEFT, 2005).

Linkages between small enterprises and large firms are significantly underdeveloped. Only 25% of large firms subcontract to other firms. Although the Egyptian Government reports that SMEs are eager to subcontract, they cite their poor managerial and technological capabilities as the major bottleneck for backward linkages (i.e. local content making) (MOEFT, 2005). In addition, SMEs have limited access to public contracts and subcontracts, often because of cumbersome bidding procedures and/or lack of information.

Government Support to SMEs

The fundamental key to a successful SME development strategy according to SME policies is the establishment of a business environment that helps SMEs compete on a more equal basis (Levy and Powell, 2005). There are many advantages to SMEs and Levy et al. (2003) and Levy and Powell (2005) highlighted some of the important points:

- Create jobs with low capital costs.
- Create conditions for development and introduction of new technologies.
- Function as subcontractors for large corporations.
- Adapt faster to the demand and fluctuations of the market place.
- Fill marginal areas of the market, which are not targeted by large corporations.
- Decentralized business activity and help foster faster development of regions, small towns and rural communities.
- Alleviate the negative impact of structural changes.

SME contributions to employment creation, productivity improvement, and income generation are under-utilized in Egypt at a time when economic transformation is shifting the onus for productivity from the public sector to the private sector. In June 1998, the Ministry of Economy and Foreign Trade (back then the Ministry of Economy) issued a "Draft National Policy for Small and Medium Enterprises in Egypt." The document was probably the first attempt at proposing such a national policy framework in response to a situation whereby, as per 1997 data, the country had more than forty different SME projects sponsored by government agencies, donor agencies, and non-governmental organisations. Back then the government found that $560 million US dollars were being invested in developing the sector in the absence of such a framework. Egypt needs consistent framework to guide and streamline these efforts and invest these resources efficiently (MOEFT, 2002).

The Egyptian Government needs to develop a strong private sector, stimulate ownership solutions, significantly increase the number of entrepreneurs, and in particular, develop the SME sector (MOEFT, 2005). The minister of economy and foreign trade in Egypt emphasises this by issuing a statement in the monthly SME policy newsletter: '*Today let me share with you a vision that I have of our society being the most apt at fostering the growth of SME, not only because of our present circumstances, or of our needs in terms of industrialisation, but most importantly because of our fabric. The fabric of our Egyptian society promotes cohesion: in self-support, cohesion in tightening the community and a tightening society is what is needed to foster the growth of a modern and capable SME sector.*' (MOEFT, 2005). It is obvious that maximum efforts are being made to increase the trade of SMEs and the Egyptian economy can benefit greatly.

A key component of a successful SME development strategy is the establishment of a business environment that helps SMEs compete on a more equal basis. To establish a level playing field for SMEs, the Egyptian governments need to (MOEFT, 2006):

- Re-evaluate the costs and benefits of regulations that place a disproportionate burden on SMEs.
- Implement regulations with the flexibility needed by SMEs.
- Place greater emphasis on competition and opening procurement practices to small firms.

ANALYSIS OF IS STRATEGY IMPLEMENTATION: THE CASE OF EGYPTIAN SMES

For the purpose of this study, four areas of IS strategy are explored namely: IS strategy decision-making, IS strategy planning, IS strategy problems and IS sourcing. The four areas to be investigated can be summarised as a formulation of a trans-national global IS. Although these areas have been found to affect IS strategy formulation, this research intends to discover if organisations from developing countries such as Egypt, consider them to be important.

In addition, a number of situational and demographic characteristics of organizations are included in the research model as contingency variables. These variables give an overview of the SME status, regarding the number of employees, how old the business is and its turnover, which can all be used as measures for analysis. In order to gain an understanding about the present IT structure of SMEs, some further contingency variables have been introduced (i.e., the number of computers). These contingency variables have been chosen with regard to secondary research and where we feel there is a need to gain information of the SMEs to gain a superior overview.

Setting the Scene for Investigation

Currently, many models and frameworks have been identified in the literature that recognise the importance of organisations aligning IS strategy with their business strategy to ensure consistency throughout implementation of projects [such as Boar (2001) and the four cycles method (Salmela et al., 2000)]. It is not yet clear whether organisations in developing countries such as Egypt follow a comprehensive, an incremental approach or a combined approach. In this section we identified four areas of IS strategy to set the scene for investigation bases on the literature review undertaken in the previous section, namely: IS strategy decision-making, IS strategy planning; IS strategy problems and IS sourcing.

IS Strategy Decision Making: Top Management Involvement

Top management support is seen as a fundamental necessity to achieve success, Ward and Peppard (2002) believes that obtaining top management commitment to the process of IS implementation is a prerequisite for success but that it is often difficult to obtain. However, they recognise that ultimately someone at the board level, even the CEO should be accountable for IS, although often that will not be their main responsibility, there is still some debate to whether someone at this level should make it their primary concern.

Top management in developing countries such as Egypt is expected to play a far more proactive and critical role than in a developed country in order to ensure a smooth and successful system implementation (Jain, 1995). This is because top management is seen as the ultimate power in Egyptian organisations, therefore they are expected to have knowledge in all areas of business (MOEFT, 2005). However, this is not the case in many

Egyptian firms as Abdul-Gader (1990) indicates that top management do not involve themselves with IT functions, as they lack the knowledge in this area. From the varied amount of views regarding this topic, it is seen as an area that needs more investigation.

IS Strategy Planning

By improving the complex relations between the IS function and other business functionsin a firm, IS strategy planning could, in the long run, become a unique capability and a source of sustainable competitive advantage (Wynn, 2009). Many organisations operate with different departments that need to be aligned to channel their effort toward one organisational goal. Willcocks and Lester (1999) indicate that spending on IS and in particular IT capital, is widely regarded as having enormous potential for reducing costs and enhancing the competitiveness of firms.

Whether organisations have an IS manager, an IS department and a specific IS budget is an issue that must be investigated. IS is regarded as a tool that can enhance business performance and to make this as efficient as possible, an IS manager is needed, whose primary task it to coordinate all the organisations IS activities. This can be reinforced as argued by Ward and Peppard (2002) by devoting a department solely to IS. Organisations that become increasingly efficient are usually associated with larger turnovers per employees, so organisations of different size can be compared (Belleflamme, 2001). By determining whether SMEs in Egypt recognise the importance of IS strategy planning and whether they continually seek to improve will provide relevant information to analyse this issue.

IS Strategy Problems

The actions of others may well affect what the firm has to do or can do regarding IS (Ward, 1995). It is important for organisations to recognise that IS is a fundamental function and they can control this now more than ever. It is then necessary for SMEs to gain the expertise needed to enhance their performance in this area. Ward and Peppard (2002) stated that IS knowledge ensures the conception of strategies to utilize technological innovation, to seize opportunities quickly and to implement these strategies successfully.

In this emerging new economy, IS is expected to significantly contribute to the managerial modernisation of Egyptian SMEs which are under increasing pressure from the global economic competitiveness and face problems of low productivity (Salmela and Spil, 2002), difficulty in gaining new technologies and adequate expertise (MOEFT, 2002). It is necessary to investigate into this topic to gain an understanding as to the IS problems of Egyptian SMEs.

IS Sourcing

To remain competitive and ever increasingly sophisticated in the marketplace, businesses must invest in IT if they are to survive in the long-term, whether this is through outsourcing or internal solutions. Many organisations choose a 'best of breed' approach to their outsourcing strategy, contracting with a variety of vendors for the delivery of IT services (Ward and Peppard, 2002).

It is now easier than ever to gain the relevant advice and find external firms to assist in the IS of organisations. Managers should not make a one-time decision whether to outsource or not. Organisations should choose to outsource carefully selected, non-core activities that can be accomplished quicker, cheaper and better by external companies (Ward and Peppard, 2002). Earl (1996) argues that companies should first ask why they should not in-source IT services. Justification of the IS budget need to be considered as it is quite common for IS managers to be under attack from senior management for seemingly endless rapid increases in IS budgets (Ward and Peppard, 2002). It is necessary to investigate into this topic to gain an understanding as to the outsourcing activity of Egyptian SMEs.

The Investigation Tools

This study uses a variety of methods to investigate the four areas of IS strategy, namely: IS strategy decision-making, IS strategy planning; IS strategy problems and IS sourcing. This includes questionnaires and interviews in order to collect relevant data to compile case studies and discussions. The questionnaire was firstly piloted to ten accounting professors to test for validity, reliability and the method of analysis. The importance of this was highlighted by Saunders et al. (2009) stating that questionnaires have to be tried out, improved and then tried out again. It is inevitable that bias will be experienced (Marshall and Rossman, 2006) and to alleviate this, the questions were constructed in a way, which minimised bias by not including leading questions, which guide respondent to a certain answer (Belson, 1982). To avoid a low response rate, the questionnaire was aimed at the IS manager or someone nearest to that position, as it was realised that IS managers may not be available to complete the questionnaire.

Secondary research was carried out in order to gain an understanding of the issues regarding ISS, Egypt and SMEs. Much secondary research was done in the area of IS and many factors were identified as important to organisational success. Different models and frameworks were investigated, accumulating to a theory of trans-national IS. The hypotheses including the contingency independent variables were considered based on the literature review and the secondary research. Other secondary research was done trying to discover different elements, including economic, cultural and social perspectives to aid with the analysis of Egyptian SMEs. Any information gained from organizations from Egypt are fully referenced and used only with prior consent. All the information is protected by copyright; however the documents have been used with adequate referencing and permission has been granted.

Initially, a sample of all SMEs within Egypt was envisaged, however, problems were encountered while undertaking the research and changes had to be made. Initially, a meeting was arranged with the Minister of Information, where a list of SMEs in Egypt would have been obtained and a sample could have been chosen. However, due to the meeting being cancelled, a sample was taken

from other resources. A mixture of haphazard sample and random sample was used for selecting the sample for the current study.

The sample was selected from Misr for Construction and Building Information (MCBI), who collaborate with construction SMEs within Egypt; one objective of MCBI is to assist their clients in developing their internal operation and decision-making systems through the use of IT. There are 30 SMEs within their database, which represents approximately 50% of all SMEs within this sector as indicated by the Managing Director of MCBI. Therefore, this represents a haphazard sample from which the research can be done, however, giving a random sample with the resources at hand. The SMEs can be described as random as they have not been pre-chosen by the researcher (Marshall and Rossman, 2006). Therefore, the sample was drawn from all the 30 SMEs and aimed at the person who deals with the IS within the company or the nearest to that position. There are some practical reasons for using a haphazard sample. First, the unavailability of published data on companies' sampling frame in Egypt (Abou Aish, 2001); second, lack of cooperation of organisations with the researchers and problems through direct contact with members of the Ministry of Information and finally, this method of sampling was forced upon this investigation as the meeting with the Ministry of Information being cancelled.

Taking into account the above, convenience sample becomes a necessity. As Tuncalp (1988) highlighted in reference to a neighbouring Arab country 'it is a formidable, if not impossible, task to draw probabilistic samples in Saudi Arabia'. In the same vein, Al-khatib et al. (1997) conducted a cross-cultural investigation of consumer ethics between Egypt and the USA. Also, Abou Aish (2001) conducted a cross-national research of bank selection decision and implications for positioning comparing between Egypt and the UK. Both studies highlighted the difficulty of conducting a survey research depending on a random sample in Egypt. We decided to employ

Figure 3. Number of employees

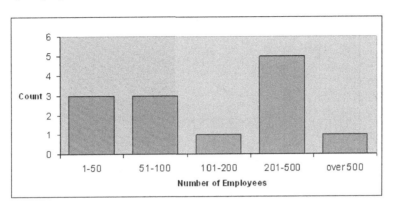

partially a haphazard sample in the current study especially that this approach was used successfully in the above mentioned studies. In those two studies, the researchers used a random sample in the USA and the UK respectively and a non-random sample in Egypt as a consequence of the sampling difficulties in Egypt.

We received 13 questionnaires representing a response rate of 43%. Three SMEs from the returned questionnaires were chosen to compile case studies to gain a more in-depth insight into their IS behaviour. The SMEs for the case studies were chosen based on the ease of accessibility representing a haphazard sample and size. One SME was from the smaller end bracket as defined by the questionnaire (as measured by the number of employees) and one from the larger size bracket. It is worth noting that the smaller bracket is taken from between 1-100 employees, and the larger taken from 201 and over. The third firm was chosen on the basis of haphazard sampling, as it was accessible to the author. The organisations give an overview of the SMEs in Egypt as they represent a wide range of expertise in IS. The SMEs were chosen to gain a wide variety of knowledge regarding the issues identified in the hypotheses. We recognise that the building and construction industry is not in the leading edge of technology and is regarded as underdeveloped with regard to IS, however, due to forced changes

this industry was accessible, hence using the haphazard sampling method.

The Investigation Results: Questionnaires

Descriptive statistics in the form of frequencies and percentages were calculated to summarise the contingency variables, including situational and demographic characteristics of the organisations.

The results show that 84.6% of the SMEs were from the private sector and just 15.3% was from the public sector. IS managers made up 38.5% of the SMEs, managing directors 30.8%, secretaries 7.7%, internal consultants 7.7% and others were 15.4%. Regarding the number of employees in each SME (Figure 3), the results show that 23.1% between 101–200 personnel, the major share (38.5%) consisted of 201–500 employees and 7.7% employed over 500 staff.

The annual turnover was calculated in US dollars in thousands. 15.4% of the SMEs had a turnover of 50–250 thousand dollars, 15.4% had a turnover of 250–750, 23.1% had a turnover of 750–1000, only 7.7% had a turnover of one million to 2 million and the majority of SMEs had a turnover of over 2 million (38.5%).

The percentage of the annual budget (Figure 4) for IS was dominated by SMEs investing between 1%–10% of their budget, 53.8% investing

Figure 4. Percentage of the annual budget for IS

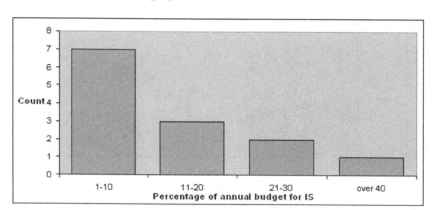

Figure 5. Number of computers that operate in the organisation

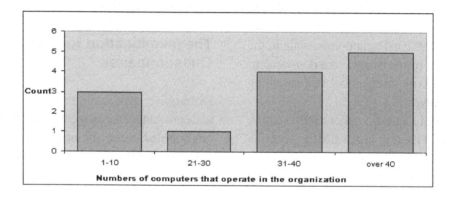

within this bracket, 23.1% between 11%–20%, 15.4% between 21%–30% and only 7.7% over 40%, however this seems to be against the norm and is thought that this result be ignored, as it is possible that the question was not understood by the respondent.

The results relating to the age of each SME revealed that only 7.7% has an age of less than five years, which was the same for SMEs between 6–10 years, 15.4% were 11–15 years and this was the same for SMEs between 15–20 years. The majority of SMEs (53.8%) were over 20 years of age.

Regarding the general information about the SMEs hardware, it was found that 23.1% are operating between 1–10 computers, 7.7% had between 21–30 computers, 30.8% between 31–40 computers and the majority of SMEs 38.5% had

over 40 computers operating in the organisation (Figure 5).

IS Strategy Decision-Making

The frequency results show that 46.2% of the SMEs had an IS manager. This was also consistent with SMEs reporting that 46.2% of SMEs had a separate department for IS. Regarding the organisational structure, 92.3% recognised that they had one, with one organisation apparently not operating with any type of structure. Of the 12 organisations that have a structure, 69.2% of them operate with the 'deep and narrow' style hierarchy and the remaining three organisations operate with a 'shallow and wide' style. Regarding the ISS within the organisation, 76.9% recognised

Table 2. Perceived importance of the factors affecting ISS decision making as mean scores (rank in parentheses): All companies

Factors affecting ISS decision making	Min	Max	Mean	Std. Deviation
IS Project must include top management	3	5	*4.15 (4)*	.899
Communication is a key part of any IS project	3	5	*4.31 (3)*	.855
It is essential to acquire qualified personal	3	5	*4.54 (1)*	.660
Empowering employees is necessary to gain motivation	2	5	*4.00 (5)*	.816
Employees gain feedback after project implementation	2	5	*4.46 (2)*	.877

Table 3. Perceived importance of the factors affecting ISS planning as mean scores (rank in parentheses): All companies

Factors affecting ISS planning	N	Min	Max	Mean	Std. Deviation
Projects require planning to ensure consistency	13	3	5	*4.46 (1)*	.776
IS projects need to be aligned to corporate strategy	13	3	5	*4.08 (4)*	.760
Regular checks throughout the project are needed to ensure corporate goals are met	13	3	5	*4.23 (3)*	.832
Outsourcing is essential to the success of the organization	13	2	5	*3.85 (5)*	.987
Information needs to be identified first, and then technology developed to satisfy them, second	13	3	5	*4.38 (2)*	.650
IS projects are regularly updated after completion	13	2	5	*3.85 (5)*	.987

it as an important factor in organisational success and 76.9% believe that top management within the organisation realise the importance of IS (they were not the same SMEs in each case). However, 92.2% believed that peoples IS knowledge can be improved within the organisation; of those 40% felt training was the best way, 30% reading and 30% thought practice. Table 2 shows the results of the perceived importance (judged by a 1–5 Likert scale)14 of the factors affecting ISS decision-making. The results indicated that acquiring qualified personnel is seen as the key element in the success of the ISS decision-making.

Information System Strategy Planning

The frequency results show that 46% indicated that it was the IS manager who made the decisions on ISSP, 46% managing director and 8%

advisors. This indicates that the decision in some SMEs was made by both the IS manager and the managing director. It was found that 76.9% of the SMEs indicated that they plan their ISS and 84.6% recognise the importance of ISSP. Also, 84.6% aligned their ISS with corporate/business strategy and 61.5% alleged that their ISS is regularly updated. In addition, 61.5% of SMEs make regular checks while carrying out ISS to ensure objectives are being met. Of those, 50% indicated that it was the IS manager who carried out the checks, 37.5% managing directors and 12.5% advisors. Table 3 shows the results of the perceived importance (judged by a 1–5 Likert scale) of the factors affecting ISSP. The results indicated that planning the IS project and identifying the needs are the key elements to pursue the ISSP process.

Table 4. Perceived ISS Problems as mean scores (rank in parentheses): All companies

ISS problems	N	Min	Max	Mean	Std. Deviation
There is a lack of expertise within the organization	13	1	5	*3.31 (1)*	1.182
Management fail to recognize the benefits of IS	13	2	5	*2.92 (2)*	1.115
IS are viewed as unnecessary expenses	13	1	5	*2.69 (4)*	1.032
IS are not used to maximum effectiveness	13	1	5	*2.77 (3)*	1.363

IS Strategy Problems

The frequency results show that one major problem found in Egyptian SMEs is a possible lack of expertise within the organisation, with 69.2% agreeing to this statement. In addition, it was found that 46.2% felt that IS was viewed as an unnecessary expense within the organisation and 53.8% thought that IT/IS was used to maximum effectiveness within the organisation. Table 4 shows the results of the perceived ISS problems (judged by a 1–5 Likert scale). The results indicated that lack of IT expertise within the organisation is the major problem found in Egyptian SMEs.

Information System Sourcing

The frequency results show that IS managers managed the process of sourcing in 46.2% of the SMEs, managing directors 38.5%, advisors 7.7% and one respondent answered other. When asked whether they bought their hardware or had it been made to certain specifications, 69.2% indicated that they buy from manufacturers and 30.8% informed that it had been made to specification. While 69.2% purchase their IT material from multinational businesses, 30.8% bought from local manufacturers. The maintenance of computers within the organisation was done through outsourcing in 53.8% of the SMEs and in 46.2% it was done partly in-sourcing and partly outsourcing. In addition, 76.9% had their programs written by an external company and in 23.1% it was done internally (in-sourcing). Regarding the software used, 69.2% used commercial 'off the shelf' solutions and 30.8% had customised solutions made.

The Investigation Results: In Depths Case Studies of 3 Egyptian SMEs

Hamza Associations (Firm A)

Hamza Associations (HA) was founded in 1979, and has grown to an award-winning organisation whose design and technical expertise extends over a comprehensive range of engineering, construction supervision, and project management activities. By continually monitoring industry developments worldwide, they incorporate the latest design and engineering techniques into every project, creating innovative and economical solutions that are fully responsive to clients' needs. They operate with a deep and narrow hierarchy, which can be seen in Figure 6.

Besides being well known in Egypt, HA has increasingly taken on projects internationally in Africa, the Middle East and Europe. The computer facilities of HA do not lack depth, where communication through an internal network is used throughout the organisation. The internal network used is a Local Area Network (LAN), which consists of 4 severs and 160 PC workstations. HA invests approximately 12.5% of their $3 million annual turnover to IS. Appendix F shows a diagram of the network map used within the organisation.

HA employs 380 staff which consists of engineers, architects, and technicians, supervised and

Figure 6. Hamza association organizational hierarchy

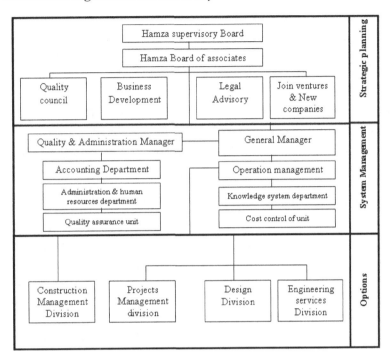

directed by 32 key managers, most with PhDs covering the full scope of engineering, architectural, and planning disciplines. This indicates that there is a high level of education within the organisation. HA possesses an extensive range of computer facilities to fulfill its working requirements including a computer center, consisting of a variety of computer software (i.e. CAD Applications: AutoCAD 2000, AutoCAD LT, 3D Studio and Turbocad 2D/3D. Project Management: MS Project, Primavera. Standard Software: MS Word, MS Excel, MS Power Point, MS Access. Graphics Programs: Corel Draw, Harvard Graphics, Adobe Photo Shop, Adobe Deluxe. Internet Programs: Adobe Page Maker, MS Front Page, MS Internet Explorer, Netscape Navigator, Eudora. Engineering Software: Specific Software for each department) to provide the departments with the necessary tools that ensures the autonomy and performance of outputs, and several computers are linked to printers, plotters and digitizer, with a full range of up-to-date computer software. The

computer network links all HA offices, which are outfitted with the latest engineering and management software, field and laboratory testing equipment for geo-technical investigations and material quality control, as well as topographic survey and mapping facilities. The IS section of the organisation is within the knowledge department of HA and can be seen in the organisations chart, Figure 6.

IS Strategy Planning of Hamza Associates
Much of the ISSP is undertaken by the IS manager within the organisation, however major decisions are discussed with the board of directors in the organisation and the final verdict is determined by them. The IS department consists of 10 employees including the IS manager. During implementation of an IS project the IS manager usually undertakes any checks to ensure the organisational goals are being met, this includes regular assessment after project completion to ensure the IS is being used to maximum effectiveness. The IS manager

still believes that there is room for improvement with regard to the knowledge of IT of employees within the organisation, and believe this can be improved with regular up-to-date training, giving an opportunity for employees to gain the relevant knowledge.

With regard to the sourcing of materials within HA, much of it is purchased from multinational companies (approximately 70%); however they also use local manufacturers if the need arises. Much of the IT materials is purchased over the Internet, with a company credit card, and is usually done by the IS manager personally after permission from the Managing Director has been granted. The software used is usually bought from manufacturers however some Engineering software is made to specifications depending on the intended usage. The maintenance of the computers within the organisation is generally undertaken within the organisation (90%); however 10% is outsourced when the problem is too demanding for the organisations expertise. The maintenance team consists of 5 personal who ensure the smooth running of the organisation computers. The maintenance team operate within the IS department and are guided by the IS manager. The maintenance team can be contacted through the secretary of the department as and when needed.

HA evidently has a good knowledge of ISSP and top management involvement is viewed as an important part of the process. The decision making usually lies with the IS manager, however major decision about the system must be discussed and verified with the board of directors. This shows that top management involvement is seen as a major part of the IS strategy. It is important as they are aware of the significance of aligning all departments and the impact ISSP has on the organisation.

Regular communication between departments is present through networks, and changes take place keeping up with the dynamic business environment. It is evident that the communication of the organisation is efficient, which is an important aspect when considering the overall business strategy.

The extensive use of software indicates a certain level of expertise within the organisation, and is used to its full potential, however it is felt that there is still a need for regular training, as technology is an ever-moving commodity. HA continually aims to improve their hardware and software, and realise the importance of updating there information systems regularly.

Firm B

Due to the confidentiality rights of the organisation they will be referred to as Firm B. Firm B was established in 1995 and employs 105 staff: 90 Professionals, 5 Technicians and 10 Administrative. They are a development consulting company committed to improving the quality and economic welfare of people and communities throughout the Middle East. They are funded partially by the government, and privately by organisations that require their services. The efforts centre on providing a range of professional services to help organisations succeed in achieving their public policy and developmental objectives. They support clients with tailored technical assistance, marketing and training services. A key function of the work is to organize research missions, which contribute to the development and implementation of the clients' strategic and tactical goals, and external and internal quality improvement programs.

Firm B operates with a deep and narrow organisational hierarchy, as can be seen in Figure 7. Although at first glance Figure 7 seems to adopt the 'shallow and wide' hierarchy, the vice president of each department is responsible for their own team of employees.

The computer facility of Firm B consists of 40 PC workstations, where communication between departments is via e-mails and file transfer is done through 3.5 Floppy Disk or Zip Disks. Each computer is equipped with a Zip drive. Firm B

Figure 7. Firm B organizational hierarchy

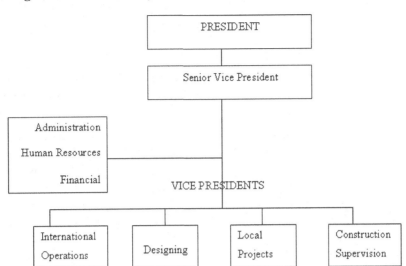

invests approximately 2% of their $1 million annual turnover to IS, and believe this will not be needed each year, as they suggest that the organisation is able to operate sufficiently with the present IS. However, they realise technology is rapidly changing and therefore state they will update once the need arises. If the organisation can operate with the current facilities they believe there is no need to invest, unless it can significantly increase their turnover.

Firm B currently operates with standard manufactured software, and do not need to have any made to specification. Within each department there are two computers that are connected to the Internet, and this is seen as sufficient. Each computer would have the opportunity to be connected; however there is reason to believe that this would distract individuals from their daily tasks. Each computer is connected to two printers that are present in each department. The design department has additional hardware, including scanners and CD-writers. The software presently in Firm B seems to be adequate for their purpose, which indicates they do not posses much experience in this area. There is no separate department within

the organisation therefore there is no such position as IS manager.

IS Strategy Planning of Firm B

Much of the IS strategy planning is undertaken by senior vice president, and makes all major decisions concerning IS. Any implementation of IS is outsourced to specialised organisations; however this is only done when necessary. Top management support is imperative within this organisation as they are the ones making the decisions. The organisation seems to be under developed with regard to ISSP; however they don't believe that it is a major problem. It is apparent that the president of Firm B does not believe that investing in IS will give a significant financial return. This shows a lack of knowledge in this area, and an inability to forecast the long term benefits of IS.

The vice president believes they posse adequate hard/software. All of the software is purchased form manufacturers and no customised software is needed. Any maintenance the organisation needs is done through external firms. They consider this as the most efficient option as it would not be cost effective to employ staff to fill this post. Firm B's long term aim is to eventually make IT training available for all employees, and believe this will help the organisation run more efficiently if all employees have some knowledge of IT.

Firm C

Firm C was established in 1957 with the aim of participating in the development of Egypt and other Arab countries, by providing professional Engineering Services. The firm is mainly established and structured to fulfill the specific needs of local/regional programs related to public utilities, community services, industrial facilities and infrastructure projects. Firm C maintains an excellent reputation with over 200 clients in 5 countries, ranging from private Sector, public Sector Companies, Governmental organisations and International Funding Agencies.

Firm C has always aspires to achieve its objectives by carefully selecting highly qualified professionals with academic and practical experience. Firm C has more than 25 years of experience in providing a wide range of consulting services, by utilizing the modern information technology software and hardware. Firm C employs 345 staff; 245 professionals, 26 Technicians and 74 administrative.

The computer facility of Firm C consists of 150 PC workstations, where communication between departments is through a Wide Area Network (WAN), as offices are not within the same building. Each workstation within each department is connected to a LAN. The internal networks (LAN) of each department are connected to the WAN. This creates an efficient manner of communication throughout the organisation, irrespective of the positioning of the departments.

Firm C invests approximately 11% of their $4 million annual turnover to IS, and believe this should be continually assessed to ensure they are up-to date with technology. Firm C have an IS department that is coordinated by an IS manager and 20 staff. Included within the IS department

is a helpdesk for any maintenance requirements other departments require.

IS Strategy Planning of Firm C
Within the IS department IS staff specialise in engineering design software ensuring that the firm stays on the cutting-edge of computer-assisted design technology. They provide training and support in the use of customised design software and maintain the internal and external networks. They also train client's staff in the use and maintenance of management software.

Firm C don't believe that top management involvement is necessary, and operate self-sufficiently unless decisions need to be made regarding important issues that will affect the organisations turnover. This includes major investments of IS materials, where approval from top management is necessary. Implementation of IS is undertaken by the IS manager personally and any training to other departments is done by the IS staff.

The IS manager recommends ways to improve the knowledge of IS within the organisation; to exchange business plans with world class organisations. Attending fairs and exhibitions related to IT, visits to foreign associations and engineering industries, and gaining feedback from external communications abroad. Evidently the IS manager realises that communication between organisations not only within Egypt can be of benefit. Seeking to share methods and gain enhanced practices and procedures to improve the knowledge of ISSP within the organisation.

IN DEPTHS DISCUSSION: LINKING THE RESULTS FROM THE QUESTIONNAIRES AND CASE STUDIES

This section discusses the results supplemented by evidence from the three case studies. First, it appears from the results of the questionnaire that 76.9% of SMEs recognised the importance of top management support in IS. Top management support means active top management participation and involvement (Teo et al., 1997). This may prove to be due to the fact that SME usually have a flatter hierarchy, therefore not as many levels as large organisations. The minimum levels of hierarchy may prove to be a reason that many organisations do not have an IS department, as it is not seen as a necessity. Many of the SMEs investigated were found not to have an IS department (53.8%) and 53.8% do not have an IS manager. It would leave the responsibility of IS decision-making to the general manager of the organisation, increasing the participation and involvement.

As the case study of Firm B shows, top management support is imperative as they have no such position as an IS manager, therefore all decisions are down to the senior vice president. Delone and Mclean (2003) believe that top management support is an important variable for success. If IS is to be a strategic tool, it is important for top management to understand and appreciate IS and control it as a strategic resource. Gunasekaran et al. (2001) argued that SMEs that do not include top management in IS decision are underdeveloped when considering ISS, unless top management are fully convinced of the benefits of to deliver quality applications on time, resources necessary to translate IS plans into actual implementation are likely to be used for other projects. There are, however, SMEs that leave all the IS decision-making to the IS manager (53.8%), as in the case study of Firm C. Firm C do not believe that top management involvement is necessary and operate self-sufficiently unless decisions need to be made regarding important issues that will affect the organisations turnover. Many reason can contribute to top management not getting involved with IS decisions. Either top management does not appreciate the impact the IS planning process has on the outcome of the company's total performance or if it does, top management does not deem it sufficiently important enough to warrant their direct involvement (Teo and Ang, 2001).

Ward and Peppard (2002) add that it is probable that this problem occurs because top management are not adequately briefed regarding the scope and importance the IS planning process has on the total bottom-line performance of the company. If this is so, then an essential task is to ensure that top management know first-hand the scope and nature of the IS planning process.

However, some SMEs reported that both IS managers and top management made decisions together as in Case Study A. Teo and Ang (2001) reinforce this by pointing out that while aspects of IS/IT will be managed by the IS function, there is generally someone in the organisation who has overall authority for IS. All-important decisions in Firm A are made by the board of directors on recommendations from the IS manager. This was not the case with all SMEs. Secondary research on Egypt shows us that Egyptians demonstrate more power distance (reflected in high centralisation and autocratic leadership). This is manifested in high formalisation and low tolerance to ambiguity (Abdul-Gader, 1990). Firm B has two layers of hierarchy and top management is seen as the ultimate power in the organisation. However, some SMEs such as Firm A, value the opinion of top management who get involved with IS decisions. It can be seen from the investigations that organisation that have a structured hierarchy involve top management and they are more advanced with regard to IS knowledge.

From Table 2, it can be seen that respondents believed that IS projects must include top management with an average of 4.15, this indicates that it is regarded as an important factor. However, Teo and King (1996) considers that sound technical knowledge of external IS experts can compensate for lower top management support. While top management should be involved in key decisions affecting the business and business processes, they need not be actively involved throughout the implementation process. The results revealed that in 42.9%, top management carried out regular checks throughout ISS implementation to ensure that objectives are being met. This result agrees with Delone and Mclean (2003), by suggesting that IS is important to organizational success and top management involvement is an important part in the process. While not in line with Teo and King (1996), it appears that top management involvement is present at the decision making stages and through implementation. Thus, the extent of support given by top management to the organisational IS could become a very important factor in determining the success of all IS related activities and the success of the organisation. This provides support for the fact that top management support is necessary for success of IS strategy.

Second, it appears from the results that 46.2% of SMEs reported that they had an IS department and 46.2% had an IS manager, however, this does not indicate that all SMEs with an IS department have an IS manager. An IS department and IS managers are important resources to enable organisations to plan their ISS. It was found that only 30.8% of SMEs had both an IS department and an IS manager. This indicate that some of the SMEs were operating their IS department without an IS manager. There is evidence to indicate that past failures reduce the credibility of IS departments and the confidence line managers have in the competence of IS departments (Reich and Benbasat,

2000). From this, it can be seen that some of the organisations operated their IS departments using other figureheads, i.e., top management. It was found that in 46% of the SMEs, it was generally a managing director who made the decision on ISSP, in 46% it was the IS manager and in 8% it was the advisors. Of these, 23.1% proved to be both the IS manager and the managing director. Rockart and Earl (1996) argued that a successful history of IS contribution is expected to increase the interest of business executives to communicate with IS executives and to have IS considered more fully and carefully in business planning because of the high value expected from IS utilisation, they also noted that a successful IS track record improves business relationship.

Regarding the ISSP, 76.9% of SMEs were found to plan before implementation and 84.6% recognised the importance of ISSP. More importantly, 61.5% of SMEs indicated that they regularly updated their ISS, which is an important process in the ever moving business world of today. Figure 8 shows that there is adequate resources for ISSP, when organisations have an IS department. SMEs that have an IS departments were found to have bigger turnovers per employees, although this was not the case in every SME. In Figure 9, SMEs with an IS department show a

Figure 8. Organisations that have an IS department and turnovers per employees

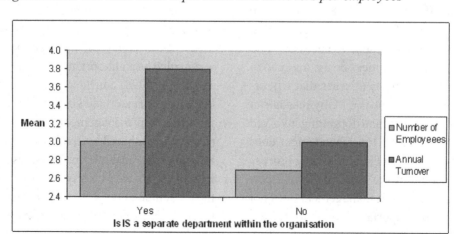

bigger turnover in comparison to SMEs that had an IS manager as Figure 9 shows less of a margin between employees and turnover. This, therefore, indicates that having an IS department is a more effective resource to IS strategy planning.

SMEs without an IS manager and an IS department showed small turnovers compared to those with. In conclusion, it seems that an IS department is more important in relation to the turnover per employees, however, SMEs that posses both an IS department and an IS manager showed larger turnovers with respect to employees (this can be seen from Figure 10; case numbers 2, 4, 8, 11 were SMEs with both an IS department and an IS manager). It is evident that organisations that posses both resources (IS manager and IS department) are more successful with a view to ISSP.

Third, it was found that Egyptian SMEs do not posses adequate resources to successfully carry out ISSP. ISSP is a fundamental necessity to suc-

Figure 9. Organisations that have an IS manager and turnovers per employees

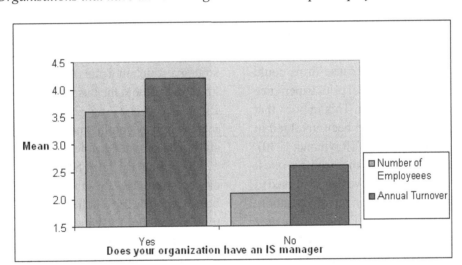

Figure 10. SMEs with both IS departments and IS managers

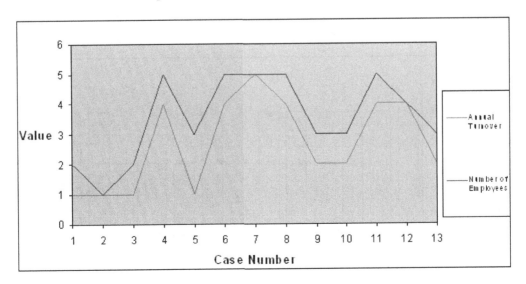

ceed in the area of IS and Egyptian SMEs need to realise this as a problem if they intend to progress with the dynamic changing environment (Levy et al., 1999). From the results of the questionnaire, it was found that 69.2% felt there was a lack of IT expertise within the organisation, however, Willcocks and Lester (1991) states that expertise only becomes critical when large-scale IT-based projects are being designed and implemented. The rest of the time IS expertise is primarily engaged in a support role to the organisation and is only used when top management believe it necessary. This indicates that SMEs in Egypt must invest more in this area to effectively implement ISS.

Technical competence is crucial to the success of any IS planning efforts. For example, many large IS projects were cancelled because firms could not employ IS staff with the real prior experience on new systems development. This implies that most of their experience 'had been involved in maintenance-related activities' (Raymond, 1990). This is consistent with the findings from the questionnaire, as only 53.8% believe that IS is used to maximum effectiveness within the organisation. Although many Egyptian SMEs posses IS, they are not being used to their full potential, which waste valuable time and money. In addition, it was unexpectedly found that 46.2% of SMEs viewed IS as an unnecessary expense.

Firm B emphasises this fact as the president does not believe that investing in IS will give a significant financial return. However, this may be due to the lack of expertise within the firm, as top management makes decision regarding IS as no IS manager is employed. Brooks (1987) suggested that the success of any IS endeavour depends on the availability of qualified personnel. One solution to the problem of not having qualified personnel is to recruit new staff. Another solution is to provide training for existing staff. Figure 11 shows that many of the SMEs regarded it as essential to acquire qualified IS personnel. This shows that 61.5% regarded it as very important to acquire qualified personnel. For IS to become effective, it must be aligned with the organisations strategy, which indicates that a certain amount of knowledge about the business is required among IS staff. Teo and Ang (2001) suggest that it is increasingly becoming more important for the IS staff to be knowledgeable about business. Figure 12 shows how Egyptian SMEs think IS expertise can be improved, 35% thought training was the best way with 25% believing that reading and training was the ideal way to improve IS expertise.

Although Teo and King (1996) found that business competence is more important than technical competence in facilitating greater integration between the companies and IS planning processes, it

Figure 11. Importance of acquiring qualified IS personnel

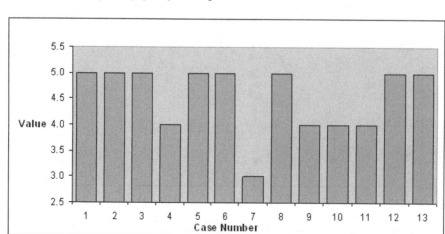

is evident that Egyptian SMEs lack the expertise needed to effectively implement ISS. Therefore, there is a great emphasis on management to support IS practices and procedure to ensure ISSP is carried out efficiently.

Finally, 69.2% of the SMEs investigated purchased their hardware from manufacturers instead of having it made to specification. However, Downing et al. (2003) suggests that there is no significant difference in process performance between outsourcing and in-sourcing. He implies that building a system from scratch will always be superior, from the viewpoint of the needs of the end user. Therefore, Egyptian SMEs will not be maximising their potential by purchasing their hardware off the shelf from manufacturers. Concerning the IS maintenance service, Earl (1996) suggests that outsourcing of the IT functions can be viewed within the context of a firm's downsizing in which multiple functional areas are affected or as a strategy in which only the functions are involved. It is apparent then, that IT outsourcing, not being an end in itself, is a part of the broader context of the firm restructuring. Figure 13 shows that of the organisations who undertake outsourcing a large percentage invest between 1-10%, with the others generally constant. This is not consistent with the thought that the bigger the budget the higher the outsourcing activity. Much of the reasoning as to

whether a firm should partake in outsourcing will be down to the needs of the firm and their overall corporate strategic plans, and not the budget at their disposal. Udo (2000) states that while it is inevitable that IS planners have to work with IT vendors at some point, it is imperative for them to pick a vendor, who understands and knows the business aspects. The vendors must be willing to do whatever is required to help the planners develop an IS plan that supports the corporate plan. However of the SMEs that carry out their sourcing activities internally it can be seen form Figure 14 that again the majority of them invest between 1-10%, with some investing between 11-20%. This shows either a higher level of expertise within the organisation such as firm A in the case study, therefore being able to internally carry out sufficient IS requirements, or a resistance from management to invest in external vendors. Of the firms investigated, graphs 13 and 14 represent the budget of IS invested in either outsourcing or in-sourcing.

CONCLUSION

Conclusions from the research undertaken on Egyptian SMEs, suggests that a theory of transnational ISS could be applied to the context,

Figure 12. Methods of improving IS expertise

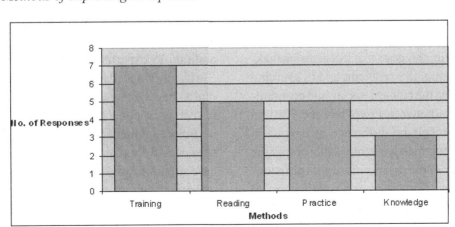

Figure 13. Budget of IS invested in outsourcing

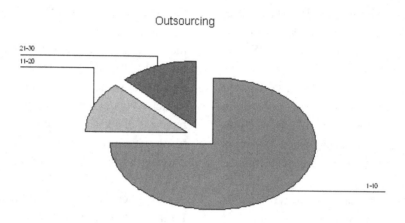

Figure 14. Budget of IS invested in in-sourcing

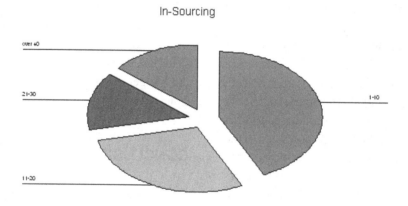

however with some modifications. The evidence provided by this study came from an environment that is socially, economically, and culturally different from the Western environment where most of the prior IS research is based. The findings of this investigation suggests that ISS decision making, ISS planning, ISS problems and IS sourcing appear to widen the cultural, social, and economical differences between Egypt and the Western countries. The cultural difference in Egypt is a major factor, top management is still seen as the ultimate force within organisations with decisions being made by them. There is a rigid hierarchal structure where management has the overall command over all processes within the organisation. As in other developing countries, lack of knowledge on the potential uses of new IT tools and shortage for highly skilled IT professionals are two concerns for IS management in Egypt. In addition IS expertise is lacking considerably in SMEs investigated in this research, this is mainly due to management not understanding the need to recruit experienced individuals.

Some Egyptian SMEs lack the structure needed to successfully plan an ISS. However, from the case studies it was discovered that organisations operating with a structured hierarchy proved to be far more advanced with regard to ISSP. In addition, communication between levels was more efficient; therefore alignment of ISS with business strategy was inevitable. The more advanced SMEs regarding IS within the Building and Construction industry, profitably gain from continuously improving their IT knowledge, and realise the advantages of outsourcing to specialised vendors, who can extensively advise in new methods and products. In many SMEs this was seen as inappropriate, and preferred to carry out their sourcing internally, or to purchase off the shelf solutions.

Incremental approaches can be seen as the pattern in most Egyptian SMEs where key personnel undertake decisions measured on their own judgments. Although this method has proved to be successful in previous literature, it is understood that incremental planning could benefit from some formal planning structure (Salmela et al 2002). Egyptian SMEs need to begin to realise the extent of possible benefits to an Information Systems Strategy, then cultural barriers can gradually be reduced by understanding practice and procedures from more advanced IS oriented countries. Due to the time limitations of the project, many issues still require supplementary investigation, however given the duration of the project; the information gained provided meaningful results that were conclusive. Additional research in this area would enhance the results gained, and are discussed in 'Further Research'.

FUTURE TRENDS

Although this project revealed relevant information for the purpose, there are areas that can be recognised to need further investigation. Firstly the area of top management support can be further analysed. A larger sample would give a better overview, detailed interviews and possibly shadowing to get involved with the day to day operations of top management. Secondly, further investigation into other industrial sectors would be appropriate. As initially conceived the investiga-

tion was to find out about SMEs in any sector, however given time constraints and problems while in Egypt this was narrowed to one industry. Different industries could then be compared, to gain an insight to SME activity in the whole of the Egyptian economy. In addition, the findings suggest that future Egyptian based research models should include other contingency variables such as size of IS department, in an attempt to increase the knowledge in this area.

Future research models should also focus on the question of whether there are relationships between SMEs and large organisations. This can be investigated in the area of sourcing to gain an idea into whether larger organisation outsource to SME and vice versa. Finally further investigation into IS expertise, discovering the academic level of individuals within SMEs in Egypt of all levels of hierarchy, in addition discovering the training that is available.

REFERENCES

Abdul-Gader, A. H. (1990). End-user computing success factors: further evidence from a developing nation. *Information Resources Management Journal*, *3*(1), 1–13.

Abdul-Gader, A. H. (1999). *Managing Computer Based Information Systems in Developing Countries: A Cultural Perspective*. Hershey, PA: Idea Group Publishing.

Abou Aish, E. (2001). *A cross-national analysis of bank selection decision and implications for positioning*. Unpublished PhD thesis, The University of Nottingham, UK.

Al-Khatib, J. A., Rawwas, M. Y. A., & Vitell, S. J. (1997). Consumer ethics: a cross-cultural investigation. *European Journal of Marketing*, *31*(11–12), 750–767. doi:10.1108/03090569710190514

Ball, D., & McCulloh, W. (1990). International Business (4th ed.). Chicago: Homewood.

Ballantine, J., Levy, M., & Powell, P. (1998). Evaluating information systems in small and medium-sized enterprises: issues and evidence. *European Journal of Information Systems*, *7*(4), 241–251. doi:10.1057/palgrave.ejis.3000307

Belleflamme, P. (2001). Oligopolistic competition, IT use for product differentiation and the productivity paradox. *International Journal of Industrial Organization*, *19*(1–2), 227–248. doi:10.1016/S0167-7187(99)00017-X

Belson, W. (1982). *The Design and Understanding of Survey Questions*. Aldershot, UK: Gower.

Bentley, T. (1998). *Information Systems Strategy for Business*. London: CIMA.

Boar, B. H. (2001). *The Art of Strategic Planning for Information Technology*. New York: John Wiley & Sons Inc.

Brooks, F. P. Jr. (1987). No silver bullet: essence and accidents of software engineering. *IEEE Computer*, *20*(4), 10–19.

Camfferman, K., & Cooke, T. E. (2002). An analysis of disclosure in the annual reports of UK and Dutch companies. *Journal of International Accounting Research*, *1*, 3–30. doi:10.2308/jiar.2002.1.1.3

Cooke, T. E. (1998). Regression analysis in accounting disclosure studies. *Accounting and Business Review*, *28*(3), 209–224.

De Boer, S. J., & Walbeek, M. M. (1999). Information technology in developing countries: a study to guide policy formulation. *International Journal of Information Management*, *19*(3), 207–218. doi:10.1016/S0268-4012(99)00014-6

Delone, W. H., & Mclean, E. R. (2003). The Delone and Mclean model of information systems success: a ten year update. *Journal of Management Information Systems*, *19*(4), 9–30.

Downing, C. E., Field, J. M., & Ritzman, L. P. (2003). The value of outsourcing: a field study. *Information Systems Management*, *20*, 86–91. doi:10.1201/1078/43203.20.1.20031201/40088.11

Duhan, S., Levy, M., & Powell, P. (2001). Information systems strategies in knowledge-based SMEs: the role of core competencies. *European Journal of Information Systems*, *10*(1), 25–40. doi:10.1057/palgrave.ejis.3000379

Earl, M. J. (1989). *Management Strategies for Information Technology*. Englewood Cliffs, NJ: Prentice-Hall.

Earl, M. J. (1993). Experiences in strategic information systems planning. *Management Information Systems Quarterly*, *17*(1), 1–24. doi:10.2307/249507

Earl, M. J. (1996). *Information Management: The Organizational Dimension*. Oxford, UK: Oxford University Press.

Ergazakis, E., Ergazakis, K., Flamos, A., & Charalabidis, Y. (2009). KM in SMEs: a research agenda. *International Journal of Management and Decision Making*, *10*(1/2), 91–110. doi:10.1504/IJMDM.2009.023916

Field, A. (2003). *Discovering Statistics Using SPSS for Windows: Advanced Techniques for the Beginner*. London: Sage Publications.

Galliers, R. D. (1991). Strategic information systems planning: myths, reality and guidelines for successful implementation. *European Journal of Information Systems*, *1*(1), 55–64. doi:10.1057/ejis.1991.7

Grover, V., Cheon, M. J., & Teng, J. T. C. (1996). The effect of service quality and partnership on the outsourcing of information systems functions. *Journal of Management Information Systems*, *12*(4), 89–116.

Gunasekaran, A., Love, P. E. D., Rahimi, F., & Miele, R. (2001). A model for investment justification in information technology projects. *International Journal of Information Management, 21*(5), 349–364. doi:10.1016/S0268-4012(01)00024-X

Hagmann, C., & McCahon, C. S. (1993). Strategic information systems and competitiveness. *Information & Management, 25*(4), 183–192. doi:10.1016/0378-7206(93)90067-4

Henderson, J. C., & Sifonis, J. G. (1988). The value of strategic IS planning: understanding consistency, validity and IS markets. *Management Information Systems Quarterly, 12*(2), 187–200. doi:10.2307/248843

Hochstrasser, B., & Griffiths, C. (1991). *Controlling IT Investment, Strategy and Management*. London: Chapman & Hall.

Hogbin, G., & Thomas, D. V. (1994). *Investing in Information Technology: Managing the Decision-making Process*. Cambridge, MA: McGraw-Hill/IBM Series.

Jain, R. (1995). MIS in large public programs: the literacy program in India. *Journal of Global Information Management, 3*(1), 18–30.

Kirytopoulos, K., Voulgaridou, D., Panopoulos, D., & Leopoulos, V. (2009). Project termination analysis in SMEs: making the right call. *International Journal of Management and Decision Making, 10*(1/2), 69–90. doi:10.1504/IJMDM.2009.023915

Lederer, A. A., & Salmela, H. (1996). Toward a theory of strategic IS planning. *The Journal of Strategic Information Systems, 5*(3), 237–253. doi:10.1016/S0963-8687(96)80005-9

Lederer, A. L., & Sethi, V. (1988). The implementation of strategic information systems planning methodologies. *Management Information Systems Quarterly, 12*(3), 445–461. doi:10.2307/249212

Levy, M., Loebbecke, C., & Powell, P. (2003). SMEs, co-opetition and knowledge sharing: the role of information systems. *European Journal of Information Systems, 12*(1), 3–17. doi:10.1057/palgrave.ejis.3000439

Levy, M., & Powell, P. (2005). *Strategies for Growth in SMEs: The role of information and information systems*. Amsterdam: Elsevier.

Levy, M., Powell, P., & Galliers, R. (1999). Assessing information systems strategy development frameworks in SMEs. *Information & Management, 36*(5), 247–261. doi:10.1016/S0378-7206(99)00020-8

Marshall, C., & Rossman, G. B. (2006). *Designing Qualitative Research* (4th ed.). London: Sage Publications.

Mata, F. J., Fuerst, W. L., & Barney, J. B. (1995). Information technology and sustained competitive advantage: a resource-based analysis. *Management Information Systems Quarterly, 19*(4), 487–505. doi:10.2307/249630

Merrill Lynch. (2006). Egypt: The Investment, Jewel on the Nile. *Global Securities Research and Economic Group of Merrill Lynch*, June.

Metaxiotis, K. (2009). Editorial to the Special Issue on Decision Support Systems and Knowledge Management in SMEs. *International Journal of Management and Decision Making, 10*(1/2), 1–3.

MOEFT. (2002). *Streamlining the Regulatory Procedures for Small and Medium Enterprises (The One-Stop-Shop Model). Workshop report*. Ministry of Economy and Foreign Trade – Egypt.

MOEFT. (2004). *Priority Policy Issues for the Development of the Micro, Small and Medium Enterprises Sector in Egypt. Workshop report*. Ministry of Economy and Foreign Trade – Egypt.

MOEFT. (2005). *Small and medium enterprises policies. MOEFT Newsletter, 5*. Ministry of Economy and Foreign Trade – Egypt.

MOEFT. (2006). *Research Policy Priorities for SME Development. Workshop report.* Ministry of Economy and Foreign Trade – Egypt.

Niederman, F., Brancheau, J. C., & Wetherbe, J. C. (1991). Information systems management issues for the 1990s. *Management Information Systems Quarterly, 15*(4), 475–500. doi:10.2307/249452

Palvia, P., Midha, V., & Pinjani, P. (2006). Research models in information systems. *Communications of the Association for Information Systems, 17,* 1042–1063.

Parker, M., & Benson, R. (1989). Enterprise wide information economics: Latest concepts. *Journal of Information Systems Management, 6*(4), 7–13. doi:10.1080/07399018908960166

Porter, M. E. (1980). *Competitive Strategy.* New York: The Free Press.

Raymond, L. (1990). Organisational context and information systems success: a contingency approach. *Journal of Management Information Systems, 6,* 5–20.

Reich, B. H., & Benbasat, I. (2000). Factors that influence the social dimension of alignment between business and information technology objectives. *Management Information Systems Quarterly, 24*(1), 81–113. doi:10.2307/3250980

Rockart, J. F., & Earl, M. J. (1996). Eight imperatives for the new IT organisation. *Sloan Management Review, 38*(1), 43–56.

Salmela, H., Lederer, A. L., & Reponen, T. (2000). Information systems planning in a turbulent environment. *European Journal of Information Systems, 9*(1), 3–15. doi:10.1057/palgrave.ejis.3000339

Salmela, H., & Spil, T. A. M. (2002). Dynamic and emergent information systems strategy formulation and implementation. *International Journal of Information Management, 22*(6), 441–460. doi:10.1016/S0268-4012(02)00034-8

Samaha, K., & Stapleton, P. (2008). Compliance with international accounting standards in a national context: some empirical evidence from the Cairo and Alexandria stock exchanges. *Afro-Asian Journal of Finance and Accounting, 1*(1), 40–66. doi:10.1504/AAJFA.2008.016890

Saunders, M. N. K., Lewis, P., & Thornhill, A. (2009). *Research methods for business students. Financial Times* (5th ed.). Upper Saddle River, NJ: Prentice Hall.

Seliem, A. A. M., Ashour, A. S., Khalil, O. E. M., & Millar, S. J. (2003). The relationship of some organisational factors to information systems effectiveness: a contingency analysis of Egyptian data. *Journal of Global Information Management, 11*(1), 41–70.

Straub, D. W., Loch, K. D., & Hill, C. E. (2001). Transfer of information technology to the Arab world: a test of cultural influence modelling. *Journal of Global Information Management, 9*(3), 6–28.

Teo, T. S. H., & Ang, J. S. K. (2001). An examination of major IS planning problems. *International Journal of Information Management, 21*(6), 457–470. doi:10.1016/S0268-4012(01)00036-6

Teo, T. S. H., Ang, J. S. K., & Pavri, F. N. (1997). The state of strategic IS planning practices in Singapore. *Information & Management, 33*(1), 13–23. doi:10.1016/S0378-7206(97)00033-5

Teo, T. S. H., & King, W. R. (1996). Assessing the impact of integrating business planning and IS planning. *Information & Management, 30*(6), 309–321. doi:10.1016/S0378-7206(96)01076-2

Thompson, J. L. (2001). Strategic Management (4th Ed.). Pacific Grove, CA: Thompson learning.

Tuncalp, S. (1988). The marketing research scene in Saudi Arabia. *European Journal of Marketing, 22*(5), 15–22. doi:10.1108/EUM0000000005282

Udo, G. G. (2000). Using analytic hierarchy process to analyze the information technology outsourcing decision. *Industrial Management & Data Systems*, *100*(9), 421–429. doi:10.1108/02635570010358348

Ward, J. (1995). *Principles of Information Systems Management*. London: Routledge.

Ward, J., & Peppard, J. (2002). *Strategic Planning for Information Systems* (3rd ed.). Chichester, UK: Wiley Series.

Willcocks, L., & Lester, S. (1991). Information systems investments: evaluation at the feasibility stage of projects. *The International Journal of Technological Innovation and Entepreneurship (Technovation)*, *11*(5), 283–301.

Willcocks, L., & Lester, S. (1999). *Beyond the IT Productivity Paradox: Assessment Issues*. Chichester, UK: Wiley.

Wynn, M. (2009). Information system strategy development and implementation in SMEs. *Management Research News*, *32*(1), 78–90. doi:10.1108/01409170910922041

Chapter 6
Broadband Development Challenges and Measures:
The Analysis of EU Countries[1]

Peter Trkman
University of Ljubljana, Slovenia

Tomaž Turk
University of Ljubljana, Slovenia

ABSTRACT

The chapter analyses the use of broadband in EU countries in an attempt to find the main reasons, which explain the differences among countries. With the use of factor analysis the underlying factors were identified as: 1. enablers and means; 2. the use of services; and 3. the ICT sector's development. Cluster analysis was used to identify similar countries. Based on these findings, a two-dimensional framework that enables the classification of policy actions depending on the influencing factor and type of influence was developed. Finally, a novel conceptualization of the field of broadband and e-commerce/e-government is proposed.

INTRODUCTION

Broadband development (defined for the purpose of this chapter as the use of broadband (BB) technology & services) can bring substantial benefits to the productivity, education, e-inclusion and economic development of society in general. Innovative productive practices in business, government, education, health care and daily life are now critically dependent on the ability to communicate information quickly and independently. The BB readiness of a country affects its ability to compete globally (Lee & Chan-Olmsted, 2004) since the Internet is becoming a significant component of society's communications infrastructure (Gillet, Lehr, & Osorio, 2004). The BB connection technology is defined for the purpose of this chapter as technologies such as DSL, cable, fiber, wireless (like WiMAX, but the definition excludes 3G and Wi-Fi) and BPL (BB over power lines) with a download speed of at least 256 kbit/s.

Various aspects of BB has been studied in the past; they can be classified to the following areas: public communications infrastructure and tariffing principles, sales of communications services, public access and equal access policies, competi-

DOI: 10.4018/978-1-60566-388-3.ch006

tive access pricing, communications industry finance, engineering-economic studies, information contents, macroeconomic issues (Pau, 2002). In addition, a number of more technically oriented topics were also discussed (Chanclu, Gosselin, Fernandez, Alvarez, & Zouganeli, 2006); see e.g (Giuliano et al., 2008) as an example of a recent study on interoperability between WiMAX and BB mobile space networks.

Together, the potential benefits at national, individual and organisational levels contribute to something of a consensus that the adoption of BB should be promoted (Xavier, 2003) because its development as a means of promoting new applications is said to provide the basis of knowledge-based economies (Cava-Ferreruela & Alabau-Munoz, 2006). Although Europe is becoming the leading region in terms of BB development (Marcus, 2005), possibilities to boost the BB development even further are being extensively studied. There are two main observations concerning the BB development in EU countries. On one hand, the growth rate is relatively high while, on the other, there is a highly unequal distribution among the various EU countries (Eurobarometer, 2006). Even bigger differences can be found at the international level (Milner, 2006). Therefore, different stakeholders (EU institutions, national and regional governments, education and research institutions, infrastructure and services providers etc.) are facing the challenge of how to identify the hindrances to the wider adoption of the Internet and BB services and consequently how to stimulate quicker progress. The development of new policies within a new regulatory framework in order to achieve the timely BB development is needed (Chanclu et al., 2006).

This question has been attracting growing attention in both the scientific and governmental communities and several research studies have been performed in the last few years (either for the adoption of BB or Internet services in general), e.g. (Savage, Waldmann, 2005, Bread, 2006). While the results of these studies show the prevailing

influence of GDP and economic development on the adoption of BB/the Internet, studies of other possibly influential variables have been inconclusive. According to Dutta and Roy (2004-2005), many studies link the Internet's diffusion with a variety of technical and social factors but do not reveal the interplay among them that generates diffusion behaviour. Without understanding these mechanics, it is difficult to develop policies to accelerate the diffusion of the Internet within a developing country.

Our main research question focuses on these mechanics. Namely, our goal is to find the underlying factors, which explain BB development at the country level, specifically within the group of EU-25 countries. The underlying factors behind the differences between EU-25 countries were identified through factor analysis based on various information society and economic indicators. Moreover, on this basis we developed a strategic policy framework in which different policies can be evaluated against these latent factors. Finally, the conceptual framework that enables a better overview of the complex field is proposed.

RELATED WORK AND MOTIVATION

The question about the factors causing the differences seen between various countries or regions has attracted considerable attention from researchers, policy-makers and other stakeholders.

In recent years several surveys have been conducted that mainly gathered data, possibly along with a basic statistical analysis. The analysis of the growth of BB adoption in various European countries is presented in (Marcus, 2005). The European Commission (Eurobarometer, 2006) published a comprehensive review of the situation in all 25 EU countries in the various categories (telephone, TV and Internet access), while Pew regularly publishes access data for the US market – see (Pew Internet, 2005). Several other organisations (i.e. Eurostat, ITU, OECD, UN,

Table 1. BB penetration (in %) by type of access in OECD countries (June, 2008) (OECD, 2008)

Rank	Country	DSL	Cable	Fibre/LAN	Other	Total
1	Denmark	22,5	9,8	3,2	1,1	36,7
2	Netherlands	21,2	13,7	0,4	0,2	35,5
3	Norway	24,1	5,9	2,6	0,7	33,4
4	Switzerland	22,5	9,7	0,3	0,3	32,7
5	Iceland	31,2	0,0	0,5	0,6	32,3
6	Sweden	19,9	6,4	6,0	0,1	32,3
7	Korea	8,4	10,5	12,2	0,0	31,2
8	Finland	26,1	4,0	0,0	0,5	30,7
9	Luxembourg	24,8	3,4	0,1	0,1	28,3
10	Canada	12,6	14,9	0,0	0,4	27,9
11	United Kingdom	21,7	5,9	0,0	0,1	27,6
12	Belgium	15,8	10,4	0,0	0,2	26,4
13	France	25,1	1,3	0,0	0,0	26,4
14	Germany	24,6	1,6	0,0	0,1	26,2
15	United States	10,1	13,2	0,9	0,8	25,0
16	Australia	18,6	4,2	0,0	0,8	23,5
17	Japan	9,6	3,1	10,2	0,0	23,0
18	Austria	12,9	7,1	0,1	0,5	20,6
19	New Zealand	18,2	1,2	0,0	0,9	20,4
20	Spain	15,5	3,9	0,1	0,3	19,8
21	Ireland	14,0	2,1	0,1	2,8	19,1
22	Italy	17,6	0,0	0,5	0,2	18,2
23	Czech Republic	6,3	3,4	0,6	5,5	15,8
24	Hungary	7,8	6,5	0,0	1,3	15,7
25	Portugal	8,6	6,0	0,0	0,2	14,8
26	Greece	11,2	0,0	0,0	0,0	11,2
27	Poland	6,7	2,7	0,0	0,1	9,6
28	Slovak Republic	6,0	1,0	1,6	0,3	8,9
29	Turkey	6,7	0,1	0,0	0,0	6,8
30	Mexico	3,1	1,4	0,0	0,2	4,7

UNCTAD) also publish various relevant statistics that are used to develop different rankings, e.g. the Networked Readiness Index (Sciadas, 2004). The transition from narrowband to broadband is now well-advanced - there were some 216 million broadband subscribers across the world at the end of 2005 amounting to just over half the total num-

ber of Internet subscribers and around one-fifth of total fixed lines (ITU Internet Report, 2006).

Table 1 shows the most recent data about broadband adoption around the world by country. It reveals that the leading EU countries in terms of BB adoption (Denmark, Netherlands) are also among the world leaders; however, most of the new member states along with Greece are at the

Figure 1. Relation between BB penetration and GDP per capita

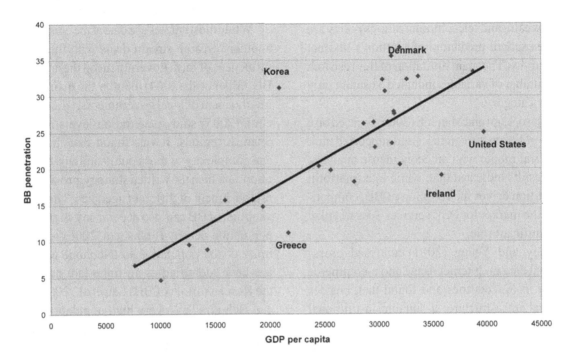

bottom at the list, while even well-developed countries such as Spain and Austria are below the average. Fransman (2006) provides an in-depth analysis of the BB situation and development in the most countries of interest (e. g. Korea, Japan, US, main EU countries)

Two basic methodological approaches to explaining the differences noted between countries are in use. Many analyses are based on cross-section or time-series data and employ different statistical techniques to either confirm the hypotheses or explore the relationships between different phenomena. Another research approach is to use case studies to analyse the situation in a certain country/region. Most studies concentrate on inter-country differences although there are notable exceptions such as the study of regional policies in Spain (Jordana, Fernandez, Sanchez, & Welp, 2005).

The common findings are that the diffusion of Internet services/BB use is increasing all over the world and that economic development (per-

sonal income, GDP or a similar indicator used to measure it) is the main influencing factor. Figure 1 shows the relation between BB penetration and GDP per capita (including all OECD countries, except Luxembourg; most interesting countries are identified). It can be seen that GDP is strongly correlated with BB use. However, the fact that several countries have considerably higher or lower penetration that would be expected based on the level of their economic development motivates further research.

The prices are usually found to be the second most influential factor. Effective regulation is also often (although not always) cited as an important issue. On the other hand, the results differ on the importance of factors such as competition, education level, English-language proficiency, level of democracy, social networks, age and appeal of the contents.

The work of Hargittai (1999) is a seminal paper on the topic of Internet adoption – her main research question sought to explain the differences between Internet adoption levels seen among OECD countries. Her main findings are that economic wealth and telecommunications policy are the most salient predictors of a nation's Internet connectivity. The main limitation of this research is the number of variables included – usually only one per category.

Distaso, Lupi and Manenti (2006) focused on a sample of European countries and supported their theoretical model with an econometric analysis. Their results indicated that, while inter-platform competition drives the adoption of BB, competition in the market for DSL services does not play any significant role.

Oxley and Yeung (2001) analysed cross-sectional data on Internet usage and e-commerce activity in 62 countries and found that, besides technical infrastructure, a suitable institutional environment ('rule of law', credible payment channels etc.) is also vital for the development of e-commerce activities.

Savage and Waldman (2005) presented an econometric analysis based on nationwide data for USA households. They found that, apart from the usual important characteristics of BB (speed, always-on connectivity), the reliability of the services offered is an important Internet access attribute. A similar approach was taken by Chaudhuri, Flamm and Horrigan (2005) who analysed the influence of various socio-economic characteristics of a household on their decision to adopt BB. They found that among standard indicators income and education are the most important, while the subscription decision is only modestly sensitive to price.

These two studies confirmed the earlier finings of Madden & Simpson (1996). Their results were obtained by using the probit regression model and suggest that household characteristics, e.g. measures of social disadvantage, are strong predictors of network subscription intentions. According to this, it is very unlikely that standard approaches (e.g. direct subsidisation, implicit cross-subsidisation) to addressing access-disadvantage problems

will be successful without ancillary measures such as targeted education programmes.

While most studies use data at the country level, another research stream deals with the possible influences of local government on the adoption of BB. Gillet et al. (2004) identify the main possible involvement of local governments, while Jordana et al. (2005) study penetration levels in various Spanish regions. It was found that the number and complexity of those public initiatives is more important than the written strategy, promotion and establishment of different agencies. The regional adoption of BB can also depend on geography and population density (Fransman, 2006) – the proximity of the population to telephone exchanges has been identified as an important enabler for the Korean rollout of BB (Lau et al., 2005), while e.g. Belgium has a very high population density yet many people live in single-family houses in the suburbs (Bread, 2006).

Several studies have specifically tackled the question of the digital divide. Similar to other technologies, the Internet has spread diffused unevenly across countries raising concerns over a 'digital divide'. The digital divide is the result of the economic, regulatory and socio-political characteristics of countries and their evolution over time (Guillen & Suarez, 2005). Obviously, differences in Internet use are the result of an array of forces over which governments have varying degrees of influence. That paper supplements earlier research by the same authors (Guillen & Suarez, 2001), where they found, after controlling for per capita income and installed telephone lines, cross-national differences in numbers of Internet users and hosts have to do with favourable conditions for entrepreneurship and investment.

Norris (2000) finds that while Internet use was found to be positively correlated with 'old' media usage (TV, radio), unsurprisingly economic development has by far the largest influence on the number of Internet users and that literacy, education and the level of democratisation do not hold any additional explanatory power. However, over a certain minimal level (approximately USD 8000 GDP per capita), economic development is no longer necessarily essential to bring about greater online use.

Contrary to those findings, Milner (2006) finds that besides technological and economic factors political factors also exert a powerful influence. She shows that a country's regime type matters greatly, even when controlling for other economic, technological, political and sociological factors. The probable reason for this finding is that autocratic governments seek to hinder the development of electronic networks because that could reduce their power.

Kiiski and Pohjola's (2002) findings are similar to the previously mentioned study (Norris, 2000). Kiiski and Pohjola found that the GDP level and the cost of Internet access are the most influential variables, while education level and English proficiency have no additional influence. Similarly, the level of competition in the telecommunications market does not have any additional explanatory value since the only effect of the competition should be reflected through the price. As this conflicts with some later studies it could be argued that, besides price, competition also has an influence on quality, technology and services development, the promotion of services etc. The research results set out in Bauer, Berne & Maitland (2002) confirm our claim since they found that, in addition to income and cost, competition in telecommunications services also increases Internet usage.

Vicente Cuervo and Lopez Menendez (2006) used a similar approach to ours to analyse the digital divide in EU-15 countries. They combined a factor analysis with clustering to identify the main influential factors as: 1. ICT infrastructure and diffusion; and 2. e-government and Internet access costs. However, their analysis is limited to 10 variables and does not provide more than a few basic strategic considerations for the countries under study.

In addition to statistical analysis a case study approach has also been frequently used. Lee and Chan-Olmsted (2004) analysed the main differences in BB Internet readiness between the USA and South Korea and found the difference lies in a combination of policy, consumer demands and supporting/related technologies. A similar approach is taken by Frieden (2005) who analysed the situation in four countries (Canada, Japan, United States, South Korea). The finding that BB development can be stimulated through either supply-side or demand-side support is important to substantiate the approach taken in the continuation of this chapter.

The heterogeneity of studies related to BB penetration indicates the complexity of the subject since it has already been studied from economic, technological, sociological, political etc. points of view. As shown, the results of previous research results were very relevant yet inconclusive and sometimes in contradiction with each other. Most of the research work has focused on BB/Internet adoption per se and not sufficiently included a study of the usage of the services – it is the usage not the access that brings most of the economic benefits.

In addition, the main deficiency of the previous research is that it usually just analyses/summarises the situation in various countries and does not provide guidance about how to analyse actions designed to stimulate BB development, which is our intent. The earlier research, however, does offer a valuable insight into various aspects of BB development and was partly used to guide the selection of the variables.

METHODOLOGY AND RESULTS

The main focus of our analysis prior to designing a framework is to identify common underlying factors (if any) that can explain the differences seen between countries. Specifically, we try to identify the underlying dimensions that are common among

Table 2. Description of variables and codes

Code	Variable
BB	Percentage of households with BB access [1]
PURCH	Electronic purchasing (percentage of individuals having ordered/bought goods or services for private use over the Internet in the last three months) [1]
GAM	Percentage of individuals using the Internet for gaming in the previous three months [1]
INFRET	Percentage of individuals who used Internet, in the last 3 months, for finding information about goods and services [1]
ITEXP	Information technology expenditures as a percentage of GDP [1]
CTEXP	Communications technology expenditures as a percentage of GDP [1]
HHINC	Household income (average annual gross earnings) [1]
PCACC	Percentage of households having access to, via one of its members, a PC [1]
PCFREQ	Percentage of individuals who used a PC in the last three months [1]
INTACC	Percentage of households having access to the Internet at home [1]
INTFREQ	Percentage of individuals who accessed the Internet, at least once a week [1]
INTDIAL	Percentage of households using a modem/dial-up access over a normal telephone line [1]
GDP	Gross Domestic Product per capita [1]
BBPRICE	Price of broadband access [2]
PHONES	Number of phones per 1,000 citizens [1]
TELEW	Percentage of households which use telework (at least one member) [1]
POPDENS	Number of people per square kilometre [1]
EDULEV	Number of years spent in formal education programmes [3]

[1] Source: Eurostat, 2006

[2] Source: OECD, 2005

[3] Source: Eurydce, 2005

a chosen set of BB development indicators. In this respect, we used exploratory factor analysis to find out whether there are any latent variables behind a chosen set of variables. The main advantage of this kind of approach is that no prior assumption is made about constraints on the estimation of factors or the number of factors to be extracted.

To achieve this, a set of variables at the country level was selected while focusing on countries within the European Union. This dataset was screened to check for outliers and any problems regarding the missing values. Further, we studied the correlation between variables – an approach that is often neglected in other studies (Dutta & Roy, 2004-2005). This was done together with checking for the appropriateness of factor analysis. Factor analysis can suggest the number of under-

lying factors and provide the means to further elaborate the meaning of factors.

Based on the above review of previous work in this field, a specific set of variables that reflect the situation in EU-25 countries was selected (Table 2).

Unless otherwise stated, we used data for 2004 from one source – Eurostat – since we tried to avoid the use of different sources as much as possible because the methodology of data collection is crucial and can greatly affect the quality of results. We only deviated from this approach for certain variables that were unavailable in the Eurostat data collection.

France and Malta were excluded from the analysis since many values in the Eurostat data were missing so the dataset contains 23 cases. This relatively small sample size might present difficulties with the statistical inference. Our solution has several high loading marker variables with loadings > 0.8, so the solution is reliable (Tabachnick, 2001), although we should stress that larger datasets (i.e. on regional level) are needed if our approach to policy assessments would be used in practice. In our case, there were no specific problems with outliers and hence no cases were dropped in this regard. Since the variables differ in scales and metrics (e.g. telework usage in % of the population vs. gross domestic product per capita), we applied a standardisation technique and used mean-corrected data in further calculations because there is a reason to believe that the variances of the variables indicate the importance of a given variable (this information is lost when using standardised values).

The correlation matrix showed that the variables are relatively well-related and that the correlation coefficients are quite high (Trkman et al., 2008). Since we are first interested in BB penetration, we noticed the fact that Internet gaming is not directly correlated to BB. One can also notice low values of correlation coefficients between BB adoption and communications technology expenditures, dial-up Internet access, number of phones, population density and education level. From the correlation matrix, it can be seen that these variables are cross-correlated with other variables. As the correlation matrix revealed the existence of strong and significant relationships between some variables, we decided that a factor analysis was suitable. The only exception is the education level with relatively low values of correlation coefficients, but we decided to keep it within the analysis since many authors have reported its relevance.

Besides the correlation matrix, the Bartlett test of sphericity and the Kaiser-Mayer-Olkin (KMO) measure of sampling adequacy were also checked. The Bartlett test examines the null hypothesis that the correlation matrix is an identity matrix, which implies that there is no correlation between the variables. The KMO measure requires values greater than 0.5 for a satisfactory factor analysis

to proceed. In our case, the Bartlett test shows that factor analysis is appropriate (with an χ^2 value of 482.09 and a significance level below 0.001 at 153 degrees of freedom). The KMO measure with a value of 0.72 suggests that the data structure is adequate for the factor analysis. PAF technique was chosen to estimate the number of factors and to find their plausible interpretation.

The factors were ranked according to their strength or the share of variance they explain (Table 3). The first factor explains 58.7% of the variation in the original variables. The second factor explains 13.8% of the variance, the third factor 6.26% etc. There are several criteria to choose the most important factors, thus to reduce the complexity of the results, with the most used being the factor eigenvalues together with scree plot and percentage of explained variance criterion.

Table 3. Results of factor analysis

Factor	Eigenvalue	Percent of variance	Cumulative percent of variance
1	10.56	58.7	58.7
2	2.48	13.8	72.4
3	1.11	6.2	78.6
4	0.87	4.8	83.5
5	0.78	4.3	87.8
6	0.53	2.9	90.7
7	0.39	2.2	92.9
8	0.32	1.8	94.7
9	0.28	1.6	96.3
10	0.24	1.3	97.6
11	0.16	0.9	98.5
12	0.12	0.7	99.2
13	0.06	0.3	99.5
14	0.05	0.3	99.8
15	0.01	0.1	99.9
16	0.01	0.1	100.0
17	0.00	0.0	100.0
18	0.00	0.0	100.0

Note: Extraction method was principal axis factoring. Extracted factors are marked.

The first 'rule of thumb' regarding the eigenvalues is their threshold value; three factors have their eigenvalues above 1. The scree plot of eigenvalues and a parallel analysis according to the technique given by Sharma (1996) was also performed (see Trkman et al., 2008). It suggests three factors with a cut-off point between the second and third factor. Besides, with three factors we can explain 78.6% of the variation in the original variables.

To provide for the interpretability of results, we used the varimax orthogonal rotation where the goal is to achieve factor loadings in such a way that each variable loads highly on one and only one factor, so that each factor represents a distinct construct.

The three factors from Table 4 can be interpreted as:

1. 'enablers and means', including the variables BB penetration, PC access, telework usage, household income, BB service price;
2. 'usage of information services', including the variables electronic purchasing, Internet usage for information retrieval; Internet usage for gaming; and
3. 'ICT sector environment', including the variables communications technology expenditures, number of phones, Internet access over phone, population density, and education level.

The first factor is strongly connected to economic factors like household income and BB service prices, with the latter being negatively correlated (as expected). The mixture of these economic indicators provides information about the influences that enable people to use advanced ICT services. The first factor also includes variables which directly express the means for access to information services, which is represented by the high loadings of PC access and Internet access, and especially BB penetration and telework. Telework can be regarded as a 'general platform'

Table 4. Varimax rotated factor matrix

Variable	Factor 1	Factor 2	Factor 3
BB	**0.904**	0.243	0.066
PURCH	**0.542**	**0.661**	0.403
GAM	0.114	**0.827**	-0.048
INFRET	**0.460**	**0.821**	0.261
ITEXP	**0.589**	**0.631**	0.212
CTEXP	-0.326	0.078	**-0.788**
HHINC	**0.797**	0.262	0.409
PCACC	**0.698**	0.345	**0.560**
PCFREQ	**0.605**	**0.705**	0.153
INTACC	**0.568**	0.436	**0.591**
INTFREQ	**0.531**	**0.800**	0.081
INTDIAL	0.219	0.224	**0.865**
GDP	**0.492**	0.398	**0.499**
BBPRICE	**-0.693**	-0.279	-0.284
PHONES	0.261	**0.482**	**0.586**
TELEW	**0.780**	0.267	0.132
POPDENS0	0.303	-0.376	**0.772**
EDULEV	-0.078	0.199	**0.617**

and strong incentive to ensure the possibility to reach information services. Telework is more than just the intensive usage of services and it is not an information service, but rather its foundation. It also requires a new job organisation paradigm (Perez, Sanchez, & Carnicer, 2002) and poses several non-technology related questions (Kurland & Bailey, 1999).

The second factor (usage of services) is correlated with variables which express the use of information services (e.g. electronic purchasing, Internet usage for gaming, Internet usage for information retrieval). It also shares some variables with the first factor (e.g. IT expenditures, frequency of PC usage, frequency of Internet usage). This shows that these variables reflect both components of the information society (enablers & means and usage). With the second factor, we can also explain the nature of the relationship between Internet usage for gaming and BB penetration as being indirect. The split number of phones variable between the second and third factors shows a similar picture – the use of information services by citizens and the infrastructural development within each country.

Namely, the third factor is connected to indicators which show the state of the ICT environment within a country (like PC and Internet access, number of phones, Internet access over the phone) and other facts about the environment. There are variables such as population density and education level which greatly influence the 'absorption capabilities' of the given society. On the other hand, expenditures on communication technologies (CT expenditures as a percentage of GDP) are correlated with the third factor only (ICT sector environment), but negatively. Since the third factor is positively oriented this looks a little strange at first glance. Behind these findings probably lies the fact that countries with a less developed CT sector have relatively large

investments for providing the core communication infrastructure.

GDP per capita is almost equally distributed among all three factors, although it is relatively weakly correlated with the second component. This confirms the findings of previous researchers that economic development is behind all the studied factors (enablers and means, usage of services, ICT sector environment) – unsurprisingly 'GDP is everywhere'.

The interplay between factors and variables is represented in Figure 2 (BB penetration is emphasized), where variables are grouped together if they are related to the same factors. The arrows denote a factor's direct relationship with these groups. Three groups of variables are strongly bonded to corresponding factors (like Internet usage for gaming and information retrieval to the factor 'usage of information services'). These groups explain the nature of the factors. Other 'mixed' groups of variables are connecting two factors together, like

Figure 2. Structure of relationships between variables important for the adoption of BB

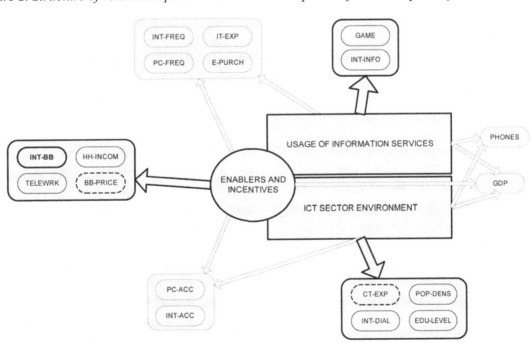

Note: statistically stronger relations are represented with thick arrows. BB development indicators with negative correlations to related factors are shown with a dashed border.

frequency of Internet and PC usage, IT expenditures and electronic purchasing connect the factors 'usage' and 'enablers & incentives'. These groups show how the factors are related to each other. For instance, the PC and Internet access mixed group shows that, for enablers and incentives to be successful, the development of infrastructure is important not only in a technological sense but also in the form of the acceptance of previously developed technologies

DEVELOPMENT OF THE FRAMEWORK

It is important to bear in mind that meaningful analyses require a conceptual framework (Vicente Cuervo & Lopez Menendez, 2006) that has not previously been developed. It is obvious that a strategic framework must address all the factors identified in the previous section along with a combination of different policies.

This is reflected in the proposed framework that has two main dimensions:

1. influencing factor: which of the three factors does the action attempt to influence? and
2. type of influence: in general, the economic laws of supply and demand also apply to the adoption of BB technology and services. Therefore, either demand- or supply-side stimulation (Frieden, 2005; Cava-Ferreruela, Alabau-Munoz, 2006) can be used:
   a. supply-side: to either influence the business orientation and diversity of the business models of providers with incentives or other actions (supply-side economic influence) or to directly influence the supply-side with legislative or regulative acts (supply-side social influence); or
   b. demand-side: to increase the demand for services by consumers either the real (demand-side economic influence)

or perceived (demand-side social influence) value of BB should be increased.

The two-dimensional framework is shown in Figure 3. It can be applied at various layers, e.g. national, regional or micro (e.g. municipal) level (for a complete framework at national level see (Trkman et al., 2008) or (Turk et al., 2008)). The actions listed in each quadrant do not provide a complete list of all possible ways of influencing each factor but should serve as a possible example of such policies. Although certain actions might influence several factors (in that case they might appear in various fields of the framework), a single most important influence should be found for generic actions. Those actions that influence several factors or exert different types of influence can probably be decomposed into more generic actions for the purpose of analysing them. In such a way the framework recognises that stakeholders have different methods to influence the BB development. The framework can serve as a tool to classify these diverse paths of influence. Besides the strategic policies which can be studied with this kind of framework, the framework itself can be used to study policies and actions at other 'layers' of national economies and societies (Breath, 2006).

Obviously, the framework presented above does not intend to list all possible types of influence or all possible individual influences within each type. A more detailed description of proposed actions is found in (Turk et al., 2008). However, it provides a valuable resource for strategy-makers at all levels in the consideration, identification and classification of their efforts. It can be used for country-level analysis, for analysing case studies or as a tool to help planners approach their task in a more comprehensive and systematic way.

Although other aspects should not be forgotten, special attention must be paid to the importance of competition – it has an impact on all three factors in the framework, while the entry of new firms influences both the demand and supply side

Figure 3. Structure of relationships between variables important for the adoption of BB

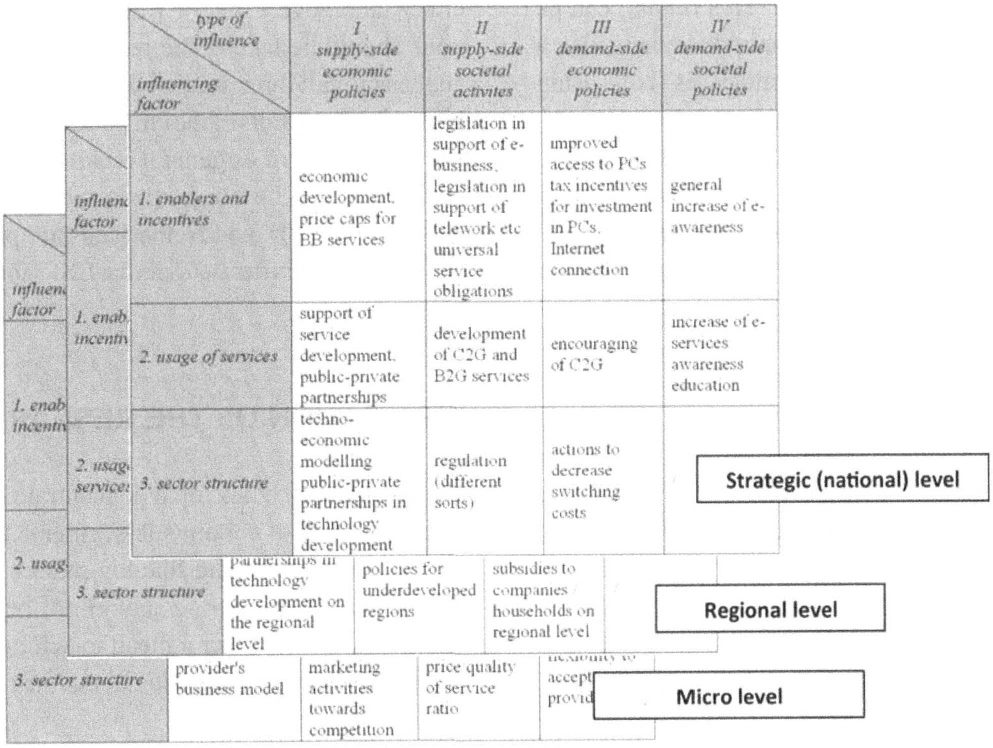

type of influence / influencing factor	I supply-side economic policies	II supply-side societal activities	III demand-side economic policies	IV demand-side societal policies	
1. enablers and incentives	economic development, price caps for BB services	legislation in support of e-business, legislation in support of telework etc universal service obligations	improved access to PCs tax incentives for investment in PCs, Internet connection	general increase of e-awareness	
2. usage of services	support of service development, public-private partnerships	development of C2G and B2G services	encouraging of C2G	increase of e-services awareness education	
3. sector structure	techno-economic modelling public-private partnerships in technology development	regulation (different sorts)	actions to decrease switching costs		**Strategic (national) level**
3. sector structure	partnerships in technology development on the regional level	policies for underdeveloped regions	subsidies to companies households on regional level		**Regional level**
3. sector structure	provider's business model	marketing activities towards competition	price quality of service ratio	flexibility to accept provid…	**Micro level**

(Agarwal, Bayus, 2002). For example, new entrants in the market can increase e-awareness due to an increase in promotional activities (Agarwal, Bayus, 2002), while competition is also one of the important incentives for using services (Hackney et al., 2006). Therefore, effective competition and the continued liberalisation of infrastructure, network services and applications were recommended as being crucial to stimulating broadband development (OECD, 2004). While a full analysis of the effects of competition would be beyond the scope of our research focus - see e.g. (Cave et al., 2006) for a review of various issues - we point out some of the most relevant areas for policy-makers.

On the supply side, regulation at different layers (Mindel, Sicker, 2006) is important. The focus should be on those specific layers where there are big economies of scale, or where positive network externalities can lead to under provision (compared to the social optimum) (Botterman

et al., 2003) Access to infrastructure, competition between different technologies (Fransman, 2006) and the relationship between content and infrastructure providers has attracted most attention in the regulation/promotion of competition.

Local Loop Unbundling (LLU) is another important issue since it can offer BB access to end-users for entrants without their own local networks (Fransman, 2006). Therefore, LLU is likely to lead to more competition probably faster than would have happened without regulatory intervention (De Bijl, Petz, 2005). See (De Bijl, Petz, 2005) for an overview of EU countries' experiences with unbundling, while limited success in LLU has been identified as one of the main reasons for Ireland's lag in adopting broadband (Analysys White Paper, 2006).

Further, it was shown (in the case study of Spanish geographical regions) that the number and complexity of initiatives is more important than the accepted strategic plan on the national level (Jordana et al., 2005). This finding can be well explained by our framework: namely, that a complex mix of different initiatives (both using different ways of influencing and influencing different factors) is needed. This is even more true as diffusion behaviour is not the consequence of a single action or factor but instead happens as a result of the interplay of different factors (Dutta & Roy, 2004-2005).

It must be emphasised that it is extremely important that when preparing a detailed strategic plan or initiatives at either the country or regional level, all factors should be considered while the critical success factors ('CSFs') for a strategic programme should also be identified. CSFs can vary considerably between different countries or regions. Cluster analysis (Vicente Cuervo & Lopez Menendez, 2005; Breath, 2006) can be used to identify countries that probably have similar

CSFs. After that, an appropriate combination of either the above listed or further developed actions should be taken. The results of the cluster analysis for all three studied factors are shown in Figure 4. The results of the cluster analysis should not be interpreted as general ranking instrument but specifically for our purposes - e.g. Belgium, Austria, Denmark and Netherlands are probably comparable countries with similar CSFs for further development.

IMPLICATION OF THE RESEARCH

Previous research has often concentrated on detailed analyses of certain sub-segments of these topics, while neglecting 'the big picture'. However, BB adoption *per se* should not be a final political goal but rather a mean to achieve other goals. The important question about the relation-

Figure 4. Cluster analysis – 3 factors

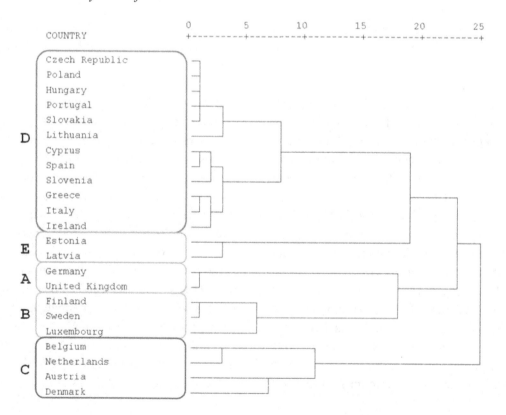

ship between BB/e-government ('EG') adoption and the possible influences of governmental strategy has to be resolved in order to efficiently streamline governmental efforts towards the final goal (the welfare of citizens, efficiency of companies). A conceptual framework that enables an overview of several important concepts (e.g. BB adoption and development, EG/EC service development and usage) and their proposed interconnections is shown in Figure 5. The purpose of the proposed conceptual framework is to tackle the often neglected: "so what" question. Often the efforts of government around the world center on the development of infrastructure (Cawley & Preston, 2007) or the quick informatization of government front offices. While this is undoubtedly important, sometimes the realization of underlying goals is lost either in research efforts or in the political process.

The main difference between the presented framework and those previously developed (e. g. (Venkatesh, Morris, Davis, & Davis, 2003); (Trkman, Jerman-Blažič, & Turk, 2008)); (Choudrie & Dwivedi, 2004)) is that the point of interest is not an individual decision to adopt BB, e-commerce (EC) or an EG service, but rather an identification and structured analysis of the causal relationship between the concepts and consequently possible governmental policy interventions. A better understanding of the underlying relations would thereby be enabled, while a more structured approach to preparation of the strategy is possible.

In Figure 5 the studied constructs and their proposed relation are shown. The arrows denote the proposed interconnections, while the stars indicate the possible ways of public policy intervention. As found in earlier research, e.g. (Cava-Ferreruela & Alabau-Munoz, 2006), (Sawada, Cossette, Wellar,

Figure 5. Conceptual framework for the adoption of BB/EG (Trkman, Turk, 2010)

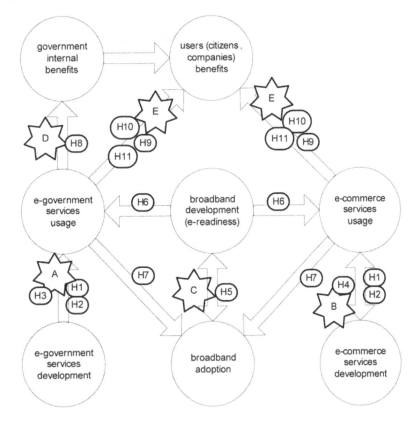

& Kurt, 2006), (Choudrie & Papazafeiropoulou, 2007), (Trkman et al., 2008) and in the previous chapter as well, these ways of influence can be either on the supply or demand side. Following (Trkman et al., 2008), some actions are also distributed in either social or economic influences. Infrastructure development was not included in the framework, although it is obviously a prerequisite for development of studied constructs. While this is the focus in less developed (e.g. African) countries and also in certain rural areas in Europe and US, the focus has mostly moved from infrastructure development towards the use and impact of new technologies (Ramos et al., 2004). The proposed hypotheses are theoretically grounded in (Trkman, Turk, 2009).

The implications from the proposed conceptual framework and the meaning of BB development studied in this chapter are shown with the explanation of one of the proposed interconnection; hypothesis 6: BB development will have a positive impact on the use of EC and EG services (see (Trkman, Turk, 2009) for a detailed explanation of other hypotheses).

Although several EG and EC services can also be used with a narrowband connection (Bauer et al., 2002), BB certainly enhances the user experience. It can reduce the costs of its usage with its always-on connectivity and basically eliminates marginal financial costs if no bit/datacap system is used.

Indeed, (Hitt & Tambe, 2007) proved that the adoption of BB considerably increases use of the Internet. The variability of the accessed content also grows. However, BB does not appear to be shifting the broad usage patterns involving the most popular applications of email, gaming, gambling, adult entertainment, online news, travel, and information searches (Cawley & Preston, 2007). The very strong influence of BB/Internet diffusion on the use of services has been proven in various fields – see e.g. (Centeno, 2004) for an analysis of the interconnection of e-banking and Internet adoption. Most importantly, (Choudrie

& Dwivedi, 2005) revealed in an analysis of the United Kingdom Government Gateway that citizens with home BB access are more likely to be aware of and adopt e-government services. There are differences in socioeconomic characteristics between citizen BB adopters and non-adopters that will affect the ability of the different citizen groups to also adopt e-government. Therefore, BB development is considered vital for the diffusion of EG services (Choudrie & Dwivedi, 2006).

However an important distinction between e-commerce, e-government and BB adoption should be drawn. BB development is a matter of ICT sector infrastructure and use of services (Trkman et al., 2008) and e-commerce adoption often relies on market mechanism. On the other hand, e-government adoption is much more complex and contingent on political culture and its effect on perception of right to freedom of information. E-government adoption is thus a systematic issue related to political demand for this type of service.

CONCLUSION AND FURTHER WORK

The diffusion of Internet technology and services is a complex process and the presented study offers new insights into the reasons underlying the differences seen among EU countries. The use of factor analysis enables an investigation of the nature of relations among variables instead of just a study of casual relationships involved in adoption of the Internet and BB access. The study discovered three underlying factors: 1. enablers and means; 2. usage of information services; and 3. the ICT sector environment. It confirmed the importance of making a distinction between 'access' and actual 'usage'. The analysis revealed that there are also other interesting facts, for instance the importance of a more complex utilisation of ICT services, such as telework.

In addition, since many governments at regional, national and international (e.g. EU) levels are developing various strategies for stimulating progress in this area, the development of a tool for planning and evaluating those strategies is of the utmost importance. The results of these research efforts and studies in this field should be joined together to develop an appropriate framework acting as a tool to study and implement strategic policies based on the identified factors along with possible ways to influence these factors. We presented one possible approach, where both strategic framework and a conceptualization of the connected fields (e.g. EG and EC adoption and finally users' or companies' benefits) were provided.

Our analysis was performed at the level of EU-25 countries. One of the possibility for further research is to apply this kind of approach to other levels, for instance for the global assessment of BB adoption and use. It is also possible to further investigate the connection between different factors with linear structural equation models (SEM), which could provide the knowledge needed to refine the presented strategic policy framework. In addition, a time-series analysis could reveal the dynamic nature of the relationships between latent factors and BB development indicators. A study of the efficiency of different actions (within the presented framework), especially the regulation/attempts to increase different sorts of competition, would also be beneficial.

On the other hand, employing the framework for various case studies at different levels to test the validity of underlying factors at the regional/micro level and the applicability of the framework is another interesting area worth exploring. Moreover, the study of the adoption process at the micro level could be supplemented with research into adoption patterns involving the use of micro-simulations.

REFERENCES

Agarwal, R., & Bayus, B. (2002). The Market Evolution and Sales Takeoff of Product Innovations. *Management Science*, *48*(8), 1024–1041. doi:10.1287/mnsc.48.8.1024.167

Analysys White Paper. (2006). *The Importance of Local Loop Unbundling in Ireland*. Analysys Consulting Limited. Retrieved from http://www.analysys.com/

Bauer, J., Berne, M., & Maitland, C. (2002). Internet access in the European Union and in the United States. *Telematics and Informatics*, *19*, 117–137. doi:10.1016/S0736-5853(01)00009-0

Botterman, M., Anderson, R., van Binst, P., et al. (2003). *Enabling the Information Society by Stimulating the Creation of a Broadband*. Rand Europe. Retrieved from http://www.rand.org

BREAD project. (n.d.). *Broadband in Europe for All: a multi-Disciplinary approach*. Retrieved September 20, 2008 from www.ist-bread.org

BReATH - Broadband e-Services and Access for the Home. (2006 October). *Breath, WP4 Report: Sustainable strategies and service evolution scenarios for broadband access*. Retrieved from http://www.ist-breath.net/

Cava-Ferreruela, I., & Alabau-Munoz, A. (2006). Broadband policy assessment: A cross-national empirical analysis. *Telecommunications Policy*, *30*, 445–463. doi:10.1016/j.telpol.2005.12.002

Cave, M., Prosperetti, L., & Doyle, C. (2006). Where are we going? Technologies, markets and long-range public policy issues in European communications. *Information Economics and Policy*, *18*, 242–255. doi:10.1016/j.infoecopol.2006.06.002

Cawley, A., & Preston, P. (2007). Broadband and digital 'content' in the EU-25: Recent trends and challenges. *Telematics and Informatics*, *24*(4), 259–271. doi:10.1016/j.tele.2007.01.015

Centeno, C. (2004). Adoption of Internet services in the Acceding and Candidate Countries, lessons from the Internet banking case. *Telematics and Informatics, 21*(4), 293–315. doi:10.1016/j.tele.2004.02.001

Chanclou, P., Gosselin, S., Fernández Palacios, J., Alvarez, V., & Zouganeli, E. (2006, August). Overview of the Optical Broadband Access Evolution: A Joint Article by Operators in the IST Network of Excellence e-Photon/ONe, Telenor R&D. *IEEE Communications Magazine, 44*(8), 29–35. doi:10.1109/MCOM.2006.1678106

Chaudhuri, A., Flamm, K., & Horrigan, J. (2005). An analysis of the determinants of internet access. *Telecommunications Policy, 29*, 731–755. doi:10.1016/j.telpol.2005.07.001

Choudrie, J., & Dwivedi, Y. (2004). Towards a conceptual model of broadband diffusion. *Journal of Computing and Information Technology - CIT, 12*(4), 323-338.

Choudrie, J., & Dwivedi, Y. (2005). *A Survey of Citizens' Awareness and Adoption of E-Government Initiatives, the 'Government Gateway': A United Kingdom Perspective.* Paper presented at the E-government workshop, London, UK.

Choudrie, J., & Dwivedi, Y. (2006). *Examining the Socio-economic Determinants of Broadband Adopters and Non-adopters in the United Kingdom.* Paper presented at the Proceedings of the 39th Annual Hawaii International Conference on System Sciences (HICSS'06) Track 4, Hawaii.

Choudrie, J., & Papazafeiropoulou, A. (2007). Assessing the UK policies for broadband adoption. *Information Systems Frontiers, 9*(2-3), 297–308. doi:10.1007/s10796-006-9022-3

De Bijl, P., & Peitz, M. (2005). *Local Loop Unbundling in Europe: Experience, Prospects and Policy Challenges.* Working Paper 29/2005, Bruchsal, February 2005.

Distaso, W., Lupi, P., & Manenti, F. (2006). Platform competition and broadband uptake: Theory and empirical evidence from the European Union. *Information Economics and Policy, 18*, 87–106. doi:10.1016/j.infoecopol.2005.07.002

Dutta, A., & Roy, R. (2005). The Mechanics of Internet Growth: A Developing-Country Perspective. *International Journal of Electronic Commerce, 9*, 143–165.

Eurobarometer: E-communications household survey. (2006 July). European Commission. Retrieved from http://ec.europa.eu/information_society/policy/ecomm/doc/info_centre/studies_ext_consult/ecomm_household_study/eb_jul06_main_report_en.pdf

Eurostat. Statistical Office of the European Communities. (2006). Retrieved from http://epp.eurostat.ec.europa.eu

Eurydce (2005). *The information network on education in Europe.* Retrieved from http://www.eurydice.org/Doc_intermediaires/indicators/en/key_data.html

Firth, L., & Mellor, D. (2005). Broadband: Benefits and problems. *Telecommunications Policy, 29*, 223–236. doi:10.1016/j.telpol.2004.11.004

Fransman, M. (Ed.). (2006). *Global Broadband Battles – Why the U. S. and Europe Lag While Asia Leads.* Stanford, CA: Stanford University Books.

Frieden, R. (2005). Lessons from broadband development in Canada, Japan, Korea and the United States. *Telecommunications Policy, 29*, 595–613. doi:10.1016/j.telpol.2005.06.002

Gillet, S., Lehr, W., & Osorio, C. (2004). Local government broadband initiatives. *Telecommunications Policy, 28*, 537–558. doi:10.1016/j.telpol.2004.05.001

Giuliano, R., Luglio, M., & Mazzenga, F. (2008). Interoperability between WiMAX and Broadband Mobile Space Networks. *IEEE Communications Magazine*, *46*(3), 50–57. doi:10.1109/MCOM.2008.4463771

Guillen, M., & Suarez, S. (2001). Developing the Internet: entrepreneurship and public policy in Ireland, Singapore, Argentina, and Spain. *Telecommunications Policy*, *25*, 349–371. doi:10.1016/S0308-5961(01)00009-X

Guillen, M., & Suarez, S. (2005). Explaining the Global Digital Divide: Economic, Political and Sociological Drivers of Cross-National Internet Use. *Social Forces*, *84*, 681–708. doi:10.1353/sof.2006.0015

Hackney, R., Xu, H., & Ranchhod, A. (2006). Evaluation Web Services: Towards a framework for emergent contexts. *European Journal of Operational Research*, *173*, 1161–1174. doi:10.1016/j.ejor.2005.07.010

Hargittai, E. (1999). Weaving the Western Web: explaining differences in Internet connectivity among OECD countries. *Telecommunications Policy*, *23*, 701–718. doi:10.1016/S0308-5961(99)00050-6

Hitt, L., & Tambe, P. (2007). Broadband adoption and content consumption. *Information Economics and Policy*, *19*(3-4), 362–378. doi:10.1016/j.infoecopol.2007.04.003

ITU Internet Report: Digital.Life. International Telecommunications Union, December 2006.

Jordana, J., Fernandez, X., Sancho, D., & Welp, J. (2005). Which Internet Policy? Assessing Regional Initiatives in Spain. *The Information Society*, *21*, 341–351. doi:10.1080/01972240500253509

Kiiski, S., & Pohjola, M. (2002). Cross-country diffusion of the Internet. *Information Economics and Policy*, *14*, 297–310. doi:10.1016/S0167-6245(01)00071-3

Kurland, N., & Bailey, D. (1999). Telework: The Advantages and Challenges of Working Here, There, Anywhere, and Anytime. *Organizational Dynamics*, *28*(2), 53–68. doi:10.1016/S0090-2616(00)80016-9

Lau, T., Kim, S., & Atkin, D. (2005). An examination of factors contributing to South Korea's global leadership in broadband adoption. *Telematics and Informatics*, *22*, 349–359. doi:10.1016/j.tele.2004.11.004

Lee, C., & Chan-Olmsted, S. (2004). Competitive advantage of broadband Internet: a comparative study between South Korea and the United States. *Telecommunications Policy*, *28*, 649–677. doi:10.1016/j.telpol.2004.04.002

Madden, G., & Simpson, M. (1996). A probit model of household broadband service subscription intentions: A regional analysis. *Information Economics and Policy*, *8*, 249–267. doi:10.1016/0167-6245(96)00008-X

Marcus, S. (2005, April). Broadband adoption in Europe. *IEEE Communications Magazine*, *43*(4), 18–20. doi:10.1109/MCOM.2005.1421895

Milner, H. (2006). The Digital Divide: The Role of Political Institutions in Technology Diffusion. *Comparative Political Studies*, *39*, 176–199. doi:10.1177/0010414005282983

Mindel, J., & Sicker, D. (2006). Leveraging the EU regulatory framework to improve a layered policy model for US telecommunications markets. *Telecommunications Policy*, *30*, 136–148. doi:10.1016/j.telpol.2005.11.004

Norris, P. (2000). The Global Divide: Information Poverty and Internet Access Worldwide. Internet Conference at the International Political Science World Congress in Quebec City, 1-6 August 2000.

OECD. (2004, February 12). Recommendation of the OECD council on broadband development. Retrieved from http://www.oecd.org/document/36/0,2340,en_21571361_34590630_34238436_1_1_1_1,00.html

OECD. (2005). *Multiple play: pricing and policy trends*. Working Party on Telecommunication and Information Services Policies. Retrieved from http://www.oecd.org/dataoecd/47/32/36546318.pdf

OECD. (2008). *OECD Broadband Portal*. Retrieved from http://www.oecd.org/sti/ict/broadband

Oxley, J., & Yeung, B. (2001). E-commerce readiness: Institutional environment and international competitiveness. *Journal of International Business Studies, 32*, 705-723. doi:10.1057/palgrave.jibs.8490991

Pau, L. F. (2002). The communications and information economy: issues, tariffs and economics research areas. *Journal of Economic Dynamics & Control, 26*(9-10), 1651–1675. doi:10.1016/S0165-1889(01)00089-6

Perez, M., Sanchez, A., & Carnicer, M. (2002). Benefits and barriers of telework: perception differences of human resources managers according to company's operations strategy. *Technovation, 22*, 775–783. doi:10.1016/S0166-4972(01)00069-4

Pew Internet. *Digital divisions*. (2005, October 15). Retrieved from http://www.pewInternet.org/

Ramos, S., Feijóo, C., Pérez, J., Castejón, L., González, A., & Rojo, D. (2004). New perspectives on broadband development and public policies. *The Journal of the Communications Network, 3*(1), 28–33.

Savage, S., & Waldman, D. (2005). Broadband Internet Access, Awareness and Use: Analyses of United States Household Data. *Telecommunications Policy, 29*, 615–633. doi:10.1016/j.telpol.2005.06.001

Sawada, M., Cossette, D., Wellar, B., & Kurt, T. (2006). Analysis of the urban/rural broadband divide in Canada: Using GIS in planning terrestrial wireless deployment. *Government Information Quarterly, 23*(3-4), 454–479. doi:10.1016/j.giq.2006.08.003

Sciadas, G. (2004). *International benchmarking for the information society*. Presented at ITU-KADO Digital Bridges Symposium, Asia Telecom 2004, Busan, Republic of Korea.

Sharma, S. (1996). *Applied Multivariate Techniques*. New York: John Wiley & Sons.

Tabachnick, B., & Fidell, L. S. (2001). *Using Multivariate Statistics*. Boston: Allyn and Bacon.

Trkman, P., Jerman-Blažič, B., & Turk, T. (2008). Factors of broadband development and the design of a strategic policy framework. *Telecommunications Policy, 32*(2), 101–115. doi:10.1016/j.telpol.2007.11.001

Trkman, P., & Turk, T. (2009). A Conceptual Model for the Development of Broadband and E-Government. *Government Information Quarterly, 26*(2), 416–424. doi:10.1016/j.giq.2008.11.005

Turk, T., Jerman-Blažič, B., & Trkman, P. (2008). Factors and sustainable strategies fostering the adoption of broadband communications in an enlarged European Union. *Technological Forecasting and Social Change, 75*(7), 933–951. doi:10.1016/j.techfore.2007.08.004

Venkatesh, V., Morris, M., Davis, G., & Davis, F. (2003). User acceptance of information technology: Toward a unified view. *Management Information Systems Quarterly, 27*(3), 425–478.

Vicente Cuervo, M., & Lopez Menendez, A. (2006). A multivariate framework for the analysis of the digital divide: Evidence for the European Union-15. *Information & Management, 43*, 756–766. doi:10.1016/j.im.2006.05.001

Xavier, P. (2003). Should broadband be part of universal service obligations? *Info - The journal of policy, regulation and strategy for telecommunications, 5*, 8-25.

ENDNOTE

[1] The content of this chapter is based on Trkman, P., Jerman-Blažič, B., & Turk, T. (2008). Factors of broadband development and the design of a strategic policy framework. Telecommunications Policy, 32(2), 101-115. It was cosiderably improved and extended with new research findings in the process of the preparation of this book.

Chapter 7
Assessing Electronic Government Readiness in Egypt:
Comparison between Two Public Organizations

Nahed Amin Azab
The American University in Cairo, Egypt

ABSTRACT

Electronic Government (e-Government) has rapidly become a political imperative at local, national and international level. The drive to implement e-government has become of critical importance globally. The e-government revolution offers the potential to reshape the public sector and remake the relationship between citizens and government. Several developing nations, including Egypt, having witnessed the benefits realized by e-Government in developed countries, took e-Government initiatives and achieved different success rates. It is frequently claimed that proving an effective e-government assessment framework is a necessary condition for advancing e-Government. The objective of this chapter is to present a framework that assesses e-Government readiness (EGR) in Egypt, focusing on electronic administration (e-Administration) within a public organization through obtaining its employees' feedback. The suggested framework investigates the internal factors affecting e-Government readiness which are: strategy, processes, people, and technology. The chapter applies this framework on 2 public organizations in Egypt to test it and to set a comparison between both organizations in terms of the internal factors effect on e-Government readiness.

INTRODUCTION

Increasing awareness and interest in e-Government drive governments to implement e-Government initiatives worldwide (Nour et al., 2008) at local, national, regional and global levels, and gaining

DOI: 10.4018/978-1-60566-388-3.ch007

further support from different stakeholders in each community (Salem, 2007). The transition from conventional government to e-Government provides an opportunity for the government to improve its services and reduce, or even eliminate expenditure and ineffectiveness that may exist in its traditional services (Bakry, 2004). e-Government can also have a great effect on modernizing governments through restructuring of public organizations, re-engineering of business processes, and fostering communication between government and citizens over time and distances (Krishnaswamy, 2005).

Although most e-Government research express optimistic views regarding the impact of e-Government (Heeks and Bailur, 2007), e-Government benefits are still difficult to reap. This is attributed to the absence of a clear roadmap to be followed to realize success because e-Government is still in an early stage (Moon, 2002). This highlights the importance of defining measures of success (Stowers, 2004) to raise awareness, elucidate e-Government development environment, and to confirm the feasibility of selected e-Government approaches (UNDESA, 2003).

Available benchmarking e-Government initiatives do not provide a comprehensive framework for assessing, classifying and comparing different e-Government programs (Hu et al., 2005; Grant and Chau, 2005). Most appraisal models are more suitable for the appraisal of the overall development of e-Government in each country; they are not directly focusing on the problems that exist in individual e-Government projects or on the internal factors affecting transformation of a government organization due to information and communication technology (ICT) adoption. In addition, the majority of such appraisals address the electronic service (eService) view of e-Government ignoring its electronic administration (eAdministration) aspect despite its importance on e-Government success (Dawes, 2002). Moreover, most of these approaches ignore the view of civil servants, even though they constitute the cornerstone in the success of any e-Government project as the direct users.

This chapter suggests an electronic government readiness (EGR) framework of e-Government project assessment focusing on eAdministration. The suggested framework encompasses all internal factors affecting a public organization categorized into four main dimensions: strategy, processes,

technology, and people. All measuring constructs under each dimension are derived from available literature on the assessment of eReadiness and EGR, as well as on information systems (IS) and eCommerce success.

The suggested EGR framework is evaluated against feedback of employees working in two public sector organizations in Egypt. Comparison of findings reveals the relationship between these four dimensions, and the weight of each dimension in affecting EGR in both organizations.

The chapter starts first by an introduction of the research philosophy selected, followed by an explanation of the framework suggested for assessing EGR, describing its different four dimensions: strategy, processes, technology, and people. Next, an overview of the Egypt's overall e-government strategy is presented, highlighting the link between the national e-government strategy and e-government readiness study, which is the main focus of the chapter. The two public organizations used as case studies for assessing EGR in Egypt are then described, followed by an explanation of the methodology used, and an analysis of the data collected from the empirical research. Finally findings are discussed along with the research limitations, leading to the conclusion derived from the study.

RESEARCH PHILOSOPHY

The focus of the study is on the internal factors affecting EGR in a public organization. Following an in-depth review of different research philosophies, positivist was the most appropriate approach that serves in reaching the research aim. Since the research addresses the factors affecting EGR, the weight of each factor as well as the relation that exists between them, there was a need to develop a framework to: i) conceptualize the suggested ideas, ii) identify variables, iii) set hypothesis, iv) focus on observable aspects, and v) adopt a testability principle. This is completely compatible with the

Figure 1. E-government readiness (EGR) framework

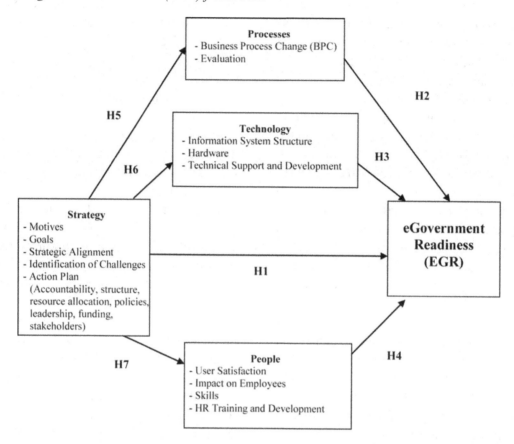

description of the positivist approach mentioned by many researchers (Myers and Avison, 2002; Creswell, 2002; Khazanchi and Munkvold, 2003; Clarke, 2000). Positivist research was also selected because it is characterized by its objectivity, generalization, and the separation of the researcher from the observed (Wilford, 2004).

A SUGGESTED FRAMEWORK FOR ASSESSING EGR

The suggested framework derives its dimensions from previous research on IS and eCommerce success, eReadiness, and EGR. The following lines present an explanation of the different dimensions of the framework.

The proposed framework adopts the four-phase model of e-Government (Baum and Maio, 2000) that classifies e-Government into four dimensions: strategy, processes, technology, and people. In addition, the research suggests a number of constructs under each dimension in the framework. Aiming to overcome the several shortcomings that exist in previous EGR assessment models, the framework covers all internal factors that affect EGR (see figure 1). It acts as a checklist; a public organization can verify the presence or absence of each construct under each dimension.

Although external factors such as environment, IT infrastructure, regulations, etc. are proved to be important in assessing EGR, they are not investigated in this research. The emphasis is instead on the internal factors that exist within a public organization because previous studies in eReadiness and EGR had already addressed them (e.g., CID, CIDCM, KAM, NRI, USAID, and WITSA (Bridges.org, 2005), UNDESA (2005, 2008)). Also, it is preferable to develop an in-depth analysis of all internal factors, which contains a rather large number of measures. Adding external factors leads to a cumbersome and complicated framework shifting the attention from the internal factors that are the main concern of the study.

The following lines explain the theoretical background from which all constructs under each dimension are derived.

Strategy

The need to set out a robust strategy for e-Government is a major factor in reaching a successful e-Government adoption (Reffat, 2003; Fletcher, 1999). An efficient strategy should identify first the main drivers for implementing e-Government (Working Group on e-Government in the Developing World, 2002). Recognizing these drivers highlights their importance, and helps in setting an appropriate action plan. e-Government strategy should also set a number of goals (Forman, 2002) -to justify its cost and to check the extent to which these goals were achieved - and should identify potential challenges (Margetts and Dunleavy, 2002): technological, administrative, legislative, economic, and political (Pilipovic et al., 2002). Highlighting challenges at an early stage helps in setting appropriate solutions (Weerakody et al., 2005) with the right priorities (Chen and Knepper, 2005). An e-Government strategy should also be aligned with the organization's business strategy, referred as strategic alignment, (Beaumaster, 2002; Baets, 1992; Bowman et al., 1983; Das et al., 1991; Henderson and Venkatraman, 1993). Strategic alignment impacts overall organization and business performance (Xia and King, 2002; Croteau et al., 2001), and helps in perceiving higher payoffs from IT (Tallon et al., 2000).

Table 1. Main constructs of "strategy"

Strategy
Motives
Goals
Strategic Alignment
Identification of Challenges
Action Plan
Organization
(Accountability, Structure, Resource allocation, IT policies and procedures, Leadership)
Funding resources
Stakeholders
(Identification, Role, Value on each one)
Promotion

In addition, an e-Government strategy should set an action plan (UNDESA, 2003; WASEDA University, 2006) including accountability (Navarra and Cornford, 2003; Heeks, 2001), organization's structure (Snellen, 2000; Baum and Maio, 2000), resource allocation (Fletcher, 2003), IT policies and procedures (Powell and Dent-Micallef, 1999; Zahra and Covin, 1993), and leadership (WASEDA University, 2006; NSW, 2001). Action plan should also investigate funding sources (WASEDA University, 2006; NSW, 2001), and identify e-Government different stakeholders (Mitchell et al., 1997; Tennert and Schroeder, 1999) in order to determine their roles (Frooman, 1999; Bryson and Alston, 1996) as well as the value to be reflected on each of them (Aldrich et al., 2002; Traunmüller and Wimmer, 2003; Sprecher, 2000; West, 2000). Finally, an action plan should develop means to promote e-Government to build awareness among all stakeholders (Hu et al., 2005; WASEDA University, 2006). Table 1 presents the various suggested constructs of the e-Government strategy dimension.

Showing the value of e-Government strategy along with its different underlying items leads us to the following hypothesis:

Table 2. Main constructs of "processes"

Processes
Business Process Change (BPC)
Motives of BPC
Focal areas of BPC
Definition, documentation and streamlining of Business processes
Vertical integration
Horizontal integration
Evaluation
Design/reality gap
Usage
(Citizens, Employees)
Citizens' feedback
(Perceived usefulness, Perceived ease of use, Satisfaction, Trust)
Employees' feedback
(Perceived usefulness, Perceived ease of use, Satisfaction)
Impact on stakeholders

- **Hypothesis 1 (H1):** e-Government strategy impacts EGR of the organization

Processes

Processes to be undertaken by an e-Government initiative are classified into two main categories: business processes change and e-Government evaluation (see table 2). Several studies highlight the value of business process change in e-Government success (Scholl, 2003; Kettinger et al., 1997; Pardo and Scholl, 2002; Heeks, 2001; Seybold, 1998). First, the motives for change should be determined (Scholl, 2005), and the focal areas where these change should take place (Harkness et al., 1996; Kettinger and Grover, 1995; Balutis, 2001). Business processes should also be defined, documented and streamlined (Rimmer, 2002; Guo and Lu, 2005; Baum and Maio, 2000) to improve information flow within the organization.

Business processes should also be integrated internally, and with other public agencies as well (Accenture, 2005; Ho, 2002; Moon, 2002; Tapscott, 1995; Chen and Knepper, 2005; Rimmer, 2002; Layne and Lee, 2001).

Furthermore, the framework considers evaluation of e-Government performance as a systematic approach to be performed periodically. Evaluation should always compare plans with real situations (Heeks, 2003); this aids in rectifying deviations from the plans at an early stage. Evaluation should also take into account the use of e-Government services by citizens (Gefen et al., 2002) and ICT usage by the employees in the organization (CSPP, 2000; Liu, 2001; DeLone and McLean, 1992; Marchionini et al., 2003; Schedler and Scharf, 2001). It is also essential to conduct periodic evaluations to understand how citizens perceive e-Government from different perspectives such as usefulness and ease of use (Davis, 1985, 1989), satisfaction (DeLone and McLean, 1992; Iivari and Ervasi, 1994; Cyert and March, 1963; Downing, 1999; Bailey and Pearson, 1983; Igbaria and Nachman, 1990), and trust (Adams, 1999; Edmiston, 2003; Chen and Knepper, 2005; Gefen et al., 2002; Tassabehji, 2005). Periodic evaluations should also be extended to investigate employees' perceived usefulness and ease of use (Davis, 1985, 1989), and satisfaction (DeLone and McLean, 1992; Bailey and Pearson, 1983; Davis, 1985, 1989; Igbaria and Nachman, 1990; Rai et al., 2002; Seddon, 1997; Seddon and Kiew, 1996; Seddon et al., 1999; Wilkin and Castleman, 2003). Finally, evaluations should be performed to assess the development of the impact of e-Government on all stakeholders (DeLone and McLean, 1992; Seddon, 1997). Table 2 shows the main constructs of the processes dimension.

Highlighting the importance of processes as an integral factor in affecting e-Government enables us to set the second hypothesis:

- **Hypothesis 2 (H2):** Organizational processes impacts EGR

Technology

Evidently, technology constitutes an important factor influencing e-Government success (NSW, 2001). Technology comprises IS structure, hardware, and service quality (see table 3). Information systems structure covers information quality (DeLone and McLean, 1992; Bailey and Pearson, 1983; Ahituv, 1980), system quality (DeLone and McLean, 1992; Bailey and Pearson, 1983; Bhimani, 1996), Web presence quality (UNDESA, 2005; West, 2000, 2006; WASEDA University, 2006; Accenture, 2002, 2005; Turban et al., 2002; Liu and Arnett, 2000; DeConti, 1998; Eschenfelder et al., 1997; Burgess and Cooper, 1990; Smith, 2001; Boon et al., 2000; Farquhar et al., 1998; Fogg, 2002; Fogg, et al., 2002; Hamilton and Chervany, 1981; Ho and Wu, 1999; Kossak et al., 2001; Swanson, 1986; Wan, 2000), and security measures (NSW, 2001; Ben Abd Allah et al., 2002; Conklin and White, 2006; Boudriga, 2002). Technological dimension should also consider the quality of the hardware (Victoria, 2002), and the technical support and development provided by the IT department to the entire organization referred as service quality (CSPP, 2000; Woodroof and Burg, 2003; Pitt et al., 1995; Li, 1997; Wilkin and Hewett, 1999; Wilkin and Castleman, 2003).

The effect of technology on EGR presented in the literature directs us to the third hypothesis:

- **Hypothesis 3 (H3):** Technology in the organization impacts EGR

People

People are one of the main factors in the success of e-Government (NSW, 2001). Several constructs exist in this dimension such as, user satisfaction (DeLone and McLean, 1992; Bailey and Pearson, 1983; Davis, 1985, 1989; Igbaria and Nachman, 1990; Rai et al., 2002; Seddon, 1997; Seddon, and Kiew, 1996; Seddon et al., 1999; Wilkin and Castleman, 2003), assessing satisfaction of

Table 3. Main constructs of "technology"

Technology
Information Systems Structure
Information quality
(Content, Availability, Accuracy, Timeliness, Convenience, integration [vertical, horizontal, Internet])
System quality
(Reliability, Ease of Use, Accessibility, Usefulness, Flexibility, integration [vertical, horizontal, Internet])
Web presence quality
(Usability, Layout, Navigation, Consistency, Content, Number of services, Stage [presence, interaction, transaction, transformation])
Security measures
(Data and software protection, data transfer over networks, Safety of electronic payment)
Hardware
(Quality, Integration [vertical, horizontal])
Technical Support and Development
(Reliability, Competence, Responsiveness, Timeliness, Communications, Commitment, Access)

e-Government from the part of employees using IT. Also, it is vital to detect the impact of e-Government on them (DeLone and McLean, 1992; Seddon, 1997). Also, employees' skills should be taken into account such as, adaptation to change (Bertelsmann Foundation, 2002), proficiency in using IT (ICMA, 2002); ability to communicate with other employees within and outside the organization (Powell and Dent-Micallef, 1999), and providing an adequate service to citizens (Accenture, 2002, 2005). Finally, there should be a special focus on the training to be provided to the employees in order to develop their various skills (Baum and Maio, 2000). Table 4 presents the various suggested constructs under the people dimension.

Recognizing the value of people in e-Government readiness guides us to the fourth hypothesis:

- **Hypothesis 4 (H4):** People in the organization impact EGR

Table 4. Main constructs of "people"

People
User Satisfaction
Impact on employees
Skills
(Adaptation to change, Use of technology, Integration, Customer service)
HR Training and Development

Relation Between Strategy, and Processes, Technology, People

The study argues that all three factors: processes, technology, and people, are affected by e-Government strategy since this strategy comprises a number of aspects that cause major changes in the mentioned three factors. An efficient e-Government strategy, if followed, should have a direct impact on them, which leads to the following three hypotheses:

- **Hypothesis 5 (H5):** e-Government strategy impacts processes in the organization
- **Hypothesis 6 (H6):** e-Government strategy impacts technology in the organization
- **Hypothesis 7 (H7):** e-Government strategy impacts people in the organization

COUNTRY PROFILE

Egypt has taken an e-Government initiative since the introduction of the Ministry of Communication and Information Technology (MCIT) in 1999, as part of its plan to turn Egypt into an information-based society. The vision of e-Government initiative in Egypt is "delivering high quality government services to the public in the format that suits them". Such vision relies mainly on three principles that include: 1) citizen centric service delivery; 2) community participation; and 3) efficient allocation of government resources. Such vision led to formulate Egypt's e-government strategy directed mainly towards utilizing ICT to enhance government readiness to accept a strong local program and to smoothly integrate in the global community (Darwish, 2007). Egypt IT strategy should be based on the building blocks: people, training, information, technology and the partnership between the public and private sector (Kamel et al., 2002). The main projects guided by this strategy - related to the third principle of the national vision (efficient allocation of government resources) - are back office automation and automation of local governorates (EISI-Government Team, 2003). This proves the focus on automating back office over both central and local governmental agencies since the beginning of the Egyptian e-government program.

The official inauguration of the Egyptian e-Government portal (www.egypt.gov.eg) took place in 25 January 2004 and was attended by Bill Gates during his first visit to Egypt, as Microsoft was chosen to be in charge of the project's implementation. Some services were placed in the portal to pilot test the project such as telephone e-billing, birth certificate issuing, etc. With the new cabinet announced in Egypt in July 2004, the e-government program became the responsibility of the Ministry of States for Administrative development (MSAD) instead of MCIT. This decision indicates the clear vision of e-government program perceived as a transformative project affecting all government organizations rather than a technological one.

Egypt's e-Government program has identified a number of objectives to realize a successful implementation of e-Government and that includes (but not limited to): 1) tailoring government services to meet citizens expectations; 2) creating a conducive environment to investors (local and international); 3) availing accurate and updated government information; 4) increasing government efficiency through modern management techniques and new working models; 5) reducing government expenditure; and 6) fostering local competitiveness and increasing globalization readiness.

The above objectives cannot be realized without considering ICT readiness on a macro level (i.e., of the overall country) as well as on a micro level (over public organizations). E-government policy makers in Egypt were interested in assessing the country's overall e-government readiness since 2003 through undertaking a qualitative comparison of UN e-government readiness criteria with ICT readiness of Egypt (EISI-Government Team, 2003). Assessing e-government readiness of public organizations is largely considered also; this can be deduced from the interest of e-government responsibles in this research (Dr. Hatem elKady, e-government program manager, expressed his interest in getting the research findings). In addition, MSAD performs a yearly survey to assess e-government readiness of public organizations (see the fifth issue of this survey on http://www.msad.gov.eg). The survey provides an insight about the skills of the employees and the technology components within each organization. MSAD responsibles send one questionnaire to each organization's manager asking him to provide MSAD with the information required in the questionnaire. Such information is aggregated and serves as a documentary source to determine the skills of employees and the technology standards in Egyptian public organizations.

Egypt e-Government program is in continuous progress; this can be deduced by monitoring its rank in several studies conducted regularly to evaluate EGR worldwide. For example, in the global e-Government readiness by Darrell West, Brown University - evaluating 198 around the world based on their national websites - Egypt ranks 73rd in 2008 compared to 81st in 2007. Furthermore, in the UN e-Government readiness report (2008), Egypt ranks 79th over 193 countries compared to 99th in 2005 (no UN ranking reports were issued in 2006 and 2007).

It is expected that citizens will rely more on online services due to the growing number of:

Internet users (increased from 300,000 in October 1999 to 11.3 million in April 2008), fixed telephone lines (increased from 4.9 million in October 1999 to 11.3 million in December 2008), and mobile users (increased from 654 thousands million in October 1999 to 35.09 million in December 2008) (MCIT, 2008).

CASE STUDIES

A contextually specific empirical study was undertaken in cooperation with Montaza District (MD), Alexandria, and the Tax Unit for Non-Commercial Professions (TUNC). Further studies are already taking place on additional cases in other contexts to produce results that can be compared with those obtained from this study.

Case Study 1: Montaza District (MD)

Montaza district is located in Alexandria (one of Egypt's 29 governorates located in North Egypt on the Mediterranean). MD's area is 92 square kilometers; it has a population of 1.023 million, which is the highest population among the other five districts of Alexandria, constituting around 25% of the total population of Alexandria (4.110 million). MD offers a total of 69 services to citizens such as, issuance and renovation of permits (stores, buildings, digging), issuance and re-issuance of certificates, etc.

The district started its e-Government program since 2003 focusing on using ICT to reach two main objectives: simplify and speed-up the procedure in providing services to the citizens in case of physical interaction, and enable citizens to get the services remotely. The first objective was realized to a great extent by placing public kiosks, in several convenient locations, doing any service with MD on behalf of the citizen; and by making 38 services (around 55% of total services offered) instant ones, i.e. to be completed in 30 minutes only or less. More services are to be transferred to instant ones. The second objective was attained by launching a Web site for MD (www.montazaonline.com). Most services are offered online, but electronic payment is still not implemented, which means that for services requiring fees, payment could be upon delivery, or citizens have to go to MD for payment. Also, citizens cannot submit documents electronically, but they can see the documents required for each service to be prepared before visiting MD. Other important services are provided through the website such as, check the status of a property, track the status of the services applied for, apply and follow-up services from other public entities making MD play an intermediary role. The website gives also its visitors insight on most issues related to the district such as events and attraction places.

Case Study 2: Tax Unit for Non-Commercial Professions (TUNC)

Tax Unit for Non-Commercial Professions (TUNC) is one of five tax units in Cairo 8th area. In fact, Egyptian Tax Authority (ETA) of has divided each governorate geographically into several areas. For example Cairo, the capital and main governorate is divided into eight main areas, and each area comprises several tax units.

TUNC was founded in November 2004 in an attempt to separate the tax collection of non-commercial professions from others. Non-commercial professions comprise citizens working as physicians, lawyers, pharmacists, engineers, etc. who run their private business. TUNC serves now 58000 financers whose businesses are in its geographic area.

TUNC was among the first tax units to adopt the e-Government program set by the ETA. ETA started this program in 2006 on a small number of tax units and plans to implement it over all tax units in Egypt in the future. The main objective of implementing e-Government is to enhance the services provided to citizens, hence being in accordance with the national e-Government program. The first implementation stage was through improving eAdministration in several tax units by providing a computer to each employee especially those who have a direct contact with the citizens. The second stage was performed by enabling financers to communicate with ETA over the Internet. ETA added different services through the Egyptian e-Government portal.

Several eServices are provided such as registering a new activity, notifying ETA of a temporary or permanent halt, applying for a tax ID, or presenting income statements. Citizens can even send a check number for payment without having to go to the correspondent tax units for payment. All communications with ETA are sent first to the central administration, and are then directed electronically to the correspondent tax unit through a wide area network that connects the central administration with all tax units. ETA is planning to implement a full ePayment solution through providing a digital signature by the end of 2008.

Methodology

The following methodology was undertaken in both case studies. A conceptual framework is proposed to investigate the factors affecting EGR. In order to validate it, a case study research strategy is selected since it is a well known approach for exploratory, theory-building research (Eisenhardt, 1989) allowing in depth investigation (Yin, 1993; Walsham, 1993; Pettigrew, 1990). Both qualitative and quantitative data were combined. Qualitative data was collected through in-depth unstructured and semi-structured interviews (Yin, 1994) with top management, key people (IT managers and webmasters official websites), and with a number of employees. Interviews were combined with observations and a review of the documentation and archival records to enable validation of the questionnaire findings through triangulation (Yin, 1994; Saunders et al., 2000; Ragin, 1987). Quantitative data was collected through distributing a questionnaire on a sample representing employees working in administrative positions.

Based on the interviews conducted with e-Government responsibles, and on observation of the work environment, the number of employees suitable to participate in each case was identified (computer users, senior management, IT specialists, and administrators). The rest of employees are computer illiterate which makes them unable to respond to the different parts of the questionnaire. The small number of respondents enabled a direct contact with the employees while answering the questionnaire.

Questionnaire Structure

The questionnaire used in this research is adopted from three previous studies: Koh and Prybutok (2003) and Liu (2001), developed to measure EGR in City of Denton, Texas, and UNDESA (2003), addressed to public agencies in any country to assess EGR. Several questions were modified and others are added to reflect all the measuring constructs that exist in the suggested EGR framework.

The questionnaire consists of six sections: the first four sections measure employees' perceptions toward the four suggested dimensions of the model: strategy, processes, technology, and people. Each question in each section reflects a measurement construct under each dimension. The research variables are measured in a 7-point Likert's scale, with 1 as *strongly disagree*, and 7 as *strongly agree* for some constructs, or with 1 as *far short of expectations*, and 7 as *greatly exceeds expectations* for other constructs (see appendix A). The fifth section contains only one question requesting employees to express their view regarding the extent to which their organization is ready for e-Government. Finally, the sixth section contains personal questions about each subject (e.g. age range, gender, experience with IT, etc.). The questionnaire was translated to the Arabic language because the majority of the

employees do not have adequate proficiency in the English language.

Study Findings

Demographics

Table 5 shows that the response rates in both cases are relatively high (87.6% and 89%). Invalid responses were discarded because they were incomplete due to three reasons: the first reason is related to the first section concerning the strategy dimension, which was hard for the employees to reply to because most of them do not have a complete idea about all the issues stated under it. Some of them left this section because they could not perceive its relevancy to them. The second reason was due to the length of the questionnaire (consisting of 11 pages). Some of them completed 4 or 5 pages and were not interested in terminating it. The third reason is due to their fear to express any negative perception towards any item raised in the questionnaire.

Comparing the samples in both cases reveals that the percentage of females is high at MD (84.5%) in contrast with TUNC where both genders are almost equally distributed. Also, the percentage of four-year graduate employees at TUNC is much higher than at MD (96% versus 49%). Experience in IT is almost the same in both cases, but the difference lies in the time spent in using IT during the working hours. MD employees use computers longer than those at TUNC (80% versus 53% of working time). Table 5 presents a description of the sample used in each case.

Concerning IT skills, respondents in each sample rated their personal computers skills above average in contrast with their below average skills in using both Internet and email. Around 80% of respondents in both cases have access to personal computers as opposed to a relatively low percentage having access to Internet (around 20%) or email (around 10%). Software training and usage is mainly on Microsoft Word followed

Table 5. Description of the sample used at MD and TUNC

	Montaza District (MD)	**Tax Unit for Non-Commercial Professions (TUNC)**
Sample	No. of prospect respondents: 140 No. of respondents: 81 Invalid responses: 10 Response rate: 87.6%	No. of prospect respondents: 70 No. of respondents: 55 Invalid responses: 6 Response rate: 89%
Gender	Female: 84.5%	Female: 51%
Highest Age Range	From 20-30: 45%	From 31-40: 38%
Education	Four-year college degree: 49%	Four-year college degree: 96%
Average IT Experience	6 years	5 years
Managerial Positions	18%	33%
Working Hours/week	35.6 (6 hrs/day – 6 days/wk)	45 (9 hrs/day – 5 days/wk)
Use of IT/Working Time	80%	53%

Table 6. Software usage and training at MD and TUNC

	Montaza District (MD)	**Tax Unit for Non-Commercial Professions (TUNC)**
Use of Word/Excel	Word:88.7% Excel: 52.1%	Word:63.3% Excel: 55.1%
Training Attended	Word:70.4% Excel: 43.7%	Word:69.4% Excel: 51%
Training Needed	Word:70.4% Excel: 83.1% Power Point: 94.4% Access: 54.9%	Word:26.5% Excel: 42.9% Power Point: 38.8% Access:40.8%

by Microsoft Excel. As of the required training Microsoft PowerPoint has the first priority for the respondents at MD (94.4%) as opposed to Microsoft Excel at TUNC (42.9%). Table 6 shows the software mostly used, the most training courses provided as well as the most requested training courses.

Testing Research Model

When investigating employees' knowledge about the four dimensions of the proposed research model: strategy, processes, technology, and people, and their perception towards e-Government readiness (EGR) in both cases, many employees were unaware of many issues related to IT strategy at MD and TUNC. Table 7 presents the four dimensions and the level of EGR, their corresponding: scales,

average scores, standard deviation (SD) values, and results of student's t-test for the comparison between both organizations. The results obtained prove that there is no statistically significant difference between the two case studies.

Testing the research model in each case study is performed following the four following steps adapted from the study of Liu (2001): 1) carry out a factor analysis to extract and group dimensions in each construct, 2) test multi-collinearity among these dimensions to determine the strength of the relationship between them, 3) check reliability and validity of the model, and 4) test the partial models.

Factor Analysis

Using SPSS version 13.0, a factor analysis was performed, and resulted in an elimination of a number of constructs extracted under each dimen-

Table 7. Comparison of the average of the four dimensions between MD and TUNC

Group / Construct	Scale 1 to 7	MD (n = 71) Mean	MD (n = 71) SD	TUNC (n = 49) Mean	TUNC (n = 49) SD	T-Test (P-value)
Strategy	Strongly disagree to Strongly agree	5.9	0.6	5.3	1.4	0.127
Process		5.3	1.1	4.8	1.5	0.073
Technology	Far short of expectations to Greatly exceeds expectations	5	1.2	4.8	1.4	0.885
People	*1st Section:* Strongly disagree to Strongly agree *2nd Section:* Far short of expectations to Greatly exceeds expectations	5.2	1.1	5.3	1.3	0.975
EGR	Extremely unready to Extremely ready	5.95	2.1	5	1.5	0.471

sion. Using Varimax with Kaiser Normalization rotation method, items with a loading number greater than 0.5 on one factor, and less than 0.5 on all others were retained.

Degree of Multi-Collinearity

Presence of a high degree of multi-collinearity among constructs in each dimension results in several problems (Dielman, 1996); this dictates the need to investigate the strength of relationships between them. Correlation tests show that all construct pairs are not highly correlated (all pair correlation is less than 0.5), proving the absence of multi-collinearity since many researchers suggest that multi-collinearity exist if correlation between each determinant pair is greater than 0.75 (Liu, 2001).

Reliability and Validity

To assess the reliability of the model, a Cronbach's alpha is used since it is the most common method of estimating the reliability of an instrument (Zmud and Boynton, 1991). Results obtained show that all alpha coefficients exceed 0.80 (Nunnally, 1978), indicating a high level of internal consistency or homogeneity among the constructs under each dimension (Straub, 1989).

Convergent validity is also checked to ensure the extent to which all group of constructs indicate the same dimension as well as the degree of compatibility of multiple measures within the same dimension (Kerlinger, 1986). Table 8 shows that all correlations between these constructs are higher than 0.568, ranging from 0,568 to 0.996 proving the existence of convergent validity.

Partial Models

Testing research hypotheses was performed using LISREL version 8.72 due to its powerful ability in identifying relations among dimensions (or latent variables), each comprising several measurable constructs (or observed variables). Findings are presented in table 8.

Discussion

The average score of each of the four research dimensions in both cases and the level of EGR is relatively high, ranging from 4.8 to 5.95, contradicting some of the data collected from the interviews that reveal employees negative impressions towards IT and integration of processes. This high average score could be attributed to a cultural aspect that characterizes Egyptians when responding to surveys; feeling uncomfortable in expressing negative impressions towards a person or even a concept (Manawy, 2006) especially in case of surveys related to their work environment.

Comparing the results obtained in both cases with the research hypotheses shows that findings confirm all research hypotheses. The weights of the factors in each hypothesis are the same in both case

Table 8. Partial research model results (rows showing different results in both cases are highlighted)

Hypothesis	Montaza District (MD)			Tax Unit for Non-Commercial Professions (TUNC)		
	P-Value	Significance	Result	P-Value	Significance	Result
H1 **Strategy→EGR**	**0.44116**	**Modest impact**	**Accepted**	**0.84327**	**High impact**	**Accepted**
H2 Processes→EGR	0.87330	High impact	Accepted	0.91212	High impact	Accepted
H3 Technology→EGR	0.65767	High impact	Accepted	0.88842	High impact	Accepted
H4 People→EGR	1.00000	High impact	Accepted	0.90125	High impact	Accepted
H5 **Strategy→Processes**	**0.16749**	**Weak impact**	**Accepted**	**0.41201**	**Modest impact**	**Accepted**
H6 Strategy→Technology	0.54218	Modest impact	Accepted	0.44006	Modest impact	Accepted
H7 Strategy→People	0.82310	High impact	Accepted	0.85100	High impact	Accepted

studies except in the effect of the strategy factor first on EGR (H1) and second on processes (H5).

The difference in H1 lies in its modest impact on EGR at MD compared with its high impact on EGR at TUNC. This could be due to the unperceived value of IT strategy by MD employees because almost half of the sample is not highly educated as opposed to the sample taken at TUNC (51% do not hold four-year college degree at MD versus 4% at TUNC). In addition, the percentage of employees in management positions – who are usually involved in strategic planning - is higher at TUNC than at MD. In fact, the majority of employees in non-managerial positions (subordinates) are not involved in IT strategy formulation, or even aware of its existence (as revealed by the interviews conducted with them). This ascertains the direction of the research in choosing the employees as the sample to reply to the questionnaire because their feedback and participation are rarely investigated.

The second difference in the weight of strategy between the two case studies lies in its effect on processes (H5). Strategy at MD has a weak impact on processes in contrast with its high impact on processes at TUNC. This confirms the results obtained from the interviews conducted with MD employees; they revealed that IT strategy does not put high value on changing business processes or on conducting regular evaluation of IT performance. This could be attributed to the fact that TUNC is a relatively new organization (since 2004) compared to MD (since 1982). In their early stages, usually organizations take the best practices and have clear strategies which they tend to adhere to. Furthermore, processes in new organizations can be formulated and adjusted easier than old organizations characterized by their old and rigid processes.

The strong effect of processes on EGR (H2) in both case studies is easily perceived, since improvements in services and in government internal relationships could not be realized without an attempt to examine and simplify all business processes, and to monitor continuously IT progress and impact. Also, the impact of technology on EGR (H3) proves to be high because the technology value is easily apparent to the employees; evidently e-Government could never exist without applying ICT. This is ensured through the interviews conducted with some employees who expressed that technology is main factor affecting

EGR. Finally, the effect of people on EGR (H4) has the highest weight (P-value = 1.00), ensuring that people is the major factor in the success of any information system.

Looking at the impact of IT strategy on technology (H6) and on people (H7) reveals that IT strategy has a modest effect on technology because first, there is a common understanding among many employees (determined through interviewing them) that IT strategy is not a business issue, and second, since employees are not involved during development phases, they cannot perceive a high impact of strategy in affecting ICT. The high impact on the strategy dimension on people (H7) means that IT strategy considers people as a major component focusing on improving their skills and on re-allocating them in the right places (interviews with employees confirm that training courses are easily provided especially in IT; also many employees state that they changed their positions due to e-Government program). In addition, IT strategy has a strong impact on employees' behaviors due to the hierarchical structure of the public sector which drives people to respond to changes approved by top management.

Limitations

The study investigates two cases only, with small sample sizes (71 and 49) restricting the generalization of the findings over all public organizations in Egypt. Further studies should be performed on further cases. Moreover, the data collected depends on the opinions of the employees, without considering other stakeholders, such as citizens and business partners. Additionally, employees' feedback could be incorrect due to several reasons: 1) culture: Egyptians are always reluctant to reveal any negative attitude when responding to surveys, and especially towards issues related to their work environment despite assuring them of the anonymous nature of the questionnaire; 2) skills and awareness: participants have different levels of expertise and familiarity with the

research topic; 3) questionnaire's length: which could lead to less valid answers due to fatigue or unwillingness of participants to seriously answer a large number of questions.

CONCLUSION AND FUTURE TRENDS

In order to reap e-Government benefits, policy makers should conduct regular evaluation on electronic government readiness (EGR) to pinpoint weaknesses and provide appropriate solutions. This study aims to develop a framework for assessing EGR in a public organization. The proposed framework was derived from previous appraisal models of electronic readiness and EGR in addition to the models of IS and eCommerce success available in the literature.

The suggested framework assessed EGR in a public organization covering all internal factors affecting EGR. It classified these factors into four main dimensions: strategy, processes, technology, and people. A number of measurement constructs were proposed under each dimension. Testing the framework was performed through conducting a case study approach on two public organizations in Egypt by getting their employees' perception on ICT and EGR in each organization. The study examined the weight of each of the four dimensions on impacting EGR and the relationships between them, and compared findings in both case studies. Further studies on additional cases are taking place. Comparing all findings could lead to the development of a generic framework.

The study findings confirmed the research hypotheses indicating that all four dimensions affect EGR but with different weights. Results obtained revealed the great effect of e-Government strategy dimension on the people dimension which in its turn, has a great impact on EGR. This means that e-Government strategy dimension has an indirect effect on EGR through the people dimension. Due to the high impact of people in affecting EGR, the study recommends that more awareness should be provided to employees about e-Government strategy in the organization stressing on their involvement during its formulation. This would ensure their support and willingness leading to the success of the overall e-Government project. In addition, the study highlighted the importance of the employees' education level as an integral factor in perceiving the value of e-Government strategy.

Results also showed that e-Government strategy has a higher effect on processes in the case of new organizations than old ones. In new organizations, it is much easier to integrate e-Government processes with the organization's business processes, and to promote e-Government concepts within the entire organization.

As a conclusion, the research recommends that in studying various e-Government efforts and initiatives, one should take into consideration all internal e-Government building blocks: strategy, processes, technology, and people.

Further research should be undertaken in more case studies at different maturity levels in terms of e-Government. This would lead to a common understanding of e-Government readiness level of public organizations on a national scale. This research could be applied also to other developed and developing countries to: (i) set a comparison of EGR between Egypt and other countries to spot differences and similarities in the critical success factors of e-Government, which would help in enhancing e-Government initiatives in Egypt; (ii) Develop a generic framework for assessing EGR of public organizations that could be applied worldwide.

REFERENCES

Accenture. (2002). *e-Government Leadership: Realizing the Vision*. Retrieved July 12, 2003, from http://www.gol-ged.gc.calpub/pub_e.asp

Accenture. (2005). *Leadership in Customer Service: New Expectations, New Experiences*. Retrieved June 20, 2005, from http://www.accenture.com/xdoc/ca/locations/canada/insights/studies/leadership_cust.pdf

Adams, A. (1999). The Implications of Users' Privacy Perception on Communication and Information Privacy Policies. *Telecommunications Policy Research Conference*, Washington DC.

Ahituv, N. (1980). A Systematic Approach toward Assessing the Value of an Information System. *Management Information Systems Quarterly*, *4*(4), 61–75. doi:10.2307/248961

Ahmed, F. A., & Hassan, H. A. (2007). *Local administration Regulatory Law, Number 43 of Year 1979*. Cairo, Egypt: Amiriya Publications.

Aldrich, D., Bertot, J. C., & McClure, C. R. (2002). e-Government: Initiatives, Developments, and Issues. *Government Information Quarterly*, *19*(4), 349–355. doi:10.1016/S0740-624X(02)00130-2

Baets, W. (1992). Aligning Information Systems with Business Strategy. *The Journal of Strategic Information Systems*, *1*(4), 205–213. doi:10.1016/0963-8687(92)90036-V

Bailey, J. E., & Pearson, S. W. (1983). Development of a Tool for Measuring and Analyzing Computer User Satisfaction. *Management Science*, *29*(5), 530–545. doi:10.1287/mnsc.29.5.530

Bakry, S. H. (2004). Development of e-Government – A STOPE View. *International Journal of Electronic Management*, *14*(5), 339–350.

Balutis, A. P. (2001). e-Government 2001 – Part 1: Understanding the Challenge and Evolving Strategies. *The Public Manager*, Spring, 33-37.

Baum, C., & Maio, A. D. (2001). Gartner's Four Phases of e-Government Model. *Gartner Research*. Retrieved May 4, 2006, from http://gartner3.gartnerweb.com/public/static/hotc/00094235.html

Beaumaster, S. (2002). Local Government IT Implementation Issues: A Challenge for Public Administration. In *35ᵗʰ Hawaii International Conference on System Sciences*, Hawaii.

Ben Abd Allah, S., Gueniara El Fatmi, S., & Oudriga, N. B. (2002). Security Issues in e-Government Models: What Governments Should Do. In *IEEE International Conference on Systems, Man, and Cybermatics*, Hammamet, Tunisia.

Bertelsmann Foundation. (2002). *Balanced e-Government: e-Government – Connecting Efficient Administration and Responsive Democracy*. Retrieved December 7, 2007, from http://www-it.fmi.uni-sofia.bg/eg/res/balancede-gov.pdf

Bhimani, A. (1996). Securing the Commercial Internet. *Communications of the ACM, 39*(6), 29–35. doi:10.1145/228503.228509

Boon, O., Hewett, W. G., & Parker, C. M. (2000). Evaluating the adoption of the Internet: A Study of an Australian Experience in Local Government. In *13ᵗʰ International Bled Electronic Commerce Conference*, Bled, Slovenia.

Boudriga, N. (2002). Technical Issues in Securing e-Government. In *IEEE International Conference on Systems, Man, and Cybermatics*, Hammamet, Tunisia.

Bowman, B. J., Davis, G. B., & Wetherbe, J. C. (1983). Three Stage Model of MIS Planning. *Information & Management, 6*(1), 11–25. doi:10.1016/0378-7206(83)90016-2

Bridges.org. (2005). *E-Readiness assessment: Who is Doing What and Where?* Retrieved June 19, 2005, from http://www.bridges.org/ereadiness/ereadiness_whowhatwhere_bridges_10Mar05.pdf

Bryson, J. M., & Alston, F. K. (1996). *Creating and Implementing your Strategic Plan: A Workbook for Public and Non-Profit Organizations*. San Francisco, CA: Jossey-Bass Publishers.

Burgess, L., & Cooper, J. (1990). A Model for Classification of Business Adoption of Internet Commerce Solutions. In *12ᵗʰ International Bled Electronic Commerce Conference*, Bled, Slovenia.

Chen, Y. C., & Knepper, R. (2005). Digital Government Development Strategies: Lessons for Policy Makers from a Comparative Perspective. In Huang, W., Siau, K., Wei, K. K., & Siau, K. (Eds.), *Electronic Government Strategies and Implementation* (pp. 394–420). Hershey, PA: Idea Group Publishing.

Clarke, R. (2000). *Appropriate Research Methods for Electronic Commerce*. Retrieved February 3, 2007, from http://www.anu.edu.au/people/Roger.Clarke/EC/ResMeth.html

Conklin, A., & White, G. B. (2006). e-Government and Cyber Security: The Role of Cyber Security Exercises. In *39ᵗʰ Hawaii International Conference on System Sciences*, Hawaii.

Creswell, J. W. (2002). *Research Design: Qualitative, Quantitative, and Mixed Methods Approaches*. Thousand Oaks, CA: Sage Publications.

Croteau, A., Solomon, S., Raymond, L., & Bergeron, F. (2001). Organizational and Technological Infrastructures Alignment. In *34ᵗʰ Hawaii International Conference on System Sciences*, Hawaii.

Cyert, R., & March, J. (1963). *A Behavioral Theory of the Firm*. Englewood Cliffs, NJ: Prentice Hall.

Darwish, A. (2007). *Electronic Government – Egypt*. Retrieved February 3, 2008, from http://www.egypt.gov.eg/english/documents/

Das, S. R., Zahra, S. A., & Warkentin, M. E. (1991). Integrating the Content and Process of Strategic MIS Planning With Competitive Strategy. *Decision Sciences, 22*(1), 953–984.

Davis, F. D. (1985). *A Technology Acceptance Model for Empirically Testing New End-User Information Systems: Theory and Results*. Doctoral Dissertation, MIT Sloan School of Management, Cambridge, MA.

Davis, F. D. (1989). Perceived Usefulness, Perceived Ease of Use and User Acceptance of Information Technology. *Management Information Systems Quarterly*, *13*(3), 319–339. doi:10.2307/249008

Dawes, S. (2002). The Future of e-Government. *Center for Technology in Government*. Retrieved March 10, 2007, from http://www.ctg.albany.edu/publications/reports/future_of_egov/future_of_egov.pdf

DeConti, L. (1998). Planning and Creating a Government Website: Learning from the Experience of US States. *Information Systems for Public Sector Management, Working Paper Series No. 2, Institute for Development Policy and Management*. Retrieved June 3, 2002, from http://www.amn.ac.uk/idpm

DeLone, W. H., & McLean, E. R. (1992). Information Systems Success: The Quest for the Dependent Variable. *Information Systems Research*, *3*(1), 60–95. doi:10.1287/isre.3.1.60

Dielman, T. E. (1996). *Applied Regression Analysis for Business and Economics* (2nd ed.). Belmont, CA: Wadsworth Publishing Company.

Downing, C. E. (1999). System Usage Behavior as a Proxy for User Satisfaction: An Empirical Investigation. *Information & Management*, *35*(4), 203–216. doi:10.1016/S0378-7206(98)00090-1

Edmiston, K. (2003). State and Local e-Government: Prospects and Challenges. *American Review of Public Administration*, *33*(1), 20–45. doi:10.1177/0275074002250255

Eisenhardt, K. M. (1989). Building Theories from Case Study Research. *Academy of Management Review*, *14*(4), 532–550. doi:10.2307/258557

EISI-Government Team. (2003). EISI-Government: Action Plan and Roadmap. *Ministry of Communications and Information Technology*. Retrieved May 12, 2005, from http://www.egypt.gov.eg/english/documents/

Eschenfelder, K. R., Beachboard, J. C., McClure, C. R., & Wyman, S. K. (1997). Assessing US Federal Government Websites. *Government Information Quarterly*, *14*(2), 173–189. doi:10.1016/S0740-624X(97)90018-6

Farquhar, B., Langmann, G., & Balfour, A. (1998). Consumer Needs in Global Electronic Commerce. *Electronic Markets*, *8*(2), 9–12. doi:10.1080/10196789800000017

Fletcher, P. D. (1999). Strategic Planning for Information Technology Management in State Government. In Garson, D. (Ed.), *Information Technology and Computer Applications in Public Administration: Issues and Trends* (pp. 81–89). Hershey, PA: Idea Group Publishing.

Fletcher, P. D. (2003). The Realities of the Paper work Reduction Act of 1995: A Government-Wide Strategy for Information Resources Management. In Garson, D. (Ed.), *Public Information Technology: Policy and Management Issues* (pp. 74–93). Hershey, PA: Idea Group Publishing.

Fogg, B. J. (2002). Stanford Guidelines for Web Credibility. *A Research Summary from the Stanford Persuasive Technology Lab*. Retrieved August 22, 2003, from http://www.webcredibility.org/guidelines

Fogg, B. J., Marable, L., Stanford, J., & Tauber, E. R. (2002). How do People Evaluate a Website's Credibility? Results from a Large Study. *Consumer Webwatch News*. Retrieved October 4, 2006, from http://www.consumerwebwatch.org/news/report3_credibilityresearch/stanfordPTL_TOC.htm

Forman, M. (2002). *e-Government Strategy*. Washington, DC: Executive Office of the President Office of Management and Budget. Retrieved April 7, 2006, from http://www.usa.gov/Topics/Includes/Reference/egov_strategy.pdf

Frooman, J. (1999). Stakeholder Influence Strategies. *Academy of Management Review, 24*(2), 115–191. doi:10.2307/259074

Gefen, D., Pavlou, P. A., Warkentin, M., & Rose, G. M. (2002). e-Government Adoption. In *8th Americas Conference on Information systems*, Dallas, TX.

Grant, G., & Chau, D. (2005). Developing a Generic Framework for e-Government. *Journal of Global Information Management, 13*(1), 1–30.

Guo, X., & Lu, J. (2005). Effectiveness of e-Government Online Services in Australia. In Huang, W., Siau, K., Wei, K. K., & Siau, K. (Eds.), *Electronic Government Strategies and Implementation* (pp. 214–241). Hershey, PA: Idea Group Publishing.

Hamilton, S., & Chervany, N. L. (1981). Evaluating Information System Effectiveness: Comparing Evaluation Approaches. *Management Information Systems Quarterly, 5*(3), 55–69. doi:10.2307/249291

Harkness, W. L., Kettinger, W. J., & Segars, A. H. (1996). Sustaining Process Improvement and Innovation in the Information Service Function: Lessons Learned from Bose Corporation. *Management Information Systems Quarterly, 20*(3), 349–367. doi:10.2307/249661

Heeks, R. (2001). Building e-Governance for Development: a Framework for National Donor Action. *e-Government Working Paper, No. 12*. University of Manchester, UK: IDPM.

Heeks, R. (2003). Most e-Government-for-Development Projects Fail. *iGovernment Working Paper, No. 14*. University of Manchester, UK: IDPM.

Heeks, R., & Bailur, S. (2007). Analyzing e-government research: Perspectives, Philosophies, Theories, Methods, and Practice. *Government Information Quarterly, 24*(2), 243–265. doi:10.1016/j.giq.2006.06.005

Henderson, J. C., & Venkatraman, N. (1993). Strategic Alignment: Leveraging Information Technology for Transforming Organizations. *IBM Systems Journal, 32*(1), 4–16. doi:10.1147/sj.382.0472

Ho, A. T. K. (2002). Reinventing Local Governments and the e-Government Initiative. *Public Administration Review, 62*(4), 434–444. doi:10.1111/0033-3352.00197

Ho, C. F., & Wu, W. H. (1999). Antecedents of Customer Satisfaction on the Internet: An Empirical Study of On-Line Shopping. In *32nd Hawaii International Conference on System Science*, Hawaii.

Hu, Y., Xiao, J., Pang, J., & Xie, K. (2005). *A Research on the Appraisal Framework of e-Government Project Success. In 7th international conference on Electronic commerce*. Xi'an, China.

Igbaria, M., & Nachman, S. A. (1990). Correlates of User Satisfaction with End User Computing. *Information & Management, 19*(2), 73–82. doi:10.1016/0378-7206(90)90017-C

Iivari, J., & Ervasi, I. (1994). User Information Satisfaction: IS Implementability and Effectiveness. *Information & Management, 27*(4), 205–220. doi:10.1016/0378-7206(94)90049-3

International City/County Management Association (ICMA). (2002). *Electronic Government 2002*. Washington, DC: Author. Retrieved May 13, 2006, from http://bookstore.icma.org/freedocs/e_government_2002.pdf

Kamel, S., Ghoneim, A., & Ghoneim, S. (2002). The Role of the State in Developing the eCommerce in Egypt. In *Role of the State in a Changing World Conference*, Cairo, Egypt.

Kerlinger, F. N. (1986). *Foundations of Behavioral Research* (3rd ed.). New York: Harcourt Brace Jovanovich College Publishers.

Kettinger, W. J., & Grover, V. (1995). Toward a Theory of Business Process Change Management. *Journal of Management Information Systems, 12*(1), 9–30.

Kettinger, W. J., Teng, J. T. C., & Guha, S. (1997). Business Process Change: A study of Methodologies, Techniques, and Tools. *Management Information Systems Quarterly, 21*(1), 55–80. doi:10.2307/249742

Khazanchi, D., & Munkvold, B. E. (2003). On the Rhetoric and Relevance of IS Research Paradigms: A Conceptual Framework and some Propositions. In *36th Hawaii International Conference on System Sciences*, Hawaii.

Koh, C. E., & Prybutok, V. R. (2003). The Three Ring Model and Development of an Instrument for Measuring Dimensions of e-Government Functions. *Journal of Computer Information Systems, 33*(3), 34–39.

Kossak, F., Essmayr, W., & Winiwarter, W. (2001). Applicability of HCI Research to e-Government Applications. In *9th European Conference on Information Systems*, Bled, Slovenia

Krishnaswamy, G. (2005). eServices in Government: Why We Need Strategies for Capacity Building and Capacity Utilization? In *International Business Information Management Association (IBIMA 2005)*, Cairo, Egypt.

Layne, K., & Lee, J. (2001). Developing Fully Functional e-Government: A Four-Stage Model. *Government Information Quarterly, 18*(2), 122–136. doi:10.1016/S0740-624X(01)00066-1

Li, E. Y. (1997). Perceived Importance of Information System Success Factors: A Meta Analysis of Group Differences. *Information & Management, 32*(1), 15–28. doi:10.1016/S0378-7206(97)00005-0

Liu, C., & Arnett, K. P. (2000). Exploring the Factors Associated with Website Success in the Context of Electronic Commerce. *Information & Management, 38*(1), 23–33. doi:10.1016/S0378-7206(00)00049-5

Liu, S. (2001). *An e-Government Readiness Model*. Dissertation Prepared for the Degree of Doctor of Philosophy, University of North Texas, TX.

Manawy A. (2006, October 14). For Everything not to be Fine. *Al Ahram Newspaper*, 2006.

Marchionini, G., Samet, H., & Brandt, L. (2003). Digital Government. *Communications of the ACM, 46*(1), 25–27.

Margetts, H., & Dunleavy, P. (2002). *Cultural Barriers to e-government*. Academic article for the report: Better Public Services Through e-government. Retrieved March 10, 2006, from http://www.governmentontheweb.org

Ministry of Communication and Information Technology (MCIT). (2008). Retrieved December 22, 2008, from http://www.mcit.gov.eg

Ministry of Local Development (MOLD). (2008). Retrieved June 18, 2008, from http://www.mold.gov.eg

Mitchell, R. K., Agle, B. R., & Wood, D. J. (1997). Toward a Theory of Stakeholder Identification and Salience: defining the Principle of Who and What Really Counts. *Academy of Management Review, 22*(4), 853:866.

Moon, J. M. (2002). The Evolution of e-Government Among Municipalities: Rhetoric or Reality? *Public Administration Review, 62*(4), 424–433. doi:10.1111/0033-3352.00196

Myers, M., & Avison, D. (2002). *Qualitative Research in Information Systems: A Reader*. Thousand Oaks, CA: Sage Publications.

Navarra, D. D., & Cornford, T. (2003). A Policy Making View of e-Government Innovations in Public Governance. In *9ᵗʰ Americas Conference on Information Systems*, Tampa, Florida.

Nour, M., Abdel Rahman, A., & Fadl Allah, A. (2008). A Context-Based Integrative Framework for e-Government Initiatives. *Government Information Quarterly*, *25*(3), 448–461. doi:10.1016/j.giq.2007.02.004

NSW (New South Wales) Audit Office. (2001). eReady, eSteady, e-Government. *State Library of New South Wales Cataloguing-in Publication Data*. Retrieved May 11, 2006, from http://www.audit.nsw.gov.au/publications/better_practice/2001/e_gov_bpg_sept_01.pdf

Nunnally, J. (1978). *Psychometric Theory* (2nd ed.). New York: McGraw Hill.

Pardo, T. A., & Scholl, H. J. J. (2002). Walking Atop the Cliffs: Avoiding Failure and Reducing Risks in Large-Scale e-Government Projects. In *35ᵗʰ Hawaii International Conference on System Sciences*, Hawaii.

Pettigrew, A. M. (1990). Longitudinal Field Research on Change: Theory and Practice. *Organization Science*, *1*(3), 267–292. doi:10.1287/orsc.1.3.267

Pilipovic, J., Ivkovic, M., Domazet, D., & Milutinovic, V. (2002). e-Government, eBusiness and eChallenges. Amsterdam: IOS Press.

Pitt, L. F., Watson, R. T., & Kavan, C. B. (1995). Service Quality: A Measure of Information Systems Effectiveness. *Management Information Systems Quarterly*, *19*(2), 173–187. doi:10.2307/249687

Powell, T. C., & Dent-Micallef, A. (1999). Information Technology as Competitive Advantage: The Role of Human, Business, and Technology Resources. *Strategic Management Journal*, *18*(5), 375–405. doi:10.1002/(SICI)1097-0266(199705)18:5<375::AID-SMJ876>3.0.CO;2-7

Ragin, C. C. (1987). *The Comparative Method: Moving Beyond Qualitative and Quantitative Strategies*. Berkeley, CA: University of California Press.

Rai, A., Lang, S. S., & Welker, R. B. (2002). Assessing the Validity of IS Success Models: An Empirical Test and Theoretical Analysis. *Information Systems Research*, *13*(1), 50–69. doi:10.1287/isre.13.1.50.96

Reffat, R. (2003). *Developing a Successful e-Government*. Working Paper, School of Architecture, Design Science and Planning, University of Sydney, Australia.

Rimmer, J. (2002). *e-Government – Better Government*. Retrieved May 5, 2003, from http://www.noie.gov.au/publications/speeches/Rimmer/Breakfast/egov_sep18.htm

Salem, F. (2007). Benchmarking the e-Government Bulldozer: Beyond Measuring the Tread Marks. *Measuring Business Excellence*, *11*(4), 9–22. doi:10.1108/13683040710837892

Saunders, M., Lewis, P., & Thornhill, A. (2000). *Research Methods for Business Students* (2nd ed.). London: Prentice-Hall.

Schedler, K., & Scharf, M. C. (2001). Exploring the Interrelations between Electronic Government and the New Public Management: A Managerial Framework for Electronic Government. In *Association for Public Policy Analysis & Management Conference (APPAM 2002)*, Dallas, TX.

Scholl, H. J. J. (2003). e-Government: A Special Case of ICT-Enabled Business Process Change. In *36ᵗʰ Hawaii International Conference on System Sciences*, Hawaii.

Scholl, H. J. J. (2005). The Dimensions of Business Process Change in Electronic Government. In Huang, W., Siau, K., Wei, K. K., & Siau, K. (Eds.), *Electronic Government Strategies and Implementation* (pp. 44–67). Hershey, PA: Idea Group Publishing.

Seddon, P. (1997). A Respecification and Extension of the DeLone and McLean Model of IS Success. *Information Systems Research*, *8*(3), 240–253. doi:10.1287/isre.8.3.240

Seddon, P. B., & Kiew, M. Y. (1996). A Partial Test and Development of DeLone and McLean Model of IS Success. *Australian Journal of Information Systems*, *4*(1), 90–109.

Seddon, P. B., Staples, S., Patnayakuni, R., & Bowtell, M. (1999). Dimensions of Information Systems Success. *Communications of the AIS*, *1*(20), 1–39.

Seybold (1998). *Customer.com*. New York: Random House.

Smith, A. G. (2001). Applying Evaluation Criteria to New Zealand Government Website. *International Journal of Information Management*, *21*(2), 137–149. doi:10.1016/S0268-4012(01)00006-8

Snellen, I. (2000). Public Service in an Information Society. In Governance in the 21st Century: Revitalizing the Public Service, Canadian Centre for Management Development, Montreal and Kingston.

Sprecher, M. (2000). Racing to e-Government: Using the Internet for Citizen Service Delivery. *Government Finance Review*, *16*(5), 21–22.

Stowers, G. N. L. (2004). Measuring the Performance of e-Government. *IBM Centre for the Business of e-Government*. Retrieved March 10, 2007, from http://www.businessofgovernment.org/pdfs/8493_Stowers_Report.pdf

Straub, D. W. (1989). Validating Instruments in MIS Research. *Management Information Systems Quarterly*, *13*(2), 147–169. doi:10.2307/248922

Swanson, E. B. (1986). A Note of Informatics. *Journal of Management Information Systems*, *2*(3), 86–91.

Tallon, P. P., Kraemer, K. L., & Gurbaxani, V. (2000). Executives' Perceptions of the Business Value of Information Technology: A process-Oriented Approach. *Journal of Management Information Systems*, *16*(4), 145–173.

Tapscott, D. (1995). *Digital Economy: Promise and Peril in the Age of Networked Intelligence*. New York: McGraw-Hill.

Tassabehji, R. (2005). Inclusion in e-Government: A Security Perspective. In e-Government Workshop '05 (eGOV05), Brunel University, London.

Tennert, J. R., & Schroeder, A. D. (1999). Stakeholder Analysis. In *60ᵗʰ Annual Meeting of the American Society for Public Administration*, Orlando, FL.

The Computer System Policy Project (CSPP). (2000). *Living in the Networked World Readiness Guide*. Retrieved March 10, 2006, from http://www.cspp.org/documents/NW_Readiness_Guide.pdf

Traunmüller, R., & Wimmer, M. (2003). e-Government at a Decisive Moment: Sketching a Roadmap to Excellence. In *2ⁿᵈ International Conference (EGOV 2003)*, Prague, Czech Republic.

Turban, E., King, D., Lee, J., Warkentin, M., & Chung, H. M. (2002). *Electronic Commerce 2002: A Managerial Perspective*. Upper Saddle River, NJ: Prentice-Hall.

UNDESA (United Nations Department for Economic and Social Affairs). (2003). e-Government Readiness Assessment Survey. Division for Public Administration and Development Management (DPADM), NY.

United Nations Department of Economic and Social Affairs (UNDESA). (2005). Global e-Government Readiness Report 2005: From e-Government to eInclusion. *Division for Public Administration and Development Management (DPADM)*, NY. Retrieved September 10, 2008, from http://unpan1.un.org/intradoc/groups/public/documents/un/unpan021888.pdf

United Nations Department of Economic and Social Affairs (UNDESA). (2008). UN e-Government Survey 2008: From e-Government to Connected Governance. *Division for Public Administration and Development Management (DPADM)*, New York. Retrieved September 10, 2008, from http://unpan1.un.org/intradoc/groups/public/documents/UN/UNPAN028607.pdf

Victoria, M. (2002). *Putting People at the Centre: Government Innovation Working for Victorians*. Retrieved March 10, 2008, from http://www.mmv.vic.gov.au/egov

Walsham, G. (1993). *Interpreting Information Systems in Organizations*. Chichester, UK: Wiley.

Wan, H. A. (2000). Opportunities to Enhance a Commercial Website. *Information & Management*, *38*(1), 15–21. doi:10.1016/S0378-7206(00)00048-3

WASEDA University. (2006). *The 2006 WASEDA University e-Government Ranking*. Retrieved September 12, 2008, from http://egov.sonasi.com/repository/the-2006-waseda-university-e-government-ranking/download

Weerakody, V., Sarikas, O. D., & Patel, R. (2005). Exploring the Process and Information Systems Integration Aspects of e-Government. In e-Government Workshop '05 (eGOV05), Brunel University, London.

West, D. (2008). *Improving Technology Utilization in Electronic Government around the World*. Retrieved November 13, 2008, from http://www.brookings.edu/~/media/Files/rc/reports/2008/0817_e-Government_west/0817_e-Government_west.pdf

West, D. M. (2000). *Assessing e-Government: The Internet, Democracy, and Service Delivery by State and Federal Government*. Retrieved June 12, 2002, from http://www.insidepolitics.org/egovtreport00.html

West, D. M. (2006). *Global e-Government, 2006*. Retrieved July 10, 2006, from http://www.Inside-Politics.org

Wilford, S. H. (2004). *Information and Communication technologies, Privacy and Policies: An Analysis from the Perspective of the Individual*. Doctoral Dissertation, De Montfort University, Leicester, UK.

Wilkin, C., & Castleman, T. (2003). Development of an Instrument to Evaluate the Quality of Delivered Information Systems. In *36th Hawaii International Conference on System Science*, Hawaii.

Wilkin, C., & Hewett, B. (1999). Quality in a Respecification of DeLone and McLean's IS Success Model. In *1999 IRMA International Conference*, Hershey, PA.

Woodroof, J., & Burg, W. (2003). Satisfaction/Dissatisfaction: Are Users Predisposed? *Information & Management*, *40*(4), 317–324. doi:10.1016/S0378-7206(02)00013-7

Working Group on e-Government in the Developing World. (2002). Roadmap for e-Government in the Developing World – 10 Questions e-Government Leaders Should Ask Themselves. *Pacific Council on International Policy*. Retrieved May 10, 2006, from http://www.pacificcouncil.org/pdfs/e-gov.paper.f.pdf

Xia, W., & King, W. R. (2002). Determinants of Organizational IT Infrastructure Capabilities. *MIS Research Center Working Papers*. University of Minnesota.

Yin, R. K. (1993). *Applications of Case Study Research*. London: Sage Publications.

Yin, R. K. (1994). *Case Study Research: Design and Methods*. Thousand Oaks, CA: Sage Publications.

Zahra, S. A., & Covin, J. G. (1993). Business Strategy, Technology Policy and Firm Performance. *Strategic Management Journal, 14*(6), 451–478. doi:10.1002/smj.4250140605

Zmud, R. W., & Boynton, A. C. (1991). Survey Measures and Instruments in MIS: Inventory and Appraisal. *Harvard Business School Research Colloquium, 3*, 149–180.

Chapter 8
An Information Communication Technology Adoption Model for Small and Medium Sized Enterprises

Dan J. Kim
University of Houston - Clear Lake, USA

ABSTRACT

Despite the increased number of SME adopters of information communication technology (ICT) for their business, there are limited studies that address the factors affecting SME's adoption decision. Especially, a theoretical perspective on E-business adoption model for SMEs is required to better understand the SME's complex adoption decision process and, in turn, to provide a realistic means of creating guidelines for other SME's to consider when making their adoption decision. Thus, the goal of this chapter is three-fold: i) to review key literature of the factors affecting SME's adoption decision and then summarize major determinants of key dimensions with definition and literature sources, ii) to propose a theoretical framework of e-business adoption for SMEs, namely an OBTG (Organizational, Business, Technological, Governmental) e-business adoption model for SMEs, and finally iii) to provide insightful discussions on the driving factors and barriers of the SMEs' e-business adoption decision.

INTRODUCTION

Small and medium size enterprises (SMEs)[1] play significant roles in the economy of many countries by providing employment opportunities and supporting large-scale firms. According to the literature (Chau & Jim, 2002; KIMI, 2002; OECD, 1997; Towler, 2002), SMEs comprise 99.7%, 92%, 90%, 98% and 99.7% of the enterprises in

the US, Singapore, the UK, Hong Kong, and the Republic of Korea (hereafter Korea) respectively. However, only about 25% and 26% of SMEs in the US and Korea respectively are using the Internet for business (MIC, 2002; Nua_Internet_Surveys, 2001). In light of the fact that Korea has the world's fifth largest Internet market and the highest Internet penetration in the world (ITU, 2003), the percentage of SMEs in other countries using the Internet for business is perhaps lower than 26%. Moreover, the penetration rate of other Information

DOI: 10.4018/978-1-60566-388-3.ch008

and Communication Technology (ICT) is lower than that of Internet use.

In the SME sector, the rate of ICT adoption, which is also described as computerization, E-commerce, Internet business, etc. is lower than that of big companies. This is mainly because of their characteristic "resource-poverty," which includes a lack of finances, ICT experts, time and planning (Blili & Raymond, 1993; Paraskevas & Buhalis, 2002; Soh, Mah, Gan, Chew, & Reid, 1997). This phenomenon is also seen in other countries (OECD, 2003). For these reasons, governments of some countries have made an effort to initiate a wider diffusion of ICT for the SME sector. The Korean Government, for example, has taken a direct and indirect role to lead the ICT diffusion for SME since 2001 (KIMI, 2003). Under the government's plan, 3 Telcos and about 130 application service providers (ASPs) including IT ventures, which are developing their own business models of application programs and ASP solutions (i.e., the ICT service platforms in this study) are composed of a consortium to promote the adoption of ICT and to create business models suitable for SMEs. The biggest benefit of the construction of the consortium is to provide a service platform at an extremely low cost with the government support.

Despite the increased number of SME adopters of ICT for their business, there are limited studies that address the factors affecting SME's adoption decision. Especially, a theoretical perspective on E-business adoption model for SMEs is required to understand better the SME's complex adoption decision and, in turn, to provide a realistic means of guidelines for other SME's for their adoption decision. Thus, the goal of this chapter is three-fold: i) to review key literature of the factors affecting SME's adoption decision and then summarize, with definition and literature sources, major determinants of key dimensions, ii) to propose a theoretical framework of e-business adoption, namely an OBTG (Organizational, Business, Technological, Governmental) e-business adoption model for SMEs, and finally iii) to

provide an insightful discussion on the driving factors and barriers of the e-business adoption decision by SMEs.

The reminder of this chapter is organized as follows. The next section briefly discusses SMEs in the Korean environment as a background. The third session reviews key SME studies on various dimensions affecting the SME's ICT adoption decision and summarizes major determinants of each dimension with definition and literature sources. Then the section four proposes a theoretical framework for SMEs' CIT adoption decision. Shortly after the description of the cases that are collected by the National Computerization Agency, one of the executive agencies of the South Korean government, section five presents the case analysis, results, findings, discussion to validate the proposed framework. Lastly, the chapter is concluded with limitation and future directions.

BACKGROUND: SMES IN THE KOREAN ENVIRONMENT

South Korea (Korea hereafter) was noted as one of the Asia Tigers, and successfully maintained a high level of GDP growth throughout the first half of the 1990's while the same time keeping inflation at around 4% and unemployment below 3% (Hsiao & Hsiao, 2001). For its rapid economic development over recent decades, Korea joined the OECD in 1996. Until the mid-1990s, Korea's economic growth was based primarily on traditional manufacturing industries such as shipbuilding and automobile industries. Since the early 1990s, the Korean government has continually expressed its intention to centralize policy coordination and has invested in the IT industry based on the view that IT will help the Korean economy as a driving force of economic growth.

The Korean government defines SMEs in terms of the number of employees and the amount of sales. The upper limit for an SME in manufacturing, mining, construction and transportation is

Table 1. Definition of Korean SMEs[2]

Sector	SMEs		Small Business	Micro-enterprises
	No of Workers	Capital & Sales	No. of Workers	
I. Manufacturing	Less than 300	Capital worth $8M or less	Less than 50	Less than 10
II. Mining, construction and transportation	Less than 300	Capital worth $3M or less	Less than 50	Less than 10
III. Large general retail, hotel, communications, information processing and other computer-related industries, engineering service, hospital, etc.	Less than 300	Sales worth $30M or less	Less than 10	Less than 5
IV. Fishery, film, seedling production, electrical, gas and waterworks, medical and orthopaedic products, etc.	Less than 200	Sales worth $20M or less	Less than 10	Less than 5
V. Wholesale and product intermediation, machinery equipment rent for industrial use, R&D for natural science, public performance, news provision, etc.	Less than 100	Sales worth $10M or less	Less than 10	Less than 5
Other sectors	Less than 50	Sales worth $5M or less	Less than 10	Less than 5

300 employees. When SMEs in these areas have less than 50 or 20 workers, they are classified as small business or micro-enterprises, respectively (See Table 1).

The Korean government intensively fosters the IT-based innovative businesses as a growth engine of the national economy by designating SMEs with technological competitiveness and growth potentials (Lallana, 2004). Based on an excellent network infrastructure Korea has built, following the previous master plans for Informatization promotion in 1996, Cyber Korea 21 in 1999, and e-Korea VISION in 2007, Korea's IT strategy could promote the infrastructure to quality of services and practical applications. As a result, the Organization for Economic Cooperation and Development (OECD, 2004) and the International Telecommunication Union (ITU, 2005; OECD, 2004) report that Korea ranks the first in the deployment of nationwide broadband Internet and its rate of adoption far exceeding that of other developed countries. Recently, the Korean government proposed the u-KOREA Master Plan (2006-2010) to continue efforts toward shaping the nation's direction on Information Technology. As a continuous plan of the 'Broadband IT

Korea VISION 2007,' the master plan provides a blueprint that guides users in how to use IT to deal with the new social and economic demands and carry out nationwide innovation in order to become the world's leading country in terms of CIT (NCA, 2006).

Because of these government efforts and the continuous innovation in communication information technology, the number of IT-based innovative SMEs (e.g., venture businesses) is continuously growing (i.e., 2,454 in 2005 and 12,620 in 2008). Along with technological innovation, Korean SMEs have endeavored to upgrade their productivity and create new values by innovating non-technological aspects of their business, which allows that they have higher added value than ordinary businesses in Korea.

According to the Small and Medium Business Administration (SMBA) of Korea, the contributions of SMEs in the Korean economic are about 99.9% of all enterprises (3 million SMEs); 87.5% of all employees (10.8 million employees); 52.7% ($97.3 billion) of the total value added in the manufacturing industry; 85.1% ($517.4 billion) of the gross domestic product (GDP); and 42.2% ($81.7 billion) of the total exports. Korean economies have relied heavily on SMEs for their marked success in development over the last few decades.

LITERATURE REVIEW

Many SME studies (Chong & Pervan, 2007; Dholakia & Kshetri, 2004; McCole & Ramsey, 2005; Scupola, 2003; Seyal, Awais, Shamail, & Abbas, 2004) suggest various internal organization and technology related explanatory variables influencing the adoption of new technologies, such as inter-organizational systems, computerization of businesses, e-commerce, EDI, etc. For example, internal factors, such as a lack of technology awareness (Locke & Cave, 2002; MIC, 2002; Rogers, 1995) and implementation cost (Locke & Cave, 2002; Purao & Campbell, 1998) are crucial elements in the general adoption of ICT by SMEs. Lack of technology awareness contains several sub components which include unfamiliarity of technologies, uncertainty of ICT benefits, and lack of guidance (MIC, 2002; Purao & Campbell, 1998). Implementation cost is mostly related to technology factors including software, hardware, training, maintenance costs, etc. On the other hand, external environmental factors, such as national-level information technology infrastructure, industry-level technology availability, and market-level critical mass (Abell & Lim, 1996), are also major barriers to obstructing the ICT adoption in SME. Lefebvre and Lefebvre (1996; 1996) identify three levels of external factors (industry, macroeconomic, and national policy level) affecting the general and competitive environment where a particular firm has to operate. Iacovou et al. (1995) identify three factors of EDI adoption: external pressures (i.e., competitive pressure and requirements by trading partners), perceived benefits of the new technology, and organizational readiness. Among them, perceived benefits form a key reason why participants adopt and continue to use the Internet (Poon & Strom, 1997). Focusing on small firms

in the Netherlands, Walczuch et al. (2000) explore several benefits and barriers that influence small businesses in their choice of Internet use. The main barrier is the concern that the Internet or the Website would not lead to more efficiency or lower costs.

Rashid and Al-Qirim (2001) propose a framework for e-commerce technology adoption by New Zealand SMEs. The framework consists of four contexts: technological, organizational, environmental, and individual contexts. Kurnia and Johnston (2000) suggest a general framework including three key explanatory variables: the external environment, the technology, and the capabilities of an organization. Their model is similar to the contexts of Tornatzky and Fleischer's (1990) model. Based on Tomatzky and Fleischer's model, Scupola (2003) suggests other external factors, such as competitive pressure, government intervention, and supplier and buyers' components, influencing the adoption decision of Internet commerce. Other studies (Chong & Pervan, 2007; OECD, 2000; Scupola, 2003) suggest the role of government as a primarily external factor of the ICT adoption. Government's role is mainly related to financial support and policy, such as tax breaks, technology-adoption tax credits, financing, interventions, business regulations, and others. According to a report by OECD (2000), SMEs need more financing than big enterprises because of the structure characteristics of SMEs (e.g., lack of experience and weakness of market power). Besides, due to the development of a variety of ICT and the proliferation of ASPs, ICT outsourcing is emerging as an influencing factor and becoming suitable for many SMEs sectors (Teng, Cheon, & Grover, 1995; Turban, Lee, King, & Chung, 2000). Therefore, outsourcing elements are also considered as influencing factors for SMEs to overcome their weak positions in the market.

Emerging from the previous relevant literature (Chong & Pervan, 2007; Dholakia & Kshetri, 2004; Fink & Disterer, 2006; McCole & Ramsey, 2005; Rashid & Al-Qirim, 2001; Scupola, 2003;

Seyal et al., 2004), a number of factors influencing the adoption decision of information communication technology (ICT) in SMEs are identified. Basically, there are two different groups of factors: organization-related internal factors and business environment-related external factors. Further, these two factor groups are classified into four dimensions influencing the e-business adoption decision by SMEs: the internal organizational, external business environmental, technology-related, and government-related dimensions. Table 2 summarizes major influencing factors related to the four dimensions with definitions and literature sources.

OBTG (ORGANIZATION, BUSINESS, TECHNOLOGY, AND GOVERNMENT) MODEL FOR SMES

In order to better comprehend the driving factors and barriers that influence SMEs' ICT adoption decision, a holistic Organizational, Business, Technological, Governmental (OBTG) ICT adoption model for SMEs is proposed based on a number of factors identified by previous literature. The model is depicted in Figure 1.

Previous studies have examined a number of factors influencing the adoption decision regarding information communication technology by SMEs. On the basis of existing literature dealing with driving factors and barriers of ICT adoption by SMEs, a holistic Organizational, Business, Technological, Governmental (OBTG) ICT adoption model is proposed. The OBTG ICT adoption model is depicted in Figure 1.

Organizational dimension refers to an organization's internal factors or attributes that affect the SME's ICT adoption decision. The factors include organizational characteristics (size, age, type of business, etc), culture, technological awareness and motivation, technical capability, management support, and others.

Business dimension refers to the external factors or attributes that influence the SME's ICT adoption decision. The factors of this category are related to the general business environment within which a particular SME has to operate. The factors include business related pressure, competition, and relationships with stakeholders and outsourcing partners.

While factors in both internal and external dimensions directly influence SMEs' ICT adoption decision, there are other factors that indirectly affect SMEs' ICT adoption decision. These factors can be categorized as technology and government dimensions. *Technology dimension* refers to the factors ICT related attributes that promote or deter the ICT adoption, which includes availability of technology, technology-business fit, cost, and fear factors.

Government dimension is another key dimension which few studies have identified as a factor influencing the SME's ICT adoption decision. The role and leadership of government in ICT adoption and implementation is very important, especially for SMEs in developing and under-developed countries. The government can help SME's ICT adoption directly, by giving financial subsidies and making favorable regulations and policies for SMEs, and indirectly, by conducting informational campaigns to increase awareness, and facilitating the access to related technologies for SMEs through ICT infrastructure.

RESEARCH METHODOLOGY: CASE STUDIES

As a form of qualitative descriptive research that is used to look at individuals, a small group of participants, or a group as a whole, case study is an ideal research methodology when a holistic and in-depth analysis is needed (Feagin, Orum, & Sjoberg, 1991). Unlike more statistically-based studies (e.g., survey methodology) which search for quantifiable data, case studies seek a qualitative

Table 2. Factors affecting SMEs' ICT adoption decision

Types	Definition	Major Determinants (Literature source)
Organizational factors (internal)	Organizational (internal) attributes that affect the ICT adoption decision of the SME	• Organization characteristics (e.g., size, age, type of business, past experience, centralization, formalization, technocratization, etc) (Dholakia & Kshetri, 2004; É. Lefebvre & Lefebvre, 1996; L. A. Lefebvre et al., 1996) • Technological awareness and motivation (É. Lefebvre & Lefebvre, 1996; L. A. Lefebvre et al., 1996; Locke & Cave, 2002; Rogers, 1995) • Technical capabilities (É. Lefebvre & Lefebvre, 1996; L. A. Lefebvre et al., 1996; MIC, 2002; Purao & Campbell, 1998) • Strategic motivations in terms of costs, productivity, quality, flexibility (É. Lefebvre & Lefebvre, 1996; L. A. Lefebvre et al., 1996) • Lack of guidance about how to start the process (MIC, 2002; Purao & Campbell, 1998) • Management support (Palvia & Palvia, 1999; Rashid & Al-Qirim, 2001; Thong, 1999) • Users' knowledge and involvement (Kwon, 1990; Rashid & Al-Qirim, 2001) • Organizational culture (Seyal et al., 2004) • Communication effectiveness (Ball, Dambolena, & Hennessey, 1987) • Information intensity (Rashid & Al-Qirim, 2001) • Perceived readiness (Iacovou et al., 1995) • Perceived relative advantage (Soh et al., 1997)
Business environment factors (external)	External business attributes that influence the SME's adoption decision	• Electronic and telecommunications environment (e.g., IT infrastructure) (Dholakia & Kshetri, 2004) • Pressure from competitors (É. Lefebvre & Lefebvre, 1996; Premkumar & Roberts, 1999; Scupola, 2003; Thong, 1999) • Outsourcing elements (Teng et al., 1995; Turban et al., 2000) • Buyers and Suppliers' pressure (Abell & Lim, 1996; Premkumar & Roberts, 1999; Rashid & Al-Qirim, 2001; Scupola, 2003) • Business Partner (Iacovou et al., 1995) • E-Commerce Benefits (Scupola, 2003) • Availability of capital, inflation (É. Lefebvre & Lefebvre, 1996; L. A. Lefebvre et al., 1996)
Technology related factors	Information technology related attributes that promote or deter the SME's adoption decision	• Technology availability (Scupola, 2003) • Complexity (Rashid & Al-Qirim, 2001) • Benefits: usefulness (Iacovou et al., 1995; Poon & Strom, 1997; Rogers, 1995; Vickery, 2002) • Adoption Risk/Cost: (KIMI, 2002; Locke & Cave, 2002; Purao & Campbell, 1998; Rashid & Al-Qirim, 2001) • Security Hazards: (Abell & Lim, 1996; MIC, 2002; Purao & Campbell, 1998)
Government related factors	Government related attributes (e.g., polities, leadership, initiatives, IT infrastructure, etc.) that affect the adoption decision of the SME	• Government Role: leadership, tax break, technology-adoption tax credits, financing, intervention (Jutla, Bodorik, & Dhaliwal, 2002; É. Lefebvre & Lefebvre, 1996; OECD, 2000; Scupola, 2003) • Information channel & trade policies (Kettinger, 1994; É. Lefebvre & Lefebvre, 1996; Rashid & Al-Qirim, 2001) • Level of support (Chong & Pervan, 2007) • Control industry regulation (É. Lefebvre & Lefebvre, 1996)

and holistic understanding of the event or situation in question using inductive logic-reasoning from specific to more general terms. Most notably, case studies are preferred research methodology when the researcher has little control over the events and when there is a contemporary focus within a real life context (Becker et al., 2005).

To investigate the effects of the OBTG (Organizational, Business, Technology and Government) dimensions of ICT adoption for SMEs, an exploratory case study with 10 SMEs was conducted using the data collected by the National Computerization Agency, one of the executive agencies of the government of South Korea. The sample SMEs used the ICT service platform developed by the ICT consortiums under the support of the Korean government. They are primarily small SMEs in a variety of business areas. They also have the common characteristics of resource poverty[3] (Welsh & White, 1981). Nonetheless,

Figure 1. OBTG adoption model for SMEs

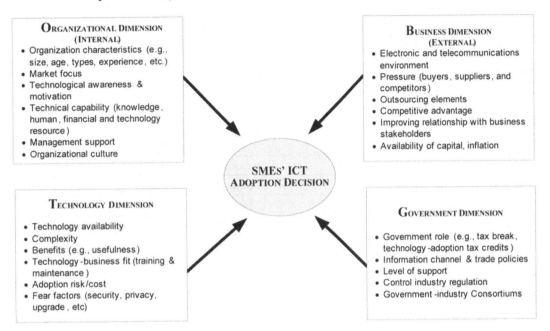

they continue to try to adopt ICT to facilitate their business, to save time, or to reduce cost.

Structured interview questions were formulated to gather information about the driving factors and barriers of ICT adoption for e-business in SMEs. The interviews were conducted face-to-face at the company's site. Brief descriptions of all ten companies are summarized in Table 3.

Case Analysis and Results

Using the OBTG (Organizational, Business, Technology and Government) framework, each case was analyzed to identify factors. The SMEs have experienced various benefits from the usage of the ICT service platforms. There are three main reasons why the SMEs adopt ICT: savings of maintenance cost, reduction of transaction time, and increasing efficiency of work. Those are very similar to the benefits found in other literature: increased productivity (Abell & Lim, 1996), distance related barrier disappearance (Walczuch et

al., 2000), and ease of access to potential customers (Poon & Strom, 1997).

Depending on the goal and the capability of SMEs, the ICT choice and its usage are diverse. The usage areas on which the SMEs have applied the ICT service platform can be categorized into two areas: non-core business and core business activity. Non-core business consists of accounting and insurance management of employees and core-business activity consists of web-storage services for internet transaction, materials management application for body shops, sales analysis for beauty shops, and more. Most IT ventures (C2, C3, C4, and C6) have only chosen an accounting service platform as a non-core business. On the other hand, other SMEs have used the Internet based service platforms to extend their market as core business activity. However, even the same solutions have different usage in the SMEs. For example, the homepage in C8 is used for mere public information while C2 uses its homepage for Internet business.

Table 3. Brief descriptions of the 10 cases

Case Company[4]	Type of business	Number of Employees	Year of ICT Adoption	Using ICT service Application
C1	IT consulting	15	2002	Insurance (Health, life, pension) management, Homepage
C2	Server Hosting	4	2002	Accounting, Internet billing, Homepage
C3	Private Exchange management	4	2001	Accounting
C4	Computer training	N/A	1997	Accounting, Internet billing, Homepage
C5	Body shop, Car repair	8	2002	Accounting, Total management, CRM, Job scheduling. Homepage
C6	Web Magazine	4	2002	Accounting
C7	Furniture design & sale		2001	Web storage, E-mail hosting
C8	Dental clinic	33	2001, 1998	EDI(insurance), Homepage
C9	Beauty shop	20	1998, 2001	Sale analysis, DB marketing, Customer Management program
C10	Printing, publishing	N/A	N/A	FTP, email, Homepage

Organizational Environment-Related Factors

Awareness: Four SMEs (C1, C2, C3, and C4) have the positive awareness of ICT adoption in the light of their intention and effort of other ICT adoption and pursuit of business extension via ICT service platform (C5, C8, C9, and C10). The result shows that higher awareness about ICT has played a very important role in ICT adoption and extension.

Perceived benefit: Five SMEs (C1, C2, C3, C4, and C6) have known the benefit of ICT adoption through previous experience. Therefore, they are highly willing to adopt new ICT service platforms with the expectation of benefit (C8). The perceived benefit is highly related to new ICT adoption.

Business-Related Factors

Outsourcing element: Some SMEs (C3, C4, C6, and C10) are dependent upon an agent to fill in the part of the business process that they cannot perform or deal with. They use an accounting service application customized to their business. They call it "simple bookkeeping", which provides an account form balance sheet and makes it easier for their users to write and report their accounting.

For example, in C3, one of IT ventures having 4 employees, used to pay about $250 per month to an agent for tax accounting. However, after using the ICT service platform, they now pay only about $15 (not including broadband Internet service) per month.

Buyer and Supplier: C7 has difficulty sending its estimate and blueprint to the customers on the Internet, because their main customers are women in their 50s, who are not familiar with the Internet. Therefore, it has to retain both online and offline business structure. C2 has used an accounting program that enables it to do Internet transactions according to the increasing trends of Internet business. However, since many people in Korea think that the receipt issued on the Internet is not trustworthy, the C2 has sent the receipt to their customers by mail. This type of problem can be a barrier to the extension of the Internet business.

Business partner: SMEs, which are subcontractors or agents of the big enterprises that use EDI or e-commerce, generally adopt an EDI system or e-commerce solution (Abell & Lim, 1996; KIMI, 2003). C7, which is an agent and is associated with its major business partner (a big enterprise), transacts e-business with its partner on the Internet by the major partner's request.

Among the business related factors, the outsourcing element seems to be an important factor to initiate ICT adoption in SMEs because most SMEs cannot implement the ICT project by themselves due to costs. The outsourcing element differs greatly by the characteristics and the types of business in SMEs. Therefore, this factor is highly related to technology availability as a substitute of an outsourcing element. In conclusion, the results suggest that certain outsourcing elements with reasonable costs can provide the motivation of ICT adoption to many SMEs.

Technology-Related Factors

Cost: Even in the SMEs already using ICT, cost is still a critical barrier (C1). The lowered price of ICT service platforms caused SMEs (C3, C4, and C9) to change their business partners or disconnect them. Due to the limitation of capability or time, they outsourced a part of their business to accountants (C3 and C4) and private consultants (C9). In short, the lowered cost of ICT causes SMEs to adopt ICT. The lowered cost is a driving factor to adopt ICT by SMEs.

Maintenance and Training: The limited technological knowledge of employees and their management capability can be a barrier to adoption and extension of the information systems. Some CEOs (C1 and C2) are worried about the introduction of ICT because of the fear that their employees might be not familiar with it. C1 and C2 complain about the lack of training for their employees from the ICT service providers. Nonetheless, this factor seems not to be a critical one because they can ask the ICT service providers for training.

Fear factor (security and privacy): The fear of the possibility of leaking company's valuable information can be a critical barrier to adopting and extending implementation of new ICT service applications. Two companies (C3 and C7) are afraid of exposing their company information to outsider. C3 is unwilling to adopt new ICT because

of this reason. In C7's case, since most business activities are processed and arranged through the Internet, the security and privacy concerns about its business information and marketing strategy are the major fear factors of their new ICT adoption decision.

Technology availability (Hard to find solution & Customization): This is a crucial barrier that directly influences SME's ICT adoption decision. The CEOs of C2 and C6 insist that the sample accounting program provided by the ICT consortiums needs to be more developed and customized, although they are satisfied with the function and the price. The CEO of C2 points out that "the absence of a suitable application program is one of the barriers to adopt new ICT by SMEs." The CEO of C1 tried to use a personnel management application program of the consortium. However, he could not use it because the program was not suitable for his business practice.

In conclusion, the result shows that high cost is still a main barrier in some SMEs in the extension of ICT adoption like initial adoption. The results also show that the cost of ICT adoption could be decreased gradually, depending on the level of ICT development and the degree of the assistance of external environment. The lowered cost of ICT might influence more on the wider adoption of ICT in the SME sectors.

Government-Related Factors

Cost related financing: Many SMEs have used one of the ICT service platforms developed by the support of the government. They are satisfied with the price of the ICT service platforms. This factor might come from the government's support.

Cooperation Work: All SMEs have used an ICT service platform provided by the consortiums, which have played an important role in ICT adoption in the SME sector. They were organized in 2001 by the enforcement of government legislation to promote ICT adoption in SMEs. They are divided into five-business domains: content service, telecommunication service, application service, web-hosting, and on-line training. Owing to the sharing work between the members of the consortiums, ASPs and other service providers can reduce the development cost of ICT service platforms. Moreover, they do not need additional labor for marketing and billing because Telcos and ISPs, as the leaders, are in charge of the management and operation of the consortium. Therefore, they can not only reduce the cost of outsourcing, but also focus more on their core business.

Information channel: The result shows that SMEs got the ICT information through various channels: an acquaintance (C10), customers (C4), the Internet (C3), newspapers (C6), etc. Ironically, many SMEs can reach the information of ICT service platforms not from marketers or advertisement of the ICT service providers, but from their acquaintances and other parties.

Discussion

In the technology dimension, the cost related to ICT usage does not seem to be a barrier currently in most SMEs, because it is an investment for the future. This seems to drive from the higher awareness after they achieved the benefit and satisfaction of ICT usage. In addition, they are willing to adopt other ICT service platforms to extend the market and to pursue the efficacy of business. In this case, however, cost is still a crucial barrier to adopting ICT even though their awareness and the intention of ICT adoption are getting broader. As an influencing factor of ICT adoption, the existence of an alternative to high management cost brought the ICT adoption to the SMEs. Some SMEs change their business partners who use the ICT service platforms to reduce the management cost. Consequently, the result shows that high cost is still a main barrier in some SMEs in the extension of ICT adoption like initial adoption. The results also show that the cost of ICT adoption could be decreased gradually, depending on the level of ICT development and the degree of the

assistance of external environment. The lowered cost of ICT might influence more on the wider adoption of ICT in the SME sectors.

Among the business-related factors, outsourcing elements are important factors in initiating ICT adoption in SMEs because most SMEs cannot implement the ICT project by themselves. These outsourcing elements differ greatly by the characteristics and the types of business in SMEs. Therefore, this factor is highly related to technology availability as a substitute of an outsourcing element. For example, "Simple bookkeeping", which is one of the outsourcing elements, became one of the most popular service applications in many SMEs as a great deal of companies in the USA have been outsourcing payroll and accounting. With the development of various ICT products in the market and the proliferation of ASPs, outsourcing became suitable for SMEs with limited ICT capability (Teng et al., 1995; Turban et al., 2000). In conclusion, this study suggests that certain outsourcing elements with reasonable costs can provide the motivation of ICT adoption to many SMEs. Furthermore, the ICT adoption by the elements and the satisfaction with it can initiate an additional ICT adoption in the near future regardless of whether the ICT is for non-core or core business activity.

As an indirect factor impacting ICT adoption in the SMEs, cooperation work created by the ICT consortiums has an important role in the process of ICT adoption in Korea. All SME cases in the study have used the ICT service platform provided by one of the consortiums, whose main function is to provide the particular ICT service applications to the SMEs at lower prices. Due to the division of the work between the members of the ICT consortiums, each company can concentrate on its core business. For example, ASPs, which are also one of the representatives of SMEs in Korea, can focus on the development of ICT service applications without being concerned about the marketing or the advertisement of their products. Instead, Telcos and ISPs, which are leaders of the

ICT consortiums, are in charge of marketing and management of the ICT service platforms, and they also sell their own products, such as leased lines or the broadband Internet, with the ICT service applications. Therefore, ASPs and other service providers can reduce the cost of development of ICT service platforms and secure more customers. Accordingly, this type of cooperation would result in economies of scale that help the developers of ICT service platforms to deliver the advanced and customized applications to much larger number of SMEs' businesses at very lower prices (Beaumont & Costa, 2002). As a result, it would be helpful to reduce or break up the cost barrier and technology availability barrier.

Nevertheless, the cost issue resists resolution, because of the inferiority of SMEs' environment. As many studies suggested the importance of the government's role, as one of external environment related factors, government support is key to breaking through the barriers of ICT adoption in SMEs. Government support that SMEs wishes in the study, like other countries, are mostly related to the reduction of cost burden: financial support of development of ICT service platform, funds for training, tax cut, etc. Therefore, the intervention of government is thought to be inevitable in the SME sector. The main role of government is to open the way of using ICT without the burden of cost and to create the atmosphere of ICT usage through the systemically support to let the SMEs realize the benefits of ICT and to give more motivation in all possible areas. One thing that the Korean government did for the promotion of ICT adoption was to create the ICT consortiums and to provide financial support for the development and the training of ICT service platforms in the early stages. The creation of ICT Consortiums seems to be especially meaningful in terms of the improvement of the SMEs' atmosphere to diffuse the ICT.

In addition, another issue that the case study identifies is the lack of information channels to allow the SMEs to reach the ICT service platforms.

The channels were mainly the word of mouth from an acquaintance and the third parties, not the marketers or advertisement of the ICT consortiums. Although the SMEs have high awareness and interest about ICT adoption, they have not gotten the information directly from the government or the ICT Service providers.

Consequently, it suggests that more channels are necessary for ICT adoption. As a good example of the channel, the excavation and diffusion of successful cases through diverse channels such as magazines made by the same business groups or their associations can be good resources. These channels might be worked as an influencing factor to help SMEs to adopt ICT more rapidly. The excavation of various channels and the successful cases could be a crucial portion of the government.

CONCLUSION AND FUTURE DIRECTIONS

The preliminary analysis results of the ten cases show the barriers related to cost and technology availability are the most crucial factors which affect the SME's e-business adoption decision. Among the business-related factors, outsourcing elements are emerging as influencing factors to adopt ICT. The government-related factors are also important factors in the reduction of the main barriers and the creation of atmosphere of e-commerce adoption in the SME sector. In particular, the governmental role is important if there is to be a break in the barriers of ICT adoption in SMEs. The primary role of government is to open the way to using ICT without the burden of cost and to create the atmosphere of ICT usage through systemic supports. The results also show that even the SMEs already adopting ICT have many barriers. In addition, there is no big difference between the pre-adopters and post-adopters in terms of the type of barriers except awareness and perceived-benefits comparing the previous literature.

There are several limitations of this study. The first limitation is that this study focuses only the successful SMEs using the ICT service platforms. Second, the sample case of the SMEs is relatively small to generalize for all SMEs' environments. Third, only the qualitative view of cases is considered in this study. Therefore, a resech using quantifiable empirical data needs to support the findings of this study.

Nonetheless, there are several contributions. Unlike more statistically-based studies (e.g., survey methodology) which search for quantifiable data, case studies seek a qualitative and holistic understanding of the event or situation in question using inductive logic--reasoning from specific to more general terms. The major contribution of this chapter is to propose an OBTG (Organizational–Business–Technological-Governmental) e-business adoption model for SMEs and to preliminary validate the model using the ten cases of SMEs data collected by an information communication technology (ICT) consortium. Although the number of cases is limited to generalize for all SMEs' environments, this study reveals important factors which affect ICT adoption decision in SMEs. It is expected that the proposed model will be tested empirically in the future.

ACKNOWLEDGMENT

An earlier version of this chapter was presented in the 2008 Americas Conference on Information Systems (AMCIS), Toronto, Ontario

REFERENCES

Abell, W., & Lim, L. (1996). *Business Use of the Internet in New Zealand: An Exploratory Study.* Paper presented at the Second Australian World Wide Web Conference.

Ball, L. D., Dambolena, I. G., & Hennessey, H. D. (1987). Identifying early adopters of large software systems. *Database*, *19*(1), 21–27.

Beaumont, N., & Costa, C. (2002). Information technology outsourcing in Australia. *Information Resources Management Journal*, *15*(3), 14–31.

Becker, B., Dawson, P., Devine, K., Hannum, C., Hill, S., Leydens, J., et al. (2005). *Case Studies*. Retrieved from http://writing.colostate.edu/guides/research/casestudy

Blili, S., & Raymond, L. (1993). Information technology: Threats and opportunities for small and medium-sized enterprises. *International Journal of Information Management*, *13*(6), 439–448. doi:10.1016/0268-4012(93)90060-H

Chau, P. Y. K., & Jim, C. C. F. (2002). Adoption of Electronic Data Interchange in Small and Medium-Sized Enterprises. *Journal of Global Information Management*, *10*(4), 61–85.

Chong, S., & Pervan, G. (2007). Factors Influencing the Extent of Deployment of Electronic Commerce for Small- and Medium-sized Enterprises - An Exploratory Study. *Journal of Electronic Commerce in Organizations*, *5*(1), 1–29.

Dholakia, R. R., & Kshetri, N. (2004). Factors Impacting the Adoption of the Internet among SMEs. *Small Business Economics*, *23*(4), 311–322. doi:10.1023/B:SBEJ.0000032036.90353.1f

Feagin, J., Orum, A., & Sjoberg, G. (1991). *A case for case study*. Chapel Hill, NC: University of North Carolina Press.

Fink, D., & Disterer, G. (2006). International case studies: To what extent is ICT infused into operations of SMEs? *Journal of Enterprise Information Management*, *19*(6), 608–625. doi:10.1108/17410390610708490

Hsiao, F. S. T., & Hsiao, M.-C. W. (2001). Capital flows and exchange rates: recent Korean and Taiwanese experience and challenges. *Journal of Asian Economics*, *12*(3), 353–381. doi:10.1016/S1049-0078(01)00092-6

Iacovou, C. L., Benbasat, I., & Dexter, A. S. (1995). Electronic Data Interchange and Small Organizations: Adoption and Impact of Technology. *Management Information Systems Quarterly*, *19*(4), 465–485. doi:10.2307/249629

ITU. (2003). *World Telecommunication Indicators database*. Retrieved from http://www.itu-t.org

ITU. (2005). *ITU's New Broadband Statistics*. Retrieved from http://www.itu.int/osg/spu/newslog/ITUs+New+Broadband+Statistics+For+1+January+2005.aspx

Jutla, D., Bodorik, P., & Dhaliwal, J. (2002). Supporting the e-business readiness of small and medium-sized enterprises: approaches and metrics. *Internet Research: Electronic Networking Applications and Policy*, *12*(2), 139–164. doi:10.1108/10662240210422512

Kettinger, J. (1994). National Infrastructure Diffusion and US Information Super Highway. *Information & Management*, *27*(6), 357–369. doi:10.1016/0378-7206(94)90016-7

KIMI. (2002). *The evaluation of ICT adoption in SMEs*. Retrieved from www.kimi.or.kr

KIMI. (2003). *Whitepaper of ICT Adoption of SME 2003*. Retrieved from http://www.kimi.or.kr/pds/2003w-paper/sub/header.html

Kurnia, S., & Johnston, R. B. (2000). The Need of a Processual View of Inter-organizational Systems Adoption. *The Journal of Strategic Information Systems*, *9*(4), 295–319. doi:10.1016/S0963-8687(00)00050-0

Kwon, T. H. (1990). *A diffusion of innovation approach to MIS diffusion: conceptualization, methodology, and management strategy*. Paper presented at the 11th International Conference on Information Systems, Copenhagen, Denmark.

Lallana, E. C. (2004). *An Overview of ICT Policies and e-Strategies of Select Asian Economies*. Bangkok, Thailand: United Nations Development Programme-Asia Pacific Development Information Programme.

Lefebvre, É., & Lefebvre, L. A. (1996). *INFORMATION AND TELECOMMUNICATION TECHNOLOGIES: The Impact of their Adoption on Small and Medium-sized Enterprises*. Ottowa, Canada: IDRC.

Lefebvre, L. A., Lefebvre, E., & Harvey, J. (1996). Intangible assets as determinants of advanced manufacturing technology adoption in SME's: toward an evolutionary model. *IEEE Transactions on Engineering Management*, *43*(3), 307–322. doi:10.1109/17.511841

Locke, S., & Cave, J. (2002). Information Communication Technology in New Zealand SMEs. *Journal of American Academy of Business*, *2*(1), 235–240.

McCole, P., & Ramsey, E. (2005). A Profile of Adopters and Non-adopters of eCommerce in SME Professional Service Firms. *Australasian Marketing Journal*, *13*(1), 36–48.

MIC. (2002). *The planning of development of ICT in SME*. Retrieved from http://www.mic.go.kr

NCA. (2006). *2006 Informatization White Paper*. Seoul, Korea: Author.

Nua Internet Surveys. (2001). *The Kelsey Group: US Small Businesses Move Online*. Retrieved from http://www.nua.ie/surveys/?f=VS&art_id=905356432&rel=true

OECD. (1997). *Globalization and Small and Medium Sized Enterprises (SMEs)*. Paris: Organization for Economic Cooperation and Development.

OECD. (2000). *Small and Medium-sized Enterprises: Local Strength, Global Reach*. Retrieved from http://www.oecd.org

OECD. (2003). *OECD Science, Technology and Industry Scoreboard*. Retrieved from http://www1.oecd.org/publications/e-book/92-2003-04-1-7294/PDF/B45.pdf

OECD. (2004). *OECD Broadband Statistics*. Retrieved from http://www.oecd.org/document/60/0,2340,en_2825_495656_2496764_1_1_1_1,00.html

Palvia, P. C., & Palvia, S. C. (1999). An Examination of the IT Satisfaction of Small-Business Users. *Information & Management, 35*(3), 127–137. doi:10.1016/S0378-7206(98)00086-X

Paraskevas, A., & Buhalis, D. (2002). Outsourcing IT for small hotels: The opportunities and challenges of using application service providers. *The Cornell Hotel and Restaurant Administration Quarterly, 43*(2), 27–39. doi:10.1016/S0010-8804(02)80029-5

Poon, S., & Strom, J. (1997). *Small Business Use of the Internet: Some Realities*. Paper presented at the Association for Information Systems Americas Conference, Indianapolis, IN.

Premkumar, G., & Roberts, M. (1999). Adoption of new Information Technologies in rural small businesses. *Omega. The International Journal of Management Science, 27*(4), 467–484.

Purao, S., & Campbell, B. (1998). *Critical Issues for Small Business Electronic Commerce: Reflections on Interviews of Small Business in Downtown Atlanta*. Paper presented at the Proceedings of the AIS Americas Conference on Information Systems, Baltimore, MD.

Rashid, M. A., & Al-Qirim, N. A. (2001). E-Commerce Technology Adoption Framework by New Zealand Small to Medium Enterprises. *Research Letters Information Mathematical Science, 2*(1), 63–70.

Rogers, E. M. (1995). *The diffusion of Innovation* (4th ed.). New York: Free Press.

Scupola, A. (2003). The adoption of Internet commerce by SMEs in the south of Italy: An environmental, technological and organizational perspective. *Journal of Global Information Technology Management, 6*(1), 52–71.

Seyal, A. H., Awais, M. M., Shamail, S., & Abbas, A. (2004). Determinants of Electronic Commerce in Pakistan: Preliminary Evidence from Small and Medium Enterprises. *Electronic Markets, 14*(4), 372–387. doi:10.1080/10196780412331311801

Soh, C., Mah, Q. Y., Gan, F. Y., Chew, D., & Reid, E. (1997). The use of the Internet for business: The experience of early adopters in Singapore. *Internet Research: Electronic Networking Applications and Policy, 7*(3), 217–228. doi:10.1108/10662249710171869

Teng, J., Cheon, M., & Grover, V. (1995). Decisions to outsource information systems functions. Testing a strategy-theoretic discrepancy model. *Decision Sciences, 26*(1), 75–103. doi:10.1111/j.1540-5915.1995.tb00838.x

Thong, J. Y. L. (1999). An Integrated Model for Information Systems Adoption in Small Businesses. *Journal of Management Information Systems, 15*(4), 187–214.

Tornatzky, L. G., & Fleischer, M. (1990). *The Process of Technological Innovation*. Lexington, MA: Rowman & Littlefield, Lexington Books.

Towler, D. (2002). Digital Revolution or Digital Divide. *Journal of Vocational and Technical Education and Training, 2*, 41–45.

Turban, E., Lee, J., King, D., & Chung, H. M. (2000). *Electronic Commerce: A Managerial Perspective*. Upper Saddle River, NJ: Prentice Hall.

Vickery, G. (2002). *E-business Experience in the OECD Countries: Results of a Multi-Country, Multi-Sector Study*. Retrieved from http://www.oecd.org

Walczuch, R., Braven, G. d., & Lundgren, H. (2000). Internet Adoption Barriers for Small Firms in the Netherlands. *European Management Journal*, *18*(5), 561–572. doi:10.1016/S0263-2373(00)00045-1

Welsh, A. H., & White, J. F. (1981). A small business is not a little big business. *Harvard Business Review*, *59*(4), 18–32.

ENDNOTES

[1]   OECD (1997) defines SMEs as enterprises with number of employees less than 500.

[2]   Source: Small and Medium Business Administration of Korea (www.smba.go.kr)

[3]   Compared to big companies, SMEs have a special characteristic that distinguishes them from their larger counterparts. They tend to be clustered in highly fragmented industries; SMEs cannot usually afford to pay for the kinds of necessary services such as accounting and bookkeeping that they need; the owner's salary in a SME represents a much larger fraction of revenues than in a big company; External forces tend to have more impact on SMEs; and so on, Such limitations creates a special condition namely resource poverty (Welsh & White, 1981).

[4]   The companies are renamed for the privacy purpose.

Chapter 9
ICT for Development (ICT4D) Projects in Developing Countries:
A Proposed Conceptual Framework

Md. Mahfuz Ashraf
University of Dhaka, Bangladesh

Bushra Tahseen Malik
Brainstorm Bangladesh, Bangladesh

ABSTRACT

It is argued that Information and Communication Technologies (ICT) can lead to the socio-economic development of people, especially in developing countries. Hence, developing countries have been rushing to implement ICT for Development (ICT4D) projects in rural areas through the direct-indirect supervision of institutions such as the World Bank, the United Nations (UN) and other donor/local agencies. While there is considerable interest regarding donor agencies or funding bodies and the ways ICT can be deployed in developing countries, identifying the actual impact at the micro (community) level is less observed in the literature. The aim of this chapter is to understand ICT4D project/research in developing countries, presenting key challenges which influence the success of ICT4D projects. In this chapter, the authors propose a conceptual framework aimed to improve this understanding at the micro (community) level.

INTRODUCTION

In general, ICT projects towards development in developing countries are typically guided and designed at the macro level (national strategic), adopted at the meso level (organization), implemented at the micro level (individual/group/community), and are exclusively dependent on the interests and funding from the international development agencies. Therefore, ICT4D research can be understood at the above three levels. While researchers and international donor agencies report on the implementation of ICT interventions (Adam & Wood, 1999; Madon, 1991) with the hope of bridging so called digital divide, the ICT impact research towards development in rural areas of

DOI: 10.4018/978-1-60566-388-3.ch009

developing countries is scarce (Mbarika et al., 2005; Meso, Datta & Mbarika, 2006).

In recent years, international donor agencies and non-government organizations (NGO) have been attempting to fill this gap, as are key researchers and academicians such as Walsham (2006), Avgerou (2006), Madon (1997), Sein and Ahmed (2001), Heeks (2002), and Harris (2005), to name a few. In this chapter, we highlight concepts of ICT4D project/research and present a proposed conceptual framework to understand impact which may form the basis of further research effort at the micro level.

ICT4D RESEARCH

The literature of ICT4D is clearly divided into two streams of thought — the optimistic and the pessimistic viewpoints. The optimistic viewpoint suggests that ICT can act as a catalyst for development by making information exchange faster and more frequent, and by reducing costs. In developing countries, telecentres and information kiosks enable poor people to receive information about their governments, market prices, health and education (Amariles et al. 2006; Kumar & Best 2006): this means of providing ICT services to poor communities helps them to become active citizens of a country. Such a viewpoint supports the idea of modernisation where developing countries do not have sufficient skills, knowledge, or ability to produce. To become developed, these countries need to seek assistance — capital, technology, skilled workforce — and to hire concepts from western countries. In addition, they can enjoy the benefit of low cost technology because of being late adopt ICT originating from the western countries where it was developed (Soeftestad & Sein 2003).

On the other hand, the pessimistic viewpoint expresses little hope that ICT will lead to national development in developing countries. Those who hold it consider that ICT will not be of help be-

cause of deep-rooted problems such as poverty, poor telecommunications infrastructure and lack of IT investment (Cecchini & Scott 2003; Macome 2002). Further, the competitive advantage of ICT in Western countries enables them to enjoy a superior level of economic growth at the cost of poor countries (Sein & Ahmad 2001): for example, offshore software industry is mainly feeding rich nations — a view from the dependency perspective of development (Krishna & Madon 2003; Sein & Harindranath 2004). The following comment by Heeks (2001) is useful in this regard;

Academics may be seen as taking data and value from developing countries and repackaging them for the (limited) benefit of a small clique of other Western/Western-oriented theoreticians. If so, they differ little from the exploitative colonialists and capitalists extracting resources and labour value from developing countries for the benefit of Western elites. If this is to be avoided, a question for all those involved in IS and development must therefore surely be, *What benefit is being returned to the individuals and organisations and communities from whom my data was drawn?"* (Heeks 2001, p.3).

These two schools of thought take extreme position on two core issues: the optimistic school of thought postulates a global agenda on development, while the pessimistic school of thought concentrates on local issues rather than on the global context.

This discourse of ICT4D in developing countries has been shaped by an alternative perspective of development thought, that of human development. Another group of IS researchers emphasises that the social factors are separate from technological factors — themselves similar to the economic indicators — while studying IS in developing countries (Avgerou 2003; Harris & Bhatarai 2003; Heeks & Kenny 2002; Krishna & Madon 2003; Madon 2000; Sein & Ahmad 2001). According to this group, the important challenge is the assessment of meaningful information for knowledge-building by the use of social resources, rather than by providing simply technology to a community (Johnston 2003; Mansell & Wehn 1998; RIRDC 1997); and assessment and transformation of information requires people's capabilities to access and assess data and to acquire and share knowledge.

A PROPOSED CONCEPTUAL FRAMEWORK

In this section, we begin to construct a conceptual framework to identify the ICT-led developmental impact, and to understand such impact at micro level (i.e., from the participants' perspective).

Traditionally, ICT4D impact research towards development has been carried out in order to:

- understand the economic/social developmental impact (Adam & Wood, 1999), or
- assess or measure the impact (impact assessment) considering different quantifiable indicators (ITU 2006).

Our research supports the first of these two perspectives — to understand the economic and social developmental impact of ICT interventions on the rural areas of a developing country — for the reasons we will put forward.

Impact assessment requires a lengthy period for understanding possible changes that can occur as a result of the intervention. Moreover, many aspects of the initial situation must be known in order for the outcome to be compared with the intervention's objective/s (Menou & Potvin, 2007). In many cases, changes the researchers would like to know about may occur quickly; but many social changes are likely to take longer to unfold. Therefore, impact assessment is a continuous, long-term process that depends upon a variety of factors and requires rigorous monitoring at field level. Even research undertaken over two or three

years is relatively brief in the societal context, especially when there is little previous ICT4D impact research in a particular social context.

Our research stands on the understanding of economic/social developmental impact, while recognising that the impact of ICT4D interventions goes beyond simple economic factors, affecting also human, social and political structures, both within the communities which are directly affected by the intervention and an expanding area surrounding those communities. In essence, we argue that for an assessment framework to be robust, it must be founded upon an holistic understanding of the impact of ICT4D on communities. Robust frameworks must recognise the complex nature of such projects. Too often, impact assessment frameworks focus on the efficiency and availability of computer hardware and software, 'paying insufficient attention to the human and social systems that must also change for technology to make a difference' (Warschauer, 2002, p.4).

ICT4D projects are embedded in a complex array of factors, encompassing physical, digital, human and social resources and relationships that exist across the intervention: so our work provides some broader insights into ICT4D impact research.

After the identification of these two broad ICT-led development types, the next step is to understand their impact on social and economic development from the participants' perspectives. This can be done by adopting a conventional 'input-output' model (ITU, 2006): here, *input* is defined as the program itself (ICT intervention) and *output* as the results of the *input*. Traditionally, the input-output model can be used in many ways, and for our research the model can assist us to understand and compare a particular programme's objective/s with its potential or actual outcomes.

In the next sub-section, we focus on the level/ perspective of and the mechanism for understanding the impact/s (output) of ICT interventions on development.

Understanding Impact for the Conceptual Framework

ICT4D impact studies can be investigated within their local context, and best understood from the participants' viewpoints; so it is our intention to understand ICT impact on development at micro level from that perspective. Because we need a mechanism to understand the possible impacts, we turn to discussing that — an important aspect of our conceptual framework.

Heeks's (2005a) information chain model and Sen's (2000) notion of 'development as freedom' are two useful mechanisms to understand economical and social impact within a particular context and from the participants' viewpoints. To ensure this process and achieve successful implementation of ICT projects, Heeks' (2005a) information chain model provides a mechanism to;

- access data from the appropriate sources,
- assess the data relevance,
- apply the relevant data to a specific decision, and
- act upon the decision.

Heeks (2005a) suggests that it is necessary to follow the entire information chain while understanding ICT-led development projects. He lists several different types of resources as essential for humans to process information. These are;

a.   data resource (relevant data),
b.   economic resource (money, skills, technology),
c.   social resource (motivation from social setting, confidence to data source, knowledge to access), and
d.   action resource (skills and empowerment to act on decisions).

Our research/conceptual framework looking at these issues uses Heeks' (2005a) information chain model as a basis for the improvement of

understanding the process of outcome from/impact of ICT4D projects from the participants' perspectives. However, one way uni-directive information chain model is not sufficient to postulates the impact of ICT4D project (Ashraf, Swatman & Hanisch 2008) if the scenario becomes critical. For example, 'action' may not lead ultimate development until 'social constraints' have been removed. Therefore, we adopt Sen's (2005) theory to shape our framework.

According to Sen (2000), development is the process of expanding human freedoms that a person can value and enjoy, and 'the assessment of development has to be informed by this consideration' (Sen 2000b, p 36). Sen (2000) views expansion of freedom as the means and the end of development in general, and of capacity development in particular. Sharing Sen's viewpoint, Fakuda-Parr, Lopes and Malik (2002, p.20) write that the expansion of freedom ' *is not merely a stepping-stone towards higher levels of human development; it is an end in itself'.*

Sen's (2000) notion of development as freedom, popularly known as 'the capability approach', has added a new dimension to thinking on the subject — e.g., adding health care facilities, education attainment, political participation and civil rights to conventional economic development issues like rise in income, technological advancement and so on (Kvasny, Payton, Mbarika & Chong 2006). Sen (2000) suggests that the assessment of development has to be informed by the process of enlargement of freedom through eradication of different forms of oppression — social and economic deprivation, censored speech, and so on (Kvasny et al. 2006). Following Sen's research, there have been attempts to redefine development from human capital (skills and education), household facilities (resources), and its social capital (Madon, 2003). Sen's viewpoint of the broader perspective of development has gained favour amongst academics and policy-makers (Madon, 2003).

A number of studies has referred to the relationship between ICT and Sen's (2000) notion of 'development as freedom' (Gigler, 2004, Walsham & Sahay, 2006, Garai and Sahadrach, 2006). Madon (2003) has provided an exploratory framework for assessing impact of three e-governance projects in India, taking a social constructivist perspective; her framework for analyzing field data is broadened by her use of wider definitions of 'development as freedom'. Gigler (2004) also conceptualized development from the same perspective (capability approach) for assessing ICT impacts on indigenous peoples' empowerment in Peru. Gigler (2004) provided a set of capabilities/number of instrumental freedoms as outcome indicators of ICT interventions to measure empowerment at the individual and community levels.

It is worth mentioning that Sen (2000) classifies instrumental freedom into five different perspectives:

- political,
- economic,
- social,
- security and
- transparency;

for, according to Sen (2000), these distinct types of rights and opportunities help to advance a person's general capability. Inspired by Madon (2003) and Gigler (2004), Garai and Sahadrach (2006) have attempted to extend Gigler's (2004) previously developed capabilities/instrumental freedoms set by testing them in rural India. Sen (2000) believes it important to consider a number of instrumental freedoms that contribute, directly or indirectly, to the overall freedom to live the way they would like to that people have (Sen, 2000, p 38).

While significant attention to Sen's notion of development as freedom/the capability approach has been paid by economists, philosophers, academicians and development agencies after Sen (2000) won the Nobel prize for economics in 1998, operationalising his theory or approach is not straightforward; researchers are yet to reach any decisive conclusions on the process of assessing an individual's capability or freedom. It is easy to measure the 'income' of an individual rather than his/her 'self-esteem', for example; and people's capabilities are affected in different ways by weightings (a small income increase will affect the poor and the rich capability sets in different ways, e.g.). As a remedy, Sen (2000) calls for self-defined instrumental freedoms for individuals: individuals are responsible for their own well-being, so it is up to each to decide what capabilities and functionings towards achieving instrumental freedoms are important to enable him or her to lead the life desired. Sen (2000) argues that selection and weighting of individuals' capabilities are subject to personal value judgment.

Although Gigler (2004) and Garai and Sahadrach (2006) have attempted to provide a list of capabilities as output indicators to measure ICT impact on individual/community empowerment, Sen (2000) does not subscribe to a fixed or definitive list of capabilities (Clark 2005). However, it is easy to identify five distinct types of instrumental freedom — as mentioned earlier — but by no means is this list exhaustive. Those five distinct but interrelated instruments may help to focus on some particular policy issues that demand special attention.

We propose that our conceptual framework can be used for deductive study purposes. When using this framework, researchers may follow a systematic and iterative process where the conceptual framework guides the collection and analysis of field data, which in turn may shape the framework.

CONCLUSION

In this research, we propose a conceptual framework to understand ICT4D projects in developing countries. To support our conceptual framework, it was considered important to conduct an empirical study, which was used to further refine the framework. Our proposed model may be used as a normative tool for the academicians, development agencies and international donor agencies who wish to understand the impact (s) of ICT4D projects. The framework not only describes existing concepts of developments and Heeks' (2005a) information chain, but goes beyond to integrate developmental agendas with ICT enabled initiatives.

REFERENCES

Adam, L., & Wood, F. (1999). An investigation of the impact of information and communication technologies in sub-Saharan Africa. *Journal of Information Science, 25*(4), 307–318. doi:10.1177/016555159902500407

Ashraf, M., Swatman, P., & Hanisch, J. (2008). *An extended framework to investigate ICT impact on development at the micro (community) level.* Presented and published in 16th European Conference on Information Systems (ECIS) 2008, (9-11 June 2008), Galway, Ireland.

Avgerou, C. (2003). The link between ICT and economic growth in the discourse of development. In Korpela, M., Monetealerge, R., & Poulymenakou, A. (Eds.), *Organizational information systems in the context of globalization* (pp. 373–386). Amsterdam: Kluwer.

Avgerou, C. (2006). *Taking into account Context in IS research and practice.* London: London School of Economics and Political Science. Retrieved May 13, 2006, from http://www.dmst.aueb.gr/gr2/diafora2/Prosopiko2/visitors_ppts/Avgerou-research-pre-Framing.ppt

Bhatnagar, S. C. (2000). Social Implications of Information and Communication Technology in Developing Countries: Lessons from Asian Success Stories. *Electronic Journal of Information Systems for Developing countries, 1*(4), 1-9.

Cecchini, S., & Scott, C. (2003). Can information and communications technology applications contribute to poverty reduction? Lessons from rural India. *Information Technology for Development, 10*(2), 73–84. doi:10.1002/itdj.1590100203

Clark, A. D. (2005). The capability approach: its development, critiques and recent advances. Manchester, UK: Institute for development policy and management, University of Manchester.

DFID. (2005). *Monitoring and evaluating Information and Communication for Development (ICD) programmes: Guidelines. Information and communication for development.* UK: Department for International Development.

Fukuda-Parr, S., Lopes, C., & Malik, K. (2002). *Capacity for Development: New Solutions to Old Problems.* London: Earthscan Publications.

Garai, A., & Sahadrach, B. (2006). *Taking ICT to every Indian village: opportunities and challenges.* New Delhi: One World South Asia.

Gigler, B.-S. (2004). Including the Excluded - Can ICTs empower poor communities? In *Proceedings of the 4th International Conference on the Capability Approach*, Italy, 5-7 September, 2004.

Harris, R. W. (2005). Explaining the success of rural Asian telecentres. In Davison, R. M., Harris, R. W., Qureshi, S., Vogel, D. R., & Vreede, G.-Jd. (Eds.), *Information systems in developing countries: theory and practice* (pp. 83–100). Hong Kong: City University of Hong Kong Press.

Harris, R. W., & Bhatarai, M. (2003). *Fact-Finding Review of ICT in Development in a Rural-Urban Setting. UN-HABITAT and Roger Harris Associates. Rural-Urban Partnerships Programme (RUPP) under Support Services Policy and Programme Development.* SPPD.

Heeks, R. (1998). Foundation of ICTs in Development: Pushing and Pulling. *Information Technology in Developing Countries Newsletter, 4*(1), 1–2.

Heeks, R. (2002). Information Systems and Developing Countries: Failure, Success, and Local Improvisations. *The Information Society, 18*(2), 101–112. doi:10.1080/01972240290075039

Heeks, R. (2005a). Foundation of ICTs in Development: The information chain. *e Development Briefing, 3*(1), 1-2.

Heeks, R. (2005b). *ICTs and the MDGs: On the Wrong Track?* UK: Development Informatics Group, University of Manchester.

Heeks, R., & Kenny, C. (2002). *ICTs and development: Convergence or divergence for developing countries?* Paper presented at the Norwegian Association for Development Research Conference, Trondheim, Norway, November 14-15, 2002.

IDRC. (1993). *Measuring the impact of information on development.* Ottawa, Canada: The International Development Research Centre.

IICD. (2007). *IICD supported project: Eastern Corridor Agro-Market Information Centre (ECAMIC).* Retrieved July 10, 2007, from http://www.iicd.org/projects/articles/Ghana-ECAMIC

ITU. (2006). *World Telecommunication/ICT Development Report.* Geneva, Switzerland: International Telecommunication Union.

Jerinabi, U., & Arthi, J. (2005). Impact of Information Technology and Globalisation on Women's career, In *Proceedings of the International Conference on Information and Communication Technology of Management,* Melaka, Malaysia.

JIVA. (2007). *TeleDoc: Healthcare to touch everyone.* Retrieved July 10, 2007, from http://www.jiva.com/teledoc/

Johnston, J. (2003). *The Millennium Development Goals and Information and Communications Technology.* Berlin: United Nations Information and Communication Technologies Task Force.

Krishna, S., & Madon, S. (Eds.). (2003). *Digital Challenge: Information Technology in the Development Context.* Aldershot, UK: Ashgate.

Kumar, R., & Best, M. L. (2006). Social Impact and Diffusion of Telecenter Use: A Study from the Sustainable Access in Rural India Project. *Journal of Community Informatics, 2*(3). Retrieved February 12, 2008, from http://www.ci-journal.net/index.php/ciej/article/view/328

Kvasny, L., Payton, F. C., Mbarika, V., & Chong, J. (2006). *Information technology education and employment for women in Kenya.* Paper presented at the SIGMIS-CPR, Claremont, California, USA.

Macome, E. (2002). *The dynamics of the adoption and use of ICT-based initiatives for development: results of a field study in Mozambique.* PhD thesis, Faculty of Engineering, Built Environment and Information Technology, University of Pretoria.

Madon, S. (1991). *The impact of computer-based information systems on rural development: A case study in India.* PhD thesis, Imperial College of Science, Technology & Medicine.

Madon, S. (1997). Information-Based Global Economy and Socioeconomic Development: The Case of Bangalore. *The Information Society, 13*(3), 227–244. doi:10.1080/019722497129115

Madon, S. (2000). The Internet and socio-economic development: exploring the interaction. *Information Technology & People, 13*(2), 85–101. doi:10.1108/09593840010339835

Madon, S. (2003). Studying the developmental impact of e-governance intitatives. In *Proceedings of the Internationals Federation of Information Processing, IFIP*, Working Group 8.2 and 9.4, Athens,Greece, 15-17 June 2003.

Mansell, R., & Wehn, U. (1998). *Knowledge societies: information technology for sustainable development. Published for and on behalf of the United Nations*. New York: Oxford University Press.

Mbarika, V. W. A., Okoli, C., Byrd, T. A., & Datta, P. (2005). The Neglected Continent of IS Research: A Research Agenda for Sub-Saharan Africa. *Journal of the Association for Information Systems, 6*(5), 130–170.

Menou, M. J., & Potvin, J. (2007). *Toward A Conceptual Framework For Learning About ICT's And Knowledge In The Process Of Development A GK LEAP Background Document*. Retrieved January 22, 2007, from http://www.cidcm.umd.edu/ICT/research/ICT_and_Conflict/Resources%20About%20Assessments/LEAP_Conceptual_Framework.doc

Meso, P., Datta, P., & Mbarika, V. (2006). Moderating information and communication technologies' influences on socioeconomic development with good governance: A study of the developing countries. *Journal of the American Society for Information Science and Technology, 57*(2), 186–197. doi:10.1002/asi.20263

Midgley, J. (1995). *Social Development: The developmental perspective in social welfare* (1st ed.). New Delhi: Sage Pulication.

RIRDC. (1997). *A framework for developing regional communications initiatives*. Melbourne: Centre for International Research on Communication and Information Technologies.

Roman, R., & Colle, R. D. (2003). Content creation for ICT development projects: Integrating normative approaches and community demand. *Information Technology for Development, 10*(2), 85–94. doi:10.1002/itdj.1590100204

Sein, M., & Ahmad, I. (2001). A Framework to Study the Impact of Information and Communication Technologies on Developing Countries: The Case of Cellular Phones in Bangladesh. In *Proceedings of the BITWORLD 2001*, Cairo, Egypt.

Sein, M., & Harindranath, G. (2004, January). Conceptualizing the ICT Artifact: Toward Understanding the Role of ICT in National Development. *The Information Society, 20*(1), 15–24. doi:10.1080/01972240490269942

Sen, A. (2000). *Development as freedom* (1st ed.). New Delhi: Oxford University Press.

Soeftestad, L. T., & Sein, M. K. (2003). ICT and Development: East is East and West is West and the Twain may yet Meet. In Krishna, S., & Madon, S. (Eds.), *Digital Challenge: Information Technology in the Development Context* (pp. 63–83). Aldershot, UK: Ashgate.

Wagner, D. A., Day, B., James, T., Kozma, R. B., Miller, J., & Unwin, T. (2005). *Monitoring and Evaluation of ICT in Education Projects: A Handbook for Developing Countries*. Tunis: InfoDev.

Walsham, G., & Sahay, S. (2006). Research on information systems in developing countries: current landscape and future prospects. *Information Technology for Development, 12*(1), 7–24. doi:10.1002/itdj.20020

Warschauer, M. (2002). *Technology and social exclusion: Rethinking the digital divide*. London: MIT Press.

Warschauer, M. (2003). *Technology and Social Exclusion: Rethinking the Digital Divide*. London: MIT Press.

Chapter 10
The Challenges of the National ICT Policy Implementation Process:
A Comparative Study of Malaysia and Thailand

Nicholas C. Maynard
RAND Corporation, USA

ABSTRACT

Thailand and Malaysia have both undergone a rapid transformation of their ICT sectors, including their telecommunications networks, national policies, institutions, and regulatory regimes. The author contends that the privatization of the monopoly telecommunications operator and the creation of a regulatory agency are the foundation for all other governmental ICT initiatives designed to accelerate telecommunications adoption. This is a difficult process to successfully implement, with many countries unable to sufficiently reduce the authority of the postal, telegraph & telephone (PTT) agency to develop a new entity that is politically independent. Despite these difficulties, this process is vital to the success of a national ICT market. The creation of a competitive market and a government regulator is the basis on which all other regulatory reforms, institutional reforms, and national ICT policies must rest. If a country cannot achieve a politically sustainable balance of power between the government, the former monopoly, and the competitive players, then that country cannot sustain its rapid ICT adoption. A number of national initiatives are currently under way to develop technology sectors and increase adoption rates in developing countries, but many of these initiatives do not have a clear understanding of their potential impact and benefit on the economy – and are therefore difficult to justify politically or economically (Docktor, 2004). The stated goal of this research was to provide a set of tools for local and international policy makers and technology providers to help assess the benefits of technology initiatives while tying them to the larger issue of economic development.

DOI: 10.4018/978-1-60566-388-3.ch010

INTRODUCTION

ICT development requires acknowledgement of societal diversity across countries and within regions. Although overarching models for deployment and utilization can be developed, these models need to be flexible enough to be tailored to the national and regional requirements of the end users (Hossain, 2003). This customization of ICT deployment models is based on a country's social, historical, economic, political, and cultural environment. ICT projects that are likely to succeed will build upon existing formal and informal structures in the region. Projects that are not tailored to the society may be unsuited to meet the region's needs at launch and lack the required local support to achieve sustainability.

As countries privatize their monopolies, governments must work to open their telecom market to new entrants while supporting new infrastructure deployments – in short, helping to drive demand while supporting the development of the ICT sector (Gasmi, 2000). However, the policy initiatives underpinning these regulation and utilization efforts must be precisely sequenced to support a thriving ICT sector within a developing country (Wallsten, 2002). Governments that have been successful in their ICT initiatives have closely coordinated their ICT market policies with the private sector to achieve regulated and sustainable competition.

Within this institutional and market context, I examine the ICT adoption paths of Malaysia and Thailand. Both of these countries are at similar levels of economic and political development, although Malaysia has had a more stable macroeconomic and political environment since the Asian financial crisis of 1997 (Jomo, 2003). Each country has modeled its ICT institutional structure and policies on the successful example of Singapore, along with South Korea and Japan, for their national broadband and infrastructure initiatives (Lee, 2004). Despite these similarities, political considerations in Thailand have influenced the

privatization of the monopoly operator and the creation of the regulatory agency according to government officials interviewed for this case study. These considerations have led to a less competitive environment for the ICT market and the country has not been able to sustain its pace of ICT adoption, resulting in a plateau in Thailand's ICT development progress.

This chapter discusses and compares the ICT market, regulation, and policies of Thailand and Malaysia. The section is divided into six parts. The first includes a review of the current literature while the second provides an overview of the case study methodology. The third covers the economic conditions within Malaysia and Thailand as well as provides a discussion of the current conditions of the ICT sectors in Thailand and Malaysia, including an examination of adoption levels. The fourth part covers a comparison of Thailand and Malaysia to other middle-income and rural countries. The fifth part studies the universal service regimes of both of these middle-income countries. The last part offers a broader discussion on about Thailand's and Malaysia's ICT policies and institutions.

LITERATURE REVIEW

This section focuses on the large body of literature devoted to explaining the rapidly industrializing economies of East Asia, which include Thailand and Malaysia. This development literature is used as a basis for understanding the role of the state within the economy at large and the ICT sector in particular. These past studies from the literature provide a foundation for understanding the critical role the government plays in ICT development even after a sector has been privatized.

There has been a lengthy debate within economic development literature over the active role of the state as a key factor behind the success of the East Asian Newly Industrialized Economies, including Singapore and South Korea (Ranis, 1989;

Lim, 2000). There have been significant hurdles and setbacks; but both Thailand and Malaysia have successfully transitioned from an agrarian economy, to an import substitution, and finally to a technologically advanced economy (Amsden, 1989). A key component of this shift has been the creation of national ICT policies and institutions to support ICT adoption. By advancing national technological capacity, a country's technology institutions are an important contributor to larger economic development efforts (Feinson, 2003).

One of the most important institutions to support ICT sector development is the national telecommunications regulator. Levy (1994) argues that while performance of the telecommunications sector can be satisfactory under a wide range of regulatory conditions, these conditions must be stable to allow long-term investment into the sector. With arbitrary or volatile regulatory conditions, and without a credible commitment to enforce and maintain the regulatory regime, the necessary long-term investment will not be available to the telecommunications industry (Weingast, 1995). In this highly volatile regulatory environment, public ownership may be the only feasible option to achieve this credible commitment, given a country's economic and political environment (Levy, 1994).

Under a more stable regime and private provisioning, Levy suggests there is a need for an independent regulatory agency to sustain a competitive market and ensure the benefits of ICTs are diffused throughout the population. An independent institution in the sector increases market certainty and long-term stability, which in turn opens the sector to investment and increases its potential for benefiting the country's economic growth. Private telecommunications operators invest heavily in their infrastructure if the necessary regulatory constraints are in place; otherwise, the private investment is minimal (Levy, 1994).

Policy and institutional reforms are the critical success factors for growth in ICT penetration rates within developing countries, whose governments currently face a myriad of policy options (Wilson, 2003). These regulatory policy issues include public versus private initiatives, monopoly versus competitive markets, domestic versus foreign ownership, and centralized versus decentralized administrative controls. Until the late 1990s, a vast majority of countries opted for public provisioning of telecommunications services. Wilson suggests today a vast majority of governments have, to greater or lesser degrees, begun to shift toward more private, more international, more competitive, and more de-centralized management of their ICT sectors. However, compared to developed countries, developing country governments are neither moving at the same pace nor have they developed the same level of institutional support (Wilson, 2003).

METHODOLOGICAL APPROACH

This chapter outlines and compares the ICT adoption trajectories and policies of Thailand and Malaysia as well as the hurdles that impeded implementation. Data sources for these country studies include international indices, secondary surveys, governmental reports, and third-party research on ICT industries, government regulations, and ICT policies. The research also includes fieldwork in Thailand and Malaysia, completing 21 interviews with key officials responsible for design and implementation of the national ICT strategies. Using the results of these interviews, I examined the commonalities between Thailand and Malaysia in their ICT policies and differences in adoption rates.

My interviews for this research were completed with a wide range of stakeholders in the public and private sector. These government interviewees included officials at ministries of communication, the technology policy agency, and the telecom regulator. From the private sector, these interviews focused on local telecommunications firms to understand their plans for ICT investment and their

Table 1. Economic and ICT indicators by country, for Thailand, Malaysia, and Singapore

Economic Indicators 2005	Thailand	Malaysia	Singapore
GDP per capita, PPP (constant 2000 international $)	$7,740	$9,685	$26,550
Services, etc., value added (% of GDP)	46	40	66
Foreign direct investment, net inflows (% of GDP)	3	3	17
Urban population (% of total)	32	67	100
Technology Indicators 2005			
Fixed and mobile telephone subscribers per 1,000 inhabitants	653	943	1435
Internet users per 1,000 inhabitants	110	435	640
Broadband subscribers per 1,000 inhabitants	1	19	153
ICT expenditures (% of GDP)	4	7	9
High-technology exports (% of manufactured exports)	27	55	57

Source: World Development Indicators, 2007.

support for the national strategy. In addition, my interviews were completed with outside experts and additional officials, including those in the Ministry of Finance.

ECONOMIC AND ICT BACKGROUND

Many developing countries, such as Malaysia and Thailand, have announced their national policies within the last ten years (Ramasamy, 2004). Because both were modeled after Singapore's national ICT policies and institutions, the national plans and ICT institutions of both countries are very similar. However, the implementation and success of the two countries have differed considerably. A series of interviews were completed with government, private sector, and university stakeholders in Thailand and Malaysia to examine the cause behind these two differing experiences.

Both countries are at a crossroads in their development; each is attempting to shift their economy from agriculture and manufacturing to advanced services. Table 1 summarizes key national indicators for the two countries in addition Singapore's indicators for comparison. All figures within this chapter are reported in US dollars. The national ICT policies are at the center of the

government's attempt to create new economic opportunities while improving the country's ability to compete globally.

Malaysia is one example of a developing country that has focused almost singularly on technology development through foreign investment. While attracting a great deal of FDI, the country's economy has grown dependent on exporting multinational corporation (MNC) products to foreign markets (Blomstrom, 1998). Industry is moving slowly toward designing and innovating its own products. However, many of Malaysia's manufacturing facilities are still low-skilled components within the global supply chain.

Many developing countries have shifted their focus from deploying fixed lines to wireless penetration. Malaysia has managed to maintain a relatively high level of wireline adoption while driving wireless infrastructure, with average penetration for wireline doubling during the 1990s before reaching a plateau (World Development Indicators, 2007). Despite a slowdown in overall economic growth during the Asian financial crisis, wireless penetration grew rapidly, outnumbering landlines in less than a decade. Unfortunately, some areas within the country have been neglected during the rapid increase in teledensity. This lack of telecommunications infrastructure in these areas also highlights a larger problem of concentrated investment and governmental support to Kuala Lumpur metropolitan area in comparison to the rest of the economy (James, 2003).

Thailand has closely studied its neighbors to benchmark its own ICT policies and institutional structure (Lallana, 2004). When Thailand was implementing structural reforms in 2002, Malaysia was undergoing a similar effort – causing Thailand to mirror its ICT institutional restructuring closely after Malaysia's. Now that Thailand is working on a second round of ICT reforms, it has looked to Malaysia and Singapore again for guidance on evolving its ICT structures. In the ICT-related industries, Thailand is currently competing with countries that have low-cost labor, such as China, as well as countries with high levels of skilled labor, such as Singapore. Unlike Malaysia, Thailand does not have the high levels of governmental coordination and marketing required to compete against these other Asian economies.

Fixed line telephony penetration and broadband penetration are below average for Thailand, given its level of economic and technological development. This situation was significantly worse in 2000, when the government began working to catch up through its ICT Master Plan (Intarakumnerd, 2004). Although broadband penetration rates are improving, it may not be due to government intervention but higher demand by more affluent customers.

ICT CHALLENGES FACING DEVELOPING AND RURAL COUNTRIES

Although the institutional, economic, and technological environments of Thailand and Malaysia are similar, there are two key differences between the countries that impact their ability to adopt ICTs: a disparity in GDP per capita that has grown in recent years, and an increasing gap in rural population as a share of the total population. Thailand's GDP

per capita is nearly $2,000 lower than Malaysia's while its rural population is almost 68 percent of the total (World Development Indicators, 2006). This is over twice as high as Malaysia's rural population, which was at 33 percent in 2005 after declining from 50 percent in 1990 (World Development Indicators, 2006).

A country's GDP per capita has a strong and positive relationship with ICT adoption; increases in GDP per capita can lead to higher disposable incomes, which can be spent on new ICT services (Bassanini, 2002). In addition, as a country improves its GDP per capita, it is likely to shift from an agrarian economy to one that focuses on manufacturing and service sectors (Wong, 2002). These sectors, particularly in advanced services, have higher levels of ICT adoption, which assists in accelerating national penetration. However, GDP per capita increases do not account for the wide variation in ICT adoption across countries – resulting in many example countries with lower incomes but higher ICT penetration rates than Thailand.

There is also a positive relationship between ICT penetration and population density, due to a number of factors that increase the costs of serving rural areas and potentially limit penetration rates (Galperin, 2005). Network infrastructure deployment costs will be higher in comparison to urban areas due to lower density in rural areas; this increases the length of last mile access networks. This lower density also increases the operational costs of carriers, requiring them to cover a larger area with a scarce number of technicians. In addition, the income disparity between rural and urban areas also presents a significant challenge, with carriers experiencing lower revenues per person in rural areas (Li, 2005). None of this suggests that carriers cannot find a financially sustainable business model serving rural subscribers; but it does suggest that there are additional hurdles to increasing penetration rates within these areas.

It is important to note that these rural population and GDP per capita metrics do not account for all of the variance in ICT penetration rates. In fact, several example countries have low levels of urbanization similar to Thailand's or a similar GDP per capita, but have managed to successfully accelerate their ICT penetration rates (World Development Indicators, 2006).

Rural and Middle-Income Case Countries

Several countries that have levels of rural population and GDP per capita similar to Thailand's have successfully initiated and sustained rapid ICT adoption. This suggests that factors such as ICT policies and implementation played a significant role in Thailand in addition to these geographic and economic factors. The charts in Exhibits 2 and 3 depict the ICT adoption rates in countries selected for their appropriate levels of GDP per capita and rural populations.

Thailand vs. Countries with Similar GDP per Capita

Each of the countries included in Figure 1 have levels of GDP per capita that are similar to or lower than Thailand's. For example, in 2005, Thailand's GDP per capita was $7,740, while Algeria's was $6,283, Ecuador's was $3,863, and Jamaica's was $3,819 (World Development Indicators, 2006). Despite being low- or middle-income countries, several have been able to maintain rapid growth rates within their ICT sectors. Thailand's ICT adoption rate has been surpassed recently by Belarus, Colombia, Ecuador, and Venezuela. Algeria is also on pace to overtake Thailand's penetration rate in 2007, while additional countries, such as Jamaica and Macedonia, have lower GDP per capita but have maintained a higher rate of adoption for the past 10 years. The chart in Figure 1 depicts the trends for fixed and mobile subscribers per 1,000 people for the countries discussed above.

Thailand vs. Countries with Similar Rural Populations

With 68 percent of its population living in rural areas, Thailand has one of the lower levels of urbanization for a middle-income country. However, several countries that have similar-sized rural populations have managed to successfully accelerate their ICT adoption rates (see Figure 2).

Figure 1. Mobile phone adoption rates in middle-income countries

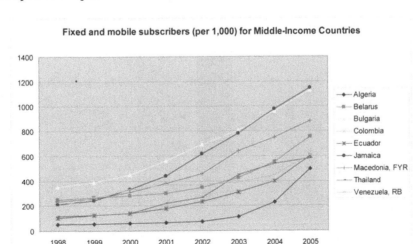

Source: World Development Indicators, 2006.

With more than 50 percent of their populations in rural areas, all of the countries included in the chart below have rural populations of a similar size to Thailand. For example, in 2005, China's rural population was 60 percent of the total, Bosnia's was 54 percent, Guatemala's was 53 percent, Guyana's was 72 percent, and Moldova's was 53 percent (World Development Indicators, 2006). Each of these countries has managed to accelerate and maintain its accelerated ICT adoption rates, with several countries on track to overtake Thailand by 2007.

The most notable is China, which has a similar-sized rural population and a lower level of GDP per capita, at $6,011 in 2005 (World Development Indicators, 2006). The country has been able to foster accelerated growth in its ICT sector, with its fixed and mobile subscribers estimated to reach 626 per 1,000 inhabitants in 2006 (Yankee Group, 2007). In contrast, Thailand's ICT adoption rate is estimated to be 618 in 2006 (Yankee Group, 2007). The chart below presents the ICT adoption trends of countries with similar levels of rural population.

UNIVERSAL SERVICE GOALS AND POLICIES

One of the more important policies for increasing ICT adoption rates is developing a universal service policy and public-private mechanism for supporting ICT access (Frieden, 2005). This section examines the universal service obligations (USO) placed by the national regulators on the incumbent and competitive operators in Thailand and Malaysia. These obligations can raise the necessary funds for rapidly expanding access within a developing country, if the mechanisms for raising and disbursing the monies are carefully designed and implemented.

Thailand

A key component to Thailand's effort to bolster ICT adoption is the launch and management of the universal service fund (Intarakumnerd, 2004). According to officials with the national regulator, the obligation is set at four percent; but it is unclear how growing broadband revenues will be dealt with or if the universal service fund will be used

Figure 2. Fixed and mobile phone adoption rates in rural countries

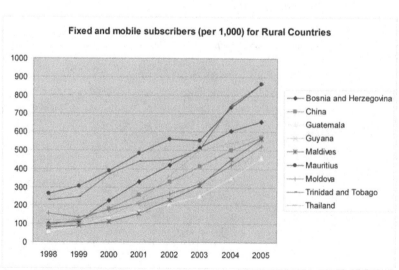

Source: *World Development Indicators, 2006.*

to deploy broadband infrastructure in addition to traditional fixed line infrastructure. The universal service obligation for carriers was a requirement under the telecom legislation. However, there is little guidance to the national regulator on implementation.

Several open questions remain, including whether all carriers should pay into the fund; and of those that are included, whether the treatment of wholesale carriers should differ from retail providers. Another key question is the implementation of the tax on a sliding scale that depends on the current levels of infrastructure deployment within rural areas, which allows providers to reduce their USO from the full 4 percent. Most important, the regulator still needs to define the policy mechanism for injecting the universal service funds into the market, whether that is through direct subsidy to customers or to the providers for their deployments to under-served areas (Gasmi, 2000).

Malaysia

For the Malaysian universal service fund, broadband is also part of the universal service obligation; added to the USO by the Cabinet in 2005, targeting areas with lower than average penetration rates. The USF is managed by the Malaysian Communications and Multimedia Commission (MCMC), the governmental entity that is responsible for determining the level of USF support by region and collects the six percent fees from telecom operators (Nambiar, 2006). MCMC officials stated that 89 areas within Malaysia are receiving funds, and telecom operators bid in a tender process to win the opportunity to build infrastructure within these areas, with a single winner of the tender per region. The universal service fund also continues to support deployment of the PSTN to households and payphones in low-income and rural areas.

The government has set the national goal of 25 percent broadband penetration for households based on wireline deployment of ADSL infrastructure (Malaysian Communications and Multimedia

Commission, 2006). In 2005, the MCMC stated in its report that the country had 1.3 million subscribers or 23 percent of households connected with broadband. The key component of this deployment initiative uses government intervention to spur private sector investment in areas that have little or no infrastructure. This intervention continues until the area reaches five percent penetration, which the government has determined through demand modeling as the level required to develop a critical mass of private sector support. After this five percent threshold, the government begins to throttle back its broadband support and encourages private service providers to enter the region.

ICT POLICIES AND INSTITUTIONS

Over the past two decades, telecommunications has evolved to become an essential service for the economic development of developing countries; viewed as vital for development like clean water, power generation, and new roads (James, 2003). More recently, the goal of bringing affordable telecommunications access to each household throughout entire population, particularly those in rural areas, has become a priority among national governments and within the international community as an economic development tool (Luger, 2002). Developing countries require close coordination of private and public sector resources to reach high levels of ICT adoption (Jomo, 1997). Countries with strong coordination and institutional support have been able to harness their public-private resources to produce indigenous capacity for accelerated ICT penetration, utilization, and innovation – which, in turn, directly supports the advancement of the economy.

There is no single approach that is the state's proper role in supporting ICT adoption. The role of the state is ever-changing and differs widely across countries depending on their network infrastructure, market environment, geography, and overall economy (Feinson, 2003). Despite this wide variation, it is still important to note that developing countries that have had sustained success in their ICT adoption rates have also had a strong role for the government. In most cases, a developing country's ICT sector needs to be led by the private sector. However, ICT deployment cannot be done without strong government regulation and either direct or indirect financial support (Nambiar, 2006). Without this level of government participation in the sector, the challenges of an unstable environment can severely limit investment and competition.

As countries develop their ICT policies, the role of the state must evolve further. Public-private collaboration is key for innovating and customizing ICTs for domestic use, which is essential to increasing adoption within developing countries (Frieden, 2005). Relying too heavily on international technologies, content, and applications will hamper utilization because these ICTs will not be tailored to the local environment. Developing country governments must take an active role to support the process while allowing the private sector enough flexibility to thrive.

The government plays a vital role in the deployment of ICT infrastructure and the development of ICT-related industries. This role is constantly evolving to match the changing demands of the sector and shifts in technology options. The deployment of infrastructure may have a government fill several roles simultaneously, from directly running municipal networks to offering indirect subsidies to carriers for deploying national ICT infrastructure (Mariscal, 2005). Although these efforts require significant resources and institutional support, they still do not require the same level of effort as ICT-sector development.

As the technological capabilities of local firms and ICT providers become more advanced, governments must transition to a secondary role within the sector while simultaneously providing a more complex set of policy supports. This can include a range of public-private R&D efforts, the creation of a technology park, or providing venture capital to technology start-ups (Amsden, 1997). All of these efforts can support the development of clusters of innovative ICT firms. However, they require significant budget and resources, and policymakers must choose from a wide array of policy options for effort.

ICT Institutions

ICT policies also necessitate strong institutional structures to implement and maintain these efforts, requiring a significantly higher level of governmental response than was seen when the government had the primary role as monopoly operator in the sector (Levy & Spiller, 1996). As a result, it is a real policy challenge for developing country governments to be nimble enough in adapting to the changing domestic ICT sector and global technology market, while giving the private sector enough flexibility to pursue many different technology avenues instead of following government-led ICT decisions.

The development of a national ICT institution within a developing country assists in creating a critical mass of expertise and funding capable of implementing complex sector support policies that are necessary for accelerating adoption rates. However, while creating an institution or national ICT policy based on international best practices is a necessary step, it is not sufficient to ensure successful implementation. In Thailand, the government has experienced difficulties in funding, implementing, and evaluating ICT policies due to a weakness in its institutions and instability in its political environment (Intarakumnerd, 2004).

Once an ICT institution has been created, the government must set a clear national goal for ICT adoption and innovation that incorporates input from the private sector. This public-private coordination can assist in designing policy goals that are feasible (a problem in Thailand) but also target the most appropriate regions and sectors (Frieden, 2005). This cooperation can also help ensure that the policy or initiative is designed to fill a gap left by the market or by other public sector efforts, avoiding policy overlap and competing initiatives. The necessary budgeting and authority must be given to the government ministry to ensure that program monitoring and evaluation are completed regularly.

Only after these national goals and policies have been set should the ICT ministry determine the most appropriate technology options to fit the needs of residents and domestic firms. These technology deployments should also offer an attractive environment to foreign companies, while avoiding the trap of placing the ICT requirements of these MNCs above the needs of domestic users. Allowing the needs of MNCs to influence national ICT goals and policies too heavily can lead to limited ICT diffusion in developing countries, particularly to rural or low-income areas.

ICT ADOPTION CHALLENGES

One of the largest hurdles facing many developing countries is the creation of a regulatory regime that is politically independent and a privatized monopoly operator that does not hamper competition. The creation of a regulatory agency and the privatization process are the foundation for all other ICT policies, including universal services programs, competitive market regulation, and ICT cluster development (Weingast, 1995). If these two foundational reforms are not completed or become too heavily skewed by the political process, the resulting market conditions will hamper ICT adoption dramatically. This was the case in Thailand, which saw its ICT adoption rates stall. But similar challenges have plagued the US, which has seen its broadband market become a global laggard thanks in part to the weaknesses of the Telecommunications Act of 1996.

Another significant challenge for developing countries is their lack of ICT wireline infrastructure, particularly in low-income areas that do not have the necessary networks to support rapid ICT

adoption. This lack of a network infrastructure can become self-reinforcing, as the poor infrastructure leads to poor services, and residents postpone adoption until utilization reaches a minimum threshold due to network effects (Indjikian, 2005). This can further dampen demand and starve networks of needed investment for improvements and expansion. Poor infrastructure can also translate into a lack of local technological expertise, limiting the ability of operators, firms, and residents to utilize ICTs. With low levels of domestic ICT expertise, developing countries may find it difficult to support a domestic ICT industry or the creation of local content. In turn, this can hamper ICT adoption by limiting the availability of technology, content, and applications tailored to the local environment.

FURTHER RESEARCH

Although this research covers a wide range of topics within the area of ICT diffusion, several opportunities still remain for additional study in the area of institutional development and ICT adoption in developing countries. This section offers some initial thoughts on topics and methods that could be utilized for additional study of these two national case studies.

Although it may certainly be time consuming, additional developing country case studies would be beneficial for this research area. One approach would be to complete another round of interviews in Asian countries that have a larger variance in their ICT adoption rates, policies, and institutions. This variance in ICT adoption would offer a larger range of economic development levels among the study countries, allowing for a more in-depth study of the influence of economic development on evolving ICT policies and institutions. In addition, because the study countries would still be in Asia, further research could be completed on the policy influence between countries

REFERENCES

Amsden, A. (1989). *Asia's Next Giant: South Korea and Late Industrialization*. New York: Oxford University Press.

Amsden, A. H., & Mourshed, M. (1997). Scientific publications, patents and technological capabilities in late-industrializing countries. *Technology Analysis and Strategic Management, 9*(3), 343–359. doi:10.1080/09537329708524289

Bassanini, A. (2002). Growth, Technology Change, and ICT Diffusion: Recent Evidence from OECD Countries. *Oxford Review of Economic Policy, 18*(3), 324–344. doi:10.1093/oxrep/18.3.324

Blomstrom, M., & Kokko, A. (1998). Foreign Investment as a Vehicle for International Technology Transfer. In Navaretti, G. B. (Eds.), *Creation and Transfer of Knowledge: Institutions and Incentives*.

Docktor, R. (2004). *Successful Global ICT Initiatives: Measuring Results Through an Analysis of Achieved Goals, Planning and Readiness Efforts, and Stakeholder Involvement*. Presentation to the Council for Excellence in Government.

Feinson, S. (2003 June). National Innovation Systems Overview and Country Cases. In Bozeman, B. (Eds.), *Knowledge Flows and Knowledge Collectives: Understanding The Role of Science and Technology Policies in Development. Synthesis Report on the Findings of a Project for the Global Inclusion Program of the Rockefeller Foundation*.

Frieden, R. (2005). Lessons from broadband development in Canada, Japan, Korea and the United States. *Telecommunications Policy, 29*, 595–613. doi:10.1016/j.telpol.2005.06.002

Galperin, H. (2005). Wireless Networks and Rural Development: Opportunities for Latin America. *Information Technologies and International Development, 2*(3), 47–56. doi:10.1162/1544752054782420

Gasmi, F., Laffont, J. J., & Sharkey, W. W. (2000). Competition, universal service and telecommunications policy in developing countries. *Information Economics and Policy, 12*, 221–248. doi:10.1016/S0167-6245(00)00016-0

Hossain, L. (2003). Is a formalized structure a necessary prerequisite for implementing national telecommunication plan developing and developed economies? *Technovation, 23*, 39–49. doi:10.1016/S0166-4972(01)00084-0

Indjikian, R., & Siegel, D. S. (2005). The impact of investment in IT on economic performance: implications for developing countries. *World Development, 33*, 681–700. doi:10.1016/j.worlddev.2005.01.004

Intarakumnerd, P. (2004 April). *Thailand's National Innovation System in Transition*. Presented at the First Asialics International Conference on Innovation Systems and Clusters in Asia: Challenges and Regional Integration, National Science and Technology Development Agency, Bangkok, Thailand.

James, J. (2003). *Bridging the Global Digital Divide*. Cheltenham, UK: Edward Elgar.

Jomo, K. S. (2003). Growth and Vulnerability Before and After the Asian Crisis: The Fallacy of the Universal Model. In Andersson, M., & Gunnarsson, C. (Eds.), *Development and structural change in Asia-Pacific: globalising miracles or end of a model?* (pp. 171–197). London: Routledge.

Jomo, K. S. (1997). *Southeast Asia's Misunderstood Miracle: Industrial Policy and Economic Development in Thailand, Malaysia, and Indonesia*. Boulder, CO: Westview.

Lallana, E. C. (2004). *An Overview of ICT Policies and e-Strategies of Select Asian Economies*. United Nations Development Programme-Asia Pacific Development Information Programme, Reed Elsevier India Private Limited.

Lee, C., & Chan-Olmsted, S. M. (2004). Competitive advantage of broadband Internet: a comparative study between South Korea and the United States. *Telecommunications Policy*, *28*, 649–677. doi:10.1016/j.telpol.2004.04.002

Levy, B., & Spiller, P. T. (1994). The Institutional Foundations of Regulatory Commitment: A Comparative Analysis of Telecommunications Regulation *Journal of Law, Economics and Organization.*

Levy, B., & Spiller, P. T. (1996). *Regulations, institutions, and commitment: Comparative studies in telecommunications*. London: Cambridge University Press.

Li, W., Qiang, C. Z.-W., & Xu, L. C. (2005). Regulatory Reforms in the Telecommunications Sector in Developing Countries: The Role of Democracy and Private Interests. *World Development*, *33*(8), 1307–1324. doi:10.1016/j.worlddev.2005.03.003

Lim, P. W. (2000 May). Path Dependence in Action: The Rise and Fall of the Korean Model of Economic Development. *Korea Development Institute.*

Luger, M. I., & Stewart, L. S., & Traxler, J. (2002 July). *Identifying Technology Infrastructure Needs in America's Distressed Communities: A Focus on Information and Communications Technology.* Report for the U.S. Economic Development Administration. Office of Economic Development Kenan Institute for Private Enterprise at the University of North Carolina at Chapel Hill.

Malaysian Communications and Multimedia Commission and Ministry of Energy, Water and Communications. (2006). *The National Broadband Plan: Enabling High Speed Broadband Under MyICMS 886.* Cyberjaya, Malaysia: Malaysian Communications and Multimedia Commission. Retrieved from http://www.mcmc.gov.my

Mariscal, J. (2005). Digital divide in a developing country. *Telecommunications Policy*, *29*, 409–428. doi:10.1016/j.telpol.2005.03.004

Nambiar, S. (2006, November). Enhancing Institutions and Improving Regulation: The Malaysian Case. *EABER Working Paper Series Paper No. 4.* Paper prepared for discussion at the Microeconomic Foundations of Economic Performance in East Asia Conference, Manila.

Ramasamy, B., Chakrabarty, A., & Cheah, M. (2004). Malaysia's leap into the future: an evaluation of the multimedia super corridor. *Technovation*, *24*, 871–883. doi:10.1016/S0166-4972(03)00049-X

Ranis, G. (1989, September). The Role of Institutions in Transition Growth: The East Asian Newly Industrializing Countries. *World Development*, *17*(9), 1443–1453. doi:10.1016/0305-750X(89)90085-5

Wallsten, S. (2002 February). *Does Sequencing Matter? Regulation and Privatization in Telecommunications Reforms.* World Bank Working Paper.

Weingast, B. (1995). The Economic Role of Political Institutions: Market-Preserving Federalism and Economic Development. *Journal of Law Economics and Organization*, *11*(1), 139–152.

Wilson, E. J. III, & Wong, K. (2003). African information revolution: a balance sheet. *Telecommunications Policy*, *27*, 155–177. doi:10.1016/S0308-5961(02)00097-6

Wong, P.-K. (2002). ICT production and diffusion in Asia: Digital dividends or digital divide? *Information Economics and Policy*, *14*, 167–187. doi:10.1016/S0167-6245(01)00065-8

World Bank. (2006). *World Development Indicators*. Washington, DC: IBRD, World Bank.

Yankee Group. (2007). *Asia Mobile Forecast 2007*. Boston, MA: Yankee Group.

Chapter 11
Business Models for Development:
The Global Capability Sourcing Model

Sajda Qureshi
University of Nebraska at Omaha, USA

Peter Keen
Keen Innovations, USA

Mehruz Kamal
University of Nebraska at Omaha, USA

ABSTRACT

Organizations are increasingly inter-connected as they source talent, goods and services from other organizations located in disparate parts of the world and enable social and economic development to take place. They seek new ways of creating value for themselves, customers and partners, increasingly operating outside and across traditional industry boundaries and definitions. These innovations have lead to a focus on business models as a fundamental statement of direction and identity as they enable development to take place. This chapter considers the fundamental tenets of the business model concept and ways in which value can be created for development efforts. The contribution of this chapter is the application of Global Capability Sourcing Model to enable businesses to compete globally. This chapter concludes with insights into the sustainability of business models for development.

INTRODUCTION

Development is improvement in the lives of people. The effects of information technology on development have been studied by assessing improvements in the lives of people in their communities, regions, countries or even groups of countries. This can be studied by investigating the social impacts on development of the technologies. The social concept of development suggests that people participate in improving their circumstances through the development of healthcare, education, environment and community services (Apthorpe 1999, Arce 2003, and Midgley 2003). Social development considers improvements in the lives of people through programs in healthcare, education, and the environment that are often

DOI: 10.4018/978-1-60566-388-3.ch011

implemented by governments. When governments make use of information and communication technologies to improve their services, they might also contribute social development. Some authors suggest that governments make policy based on discourse that has recourse to neat, easily available and powerfully constructed sets of institutional, legislative and financial resources (Apthorpe 1999, Midgley 2003). These policies are implemented to bring about social development. Social development activities are designed to raise living standards, increase local participation in development and address the needs of vulnerable and oppressed groups (Midgley 2003).

Economic development is a means of studying development that considers improvements in the lives of people through income generation, job creation, and other factors such as trade and migration. Theories of economic development try and predict the choices people make in order to improve the quality of their lives and offer tools that policy makers can use to balance the cyclical changes in economies. Development theorists such as Schumpeter (2002) offer empirical evidence of how economies can benefit from innovation, education and foreign investments. In particular the effects of ICT on economic growth have been studied by authors such as Avgerou (1998), Qiang et al (2003), Baliamoune Lutz (2003), Cecchini and Scott (2003), and Kottemann and Boyer-Wright (2009). It seems that while there is a relationship between ICT and growth in countries, the gains from ICTs are not always as expected. It seems that more open government policies can be conducive for the uptake and use of ICTs for economic and social development.

This suggests that current business models may not be suited helping businesses use ICTs for growth. In particular, when businesses grow using ICTs they generate income and opportunities for the people their communities and can potentially support social development. This chapter reviews business model thought and practice in terms of its contributions and illustrates how these may be used to support development efforts. The term "business model" is a recent addition to the management literature and needs to address the needs of businesses in developing regions. The aim of this chapter is to point towards an agenda for building such a base. Following an overview of key concepts underlying business models, this chapter highlights the basic principles upon which business models can be designed and provides an example of a business model that addresses these principles to support social and economic development. The implementation of business models influences the ways and degree to which organizations transform their structures to ensure the capabilities needed to move to capture value. The contribution of the chapter is in the insight it provides into the many applications of business models and their effects on social and economic development. It concludes with implications for research and practice.

CONCEPTS UNDERLYING BUSINESS MODELS

We examine business models from the perspective of necessary construct versus superfluous neologism. This requires filtering out the signals from a great deal of noise. As Hawkins states: "as the [dot com] bubble grew, the market filled up with books and articles about business models, ranging from the vaguely analytic to the *quasi* instructional.... .... The business model seemed to fill a niche even if no one could explain exactly what it was." (Hawkins, 2004, page 65). Even today, most work on business models is taxonomic and descriptive, classifying types of business model in lists, heavily derived from multiple case examples. Typical is Afuah and Tucci's eight categories: brokerage, advertising, intermediary, merchant, manufacturing, affiliate, community, subscription, and utility (Afuah and Tucci, 2000). Timmers' classification is very different: e-shop, e-mail, information services provider, e-auction, value-chain services provider, virtual community, third-party marketplace, value-chain integrator. (Timmer, 1999) Chesbrough classifies them in terms of their explicit reliance on "open" sources of ideas and information for innovation (Chees-brough, 2006) Mahajan's analysis of innovation in Africa views business models as the embodiment of entrepreneurial initiatives (Mahajan, 2009). Haaker et al adopt a four component taxonomy of organizational resources (Haaker, Faber and Bouwman, 2006) Ballon's framework reviews them as the (re)configuration of control and value parameters. None of these or other comprehensive taxonomic analyses are directly comparable. There is no established general classification, which means that there is as yet little theoretical base for business model research and application.

"Logic" and "value" are core words in the literature on business models. Basically, the emerging consensus is that a business model is a hypothesis (i.e., a model) of how to generate value in a customer-driven marketplace. Keen and Williams argue that three main forces of external change—deregulation/trade liberalization, technology as a coordination base, and modularity and standardization of interfaces—shift the nature of value generation, in many cases leading to commoditization, with value passing to the customer at the expense of the provider; this demands a business model shift for the firm to grow. (Keen and Williams, 2008) Such a shift is a highly focused "public" declaration intended to help identify and build relationships that are core to turning the model into reality. Magretta (2002) highlights the "narrative" element of business models: "The business model tells a logical story explaining who your customers are, what they value, and how you'll make money providing them that value." It is in this sense that we view a business model as a *hypothesis* of value creation, to be tested in the marketplace and often subject to public scrutiny particularly by investors. Hawkins (2004) makes the interesting point that a business model may become a product in

and of itself. Certainly, in the dot com era the business model was the selling point for most startups and it is very much the "brand" for such successful e-commerce firms as Amazon, eBay and Priceline. Keller et al suggest that there is a direct link between identity and branding as a "frame" that "signals to consumers the goal they can expect to achieve by using a brand." (Keller, Sternhal and Tybout, 2002)

The most parsimonious definition of business model is by Rappa (2002): it "spells out how the company makes money." Betz (2002) similarly states that it is "an abstraction of a business identifying how [it] profitably makes money." "A business model is a blend of three streams that are critical to the business. These include the value stream for the business partners and the buyers, the revenue stream, and the logistical stream." (Mahadevan, 2000). Linder and Cantrell, (2001) extend their own definition of a business model as "the organization's core logic for creating value" to its including within it: "the set of value propositions an organization offers to its stake-holders, along with the operating processes to deliver on these, arranged as a coherent system, that both relies on and builds assets, capabilities and relationships to build value."

There are several common themes running through these conceptions. The most distinctive is the focus on "value." When the factors affecting value generation (producer operating and capital investment costs and customer prices) remain stable or under the control of a protected economy, regulated industry or owner of a scarce resource, leading players will tend to protect their existing models, while new entrants must offer a new value base. This leads to what Keen and Williams describe as industry decomposition and convergence, illustrated by the twenty erosion of the established telecommunications establishment models, the emergence of innovators in mobile communications and the convergence of firms from many industries on the same customer target, creating what is loosely termed the digital media market: Google, Apple, Amazon, Vodafone, Face-book, Bharti (India), Hulu, Sony, and Comcast, to name just a few instances. If the dot coms were the stimulator of interest in and launching of the business model concept, digital media may be its fuller embodiment in sustained and massive industry decomposition/convergence, with the customer very much in control of the value calculus (Cairncross, 2001; Keen and Williams, 2008; Kaul et al, 2008). This means that any business model that can sustain social and economic development must have value to the customer.

The second theme underlying the standard conceptions of business models is that they all stress that a business model is a statement of the basic "logic" of the business; it is an abstraction of propositions, articulated as claims and intentions. In some regards, this intellectual base for business models contrasts usefully with the less rigorous conception of business vision that preceded it; both of these are intended to set the framework for strategies for market innovation and/or orga-nizational transformation. This relates to the third common theme: the separation of business model from business strategy and also from organiza-tional structure. The business model establishes the principles and axioms on which strategy is built; the distinction is between value generation, the potential enabled by the business model principles, and value capture, the realization of the potential. Strategy follows on from the business model and is targeted to achieve competitive differentiation. To some degree, the business model is the "what" of business innovation and strategy the "how." As a number of commentators observe, the two terms business model and strategy are often used interchangeably. This both weakens the value of the sharp logic of an effective business model and makes it a redundant concept if it is just a variant on strategy.

The separation of business model from strategy has far-reaching impacts. The most consequential is that the *logic* of value-generation is the core of a business model; the details of how to realize

that value are in the domain of strategy. Many of the dot com models were hypotheses of value-generation that may have looked accurate in the laboratory stage of the startup but were not sup-ported in the large-scale application of the model in the marketplace. These are often referred to as "broken" models. Others were perhaps valid hypotheses but were undermined by inattention to execution. Many commentators argue that too many companies and their investors saw their business model almost as self-implementing. Strategy and execution were ignored. An in-depth series of research studies of e-commerce retail-ing innovations in eight countries ranging from Australia to Hong Kong to Greece to Denmark to the United States, concludes that a clearly stated and understood business model is a prerequisite for success, but ultimate success of failure rests on the capability of the firm to customize both model and follow-on strategy to the dynamics of the market (Elliot, 2002). This suggests that there is a sharp distinction between model and strategy that may be characterized as innovation plus discipline.

BUSINESS MODELS FOR DEVELOPMENT

A business model should enable development to be undertaken if it enables communication and knowledge networking among a diverse set of stakeholders. There is a trend in the literature to suggest that that knowledge is communicative action and is needed if development efforts are to suceed. Richard Rorty captures its general trend in his phrase "the linguistic turn." (Rorty, 1991) Rather than defining knowledge in terms of infor-mation, the linguistic turn examines how language shapes "reality." Key thinkers in this regard who provide many new avenues of exploration for KM/IS include Habermas, who is increasingly cited in the field for his work on communicative rationality and the "public sphere" as a space of discourse that, in KM/IS terms, builds communities of practice (Habermas, 1989); Wittgenstein whose "meaning as use" contrasts strongly with the standard KM/IS conception of information as representation (Wittgenstein, 1958); Searle, whose speech act theory has directly led to promising lines of development in coordination technology (Searle, 1995); Keen, (1992) provides a discussion of the application of Searle's line of thought to software designed to coordinate business processes; and the postmodernists who challenge the conception of "objective" and absolute truth, unitary personal identities and "grand narratives". Postmodernists see a new world of simulacra and hyperreality (Baudrillard, 1994) marked by fragmentation of authority, commoditization of knowledge, and deep skepticism about official truths. In a world of constant change, we adopt multiple identities (including online persona in chart rooms and games) and mass media generates an "information" world of irony, pastiche, playfulness and magical realism. That is a far more accurate description of blogs than standard KM/IS conceptions of modernist rationality and objectivity in publishing.

The sharing and use of knowledge among diverse stakeholders is not straightforward. Qureshi and Keen (2005) suggest that in their everyday work, individuals distinguish between their "accountable" that is part of their professional identity and responsible and that needs to be well-articulated and shared, their "discretionary" knowledge that they share with trusted associates, and autonomous knowledge that is none of anyone else's business. They argue that organizations are most anxious to stimulate the sharing of discretionary knowledge but that to achieve this they need to separate the technology platforms and modes of invitation, access and use from those designed for sharing accountable knowledge. In a case study, they show that this separation can vanquish the "knowledge paradox" of all parties agree that knowledge-sharing and

collaboration are vital for innovation but most of them resisting doing so.

Given that knowledge networking is a challenge, operational tactics handle outsourcing as a make-buy, largely cost-based option. Commentators here draw heavily on transaction cost economics. The choice of in-house operations versus outsourcing fits well in that theory, trading off purchase costs and coordination costs. The business strategy level of analysis is more radical and often involves contracting for a services provider to take over a whole function, such as back office administration and data centers. The strategic emphasis here is often on core versus non-core activities. We present below a framework that may help companies in addressing the knowledge networking dilemma. It is a conceptual model of global sourcing of talent and capabilities, developed from a wide range of studies of e-commerce and international business. (Keen, 2004, 2004a; Williams and Keen, 2005).

One issue for research is the extent to which investment in ICT should now be built around bottom-up, localized initiatives aimed at collaborative knowledge networking rather than planned and implemented on a top-down, national basis. Knowledge networking brings into the digitally-enabled economy many individuals and communities that may not be ICT-adept and whose work in no way involves ICT. (Madon, 2000) similarly concludes that "effective participation in current globalization must be based on adaptation and learning.......", rather than on technology supply. Two simple and fairly typical instances of knowledge networking are quoted in Qureshi, Keen and Kamal, (2007):

Daniel Mashva heaves his sack of cabbages and sweet potatoes into a rickety shared taxi and travels nine hours under the scorching sun to the market in Johannesburg. By the time he arrives, half his tiny harvest is rotten and the 48-year-old father of five returns to his impoverished village just a few pennies richer. That was before new cell phone technology changed his life. Mashva now dials up to a virtual trading platform on his new high-tech phone and sells his produce direct from his small thatched hut on the fringe of the vast Kruger National Park. "I check the prices for the day on my phone and when it's a good price I sell," he told reporters from his village in the remote Northeast of South Africa. "I can even try to ask for a higher price if I see there are lots of buyers." Mashva is one of around 100 farmers in Makuleke testing cell phone technology that gives small rural farmers access to national markets via the Internet, putting them on a footing with bigger players and boosting profits by at least 30 percent." [Our emphasis added] Here, the mobile phone is the enabler of access to and use of a knowledge resource, the trading platform, which is an Internet portal.

The new technology has had a bigger impact on shopkeepers and tradesmen, who use it to keep in touch with suppliers and customers. "Before we got a signal here, I was doing five or six jobs a week," said electrician Isaac Kamanda. "Now I'm doing 20 or 30 jobs a week. Before, people had to call the landline, which was not at all that reliable. Maybe there would be an emergency, but customers couldn't reach me – they had to send somebody with a message." Here, the innovation is the ability of customers and providers to interact. That seems a trivial issue for anyone living in an advanced economy but it illustrates the extent to which coordination and communication are often more of an enabler to innovation than information.

These examples bring rural entrepreneurs and laborers into the wider economy. At the next level of aggregation, the urban complex has become the focal point for innovation via talent pools through policies aimed at building "cities of knowledge." In many instances, these initiatives are driven by the need to escape from being dependent on eroding "smokestack" industries with declining employment and consequent growing poverty traps. Keen

(2006) describes "hidden jewels", cities such as Jena, Germany, and Monterrey, Mexico, that are not as well-known or their companies as sought after as business "spokes" as Bangalore, Singapore, Shanghai or Silicon Valley but that offer valuable capabilities to company "hubs" across the world. Just ten years ago, it would be implausible to suggest that war-wrecked and economically lagging Eastern Europe would become a major growth area in engineering, IT and back offices.

In this way the business model conceptualizes this logic of value. The network-based model assumes a multiplicity of supplier/partner relationships and a dynamic interaction with customers. This demands a new perspective on value-creation, since obviously they must all gain some additional value for them to choose to be suppliers to or users of the value complex.[1] Parilini captures the issue: "The growing competitive pressures characterizing many sectors are forcing companies to adopt the perspective of their final customers in an attempt to what they consider to be key elements in a supply system and thus determine the value received." (Parolini, 1999, page 55.)

CREATING VALUE THROUGH BUSINESS MODELS FOR DEVELOPMENT

Roller and Waverman (2001) investigated economic growth of 21 OECD countries resulting from ICT investments. The findings from that study shows that the more people use ICT products, the more that those products will increase in value resulting from the phenomenon of network externalities. Castells (1999) argues that globalization leads to polarization, or in other words, a further division between the haves and have-nots. He suggests that in a global world, people must cooperate to raise living standards. He emphasizes that it is urgently necessary to reverse the downward spiral of exclusion and to use information and communication technologies to empower

Table 1. Principles of business model design

	Novelty	Efficiency	Complementarities	Lock-in
Schumpeterian analysis	High	Low	Low	Low
Value chain analysis	Medium	Medium	Medium	High
Strategic network theory	Medium	Medium	Medium	
Resource-based theory	Medium	Low	High	Medium
Transaction cost economics	Low	High	Low	Medium

humankind. Phillips et al. (2007) examine the practices of Zambian entrepreneurs and discovers that their primary difficulty of growing their businesses lies in the area of risk assessment. The entrepreneurs, she discovers, have been making poor decisions based on inadequate information obtained from informal sources. Her research suggests that training and information availability provide the keys to business expansion for microenterprises (Phillips et al. 2007). It is clear that value creation from the business models are needed to support such businesses.

Amit and Zott identify theoretical work on value creation that provides some inputs to business model thinking (Amit and Zott, 2001, page 511). These are value chain analysis, Schumpeterian innovation, Resource-based theory, Strategic network theory, and Transaction cost economics. They map these against four design schemes, as shown below (our table is adapted from the original) that the researchers identify from their empirical surveys: efficiency, innovation, complementarities (the firm's bundling of capabilities and resources and its bundling of products and services) and customer lock-in. The table entries describe the degree to which the different theoretical frameworks view each of the design schemes as important for value creation. Schumpeter's "creative destruction", for instance, views innovation as a high value generator. Transaction cost economics, which has been the underlying intellectual underpinning of many brokerage, value-adding intermediary and

business-to-business initiatives, regards innovation as of low importance.

The above analysis points to Efficiency and Innovation as the two main distinguishing features of successful business models. This table suggests that designers will not gain much practical guidance from strategic theory. The focus on Efficiency leads to transaction cost economics as a rich source of guidelines, but at the expense of Innovation. Schumpeterian innovation points to the exactly the opposite path for design. It is a testable proposition that any business model that can successfully combine the four design themes does not need theory and will not fit into existing theory. In this sense, an agenda for study is the role of truly innovative business models in theory-making.

"Value" in this context means value to the company as the goal, with that value depending on consumer satisfaction. Cost, market share and price were the main variables of value management. Relationships with suppliers were very much based on bargaining and contracts, with power customers playing off suppliers and vice versa. A well-documented analysis of Wal-Mart describes its dominance of its supply chain (Fishman, 2008). Basically, value generation in this context was a battle for market share, reliance on advantages of scale, access to investment capital, tight cost management, protection of brands, distribution and intellectual property. Value is captured through revenue growth and protection of operating margins. It is the stereotype of "Big Business."

The primacy of this perspective in which the customer plays a relatively passive role as a buyer and suppliers are just suppliers is apparent in Porter's influential value chain framework. (See Porter 1994) for his own synthesis of the evolution of his thinking on competitive strategy, which aimed at fusing what he describes as the two main and contrasting views of strategy, one that emphasizes organizational differentiation via what is now termed core competencies and one where "competitive advantage was defined by a single variable: cost.") Porter's own conclusion is that strategy "must begin by declaring a clear goal for the enterprise: in my view, this should be superior, long-term return on investment." (Porter, 1994, page 251). Out of this perception came his five forces of industry model, followed by the value chain. One of Porter's most central tenets hints at one reason for the emergence of business model conceptualization: "the fundamental unit of analysis for developing strategy is the industry." (Porter, 1994, page 290).

One of the most striking examples of innovation through an unlikely business model is India's Bharti Airtel offering the lowest prices for mobile phone service in the world with its market being the rural poor who cannot the services and subscriptions that are the value-generating base for its established competitors, most obviously Reliance, the old government telecommunications monopoly. (Bharti is as yet not at all analyzed in depth in available research on business models, but is very prominent in business publications and several detailed Harvard Business School cases. Keen and Williams provide summary data on mobile banking, yet another customer-creating value generator that amounts to a potential mkyt of 5 billion people and $3 trillion a year of annual remittances. Vodafone, Citicorp and mCheck are global companies that have joined with such organizations as Grameen Microfinance and MFI, Afghanistan's leading microfinance institution (MFI); Afghanistan is rapidly expanding in its mbanking operations via Roshan Bank, with sub-

stantial social and economic impacts in a nation that has under 50,000 phone lines but 5 million mobile phones. Note that all the examples in the above paragraph do not fit into the industry model: Porter's assertion that the fundamental unit of analysis for developing strategy is the industry needs complementing by one that states that the unit for analysis is the customer in a world of choices and hence value options.

THE GLOBAL CAPABILITY SOURCING MODEL

A way of bridging the gap between business model and strategy is to recognize that an effective business model must first be supported by effective strategy and over time become embedded in the strategy. McDonald's, Wal-Mart, FedEx, Cisco and Dell were built on their founder's insights that were crystallized in what was clearly a business model (Michael Dell appears to be one of the earliest chief executives to use the term). Now the model is still the reference point for strategic planning but just that: a reminder of the founding principles – and the logic of value-generation.

This suggests that, as Magretta states, there is a public narrative element to business models. (Magretta, 2002) and that they serve a different purpose than a comparable statement of strategy. The audience for these narratives is often the investment community, who tear apart the logic of the model and the detailed economic justification of its value-generation. In other instances, it is the base for building a culture and for getting everyone on the same page. This suggests that there may be a fruitful link in assessing the role of business models in terms of stories being the "life-blood" of an organization. (Mitroff and Kilmann, 1975). Boje (1991) states that organizations are essentially story-telling systems. Siehl and Martin (1982) argue that stories are key indicators of underlying cultures and that socialized members of an organization are knowledgeable about its main stories. Stories are scripts in organizational settings (Martin, 1982). Quinn and McGrath view stories as part of the transformation of organizational cultures. (Quinn and McGrath, 1985).

We present below a framework that may help companies to enter into emerging markets. It is a conceptual model of global sourcing of talent and capabilities, developed from a wide range of studies of e-commerce and international business. (Keen 2004, 2004a; Earle and Keen, 2000; Keen and Williams, 2005, 2008). We use it here to capture the key link in moving from the business model as a hypothesis of how to generate value to the strategic and operational practicalities of value-capture. Value demands capabilities. Capabilities must be sourced either through in-house resources or outside relationships that range from traditional supplier contracts to tight collaborations.

A general trend in business model designs is towards value webs of what amounts to "co-sourcing" rather than "outsourcing." To take one just one example, Apple brands its iPhone but does not make it; manufacturing and many elements of technical design are handled by HTC, the Taiwanese technology leader in mobile phones. By finally opening up its proprietary operating system to third party designers, Apple gains a growing range—tens of thousands—of applications (for games, search, personal productivity, location srevs, etc.) that it sells through its App Store. It does not offer mobile communications service; that is provided on a country by country basis, with AT&T its US partner and Softbank its Japanese one; Vodafone provides iPhone service in ten countries, including India. This is an extraordinary complex of capabilities. Apple brings design. HTC provides the handset technology. AT&T provides the network and billing, subsidizing the purchase price of the iPhone in the hopes of generating a new revenue stream in the mobile data communications market, which has been a large profit drain for a decade. Apple benefits from this subsidy, of course, and so does the customer if but only if the purchase price is the main measure of value rather than total cost per year. App developers gain access to a huge market at no cost to Apple. Product design, network infrastructure, manufacturing, software development are all essential capabilities for Apple's business model value creation and capture. No one company in the world has all of these capabilities and many are notorious for their weaknesses in trying to add them. Apple was once in the telecommunications business; veterans will recall with nostalgia it's noted "zip clouds" that brought corporate networks to a contemplative halt. AT&T has not stood out as an innovator.

Bringing these capabilities together is very different from outsourcing them. Any focus on operational tactics treats outsourcing as a make-buy, largely cost-based option. Commentators here draw heavily on transaction cost economics. The choice of in-house operations versus outsourcing fits well in that theory, trading off purchase costs and coordination costs. The business strategy level of analysis is more radical and often involves contracting for a service provider to take over a whole function, such as back office administration and data centers. The strategic emphasis here is often on core versus non-core activities. In both instances the outsourced area of activity is not seen an integral to the business model and to value-building rather than cost reduction and process streamlining.

Combine all these factors – the problem of costs and the China Price plus the opportunity opened up by coordination technology to move the work to where the people are instead of the other way round, the eBig supply of skills, a large global pool of well-educated labor, and the result is a new segmentation of global business sources of capabilities, as shown in the figure 1.

The cells of this matrix enable a better understanding to be developed of the social and economic implications of entering new markets. This matrix offers guidance in developing business models for succeeding in emerging economies while avoiding the traps of crisis creators in highly

Figure 1. Global capability sourcing

Labor Cost Burden

	Low	High
Premium	**1.** Specialist Services	**4.** Creative Economy
Commodity	**2.** Assembly Economy	**3.** Outsourcing Crisis Generator

Skills

commoditized, high cost markets. The following sub-sections address each of the quadrants in turn and provide insight into how businesses can position themselves in the quadrant of their choice.

1. Specialist services offer premium skills at (for now at least) a low cost burden. Engineering, research, architectural design, electronic records management, computer systems development and operations, drug testing, telemarketing….. The list grows. Cost is obviously a key factor here but it is the quality at low cost that is the main attraction. Many specialist services firms combine low labor costs with low overhead because of their specialization. Flextronics, for instance, is the contract manufacturer whose production is larger than the sales for most of the consumer electronics and computer hardware brands for whom it is the manufacturer, assembler and in many instances design partner. Its overhead is in the 2-3 percent range versus the more typical 15-20 percent for its customers. Such firms take on much of the business risk of their clients, converting the fixed costs of their in-house manufacturing to a variable cost pay-as-you-go.

2. The assembly economy is the sad area of lesser developed countries. Here, low cost workers handle commodity tasks. Many of the widely-reported abuses of workers in the textile and apparel industry reflect the fact that this segment is price-based with no premium offer to add. Every month, there is a buyer looking to cut prices and a factory having to do so to stay in business. It is interesting to note how China, which has been the main beneficiary of the World Trade Organization's removal of all tariffs on apparel goods for its members, has responded to the threat of new restrictions being imposed on it after its exports to the U.S. increased by as much as 1,000 percent in some categories in the first three months of the new regime. It is moving out of the bottom end of the market – the $3 t-shirt and bundle of six pairs of socks for $2. They will leave that to the low cost assembly economy of such countries as Bangladesh and El Salvador. China's edge is quality and education, not just cost.

3. The outsourcing crisis creator is the sad area of many developed countries: high labor cost burdens for commodity skills applied to commodity tasks. A commodity task may

be defined as one that can be learnt in weeks and that is a strong candidate for automation: back office administration is the obvious example, along with routine telemarketing, machine-tending and customer phone service. These are jobs that are increasingly also candidates for contract- and price-based outsourcing to specialist services, wherever those may be located. It is distressing to many IT professionals to hear much of their own work described as "commodity" in nature but many activities are just that. They can be well-handled by educated foreigners who often earn one tenth the amount they do. Where the labor burden is high, these jobs will be moved and new ones not created to replace them. Germany, for instance, has not generated a net increase in manufacturing workers in over a decade.

4. The fourth quadrant is the Creative Economy, our term that parallels the concept of the Creative Class (Florida, 2002). Florida claims that in cities and regions of the U.S. that are dominated by design companies, researchers, the arts, higher education, media firms and other creative communities, earnings are around 35 percent higher than the average. The corollary of this is that the only way a company can escape the commodity trap of eroding margins, the China Price and the outsourcing crisis creator is to be part of the Creative Economy: design, invention, innovation and skilled customer relationships and experience-building. That is how high labor cost burden areas can maintain their standard of pay and living. The alternative is to narrow down the business model and focus on creating roles as specialized services as part of a value complex. Maga Steyr is part of BMW's value complex or value web, for instance. (We prefer the term complex because such supply chains as, say, that of Dell involve multiple procurement, production, distribution and service webs.)

The Creative Economy is closely tied to the other cells, especially specialized services. Apple, for example, is a design company not a consumer electronics manufacturer that co-sources and outsources many functions. HP takes this to an extreme with its printers, by far the most profitable of all its products. HP neither makes nor repairs its printers. Contract manufacturers make them and UPS picks them up and services them in UPS warehouses.

The GCS framework is evocative in its implications for business model versus strategy. If our analysis is correct, many firms will soon find that their existing model is not sustainable in the longer-term. Many are stuck in Cell 3 – the outsourcing crisis creator – and, as suppliers, vulnerable to the specialist services innovators. They are vulnerable as producers to commoditization. They are in a value-eroding not value-generating position. The question that the framework raises is what role does a particular company most effectively play in the global sourcing economy? Many of the most effective business models of the past two decades have been ones where a company builds a distinctive role in an expanding company/customer/business partner complex, often by surrounding a commodity transaction with value-adding services. UPS is one example of surrounding the basic package delivery with third party logistical services that include repairs, financing, international customs and payments, and many others. Consumer electronic and cell phone manufacturers are extending their value web roles by allowing 60% of their products to be made by third parties.

SUMMARY AND CONCLUSION

Sustainability of these models depends upon their applications. New technologies have strengthened our ability to develop new solutions. For example mobile communications technologies have provided people with addresses and network of social active support. In an African village a number of people can be drawn upon for support when making payments through the cell phone. According to the World Bank, sustainable development entails the simultaneous achievement of economic (growth, equity and efficiency), social (empowerment, participation, social mobility, social cohesion, cultural identity and institutional development) and ecological objectives (ecosystem integrity, carrying capacity, biodiversity and protection of global commons) (Vargas 2000).

The sustainability of business models depends upon the simultaneous achievement of these economic and social goals. Regardless of the specific applicability of the GCS framework, it highlights the major difference between viewing sourcing as a tactical matter and that of developing strategies that address the social and economic needs of the businesses. The choice of perspective is a choice of transformation target and opportunity: tactically transform selected operations costs, strategically improve overall company efficiency, or redefine identity, roles and value complex/web. This choice of transformation response has profound implications for the structure of organizations. Modern businesses are increasingly sourcing processes to other organizations, often located in developing parts of the world. The concept of the value web has come to denote a demand-driven organization that re-configures its business partners to adapt to changes in customer demand and/or economic conditions. This nonlinear form of organization needs to be able to coordinate increasingly dispersed processes, while continuing to create value.

REFERENCES

Abraham, R. (2007). Mobile Phones and Economic Development: Evidence from the Fishing Industry in India. *Information and Technologies and International Development, 4*(1).

Afuah, A., & Tucci, C. (2001). *Internet Business Models and Strategies*. Boston: McGraw-Hill Irwin.

Amit, R., & Zott, C. (2001). Value Creation in E-Business. *Strategic Management Journal, 22*, 493–520. doi:10.1002/smj.187

Apthorpe, R. (1999). Development Studies and Policy Studies: In the Short Run We are All Dead. *Journal of International Development, 11*(4). doi:10.1002/(SICI)1099-1328(199906)11:4<535::AID-JID603>3.0.CO;2-U

Arce, A. (2003). Re-approaching Social Development: A Field of Action between Social Life and Policy Processes. *Journal of International Development, 15*(7). doi:10.1002/jid.1039

Avgerou, C. (1998). How can IT Enable Economic Growth in developing Countries? *Journal of Information Technology for Development, 8*(1).

Baliamoune-Lutz, M. (2003). An analysis of the determinants and effects of ICT diffusion in developing countries. *Information Technology for Development, 10*(3), 151–170. doi:10.1002/itdj.1590100303

Baudrillard, J. (1994). *Simulacra and Simulation* (Glaser, S. F., Trans.). Ann Arbor, MI: University of Michigan Press.

Betz, F. (2002). Strategic Business Models. *Engineering Management Journal, 14*(1), 21–34.

Boje, D. (1991). The Storytelling Organization: A Study Of Story Performance In An Office-Supply Firm. *Administrative Science Quarterly, 36*, 106–126. doi:10.2307/2393432

Cairncross, F. (2001). *The Death of Distance*. Cambridge, MA: Harvard Business School Press.

Castells, M. (2004). The Information Age Economy, Society and Culture: *Vol. 1. The Rise of the Network Society*. Oxford, UK: Blackwell.

Cecchini, S., & Scott, C. (2003). Can information and communications technology applications contribute to poverty reduction? Lessons from rural India. *Information Technology for Development*, *10*(2), 73–85. doi:10.1002/itdj.1590100203

Chesbrough, H. (2006). *Open Business Models*. Cambridge, MA: Harvard Business School Press.

Davidow, W., & Malone, M. (1992). *The Virtual Corporation: Structuring and Revitalizing the Corporation for the 21st Century*. New York: HarperBusiness.

Earle, N., & Keen, P. (2000). *From. Com to. Profit: Inventing Business Models That Deliver Profit And Value*. San Francisco: Jossey-Bass.

Elliott, S. (Ed.). (2002). *Electronic Commerce B2C Strategies and Models*. Chichester: John Wiley.

Fishman, C. (2008). *The Wal-Mart Effect*. New York: Penguin Press.

Florida, R. (2002). *The Rise of the Creative Class*. New York: Basic Books.

Haaker, T. E. F., & Bouwman, H. (2006). Balancing Customer and Network Value in Business Models for Mobile Services. *International Journal of Mobile Communications*.

Habermas, J. (1989). *The Structural Transformation of the Public Sphere: An inquiry into a category of Bourgeois Society*. Cambridge, MA: MIT Press.

Hawkins, R. (2004). Looking Beyond The Dot Com Bubble: Exploring The Form And Function Of Business Models In The Electronic Marketplace. In B. Preisel, H. Bouwman & C. Steinfeld (Eds.), E-Life After The Dot Com Bust. Heidelberg, Germany: Physica-Varlag.

Kaul, S., Ali, F., Janikiram, S., & Wattenstrom, B. (2008). *Business Models for Sustainable Telecommunications Growth in Developing Countries*. Oxford, UK: Wiley-Blackwell. doi:10.1002/9780470987759

Kavajecz, K., & Keim, D. (2003). *Packaging Liquidity: Blind Auctions and Transaction Cost Efficiencies*. Wharton School working paper reprints.

Keen, P. (2004). *A Manifesto for Electronic Commerce*. Presented at Bled Electronic Conference.

Keen, P. (2004). Building New Generation E-Business: Exploiting the Opportunities of Today. In Preisel, B., Bouwman, H., & Steinfeld, C. (Eds.), *E-Life After The Dot Com Bust*. Heidelberg: Physica-Varlag.

Keen, P., & Sol, H. (2005). *Coordination by Design: Escaping the Commodity Trap*.

Keen, P., & Williams, R. (2005). Is Industry Thinking Inhibiting Value Creation? Paper to be presented at ICE2005 conference, Xi'an, China.

Keen, P., & Williams, R. (2008). *The Innovation Path: Connecting Business Model Opportunities with Value-Creating Capabilities*.

Keller, K., Sternhal, B., & Tybout, A. (2002 September). Three Questions You Need To Ask About Your Brand. *Harvard Business Review*.

Kottemann, J. E., & Boyer-Wright, K. M. (2009). Human resource development, domains of information technology use, and levels of economic prosperity. *Information Technology for Development*, *15*(1), 32–42. doi:10.1002/itdj.20114

Linder, J., & Cantrell, S. (2001). *What Makes a Good Business Model, Anyway?* Madon, S. (2000). The Internet and Socio-economic Development: Exploring the Interaction. *Information Technology & People, 13*(2).

Magretta, J. (2002). *Why Business Models Matter*. Harvard Business Review.

Mahadevan, B. (2000). Business Models for Internet-based E-commerce. *California Management Review, 42*(4), 55–69.

Mahajan, V. (2009). *Africa Rising*. Upper Saddle River, NJ: Wharton Publishing.

Martin, J. (1982). Stories As Scripts In Organizational Settings. In A. Hasdorf & A. Isen (Eds.), Cognitive Social Psychology. New York: Elsevier-North Holland.

McCaney, K. (2000). Reverse Auction. *Government Computer News, 19*(13), 1–3.

Midgley, J. (2003). Social Development: The Intellectual heritage. *Journal of International Development, 15*(7). doi:10.1002/jid.1038

Mitroff, I., & Kilmann, R. (1975, July). Stories Managers Tell: A New Tool For Organizational Problem Solving. *Management Review*, 18–28.

Parolini, C. (1999). *The Value Net: A Tool for Competitive Advantage*. New York: John Wiley.

Phillips, C., & Bhatia-Panthaki, S. (2007, August). Enterprise development in Zambia: reflections on the missing middle. *Journal of International Development, 19*(6), 793. doi:10.1002/jid.1402

Porter, M. (1994). From Strategy to Advantage: The Evolving Competitive Paradigm. In Duffy, P. (Ed.), *The Relevance of a Decade*. Cambridge, MA: Harvard Business School Press.

Qiang, C. Z., Clarke, G. R., & Halewood, N. (2006). The Role of ICT. In *Doing Business Information and Communications for Development—Global Trends and Policies*. Washington, DC: World Bank.

Quinn, R. E., & McGrath, M. R. (1985). The Transformation of Organizational Cultures: A Competing Values Perspective. In Frost, R., Moore, L. F., Louis, M. R., Lundberg, C. C., & Martin, J. (Eds.), *Organizational Culture* (pp. 315–334). Beverley Hills, CA: Sage.

Qureshi, Q., Keen, P., & Kamal, M. (2007). Knowledge Networking for Development: Building Bridges across the Digital Divide. In *Proceedings of the 40th Annual Hawaii International Conference on System Sciences (HICSS-40)*, Waikoloa, Hawaii.

Qureshi, S., & Keen, P. (2005). Activating Knowledge through Electronic Collaboration: Vanquishing the Knowledge Paradox. *IEEE Transactions on Professional Communication, 48*(1). doi:10.1109/TPC.2004.843296

Rappa, M. (n.d.). *Managing the Digital Enterprise, Web site courseware*. Retrieved from http://www/digitalenterprise.organization/models/models.html

Röller, L., & Waverman, L. (2001). Telecommunications Infrastructure and Economic Development: A Simultaneous Approach. *The American Economic Review, 91*(4), 909–923.

Romer, P. (1998). Innovation: The New Pump of Growth. *Blueprint: Ideas for a New Century*.

Rorty, R. (1991). *Objectivism, Relativism, and Truth: Philosophical Papers (Vol. 1)*. Cambridge, UK: Cambridge University Press.

Schumpeter, J. A. (2002). The economy as a whole: Seventh chapter of The Theory of Economic Development. *Industry and Innovation, 9*(1/2), 93–145.

Searle, J. R. (1995). *The Construction of Social Reality*. New York: Simon and Schuster.

Siehl, C., & Martin, J. (1982). *Learning Organizational Culture*. Research Paper 654, Stanford Graduate School of Business.

Tapscott, D., & Caston, A. (1993). *Paradigm Shift: The New Promise of Information Technology*. Boston: McGraw-Hill Irwin.

Timmers, P. (1999). *Electronic Commerce Strategies and Models for Business-to-business Trading*. Chichester: John Wiley.

Vargas, C. M. (2000). Community development and micro-enterprises: fostering sustainable development. *Sustainable Development, 8*(1), 11. doi:10.1002/(SICI)1099-1719(200002)8:1<11::AID-SD119>3.0.CO;2-7 von Mises, L. (1998). National Economy: Human Action. Auburn, AL.: Von Mises Institute. (Original manuscript published in 1949).

Wittgenstein, L. (1958). *The Blue Book*. New York: Harper.

ENDNOTE

[1] Value complex is Keen and Sol's term (2005). It views business increasingly as open systems comprised of a mix of chains and webs. A "manufacturer" like Dell is linked to UPS's value web, specialist firms' value chains, large business customers each with their own internal networks, and consumers.

Chapter 12
Citizens' Readiness for E–Government in Developing Countries (CREG)

Hany Abdelghaffar
Middlesex University, UK

ABSTRACT

Many developing countries are facing difficulties in applying successful electronic government (e-government) projects. A major part of these difficulties that they are not used by citizens due to the lack of appropriate ICT infrastructure that support e-government services; in addition to the existence of a small percentage of citizens who are able to deal with such technology. This chapter introduces an empirical research that closely investigates the e-government weaknesses in developing countries from two major perspectives: e-readiness and trust. The research proposes a model based on e-readiness assessments and relevant literature that investigates the impact of citizens' readiness for e-government (CREG) on e-government success within developing countries. The model was tested on the Egyptian e-government project as a sample of developing countries. The research findings confirmed the importance of the CREG model to achieve successful e-government projects in developing countries.

INTRODUCTION

E-government could simply defined as "the use of information and communication technologies (ICT) in improving the activities and services of government" (Heeks, 2004). Its remarkable benefits encouraged most governments in both developed and developing countries to launch e-government projects (Liikanen, 2003). However,

few of them have succeeded in achieving their set targets. In developing countries, Heeks (2003a) reports in his survey on 40 e-government projects that 35% totally failed as they were terminated or never used by users, 50% partially failed to achieve their goals and only 15% succeeded. Furthermore, the failure rate of e-government projects worldwide is identified by Gartner Group (2002) as 60%. The cost of failed e-government projects is high, including not only tangible costs such as wasted project expenditure and employee time,

DOI: 10.4018/978-1-60566-388-3.ch012

but also intangible costs such as loss of citizen trust (Heeks, 2003c).

In many cases, countries which achieved their set targets for e-government projects (Accenture, 2004; Blakemore & Lloyd, 2007) had high levels of e-readiness. Examples are Canada, USA and UK which got the highest ratings for e-readiness (DAI, 2003; EIU, 2006). Conversely, developing countries are typically reported as having low levels of success in e-government and low e-readiness ratings (DAI, 2003; UNDESA, 2005). This is because they were not electronically ready 'e-ready' in terms of ICT and had major problems with regard to their ICT fundamentals.

Many developing countries have accordingly launched strategic plans to enhance their e-readiness. These plans usually start with an essential step, undertaken in 188 countries (Bridges, 2005b), to measure their current e-readiness and decide how it could be improved. This was followed by developing action plans (Brown, 2002) to enhance their citizens' capabilities in ICT as well as enabling their businesses and governments to take the opportunities offered by ICT. Nevertheless, these plans did not lead to more successful e-government projects used by citizens. That is because the available e-readiness assessments are designed to assess countries' e-readiness in general without a specific focus on the issues that affect e-government projects in particular (Ojo et al, 2007). Furthermore, these assessments do not identify how their factors affect citizens' usage of e-government services.

The research investigates *citizens' readiness for e-government (CREG) in development countries,* the factors that influence it, and the extent to which it affects e-government success, form a primary focus of the research.

The research investigates the following question and its sub-questions:

RQ: What are the factors that affect citizens' readiness for e-government (CREG) in developing countries?

SQ1: How do factors from e-readiness assessments affect citizens' usage of e-government?

SQ2: How do trust factors affect citizens' usage of e-government?

SQ3: How do other factors affect citizens' usage of e-government?

SQ4: How do e-readiness assessments affect e-government projects?

SQ1 was introduced as a result of reviewing the current e-readiness assessments that show e-ready citizens who have appropriate ICT infrastructure and have computer and internet skills are using e-government services more than non e-ready citizens. Consequently, it becomes crucial to identify the e-readiness factors that citizens' in developing countries should have to be ready for e-government.

Identifying e-readiness factors was not sufficient to have successful e-government projects in developing countries. This is because there are some developing countries with reasonable levels of e-readiness but nevertheless with low levels of e-government success (Prattipati, 2003) which draws the attention to the existence of other factors. Reviewing the literature showed that many researchers report that citizens' trust in e-government is important in encouraging their usage of e-government services (Al-adawi et al, 2005; Gefen et al, 2002; Otto, 2003). Identifying these factors, based on the discussion about them in the published literature, forms a second and crucial category of factors influencing CREG and is thus presented in **SQ2**.

Conducting a pilot study with citizens showed the existence of other factors including awareness, perceptions of e-government services and non-resistance to use (or conversely resistance to use) that affect citizens' usage of e-government. These formed the third group of factors affecting CREG and are investigated in **SQ3**.

The pilot study with managers, on the other hand, demonstrates the importance of understanding how e-readiness assessments, which e-readiness factors are drawn from, influence government strategy on e-government as appears in **SQ4**.

All the identified CREG factors from e-readiness assessments, literature review and citizens' and managers' experiences (in the pilot study) formulated the proposed CREG model which is tested in the main study. The results which formed the final model will lead to more successful e-government projects in developing countries.

For clarity, the research focuses on e-government and not e-governance. Also, the research focuses on central government services provided for citizens (G2C).

BACKGROUND

A number of researchers have discussed factors that might help reducing failure rates and achieving higher success rates in e-government projects. Their focus is mainly related to how government could improve its own e-government processes (the supply side). In this context, many researchers, such as Papantoniou, et al (2001), Cohen and Eimicke (2002), Burn and Robins (2003), Hackney and Jones (2002) and Reffat (2003) agree on the importance of change management as a success factor for e-government. Oberer (2002) adds that the changes in organizational conditions should include administrative measures for adapting to the new e-government process.

Although there are a number of approaches that focus on how government could improve its own e-government processes (the supply side) to achieve successful e-government projects, few researchers have studied the factors that affect citizens' usage of e-government (demand side). Bélanger and Carter (2006), and Choudrie and Dwidedi (2005) conducted an empirical study to define the impact of the digital divide on e-government in developed countries only.

From the government viewpoint (the viewpoint taken by most researchers), e-government

success factors may be partitioned into internal (government-related) and external (for instance, society and the technology environment). Huijboom and Hoogwout (2004) emphasize the importance of taking external factors into account in the development of e-government projects. The main problem of external factors is that government has less control over them (Garner, 1986). Both society (citizens) and the technology environment need to be e-ready, otherwise there is a high risk of e-government failure.

The few studies that discuss the impact of e-readiness on citizens' usage of e-government take into account relatively few e-readiness factors, and omit consideration of other citizen-related factors found in the large number of assessments that attempt to rate or rank the e-readiness of sets of countries (Bélanger & Carter, 2006; Choudrie & Dwidedi, 2005). Further, these studies address developed rather than developing countries. This research aims to fill this gap by identifying the factors that may influence citizens to be ready for e-government (CREG) and to use it.

E-GOVERNMENT, E-READINESS AND TRUST

1. E-Readiness Assessments

As a result of the lack of basic ICT provision in developing countries (Bhatnagar & Vyas, 2001; Ndou, 2004; InfoDev, 2002; UNDESA, 2004), which might cause problems for e-government and other internet-based projects, many countries have been measuring their e-readiness using international e-readiness assessments that have predefined criteria (Bridges, 2005a; GeoSINC, 2002). Although e-readiness assessments are important as an initial step towards having a more e-ready society that is able to benefit from e-government projects, these assessments present various problems that might have a negative effect on countries' plans.

One problem is the lack of agreement on identifying what e-readiness mearuse and how. This could clearly proved by looking for the various in e-readiness definitions. According to the Centre of International Development at Harvard University (CID), which focuses on measuring the networked world, e-readiness is "the degree to which a community is prepared to participate in the Networked World" (CID, 2003). On the other hand, The CSPP (1998) defines an 'e-ready' community as "the one that has high-speed access in a competitive market; with constant access and application of ICTs in schools, government offices, businesses, healthcare facilities and homes; user privacy and online security; and government policies which are favourable to promoting connectedness and use of the Network."

Another problem is the existence of many organizations providing varied methods of assessment. These assessments have different objectives and goals for what they measure. McConnell International (2000), for instance, assesses the national economy's e-readiness to participate in the global digital economy while Asian Pacific Economic Cooperation (APEC), on the other hand, provides an assessment of e-commerce readiness and what should be focused on to improve it (APEC, 2000).

Solutions are provided by different researchers and organisations for overcoming this problem by having a taxonomy for e-readiness assessments. A classification for assessments might assist policy makers to have a clearer vision of which assessment is appropriate to achieve a country's goals (Bridges, 2005a). GeoSINC (2002) suggests an alternative approach to the problem of assessment diversity, by using combinations of different assessments, because no single assessment covers all criteria. The difficulty remains, however, of the extent to which one assessment may fit with one or more others.

A further problem arises from the existence of assessments for a single country by a number of different organisations. This problem leads to have conflicting figures for the same country.

According to Bridges (2005b), 69 countries have been assessed more than ten times by different organisations (such as Egypt, South Africa and China). Another 68 countries have been assessed between five and ten times by different organizations. Other countries (such as North Korea and Nauru) have not been assessed at all. Accordingly, government policy makers would have to choose between conflicting figures to decide their action plan, which could give rise to problems (Abdelghaffar & Bakry, 2005; Bakry, 2003).

Each assessment organization uses its own set of assessment criteria, depending on its assessment objectives, and these criteria vary between assessment organizations (Bridges, 2005a). Furthermore, even where two or more organizations apparently use the same criterion, they may use different sets of variables to measure it. For example, the *access* criterion consists of bandwidth, industry diversity, export controls and credit card regulation in the APEC assessment (2000), while in the CID assessment (2003) it consists of information structure, internet availability, internet affordability, network speed and quality, hardware and software, and service and support.

Not only this, but also, defining parameters is static in terms of neglecting the current situation for each country (Mwangi, 2006). Further, the definition of parameters is static and may neglect important differences between countries or in a single country over time (Mwangi, 2006). For example, assessments may not consider the distribution of ages in a population. In Egypt, 33.4% of the population is under fifteen and are therefore not in the work force (Gronlund et al, 2005), so that it is misleading to compare the number of personal computers per thousand population in Egypt with the number per thousand in a country with a substantially older population.

The assessments discussed so far measure e-readiness in general but not the more specific readiness for e-government (Ojo et al, 2007). There are a small number of other assessments that specifically address e-government readiness,

Figure 1. Proposed CREG model

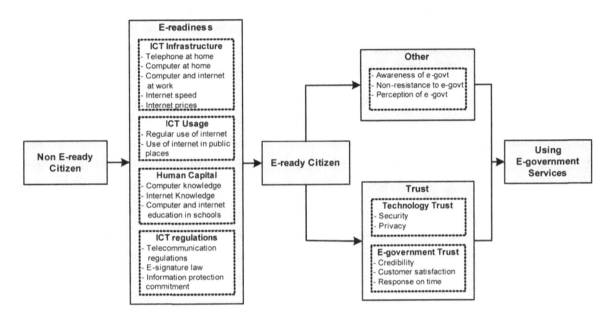

but again their different objectives and assessment criteria mean that there is no agreement between them on what should be measured.

E-Readiness Factors in CREG

Reviewing all the available assessments (28 assessments) for both e-readiness in general and e-government readiness in particular, despite the differences that have been discussed, it is possible to identify four major factors that occur pervasively. The four group factors and their sub-factors that contribute to CREG are as follows (Figure 1).

- **ICT infrastructure** mainly relates to the elements of ICT infrastructure that need to be available to citizens if they are to use e-government services. It includes the following sub-factors: telephone at home, computer at home, computer and internet at work, internet speed and prices.
- **Human capital** relates to citizens' education and knowledge on how to use computers and the internet. It includes the fol-

lowing sub-factors: computer and internet knowledge and computer and internet education in schools.
- **ICT usage** reflects how citizens use computers and the internet in their daily lives. It includes the following sub-factors: regular use of internet and use of internet in public places.
- **ICT regulations** relate to legislative provisions that affect the use of e-government services. It includes the following sub-factors: telecommunication regulations, e-signature and information protection commitment.

The existence of these factors helps to move citizens from being non e-ready to be e-ready citizens and be able to use e-government services.

2. E-Government and Trust Issues

Although the previous e-readiness factors are important for e-government success, they need to be combined with other trust factors to overcome the problem of the low level of usage for e-government services (Prattipati, 2003).

Several researchers have identified some factors that might help to increase citizens' trust in e-government. Thomas (1998) identified personal characteristic such as age and gender as a significant factor that affects trust in e-government. Parent et al (2004) mention that citizens' past experience affects their trust in e-government. For example, if citizens' experience of electronic transactions is negative, they would probably be less willing to use e-government to conduct transactions.

Srivastava and Teo (2005) who studied e-government in Singapore, confirmed that trust in both technology and government are major factors in citizens' adoption of e-government. These findings contradict Carter and Belanger (2004) study in the United States that found trust in government is not a significant factor in determining trust in e-government. The basis for their argument is that, driving licences (the example they use) must be requested from government regardless of the degree of trust in it. The issue of internet trust was in any case largely insignificant for their research as their users were mainly university students using the internet regularly anyway.

Trust Factors in CREG

Looking to the e-government definition might help to identify which factors are important for CREG. As e-government uses *ICT* to improve *government* services and deliver them over the internet, the two key components – ICT and government – provide the basis for factors affecting trust in e-government. If there is a lack of trust in either or both of these issues, it could negatively affect e-government usage (Abdelghaffar & Kamel, 2006).

ICT trust is mainly related to *technology trust* which consists of **(1)** security and **(2)** privacy as identified by many researchers as issues influenc-

ing citizens' trust in technology (InfoDev, 2002; Lau, 2004; OECD, 2003; Wimmer & Bredow, 2002).

- *Security* is important on different levels of information transmission (NECCC, 2001) and data storage (Wimmer & Bredow, 2002; Yang et al, 2005). If there is a perceived lack of either in the chain between citizens' points of access – which may be at home or work, or at third-party locations such as relatives, friends, private centres or kiosks (Baldwin et al, 2002) – citizens are less likely to use e-government to send private and financial information.

- *Privacy*, especially online privacy, has become a concern of many citizens in different countries (Irani et al, 2007). This is because of the amount of information collected about citizens, through surfing the internet or purchasing products online, without their permission or knowledge.

Trust in government might not be an important issue for developing countries. This is because achieving trust in governments might not be visible for many countries due to the lack transparency for many years (Transparency International, 2006). Consequently, building *trust in e-government is a more limited task, and may be more feasible, easier and quicker* (Pacific Council on International Policy, 2002). Even more, building trust in e-government could increase trust in government as it shows that the government works for the citizens' benefits by facilitating receiving services in a better way (Parent et al, 2004).

PROPOSED CREG MODEL

The proposed CREG model which is tested in this study consists of:

- E-readiness and trust factors which are the findings from the literature review as presented earlier.
- Other factors which are detected within the pilot study (explained in the research methods) and show an importance impact on citizens' usage of e-government (Figure 1).

RESEARCH METHODS

In order to answer the research question, a pilot study was carried out with citizens and government managers to test the significance of the proposed factors and where necessary to redefine the research question. The main empirical study was conducted using qualitative and quantitative research approaches. Egypt was selected as an example of a developing country: it has an ambitious e-government programme which began in 2001, designed to improve the delivery of government services to citizens [The Egyptian e-government programme strategy explained in the following section]. Nevertheless, Egypt faces many ICT problems similar to those in many other developing countries (Sayed, 2004). At the time of conducting the research, there were eight services available online. Three of them were selected, according to the research scope criteria, for in-depth investigation. These are:

- reissue of birth certificates;
- renewal of vehicle licences;
- Universities and Colleges Admission Services (UCAS).

The study was structured into two main data collection phases conducted in 2005 and 2006 to test the proposed CREG model. Each phase consisted of three levels of data.

- The *first level* of data addresses issues of how policy makers, project managers and executive managers in the relevant government departments in Egypt consider e-readiness within the design and implementation of e-government projects and what measures exist to increase citizens' trust in e-government.

Face-to-face interviews (Denscombe, 1999) were conducted for managers in two organizations. **(1)** The Ministry of Communications and Information Technology (MCIT) is responsible for strategy, decision making, developing of ICT plans that are related to e-readiness and conducting e-readiness assessments within Egypt. **(2)** The Ministry of States and Administrative Development (MSAD) is responsible for the initiation of e-government services through proposing them to other ministries and followed by the development of these services to be ready for implementation.

- The *second level* of data targets managers, technicians and other relevant stakeholders involved with the provision of each of the selected e-government services again using face-to-face interviews. This was important to have an in-depth understanding of the e-government project processes on the ground, to understand their experience and the lessons they have learned, and to understand how e-readiness and trust impact the services for which they are responsible.

Face-to-face interviews conducted for staff and managers responsible about the selected services in two organizations. **(1)** Reissue of birth certificates and renewal of vehicle licences online is the responsibility of the Ministry of the Interior (MI). **(2)** Online UCAS is the responsibility of the Ministry of Higher Education (MHE).

66 face to face interviews were conducted for the first and second level of data during 2005 and 2006.

- The *third level* of data addresses end-users (citizens) of the selected e-government services to evaluate the impact of the services offered to the community at large and to have a clear understanding of the impact of e-readiness within society on using e-government services.

To achieve this, a survey of end-users has been run twice (in two consecutive years: 2005 and 2006). Consequently, comparable results become available to show how progress in e-readiness and trust on the part of end-users affect e-government success and how policy makers and managers design their e-government plans to adjust to the changes in these factors.

For reissue of birth certificates and renewal of vehicle licences services, 1885 valid questionnaires collected from citizens in seven Egyptian governorates in 2005 and 2006.

For UCAS, 2018 valid questionnaires collected from high school students who applied to seven governmental universities in Egypt during the academic years 2005/2006 and 2006/2007 in 2005 and 2006. UCAS is only apply for governmental universities in Egypt.

Data analysis was designed at the following two stages.

- *Stage (1)* analyses interview and survey data for the two years separately. The interview data is from relevant government organizations (MCIT and MSAD at *level 1*, and MI and MHE at *level 2*), covering how government defines and implements its e-readiness, e-government and trust policies. The survey data is from citizen questionnaires (at *level 3*), covering how e-readiness and trust issues affect citizens' use of e-government services.
- *Stage (2)* analyses *all the levels of data* (government and citizens, both years) to investigate how government policies affect citizens and how citizens respond to e-government services, helping to identify the factors that affect CREG. This is followed by comparing the results with other studies to investigate their validity.

Reliability and Validity

Reliability achieved through using the same protocol for each of the three investigated e-government services and for the two phases of data collection (phase 2 (in 2006) followed phase 1 (in 2005) after an interval of one year). Validity is achieved by a careful triangulation between interviews, questionnaires and document study for the data collection and analysis levels.

EGYPTIAN E-GOVERNMENT PROGRAMME DESCRIPTION (WWW.EGYPT.GOV.EG)

Egypt is one of the developing countries which is considered as a low middle-income country (World Bank, 2006) with 76.7 million population (CAPMAS, 2009). The public administration sector is operated by the Council of Ministers (responsible for ministers working groups). In order to overcome the problem of increasing bureaucracy, the government launched its administrative reform programme in 1997. The Ministry of States and Administrative Development (MSAD) became responsible for the programme and its major target was to improve public service and simplify administrative procedures (Sayed, 2004). In 1999, the government launched the Egyptian Information Society Initiative (EISI) to reduce the digital divide and convert Egypt to an information society. This initiative consisted of six parts: access, government, business, learning, health and culture (Sayed, 2004). The government part is relevant to this research.

ICT is seen as important for the Egyptian economy and the Egyptian government started planning for it in 1999. A conference was held by the Cabinet of Ministers, Information and Decision Support Centre (IDSC) to define the Egyptian ICT plan for the next five years. After this conference a new Ministry of Communications and Information Technology (MCIT) was established. The main objective of the new ministry is to encourage both public and private sectors to modernise Egyptian society. IDSC and MCIT cooperated to launch the e-government programme. From 2001 to 2003, MCIT prepared for the e-government programme with some pilot projects, such as the reissue of birth certificates. By January 2004, MSAD had become responsible for the e-government programme in addition to its main goal of enhancing the efficiency of Egypt's administrative agencies (MSAD, 2006).

Through the e-government programme, the Egyptian government expects to have several direct and indirect benefits. Direct benefits have been identified as the following.

- Economic benefits from saving (a) between 1% and 3% of government purchasing costs, (b) government working hours, estimated at 900,000 per year.
- Social benefits from increasing citizens' satisfaction through better delivery of government services.

Indirect benefits have been identified (EISI-G, 2005) as the following.

- Encouragement of investment, helping to reduce unemployment.
- Bringing the national database nearer to completion.

E-Government Strategy

The e-government strategy has three parts that are applied together (EISI-G, 2005).

- *The first part* of the strategy is to change both citizens' and business perceptions of

government services changing from paper-based to electronic-based. This is followed by expanding service provision to include other parties such as the private sector and post offices rather than government only.

- *The second part* is to put in place the fundamentals of the legal framework that supports applying for services online, such as providing e-signature law. The government is also establishing a government gateway and communication network and providing standard specifications for networking and document classifications.
- *The final part* of the strategy is to automate all government ministries and organizations to provide electronically based services.

RESEARCH FINDINGS

SQ1: How do Factors from E-Readiness Assessments Affect Citizens' Usage of E-Government?

Investigate the impact of e-readiness factors (as appear in the proposed CREG model) on using e-government services in developing countries show an agreement between managers that Egypt, as a developing country, should have proper ICT fundamentals in order to have a successful e-government programme. All the proposed e-readiness sub-factors were considered important and significant to the use of e-government services (Figure 2). This was reflected on the government policies in enhancing Egyptian e-readiness (MCIT, 2005b, 2006b).

Findings from citizens' surveys showed that there is a *partial match* between what government managers expect to be important e-readiness factors for e-government and those that actually affect citizens' usage of e-government. Significant factors for citizens include: telephone at home, computer at home, computer and internet at work,

Figure 2. Managers' responses for e-readiness factors

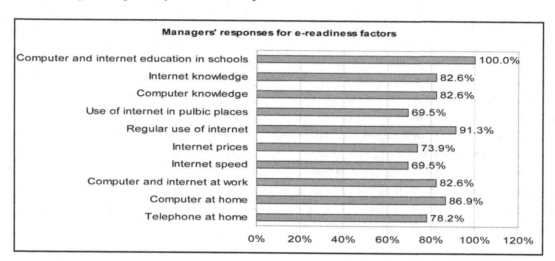

Figure 3. Citizens' responses for e-readiness factors: birth certificates and vehicle licences

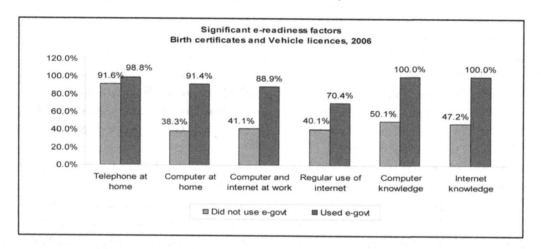

regular use of internet, computer knowledge, internet knowledge, e-signature law and information protection commitment. These factors are significant and essential to move non e-ready citizens to be e-ready and able to use e-government services (Figure 3).

On the other hand, few e-readiness factors did not have a significant impact on using e-government services and contradicted the managers' agreement regarding their impact. These factors include: internet speed, internet prices, use of internet in public places and computer and internet

education in schools. This is because, for example, once a satisfactory level of internet prices and speed is achieved citizens become more saturated towards any improvement from the government.

The improvement of e-readiness factors from one year to another has a significant impact on citizens' usage of the investigated services. Although the increase of the online usage could be a result of increasing citizens' awareness or other undetected factors, the fact is that almost all citizens who used online services were e-ready in terms of ICT. In addition, there was an improvement

Figure 4. Improvements in e-readiness factors from citizens' surveys 2005-2006: birth certificates and vehicle licences

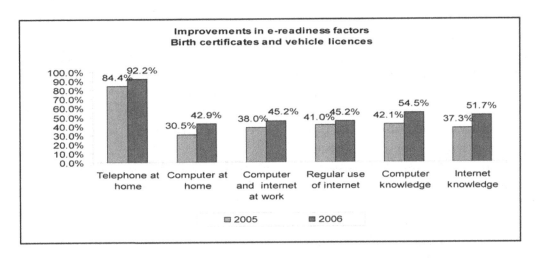

Figure 5. Citizens' responses for technology trust factors

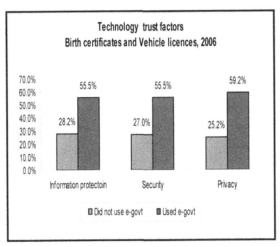 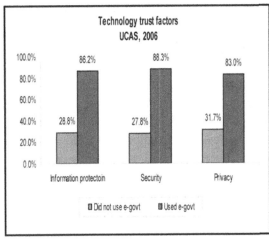

in the e-readiness level between 2005 and 2006 for citizens who used online services (Figure 4).

SQ2: How do Trust Factors Affect Citizens' Usage of E-Government?

Although e-readiness factors are important for using e-government services, they need to be combined with other trust factors to encourage citizens to use online government services. All managers and citizens who used e-government services agreed on the significance of technology trust factors *(information protection, security and privacy)* and e-government trust factors *(credibility, customer satisfaction and response on time)* (Figure 5).

On the other hand, citizens' who did not use e-government services were less trusting both the technology and government. The lack of citizens' trust in technology is a problem in both developed and developing countries (Srivastava & Teo, 2005). Although these findings contradict the Carter and Belager (2004) study conducted in the United States, this research confirms the importance of having technology trust between citizens to increase their use of e-government services.

Although appropriate security and protection measures are in place for online e-government transactions, the government does not explain its security or privacy policy for citizens. Consequently, citizens are unaware of the existence of these measures. To reassure that citizens aware of these aspects, governments need to publicize the measures taken to secure their personal information both on the e-government website and by advertising them to the public (RAND Europe, 2003) using appropriate language understood by citizens (Hackney et al, 2005; Tassabehji & Elliman, 2006). A strong legal system that has a practical impact in supporting the technical measures would also help to convince more citizens to trust the technology.

Lack of e-government trust is due to the differences between online and traditional government services such as the increased cost for a birth certificate or the lack of admission proof in the UCAS case reduce the credibility of e-government services. Consequently, e-government services do not have an advantage compared to the traditional methods in respect of citizens' satisfaction of e-government; as well as losing a major element of trust that governments work for citizens' benefits (Thomas, 1998).

SQ3: How do Other Factors Affect Citizens' Usage of E-Government?

The third part of the proposed CREG model is related to testing the impact of the other factors detected within the pilot study on using e-government services. As both e-readiness and trust factors show a significant impact on using e-government services, it becomes important to understand how *citizens' awareness* of e-government, their *willing*

to use it and *perception* of the service affect their usage. All the proposed sub-factors were showing a significant impact in citizens' surveys on using e-government services.

However, increasing citizens' awareness of e-government services needs to be combined with citizens' trust and willingness to use the service in order to have an effective impact on e-government usage.

SQ4: How do E-Readiness Assessments Affect E-Government Projects?

E-readiness factors presented in CREG had an impact on the macro level of e-government strategy resulting in a special focus on project selection. Project's selection was based on the existence of e-ready citizens who are able to use electronic services. For example, the UCAS project was selected as it targets students who are, in many cases, interested in using the internet and who had some computer and internet education at schools. Consequently, there would be more potential users of the online UCAS service.

FINAL (CREG) MODEL

RQ: What Are the Factors that Affect Citizens' Readiness for E-Government (CREG) in Developing Countries?

Answering the research sub-questions help to achieve an answer to the main research question and achieve the final model for citizens' readiness for e-government (CREG). Most of the proposed CREG factors show a significant impact on using e-government services. This was verified from both mangers and citizens perspectives.

This final CREG model (Figure 6) consists of three steps:

Figure 6. Final CREG model

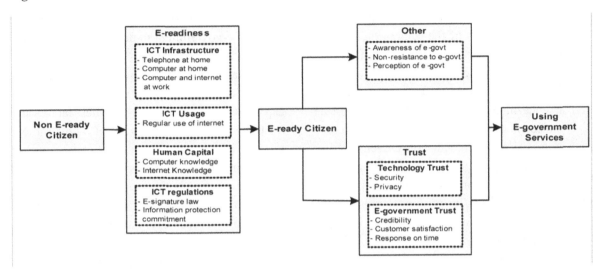

- The *first step* consists of the essential e-readiness factors (including ICT infrastructure, ICT usage, human capital and ICT regulations) that show a significant impact on moving non e-ready citizens to be e-ready for using the internet technology.

- The *second step* takes place by increasing citizens' awareness of the service existence and followed by encouraging citizens' willingness (or reducing their resistance) to use the e-government service.

- Willingness to use the service is an important step towards using e-government services. However, it should be combined with the *third step* which is encouraging trust in both the technology and e-government. Trusting the technology is achieved by providing adequate security and privacy measures. Trusting e-government is achieved by providing credibility of e-government services as in the traditional way combined with customer satisfaction of the online service.

Following these steps would help to reach the goal of having citizens who are ready to use e-government services in developing countries. It also helps to bridge the gap between the impact of e-readiness and trust factors together on citizens' usage of e-government services in developing countries.

RESEARCH RECOMMENDATIONS

The findings of the research recommend that governments in developing countries, need to take into account the following key points.

- E-government projects need to be sure that all the significant e-readiness factors presented within the CREG model exist to ensure that citizens are able to use the technology and appropriate ICT infrastructure exist. E-readiness factors have different impacts on e-government projects. Consequently, each government should prioritize, depending on its objectives, the factors that they consider are more important and focus on them rather than attempting to cover all factors. E-government projects should not be postponed until the whole society becomes e-ready as in developed countries but only until a mass level of distribution of e-ready citizens is reached. This distribution should reach different categories of the society that allow e-government projects to have enough users of different services.

- Increasing citizens' awareness of the existence of e-government services is not a sufficient factor for e-government success unless it is combined with citizens' willingness to use online services and trust receiving e-government services online.

- Gaining citizens' trust for e-government projects could be achieved by having appropriate privacy and security measures at both e-government and government levels. This should be supported by having credibility for e-government services by having online services offering preferences regarding cost and time that are equivalent to traditional services, or even better. Furthermore, this should be applied to all e-government services equally.

- E-government managers need include e-readiness assessments at different levels of decision making within projects rather than focusing only on the design level. Reviewing e-readiness assessments needs to be done annually. Consequently, managers would be able to define what needs to be improved or adjusted within their projects. Also, a citizens' survey should be conducted annually to identify the impact of e-readiness and trust factors on citizens. Citizens' feedback provides an important evaluation on the project's success and enables an appropriate readjustment to e-government plans.

RESEARCH CONTRIBUTION

The work carried out for this research makes a *contribution* to the e-government field by introducing a formalized concept of citizens' readiness for e-

government (CREG) which includes e-readiness, trust and other factors that contribute to citizens' usage of e-government in developing countries.

The CREG model that has been derived from this research *contributes* to the information systems field by providing a model that bridges the gap between the impact of e-readiness factors and trust factors on citizens' usage of e-government services in developing countries.

Closing the gap between e-readiness and trust factors widens the scope of e-readiness assessments to include other trust factors that are related to e-government trust rather than technology trust only.

A secondary contribution from this model is in providing a foundation for other researchers to build on by considering both trust and e-readiness together when investigating e-government projects in developing countries.

CONCLUSION

In conclusion, the research investigates the impact of CREG factors on e-government in developing countries and focussed on the Egyptian e-government programme as an example of e-government in developing countries. In line with the scope, three e-government services were selected to study.

Data was collected by conducting interviews with government managers and surveys with citizens. Obtaining managers' and citizens' opinions was vital to see how they matched in order to bridge the gap between the *provision* of e-government services and the *use* of e-government services. The research validity was achieved by triangulating the findings from different sources (primary and secondary) together.

The research recommends having appropriate e-readiness levels within a community is an essential step for citizens to use e-government services but is not sufficient unless it is combined with citizens' trust of receiving services online. Achieving citizens' trust in e-government is a complicated process and requires governments to provide protection for citizens' information and to convince citizens of e-government credibility by providing services that have at least as good, or better, conditions than the traditional ways. By announcing these procedures to citizens, governments would be able to overcome the problem of invisibility and minimize the risk of requesting government services online.

FUTURE TRENDS

This research is an exploratory research which focused on identifying the impact of citizens' readiness for e-government factors in developing countries. The findings have proven the importance of certain e-readiness and trust factors on e-government usage.

The work presented has been limited to three e-government services and to central government projects only. Future work investigating the significant factors on a large scale to include more selected e-government services would further add to the understanding of e-government projects in developing countries. Similar research covering local e-government projects at local council level would also be valuable in extending the scope of citizens' use.

Furthermore, as the improvement of e-readiness and trust factors helps to increase usage of e-government services, there will be a need to understand their impact on society from the social, economic and governance perspectives.

REFERENCES

Abdelghaffar, H., & Bakry, W. (2005). Defining E-government and E-readiness. In *Proceedings of the Information Resources Management Association (IRMA)*, San Diego, USA.

Abdelghaffar, H., & Kamel, S. (2006). The Impact of E-readiness on E-government in Developing Countries: The Case of Egypt. In *Proceedings of the Information Resources Management Association (IRMA)*, Washington, USA.

Accenture. (2004). *E-government Leadership: High Performance, Maximum Value*. Retrieved September 29, 2006, from http://www.accenture.com

Al-adawi, Z., Yousafzai, S., & Pallister, J. (2005). Conceptual Model of Citizen Adaptation of E-government. In *Proceedings of the 2nd International Conference on Innovations in Information Technology*, Dubai, UAE.

APEC (Asian Pacific Economic Cooperation). (2000). *APEC's E-commerce Readiness Assessment*. Retrieved March 12, 2006, from http://www.apec.org

Bakry, S. (2003). Toward the Development of a Standard E-readiness Assessment Policy. *International Journal of Network Management, 13*(2), 129–137. doi:10.1002/nem.466

Baldwin, A., Simon, S., & Mont, M. (2002). Trust Services: A Framework for Services-Based Solutions. In *Proceedings of the 26th Annual Computer Software and Applications Conference*, IEEE, UK.

Bélanger, F., & Carter, L. (2006). The Effects of the Digital Divide on E-government: An Empirical Evaluation. In *Proceedings of the 39th Hawaii International Conference on System Sciences*, IEEE, USA.

Bhatnagar, S. (2002). E-government: Lessons from Implementation in Developing Countries. *Regional Development Dialogue, United Nations Centre for Regional Development (UNCRD), 24*(Autumn).

Bhatnagar, S., & Vyas, N. (2001). Community-Owned Rural Internet Kiosks. *The World Bank*. Retrieved March 12, 2006, from http://www1.worldbank.org

Blakemore, M., & Lloyd, P. (2007). *Trust and Transparency: Pre-Requisites for Effective E-government, Organizational Change for Citizen-Centric E-government*. European Commission.

Bridges. (2002). E-readiness as a Tool for ICT Development. *Bridges Organization*. Retrieved February 2, 2006, from http://www.bridges.org

Bridges. (2005a). *E-readiness Assessment Tools Comparison*. *Bridges Organization*. Retrieved May 20, 2006, from http://www.bridges.org

Bridges. (2005b). E-readiness Assessment: Who is Doing What and Where. *Bridges Organization*. Retrieved June 22, 2006, from http://www.bridges.org

Brown, C. (2002). G-8 Collaborative Initiatives and the Digital Divide: Readiness for E-government. In *Proceedings of the 35th Annual Hawaii International Conference on System Sciences*, IEEE, USA.

Burn, J., & Robins, G. (2003). Moving Towards E-government: A Case Study of Organisational Change Process. *International Journal of Logistics Information Management, 16*(1), 25–35. doi:10.1108/09576050310453714

CAPMAS (Central Agency for Public Mobilization and Statistics). (2009). *Population Statistics in Egypt*. Cairo, Egypt: Central Agency for Public Mobilization and Statistics.

Carter, L., & Belanger, F. (2004). Citizen Adoption of Electronic Government Initiative. In *Proceedings of the 37th Hawaii International Conference on System Sciences*, IEEE, USA.

Choudrie, J., & Dwiedi, Y. (2005). A Survey of Citizens' Awareness and Adoption of E-government Initiatives. In *E-government Workshop 2005*. London, UK: Brunel University.

CID (Centre for International Development). (2003). *Readiness for the Network World: A Guide for Developing Countries*. Cambridge, MA: Harvard University.

Cohen, S., & Eimicke, W. (2002). The Future of E-government: A project of Potential Trends and Issues. In *Proceedings of the 36th Hawaii International Conference on System Sciences*, IEEE, USA.

CSPP. (n.d.). *Readiness Guide for Living in the Networked World*. Retrieved March 20, 2006, from http://www.cspp.org

DAI (Digital Access Index). (2003). Gauging ICT Potential Around the World. *International Telecommunication Union (ITU)*. Retrieved July 23, 2007, from http://www.itu.int/ITU-D/ict/dai/material/DAI_ITUNews_e.pdf

Denscombe, M. (1999). *The Good Research Guide for Small Scale Social Research Projects*. Buckingham, UK: Open University Press.

EISI-G (Egyptian Information Society Initiative-Government). (2005). *Egyptian Information Society Initiative- Government*. Cairo, Egypt: Ministry of States and Administrative Development.

Europe, R. A. N. D. (2003). *Benchmarking Security and Trust in the Information Society in Europe and the US, Information Society Technologies*. European Commission.

Garner, L. (1986). Critical Success Factors in Social Services Management. *New England Journal of Human Services, 6*(1), 27–30.

Gartner Group. (2002). Majority of E-government Initiatives Fail or Fall Short of Expectations. In *E-government at Gartner Symposium*, San Diego, USA. Retrieved July 9, 2007, from http://symposium.gartner.com/story.php.id.1367.s.5.html

Gefen, D., Warkentin, M., Pavlou, A., & Rose, G. (2002). E-government Adoption. In *Proceedings of the 8th Americans Conference on Information Systems*, USA.

GeoSINC International. (2002). E-readiness Guide: How to Develop and Implement a National E-readiness Action Plan in Developing Countries. In *Information for Development Program (InfoDev)*. Washington, DC: The World Bank.

Gronlund, G., Andersson, A., & Hedstrom, K. (2005). NextStep E-government in Developing Countries. In *The Swedish Program for Information and Communication Technology in Developing Regions*. Sweden: Orebro University.

Hackney, R., & Jones, S. (2002). Towards E-government in the Welsh (UK) Assembly: An Information Systems Evaluation. In *ISOneWorld Conference and Convention*, Nevada, USA.

Hackney, R., Jones, S., & Irani, Z. (2005). E-government Information Systems Evaluation. In *Conceptualising Customer Engagement, E-government Workshop (eGOV05)*. London, UK: Brunel University.

Heeks, R. (2003a). Most E-government for Development Projects Fail: How Can Risk Reduced. In Institute for Development Policy and Management (IDPM), University of Manchester, UK.

Heeks, R. (2003c). E-government for Development: The Impact of E-government Failure. In Institute for Development Policy and Management (IDPM), University of Manchester, UK.

Heeks, R. (2004). E-government for Development: Basic Definitions. In Institute for Development Policy and Management (IDPM), University of Manchester, UK.

Huijboom, N., & Hoogwout, M. (2004). Trust in E-government Cooperation. In *Proceedings of the 3rd International Electronic Government Conference*, Zaragoza, Spain.

InfoDev (Information for Development Program). (2002). *The E-government Handbook for Developing Countries*. InfoDev Program, The World Bank.

Irani, Z., Love, P., & Montazemi, A. (2007). E-government: Past, Present and Future. *European Journal of Information Systems*, *16*(2), 103–105. doi:10.1057/palgrave.ejis.3000678

Liikanen, E. (2003). E-government and the European Union. [UPGRADE]. *The European Journal for the Informatics Professional*, *4*(2), 7–10.

McConnell International. (2000). Risk E-business: Seizing the Opportunity of Global E-readiness. *McConnell International*. Retrieved March 7, 2005, from http://www.mcconnellinternational.com/ereadiness/ereadinessreport.htm

MCIT (Ministry of Communications and Information Technology). (2005a). *Ministry of Communications and Information Technology Indicators, MCIT*, Cairo, Egypt. Retrieved December 1, 2005, from http://www.mcit.gov.eg/indicator

MCIT (Ministry of Communications and Information Technology). (2005b). *Egypt's Information Society (Annual Report)*. Cairo, Egypt: Ministry of Communications and Information Technology.

MCIT (Ministry of Communications and Information Technology). (2006). *Ministry of Communications and Information Technology Indicators*. Cairo, Egypt: MCIT. Retrieved November 15, 2006, from http://www.mcit.gov.eg/indicator

MCIT (Ministry of Communications and Information Technology). (2006b). *Year Book 2006, Annual Report*. Cairo, Egypt: Ministry of Communications and Information Technology.

MSAD (Ministry of State for Administrative Development). (2006). *Program of Enhancing the Efficiency of Egypt's Administrative Agencies*. Cairo, Egypt: Ministry of State for Administrative Development.

Mwangi, W. (2006). The Social Relations of E-government Diffusion in Developing Countries: The Case of Rwanda. In *Proceedings of the International Conference on Digital Government Research,* San Diego, USA.

Ndou, V. (2004). E-government for Developing Countries: Opportunities and Challenges. *The Electronic Journal on Information Systems in Developing Countries, 18*(1), 1–24.

NECCC (National Electronic Commerce Coordinating Council). (2001). *Citizen Expectations for Trustworthy Electronic Government.* USA: National Electronic Commerce Coordinating Council.

Oberer, B. (2002). International Electronic Government Approaches. In *Proceedings of the 35th Annual Hawaii International Conference on system Sciences,* IEEE, USA.

Ojo, A., Janowski, T., & Estevez, E. (2007). *Determining Progress Towards E-government: What are the Core Indicators?* Japan: Center for Electronic Governance, United Nation University.

Otto, P. (2003). New Focus in E-government: From Security to Trust. In M. Gupta, (Ed.), *Proceeding of International Conference on E-governance, Promises of E-governance: Management Challenges,* New Delhi, India.

Papantoniou, A., Hattab, E., Kayafas, E., & Loumos, V. (2001). Change Management, a Critical Success Factor for E-government. In *Proceedings of the 12th International Workshop on Database and Expert Systems Applications,* IEEE, Germany.

Parent, M., Vandebeek, C., & Gemino, A. (2004). Building Citizen Trust Through E-government. In *Proceedings of the 37th Hawaii International Conference on System Sciences,* IEEE, USA.

Prattipati, S. (2003). Adoption of E-governance: Differences Between Countries in the Use of Online Government Services. *Journal of American Academy of Business, 3*(1), 386–391.

Reffat, R. (2003). Developing a Successful E-government. In *Proceedings of the Symposium on E-government: Opportunities and Challenge,* Muscat, Oman.

(2002). Roadmap for E-government in The Developing World – 10 Questions E-government Leaders Should Ask Themselves. In *Pacific Council on International Policy.* Los Angeles, USA: Pacific Council on International Policy.

Sayed, F. (2004). *Innovation in Public Administration: The Case of Egypt. United Nations Department for Economic and Social Affairs.* UNDESA.

Srivastava, S., & Teo, T. (2005). Citizen Trust Development for E-government Adoption: Case of Singapore. In *Proceedings of the 9th Asia Pacific Conference on Information Systems,* Bangkok, Thailand.

Tassabehji, R., & Elliman, T. (2006). Generating Citizen Trust in E-Government Using A Trust Verification Agent. In *Proceedings of the European and Mediterranean Conference on Information Systems (EMCIS)*, Spain.

Thomas, W. (1998). Maintaining and Restoring Public Trust in Government Agencies and Their Employees. *Administration & Society, 30*(2), 166–193. doi:10.1177/0095399798302003

Transparency International. (2006). *Transparency International Corruption Perceptions Index,* Germany. Retrieved June 14, 2007, from http://www.transparency.org

UNDESA (United Nations Department for Economic and Social Affairs). (2004). *Global E-government Readiness Report 2004.* Division for Public Administration and Development Management.

UNDESA (United Nations Department for Economic and Social Affairs). (2005). *Global E-government Readiness Report 2005.* Division for Public Administration and Development Management.

Wimmer, M., & Bredow, B. (2002). A Holistic Approach for Providing Security Solutions in E-government. In *Proceedings of the 35th Hawaii International Conference on System Sciences, IEEE, USA.*

World Bank. (2008). *Country Classification: Data and Statistics.* The World Bank. Retrieved November 2, 2008, from http://web.worldbank.org

Yang, L., Lu, Y., & Fu, G. (2005). Study on E-government Construction. In *Proceedings of the 7th International Conference on Electronic Commerce (ICEC)*, Zi'an, China.

Chapter 13
Do Insecure Systems Increase Global Digital Divide?

Jawed Siddiqi
Sheffield Hallam University, UK

Ja'far Alqatawna
Sheffield Hallam University, UK

Mohammad Hjouj Btoush
Sheffield Hallam University, UK

ABSTRACT

This chapter surveys the issues concerning the digital divide facing developing nations. The authors assert that "insecurity" and the "digital divide" are highly dependent on each other and as insecurity increases so does the digital divide. Therefore, the authors propose to extend the concept of the digital divide to include information security features by putting forward a new model or paradigm of security that is multi-faceted and is able to assist in bridging the digital divide gap. They argue that a lack of attention to security reduces the access to and use of resources with which to attack the digital divide. In particular, for e-business, the authors conclude that in developing countries having security issues at the forefront would encourage engagement with e-initiatives, or restrain it if there is an absence of security.

INTRODUCTION

Without doubt information and communication technologies (ICTs) continue to change the world to varying degrees from one place to another, depending on a number of technological and socio-economical factors such as: physical access to technology, education, geographical locations, language and gender (Warschauer, 2002; Chen & Wellman, 2003; Nahon, 2006). As a result of these factors the rates of adopting ICTs are different between countries. Accordingly, this creates a disparity between communities, or a gap commonly known as Global Digital Divide.

The term digital divide is claimed to have been first used a decade ago by US Department of Commerce's National Telecommunication and Information Administration (NITA, 1999). Since then, the term has been extensively discussed by scholars and politicians in order to propose strategies and recommendation for bridging the

DOI: 10.4018/978-1-60566-388-3.ch013

digital gap and helping nations to fully benefit from ICT diffusion.

Different types of inequalities which contribute to increasing the digital divide have been discussed in the literature (van Dijk, 2006). However, we believe that information and communication systems security aspects, which in our opinion can no longer be add-on features, are often overlooked. Moreover, they come as an afterthought when researchers and politicians talk about ICT adoption, and the issues of global digital divide. In this chapter, we argue that a new type of inequality is emerging because many companies are increasingly off shoring and outsourcing part of their businesses to many developing nations resulting in an increasing number of e-business transactions, which are conducted across the borders. Hence, inequality is related to aspects of information security that are rarely addressed in the digital divide literature. We assert, therefore, that a lack of security can negatively affect national initiatives and strategies that are attempting to bridge the digital gap. Consequently, this absence of security would increase the chance that a country stays longer on the wrong side of the global digital divide.

EXPLORING THE DIGITAL DIVIDE IN DEVELOPING NATIONS

In order to bridge the digital divide gap and exploit the claimed benefits of ICT, many developing nations have started a number of ICT projects that are usually referred to as e-initiatives. For instance, PC@ every home, e-Health and e-Government are some examples of e-initiatives in Jordan (MoICT, 2006). Other Arab states have launched e-initiatives to bridge the gap, create technology awareness and emphasise the importance of personal computer penetration for their people (Soumitra, 2003).

According to Samer (2008), the problem with many of these countries is the lack of strong ICT foundation which leads them to follow short term plans and ad-hoc approaches, which are not based on a well defined and long term comprehensive ICT strategy. As a result, these initiatives provide relatively small achievements compared to their initial intended goals. In addition, there is a clear lack of awareness of ICT security issues in these countries' ICT strategies.

Introducing ICT in developing nations means that governmental, financial and personal information is being processed, stored and exchanged over ICT networks. Moreover, the governments of these nations have the obligation and/or the responsibility to provide their people with all the essentials of education, awareness, technology and legislations required for secure ICT environment.

Unfortunately, many studies reveal that ICT security is becoming an even lower priority and in some cases ignored completely (Tanburn et al., 2001; Bakari, et al., 2005). We argue in the next section that the reason behind this is a lack of focus on ICT security in the digital divide literature and therefore making ICT strategies for bridging the digital gap security-unconscious. As a result leading to a new unanticipated aspect of the global digital divide, and moreover, this absence of security further increases the global digital divide.

Many studies have explored the digital divide from different perspectives. In the nineties, the traditional focus was mainly on infrastructural access (Nahon, 2006). Accordingly, the term "digital divide" has been defined as the inability of citizens to have equal access to online services, either because they do not have the technical means, or the necessary knowledge and expertise (Muller & Horner, 2004). More commonly, it is defined as the gap between the 'technology haves' and 'technology have-nots' (Sipior & Ward, 2005). This distinction can be recognised at four levels: individual, organizational, national and international; the latter has been referred to as "Global Digital Divide". In earlier works, the term focused on the digital divide issue from one perspective:

that is of the physical access to computer related technologies. Even as the term has evolved to include internet access, its physical perspective has not changed. Therefore, for example, the definition from US NITA considers the digital divide as a term coined for the disparity between the *"haves"* and the *"have-nots"* in the technology revolution (NITA, 2000) - this consideration clearly emphasises the physical access perspective.

Recently, the discourse about the digital divide has become multifaceted, and other factors are considered to affect the emergence of the digital divide. Warschauer (2002) argues for redefining the digital divide concept, as not solely marked by physical access to computers and connectivity, but also by considering access to the additional resources that would allow people to use technology, such as content, language, education, literacy, or community and social resources. Realizing the narrow focus of traditional definitions, interested researchers modify the term to include capability and skills for effective use of ICT. For example, Boris and Schlüter (2007: 1) define the digital divide as:

Empirical concept that refers to new form of social inequality, regarding the access and/or use of ICT and/or skills of using ICT (especially internet) at various level of society.

This shift towards including different factors in studying the digital divide beyond the accessibility offers a social perspective that puts users/people at the heart of the debate. For example, Chen & Wellman, (2003) contend that there are multiple digital divides, not even one; hence, they have pointed out that socio-economic status, gender, life stage, and geographic location significantly affect people's access to and use of the Internet. Other studies refer to factors such as language; time online, skills, ethnicity, and frequency of use (Nahon, 2006).

Furthermore, from a developing versus developed nations' perspective, the global digital divide points to great cross-national differences in IT resources and capabilities. These IT resources are concentrated in the hands of a few western, affluent countries, whereas the rest of the world lags behind them (Drori & Jang, 2003). However, following what has become a well-established argument by Rogers (1995): that diffusion of innovations in general follows complex patterns shaped not only by the technical side of the innovation itself, but also by the economic, political, and sociological context in which it occurs, the parameters that affect the global digital divide need to account for trends of politics, economy, culture, and security.

Some studies offer an in-depth investigation of the influence of political, economic, and social factors in creating and sharpening the global digital divide. Drori & Jang (2003) argue that despite the economic and political nature of the justifications for IT connections, it is primarily the connectedness with global society and local cultural changes—expressed by education and science penetration—that serves as the critical antecedents for any change in the global digital divide. Their findings were based on empirical analysis of data collected over time, and according to them, economic openness and democracy have no effect on global digital divide, whereas, permeation of IT into the whole society is the key to bridging the global digital divide.

However, we would argue that social and cultural changes, especially in developing countries, are closely linked to political will and economic development. Thus, we would contend that it does not make sense to refer to the global digital divide simply as "a product of networking into a global society" (Drori & Jang, 2003: 144) that is detached from political and economic national characteristics. Reinforcing our viewpoint, a study by Guillén & Suárez (2005) contends that many of the cross-national differences in Internet use that exist today are likely to remain in place because they are the result of the fundamental economic, political and social gap that separates the advanced from the less developed countries, which to a certain degree is due to unequal power relations, as indicated by dependency and world-system status. Moreover, they argue that the Internet will not be the quick technological fix that will render disadvantaged countries and firms competitive, nor will it be the factor that helps spread the cause of democracy around the world. Currently rich, competitive, high-status countries and firms, and industrialised countries, are likely to benefit the most from the new medium at the current time.

Although these studies provide a solid foundation to understand, and in many cases, to assist in bridging the digital divide, they, nevertheless, come up short when investigating what might drive people's decision to use or not to use the Internet, or what might be the political and social roots and consequences of such decisions and their impact on increasing the global digital divide. From our perspective, a reason worthy of consideration is security, precisely that such studies seldom address the secure use of technology and the necessary skills and knowledge to securely deploy and use ICT. Hence, this absence becomes one of the major reasons for the strategic focus of our research, of which we are providing a preliminary report in this chapter. Moreover, to the best of our knowledge, no study up to date has linked security to the global digital divide.

From the above discussion it is clear that those traditional digital divide perspectives, which do not incorporate security, are inclined to increase the risk that nations will not fully benefit from the digital revolution, besides, these perspectives would hamper nations' endeavor to overcome the digital divide; consequently, rendering them unable to compete in the global information economy. Adoption of this security unconscious view will lead these nations to invest heavily in providing their citizens with physical ICT infrastructures without paying much attention to securing these infrastructures and providing a trustworthy electronic environment. This has many implications for the economies of these less-developed na-

tions internally and across the borders. One can argue that considering factors such as ICT skills, knowledge and education implies the necessity for having in place security practices to use and mange ICT, but, in fact, this is misleading and most of the time security aspects are overlooked, come as an afterthought or perceived from purely technical dimension (Alqatawna et al., 2008a).

Therefore, we argue that the definition of the global digital divide should be extended to incorporate security and focus on the effective and secure use of ICT. This will ensure that security is integrated into the national ICT strategy of these nations and not be overlooked or be an afterthought. From our perspective, effective incorporation of security in the national e-Strategy should not be perceived from a single technical point of view but from a multiplicity of views that incorporate: legal, organizational, and social aspects (Alqatawna et al., 2008b). In this way we will provide a comprehensive solution for the global digital divide, otherwise, we will solve part of the problem leaving many important issues such as security until the end; this means additional time, effort, and cost that reduces the likelihood for these nations to succeed in a digital environment.

SECURITY AS A MECHANISM FOR DECREASING DIGITAL DIVIDE

In a recent evaluation of the digital divide research van Dijk (2006) identifies ten potential inequalities and categorises them into five types (see table 1). According to this study, all these inequalities can be observed in the digital divide literature. However, the technological opportunities are still the most popular because the physical access to ICTs is getting most of the attention.

More than at any other time, the issue of information receives more attention at the national and international levels especially when ICT has become an integral part of business, finance,

Table 1. Possible types of inequality that digital divide may refer to (van Dijk, 2006)

Technological	• Technological opportunities
Immaterial	• Life chance • Freedom
Material	• Capital(economic, social, culture) • Recourse
Social	• Position • Power • Participation
Educational	• Capabilities • Skills

government, and social communication. Consequently, many countries have started to take significant steps towards secure ICT environments. For example, OECD has encouraged its member states to introduce security as an integral part of the daily routine of individuals, businesses and governments in their use of ICTs and conduct of online activities (OECD, 2002). OECD has proposed many guidelines to cultivate an information security culture in its member states. Hence, security management and security standards for managing and evaluating security practices in organisations have been developed. For instance, the BS7799 standard which has been developed by the British Standards Institute (BSI) later became an international standard (ISO/IEC 27001:2005); a well-known standard for establishing, implementing, operating, monitoring, reviewing, maintaining and improving an Information security management system (ISO, 2005). These changes, which are intended to increase ICT security in developed countries, are not limited to security technical and management solutions, but extend to reforming the legal frameworks to support security. Therefore, privacy act, data protection laws, cybercrime laws and many other regulations have been enacted to support security. An Additional fundamental aspect of these security changes is the security awareness programmes at various levels of the society.

On the other side of the security divide, there are many countries, which lag behind with respect to ICT security and, therefore, are detrimentally affected by the potential benefits of deploying ICTs in these countries. E-business is an exemplar ICT application that is everywhere transcending national boundaries. It is claimed that e-business creates great opportunities to increase income and trade flow in the developing counties (Rao, 2001). Therefore, we will use it as an example to discuss the security divide issue. There is a notable increase in utilising ICT and e-business adoption in many developing and emerging countries (Al-Jaghoub & Westrup, 2003; Gregorio et al., 2005). This appears to encourage many researchers to pay more attention to this phenomenon and to investigate many related issues in an attempt to help these countries to successfully deploy e-Business and benefit from the experience of the early adopters of e-business in developed countries. Information security and its implications on e-business in the context of these countries were among the major issues that researchers highlighted. Two key reasons as to why people in developing countries are reluctant to engage in e-Business transaction are the lack of trust in online transitions and inadequate privacy policies (Shalhoub, 2006). Consequently, people in these countries are being excluded from receiving the claimed advantages of e-Business.

Many developed world companies are off-shoring part of their business to developing countries and relying heavily on their ICT infrastructure to communicate with customers and provide services. However, e-business security seems to be overlooked. A recent report reveals that India, the world's primary locus of IT outsourcing, is lacking a basic information security practices (CIO, 2006). Other unsettling results from (VeriSign, 2004) show that the largest percentages of fraudulent transactions are coming from developing countries such as Indonesia, Nigeria and Pakistan. In contrast, Middle East countries such as UAE and Jordan enacted electronic transaction laws in order to regulate e-business and protect customers' rights. However, these laws do not have any regulation regarding cyber crimes or privacy (Shalhoub, 2006; MoICT, 2006). Other researches argue that developing countries are lacking secure communication infrastructure and trusted certificate authorities, which have a direct effect on e-business security and the willingness of foreign parties to transact online with businesses in developing countries (Aljifri et al., 2003). To this extent, it is clear that this lack of security can lead to different levels of exclusion: individual, business or even nationwide participation in the global economy.

We can conclude that "insecurity" and the "digital divide" are highly dependent on each other. As insecurity increases so, does the digital divide; leading to exclusion at various level of society from fully benefiting from the ICT revolution? Therefore, we propose to extend the concept of the digital divide to include information security features. In this way, we can ensure that security will not be overlooked in any ICT initiative that is intended to bridge the digital divide gap. Moreover, we contend that making ICT secure will increase the trust at all levels: individual, organizational, national and international, and, therefore, contribute directly to the development and increase participation of both developed, and more pertinently in the context of this chapter developing nations in the digital economy. In the next section, we put forward a new model or paradigm of security that is multi-faceted, and which is able to assist in bridging the digital divide gap.

THE WAY FORWARD

Having argued for the importance of security issues to the digital divide literature and discussed the consequences of its absence, this section will discuss how information security can be integrated at all levels – individual, organisational and national – in order to provide a trustworthy digital environment, which, we argue, can enhance developing countries' initiatives to bridge the digital gap.

The complexity of today ICT environments makes traditional security approaches and ad hoc security solutions insufficient to thwart the increasing numbers of security breaches. These approaches, which perceive security from one dimension – usually the technical one -, are unable to provide adequate security level for current complex digital environments. The large number of security breaches that we see every day provides evidence that encourages us to rethink and investigate other approaches that perceive security as an integrated part of business and hence, follow a holistic way for understanding and solving the security problem (Alqatawna et al., 2008a).

Security is a complex area, and understanding the security problem is not an easy task. It is not enough to address only technical requirements (Confidentiality, Integrity, Availability…etc) in order to increase the security bar. ICT environments have interconnecting and interacting components (people, software, hardware, procedures and data) and should be looked upon as information systems with a technological infrastructure, and an organisational framework; rather than a purely technological infrastructure (Sokratis at al., 2005). A comprehensive and interdisciplinary definition for information security emphasises both technology and strong coordination with social systems, such as that suggested by Tsujii (2004: 9), who defines information security as:

the dynamic process for establishing an integrated and complete system of social fundamentals designed to form, without infringing freedom broadened by IT (information technology), and with closer linkage and coordination among technologies, administration and management techniques, legal and social systems and information morals in order to make compatible improved usability and efficiency and enhanced security, protected privacy and minimized surveillance, or monitoring, over people

The previous definition may represent the ultimate goal of information security and give a picture for the ideal e-society. However, this might be impossible since there is a still trade-off between security and usability, and between privacy and protection. Nevertheless, the definition clearly specifies the different dimensions that influence security and it emphasises that these dimensions should be addressed in an interdisciplinary and holistic way.

In a previous research paper (Alqatawna et al., 2008b); the Informatics Research Group at Sheffield Hallam University, UK presented a framework of inquiry which is intended to be applicable for any e-Business environment. It is part of ongoing project to construct a conceptual framework, which facilitates holistic understanding of e-Business security and how it can be an integral part of an e-Business environment. We believe this framework can be generalized to provide a tool for ensuring that security will be properly addressed in any ICT initiative; whether it is at individual, organisational or national level.

The idea of the framework is to use the ''stakeholders'' concept, which represents all the interested parties in the digital environment. This digital environment has been presented as interrelated conceptual dimensions (Technical, Social, Organisational, Legal and Trust). A brief overview of this framework follows.

Government, citizens/customers, private sector e-business organizations, business partners and technology vendors are key players in the digital environment. They have different roles and goals, and together they play an important part in success of ICT diffusion in the country. For studying security requirements from a holistic perspective, we recommend the use of the stakeholder model proposed. The model will represent all the interested parties, which can benefit and therefore determine the interrelated dimensions that affect

security. These dimensions will be the building blocks for any approach to holistically integrating security with any ICT initiative. Understanding the nature of each dimension and how it affects the other dimensions is a key factor for creating secure and trustworthy digital environment:

- *The Technical Dimension:* This dimension focuses on securing the physical and the technological infrastructure that are needed by the country to participate securely in the digital environment. Thus, this dimension is concerned with issue such as: securing communication links, Cryptography and Public Key Infrastructure (PKI), as well as Authentication, Authorisation and Accounting methods.

- *The Social Dimension:* Customers, system administrators, accountants, helpdesk personnel and outsource-contactors are the heart of any security systems. Many human factors such as habits, culture and norms can potentially make people the weakest link in the security chain. Many security attacks have been committed successfully not because of the technical vulnerabilities, but because of the human errors and omissions. Education and security awareness in the society are important for successful secure ICT adoption.

- *The Organisational Dimension:* This is responsible for developing secure environments that support and enforce the technical solutions in place. This can be done by a set of policies, procedures, guidance and engagement from people at all the organisation levels, from the top management down to the employees. Our future study will investigate requirements such as: security management standards, top management participation, employees' involvement, training and awareness and other organisational requirements.

• *The Legal Dimension:* With evolution of ICT and wide spread use of Internet, the so-called "*cyber crimes*" have increased. Activities such as identity theft, credit cards fraud, phishing, child pornography, intellectual property infringements... etc, become more and more popular despite the wide use of the physical guards. Unfortunately, in many jurisdiction realms especially in developing countries the role of law against many cyber crimes is still inadequate. From a business perspective, law has an important proactive role in terms of regulation and contracts, which are important for online, as well as offline businesses. Several e-business activities such as e-contracting, e-auction and e-invoicing in developing countries should be regulated from a legal perspective.

• *Trust Dimension:* Lack of trust in technology is one of the main reasons why many people are reluctant to engage in activities or transactions over ICT networks. Therefore, understanding this dimension and its relation with the previous dimensions is very important if we look for a comprehensive solution for the security problem.

CONCLUSION

The security of any electronic environment is a crucial issue that should receive significant attention from the very beginning of any ICT initiative. With internet evolution and globalization, new forms of concerns have started to emerge, one of which is security. We have argued that it is a major concern that could widen the digital divide largely, especially when people become reluctant to engage in any transactions online due to the fear of any breaches of their security and privacy. Redefining the digital divide to include security concerns would help to highlight an unconscious aspect of the digital divide that goes beyond the physical aspects. Moreover, by incorporating these security concerns in the digital divide term we hope to be able to address a very important barrier that keeps many people, organisations and countries from using ICT initiatives worldwide.

In conclusion, a lack of attention to security in developing countries reduces the access to and use of resources with which to attack the digital divide, specifically it can lead to a lack of trust and confidence among local potential adopters of ICT and e-Business practice. Moreover, to paraphrase what one referee perceptively pointed out that the effect of poor security environments could mean that not only off-shore activities and inward investors are kept in their separate and secure systems, but that would also result in less transfer of skills and resources for local use; and thereby potentially re-creating the digital divide further within a country seeking to overcome it.

REFERENCES

Al-Jaghoub, S., & Westrup, C. (2003). Jordan and ICT-led development: towards a competition state? *Information Technology & People, 16*(1), 93–110. doi:10.1108/09593840310463032

Aljifri, H., Pons, A., & Collins, D. (2003). Global e-commerce: a framework for understanding and overcoming the trust barrier. *Information Management & Computer Security, 11*(3), 130–138. doi:10.1108/09685220310480417

Alqatawna, J., Siddiqi, J., Akhgar, B., & Hjouj Btoush, M. (2008a). Towards Holistic Approaches to Secure e-Business: A Critical Review. In *Proceedings of EEE'08*, Las Vegas, USA.

Alqatawna, J., Siddiqi, J., Akhgar, B., & Hjouj Btoush, M. (2008b). A Holistic Framework for Secure e-Business. In *Proceedings of EEE'08*, Las Vegas, USA.

Bakari, J. K. (2005). *Towards a Holistic Approach for Managing ICT Security in Developing Countries: A Case Study of Tanzania*. Retrieved May 15, 2008, from http://dsv.su.se/en/seclab/pages/pdf-files/05-011.pdf

Boris, K., & Schlüter, E. (2007). ' Reconsidered: A Country- and Individual-Level Typology of digital inequality in 26 European Countries. In *Quantitative Methods in the Social Sciences (QMSS)*. Prague: Digital Divide.

Chen, W., & Wellman, B. (2003). Charting and bridging digital divides: Comparing Socio-Economic, Gender, Life Stage and Rural-Urban Internet Access and Use in Eight Countries. *AMD Global Consumer Advisory Board (GSAB)*. Retrieved May 15, 2008, from http://www.amd.com/usen/assets/content_type/DownloadableAssets/FINAL_REPORT_CHARTING_DIGI_DIVIDES.pdf

CIO. (2006). The State of Information Security. *CIO Magazine and PricewaterhouseCoopers*. Retrieved May 15, 2008, from http://www.pwc.com/extweb/pwcpublications.nsf/docid/3929AC0E90BDB001852571ED0071630B

Drori, G. S., & Jang, Y. S. (2003). The Global Digital Divide: A Sociological Assessment of Trends and Causes. *Social Science Computer Review, 21*(2), 144–161. doi:10.1177/0894439303021002002

Gregorio, D. D., Kassicieh, S. K., & De Gouvea Neto, R. (2005). Drivers of E-business activity in developed and emerging markets. *Engineering Management. IEEE Transactions, 52*(2), 155–166.

Guillén, M. F., & Suárez, S. L. (2005). Explaining the Global Digital Divide: Economic, Political and Sociological Drivers of Cross-National Internet Use. *The University of North Carolina Press Social Forces, 84*(2), 671–708.

ISO. (2005). ISO/IEC 27001. *Information technology - Security techniques - Information security management systems - Requirements*. Retrieved May 25, 2008, from http://www.iso.org/iso/catalogue_detail?csnumber=42103

Katsikas, S. K., Lopez, J., & Pernul, G. (2005). Trust, Privacy and Security in E-business: Requirements and Solutions. In *Proceedings of the 10th Panhellenic Conference on Informatics (PCI'2005)*, Volos, Greece, November 2005 (pp. 548-558).

MoICT. (2006). *E-Initiative Database*. Ministry of Information and Communications Technology (MoICT). Retrieved April 12, 2008 from http://www.moict.gov.jo/MoICT/MoICT_Initiative.aspx

MOICT. (2006). *The e-Readiness Assessment of the Hashemite Kingdom of Jordan 2006*. Ministry of Information and Communication technology (MoICT).

Mullen, H., & Horner, D. S. (2004). Ethical Problems for e-Government: An Evaluative Framework. *Electronic. Journal of E-Government, 2*(3), 187–196.

Nahon, K. B. (2006). Gaps and Bits: Conceptualizing Measurements for Digital Divide/s. *The Information Society, 22*(5), 269–278. doi:10.1080/01972240600903953

National Telecommunications and Information Administration (NTIA). (1999). *Falling through the Net: defining the digital divide*. Retrieved May 25, 2008, from http://www.ntia.doc.gov/ntiahome/fttn00/contents00.html

National Telecommunications and Information Administration (NTIA). (2000). *Falling through the Net II: toward digital inclusion*. Retrieved May 25, 2008, from http://www.ntia.doc.gov/ntiahome/fttn00/contents00.html

OECD. (2002). *Guidelines for the Security of Information Systems and Networks: Towards a Culture of Security.* Retrieved May 25, 2008, from http://www.oecd.org/dataoecd/16/22/15582260. pdf

Rao, T. P. (2001). *E-Commerce and Digital Divide: Impact on Consumers.* Paper Presented at the Regional Meeting for the Asia-Pacific: New Dimensions of Consumer Protection in the Era of Globalization, Goa, India.

Rogers, E. M. (1995). *Diffusion of Innovations.* New York: Free Press.

Sachs, J. (2000, June 24). A New Map of the World. *Economist Magazine*, 81-83.

Shalhoub, Z. (2006). Trust, Privacy, and Security in Electronic Business: The Case of the GCC countries. *Information Management & Computer Security, 14*(3), 270–283. doi:10.1108/09685220610670413

Sipior, J. C., & Ward, B. T. (2005). Bridging the Digital Divide for e-Government inclusion: A United States Case Study. *Electronic. Journal of E-Government, 3*(3), 137–146.

Soumitra, D. (2003). ICT challenges for the Arab world. In *The Global Information Technology Report 2003-2004: Towards an Equitable Information Society (Global Information Technology Report).* World Economic Forum. Retrieved June 25, 2008, from http://www.mafhoum.com/press7/218T42.pdf

Tanburn, J., & Singh, A. D. (2001). *ICTs and Enterprises in Developing Countries: Hype or Opportunity?* Paper No. 17, International Labour Office, Geneva. Retrieved June 5, 2008 from http://www.ilo.org/dyn/empent/docs/F1089912836/WP17-2001.pdf

Tsujii, S. (2004). Paradigm of Information Security as Interdisciplinary Comprehensive Science. In *Third International Conference on Cyberworlds (CW'04)*, 2004 (pp. 9-20).

van Dijk, J. (2006). Digital divide research, achievements and shortcomings. *Poetics, 34*(4-5), 221–235. doi:10.1016/j.poetic.2006.05.004

VeriSign. (2004). *Internet Security Intelligence Briefing, 2*(2). Retrieved May 28, 2008, from http://www.verisign.com/static/017574.pdf

Warschauer, M. (2002). Reconceptualizing the Digital Divide. *First Monday, 7*(7). Retrieved May 22, 2008, from http://www.firstmonday.dk/issues/issue7_7/warschauer/#author

Chapter 14
Communicating Farm Technologies through Traditional and New Media Channels:
Lessons from India

D. Puthira Prathap
Sugarcane Breeding Institute (Indian Council of Agricultural Research), India

ABSTRACT

This chapter begins by looking at the importance of knowledge and information in agricultural development. Then the chapter discusses how the traditional mass media channels, viz., radio, print and television had been instrumental in India's agricultural technology transfer. Next, it explores the characteristics of new media, the problems associated with the advent of Internet and how self-help groups and ICTs could be effectively used in technology transfer. The focus narrows to a comparative study on the effectiveness of traditional and new media in communicating farm technologies. Finally, the chapter examines how the extension agents, based on the results could formulate communication strategies for effectively using the mass media channels.

"Slowly, the new media will cease to be thought of as new media; they will simply be additional channels of communication, earning a well deserved place in the media repertoire..."

—Sir Martin Sorrell

DOI: 10.4018/978-1-60566-388-3.ch014

INTRODUCTION

During the past century, the world has undergone a change from agriculture society, where manual labour was the critical factor, to an industrial society where the management of technology, capital and labour has provided the competitive advantage. Knowledge plays a major role here. In the words of Kofi Annan, the former UN Secretary-General, if information and knowledge are central to democracy, they are the conditions of development. Agricultural development too, depends heavily on knowledge and information, which are the least expensive inputs, but are the basic ingredients of food security. The present day farmer requires information on supply of inputs, new technologies, early warning systems (such as drought, pests, diseases), credit, market prices and his global competitors. The success of the Green Revolution in India has largely been attributed to giving rural communities access to knowledge, technology and services. Knowledge and information on important farm technologies, methods and practices need to be put in the right hands at the right time. Economists have pointed out how deficient information affects the development process in the rural sector (Ray, 1978). Since direct contacts between extension agents and farmers are few and far between, the low 'extension worker- farmer' ratio being one of the reasons for that, the mass media have to discharge this duty of technology transfer.

Mass media, popularly called the 'one-to-many' media are enormously instrumental in accelerating development in many areas of human endeavour. They can communicate with more people in less time and less cost. This strength of mass media is of great help to the change agent in providing effective service to farmers. The same content goes to all recipients and the one who sends it has absolute control over that content are a few advantages that mass media have over other forms of communication. One drawback in this form of communication is that its content cannot be individualized to each recipient's unique needs and interests. Despite this handicap, traditional mass media such as print, television and radio have been used very successfully in the developing countries. In India, the importance of utilizing mass media for communicating farm technologies was felt and has been highlighted from the III Five

Year Plan onwards. Of late, new media, internet in particular, have the potential of getting vast amount of information, individualized sometimes, to the rural population of the country in a more timely and comprehensive manner.

On one hand, therefore, the experts involved in transfer of farm technologies, have the traditional extension methodologies such as print, radio and television and on the other hand, they have the new media. A few questions are bound to arise in their minds – What is the impact of traditional media in technology transfer? Are the traditional methods of mass communication becoming insignificant with the advent of new media? Are the new media technologies out of place in a developing country like India? Are they as effective as the traditional media in influencing the knowledge gain of the farmers? Keeping these questions in mind, this chapter has been organized.

MASS MEDIA AND FARM TECHNOLOGY TRANSFER

This section discusses how the traditional mass media, viz., radio, print and television had been instrumental in India for transferring agricultural technologies over the years and the recent initiatives using the new media.

Radio Broadcasts

Radio technology was first developed during the late nineteenth century and came into popular usage during the early twentieth century. Equipped with many advantages such as, the ability to reach both literate and illiterate audiences with messages in their own language, the potential to be useful in areas without electricity, the capacity to repeat broadcasts many times during the day, and inexpensive programme production, radio remains the most powerful, and yet the cheapest, mass medium for reaching large numbers of people in isolated areas. Thanks to the revolution of the transistor, even the remotest villages in India have access to rural radio, which builds on the oral tradition of rural populations. Radio however, is not useful for teaching people how to perform an activity that requires a demonstration. The scope for feedback is also less. Despite these shortcomings, radio represents a medium, capable of reaching a wide geographic audience at a low production cost with proven results.

In India, the Radio Club of Bombay was the first to broadcast the radio programme in June 1923 (Sharma, 2002). The operations of the public broadcaster, All India Radio (AIR) began formally in 1936, with objectives to inform, educate and entertain the masses. When India became independent, the AIR network had only six stations located at the cities of Delhi, Bombay, Calcutta, Madras, Lucknow and Tiruchirappalli. As against a mere 2,75,000 receiving sets at the time of Indian independence, in 2003, there were about 111 million estimated radio sets in about 105 million households in 2003. The broadcast scenario had also drastically changed, with the country having 208 broadcasting centres, including 74 local radio stations, covering nearly 100 per cent of the country's population and 89.51% of the area today. ("All India Radio", 2003).

The experiments conducted with the medium of radio had been far more successful than those conducted with the medium of Television. The reasons were: the extent of penetration of Radio had been far greater than that of Television; radios were easily accessible and with the transistor revolution, radio as a technology had become very cheap; another factor working in favour of radio, as a medium was the low capital investment and operating costs of radio broadcast technologies (Rajesh, 2003).

Farm and Home Broadcasts of All India Radio

Since radio provides the reach, frequency and access to rural and remote areas, it makes a promising, appropriate and powerful tool of farm communication. In addition, owner-ship among poor households is relatively high compared to other media forms, particularly in rural settings. Hence, in order to tap this potential of radio, the Farm and Home project was launched by All India Radio in 1966. These broadcasts were designed to provide information and advice on agricultural and allied topics. The aim was to educate the farmers and assist them in adopting innovative practices in their fields as per the local relevance. The experts also conducted occasional farm radio schools, which proved to be very effective. It can be said that the concept of green revolution, blue revolution and white revolution that happened in the country could not have become a reality, but for the continuous efforts made by AIR. Several farm inputs had been aggressively promoted by AIR that some have radio tags attached to their names. In Tamil Nadu, a constituent State of India, for instance, ADT 27, a rice variety was popularly called *radio* rice. Taichung native -1 was rechristened *radio* rice in Orissa, another Indian State. Instances of "All India Radio" stations adopting non-descript villages have also been witnessed. ("After radio, rice Orissa will now have a radio village too," 2003). During 1995, there were 81 All India Radio stations producing and broadcasting Agricultural and rural programmes in the country. (Kaurani, 1995). The All India Radio, Tiruchirappalli in Tamil Nadu broadcasts 110 minutes of rural programmes daily, the highest in the country. Several private FM channels are coming up in the state besides the Rainbow FM channels of *Prasar Bharati* (Broadcasting Corporation of India). *Gyan Vani,* an educational FM channel run by Indira Gandhi National Open University, has been commissioned at several states of the country. A survey had showed that Coimbatore district of Tamil Nadu has a strong rural listenership with All India Radio, Coimbatore. The survey had concluded that the radio station provides valuable information to farmers with the assistance of Tamil Nadu Agricultural University, located here, with

37 per cent of listeners tuning in at least once a day, ("You cannot carry your television set to the beach", 2002) which is appreciable to note, in this information age.

Television Broadcasts

Television (TV), until recently the new medium, has been used for raising awareness, imparting training, thereby making a useful rural development tool. One of the unique advantages of TV is that it allows people know how to do something. However, some people find it costly compared to radio. Producing a TV programme too is more expensive than radio or print media. If the listener does not hear or understand the message correctly, he or she does not have an opportunity to ask for an explanation. Access to television is also highly limited in countries like India where the TV penetration is only about 80 per 1000 people. Despite all these, television has been playing a major role in the developmental efforts of the country.

There was no television in India until 1959 when an experimental educational TV system was introduced in Delhi for the benefit of school children with UNESCO's (United Nations Educational, Scientific and Cultural Organization) support. *Doordarshan*, the national television service of India devoted to public service broadcasting is one of the largest terrestrial networks in the world. The regular service of *Doordarshan* with a News bulletin was started in 1965 at Delhi. Television went to a second city, Mumbai, only in 1972, and by 1975 Calcutta, Chennai, Srinagar, Amritsar and Lucknow had television stations. Doordarshan has established programme production facilities in 46 cities across the country. Its programmes are watched in India by more than 360 million viewers in their homes and TV reaches more than 95 per cent of our population. Several private TV channels too operate in various languages. Due to the initiatives taken up by the eminent Indian scientists, Dr.M.S. Swaminathan and Dr.Vikram Sarabhai,

the innovative rural programme, *Krishi Darshan* was crystallized in 1967. The first experiment with satellite technology in India, known as the Satellite Instructional Television Experiment (SITE), was conducted in 1975-76. This was, incidentally, the first attempt anywhere in the world of using the sophisticated technology of satellite broadcasting for social education. With 562 television stations as of 1997, India ranks 8th in the list of countries by number of television broadcast stations.

We find that accessibility in rural areas is no more a problem. According to a recent survey conducted by the Broadcasting Corporation of India (Prasar Bharati) the average TV watching during was found to be 83 per cent in rural areas and 75 per cent in urban areas. Among the farm programmes, the regional agricultural programme of *Doordarshan Kendra*, Bhopal in the state of Madhya Pradesh was being watched by maximum 31-44 per cent of the rural audience, followed by the corresponding programme watching of Bhubaneswar (18-25 per cent), Guwahati (11.6-13.6 per cent), Jalandhar (7.5-19 per cent) and Thiruvananthapuram (5-6 per cent). Studies also show that television had provided more time for dairy and pet animals than radio; radio had given more importance to farmers' presentations than television (Mary and Vasanthakumar, 2001).

Publications

One of the greatest events in the history of man happens to be the invention of printing in the 15th century in Europe. In contrast to the highly centralized and capital-intensive structure of media like radio and television, print medium is ideally suited to the dissemination of localized news and information. Several strengths of this media have kept it in the reckoning all these years. Readers can read a story many times to confirm their understanding. Some experts believe that printed stories are more reliable than stories on the radio or television. Since one can keep a newspaper or magazine forever, people can hold on to important information for future reference. Though they can be only useful mainly for people who can read and who can afford to buy them, print media have been playing a major role in India's agricultural development.

The first printing press in India was the one in Goa brought by Portuguese missionaries in 1556. Printing and newspaper production in various linguistic areas of India became widespread in the nineteenth century. There is a general feeling that print media are being under-utilized due to the low literacy levels prevailing in the country. On the contrary, statistics show that rural literacy has been showing a steady progress over the years. Rural literacy, which was 12.1 per cent in 1951, had risen to 56.0 per cent in 1997 (NSSO, 1997). Newspaper readership had grown up by 20.00 per cent in the country from 1999 to 2002, which is higher than the literacy growth (Vijapur-kar, 2002). It had grown by 10.00 per cent over the last 10 years, almost half of that in the rural areas (Ninan, 2002). The importance of printed material is increasing with the increase in the rate of literacy. Apart from English and 18 principal languages enumerated in the eighth schedule of its Constitution, India has publications in 81 other languages, mostly Indian languages or dialects and a few foreign languages. Daily newspapers are being brought out in 18 principal languages and Kashmiri is possibly the only principal language that does not have a daily newspaper.

Newspapers and other periodicals are fast spreading in rural areas. Literacy and roads help their spread. Like radio and television, newspapers carry a range of information: news, gossip, entertainment and cultural topics. It is important for rural readers – and for the research and extension organizations that serve them – for agricultural and environmental information to be part of that mix. Farm publications serve as an important communication link between farmers and scientists, the advantage being they can be referred to later. National newspapers such as *The Hindu, Tribune* and so forth and regional newspapers such as *Daily Thanthi, Dinamalar* and so forth have separate sections for farmers.

Some of the few early farm publications were, the *Indian Agricultural Gazette*, published by J.C Bose, J.N Dey and H.Patra in 1885 to disseminate agricultural information among English–knowing landlords and big farmers. During the same year *Indian Agriculturist* was launched by Robert Knight, founder – editor of *Statesman,* Calcutta. (Vilanilam, 1993) and there has been a spurt in the farm publications ever since. At present, more than 465 agriculture magazines are being published in different languages. (Chandrashekara, 2001) in the country.

New Media

What are traditional mass media and what are new media? Radio was a novelty as a mass communication tool in the 1920s, after print, which was the oldest. It evolved into an important tool, and television, which followed suit, had offered the added advantage of being able to transmit motion pictures. Nevertheless, all these are technologies of the past today. They are being increasingly referred to as the traditional media leaving the mantle of 'new' media to the new emerging technologies such as, internet.

Traditional communication channels have all along been used successfully, but these have mostly been monologic and have not allowed for much interaction with users. The new media such as internet however offers great potential as an interactive mass medium. The Internet is a multifaceted mass medium, that is, it contains many different configurations of communication. Its varied forms show the connection between interpersonal and mass communication that has been an object of study since the days of the two-step flow model (Lazarsfeld, Berelson, & Gaudet, 1944).

The hallmark characteristics of this New Medium have been its ability to deliver individualized messages to an infinite number of people; each of the people involved shares reciprocal control over that content. In other words, the New Medium has the advantages of both the Interpersonal and the Mass media, but without their complementary disadvantages. No longer must anyone who wants to individually communicate a unique message to each recipient have to be restricted to communicating with only one person at a time. For instance, the millions of computers interconnected through the Internet can acquire, sort, package, and transmit information in as many ways as there are individual people. They can establish those communications simultaneously. In addition, they allow each participant (senders and receivers) to share equal simultaneous control.

All these capacities have prompted some communication experts to believe that such new communication technologies might allow the countries like India to leap frog the industrial era to become an information society. However, some feel that such new media are mainly for creating and strengthening a global market and not for benefiting the resource - poor.

Taking in to account the phenomenal growth in the number of internet users in the country (5.5 users per 100 people in 2006 as against 0.5 users per 100 people in 2000 – World Bank, 2006) during the past two decades, the Government and the private sector are supporting several Internet and development initiatives. These projects which have agriculture as one of their components are making full use of Internet tools such as the World-Wide Web and interactive discussion tools to assist in the harmonization of Internet and agricultural development efforts.

A few successful ICT projects include, the Gyandoot project (Madhya Pradesh), the MS Swaminathan Research Foundation's Information Village project (Pondicherry), e-choupals of ITC Ltd., Application of Satellite Communication for Training Field Extension Workers in Rural Areas (Indian Space Research Organization), *Tarahaat*.

com by Development Alternatives (Uttar Pradesh and Punjab), Parrys Corners by EID Parry (I) Ltd, VOICES – Madhyam Communications (Karnataka) etc.,.

The Warana Wired Project, one such initiative, launched in Madhya Pradesh provides farmers pricelists of farm produce in the region. The farmers can also access daily weather forecasts, information on cropping patterns, soil conservation and government schemes. The National Informatics Centre, a state owned technical agency is behind this. The Hyderabad-based *ikisan.com* and the Electronics Corporation of India Ltd are to set up 100 Internet kiosks in nine cotton-growing states in the country ("Nine states to get Internet kiosks with cotton focus", 2003).The banks too are in the fray. The State Bank of India has launched a financial assistance plan for setting up internet kiosks in rural areas, wherein, women will be given preference ("SBI Plans to make rural areas e-savvy." 2003).

Looking in to all these, a day may come when virtual field days for farmers can be developed on the Web, permitting those from some distance away to gain the same type of information as those who attended. These tools have potential to reduce costs and help in reaching new audiences within resource constraints.

INDIA AND ICTS

ICTs, in a broader sense, include technologies and methods for storing, managing, and processing information such as computers, digital and non-digital libraries and for communicating information such as email, radio and television, telephones, mobile phones, internet etc. Of these, in India, ownership of computers and to a certain extent, televisions, is still a major problem in the rural areas. A survey (Pigato, 2001) conducted in the Indian states of Uttar Pradesh, West Bengal and Andhra Pradesh found that only radios are owned by a majority of poor households. Televisions,

Table 1. Access to sources of information and communication for the rural households of India

Source	Personal Ownership (%)	Shared/ Communal (%)	Not Available (%)
Radio	77.3	22.7	-
Newspapers	11.3	80.0	8.7
Television	9.3	84.0	6.7
Telephone	-	63.3	36.7
Computer/ Internet	-	12.0	88.0

(Pigato, 2001)

Table 2. Internet usage in India over the years

Year	Users	Population	Penetration (%)
1998	1,400,000	1,094,870,677	0.1%
1999	2,800,000	1,094,870,677	0.3%
2000	5,500,000	1,094,870,677	0.5%
2001	7,000,000	1,094,870,677	0.7%
2002	16,500,000	1,094,870,677	1.6%
2003	22,500,000	1,094,870,677	2.1%
2004	39,200,000	1,094,870,677	3.6%
2005	50,600,000	1,112,225,812	4.5%
2006	40,000,000	1,112,225,812	3.6%
2007	42,000,000	1,129,667,528	3.7%

IAMAI (2007)

telephones and newspapers were available to the majority of households on a shared basis. Very few families have shared access to a computer or Intenet connection, and some households have never viewed television, read a newspaper or used a telephone (Table 1).

Therefore, feasibility of approaches involving modern ICTs alone in the country is questionable, as currently, more than half of the villages lack telephone connectivity, let alone internet access. The 26 million phone lines and broadband subscribers that do exist nationwide are highly concentrated in urban areas, leaving rural areas out of the loop and harming the interests of both groups.

Coupled with these is the fact that, for most modern information and communication technologies, the user charges are very high that makes their use for technology transfer a very costly affair. A case in view is that of the cost of Internet connectivity in India. It still costs as much as 15 to 20 Indian Rupees per hour for Internet access. Such prohibitive costs make the use of such technology, a luxury. Though India ranks fifth in the world ("Top 20 countries with highest number of Internet users", 2007) in terms of Internet users, the penetration percentage is only 3.7 (Table 2), compared to the country ranked sixth (Brazil) which has a penetration percentage of 21.

TECHNOLOGY TRANSFER THROUGH ICTS AMONG SELF-HELP GROUPS IN INDIA

The importance of group influence is well recognized in the field of mass communication. Because of the power of social influence, groups are being used as agents of change. Flay (1987) through his study, had suggested that if written materials accompany a TV programme, the effectiveness doubles, if group discussions are added, the effectiveness triples. Let us discuss if the Self-Help Groups (SHGs) that are being organized in large numbers in most parts of the country, can be utilized in the process of technology transfer through mass media channels.

Self-Help Groups in India

A Self-Help Group is defined by the Reserve Bank of India (RBI) as 'a registered or unregistered group of micro entrepreneurs having homogenous social and economic background, voluntarily coming together to save amounts regularly, to mutually agree to contribute to a common fund to meet their emergency needs on mutual help basis' (RBI, 2006). Small, like-minded, homogenous groups with similar socio-economic characteristics (Prathap, 1994) generally form them. A size of 'less than 20' is the usual norm for a group and sometimes mandatory, for ensuring bank linkage (MYRADA, 2006). In general, a feeling of affinity based on similar social features (such as self-reliance, voluntarism), similar structural features (such as caste, religion, ancestral village, livelihood-base) or similar entrepreneurial activities undertaken by the group members, link these small groups together (Fernandez, 2005). In Tamil Nadu, the Self-Help groups (SHGs) were launched during the late eighties and by 2003, there were around 0.136 million Self-Help Groups in the state with a total membership of 2.3 million women ("CM's pat for SHGs", 2003). The initiatives by the Government in encouraging setting up of Cyber Café / Internet *dhabas* (Kiosks) in rural and remote areas through self-help groups by offering infrastructural facilities at subsidized cost and encouraging provision of soft loans facilities to such entrepreneurs also prompted the researcher to choose self-help groups for the study ("DRDA to help SHGs to set up internet kiosks", 2003). Besides savings, SHGs are involved in multifarious economic activities such as running ration shops, internet kiosks, floriculture, dairy farming, courier services etc., with substantial success (Government of Tamil Nadu Policy note, 2006).

Hence, these SHGs can also serve as a centre for effective knowledge dissemination, thereby improving agricultural productivity. They can be used as Knowledge dissemination centres for disseminating information on livestock and agricultural activities. SHGs who have the best practices may be asked to share and demonstrate the impact of the intervention as they stand a good chance of accepted by the community for their credibility. The active members of the SHGs could be trained on best practices in farming as well as communication skills so that they can then transfer their learning to the community.

TRADITIONAL MEDIA VS NEW MEDIA IN TRANSFER OF FARM TECHNOLOGIES

The traditional media channels have been playing a major role in agricultural development, achieving the goals of green revolution, being their most significant achievement. Post-Green revolution, agriculture is being dominated by new paradigms. In 2001, India's rural population was 70 percent of the country's total but earned only 25 percent of its GDP, while in 1951, the rural population was 83 percent of the country's total and earned more than 56 percent of GDP. Growth in agriculture has decelerated from the 1990s, facilitating the need for evolving a wholesome network for dissemination of agricultural information to the farmer. And new media channels have a major role to play in this scenario, complementing the traditional channels (FAO, 1998; Forno, 1999), in the area of agricultural information delay, more specifically.

The problem of agricultural information delay could be solved by an effective use of new media. Jain & Gogia (2006) argue that under-utilization of ICTs has been one of the major factors for the information delay between farmers and agricultural researchers in India. Farmers in the developing world still predominantly use the verbal and printed means for agricultural information (Dowlath & Seepersad, 1999; Cecchini, 2002) using radio and television, to a lesser extent. So much so that surveys conducted on the information sources used by farmers in India, do not even list Internet as one of the sources. The National Sample Survey Organization's (NSSO, 2005) recent survey, which did not list Internet as a source, showed that among the mass media channels, radio was the most used source followed by television and newspaper (Table 3)

Effectiveness of Media Channels

An experimental study of the relative effectiveness of four mass media channels (radio, television,

Table 3. Percentage of farmer households accessing information on modern agricultural technologies through various sources *

Source	% of households
Radio	13.0
Television	9.3
Newspaper	7.0

* non-mass media sources are not listed here.
(NSSO, 2005)

newspaper, and Internet) on knowledge gain was conducted among 144 rural women belonging to self-help groups of three villages in the state of Tamil Nadu, India. A farm technology, viz., 'rabbit farming', was developed into parallel messages (treatment) and was delivered through these channels to assess the knowledge gain (Prathap & Ponnusamy, 2006) of farm women belonging to self-help groups.

The results of the study showed that (Table 4) the traditional media had a slight edge over the new media with a mean knowledge gain score of 14.09. New media had a mean score of 13.78. The study also compared mass media attributes and found that in the view of majority of the farmers, radio messages were 'always of adequate duration/length' and radio was the 'most credible' medium (Table 5).

In considering these results, traditional media are still effective when compared to new media despite the fact that it allows for relatively less interaction with the users. Further, the results

indicate that the traditional extension teaching methods that have evolved during the last two centuries are still effective today. With many farmers still not using the new media for any purpose (Márquez-Berber, 2003; Suvedi, Campo, & Lapinski, 1999) the change agents need to go slowly in disseminating technologies through Internet.

Though the studies discussed in this section, place the traditional media ahead of new media, it is too early to arrive at a concrete decision. Some authors feel that such a comparison itself is unnecessary. On the question of choosing a traditional or new medium for communicating farm messages, Cook (1995) had stated that no training media is inherently better than another; it is the audience, where they are, their age, literacy level language etc., which determines their appropriateness.

So, though there will be constant competitions and comparisons between traditional and new media, these studies go on to show that the traditional media cannot be displaced altogether and that communication strategies cannot be formulated without taking traditional media into account.

STRATEGIES FOR EFFECTIVE FARM COMMUNICATION

As seen through various surveys, farmers of India still use the traditional mass media channels predominantly, as sources of information. New media channels are yet to be taken seriously by

Table 4. Traditional media versus new media on mean knowledge gain due to exposure to treatments

Particulars	Knowledge gain scores	
	Traditional Media (Radio, Television, and Newspaper)	New Media (Internet)
Before exposure to treatment	22.87	23.28
After exposure	36.96	37.06
Mean knowledge gain	14.09	13.78
% of knowledge gain	64.05	62.64

(Prathap & Ponnusamy, 2006)

Table 5. A comparative analysis of mass media attributes among farm women

Attributes	Category	Radio		Television		Print		Internet	
		No.	%	No.	%	No.	%	No.	%
Length/duration	Always adequate	37	25.7	2	1.4	5	3.5	6	4.2
	Sometimes adequate	78	54.2	61	42.3	70	48.6	65	45.1
	Inadequate	29	20.1	81	56.3	67	47.9	73	50.7
Credibility	Most credible	76	52.8	62	43.0	42	29.2	24	16.6
	Moderately credible	68	47.2	78	54.2	70	48.6	60	41.7
	Not credible	-	-	4	2.8	32	22.2	60	41.7

(Prathap, 2004)

the change agents, which might be justified, if the NSSO survey and results of the experimental study discussed in the previous section are any indication. While strategies need to be formulated with this background information in mind, policy makers and development workers cannot ignore new media altogether as internet is becoming popular in the villages as a result of several governmental and non-governmental ICT projects being implemented all over the country. Based on the experiences gained in these projects and previous studies, strategies need to be evolved. Strategies, a term often used in situations like war, are formulated after the objectives to be accomplished have been determined, all aspects of the constraints have been examined, and the possible courses of action are analyzed. The experimental study on rabbit farming technologies, discussed in the previous section, had suggested some strategies (Prathap, 2004) for ensuring effective farm communication through mass media, which are discussed hereunder:

- Of the four elements in communicative act – source, message, channel and receiver – channel plays a central part. An important strategy for any communicator is to determine what channel to use and how to use it in order to affect the receiver's knowledge and behaviour. When the target groups are to be imparted with knowledge, television need to be utilized; when they are to retain the gained knowledge, internet can be utilized more extensively and when the target groups are expected to take a decision on adoption, radio need to be utilized more. The extension agency has to choose the right channel as the situation warrants.

- Irrespective of the channel, the message that carries the agricultural technology through a mass media channel needs to be need based, timely, comprehensible, practicable, complete, of adequate length/duration, credible, accessible and should have practical utility.

- The messages designed for dissemination through mass media can use 'phone-in' programmes for radio and television; 'tidbits' for print and e-magazines for internet.

- *Radio* – The non-interesting programmes of radio should be done away forthwith and interesting messages need to be developed for the listeners. The messages can be dramatized utilizing farmers' own experiences. There is a shortage of well-trained communicators in the mass media agencies who have a historic sense of the special needs of the rural poor and should give the message in a palatable way. Offering Post Graduate diploma courses in Agricultural journalism to the media personnel would help. Such courses for in-service personnel are already being offered by institutions such as MANAGE (National Institute of Agricultural Extension Management), Hyderabad and CCS Haryana Agricultural University, Hisar, Haryana. When such qualified personnel are employed, these constraints can possibly be rectified. Ayaz (1991) too had reiterated this point through a study in Pakistan. Commissioning of community radio stations, which may be run by women self-help groups may also be set up. This concept is gaining momentum and a community radio station based on this had been established in Karnataka and Andhra Pradesh states of India (Venkateshwarlu, 2002). Farm broadcasts can include more rural women-specific programmes. Taking in to consideration the FAO observation that most of the farming activities are carried out by women in India (Shiva, 1991) programmes can be conceived keeping women in mind. Cross-media announcements can be made, wherein the day's farm programme schedule can be provided in local newspapers and local television channels.

- *Television* – Community television sets can be installed in villages and they should be accessible to all farmers, including women folk so that they can save time. The duration of farm broadcast also should be increased. A right step in this direction would be to launch a rural television channel. *Doordarshan* had announced its intention to launch a rural channel ("DD seeks funds from Agricultural Ministry for its rural bonanza" 2003). Such an exclusive channel can have increased programme duration and increased frequency of farm programmes. Using more local experts

and including more farmers in television programmes is also an effective media strategy. If the 'narrowcasting' stations of *Doordarshan* are given a facelift, this strategy can be implemented in an effective manner.

- *Print* – Access to the media has been a crucial constraint among the lower socio-economic strata audiences of the third world. When a development agency decides to address these audiences, an important task, therefore is to increase their access to the media. Effective newspaper distribution in villages should be ensured. Rural libraries need to buy more farm magazines. More local newspapers should be brought out for location specific information. More success stories, cost of cultivation/production aspects of farm enterprises need to be included in farm publications.

- *Internet* – Unlike the traditional media, computers need some expertise to use. So, farmers should be given training on operating computers and local language should be widely used in internet. The major constraints in operating ICT services in India had been infrastructure related (Dossani et al, 2005) which needs to be sorted out. Setting up of internet kiosks that can be operated by SHGs is also a worthwhile strategy.

Women farmers in rural areas of India still have the restrictions in accessing public places such as community TV centres, internet centres and local libraries. Further, the attitude of the family elders too has to change so as to encourage the women to utilize such facilities. Setting up of accessible media centres with all mass media facilities can probably solve this problem. These centres should utilize both traditional and new media to impart knowledge and can double as training centres off and on with women as teachers and trainers. Dr.M.S.Swaminathan, (2003) the renowned

Table 6. Analysis of mass media innovations

Features	Merits	Gaps	Crucial factors for success
Use of internet • to disseminate market information • to provide information related to weather, technologies etc • to provide all other information needs of rural families Use of video media to telecast live interactive programmes	Widely used to provide market information Several initiatives are emerging Widely used by TV channels	Price information (though important) alone not sufficient to realize better prices by farmers Efforts at consolidating, processing and adding value to raw information and re-packaging the same in local language in an attractive format are lacking at present Though a potentially promising area for public-private partnerships, efforts are lacking	Developing appropriate programme modules is equally or more important than providing hardware and connectivity

(Sulaiman, 2003)

scientist, had also suggested setting up Media Resource Centres, which can provide credible and timely information to the print, audio, video and new (i.e., internet) media for a hunger- free India.

India's policy framework for agricultural extension developed by the Ministry of Agriculture envisages a larger role for mass media by providing for:

• online market information

• support to the private sector to establish IT information kiosks

• wider use of mass media for extension

• more farmer participation in mass media programmes (Policy framework for agricultural extension, 2000)

Farmer participation is a vital factor for a successful mass media campaign. Involving successful farmers and local experts in developing messages for mass media could help. A worthwhile strategy would be to make the rural folk themselves to write for newspapers and magazines and make radio and TV programmes. Programmes/Publications could be effective when produced with audience participation, in local languages and with consideration for cultural traditions.

A recent analysis on the mass media innovations in transfer of agricultural technologies had revealed that developing appropriate programmes

are more important than providing hardware connectivity to Indian farmers (Table 6).

Finally, mass media need not be targeted to the public as a whole. The mass medium can choose the target audiences, say farm women, for communicating the research outputs. Only then, one can decide in which publications and on which programmes from the vast range of print, broadcast and online outlets one should be aiming for coverage. The channel should address how best to publicize the farm technologies and influence debate among the target groups.

CONCLUSION

This chapter had discussed the role of traditional mass media in farm technology transfer and the emerging role of new media. The comparison studies on the effectiveness of traditional media and new media did not bring forth a clear winner in terms of different attributes of mass media. The strategies formulated suggest a judicious combination of traditional and new media based on the situation to reach the Indian farmer.

All these strategies would be effective if they were implemented along with an ongoing development programme. Such institutionalization would help in giving these strategies a sense of permanency. In addition, one- shot short-term approaches may not result in any significant behaviour change among the farmers and these strategies need to be implemented on a long-term basis.

Though there are studies available on which traditional mass medium had been successful or otherwise, among users, research on comparing the effectiveness of traditional and new media are relatively less. Conducting more and more in–depth media comparison studies alone would assist the change agents of the country in formulating appropriate extension strategies for effective farm communication.

REFERENCES

After radio rice, Orissa will now have a radio village too. (2003, June 14). *The New Indian Express,* p. 7.

All India Radio. (2003). Retrieved March 2, 2003, from http://www.air.org.in

Ayaz, M. (1991). Radio: A supplement to agricultural development in Pakistan. *Journal of Rural Development and Administration, 23*(4), 12–22.

Cecchini, S. (2002). *Can information and communication technology application contribute to 'poverty reduction? Lessons from rural India.* Retrieved August 13, 2008, from http://www.nijenrodo.nl/download/nice/anrep2000.pdf

Chandrashekara, P. (2001 January). Mass media in Agricultural extension: Best, yet to come. *Manage Extension Research Review,* 38-44.

CM's pat for SHGs. (2003, September 2). *The New Indian Express,* p. 6.

Cook, J. (1995). Training methods and media. *International Agricultural Development, 15*(4), 8–9.

DD seeks funds from Agricultural ministry for its rural bonanza. (2003, August 4). *The New Indian Express,* p. 9.

Dossani, R., Misra, D. C., & Jhaveri, R. (2005). *Enabling ICT for Rural India.* Retrieved August 13, 2008, from http://ruralinformatics.nic.in/files/4_12_0_90.pdf

Dowlath, P., & Seepersad, J. (1999). Understanding information sources in the communication process: preparing for the information revolution in extension. In *Proceedings of the 15th Annual Conference of AIEEE,* Republic of Trinidad & Tobago.

DRDA. (2006). *District Rural Development Agency of Nagapattinam.* Retrieved August 16, 2006, from http://nagapattinam.nic.in/drda.html#sgsy

FAO. (1998). Knowledge and information for food security in Africa: From traditional media to the internet. *CAB International Database.* Retrieved December 3, 2001, from http://www.cabsubsets.org/cabsbin/bw_frames_action/

Fernandez, A. P. (2005 March). *Self-Help Affinity Groups: their role in poverty reduction and financial sector development.* Paper presented at the International Conference on Micro-finance in the global strategy for meeting the millennium development goals, Dublin, Ireland.

Flay, B. R. (1987). *Seeking the smokeless society: Fifty-six evaluated mass media programs and campaigns worldwide.* Washington, DC: American Public Health Association.

Forno, D. A. (1999). Sustainable development starts with agriculture. In *Sustainable agriculture solutions: The action report of the sustainable agriculture initiative* (pp. 8–11). London: Novello Press Ltd.

Government of Tamil Nadu. (2006). *Rural Development and Panchayati Raj Department, Policy note 2006-07.* Retrieved August 16, 2006, from http://www.tn.gov.in

IAMAI. (2007). Retrieved August 13, 2008, from http://www.iamai.in/section. php3?secid=16&press_id=813&mon=2

Jain, S. P., & Goria, S. (2006). *Digital library for Indian farmers (DLIF) using open source software: a strategic planning.* Retrieved January 24, 2009, from http://www.ifla.org/IV/ifla72/index.htm

Kaurani, M. D. (1995). *Media support to Agriculture. MANAGE Occasional paper 4.* Hyderabad, India: MANAGE.

Lazarsfeld, P., Berelson, B., & Gaudet, H. (1944). *The people's choice.* New York: Duell, Sloan, & Pearce.

Márquez-Berber, S. R. (2003). *Computers and agriculture: The Mexico case.* Retrieved August 16, 2003, from http://www.agen.ufl.edu/comconf/6thproc/cahome.html

Mary, V., & Vasanthakumar, J. (2001). Analysis of farm broadcast and farm telecast with regard to time allotment to different subjects and communication sources of programmes. *Journal of Extension Education, 12*(1), 2995–3003.

MYRADA. (2006). *Characteristics that can describe a sangha as 'good'. MYRADA Rural Management Systems Series Paper No. 15.* Bangalore, India: MYRADA.

National Sample Survey Organization (NSSO). (1997). *Final population totals excluding J&K. 53rd Round NSSO, December, 1997.* New Delhi, India: NSSO.

National Sample Survey Organization (NSSO). (2005). *Access to modern technology for farmers. 59th round NSSO, December 2003.* New Delhi, India: NSSO.

Ninan, S. (2002, June 23). Rural revolution. *The Hindu,* p. 3.

Nine states to get internet kiosks with cotton focus. (2003, April 25). *The Hindu Business Line,* p. 6.

Pigato, M. (2001). *Information and Communication Technology, Poverty and Development in sub-Saharan Africa and South Asia.* Retrieved April 8, 2003, from http://www.worldbank.org/afr/wps

Policy framework for agricultural extension. (2000). Extension division, Dept. of Agriculture & Co-operation, Ministry of Agriculture, Govt. of India

Prathap, D. P. (1994). *Participation of farmers in Credit Management Groups organized by an NGO.* Un Pub. M Sc. (Ag.) Thesis. Annamalai nagar: Annamalai University.

Prathap, D. P. (2004). Relative effectiveness of farm communication through mass media including new media: An experimental approach with rural women. *Dissertation Abstracts International, 66*(10). (Publication No. AAT 3193131).

Prathap, D. P., & Ponnusamy, K. A. (2006). Effectiveness of Four Mass Media Channels on the Knowledge Gain of Rural Women. *Journal of International Agricultural and Extension Education, 13*(1), 73–81.

Rajesh, M. (2003). A study of the problems associated with ICT adaptability in developing countries in the context of distance education. *Turkish Online Journal of Distance Education, 4*(2). Retrieved June 30, 2003, from http://tojde.anadolu.edu.tr/tojde/articles.htm

Ray, H. (1978). *The basic village education project: Guatemala.* Washington, DC: Academy for Educational Development.

RBI. (2006). *Micro credit: A lifeline for the poor.* Retrieved October 4, 2006 from http://www.rbi.org.in/scripts/FAQView.aspx?Id=7

SBI plans to make rural areas e-savvy. (2003, April 13). *The New Indian Express,* p. 3.

Sharma, R. C. (2002). Interactive radio counselling in distance education. *University News*, *40*(10), 8–11.

Shiva, V. (1991). *Most farmers in India are women.* New Delhi, India: FAO.

Sulaiman, V. R. (2003). *Innovations in agricultural extension in India.* Retrieved August 16, 2006, from www.fao.org/sd/KN1_en.htm

Suvedi, M., Campo, S., & Lapinski, M. K. (1999). Trends in Michigan farmers' information-seeking behaviors and perspectives on the delivery of information. *Journal of Applied Communications*, *83*(3).

Swaminathan, M. S. (2003). Towards hunger free India: Count down to 2007. *Current Science*, *84*(10), 1297–1300.

Top 20 Countries with highest number of Internet users. (2007). Retrieved November 14, 2008, from http://www.InternetWorldStats.com.

Venkateshwarlu, K. (2002, October 6). Community Radio has villagers excited. *The Hindu*, p. 12.

Vijapurkar, M. (2002, June 18). Newspaper readership up, says study. *The Hindu*, p. 8.

Vilanilam, J. V. (1993). *Science Communication and Development.* New Delhi, India: Sage Publications.

World Bank. (2006). *ICT at a glance.* Retrieved August 4, 2008, from http://devdata.worldbank.org/ind_ict.pdf

You cannot carry your television set to the beach. (2002, July 31). *The New Indian Express,* p. 9.

Chapter 15
Strategy of Accounting Automation:
The Case of the Egyptian International Motors Company (EIM)

Khaled Dahawy
The American University in Cairo, USA

ABSTRACT

Decisions relating to choice and implementation of computerized accounting systems differ dramatically between developed and developing nations in respect to the cultural, political, economic, and environmental factors. This study aims to assess the implementation of accounting information system in a company in a developing nation; Egypt. The case indicates the importance of the integration of accounting and technology. However, in a developing nation like Egypt, characterized with over population and high unemployment, automation becomes a very sensitive issue. Therefore, there is a need for strong management support and commitment to insure successful implementation. Developing countries, especially Egypt, should direct its companies to increase its dependence on Information Communication Technology (ICT). As the case shows there are many benefits that ICT can offer to the individual companies. If each individual company can become more efficient and effective the whole economy will be better and will be able to utilize scare resources more efficiently and effectively.

INTRODUCTION

In today's world information is power (Porter and Millar 1998). Management Information System (MIS) is a man made system that usually consists of integrated sets of components established to collect, store, and manage data and to provide output information to users. MIS facilitates the operational functions of a business and supports the management decision making processes by providing information to managers. Mangers use information to plan and control the activities of their companies (Laudon and Laudon 2003). Accounting information system (AIS) is an integral specialized subsystem of MIS. The main purpose of AIS is to collect, process, and report information related to the financial aspects of business activities (Gelinas et al. 2005). AIS is compromised of:

DOI: 10.4018/978-1-60566-388-3.ch015

(1) People operating and performing the various function of the system; (2) Procedures in terms of both manual and automated; (3) Data about the organization's business processes; (4) Software used to process the organization's data and (5) the information technology infrastructure which includes computers, peripheral devices and network communication devices. The main goals of AIS are the collation and processing data about the organization's business activities efficiently and effectively; converting data into accurate, timely and useful information for management to make decisions and establish adequate controls to ensure that data about business activities are recorded and processed accurately and safeguard both data and other organizational assets. The presence of a well designed AIS in a company should lead to improving efficiency of operations by providing more timely information, improve organization profit by improving the efficiency and effectiveness of its supply chain, improve decision making by providing accurate information in a timely manner, and facilitate or make easier sharing of knowledge and expertise. AIS can stand for a manual or an automated system.

The use of computerized accounting information systems has become an integral part of accounting systems world wide. The marriage of accounting and technology is critical to the development of accounting (Adams 2008, Robson 2006, Doost 1999, Hoing 1999). The American Institute of Certified Public Accountants conclude that "… professional accounting has merged and developed with IT to such an extent that one can hardly conceive accounting independent of IT" (AICPA 1996). However, most of the research and cases that examine issues related to accounting in general and choice and implementation of computerized accounting information systems, in particular, have focused on developed nations (Dahawy and Conover 2007, Rudaki 1998). However, decisions relating to the choice and implementation of computerized accounting systems are very sensitive to cultural and environmental factors.

Therefore, such decisions should be studied within the context of their own environments (Ismail and King, 2006). Environmental factors differ dramatically between developed and developing nations. In addition, within the context of developing nations, the cultural, political, and economic realities of each country are often very different (Dahawy et al. 2002). It is better not to develop a standard prescription and make recommendations without first analyzing the specificities of each nation (Dahawy et al. 2002). Therefore, it is vital to improve our understanding of the process of choice and implementation of computerized accounting information systems in specific developing nations, such as Egypt.

The developments in both accounting and Information and Communication Technology (ICT) have made it easier for companies to migrate to computerized accounting systems. Accounting, in Egypt, has dramatically changed in the past few years by the adoption of the International Accounting Standards (IAS)[1] in 1992 followed by translation of some international accounting standards in 1996 and using them as Egyptian standards (World Bank, 2002). In 2006, the Ministry of Investment introduced a newly developed comprehensive Egyptian Accounting Standards (EAS) that are based on the International Financial Reporting Standards (IFRS) (Hassan 2008, HassabElnaby 2003). The new EAS were issued by ministerial decree number 243 in 2006 to be applied for the financial year starting from January, 1st, 2007. The new EAS differ from IFRS in four major areas; (a) Profit distribution to employees and board members are not included as expenses as required by the IFRS but are reported as profit distributions, (b) Reevaluation of assets is not allowed except in very specific and rare cases that are represented in the Egyptian company's law (e.g. mergers and acquisitions), (c) Egyptian banks, as prescribed by the Egyptian Central Bank, are required to accumulate a general provision through deductions from the income statement, in conflict with the IFRS requirements, and (d)

Leasing treatment in EAS are completely different from IFRS. The lessor keeps the asset on his/her financial accounting books and records its depreciation. The lessee reports lease payments as expenses during the payment period. This development in adoption increased the need for timely and accurate financial records, information, and statements. Integrating information communication technology (ICT) is one of the main tools to reach this end.

Egypt, as a developing nation faces many challenges in building an information society in order to bridge the digital divides (Ahmed 2007). Egypt must overcome the barriers that constrain the use and spread of the new communications technologies and their applications (Wheeler 2003, Hashem 2002). In Egypt efforts for ICT development are led by the government, in close partnership with the business community and the civil society (MCIT, 2006). The Egyptian government has focused on the development of ICT as a national priority to contribute to high and sustainable economic growth for the Egyptian economy (El Sayed and Westrup 2003). However, these efforts are faced with problems related to language, access to data, and corporate cultures (Zaidman et al. 2008). The government views the development of information and communication technology as a national priority (American Chamber of Commerce in Egypt, 2002). Egypt aims, through ICT, at building an export strategy that is based on competiveness, which will attract foreign direct investments (FDI) and allow Egypt to act as a regional hub (Sober et al. 2006, El Sherif 2004, Handoussa and Abou Shnief 2003, Porter and Millar 1998). As a result, MCIT 2007-2010 ICT strategy reports the following priorities:

- To continue development of state of the art ICT infrastructure that provides and enabling environment for government and businesses through Egypt and links it globally

- To create a vibrant and export oriented ICT industry

- To leverage public-private partnership as an implementation mechanism whenever possible

- To enable society to absorb and benefit from expanding sources of information

- To create a learning community whose members have access to all the resources and information they require regardless of gender and location, thus allowing all to achieve their full potential and play a part in the country's socioeconomic development.

- To support the development of the skills required by the ICT industry

- To support research and innovation in the field of ICT

To reach the abovementioned strategic goals, Egypt is technologically modernizing itself. During the last decade it has successfully mainstreamed ICT as part of its national development strategy (MCIT 2007). There is a low PC penetration rate although increasing at 50% growth rate annually (www.mcit.gov.eg). However, the investment and build-up of Egypt's information and communication technology infrastructure has taken massive steps since the early 1990s in different building blocks including human, systems, procedures, and hardware and information infrastructure (IDSC Annual Report, 2000). Egypt adopted many strategies to increase the diffusion of internet. The Ministry of Communications and Information Technology (MCIT) reports a significant increase in internet users from 0.65 million users in 2000 to 9.17 million users in 2008. This increase is coupled with a 92% increase in international bandwidth. MCIT also reports significant increase in firms connected to the internet, with 71% companies of companies connected to the internet having websites which they use as tools to facilitate their marketing and publicity activities. In addition, a growing number of enterprises which have websites reports receiving (34.8%)

and sending (21%) orders over the internet. Also, 26.8% of enterprises use the internet for accessing internet banking and other financial services. Furthermore, private enterprises report several benefits from use of E-commerce like; speeding up operations (94%), increase customer accessibility (51%), reduce transaction cost (31%), and increased security (16%) (MCIT 2008).

The importance of the use of technology in accounting has been internationally recognized in general (Adams 2008, Robson 2006, Horngren et al. 2000, Mia and Clark 1999), and in Egypt in particular (Osemy and Prodhan 2001). As part of a comprehensive e-government initiative, Egypt's Ministry of Communications and Information Technology (MCIT) has licensed a comprehensive range of Oracle technology to ultimately power and link up to 5000 financial units throughout the country (MCIT, 2005). In 2006, MCIT represented by Egypt ICT Trust Fund has started with the UNDP and the International Development Research Centre (IDRC) a two years pilot research project intended to study the effect of building capacity for Egyptian SMEs to leverage ICT to generate employment and create efficient, better connected and more competitive enterprises. The project then partnered with Microsoft and ICS in The Youth & SME Empowerment Program, which is a 3 years initiative Funded by Microsoft and Implemented by the Integrated Care Society, which was launched in April 2007. Particular care has been exercised to create the capacity and the institutional frameworks necessary to support the company's development. The aim is to use ICT to provide a standardized and uniform communication mechanism, while improving the capacity to carry out critical tasks such as accounting, inventory control, etc. with greater efficiency (MCIT 2008b). Researchers have acknowledged that there is a need for Egyptian accountants to understand AIS in order to meet the needs of decision makers and to develop the decision making process. Therefore, Egyptian accountants should expand their knowledge and skills beyond the traditional

disciplinary remit of accounting to encompass knowledge of ICT (Osemy and Prodhan 2001, Abd Allah 1992). The British Council in Egypt, which is the UK's leading international organization for educational and cultural relations in Egypt, has emphasized the need for the merge between ICT and accounting in Egypt by offering the Association of Certified Chartered Accountants (ACCA) certificate that equips candidates with an in-depth knowledge of accounting techniques and principles, management skills and IT, which will enable them to work in any area of accounting and finance. Furthermore, ICT developments are an urgent desired aid to help the Egyptian government in its campaign to clean accounting malpractices and corruption in Egypt (Abdel Maguid 2004) and increase the economy's ability to compete (Mia and Clarke 1999, Porter and Millard 1998).

This study aims to assess the implementation of accounting information system in a company in a developing nation. To answer this question this manuscript attempts to do the following: (1) identify the reasons for the shift to an automated system and the main goals that the company aim to achieve form this shift, (2) determine the company's strategic decisions like choices between outsourcing versus in-house development, and ready made packages versus tailor made software, (3) describe the steps of implementation, (4) understand the reaction of the employees to the new automated system, (5) study the required changes on the organizational chart and human resources qualifications that are required, (6) recognize the problems that the company met during the process, (7) point the advantages of the shift to the automated system.

The methodology of this study is through intensive interviews with the key players of the Egyptian International Motors Company (EIM). Specifically, this paper is mainly based on in depth interviews with the CEO, CFO, and the IT department manager of the company. These interviews were also supported by interviews with selected employees in the accounting and IT departments.

Figure 1.

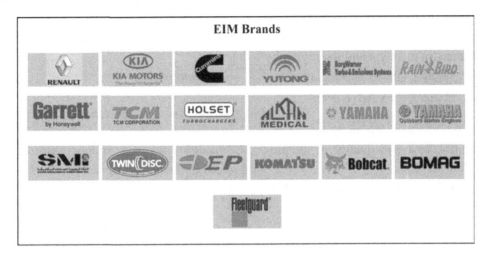

The choice of this company as a subject for this research was because it is a large local firm that implements a computerized accounting information system. The fact that the firm is a local firm and does not have an affiliation with an international firm is important to control the effect of any foreign company that might influence the choice and implementation process. If the firm had had an affiliation with a foreign company that had implemented a computerized accounting system, it would dramatically affect the choice and implementation process of the computerized accounting system of the company.

SETTING THE STAGE

EIM was established 1979 as a main business unit within Alkan group. Its remarkable growth over the years has positioned it as a market leader in various business fields. The company activities include multinational enterprise representation, lease finance services and free zone storage and clearance. The company is categorized as a commercial company that is involved in various areas/disciplines through the acquisition of licenses. This makes the company a unique company in

the sense that each acquired license is treated as a separate line of business. The company's description of line of businesses in its articles of incorporation states that it is a retail company that operates in: manufacturing, importation, export, distribution and acts as an agent of passenger cars, heavy equipment and agriculture equipment; importation of textile machinery and equipment for flour mills and crushing plants. Today the company is one of Egypt's most mature private sectors operations, exclusively distributing and servicing more than 25 world renowned brands in more than 7 business sectors, both in Egypt and in the Region (See Figure 1).

EIM has a high dynamic operational structure. Seven semi-independent business divisions organized mainly around the business sectors they serve, manage the company's different brands. EIM is able to offer its customers the superior levels of support they deserve as a result of a strong managerial and operational structure, powered by nearly 1500 employees. Each of the brands represented by EIM is a leader in its segment. These brands are served by a distribution network including EIM branches as well as extensive dealer networks and after-market services delivered through highly qualified and well trained technical staff in EIM workshops across the country or on-site wherever the customer is. EIM strives to make a distinct and profound positive difference in the trade industry in Egypt and the region by supplying the highest quality service, products and solutions to its customers. It aims to

- Achieve continuous improvements in the profitability, cost and quality of all processes and services.
- Secure the desired return on investment for shareholders
- Deliver the solutions best suited to the requirements of company clientele at commercially competitive and financially viable prices.
- Expand company markets to suit its diversified business portfolio

Company Mission

With customer satisfaction as its foremost commercial ideal, EIM will –through sophisticated and efficient distribution & servicing networks – deliver the solutions best suited to the requirements of its clientele, at commercially competitive and financially viable price, thus expanding its markets and securing the desired return on investment for its shareholder & principles.

What makes EIM unique are its strategic capabilities that allows it to pursue market opportunities in the best, most speedy manner. The company's deep local roots give it greater insight into what clients want and where opportunities for growth reside. The diversified range of businesses permits exposure to several fields of expertise, creating a knowledge base in the respective market sectors. EIM Company has nationwide presence, ensuring full local market coverage that allows for unmatched distribution. The company's broad reach of experienced and qualified employees offers an ongoing renewal of ideas, strategies and new business acquisitions. Local presence and regional

reach is made more powerful by the company's third competitive advantage; managing a portfolio of some of the most powerful brands worldwide.

Company Vision

To become the benchmark for operational efficiency and customer satisfaction in the market through providing customers with total solutions, delivered with the highest levels of performance excellence

EIM has represented diverse multinational names over the years. EIM has created a very special position for itself in the market, serving a large number of clients of various sizes, ranging from major local and international contractors to individuals. In order to preserve the company's vision and the mission, the company decided to update its manual accounting system and to introduce an electronic accounting system, and then decided to develop its accounting system to a more elaborate one. The next section presents this strategic endeavor.

The next diagram shows the extent of the complexity of the company's business by showing the breakdown of the company's business structure. It shows that the company is divided into divisions (Cost Center), which are then divided into brands. Within each brand there are several activities. The activities are performed in various branches which contains more than one point of sales (See Figure 2).

Table 1 summarizes the financial position of the company on December 2005.

THE CASE

When Tarek was hired in 2001 as the new CFO, and deputy CEO of the company he was surprised to find that the company has bought the license of Oracle financials for over a year but the program has never been implemented or used. The company

Figure 2.

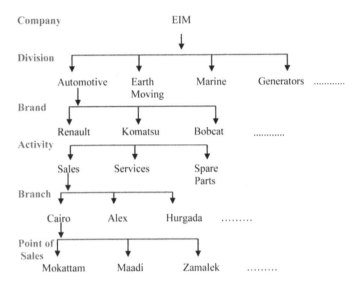

was dependent on a system of excel sheets and macros. During this period the annual sales of

Table 1.

Balance sheet (EIM) On December 31, 2005	
Assets: Current assets 384,000,000 Long term assets 37,000,000	**Liabilities:** Current liabilities 326,000,000 Long term liabilities 67,000,000 **Owner's equity** 28,000,000
Total assets <u>421,000,000</u>	Total liabilities and <u>421,000,000</u> owner's equity

the company amounted to 250 million Egyptian pounds. Tarek was hired after a vast experience as a finance and accounting manager of a multinational pharmaceutical company in Saudi Arabia and Egypt. The pharmaceutical company depended heavily on a well known accounting and finance software system. As a result, he was aware of the benefits and advantages of the presence of such developed programs.

To understand the story Tarek referred to Mohamed - head of the IT department in the company. Mohamed explained to Tarek that in the early 80s the company had depended on a very successful manual accounting system. Management had felt that this manual system is sufficient for the needs of the company in terms of technical complexity and reporting needs. Mohamed summarized the pros and cons of the manual accounting system that was used as follows:

Advantages:

- Simple to use
- No need to invest money in updating. It was very cheap to hire someone to develop
- No need to invest in training of the employees

Disadvantages:

- The reports were not offered on timely basis
- The need of high investment in internal auditing department to overcome manual human errors

- The data is recorded in the journal then posted to the ledger and the other accounting books manually until the balances reach the financial statements. These procedures are both repetitive, time consuming and has a high risk of errors

The first experience that the company had with accounting computer software came in the mid 80s when the company bought its first software that works on Vax/Vma and was installed on a mainframe and connected to a small number of terminals where the users only had a screen and a keyboard. The software was written in a language called Vax/Basic which is one of the oldest programming languages. The interface at the user terminals was text mode that was based on a question/answer interface with the user. The database depended on flat files without any relation so the integration exists in programs and not in the database. This application was designed to work on one division, so it was very difficult to make suitable integration after the company's expansion. The database was very limited, where there was very limited configuration of the fields in the files. Any change in the fields will result in huge modifications in the program code, so any expansion in the organization structure led to a huge modification by the IT department

The main advantage of the software, that the company was using, was that it was an open source software, which meant that the program codes were available and could be tailored to accept the increases in the capacities of this program. These developments were mainly administered by the IT department personnel. However, this software was designed to operate for only one division that is divided into several departments. When the company expanded to handle different licenses it was close to impossible to adjust the system to meet the needs of handling each license that the company used as a separate company within EIM. An example of the difficulties was that the code of the branches was only 0-9 which meant

that when the company had more than 9 branches they were unable to code them. In addition, the code of the customers only included 3 digits which meant that the company could not code more than 1,000customers.

In the early 1990s there was an urgent need to cover the work in the big number of branches and link them with the head office, so another application was developed by IT department by Dbase4 and installed as an isolated system in the branches and some programs created to work as a middleware between the server and the offline database in the branches to link between them and the server in the head office.

In the late 90s the company's management felt the need to change the system to a more developed system. As a result, the IT department sent a memo to the company's deputy CEO that summarized the reasons for the needed change as follows:

1. The sources that offered the needed tools for this software were fading very quickly. Therefore, it was becoming prohibitively expensive to maintain the system.
2. The development of the IT education market made it very hard to find employees who know how to work on the aging software
3. Need to develop the software to meet the problems present in the old software
4. The software interface is very user unfriendly
5. Due to the expansion of the company there is an urgent need to have new software that provides more flexible, accurate and up to date information.
6. The old software is unable to satisfy the increased management analytical requirements, reports, and analysis that are required by the decision makers in the company
7. The old software is not suitable to keep the company's competitive edge in the market

The deputy CEO acted fast and contacted Mohamed, he told him that he agreed with his assessment and that he had verbally received the

Figure 3.

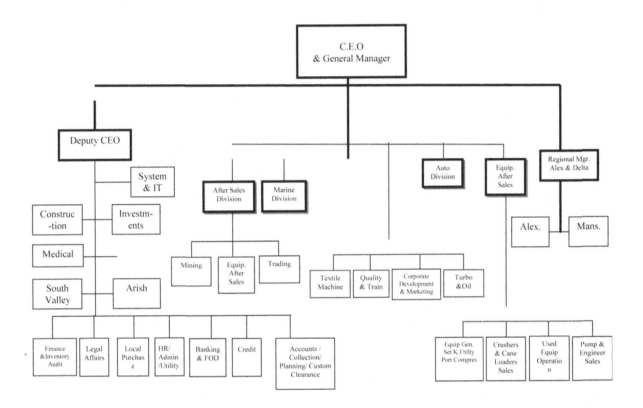

approval of the members of the Board of Directors (BOD) to proceed. He then asked Mohamed to explain to him the viable options that EIM had to proceed are.

After he researched the market and called some of his friends Mohamed informed the deputy CEO that he thinks that the company can either:

1. Buy readymade software and he recommended Oracle Financials, which he believed was the strongest and most advanced software at that time,
2. Use Oracle tools to tailor software for the specific needs of EIM.

Mohamed presented the CEO with Table 2 which summarizes the two options.

Oracle financials includes the following modules (1) General Ledger, (2) Payables, (3) Assets, (4) Purchasing, (5) Receivables, (6) Cash Man-

agement, and (7) Inventory. After a meeting with the CFO and the accounting manager, Mohamed discovered that there will be a need to adjust some of these modules to meet the detailed needs of the company. Further analysis indicated that in addition to these modules the company needs to have other modules (1) Payroll, (2) human resources, (3) call center, and (4) workshop.

After extensive meetings between the CEO, Tarek, and Mohamed they found that to get the best out of the two options they can actually combine the two options as follows:

1. Buy Oracle Financials
2. Hire Oracle Egypt company to administer GAP analysis to see the required adjustments
3. Estimate the costs of the needed adjustments
4. Support the IT department personnel with the required training for the implementation

Table 2.

	Ready Made	**Tailor Made**
Cost	High cost	Low cost
Implementation	Lower implementation time	Higher implementation time
Design	Generic design to work for large corporations	Designed based on the specific needs of the company
Adaptation	Needs several adaptations to fit EIM needs	Needs detailed analysis of the company followed by the design of the system
Details	Usually results in loss of details that are present in the current system	Includes some of the characteristics of the current system
New Ideas	Adds new ideas to the company and allows it to make appropriate decisions	If the designers do not have enough exposure to other systems the result might be a slight improvement to the current system that might not add much to the company
IT personnel	Does not depend on the IT department qualifications	Depends on the company's IT personnel abilities, knowledge and experiences
Training	Need training courses for the IT personnel	No need for training courses for the IT personnel

5. Buy the license of Oracle tools and allow the company's IT department to build the needed modules that are missing from Oracle financials

This plan seemed satisfactory and the company started implementing it. They paid the first contractual installment of 10% of the cost of Oracle financials. They then hired the Oracle engineers to apply GAP analysis and assess the required adjustments. During this time the members of the IT department of the company started taking extensive courses on how to implement, operate, and maintain the Oracle financials software. Parallel to this the members of the IT department were also taking courses to develop their abilities in using Oracle tools to produce the missing modules that are needed. Also, the IT department started preparing a list of required customizations and the costs of the needed customizations.

In mid 2002 some irritating news occurred. The problem that was not anticipated was that Oracle charged them high hourly rates to do the analysis. In addition, the findings of the GAP analysis indicated that the required adjustments would be very expensive. An example of the adjustments that were found were (1) the cash management module was not compatible with the Egyptian way of using check as a credit tool, and (2) the system treatment of inventory in branches as separate companies. Further the cost of training was very expensive. At the same time, the IT department personnel had proven their abilities and have produced the Human resources module and the Payroll module. When implemented the results were outstanding.

When Tarek and Mohamed met and added the incurred costs they decided that they rushed into their plan and that this plan turned to be a lot more expensive than what they anticipated. As a result, they decided to change their plan, to abandon the implementation process, and to build a whole tailor made software using Oracle tools without purchasing and adjusting the Oracle financials ready made software. Mohamed assured Tarek that the IT department personnel were ready to produce a tailor made program that has all the advantages of Oracle financials ready made software and at the same time specifically designed for the companies specific needs. This was possible due to two factors. First, the IT personnel have been trained very well in using the Oracle tool. Second, while being trained to use Oracle financials the IT personnel got highly accustomed with the design and interface of the ready-made program.

Mohamed was assigned to lead a team from the IT department in conjunction with a group from the various departments that are affected. The task force took the following steps:

1. Increase the number of employees of the IT department from 5 to 11.
2. The senior IT personnel would be responsible to develop a comprehensive detailed study that includes the specific needs of the current situation in every department, put solutions to the problems, and discuss these needs with the programmers.
3. Compare the current status, the problems and the Oracle financials design for the section that is studied. At that time the programmers had formulated the backbone of a system that is almost identical with the Oracle financials and were ready to adapt it to the needed adjustments to solve the needs discovered from the analysis.
4. Establish an organizational structure in a new manner that can accommodate the addition of any new company, license, department, and/or division.
5. Each IT personnel were responsible to implement a part. He/she was required to set a schedule for the implementation of his/her part in conjunction with the end users.
6. The implementation stage ended with the presence of the end user who would be actually using the part. He/she was offered detailed hands on session on how to use his/her part of the software.
7. He/she was allowed to freely state his/her remarks and/or comments on the software and the IT personnel were responsible to make the required adjustments if applicable.
8. The end user was then offered a full course in how to use the software. Concurrently the software was tested during this period by the IT personnel on a testing server after adjusting it.
9. The end users were required to spend 2 month entering their data on a test server assigned for testing purposes and training at the same time.
10. The new software would run parallel to the old software for one months for comparative purposes.

The IT department was successful in the implementation which took four full months. The system was running within one year of the inception plan. The IT department employees spent many sleepless nights in the company making sure that the software was functional in the shortest period possible. They also had to work on daily problems. However, at the end the software was a great success with many benefits for management and users. Figure 4 indicates a summary of the steps that were taken. The success of the software was echoed in the management quick acceptance of the new ICT developments in the company, as will be discussed in the next sections.

OBSTACLES IN IMPLEMENTING THE NEW SYSTEM

The implementation of the software was not as smooth as the management had expected. Several obstacles came up. There was difficulty in the integration between the software's development and implementation periods. The implementation could not be done at one time for all the diverse sections. Also, the implementation team could not shut the company during the implementation period. Instead, they implemented the software in what they called a "step by step way". For example they started by the car maintenance department. When they migrated the maintenance department system to the new software, it was hard for the updated department data to be visible to the old software. However, the actions performed in the maintenance department (for example a client brings his car for repair) would impact several

Figure 4.

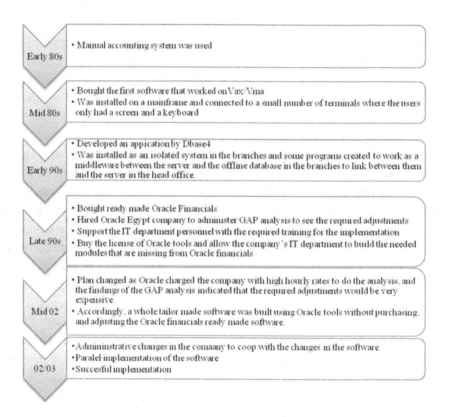

Early 80s	• Manual accounting system was used

Mid 80s
• Bought the first software that worked on Vax/Vma
• Was installed on a mainframe and connected to a small number of terminals where the users only had a screen and a keyboard

Early 90s
• Developed an appication by Dbase4
• Was installed as an isolated system in the branches and some programs created to work as a middleware between the server and the offline database in the branches to link between them and the server in the head office.

Late 90s
• Bought ready made Oracle Financials
• Hired Oracle Egypt company to administer GAP analysis to see the required adjustments
• Support the IT department personnel with the required training for the implementation
• Buy the license of Oracle tools and allow the company's IT department to build the needed modules that are missing from Oracle financials

Mid 02
• Plan changed as Oracle charged the company with high hourly rates to do the analysis, and the findings of the GAP analysis indicated that the required adjustments would be very expensive.
• Accordingly, a whole tailor made software was built using Oracle tools without purchasing, and adjusting the Oracle financials ready made software.

02/03
• Adminstrative changes in the comaany to coop with the changes in the software.
• Paralel implementation of the software
• Succesful implementation

other departments like client account, inventory, and treasury (cash). To overcome this problem the IT department had to create a middle-ware application to be able to keep the effect of the existing links between the new application and the old one. Second, the IT department recognized the need to deliver one report which includes the data from the old and the new software together. To overcome this problem the IT department created a data warehouse server and migrated daily batches from the two platforms and explored it by the Oracle discoverer tool.

Employee resistance was the main obstacle to the software and its development. Employees were afraid that the development of the software, would lead to more automation and less need for humans. This problem was intensified by the fact that many users had no experience with the basic knowledge of using WINDOWS. As a remedy the IT department made sure to involve the key users in their goals and vision. In addition, the IT department prepared the International Computer Driving License (ICDL) training to the users by dividing them into groups. The aim was to raise the level of appreciation of the technology to a level that made the employees appreciate the software as a benefit and not a threat.

The employees created another problem as the new developed software impacted the power of balance in the company. Many of the more tenured employees who had long experience with company had little computer background, while many of the younger inexperienced employees had more computer knowledge and were able to understand the changes in the system more readily. The top management had to be very careful in facing these situations on one by one case as they occur. In one case they had to hire a special secretary to one of the old employees to make sure that he/she can act as a facilitator between the manager and the software.

Another obstacle was the need to change the whole environment, especially hardware. This turned out to be expensive and sometimes led to unpleasant confrontations with management. With the exception of some incidents the IT department was able to overcome this obstacle by preparing thorough detailed budgets that included as much information as possible. In addition, Mohamed tried as much as possible to meet with the BOD members every time to explain to them any changes in the budget and the reasons for the change.

BENEFITS FROM THE NEW SYSTEM

There were several benefits that resulted from implementing the system. From the point of view of management, especially the CEO and deputy CEO, the ability to view the company information at different levels of integration on a timely basis was the top benefit. By computerizing the accounting system management was allowed full access of detailed information at different levels of aggregation, depending on the level that the decision maker needs for each decision. For example the decision maker can see financial information from a comprehensive picture, for the whole company as a whole. In the same time he/she can see the financial information by brand, site, geographical location, and/or any factor/characteristic that he/she deems necessary. Encouraged by their success, the IT department is currently working on updating this feature by using the data warehouse to create Key Performance Indicators (KPIs). This will allow the decision maker to perform sensitivity analysis (What If analysis) that would allow him/her to forecast the result of certain decision before proceeding. This will allow the decision maker to view the historical information, change any part of it, and view the impact of the change on the results in graphical, user friendly, and simple way.

Also, the data is available on timely basis. The new software allows the information to be reported and updated instantaneously on line, with not lag time. The decision maker can receive his/her information on time when he/she needs it. AIS generates real-time, comprehensive reports and ensures access to complete and critical information, instantly. Computerized accounting makes sure that the critical financial information is accurate, controlled and safe from data corruption.

AIS established the ability to handle huge volumes of transactions without compromising on speed or efficiency. Over time, this made employees more comfortable with the system as they started to view it as a friend and not as an enemy. In informal surveys that the IT department applied one year after the implementation of the new system they found that the employees actually "highly like" the new system and find it to "strongly" help them with their work. Furthermore, many employees said that the training they received made them feel more valuable.

The development of this system required large financial investments, that management initially felt was too high. However, over time management discovered that the cost cuts from using the system were a lot more than the initial amount that was spent. Cost savings came from the decrease in amount of paper used. Also, the new system included connections between the various sites of the company that are scattered all over the country. As, a result, the company shifted to Voice-Over-IP which dramatically improved the speed and accuracy of the communication and data flow.

Given the large number and variations of the licenses that the company handles, the accounting department has to handle transactions in many different currencies. Based on the Egyptian Accounting Standards the company has to report in its accounting records using the Egyptian pound. Tracking and translating transactions in various currencies and reporting them using multiple exchange rates used to put a large burden on the accounting department. The new

AIS brought with it the ability to smoothly deal in multiple currencies. It allows the company to trade in multiple currencies with ease. Therefore, problems associated with exchange rate changes are minimized.

RESULTS OF THE SUCCESS

The success of the implementation of AIS generated so much interest and genuine momentum towards applying ICT to benefit the company as much as possible through integration of the ICT power. The company took five significant steps in the area of ICT that would not be possible in their magnitude and/or rate if the AIS implementation did not succeed as it did.

First, the company implemented a customer relation management system (CRM). Based on the success of AIS implementation and the amount of data that started to be available the company decided to implement a CRM system. This system has helped the company in preparing important reports relating to its customers. These reports have allowed the company to better serve the customers and produce valuable information about how to target these customers. The IT department is currently working on transferring the CRM system into an e-CRM system to facilitate dealing with customer data through the internet. This project is only delayed by the need for detailed research of security issues.

Second, the company implemented a "Mobile-Commerce System", which is a system that is based on mobile service installed on handheld machines. This was applied in the service centers of the company. The receiving engineer can receive the equipment/car at the reception area by reading a bar code that is set on it and contains all the needed information about the equipment/car. This system has helped the company operations by reducing the wait time at the receiving area, and assures the entry of correct information of the equipment/car when received. This, system also allows the engineer to see if there was prior reservation or not and to access the history of the equipment/car, to see if there are any special notes that would help him/her. Furthermore, this system allows the information desk instantaneous information about the status of the equipment/car in repair and estimated time of end of task. As an end result this system also increased customers' satisfaction and trust.

Third, the company implemented a Voice over Internet Protocol system (VOIP), which connects the many branches, sites, buildings, and offices that the company has. This development facilitates the ability to communicate between the different parts/employees of the company with zero cost. The speed of the connection also increases the speed of business between the different departments and branches of the company, while allowing faster transfer of data.

Fourth, the company initiated an SMS server that has the ability to send thousands of messages to the customers. This server is linked to the CRM system which allows the SMS to be sent to targeted customers depending on the included information in the SMS. This system allows the company to connect more efficiently with the customers, sending customized information and offers that meet the individual customer interests and needs.

Fifth, the company linked the SMS service system with the after sales division. This link allows the creation of a report from the after sales division data that determines the needed maintenance appointment for each individual customer. This report automatically generates an individualized SMS that is sent to the customer to remind him/her of his next maintenance appointment and any needed information that he/she needs to know; like cost of the service. This service is reported to have increased customer satisfaction dramatically.

LESSONS LEARNT

The tracking of the implementation of the accounting software in the Egyptian International Motors Company can show many important lessons.

The importance of the integration of accounting and technology is an undeniable fact. The most important key to successful implementation is detailed planning. Management need to buy into the automation process and the idea of continuous development and upgrade that comes with automation. It is also important to note the snowball effect of the success of automation of one part. The success of the automation of AIS at EIM resulted in five, until today, major projects that utilized ICT to upgrade and develop the company's abilities.

In a developing nation like Egypt, that is characterized with over population and low unemployment, automation becomes a very sensitive issue. Employee's refusal of the new software could be seen as a main automation problem. To many employees automation means replacing the human employee with a machine, which is a crude and erroneous view but unfortunately is widely spread between employees. Therefore, the key to success of implementation of automation projects lies in understanding of management and IT department to this issue. In any automation project it is important for management and IT department to explain and train the employees. Step one is to meet with the employees prior to the automation project to explain to them the, extent, need and benefits of the automation. Also, they need to explain to the employees explicitly the impact of the automation on their jobs and job security. The second step is to create a well planned training system that can develop the abilities of the employees to be able to handle the new automated system.

The flexibility of management and its acceptance of the fact that they made an error was another very important reason for the success of the implementation. The management of the company is to be commended for acceptance of its role in the error of its first choice. Instead of fighting and insisting on its decision, as most managers do, the managers of EIM acknowledged that they made a mistake when they wanted to buy Oracle. They quickly changed stopped the purchase, reviewed their options and took a new course of action. This flexibility allowed the company many benefits and saved it from problems. In terms of benefits the company was able to adjust the implementation plan quickly and easily. In addition, the management avoided future costs that would have been incurred if management had refused to correct its original decision.

It is important to note how the successful implementation of software has snowball effects on the development of ICT in the company. As the case has shown the management of the company was easily convinced to upgrade the company's dependence on ICT. Increased dependent on ICT has defensibly increased the company's customer satisfaction.

From a macro perspective developing countries, especially Egypt, should direct its companies to increase its dependence on ICT. As the case shows there are many benefits that ICT can offer to the individual companies. If each individual company can become more efficient and effective the whole economy will be better and will be able to utilize scare resources more efficiently and effectively.

REFERENCES

Abd Allah, M. (1992). *Evaluating Accounting Data to Rationalize Investment Decisions: An Empirical Study*. M.Sc. Thesis, Helwan University.

Abdel Maguid, W. (2004 July). Egypt: a new government or a new approach? Is the Nazif government aware of the two main keys to reform? *Al-Ahram Center for Political and Strategic Studies*, 18.

Adams, R. (2008 January). 30 Years of IFAC: Reflections on the Global Accountancy Profession. *Journal of Association of Chartered Certified Accountants*.

Ahmed, A. (2007). Technological Transformation and Sustainability in the MENA Region. In A. Ahmed (Ed.), *Science, Technology and Sustainability in Middle East and North Africa*. London: Inderscience Enterprises Ltd Publishers American Chamber of Commerce in Egypt. (2002). *Telecommunications in Egypt*. Retrieved from http://www.amcham.org.eg/BSAC/Studies-Series/Report37.asp

American Institute of Certified Public Accountants. (AICPA). (1996). Information Technology Competences in the Accounting Profession. AICPA Implementation Strategies for IFAC International Education Guideline No. 11. New York: AICPA.

British Council. (2008). Retrieved from http://www.britishcouncil.org/egypt

Dahawy, K., & Conovere, T. (2007). Accounting Disclosures in Companies Listed on the Egyptian Stock Exchange. *Middle Eastern Finance and Economics, 1*(1).

Dahawy, K., Merion, B., & Conover, T. (2002). The Conflict between IAS Requirements and the Secretive Culture in Egypt. *Advances in International Accounting, 15*(1).

Dahawy, K., Tooma, E., & Kamel, S. (2005). The Use of IT in Teaching Accounting in Egypt: the Case of BeckerConviser. *Communications of the IIMA, 5*(3).

Doost,. R. (1999). Computers and accounting: where do we go from here? *Managerial Auditing Journal, 14*(9).

El Sayed, H., & Westrup, C. (2003). Egypt and ICTs: How UCT Bring National Initiatives, Global Organizations and Local Companies Together. *Information Technology & People, 16*(1).

El Sherif, A. (2004). FDI Profile in Egypt. Workshop on Capacity Building for Promoting FDI in Africa: Trends, Data Compilation and Policy Implications. In *United Nations Conference on Trade and Development (UNCTAD) Meeting, 22-24 November 2004, UNECA, Addis Abba*.

Gelinas, U., Sutton, S., & Hunton, J. (2005). *Accounting Information Systems* (6th ed.). Mason, OH: Thomson Southwestern.

Handoussa, H., & Abou Sheif, H. (2003). The Middle East in the Light of Change: Challenges and Opportunities of Globalization. In *Conference on the Future of Globalization: Explorations in the Light of Recent Turbulence Organized by the World Bank and the Yale Center for the Study of Globalization*, October 10-11, 2003.

Hashem, S. (2002). Bridging the Digital Divide in Egypt: Facing the Challenges. In *UNCTAD E-Commerce First Expert Meeting, 10-12 July 2002*.

Hassab El-naby, H., Epps, R., & Said, A. (2003). The Impact of Environmental Factors on Accounting Development: An Egyptian Longitudinal Study. *Critical Perspectives on Accounting, 14*(3).

Hassan, M. (2008). The development of accounting regulations in Egypt: Legitimating the International Accounting Standards. *Managerial Auditing Journal, 23*(5).

Hoing, S. (1999 May). The Changing Landscape of Computarized Accounting Systems. *The CPA Journal*.

Horngren, C., Foster, G., & Datar, S. (2000). *Cost Accounting: A Managerial Emphasis*. London: Prentice Hall International Inc.

Information and Decision Support Center. (2000). *Annual Report on Egypt*.

Ismail, N., & King, M. (2006). The Alignment of Accounting and Information Systems in SMEs in Malaysia. *Journal of Global Information Technology Management, 9*(3).

Laudon, K., & Laudon, J. (2003). *Management Information Systems* (8th ed.). Upper Saddle River, NJ: Prentice Hall.

Mia, L., & Clark, B. (1999). Market Competition, Management Accounting Systems and Business Unit Performance. *Management Accounting Research, 10*(2). doi:10.1006/mare.1998.0097

Ministry of Communications and Information Technology. (2006). *Building Digital Bridges: Egypt's Vision of the Information Society*. Retrieved from http://www.mcit.gov.eg/brochures/BuildingBridges(all).pdf

Ministry of Communications and Information Technology. (2007). *Egypt's ICT Strategy 2007-2010*. Ministry of Communication and Information Technology May, 2008.

Ministry of Communications and Information Technology. (2008a). *The Future of the Internet Economy in Egypt: Statistical Profile*. Ministry of Communication and Information Technology May, 2008.

Ministry of Communications and Information Technology. (2008b). *Egypt ICT Trust Fund: ICT for Small and Medium Enterprises*. Ministry of Communication and Information Technology. Retrieved from http://www.ictfund.org.eg/ICT4SMEs.html

Ministry of Communications and Information Technology. (2005). Retrieved from http://www.mcit.gov.eg

Ministry of Communications and Information Technology (MCIT). (2005). *Oracle technology platform drives Egypt's comprehensive e-government initiative*. Retrieved from http://www.ameinfo.com/61511.html

Nobes, C. (2001). *Introducing GAAP 2001: A Survey of National Accounting Rules Benchmarked Against International Accounting Standards*. Retrieved from http://kpmg.de/library/pdf/011120_GAAP_2001_en.pdf

Osemy, A., & Prodhan, B. (2001). *The Role of Accounting Information Systems in Rationalizing Investment Decisions in Manufacturing Companies in Egypt*. Research Memorandum. Center for International Accounting and Finance Hull University.

Peccarelli, B. (2004 June). Technology in Accounting. *Accounting Technology Magazine*.

Porter, M., & Millar, V. (1998). How Information Gives You Competitive Advantage: The Information Revolution is Transforming the Nature of Competition. In Matarazzo, J., & Connolly, S. (Eds.), *Knowledge and Special Libraries*. Oxford, UK: Butterworth-Heinemann.

Robson, C. (2006 March). It's All About Communication. *Journal of Association of Chartered Certified Accountants*.

Rudaki, J. (1998). Accounting Education in Developing Countries: Literature Review. *Journal of Social Sciences and Humanities of Shiraz University, 14*(1).

Soper, D., Demirkan, H., Goul, M., & St. Louis, R. (2006). The Impact of ICT Expenditures on Institutionalized Democracy and Foreign Direct Investment in Developing Countries. In *Proceedings of the 39th Annual Hawaii International Conference on System Sciences (HICSS'06)*, Track 4, 2006.

Wheeler, D. (2003). Egypt: building an information society for international development. *Review of African Political Economy, 30*(98). doi:10.1080/07

World Bank. (2002). *Report on the Observance of Standards and Codes*. Egypt: Accounting and Auditing.

Zaidman, N., Scwartz, D., & Te'eni, D. (2008). Challenges to ICT implementation in multinationals Education. *Business and Society: Contemporary Middle Eastern Issues, 1*(14).

ENDNOTE

[1]   Currently International Accounting Standards (IAS) has been developed to International Financial Reporting Standards (IFRS)

Chapter 16
Financial Aspects of National ICT Strategies

Melih Kirlidog
Marmara University, Turkey

ABSTRACT

All developing and industrialized countries strive to get benefits of information society and to this end almost all of them have developed strategies for effective utilization and development of Information and Communication Technologies (ICT). These strategies usually require substantial funds from domestic and international sources and national strategy documents usually pronounce the possible sources of these funds. This chapter analyzes the types of these sources for several countries.

INTRODUCTION

Information and Communication Technologies (ICT) had an unprecedented pace of development in the second half of the 20th Century and beyond. They have diffused to all aspects of life in industrialized countries where only a minority of humanity live. Yet, reflecting the broader economic and social disparities, level of diffusion of ICT in developing countries is less than ideal. As a result, a major divide that is based on the production and implementation of ICT has been formed between industrialized and developing countries. Although there are some areas where

this digital divide has the tendency to be bridged, it seems to be widening between developing and developed countries in the big picture.

Anxious for "not missing the train once more after the industrial revolution", developing countries are striving to catch up the developed world. To this end they develop strategies, plans, and blueprints for diffusing the implementation of ICT in their citizens' daily lives. Industrialized countries which do not want to be left behind are also spending the same effort. Lately, there has been a considerable effort in almost all countries to develop their ICT strategies. These efforts gained momentum with the call of First World Summit on Information Society (WSIS) that was held in Geneva in 2003 where "development of national

DOI: 10.4018/978-1-60566-388-3.ch016

Table 1. Traditional budgeting and budgeting for ICT investments

Focus of traditional government budgeting	Characteristics of high-value ICT investments
Single-year (or biennial) expenditures	Multi-year investments
Program-by-program performance	Enterprise or cross-boundary performance
Financial cost/benefits	Financial and non-financial costs/benefits
Level of effort within existing work flows	Changes in the flow of work
Ongoing operations	"Start-up" operations
Control	Innovation

e-strategies, including the necessary human capacity building" is encouraged for all countries. This call was iterated by the second WSIS conference in Tunis in 2005. The WSIS conferences regarded ICT as an important tool to achieve the Millennium Development Goals (MDG) by 2015. The MDG are about improvements in the following areas:

1. End poverty and hunger
2. Universal education
3. Gender equality
4. Child health
5. Maternal health
6. Combat HIV/AIDS
7. Environmental sustainability
8. Global partnership

National ICT strategies usually have ambitious (and sometimes unrealistic) targets about transforming the whole country towards "information society" (Machlup, 1962; Bell, 1999). Such a transformation requires massive investments not only for hardware and software acquisition, but also for diverse areas such as ICT education in different segments of the society and technology support for private firms. There are also various hidden costs such as possible tax waive for ICT hardware. Although developed countries usually do not have much difficulty for allocating some funds in the national budget for realizing their strategies, it is a challenge for developing countries to create and mobilize funds for that aim.

This chapter analyzes the sources of ICT investments for some countries in the framework of their national ICT strategies. The strategy documents usually provide adequate material for such an analysis and those documents are used as the major source of information. The effectiveness of spending large amounts is also investigated and some caveats are drawn.

The chapter is organized as follows: The next section contains literature review about some important aspects of national ICT strategies in terms of financial resources. The following section explains data collection and analysis methodology of this research and it is followed by a section which discusses domestic and international sources of ICT investments. The subsequent section depicts some attributes of the strategies of thirty countries along with their financial resources. The last section concludes the chapter.

PREVIOUS LITERATURE FOR FINANCING NATIONAL ICT STRATEGIES AND POSSIBLE PITFALLS

ICT investment can be realized with resources in or out of the national budget. National budget investments for ICT exhibit some dissimilarity from traditional types of public investments. Harvard Policy Group (HPG, 2001) lists these dissimilarities in government budgeting as in Table 1.

These dissimilarities are particularly relevant for budgeting national ICT strategies because the strategies envisage spending in diverse areas for a number of years. It is difficult to make a budget performance analysis for them because several numbers of individual programs and intersections between these programs are involved. Although many of the traditional projects allow financial cost-benefit analysis, such an analysis is more difficult in large public ICT investments because of the existence of non-quantifiable elements such as "empowering citizens with ICT literacy." Nevertheless, many countries are prepared to spend very high amounts for ICT because these investments are regarded to be *sine qua non* for transforming to an information society.

However, a caveat is required for large scale ICT investments both in firm and national level. Although there is little doubt that ICTs are contemporary tools that are regarded as prerequisites for an information society, the adequacy of ICTs for attainment to this goal is another story. In fact, contrary to the intuitive belief, ICTs' contribution to this massive transformation is neither automatic nor fast. There are even doubts about the contribution of ICT to the economic growth. In his widely-quoted sentence, Solow (1987) asserts that computers are seen everywhere except in the productivity statistics. Indeed, many economists found zero or negative productivity increases during the 1970s and 1980s when massive ICT investments were realized. Called "productivity paradox", this phenomenon has been studied by many researchers since that time (Lucas, 1999; Brynjolfsson & Hitt, 1996; Lee et al., 2005; Lin, 2008). Although there is no consensus among researchers, some later studies suggest some productivity increase due to ICT investments in industrialized countries. The productivity paradox of the previous decades is attributed to ICTs' retarded effect, methodology problems in research, and difficulty of identifying the benefits of ICT.

It must be noted that an overwhelming majority of studies related to ICTs' impact on economic growth and productivity increase have been conducted in industrialized countries. Although it can be expected that the impact of ICT on productivity would be different in developing countries where ICT diffusion is lower and there might be deficiencies in effective use of existing systems, some research shows encouraging results. For example, Kuppusamy and Santhapparaj (2005) investigated the economic growth in Malaysia during the period 1975-2002 by using secondary data. The study analyzed the impact of three independent variables, namely, investment on ICT, non-ICT investment, and total labor employed in the economy on the dependent variable Real Gross Domestic Product. It was found that ICT had contributed positively to Malaysia's economic growth over the study period. Kim (2003) examined the impact of ICT on economic growth and productivity in Korea between 1971-2000 and found that ICT capital contributed 16.3% to the output growth and had a strong positive effect on the growth of labor productivity in the long term. However, these findings contradict with some other authors' findings that revealed insignificant impact of ICT investments on productivity and economic growth in developing countries. For example, Dewan and Kraemer (2000) analyzed the returns from ICT investments of 36 developing and industrialized countries. They found that while returns from ICT capital investments are significant in industrialized countries, they are insignificant in developing countries. Lee et al. (2005) and Pohjola (2000) also contend that ICT contributes to economic growth in developed countries but not in developing economies. Lin's (2008) findings contradict this argument and suggest that productivity paradox may exist in all developing and developed countries. In an OECD report, Souter (2004) notes that this unsettled dispute is very important for developing countries where diffusion of ICT and ICT infrastructure is less advanced, thereby having a retarding effect on developing network externalities. Additionally, ICT equipment costs, connection costs, and taxes are higher in developing countries which result in significantly less ICT equipment for every investment dollar. This, in turn, results in lower rate of return.

It must also be noted that fragile economies of developing countries and the resulting crises make these types of studies extremely difficult. For example, Turkey's 1994 financial crisis resulted in 5% decrease of GDP in real terms and after the 2001 crisis Argentina's real GDP fell by 10.9% in 2002, later to be expanded by about 9% each year between 2003 and 2005. In an environment of such stark "noises" the difficulty of analyzing the impact of ICT investments on the dependent variable GDP is clear. It seems that a more reliable analysis for developing countries could only be made at the firm-level and for non-crisis periods.

Some Possible Pitfalls for Large-Scale ICT Investments

All the above facts suggest important caveats about unrealistic expectations about the transforming power of ICT both for economy and society. Nevertheless, these facts and the unsettled dispute about productivity paradox should not deter developing countries to invest in ICT. As stated above, ICTs are prerequisites for an information based society. What is meant by these caveats is that like all technologies, ICT is not a magical wand that transforms the society and improves economy immediately, and some time is needed for ICT to be effective in realizing these objectives. Further, there is evidence that this time might be longer in developing countries. Additionally, productivity paradox research is usually conducted around macro and firm-level economics where benefits are quantifiable. ICTs' long-term benefits such as improving the learning process in schools are impossible to quantify.

An important pitfall in developing ICT strategies is to regard the technology as an end rather than means to achieve national development goals. The main source of this pitfall is the unrealistic

expectations about the power of technology in transforming the society while ignoring social and historical conditions. Moodley (2005) warns about the exaggerated emphasis given to ICT for poverty reduction and general development goals in South African political discourse. According to the author this unrealistic discourse and the related policies in South Africa tend to regard ICT as an autonomous and largely unassailable agent capable for major social transformations. Souter (2004) explains the main reason of overemphasizing the importance of ICT in national ICT strategies and the tendency to detach it from overall objectives. He argues that these strategies are often designed by those who are strongly committed to the role of ICT but the participation of mainstream sectoral development planners is insufficient. It is easy in these circumstances for policy makers to exaggerate the potential benefits of ICTs and to direct investment into unproductive areas.

This techno-determinist view (MacKenzie & Wajcman, 1999) is widespread not only in developing, but also in industrialized countries and it is also one of the most important reasons of failure of large ICT projects. While the ICT strategy of a firm must be aligned to the firm's formulated strategic objectives, a country's ICT strategy must be aligned with the country's national development goals. In this context, ICT must be regarded as a strategic tool that supports the broader development goals. This is not to overlook to the strategic importance of ICT, but rather seeing it as a very important tool having a similar role with steam engine's role in the industrial revolution. Given that during the 19th Century steam engine facilitated fast transportation and efficient production in factories but acted as little more than a tool, the national strategy for ICT diffusion must aim the effective *use* of the technology within the society but not as an independent objective. Regarding ICT as an independent objective results in a flawed conception in formulating the national ICT strategy and it has the potential to waste hard-earned or borrowed resources on technological marvels that are of little use for social and economic development of the country.

An important aspect of the development strategy in developing countries should be to avoid poverty where some part of the population lives under poverty level. According to an OECD (2003) estimation only 12 of the 29 Heavily Indebted Poor Countries (HIPC) define or position ICT as a strategic component of poverty reduction and address it as an independent item in their Poverty Reduction Strategy Papers (PRSPs). Further, although 57 of the 64 national development plans make some mention of ICT as an element in national development, emphasis on ICT as well as integration of an ICT strategy (if any) with the broader development plan varies considerably. Adamali et al. (2006) analyzed the national ICT strategies of 40 countries and found that middle income countries have better linkages to their overall development strategies. They are followed by high income and low income countries. The authors also developed a framework for analyzing the national ICT strategies according to four criteria, namely, development linkages, use of indicators, implementation mechanisms, and monitoring mechanisms. The framework uses indicators "for accurately benchmarking baseline analysis, for formulating targets, and for monitoring and evaluation."

Another pitfall in allocating public resources for the national ICT strategy is to be drifted to the opposite end in the spectrum. This view tends to regard ICT only as a sector in economy that has the potential to grow. Successful software industries of some developing countries like India have boosted this trend in the last few decades. Being one of the few lucky developing countries whose ICT exports are over or close to ICT imports, India's experience is closely scrutinized by many countries which are hindered by high entry barriers of hardware production but are hopeful for developing export-oriented software industries. Although this can be an important aspect of the national ICT strategy, regarding it as the main pillar of the strategy can

be an important flaw. India has some advantages for developing a world-class software industry: Firstly, it has some high-quality ICT education and research institutions, secondly English language is commonly used among the elites and English is important not only for software development and documentation handling, but also for developing international business contacts. Thirdly, India has a very large pool of young population eager for working in any part of the world. And lastly, the country has a large Diaspora all over the world. Some of these conditions may be applicable for some countries, but there not many countries that satisfy all of them. For many countries overemphasizing the development of ICT industry to the expense of overlooking other aspects of ICT can be doomed for failure.

DATA COLLECTION AND ANALYSIS METHODOLOGY

This chapter examines the national ICT strategy documents of thirty countries and aims to investigate the declared financial resources to realize their strategies. In order to determine patterns according to income level the countries are also classified according to their per capita income.

The national ICT strategy documents are usually available on the Web and some of them are available in English along with the local language. The strategy documents of randomly chosen thirty countries are obtained from the web and a template analysis (King, 1998) was conducted on these documents. Template analysis incorporates developing codes for representing facts in textual data. These codes are used to analyze the textual data in a structured form. While most of the codes are identified a priori, some unforeseen ones are added in the course of this research.

The countries chosen are categorized as low, middle, and high income countries where low and middle income countries could be regarded as developing and high income countries could be regarded as industrialized countries. This research targets only the financial resources required by the strategy and other related financial issues such as expenditure items of the strategy are excluded from the study. Each financial resource type is given a code that is explained in Table 3. The objective of the study is to analyze the sources of strategy investments for each country.

SOURCES FOR ICT INVESTMENTS

Since their introduction in the 1950s the cost-performance ratio of ICTs has improved in such intensity that no other technology has seen in history. As commodity items, today's ordinary personal computers that cost a few hundred dollars are much more powerful than 1950s' million-dollar computers. Yet, as stated above, many developing countries have to think twice about investing in ICT where returns might have retarded effect and ICT investments have to compete with more acute needs. This is true for all sources of funds whether they have been generated domestically or acquired from abroad in the form of credit or donation.

Domestic Sources for ICT Investments

Public sources: In all countries the most important domestic source of ICT investments is the tax collected by the state. Depending on several factors such as political preferences of the government and the level of demand for ICT by the population, some part of the tax income may be allocated in the national budget for the expenses required by the ICT strategy. Use of tax for this purpose may not be a viable option in least developed countries where the population is so poor that there is little possibility for tax collection adequate for the purposes of the strategy. It may also be difficult to rely on taxes in some relatively affluent

developing and industrialized countries where tax evasion is widespread.

Until the 1990s public telecom revenues used to be an important source for ICT and other investments in several countries. For example, Turkey invested about 1% of its GNP to develop an advanced telecom network which has universal geographic coverage in the country. By 1993, over 50% of the network was digital and almost 90% of the equipment was provided by local manufacturing. According to World Bank (1993) this is a success story, and the most striking aspect of it was that it had been almost totally achieved with local resources, mainly telecom revenues. However, this is not possible in today's environment for several countries including Turkey where national telecom companies were privatized in the last few decades.

Beyond the conventional method of allocation some public funds for the strategy there are also some indirect ways such as establishment of a special fund for the expenditures of the strategy. In the same manner, tax waives for computer hardware and software must also be regarded in this respect, because this is also the diversion of some public income to the strategy requirements.

Private sector investments: Drive for profit can be an important source for realizing the requirements of the ICT strategy. Local private sector can, totally with local resources or as a joint venture with foreigners, finance major investments such as privatization of the national telecom company or buying a GSM license. For example, a local bank in Turkey bought one of the five available national GSM licenses as a joint venture with Telecom Italia for USB2.5. However, the income generated by such ICT licenses or telecom privatizations can be spent for various objectives, and ICT is only one of them. In Turkey, main part of such income is spent for easing the huge debt burden. Thus, rather than self-financing and supporting ICT diffusion in the country, ICT itself became a much needed support for the shortcomings of the economy as a whole. This scenario may be valid not only for Turkey but for many indebted countries.

Small-scale private sector can also assist the diffusion of ICT in several ways. For example, "Innovation Springboard" in Ukraine is a creative public-private partnership program that aims to involve local entrepreneurs in establishing and running Public Internet Access Points (PIAP). With financial and technical support from United Nations Development Program (UNDP, nodate), Ukrainian Computer Club acts as an umbrella organization of the local entrepreneurs who approach the local public school to establish a computer lab within the premises of the school. After the acceptance of the business plan the entrepreneur provides the equipment and the school furnishes the lab. The lab serves as computer lab for the pupils during school hour, and it becomes a PIAP and an ICT training center for the local population in the evenings and weekends (UN, 2004). This type of PIAP usage is becoming widespread in the last few years. Turkey is one of those countries that attempts to involve private sector for the PIAP. The national ICT strategy of Turkey envisages establishing 4500 PIAPs in the country (SPO, 2006a). In the "Program Description Document" of Turkey's ICT strategy, it is stated that although the government will take the initiative to establish and run the PIAP, private sector may also establish their own PIAPs provided that they will conform to the standards (SPO, 2006b). The unregulated private Internet Cafes which are widespread all over the world are also examples of private entrepreneurship for ICT access.

Joint Public and Private sector investments: Whether realized by public or private sector, ICT investments can be categorized in two main groups depending on ownership. The first group of investments targets a focused ICT system development project such as developing an e-government portal or an inventory control system in a private sector factory. In this group, the scope of the project is well determined and the system is developed by ICT professionals who are experienced in similar previous projects. Further, either there is no end-user training (e.g. in e-government systems that are used by ordinary citizens) or the user training is limited to a short period. In e-government systems the system is easy to use to the extent that it requires no end-user training. In a classical commercial inventory control system end-users are assumed to be computer literate and a short training suffices for the users who do not require a computer literacy course. The owner of these systems is either the government or the private sector, but not both. Likewise, they are either financed by government or private sector, but rarely by both. There can be cases where private sector bids to develop a system that is owned by government or the Build-Operate-Transfer model is used.

The second group of investments involves a joint public-private endeavor. Although the natural owner of such projects is the government, private sector contribution can be sought mainly due to the large size of the required resources and inadequacy of public funds. Unlike the previous type, the main tenets of this type of investments may involve providing ICT access to the broader population which might have little computer literacy. Consequently, general ICT literacy and training is important in this type. Since the user population is very broad and it is difficult to foresee how the ICT skill possession will evolve, scope of the project may not be well-defined beyond a few vague statements like "providing ICT access to the population." Some PIAP and pro-poor Community Informatics projects that aim to empower local communities with ICT (Gurstein, 2000) may be categorized in this group. This type of investments is particularly relevant for developing countries where public resources are scarce and a large majority of the population has little means of access to ICT. Although the situation is challenging in cities, it is usually more acute in remote areas where establishing communication is costly and population is poor.

Universal Access Funds (UAF) (sometimes called Universal Service Funds), a mechanism that has emerged in the last few years, seems promising to solve some of the problems of the digital exclusion (UN, 2004) of poorer countries and remote areas. The main source of the UAF is the contribution of every telecom operator in the country along with the public contribution. Beyond public sources, the high initial start-up telecommunication investments for remote areas are either funded by the private operators with a certain part of their revenues, or by international donors and financial institutions. It is assumed that the subsequent revenues generated will pay the initial investment. UAFs are usually administered by the national regulatory agency or an independent body. Although these projects usually started around telecommunications, they have been expanded to cover diverse areas such as Internet access and computer training. According to UN (*ibid.*), there were about 60 countries worldwide which had some sort of UAFs as of 2004.

Another way of public-private collaboration for ICT development and diffusion is the establishment of business incubators and techno-parks. For example, the techno-park of Middle East Technical University (METU) in Turkey is a public endeavor where several private firms employ about 1400 people 85% of whom are engineers. In the techno-park technology firms and employees enjoy several types of tax levies which constitute an important incentive. The techno-park also serves as an incubator for potential technology developers who are in need of financial support. Spatial and institutional proximity of the techno-park and the university is the main source of effective university-industry collaboration. The applications of firms that wish to join the techno-park are evaluated by a committee of academics who are experts in the relevant field. METU techno-park is one of several techno-parks in the country who are regulated by the government through "Technology Development Regions" legislation that has been passed from the parliament in 2001. Techno-parks

have little or no direct contribution for generating funds required for the ICT strategy. On the contrary, they consume some tax income that could otherwise be used for the strategy. However, they can have substantial indirect contribution to the strategy by the development of the ICT industry in the country.

International Sources for ICT Investments

Foreign Private Sector Investments: Although there could be several forms of foreign private sector investments, FDI (Foreign Direct Investment), where the foreign investor holds more than a certain threshold (usually 10%) is quite common in international telecommunications and other ICT investments. Due to the strong privatization trends in the 1980s and 1990s, there has been large scale FDI for fixed-line telecom investments in several developing and industrialized countries. A new wave of GSM investments seem to emerge in the last few years. According to a World Bank (2005) report, a significant development in these types of investments is the increasing volume of investments originated from developing countries targeting other developing countries.

The last few decades have also witnessed another important FDI trend in ICT. Mainly due to the cheaper workforce and tax advantages, large hardware and software companies establish production facilities overseas. Regarding it as an opportunity to leapfrog in ICT, potential recipient countries strive to attract this type of investments. Indeed, investments like Microsoft's and Hewlett-Packard's research labs in Bangalore, India and Intel's manufacturing and technology center in Ireland (largest manufacturing site outside the US) are seen not only facilities that create jobs, but also opportunities for participating in the international network for high technology production and distribution (Castells, 2000). Even investments for call center operations where customer calls are diverted to the recipient country are usually regarded favorably. Although this is not a high value-added operation for the recipient country it could be advantageous for creating jobs and some ICT-related tasks such as CRM software development and maintenance. Technology investments which involve high value added products and services are clearly superior for recipient countries. However, beyond tax levies and other incentives such as offering free building site, there are some prerequisites for these types of investments to occur. The most important of these prerequisites are a well educated local workforce and a domestic market large enough to absorb some part of the production.

International finance institutions and donors: Several international organizations finance ICT projects that cannot be financed by local resources. Some of them like World Bank and Asian Development Bank give loans for projects while some donor organizations and industrialized countries donate grants to developing countries without repayments. The source of loans and credits can be multilateral like the ones provided by World Bank, or bilateral like the ones provided from one government to another.

Some affluent member countries of OECD have formed Development Assistance Committee (DAC) with the stated objective of "securing an expansion of aggregate volume of resources made available to developing countries and to improve their effectiveness" (OECD, 2005). The DAC members periodically review both the amount and the nature of their contributions to aid programs and consult each other on all other relevant aspects of their development assistance policies. The members confirmed their pledges of the target of allocating 0.7% of their Gross National Incomes for Official Development Assistance (ODA) in Monterrey conference in 2002. However, although this target had first been established in 1970 in a UN General Assembly Resolution and had been re-iterated in several subsequent meetings and summits, a great majority of industrialized countries fell short of realizing

it. Given the current economic climate that is not better than the previous decades, there is little evidence that industrialized countries will keep their promise in the foreseeable future.

The share of ICT infrastructure in ODA is declining during last decade. This share fell from 4.5% in 1990 to 0.5% in 2002. This trend is largely set by Japan that was by far the largest donor over the years with a share between 30% and 68%. Japan's commitment to ICT in ODA fell from USD 550 million in 1990 to USD 40 million in 2001 (OECD, 2005). This shows the unpredictability of external support and the necessity for developing countries to rely on their own resources. This is true not only for ICT, but also for general development efforts. Nevertheless, some part of ODA goes to ICT related activities in developing countries such as infrastructure enhancement, development of an ICT industry, and even national ICT strategy formulation. Beyond grants and loans, ODA can be realized as technical cooperation or equity investment in the recipient country by directly financing companies without lasting interest in the company (UN, 2004).

Japan is active in providing ICT-related loans to other countries. Japan's "Comprehensive Co-operation Package" that was launched in 2000 has the stated objective of "bridging the international digital divide consisting of non-ODA and ODA public funding" with the view to extending a total of US$15 billion over five years (see www.mofa.go.jp/policy/economy/it/oda/role0106.html). A large scale example of these loans is the one that has been given to Malaysia in 2002 as part of the Comprehensive Co-operation Package by the Japanese government launched at the G8 Kyushu-Okinawa Summit in 2000 (OECD, 2005). The loan amounts to USD 420 million and has been realized by Japan Bank for International Cooperation with the contribution of seven private banks. The loan is primarily used for financing ICT companies and Malaysia Venture Capital Management, a public organization, oversees the usage of the funds.

This loan was followed by another one in 2004 amounting to USD 536 million.

Some affluent countries either finance or directly support developing countries for formulating their national ICT strategies. For example, Sweden has supported the development of ICT policies or ICT regulatory bodies in Sri Lanka, Rwanda, Mozambique and Tanzania (EU, nodate).

Although usually not financially, international organizations such as UN, its sub-organizations such as UNECA (United Nations Economic Commission for Africa), and some non-government organizations also provide support to developing countries in their ICT-oriented efforts. For example, UNECA assists African countries to establish their national ICT strategies (see http://www.uneca.org/aisi/nici/), and APC (Association for Progressive Communications) supports developing countries by activities like ICT strategy formulation toolkits and training materials.

There are also untraditional and creative financing mechanisms which might be helpful for developing countries. The UNDP's ICT Trust Fund and Debt-Swap are two examples for such mechanisms. Debt-Swap refers to the fact that a creditor country or organization retires some part of the debt in exchange for the debtor county's obligation for investing in local currency for local programs. In 2004, governments of Egypt (debtor) and Italy (creditor) agreed for a Debt-Swap of 48.5 million Egyptian Pounds which was used in Egypt for projects such as Smart Schools, Mobile IT Clubs, Community Knowledge Generation, Electronic Library, Illiteracy Eradication, and the Community Portal Development Projects (see http://www.ictfund.org.eg/download/FinalEng.pdf). The UNDP's ICT Trust Fund may work in coordination with Dept-Swap programs.

STRATEGIES OF SOME COUNTRIES AND THEIR FINANCIAL RESOURCES

ICT strategies usually encompass quite comprehensive actions with far-reaching effects. As a consequence they require substantial resources to be realized. Depending on the size of the country and the ambition level of the strategy, these resources can sometimes amount to billions of dollars. For example, Turkey initially envisaged spending about USD 2.3 billions during the period of 2006-2010 for the strategy (SPO, 2006c). (However, this spending was not materialized.) Although most of the national ICT strategy documents do not reveal the expenditures envisaged, it can be expected that other countries also have to mobilize extensive resources for transforming themselves on the route to the "information society." Governments either have to divert valuable resources in their budgets for the requirements of the strategy or have to be creative to secure these resources.

Table 2 depicts the chosen countries and some details of their ICT strategy documents. Most countries have developed their own strategies through diverse government agencies and some of them were supported by international organizations such UN and its agencies. Gross Domestic Product (GDP) per capita figures are of year 2005 and they are based on Purchasing Power Parity calculations. The rightmost column indicates the codes of the declared financial resources required for realizing the strategy. The codes are explained in Table 3. Many strategy documents refer to rather vague sources of funds such as "future public-private partnership." Such unclear statements are excluded from the table and only explicitly declared sources are retained.

Table 2 reveals that all of the selected strategy documents have declared some kind of resource types for financing the strategy. Although Code 1 "Some funding will be provided by the national budget" does not exist for all countries, it should be taken as granted. In other words, all countries must have allocated some budget funds and the other sources must be thought as supplements. Otherwise it would not be plausible for an affluent country like Finland not to allocate national budget funds to the strategy and to finance it only

Table 2. Some national ICT strategy documents and their financial resources

	Name of the strategy document	The main organization (government agency) that developed the strategy	Supporting international organizations	Time of the strategy document	GDP per capita-USD (UNDP, 2007)	Financial resources (codes)
Albania	National Information and Communication Technologies Strategy		Open Society Institute, UN Department of Economic and Social Affairs, UNDP Albania		5316	1, 2, 3, 4, 5, 6, 7
Azerbaijan	National Information and Communication Technologies Strategy for the development of the Republic of Azerbaijan			2003	5016	1, 2, 7, 8, 9
Bangladesh	National Information and Communication Technology (ICT) Policy	Ministry of Science and Information & Communication Technology		October 2002	2013	10
Bhutan	Bhutan Information and Communications Technology Policy and Strategies			August 2004	3413	1, 2, 10, 11
Chile	The New Information and Communication Technologies	Presidential Commission		January 1999	12027	1, 6
Czech Republic	State Information and Communications Policy			2006	20538	1, 4, 6
Dominican Republic	National Strategy for the Information and Knowledge Society	"Comision Nacional Para la Sociedad de la Informacion y el Conocimiento"		October 2005	8217	1, 2, 6, 8, 10
Egypt	National Plan for Telecommunication and Information	Ministry of Telecommunication and Information		December 1999	4337	1, 6, 10
Finland	Towards a Networked Finland	The Information Society Council		February 2005	32153	6, 4
Ghana	An Integrated ICT-led Socio-Economic Development Policy and Plan Development Framework for Ghana	Ministry of Communications and Technology	UN Economic Commission for Africa, European Union	June 2003	2480	2, 6, 7
Hong Kong	Public Consultation on Digital 21 Strategy	Commerce, Industry and Technology Bureau		October 2006	34833	10

continued on following page

Table 2. continued

	Name of the strategy document	The main organization (government agency) that developed the strategy	Supporting international organizations	Time of the strategy document	GDP per capita-USD (UNDP, 2007)	Financial resources (codes)
Indonesia	Five-Year Action Plan for the Develop-ment and Implemen-tation of Information and Communication Technologies (ICT) In Indonesia - Gov-ernment of Indone-sia's Action Plan to overcome the Digital Divide	Presidency		May 2001	3843	1, 8, 10
Ireland	New Connections – A Strategy to Realise the Potential of the Information Society: 2nd Progress Report	Ministry of the State for the Information Society		April 2004	38505	1, 10
Jamaica	A Five-Year Stra-tegic Information Technology Plan for Jamaica	Government of Jamaica	General Services Ad-ministration of the United States, United States Embassy in Jamaica	March 2002	4291	1, 6, 8
Jordan	The REACH Initia-tive: Launching Jordan's Software and IT Industry			March 2000	5530	6, 7, 10
Korea (South)	e-Korea Vision 2006: The Third Master Plan for Informatiza-tion Promotion	Ministry of Information and Communication		April 2002	22029	1
Kyrgyzstan				2002	1927	1, 2, 6, 7, 10
Namibia	Information and Communication Technology Policy For the Republic of Namibia	Prepared by Schoeman's Office Systems and sub-mitted to Ministry of For-eign Affairs, Information and Broadcasting		March 2002	7586	1, 2, 10, 11
Nigeria	Nigerian National Policy for Informa-tion Technology – Use "IT"				1128	1, 9, 10
Philippines	IT21-Phillipines: Asia's Knowledge Center	National Information Technology Council		October 1997	5137	7, 8, 10
Romania	National Strat-egy for the New Economy and the Implementation of the Information Society - Abridged version -	Ministry of Communica-tions and Information Technology		2002	9060	1, 2, 4

continued on following page

Table 2. continued

	Name of the strategy document	The main organization (government agency) that developed the strategy	Supporting international organizations	Time of the strategy document	GDP per capita-USD (UNDP, 2007)	Financial resources (codes)
Rwanda	The NICI (National Information and Communication Infrastructure) 2005 Plan		UN Economic Commission for Africa	2005	1206	1, 2, 6, 7, 10
Singapore	Innovation. Integration. Internationalization.	iN2015 Steering Committee			29663	1
Slovenia	Republic of Slovenia in the Information Society	Ministry of Information Society		February 2003	22273	1, 4, 7
Syria	National ICT Strategy for Socio-economic Development in Syria	Ministry of Communications and Technology	UNDP Syria office	2004	3808	1, 5, 6, 7, 9
Taiwan	e-Taiwan	Science & Technology Advisory Group – Executive Yuan		June 2003	-	1, 10
Tanzania	National Information and Communications Technologies Policy	Ministry of Communications and Transport		March 2003	744	1, 6, 7, 10
Thailand	Information Technology Policy Framework 2001-2010: Thailand Vision Towards a Knowledge-Based Economy	National Information Technology Committee Secretariat		2003	8677	1, 7
Turkey	Information Society Strategy	State Planning Organization		July 2006	8407	1
Ukraine	National Strategy of Information Society Development in Ukraine	The Public Working Group "Electronic Ukraine"	International Renaissance Foundation	2003	6848	1, 6, 7, 8, 10

through e-Europe funds and private investments as stated in its strategy document.

An import trend is about the variety of resources among poorer and more affluent countries. While poorer countries usually have indicated several sources of funding in their documents, more affluent ones usually have fewer types of funds. This is also plausible, because more affluent countries have the power to spend high amounts from their public treasury while poorer countries are unable to do this and they have to be creative

to find funds. For example, Albania, Azerbaijan, Kyrgyzstan, Rwanda, Syria, Dominican Republic, and Ukraine have five or more funding sources and these countries have less than USD 6000 of GDP per capita with the exception of the last two. Likewise, Czech Republic, Finland, Hong Kong, Ireland, South Korea, Singapore, and Slovenia have over USD 20000 GDP per capita and have three or less sources of funds in their documents. Although Taiwan is not included in the UNDP list it must also be included in this group because

Table 3. Codes (in Table 2) for financial resources

Code	Explanation	Domestic/ International	Public/ Private
1	Some funding will be provided by the national budget	Domestic	Public
2	Donor support will be sought for particular expenditure items in the strategy	International	Public+Private
3	Opportunity of using the ICT Trust Fund and/or Debt-Swap will be sought	International	Public+Private
4	e-Europe, e-Europe+, or some other European Union (EU) funding support will be sought	International	Public
5	Consumers will contribute to the funding of the strategy	Domestic	Public
6	Local private sector funds or investments will be used (market-driven)	Domestic	Private
7	Foreign investments	International	Public+Private
8	Purpose loans from local and international creditors	Domestic + International	Public+Private
9	Special tax or custom duty (or part thereof) for expenditures of the strategy	Domestic	Public
10	Establishment of a special fund (e.g. venture capital fund) for the purposes of the strategy in or out of the national budget	Domestic	Public
11	Universal Service Fund	Domestic	Public

of its relative affluence. Bangladesh, Chile, and Turkey are exceptions in this group.

The quest for donor support is mentioned in several poor countries' documents but it seems difficult to access this kind of support not only because of the drying up of ODA funds but also because of the high number of countries that demand it.

With the exception of Ireland, all European countries in the list seek EU funds for their strategy. This includes very affluent countries like Finland. That support is in line with the Lisbon Strategy aiming to make Europe more dynamic and competitive in the face of the competition with the US and Japan as well as the recently rising economies of China and India.

CONCLUSION

The information society that has been realized by some industrialized countries is the objective of the majority of countries in today's world. Both developing and industrialized countries are making every effort to either transforming themselves to information societies or developing smarter courses of action in the process of becoming a more effective information society. This strong desire has led almost all countries to develop national ICT strategies. Strategy development process has also been stimulated by the call of WSIS conferences and by the support of several organizations such as UN and its branches.

With their unprecedented capacity for producing, processing, storing, and disseminating information, ICTs are regarded as the most important pillar for realizing information of society. However, technology is little more than a tool in social transformations. What is important is the transformation of the society itself in such a way that in the new society ICTs will be *demanded* as a natural extension to individuals and organizations. Only *supplying* hardware to individuals and organizations with the hope of transformation to information society is not only doomed to failure, but also will end up with wasting resources. With the possible exception of India and China, this is particularly true for developing countries where ICT imports far exceed ICT exports. This is not to say that ICT expenditures are unnecessary in the face of more acute needs. On the contrary, wisely developed national ICT strategies and their

ICT expenditures are *necessary but insufficient* requirements for achieving the ultimate target of information society. What is meant is that ICT *per se* cannot realize a massive social transformation to information society which can take generations, but it is a prerequisite for such a realization. Lack of comprehension of this key point seems to be a major problem in national ICT strategy documents which usually emphasize technology to the cost of wider social transformations.

While national ICT strategies must have realistic targets and their expenditures must be wisely spent, this chapter shows that there be can be several sources for them beyond allocating some funds from the national budget. Nevertheless, a country must essentially be dependent on its domestic resources in the wake of diminishing donor support and expensive overseas credit.

REFERENCES

Adamali, A., Coffey, J. O., & Safdar, Z. (2006). Trends in national e-strategies: A review of 40 countries. In *Information and Communications for development: Global trends and policies* (pp. 87–124). Washington, DC: World Bank Publications.

Bell, D. (1999). *The coming of the post-industrial society* (Anniversary, S., Ed.). New York: Basic Books.

Brynjolfsson, E., & Hitt, L. (1996). Paradox lost? Firm-level evidence on the returns to information systems spending. *Management Science, 42*(4), 541–558. doi:10.1287/mnsc.42.4.541

Castells, M. (2000). *The rise of the network society* (2nd ed.). Oxford: Blackwell Publishers.

Dewan, S., & Kraemer, K. L. (2000). Information technology and productivity: Evidence from country level data. *Management Science, 46*(4), 548–562. doi:10.1287/mnsc.46.4.548.12057

EU. (n.d.). *Financing ICT for development: The EU approach*. Retrieved April 15, 2008, from http://www.dfid.gov.uk/pubs/files/eu-financ-wsis-english.pdf

Gurstein, M. (2000). *Community informatics: Enabling communities with information and communication technologies*. London: Idea Group Publishing.

HPG. (2001). *Improving budgeting and financing for promising IT initiatives*. Harvard Policy Group on Network-Enabled Services and Government.

Kim, S. (2003). Information technology and its impact on economic growth and productivity in Korea. *International Economic Journal, 17*(3), 55–75. doi:10.1080/10168730300080019

King, N. (1998). Template analysis. In Symon, G., & Cassell, C. (Eds.), *Qualitative methods and analysis in organizational research* (pp. 118–134). London: Sage Publications.

Kuppusamy, M., & Santhapparaj, A. S. (2005). Investment in information and communication technologies (ICT) and its payoff in Malaysia. *Perspectives on Global Development and Technology, 4*(2), 147–167. doi:10.1163/1569150054739014

Lee, S. T., Gholami, R., & Tong, T. Y. (2005). Time series analysis in the assessment of ICT impact at the aggregate level-lessons and implications for the new economy. *Information & Management, 42*, 1009–1022. doi:10.1016/j.im.2004.11.005

Lin, W. T. (2008). The business value of information technology as measured by technical efficiency: Evidence from country-level data. *Decision Support Systems, 46*, 865–874. doi:10.1016/j.dss.2008.11.017

Lucas, H. C. (1999). *Information technology and the productivity paradox*. New York: Oxford University Press.

Machlup, F. (1962). *The production and distribution of knowledge in the United States*. Princeton, NJ: Princeton University Press.

MacKenzie, D., & Wajcman, J. (Eds.). (1999). *The social shaping of technology* (2nd ed.). Buckingham, UK: Open University Press.

Moodley, S. (2005). A critical assessment of the state ICT for poverty reduction discourse in South Africa. *Perspectives on Global Development and Technology*, 4(1), 1–26. doi:10.1163/1569150053888254

OECD. (2003). *Integrating information and communication technologies in development programmes*. Retrieved April 20, 2008, from http://www.oecd.org/dataoecd/2/57/20611917.pdf

OECD. (2005). *Financing ICTs for development – Efforts of DAC members*. Retrieved May 14, 2008, from http://www.oecd.org/dataoecd/41/45/34410597.pdf

Pohjola, M. (2000). Information technology and economic growth: A cross-country analysis. Helsinki, Finland: United Nations University World Institute for Development Economics Research (UNU/WIDER).

Solow, R. (1987, July 12). We'd better watch out. *The New York Times Book Review*, 36.

Souter, D. (2004). ICTs and economic growth in developing countries. *The DAC Journal*, 5(4), 7–40.

SPO. (2006a). *Information society strategy 2006-2010*. Retrieved May 7, 2008, from http://www.bilgitoplumu.gov.tr/yayin/Information%20Society%20Strategy_Turkey.pdf

SPO. (2006b). *Program tanimlama dokumani*. Retrieved May 7, 2008, from http://www.bilgitoplumu.gov.tr/btstrateji/Program%20Tan%FDmlama%20Dokumani_Temmuz%202006%20Nihai.pdf

SPO. (2006c). *Information society strategy: Action plan 2006-2010*. Retrieved May 7, 2008, from http://www.bilgitoplumu.gov.tr/eng/docs/Action_Plan.pdf

UN. (2004). *Financing ICTD*. Retrieved April 7, 2008, from http://www.itu.int/wsis/tffm/final-report.pdf

UNDP. (n.d.). *How to build open information societies: A collection of best practices and know-how*. Retrieved April 10, 2008, from http://unpan1.un.org/intradoc/groups/public/documents/UNTC/UNPAN018476.pdf

World Bank. (1993). *Turkey: Informatics and economic modernization*. Washington, DC: World Bank Publications.

World Bank. (2005). *Financing information and communication infrastructure needs in the developing world: Public and private roles*. Draft for discussion. Retrieved December 13, 2007, from http://event-africa-networking.web.cern.ch/event-africa- networking/cdrom/Worldbank/financingICT_Draft.pdf

Chapter 17

ICT Strategy for Development:
Lessons Learnt from the Egyptian Experience in Developing Public– Private Partnerships

Sherif Kamel
The American University in Cairo, Egypt

Dina Rateb
The American University in Cairo, Egypt

ABSTRACT

Emerging information and communication technology (ICT) is setting the pace for a changing, competitive and dynamic global marketplace and representing an enabling platform for business and socioeconomic development in the 21st century. In that respect, developing nations are urged to keep pace regularly with the developments taking place in the developed world through the design and implementation of strategy, vision and detailed plans for universal access in terms of ICT literacy and its effective utilization for developmental purposes were ICT is promoted as a vehicle for development. It is important to note that building the ICT infrastructure and infostructure will not realize quantum leaps in the development process unless it is coupled with concrete projects and initiatives that engage the society at large with its multiple stakeholders from public, private, government and civil society organizations irrespective of their locations whether urban or remote, gender or background. This chapter describes the evolution of the ICT sector in Egypt over the last decade with an emphasis on national ICT strategy development and deployment as an integral element of Egypt's overall development process within the context of a an emerging economy and the various growing potentials ICT offers for its socioeconomic development.

OVERVIEW

Developing nations when addressing their future development plans, they need to develop a formula that integrates the changes and developments that are taking place globally and adapt a methodology that addresses their local changing needs while optimally allocating their limited resources to serve their business and socioeconomic development requirements. Moreover, in the case of policy-makers, promoting ICT for development has taken center stage due to its impact on development

DOI: 10.4018/978-1-60566-388-3.ch017

and on democracy across different sectors with implications on governance, better management and transparency (Frasheri, 2002). Within the context of information and communication technology (ICT) deployment in developing nations, it is worth noting that in the 1960s and 1970s the focus was more directed to the role played by the state. During the 1980s and 1990s, the attention was shifted to the role played by the private sector and ICT multinationals. In the early years of the 21st century, the attention was shifted to the role of non-governmental organizations (NGOs) and their vital involvement in diffusing ICT among different communities at urban and rural levels and especially underprivileged groups. The role of the civil society was also coupled with the growing attention being directed to corporate social responsibility (CSR) and the role of the community at large to integrate socially with the underprivileged segments in the community. Developing nations should focus on various socioeconomic needs of the society and to the benefits that could be realized from the amalgamation of the experiences and resources of the state (government), private sector, public sector and the civil society through models of partnership and collaboration such as public-private partnership (PPP). For example, in the case of Malta through their "*thesmartisland*" national ICT strategy intends by deploying a multi stakeholders approach to improve social inequality, disadvantages and disabilities while improving the quality of life of the citizens. The objective is to contribute to the long-term national development plans by capitalizing on the opportunities enabled through ICT, which led to allocate investment and ICT under the same cabinet office. A different approach deployed by Liberia looks at competition, investment, innovation and ICT as part of an overall integrated solution that needs to be formulated for ICT to have an effective impact on business and socioeconomic development and growth (Kamel, 2009).

ICT innovations are increasingly having important implications on business and socioeconomic development due to its role in introducing and diffusing the concepts of knowledge sharing, community development and equality. However, it is important to note that having the ICT infrastructure alone is not enough to solve all developmental problems; ICT should be looked at as a catalyst, a platform for development that needs the environmental and logistical setting to help the developmental process (Harris 1998; Kransberg 1991). The implications of ICT for development could be felt at the individual, organizational and societal levels. ICT advances have always changed the way human interact. While the basic needs of humankind have long been food, clothing and shelter, the time has come to add information to such invaluable list. The implications on developing nations could be remarkably effective if these technology innovations are properly introduced and managed in a world increasingly affected by access to timely, effective and accurate information. However, if the implementation process is not well supported and controlled, the result could be an increasing digital divide between developed and developing nations. It is important to avoid the fact that ICT could be marginalized in the development process. There is an urgent need to show that ICT generates the wealth of the enterprise, which in turn pays for socioeconomic development at large. Moreover, it is ICT that is delivering the productivity gains that enable lives of material comfort for many around the world that would have been unthinkable only two centuries ago (Heeks, 2005).

ICT is not an end in itself but a means towards reaching broader policy objectives. ICT main objective should be to improve the everyday lives of the community to fight poverty and to contribute towards the realization of the Millennium Development Goals-MDGs (www.wsis-online. net). WSIS also emphasized the fact that ICT has the capability to provide developing nations with an unprecedented opportunity to meet vital development goals and thus empower them to leapfrog several stages of their development far more effectively than before (Ulrich and Chacko, 2005). However, there is a lot that still needs to be done within the context of developing nations for ICT to have the real anticipated impact. For example, it is widely diffused in the literature that the developing world's lack of universal access to ICT, often labelled the digital divide. Nevertheless, it is important to note that such divide is available between nations and within nations both developed and developing despite the fact that the impact of difference of rationalities exists between the developed and developing worlds (Avgerou, 2000). The digital divide is usually due to a number of reasons including, but not limited to, expensive personal computers for most citizens of developing nations, poor or limited telecommunications infrastructure especially in remote locations, and high illiteracy rates and poor educational systems (Kamel et al, 2009; Kamel and Tooma, 2005). There are various factors that can help curb down the digital divide that relate to the legal and regulatory environment, awareness and capacity development among the community as well as the mechanisms in place for the collaboration between the different sectors in the economy. Moreover, the issue of electronic readiness takes center stage in transforming the digital divide into a platform for social inclusion. For example, in the case of Azerbaijan, the government is massively investing in rendering the population electronically ready (electronic readiness) to pave the way for electronic applications that could have implications on efficiency, transparency, rationalization of resources and social inclusion.

Since the early 1990s and with the diffusion of the Internet, millions of people around the world started relying on it for information interchange on a daily basis (Hashem, 1999). Today, the Internet represents the global medium in the new millennium (Cerf, 1999) and is a major driving force of change in the global market place (Kamel, 1995) with over one 1.4 billion Internet users exchanging around 82 billion emails and browsing the Internet almost on daily basis (www.itu.int). It is truly be-

lieved that ICT in general while neutralizing the time and distance barriers are the driving forces of globalization with great potentials for people to improve their lives (Colle and Roman, 2003).

With the growing use of ICT, it is becoming a priority to deploy them effectively to serve the socioeconomic and development objectives of the society. It is perceived that by combining emerging technology, appropriate organization, qualified human resources, capital formation techniques, and proper understanding of the needs of rural populations, this might pave the way for innovations that bring the Internet to more than 40% of the world population who live in the rural areas in developing nations (Perry and Sadowsky, 1996). According to the literature, 19% of the world's population accounts for 91% of Internet users (Samassekou, 2003). Therefore, there is an urgent need to close the technology divide through a comprehensive plan for social inclusion and by decentralizing the ICT infrastructure presence in developing nations beyond the nations' capitals and the major cities because the Internet connectivity in those areas is extremely poor and represents a compelling need to improve village life (Press, 1999a). This can only be realized through national ICT plans, strategies and policies that would characterize the needs of the community and set out initiatives and projects accordingly. It is important to note that improving ICT universal access has been one of the primary recommendations of the World Summit on the Information Society (WSIS) that was held in Geneva (Switzerland) in December 2003 and emphasized in the second summit in Tunis (Tunisia) in November 2005 (www.itu.int).

According to the study conducted in 1995-1996 by the United Nations Commission on Science and Technology for Development (UNCSTD), it underlined the importance of coordination for the formulation of national ICT strategies (Mansell and When, 1998). Moreover, the study pointed out the complexity of strategies to attract and maintain support for installation and maintenance of national ICT infrastructure in relatively low-income developing nations. The need for resources mobilization, proper environment, legislations and regulations, amongst other elements is important for building and sustaining such infrastructure. It is important to note that to promote an efficient and equitable national information infrastructure, governments of developing nations must create a negotiating environment in which banks, local telecoms, as well as other concerned parties are willing to act in a developmentally responsible way (de Alcantara, 2001).

There are four aspects to the digital divide including people, information, knowledge, and technology and these critical aspects should be developed together for an effective implementation to take place. ICT, which is a vital element of the knowledge economy, can be both a unifying and a divisive force. Its divisive aspect has come to be known as the digital divide, referring to the differences between those who have digital access to knowledge and those who lack it (Arab Human Development Report, 2002). The digital divide, also referred to as haves and have-nots, relates to the possession of ICT resources by individuals, schools and libraries to variables such as income level, age, ethnicity, education, gender and rural-urban residence (Kamel, 2005a). Reactions vary concerning the digital divide. In the final analysis, its existence is undeniable, but it is not a technological issue. Technology has always been, and will continue to be, a social product. It is important to note that the challenge has to do with the environment at large with all logistics and operational details involved and not just the technological elements (Kamel, 2009).

For societies to develop, grow, and benefit from the ICT evolution, nationwide introduction, adoption, diffusion and adaptation of technology should take place, something that is hardly seen in developing nations where most of the technology implementations and infrastructure are focused in the capital and the major cities. All these elements demonstrate the importance of developing national ICT strategies. Respectively,

based on WSIS recommendations, nations around the world since 2003 opted to develop national ICT strategy that is integral to their development process. Following is a demonstration of the efforts that were exerted by sample nations since the 1980s to formulate effective ICT vision and strategies aiming to develop the ICT sector and render it more agile and competitive in a fast and transforming global marketplace while focusing on deploying ICT capacities, tools and techniques for business and socioeconomic development. Model cases include developed and developing nations with varying sizes and different economic settings including Syria, Jamaica, India, Malta and Singapore.

In the case of Syria, the government set a national ICT strategy with specific objectives for the period 2003-2013. The strategy is more targets oriented with a focus on rendering the society more electronically ready. For example in terms of infrastructure the target by 2013 for fixed and mobile lines telephony is 30% penetration, as for Internet penetration it is 20 subscribers per 100 inhabitants and for PC penetration it is 30 PCs per 100 inhabitants with an investment plan of ICT that totals 8 billion US dollars that equals around 4% of the GDP. The 10-year investment plan is based on a PPP model with the government securing 2 billion US dollars, with an additional 2 billion US dollars from the private sector and 4 billion US dollars from the civil society and public sources (Sabouni, 2006). The government will have to overcome some of the challenges such as lack of qualified human resources due to brain drain, availing a suitable investment climate and red tape. The strategy focuses on investment in human resources and ICT deployment in urban and rural communities as well as promoting industry development through the creation of technology zones.

In the case of Jamaica, the national ICT strategic plan focuses on E-Powering the nation by 2012. It is a five-year plan that Jamaica becomes an inclusive, development-oriented, knowledge-based society that achieves economic and social growth through the integration of ICTs into all aspects of the nation's life. The objective is to magnify Jamaica's position as a leader in the delivery of ICT-enhanced services and new investment opportunities in the Caribbean (www.cito.gov.jm). The overall vision of the strategy is for Jamaica to achieve accelerated human and economic development toward global competitiveness. E-Powering Jamaica 2012 represents the foundation for the ICT sector plan within the long-term development plan for Jamaica vision 2030 (www.cito.gov.jm). The plan highlights the importance of e-Inclusion through open access to ICTs and participation in a knowledge-based society as the focal strategic mission with related objectives that addresses lifelong learning, network readiness and infrastructure development, eGovernment, ICT industry development, research and innovation, cultural content and creativity and availing a legislative and policy framework.

In the case of India, the national ICT strategy focuses on rejuvenating the economy and making it an efficient and competitive economy whereas ICT can provide a platform for development and enables policy makers to look at it from a macro-level approach. Some of the missing elements are the localization and Indianization of the nation's ICT strategies and policies. Moreover, the role of different stakeholders is not clear coupled with the fact that training and education in the ICT sector should be gender neutral, which is not the case in India. The need for a national ICT strategy that addresses the issue of women could be of massive support to the development of the nation since ICT can play a major role in women empowerment if they are provided with employment opportunities at the rural level. In the context of India, there is a need for a holistic approach where all multiple stakeholders should be playing effective roles. There are huge potentials for ICT to transform a developing into a developed nation. For India, ICT could have an effective role transforming the economy and

bringing the marginalized community into being socially included. With 15% of the role played by ICT and 85% associated with human capacities development, infrastructure deployment and an environment conducive for development; there is a need to address the needs of the citizens at large not in terms of computerization and digitization but rather in terms of effective utilization and tangible implications.

In the case of Malta, as technology becomes cheaper and more affordable coupled with the rate innovation that is growing exponentially, Malta is looking for different opportunities whereas ICT could improve the quality of life and support in the growth of its economy. The government looks to developing a strong ICT industry; transform its government through electronic applications, enhancing the citizens' quality of life, development of smart workforce, availing a connected community and establishing a robust ICT environment and next-generation ICT infrastructure. The national ICT strategy targets by 2010; broadband reaching 80% households, 75% of the population ICT-literate, 101 ICT access centers, schools interconnectivity, diffusion of real-time eGovernment services, and the creation of ICT-related job opportunities. The implementation of the overall strategy is orchestrated by the Malta Information Technology Agency (MITA) with representatives from different stakeholders in the marketplace.

In the case of Singapore, since the late 1970s ICT was identified as one key technology that would improve Singapore's economic performance by doing more with less, increasing labour productivity, making processes leaner and more efficient and delivering better services to different consumers (Hieo, 2001). Since 1980, there were 20 years of systematic evolution through 5-years national ICT development plans orchestrated by the Committee for National Computerization (CNC) headed by a cabinet minister and mandated to map out the national level strategy and policy for IT development in Singapore. It is important to note that while the period 1980-1991 targeted the national IT plan, the period 1992-2000 focused more on creating an "Intelligent Island-IT2000", and the current period that started in 2000 is targeting an "Infocomm Capital-Infocomm 21". The current plan aims to avail a nation that is dynamic and vibrant global Infocomm capital with a thriving and prosperous e-Economy and a pervasive and infocomm-savvy e-Society (Hieo, 2001). Infocomm 21 strategic objectives aim to compete in a digital future setting whereas it becomes an enabler of Singapore's competitiveness, avails information for all citizens and becomes a primary growth sector. Singapore is a model case for developing nations demonstrating that long-term iterative, dynamic and comprehensive strategies and policies can transform economies into becoming more developed while capitalizing on emerging ICT within two decades.

RESEARCH METHODOLOGY

ICT developments and their contribution to socioeconomic development are often researched and studied to assess their effectiveness and benefits on individuals, organizations and societies especially in the context of developing nations. The objective of this chapter is to demonstrate the role of partnerships between different stakeholders in rendering ICT a platform for development and its implications on the economy. The evidence compiled from the literature will be analyzed to identify a set of lessons and recommendations for future implementations in similar environments.

The research methodology followed was mainly qualitative based on a set of interviews coupled with the researcher's impressions and interpretations of the implications of ICT diffusion within the community. Additionally, a comprehensive analysis of the body of knowledge available and an extensive literature survey of published reports, articles and documents on ICT deployment and diffusion in developing nations with a focus on Egypt was conducted. The inter-

views conducted addressed different stakeholders including government officials, decision makers in public and private sector organizations as well as representatives of local ICT vendors and ICT multinational companies operating in Egypt. This chapter primarily focuses on the analysis of aggregate level information on ICT deployment in Egypt and its associated role on the economy at large given the identification of ICT as a driver for business and socioeconomic development. In the case of Egypt, the interviews targeted policy makers, CEOs and managing directors from local ICT companies, multinationals operating in Egypt as well as government officials and policy makers in the ICT sector including CEOs of IT associations and agencies. It is important to note that because ICT is looked at as a catalyst for development, non-ICT organizations yet users of ICT tools and applications in different sectors including banking, textiles, automotive, petroleum and general services were included in the sample interviewed.

EVOLUTION OF ICT IN EGYPT

ICT in developing nations is becoming a necessity for socioeconomic development (Press, 1999b). ICT are increasingly being recognized as essential tools for development, tools that can empower people, enhance skills, increase productivity, and improve at all levels (Schware, 2005). However, this can only be realized through a two-tier approaches where society will contribute in shaping the infrastructure, which will in-turn contribute in shaping the society. Egypt, as a developing country, has heavily invested in its technology and information infrastructure since 1985 to become the platform for the economy's development and growth (Kamel, 2005b). During the period 1985-1995, a government-private sector partnership had a remarkable impact on building Egypt's information (infostructure) infrastructure (Kamel 1997 and 1995). During that period, hundreds of informatics projects and centers were established in various government, public and private sector organizations targeting socioeconomic development (Kamel, 1998). These projects that included human, technology and financial infrastructure development had invaluable inputs in building a growing information technology literate society capable of leading Egypt into the 21st century from an information perspective (www.idsc.gov. eg). Such elements represented the major building blocks necessary to establish a full-fledged information infrastructure capable of keeping pace with the developments taking place globally.

In 1999, ICT was identified as a priority at the highest policy level and a new cabinet office was established namely the ministry of communications and information technology (MCIT) leading to more investments and infrastructure build-up (Kamel, 2005b). Respectively, the growth of the ICT industry took massive steps during the last decade in different aspects including human, information, legislation and infrastructure (American Chamber of Commerce in Egypt, 2007). During the 4th quarter of 2008, the number of IT companies exceeds 2,621 going up from just over 870 companies in December 1999 working in the sales and technical support of hardware, software, and in the development of IT solutions, systems integration and consultation (MCIT, 2009; Kamel, 2009). This helped create employment opportunities for fresh graduates and unemployed candidates interested in the ICT sector within major cities. More importantly, it provided opportunities for those living in the remote and underprivileged communities directly contributing to improving their economic status. Moreover, it helped ICT multinationals coming to Egypt to expand their businesses and penetrate both local and regional markets that are growing in number as the potential for a large IT marketplace grows (American Chamber of Commerce in Egypt, 2007). It is important to note that the ICT sector being a dynamic and attractive sector succeeded to attract many talented human resources working in diversified fields. Therefore,

the number of ICT employees increased to over 175,000 in December 2008 compared to 162,500 in December 2007 with an annual growth rate of 7.8% and up from just over 48,000 in 1999 (MCIT, 2009). The ICT sector is a major engine of economic growth in Egypt contributing to real gross domestic product (GDP) 3.34% in the 3rd quarter of 2008 as compared to 3.08% in the 3rd quarter in 2007. The ICT sector is one of the fastest growing sectors in Egypt reaching 14.6% in the 3rd quarter in 2008 leading all other economic sectors. The ICT sector has managed to transform itself from a sector that consumes resources in the infrastructure build-up phase into a sector that is generates revenues and provides employment opportunities and a platform for development and growth through its variety of value-added services.

During WSIS in Geneva (2003), the President of Egypt highlighted the importance the current administration is giving to ICT diffusion and its role in development reflecting the commitment of all constituencies of the collaborative efforts set to introduce and diffuse ICT in the nation. The examples demonstrated included initiatives that aimed at preparing the community for the information society such as free-Internet model, PC for every home (PC2010), establishment of IT clubs, and the introduction of broadband services in addition to projects relating to key sectors such as education, health, banking, and public administration amongst others (MCIT, 2005a). These projects have helped improve the digital demographics of the community at large especially when the infrastructure was diffused to reach communities in the remote and unprivileged areas. Table 1 demonstrates the status of electronic readiness in Egypt showing the number of Internet users, PC penetration rates and the total number of IT clubs (Kamel, 2009; 2005b and 2004).

One of the effective platforms that helped diffuse ICT in Egypt across different segments of the community during the last decade has been the models of IT clubs. There was a variety of models used but the most successful reflected a

Table 1. Electronic readiness in Egypt

Indicators	October 1999	December 2002	December 2004	December 2006	December 2008
Internet Subscribers	300,000	1.2 million	3.6 million	6 Million	11.4 million
ADSL Subscribers	N/A	N/A	N/A	206,150	593,042
Internet Penetration per 100 Inhabitants	0.38%	2.53%	5.57%	8.25%	15.59%
Mobile Phones	654,000	4.5 million	7.6 million	18 Million	38.06 million
Mobile Phones Penetration per 100 Inhabitants	0.83%	5.76%	9.74%	23.07%	50.7%
Fixed Lines	4.9 million	7.7 million	9.5 million	10.8 million	11.4 million
Fixed Lines Penetration per 100 Inhabitants	6.2%	9.8%	12.1%	13.8%	15.2%
Public Pay Phones	13,300	48,000	52,700	56,449	58,002
IT Clubs	30	427	1,055	1,442	1,751
ICT Companies	870	1,533	1,870	2,211	2,621
IT Companies	266	815	1,374	1,970	2,012
Communications Companies	59	75	152	244	265
Services Companies	88	121	148	211	242
IT Economic Indicators					
Number of Employees in the ICT Sector[1]	48,090	85,983	115,956	147,822	174,478

public-private partnership (PPP) initiative providing affordable Internet access throughout the nation's 29 provinces. The locations include youth centers, culture centers, non-governmental organizations, universities, schools, public libraries and information centers amongst other locations. The total number of clubs currently stands at 1,751 as compared to 30 in 1999 with an annual growth rate of 13.5% during the period September 2007-September 2008 (MCIT, 2009). All IT clubs are equipped with computers with Internet connectivity (MCIT, 2007a). They have the facilities to invest in human resource capacities by offering training programs to help promote ICT awareness and utilization. Among the expansion plan for the IT clubs are the provision of an electronic library, dedicated space for trainees with special needs, and

the provision of access to electronic government (eGovernment) and electronic learning (eLearning) services amongst other facilities. The target was to have one club in every village by the end of 2010. The model of IT clubs in Egypt reflects the typical telecenters available in many other developing nations (Kamel, 2004). In the case of Egypt, the objective of these telecenters goes beyond ICT diffusion with more focus on using the IT clubs as platforms supporting socioeconomic development of the local community especially in remote and unprivileged areas (Kamel, 2005a).

It is important to note that an ideal ICT strategy should guide the development of a sound information environment in order to deliver convenient and universal access to information, improve communication, support collaboration and learning and ensure flexible, responsive and above all reliable systems. The strategic objective of the strategy should be to develop and implement a business-driven institutional IT strategic plan that positions IT as a strategic asset and provides a context for institutional decisions regarding IT investments, governance and organizational structure. Being part of the global economy, Egypt has realized the importance of promoting the ICT sector and marked a new era for Egypt's ICT sector by the formation of MCIT in 1999, where the IT industry enjoyed a new and more liberalized regulatory framework.

ICT SECTOR PROFILE

The economic growth of the ICT sector during the 4th quarter of 2008 was 19.2% compared to 15.5% in 2007. It is important to note that during the 1st quarter of 2009, the indicators demonstrate the steady growth of the sector despite the implications of the global economic downturn (MCIT, 2009). Investment in the ICT sector grew from 8% to 15% annually out of the total investment compared to 3% in 2006. In 2008, 93% of total investments in the ICT sector were through private investments either local or based on foreign direct investments, which averaged 1 billion US dollars on average in 2007 and 2008. The ICT market in Egypt generates around 2.9 billion US dollars of annual revenue with almost 2.5 billion US dollars (86%) derived from the telecommunications sector. During the period 2004-2008, as indicated in the 7th World Telecommunication ICT sector meeting held in Cairo in March 2009, the ICT sector witnessed an overall 20% growth with over 7.8 billion US dollars generated to the treasury. Such investments are directed to the continuous development and improvement of the information infrastructure as well as for the investment in human resource capacities. It is important to note that projections indicate that continuous growth

derived by increasing demand in response to bold trade and tax reforms that would realize a stronger economic activity and increased disposable income for households (Kamel, 2006).

Reference Egypt's strategic vision, the government is sustaining its ongoing economic and institutional reforms, investment incentives, infrastructure development and global integration to enhance its competitiveness regionally and globally and to support investment in different fields especially in the ICT sector. Egypt is planning to increase ICT exports to 1.1 billion US dollars by 2010 (MCIT, 2005b). These projections are based on the increase in ICT investments due to the government efforts to improve the business climate, which led to foster economic growth since 2004. In terms of investment in human capacities, MCIT has made a commitment to invest in the future by working to ensure that today's students and employees receive the education and training that will prepare them to lead Egypt in the information society. MCIT in collaboration with its different partners is focusing on developing basic and professional ICT skills by collaborating with government ministries, agencies as well as multi-nationals and companies from the private sector to develop a variety of training programs designed to provide a wide range of ICT-related concepts and applications. Some of the initiatives and projects that also contributed in the investments in human capacities included the Smart Schools Network, the eLearning Competence Center as well as the support received from Egypt's ICT Trust Fund which was established in cooperation with UNDP in 2002 (ICT Trust Fund, 2007).

It is important to note that the ICT sector exports witnessed an increase from 250 million US dollars in 2005 to 750 million US dollars in 2008 mainly due to the fast growing positioning of Egypt as an outsourcing destination. Moreover, according to IDC, revenues of the ICT sector in Egypt in 2004 were about 562 million US dollars, a figure expected to increase to reach 973 million

Table 2. ICT spending as a percentage of GDP in 2007

Region	ICT Spending (Percentage of GDP)
China	7%
Canada	6.4%
Egypt	5.95%
Italy	5.79%
France	5.74%
India	5.61%
Saudi Arabia	4.71%
Chile	4.19%
Russia	4.12%
Algeria	2.51

US dollars by 2009. The analysis of these figures indicate that although the increase comes from the hardware industry, the percentage of revenues from hardware had decreased compared to software and IT services as it represented 63.6% in 2004 while it had reached 66.4% in 2000 and it is estimated to reach 62.8% in 2009. Table 2 demonstrates the ICT spending as a percentage of GDP in different regions of the world (World Bank, 2009).

In terms of ICT spending in Egypt, the highest percentage relates to hardware because of the fact that the government, the main customer, has high expenditures (63%) on this element of the industry followed by software and application software that represents about 16% and 13% respectively

(MCIT, 2009). Figure 1 demonstrates the distribution of ICT spending in Egypt.

EGYPT INFORMATION SOCIETY INITIATIVE (EISI)

The evolution in the information society heralds a new socioeconomic order. This era is witnessing the emergence of information-based economies, with traditional economic, industrial and business activities moving towards more knowledge-driven processes and the progressive transformation of advanced economies into knowledge-based, technology-driven, services-dominated economies. These shifts are increasingly laying emphasis on economic activities with intellectual content and knowledge, enabled by the development and exploitation of emerging ICTs within all spheres of human endeavour. Against that background, Egypt is recognizing the need to develop rapidly its information and knowledge base through massive investments in ICT and human capacity development, improving and broadening universal access to higher and quality education and training with an emphasis on lifelong learning and creating digital content accessible to the society.

Egypt efforts for ICT development are government-led in collaboration with the private sector and civil society. In that respect, Egypt

Figure 1. Distribution of ICT spending

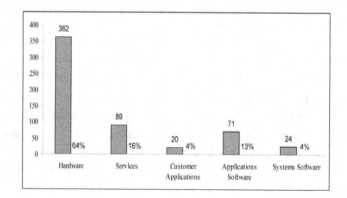

Table 3. Egypt information society initiative

eReadiness "Equal Access for All" – Enabling all citizens to have easy and affordable access to the opportunities offered by new technologies – Developing a robust communication infrastructure is key	**eLearning "Nurturing Human Capital"** – Promoting the use of ICT in education – Developing a new generation of citizens who understand and are comfortable with the use of ICT in their daily lives
eGovernment "Government Now Delivers" – Delivering high quality government services to the public in the format that suits them – Reaching a new level of convenience in government services – Offering citizens the opportunity to share in the decision making process and greatly improve efficiency and quality	**eBusiness "A New Way of Doing Business"** – Creating new technology-based firms – Improving workforce skills – Using electronic documents – Developing ePayment infrastructure – Using ICT can be a significant catalyst to increase employment, creating new jobs and improving competitiveness
eHealth "Increasing Health Services Availability" – Improving citizens' quality of life and healthcare workers work environment – Adding value using ICT through reaching remote populations – Providing continuous training for doctors, and offering the tools for building a national health network	**eCulture "Promoting Egyptian Culture"** – Documenting Egyptian cultural identity through the use of tools to preserve manuscripts, archives and index materials – Offering worldwide access to cultural and historical materials – Generate and promote interest in Egyptian cultural life and heritage
ICT Export Initiative "Industry Development" – Fostering the creation of an export-oriented ICT industry – Developing an ICT industry can be a powerful engine for export growth and job creation	

has developed a number of policies and strategies to facilitate socioeconomic development and accelerate the transformation of the nation's economy and society to become information-rich and knowledge-based. MCIT has formulated the 2007-2010 national ICT strategy. The plan paved the way for the Egyptian Information Society Initiative (EISI), which is structured around seven major tracks, each designed to help bridge the digital divide and progress Egypt's evolution into an information society. EISI represented the vision of the ICT strategy translated into initiatives and programs that targets diffusing ICT connectivity. Table 3 demonstrates the different EISI building blocks. Egypt shares with other developing nations many of the challenges of building an information society.

SWOT ANALYSIS OF THE ICT MARKET IN EGYPT

The ICT sector grew tremendously during the last 20 years going through a number of phases from introduction to adaptation to diffusion and adaptation. However, the analysis of the local and global markets showed a number of challenges that faced the growth of the sector. The following SWOT analysis has been developed based on studying the different factors related to the ICT sector and highlighting its relative and competitive advantages and its potentials for growth and contribution in overall development beyond the current capacities. It is important to note that this analysis served as a main platform for building Egypt national ICT strategy. Table 4 demonstrates the findings of the SWOT analysis.

FORMULATING EGYPT'S NATIONAL ICT STRATEGY

The government of Egypt since the late 1990s has embarked on a national effort to formulate a national ICT strategy that captures the national vision defining the introduction, use and diffusion of ICT for business and social economic development at large. The strategy that has been

Table 4. SWOT analysis of the ICT sector in Egypt

Strengths	Weaknesses
– Number of university graduates – Low employee turnover (labor laws) – Government vision and support to ICT – Political stability – Infostructure (national information infrastructure) – Telecommunication infrastructure – Low ICT infrastructure cost – Low cost of starting/doing business – Skilled, qualified and multilingual fresh university graduates	– Small market size (ICT companies and market) – Mainly hardware-dominated industry – Limited services business opportunity – Limited outsourcing projects (recently growing) – Most large bids are government-related – Bureaucratic purchasing rules (red-tape) – Fierce competition and price-driven market – Buyers market (service and quality value) – General business climate/environment (though progressing) – Import-based industry – Limited industry expertise (need for critical mass) – Non-availability of enough capital investment
Opportunities	**Threats**
– Growing economy with a focus on exports – Potentials for an ICT service-oriented hub – Possible Local market growth rate – Human capacity building programs – ICT to improve sectors competitiveness – eGovernment services and applications – Large number of private sector SMEs – Growing role of the civil society – Multinationals subcontracting national and local companies and vendors – Price-sensitive markets/lines of business – Outsourcing activities from US and EU – Buyers market created by competition – Emerging technologies adopted to increase productivity and reduce costs – Mobile technology advantages – Role of government and NGOs in supporting and promoting the ICT sector	– Availability of skills in required numbers – Perception of ICT value and delivery of required quality – Ability to cooperate between companies (legislative environment) – Competition between government and private sector companies – Competition from other nations to Egyptian exports – Minimal research and development efforts – High local software and intellectual property piracy rate (recent improvements) – Inadequate legal and regulatory climate – EU nations causing price pressures on ICT exporters to create low-cost, effective IT outsourcing to their markets

dynamically amended to reflect the changes in the global marketplace and catered for the transforming local needs was mainly related to infrastructure development, national information infrastructure build-up, investment in human resource capacities, market and environment development in the build-up to the formulation of the information society.

The guiding principle of the comprehensive national ICT strategy was that it was integrated, embedded and clearly linked to the local national development priorities. In that sense, ICT as a sector was looked as a potential for a productive sector, contributing to GDP and a facilitator for overall development. The government gave a priority to the ICT sector as a driver of economic growth. According to the World Bank, Egypt's ICT expenditure on ICT has reached 5.95% of GDP in 2007 coming ahead of many developed and developing nations (World Bank, 2009). Moreover, the government is giving priority to the ICT sector within its policy development framework scoring 4.4 on a scale of (1-7) in 2006 (World Bank, 2008). Developing national ICT strategies in recent years has been the culmination of efforts undertaken by many nations since the 1980s.

Strategies during that time were focusing on computerization of the government administrative and operational procedures, coordination of computer education and training as well as the development and promotion of a computer services industry. Highly articulated ICT policies were developed in the 1990s, inspired by the Unites States announcement of the development of a national information infrastructure (NII) plan with key focus on private investment, competition, access and universal services (UNECA, 2003a). Gradually, it was perceived that as part of their economic development strategy, governments should make substantial efforts to develop their national ICT strategies that can compete on a global scale (Neto et al, 2005). In that respect, developing nations followed two different approaches in defining their national ICT strategies. Some focused on developing ICT as an economic sector either to boost exports as in the case of Costa Rica and Taiwan or to build domestic capacity as in the case of Brazil, India and Korea (World Bank, 2006). These nations strengthened the market orientation of their economic policies and institutions, have gradually dismantled barriers to trade and investment, and facilitated rapid changes in production and telecommunications technologies. These nations made combined efforts to educate their people to keep them on track of global developments, promoted ICT as an enabler of a wider socioeconomic development, and worked on repositioning their economy to secure competitive advantage in the global economy. However, it is important to note that one common challenge for all nations was the assessment of the electronic readiness (eReadiness) of the community and having comprehensive yet accurate profiles of the status of ICT deployment especially among developing nations such as in the of Albania.

Electronic readiness is important to place nations on the global ICT "digital" map, something that not all nations, especially developing, can afford missing. In that respect, ICT strategy, vision and policies must not only be suitable but should also be embedded in a holistic application and implementation scheme. The ICT strategy, vision and policies of a nation, cannot afford to keep the different building blocks of ICT separate. Their amalgamation must be done at a priority basis otherwise, ICT as a platform for development will not bring the desired results. Moreover, successful applications of ICT for development depend on macro drivers, availing the required ecosystem as

well as the preconditions and building blocks of the required environment (Neto, 2005).

Egypt, as an African nation, was part of the framework of the African Information Society Initiative (AISI) that emerged from recommendations of the conference of African ministers of economic development and planning in 1996. Egypt among other nations strived to develop its national information and communication infrastructure (NICI) strategies and policies that articulate long-term policy, infrastructure, content and application as an integral part of overall national development (UNECA, 2003b). Egypt is considered among the nations that have advanced their national strategies from conceptualization to implementation. This was translated in the deployment of a two-tier approach, developing national strategies and harnessing ICT applications in key sectors such as education, health and commerce with an emphasis on promoting electronic commerce, attracting FDI to stimulate the knowledge-based economy and to create jobs for the youth and to harness the potential of ICT.

Egypt ICT strategy goes beyond telecom reaching a cross-sectoral approach to creating an enabling environment and mainstreaming ICT into national development policies by addressing all sectors such as trade, finance, investment, education, government, health, commerce and media amongst others. The target is to transform Egypt into becoming a vibrant and dynamic ICT hub in the Middle East with a thriving digital economy and IT-empowered citizens (MCIT, 2007b).

The national ICT strategy is a product of the collaboration of many stakeholders including the community, the government, private and public sector organizations as well as the civil society. According to WSIS in 2003 and 2005, all nations were encouraged to develop their national ICT strategies including the necessary human capacity building taking into account national local conditions. In that respect, strategies should aim to maximize the social, economic and environmental benefits of the information society, which can only

Figure 2. National ICT strategy building blocks (2000-2004)

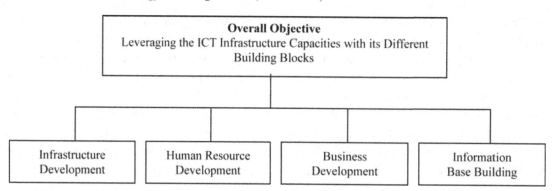

be realized if governments create a trustworthy, transparent and non-discriminatory legal, regulatory, and policy environment (www.wsis-online. net). Egypt national ICT strategy objectives were mainly formulated to promote the information society and to build an export oriented ICT industry. Such objective by nature is dynamic and changing based on emerging ICTs and its relation to socioeconomic development. Therefore, the strategy formulation process turned out to become an iterative process that aims at catering for the changing needs of the society and those that serve the development process. Figure 2 demonstrates the overall objectives of the national ICT strategy during the period 2000-2004 (MCIT, 2005a).

The national ICT strategy was formulated to encourage social inclusion in the information age. The use of ICT to minimize the creation of communities of haves and have-nots was a key-targeted outcome. At the local level, the commitment to maximum social inclusion of its population required considerable pro-active support including financial investment to ensure that Egypt is given universal access to the Internet backbone and to NII. Moreover, the strategy addressed issues such as human resources capacity development and upgrading the physical infrastructure to be able to compete in global deregulated markets. At the global level, access became invaluable in shaping the role Egypt plays in global trade and markets. Respectively, convergence became vital. The

emerging role of ICT and its integration in major sectors such as education, entertainment, health, and financial services became a prerequisite for developing nations to be able to integrate in the global information economy and Egypt factored that element in its national ICT strategy.

Egypt national ICT strategy has been dynamic and flexible adapting to the changing nature of the sector. In that respect, during the period 2004-2006 a revised strategy was formulated to include new elements such as providing an institutional support for developing electronic access (eAccess) and providing institutional development of electronic government (eGovernment) and electronic business (eBusiness). Figure 3 demonstrates the amendments that were introduced to the national ICT strategy for the period (2004-2006). The government of Egypt has made a strong commitment to advance the cause of human development in the context of an open economy. Additionally, the structural adjustment program that began in the early 1990s has caused positive and profound changes in the competitiveness of the country. Three main elements could characterize the economy being more open and that includes strengthening of market mechanisms, privatization of government enterprises and an increasing role for the private sector and the civil society (Kamel, 2006).

The role of MCIT required the provision of a policy framework for the ICT sector to grow and

Figure 3. National ICT strategy building blocks (2004-2006)

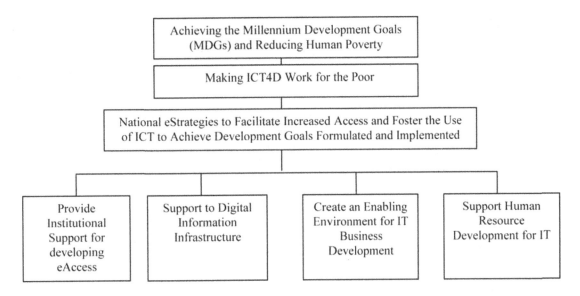

Table 5. National ICT plan projects categories

− Promoting national demand for ICT in collaboration with different stakeholders
− Focusing on an export-oriented strategy with emphasis on software development through outsourcing
− Investing in human resources as the primary building block in the ICT ecosystem
− Forging international alliances and partnerships to increase diversity, encourage FDI and create job opportunities
− Modernizing the ICT infrastructure to participate in the global ICT space
− Availing the legislative environment allowing successful implementation and sustainability of projects

become competitive both locally and globally. Table 5 demonstrates the main categories under which fall the initial 23 projects of the national ICT plan, more should be added as the need arises. The majority of the projects were implemented by the private sector with financial and technical support and guidance from MCIT (www.mcit.gov. eg). In 2006, and with the continuous development in the ICT sector in Egypt, a revisit to the strategy was conducted and a new ICT sector strategy was formulated for the period 2007-2010. The new strategy has been formulated to cater for three main components, ICT sector restructuring, ICT for reform and development and ICT industry development as demonstrated in Figure 4.

During the period 2007-2010, the focus of the amended national ICT strategy was on sector restructuring by increasing the state resources to reach 3.9 billion US dollars through restructuring the national postal service, initial public offering for Telecom Egypt (TE) and the provision of National Telecommunications Regulatory Authority (NTRA) licenses such as 3G and WIMAX services amongst others. Moreover, the government intends to exert maximum efforts to maintain the current level of investments in the ICT sector that is levelled at an annual growth rate of 20%. Finally, the government plans to help deploy state-of-the-art ICT tools and applications to serve the development in the society in different sectors.

Figure 4. National ICT strategy building blocks (2006-2010)

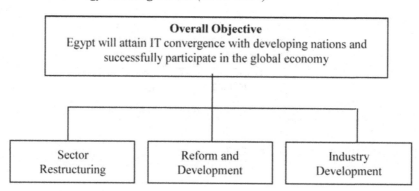

In terms of using ICT for reform and development, the strategy intends to follow three main paths. This includes; deploying ICT tools through increasing the penetration rates to mobiles, PCs, Internet usage, broadband services and ICT clubs; developing the postal services network with its 4000+ branches; and finally completing the ICT infrastructure in different institutions. Moreover, the strategy will focus on using ICT as a catalyst in reforming a number of sectors including education, health, and government institutions (ministries) amongst others.

In terms of industry development, the strategy intends to focus on innovation, research, and development in ICT through the formulation of partnership agreements with ICT multinational companies. This will include the development of different technology incubators for small and medium-sized enterprises (SMEs) in the ICT sector, investing in human capital, media convergence, development of digital Content and promoting ICT exports through outsourcing. The most recent amendments of the ICT strategy intends to look at ICT as a platform for empowering the community as a key element for socioeconomic development.

CONCLUSION

Successful ICT strategies need a number of elements in order to be effective and to realize its targeted objectives. This includes, but is not limited to, leadership from top executives and policy makers, involving all stakeholders in implementation, deploying a holistic approach covering all sectors, enabling a liberalized economy, monitoring ICT developments, tailoring towards the nation's requirements and mainstreaming ICT into national socioeconomic development plans. There is a need to emphasize the role of the government in creating the right atmosphere that encourages private sector investment in ICT related businesses. The liberalization of the telecom sector is important to encourage competition and promote FDI. The creation of a universal access policy through broadband is invaluable to induce mass-market deployment of ICT leading to improving the service quality and speed. Moreover, instituting the necessary foreign investment laws and enforcing software piracy and copyright infringement laws, which encourage ICT multinationals to establish regional operations, thus providing work opportunities for skilled individuals and limiting the brain drain effect. Egypt has already shown over the last decade some headway on the ICT development path. However, it needs to strengthen its commitment and speed its process for a long-term sector development and growth. Such a strategy would invariably drive faster growth across all economic sectors, which will lead to a sustainable socioeconomic development that can be reflected at the individual and societal level.

ACKNOWLEDGMENT

The authors would like to acknowledge the contributions of the International Relations team of the Ministry of Communications and Information Technology in Egypt for their support throughout the conduct of the research by facilitating access to different stakeholders, sharing reports and documentations, scheduling interviews and in addressing policy issues related to the ICT sector. I would also like to acknowledge the research support that was provided by my assistant Lina Nada throughout the research work.

REFERENCES

American Chamber of Commerce in Egypt. (2007 May). *Information Technology in Egypt*.

Arab Human Development Report. (2002). *Creating Opportunities for Future Generations*. United Nations Development Programme and Arab Fund for Economic and Social Development.

Avgerou, C. (2000). Recognizing Alternative Rationalities in the Deployment of Information Systems. *Electronic Journal of Information Systems in Developing Countries, 3*(7), 1–15.

Central Information Technology Office. (2009). Retrieved March 7, 2009, from http://www.cito.gov.jm

Cerf, V. (1999). *The Internet is for everyone. OnTheInternet*. July-August.

Colle, R., & Roman, R. (2003). Challenges in the Telecentre Movement. In Marshall, S., Taylor, W., & Yu, X. (Eds.), *Closing the Digital Divide: Transforming Regional Economics and Communities with Information Technology*. Westport, CT: Praeger.

De Alcantara, C. H. (2001). *The Development Divide in a Digital Age*. Issue Paper, United Nations Research Institute for Social Development, Technology, Business and Society Programme.

Frasheri, N. (2002) Critical View of e-Governance Challenges for Developing Countries. *IFIP WG9.4 Work Conference ICT and Development*, May, Bangalore, India

Harris, R. (1998). Information Technology – The New Cargo Cult? Information Technology in Developing Countries – *Newsletter of the International Federation and Information Processing (IFIP) Working Group 9.4*, Vol. 8, No. 1, January

Hashem, S. (1999, July 22). Technology Access Community Centers in Egypt: A Mission for Community Empowerment. In *Proceedings of the Internet Society Conference*.

Heeks, R. (2005). *ICTs and the MDGs: on the Wrong Track*. Information for Development Magazine.

Hieo, W. (2001). National Infocomm Strategy and Policy: Singapore's Experience, International Council for Information Technology in Government Administration. *ICA Information, 74*.

ICT Trust Fund. (2007). Retrieved January 10, 2008, from http://www.ictfund.org.eg

Information and Decision Support Center. (2005). *Annual Report on Egypt*.

Information and Decision Support Center. (2008). Retrieved June 25, 2008, from http://www.idsc.gov.eg

International Telecommunication Union. (2009, January 25). Retrieved from http://www.itu.int

Kamel, S. (1995) Information Superhighways, a Potential for Socioeconomic and Cultural Development. In M. Khosrow-Pour (Eds.), *Managing Information and Communications in a Changing Global Environment: Proceedings of the 6th Information Resources Management Association International Conference (IRMA)*, Atlanta, Georgia, USA, 21-24 May (pp. 115–124).

Kamel, S. (1997). DSS for Strategic Decision-Making. In Khosrow-Pour, M., & Liebowitz, J. (Eds.), *Information Technology Management in Modern Organizations* (pp. 168–182). Hershey, PA: Idea Group Publishing.

Kamel, S. (2004) Diffusing ICT Usage Through Technology Access Clubs: Closing the Digital Divide. In Z. Irani & S. Kamel (Eds.), *Proceedings of the Information Science, Technology and Management (CISTM) Conference on Improving Business Performance through Knowledge Management*, Alexandria, Egypt, 8-9 July.

Kamel, S. (2005a). Assessing the Impacts of Establishing an Internet Cafe in the Context of a Developing Nation. In *Proceedings of the 16th International IRMA Conference on Managing Modern Organizations with Information Technology*, San Diego, California, 15-18 May (pp. 176-181).

Kamel, S. (2005b). The Evolution of Information and Communication Technology Infrastructure in Egypt. In G. Hunter & A. Wenn (Eds.), Information Systems in an e-World (pp. 117-135). Washington, DC: The Information Institute, Kamel, S. (1998). Decision Support Systems and Strategic Public Sector Decision Making. In Egypt in Information Systems for Public Sector Management Working Paper Series. Institute for Development Policy and Management, University of Manchester, Paper No. 3

Kamel, S. (2009). The Evolution of the ICT Sector in Egypt – Partnership4Development. In *Proceedings of the 11th International Business Information Management Association (IBIMA) Conference on Innovation and Knowledge Management in Twin Track Economies: Challenges and Opportunities*, Cairo, Egypt, 4-6 January (pp. 841-851).

Kamel, S., Radwan, S., & El Oraby, N. (2009). The Experience of the Italian-Egyptian Debt Swap Program (2001-2008). Partners for Development, Technical Support Unit, Embassy of Italy (Egypt) and Ministry of International Cooperation (Egypt).

Kamel, S., & Tooma, E. (2005). *Exchanging Debt for Development: Lessons from the Egyptian Debt-for-Development Swap Experience*. Working Document, World Summit on the Information Society.

Kamel, T. (2006). *Egypt Reforms: An update from the ICT Sector*.

Kransberg, M. (1991). IT as Revolution. In Forester, T. (Ed.), *Computers in the Human Context*. Cambridge, MA: MIT Press.

Mansell, R., & When, U. (1998). *Knowledge Societies: Information Technology for Sustainable Development*. Oxford, UK: Oxford University Press.

Ministry of Communications and Information Technology. (2005a) Egypt Information Society Initiative (4th Ed.).

Ministry of Communications and Information Technology. (2005b). *Building Digital Bridges: Egypt's Vision of the Information Society*.

Ministry of Communications and Information Technology. (2007b). *Egypt's ICT Golden Book*.

Ministry of Communications and Information Technology. (2009). *The Future of the Internet Economy in Egypt*. Statistical Profile.

Ministry of Communications and Information Technology. (2007a). Retrieved February 10, 2009, from http://www.mcit.gov.eg

Neto, I., Kenny, C., Janakiram, S., & Watt, C. (2005). Look before You Leap: The Bumpy Road to E-Development. In R. Schware (Ed.), e-development from excitement to effectiveness. Prepared for the World Summit on the Information Society, Tunis, November.

Perry, J., & Sadowsky, G. (1996 November). If you build it, they will connect. *OnTheInternet*.

Press, L. (1999a January). Connecting Villages: The Grameen Bank Success Story. *OnTheInternet*.

Press, L. (1999b October). Developing Countries Networking Symposium. *OnTheInternet*.

Sabouni, I. (2006). National ICT Strategy for Syria: Methodology, Outcome and Implementation. In *Workshop on ICT Policy Making in ESCWA Member Countries*, 2-4 May, Beirut, Lebanon.

Samassekou, A. (2003). Towards a Shared Information Society for All, WSIS 2003 Connecting the World. In The World Summit on the Information Society, 10-12 December, Geneva, Switzerland.

Schware, R. (2005). Overview: E-Development: From Excitement to Effectiveness. In R. Schware (Ed.), e-development from excitement to effectiveness. Prepared for the World Summit on the Information Society, Tunis, November.

Ulrich, P., & Chacko, J. G. (2005). Overview of ICT Policies and e-Strategies: An Assessment on the Role of Governments. [JITD]. *Journal of Information Technology for Development*, *11*(2), 195–197. doi:10.1002/itdj.20011

United Nations Economic Commission for Africa. (2003a) *Policies and Plans on the Information Society: Status and Impact.*

United Nations Economic Commission for Africa. (2003b). *E-Strategies*. National, Sectoral and Regional ICT Policies, Plans and Strategies.

World Bank. (2006). *Information and Communication Technology for Development*. Global Trends and Policies.

World Bank. (2008). *Little Data Book on ICT.*

World Bank. (2009). *Little Data Book of ICT.*

World Summit on the Information Society. (2009). Retrieved February 10, 2009, from http://www.wsis-online.net

ENDNOTE

[1] There are also 14,000 indirect workers in both IT clubs and Internet cafés.

Compilation of References

Abd Allah, M. (1992). *Evaluating Accounting Data to Rationalize Investment Decisions: An Empirical Study.* M.Sc. Thesis, Helwan University.

Abdel Maguid, W. (2004 July). Egypt: a new government or a new approach? Is the Nazif government aware of the two main keys to reform? *Al-Ahram Center for Political and Strategic Studies, 18.*

Abdelghaffar, H., & Bakry, W. (2005). Defining E-government and E-readiness. In *Proceedings of the Information Resources Management Association (IRMA),* San Diego, USA.

Abdelghaffar, H., & Kamel, S. (2006). The Impact of E-readiness on E-government in Developing Countries: The Case of Egypt. In *Proceedings of the Information Resources Management Association (IRMA),* Washington, USA.

Abdul-Gader, A. H. (1990). End-user computing success factors: further evidence from a developing nation. *Information Resources Management Journal, 3*(1), 1–13.

Abdul-Gader, A. H. (1999). *Managing Computer Based Information Systems in Developing Countries: A Cultural Perspective.* Hershey, PA: Idea Group Publishing.

Abell, W., & Lim, L. (1996). *Business Use of the Internet in New Zealand: An Exploratory Study.* Paper presented at the Second Australian World Wide Web Conference.

Abou Aish, E. (2001). *A cross-national analysis of bank selection decision and implications for positioning.* Unpublished PhD thesis, The University of Nottingham, UK.

Abraham, R. (2007). Mobile Phones and Economic Development: Evidence from the Fishing Industry in India. *Information and Technologies and International Development, 4*(1).

Accenture. (2002). *e-Government Leadership: Realizing the Vision.* Retrieved July 12, 2003, from http://www.gol-ged.gc.calpub/pub_e.asp

Accenture. (2004). *E-government Leadership: High Performance, Maximum Value.* Retrieved September 29, 2006, from http://www.accenture.com

Accenture. (2005). *Leadership in Customer Service: New Expectations, New Experiences.* Retrieved June 20, 2005, from http://www.accenture.com/xdoc/ca/locations/canada/insights/studies/leadership_cust.pdf

Adam, L., & Wood, F. (1999). An investigation of the impact of information and communication technologies in sub-Saharan Africa. *Journal of Information Science, 25*(4), 307–318. doi:10.1177/016555159902500407

Adamali, A., Coffey, J. O., & Safdar, Z. (2006). Trends in national e-strategies: A review of 40 countries. In *Information and communications for development: Global trends and policies* (pp. 3–14). Washington, DC: World Bank Publications.

Adams, A. (1999). The Implications of Users' Privacy Perception on Communication and Information Privacy Policies. *Telecommunications Policy Research Conference,* Washington DC.

Adams, R. (2008 January). 30 Years of IFAC: Reflections on the Global Accountancy Profession. *Journal of Association of Chartered Certified Accountants.*

After radio rice, Orissa will now have a radio village too. (2003, June 14). *The New Indian Express,* p. 7.

Afuah, A., & Tucci, C. (2001). *Internet Business Models and Strategies.* Boston: McGraw-Hill Irwin.

Agarwal, R., & Bayus, B. (2002). The Market Evolution and Sales Takeoff of Product Innovations. *Management Science, 48*(8), 1024–1041. doi:10.1287/mnsc.48.8.1024.167

Ahituv, N. (1980). A Systematic Approach toward Assessing the Value of an Information System. *Management Information Systems Quarterly, 4*(4), 61–75. doi:10.2307/248961

Ahmad, H. (2008). History, policy and reform in Malaysian education. In Bajunid, I. A. (Ed.), *Malaysia - From Traditional to Smart Schools: The Malaysian Educational Odyssey* (pp. 35–83). Kuala Lumpur, Malaysia: Oxford-Fajar.

Ahmed, A. (2007). Technological Transformation and Sustainability in the MENA Region. In A. Ahmed (Ed.), *Science, Technology and Sustainability in Middle East and North Africa.* London: Inderscience Enterprises Ltd Publishers American Chamber of Commerce in Egypt. (2002). *Telecommunications in Egypt.* Retrieved from http://www.amcham.org.eg/BSAC/StudiesSeries/Report37.asp

Ahmed, F. A., & Hassan, H. A. (2007). *Local administration Regulatory Law, Number 43 of Year 1979.* Cairo, Egypt: Amiriya Publications.

AISI. (2003). *AISI: An action framework to build Africa's information and telecommunication infrastructure.* Retrieved January 19, 2007, from http://www.uneca.org/aisi/

Al-adawi, Z., Yousafzai, S., & Pallister, J. (2005). Conceptual Model of Citizen Adaptation of E-government. In *Proceedings of the 2nd International Conference on Innovations in Information Technology,* Dubai, UAE.

Aldrich, D., Bertot, J. C., & McClure, C. R. (2002). e-Government: Initiatives, Developments, and Issues. *Government Information Quarterly, 19*(4), 349–355. doi:10.1016/S0740-624X(02)00130-2

Aligula, E. M. (2005). Benchmarking information & communication technology (ICT) performance: Lessons for Kenya. In Etta, F. E., & Elder, L. (Eds.), *At the crossroads: ICT policy making in East Africa* (pp. 257–271). Nairobi, Kenya: East African Educational Publishers Ltd., & IDRC.

Al-Jaghoub, S., & Westrup, C. (2003). Jordan and ICT-led development: towards a competition state? *Information Technology & People, 16*(1), 93–110. doi:10.1108/09593840310463032

Aljifri, H., Pons, A., & Collins, D. (2003). Global e-commerce: a framework for understanding and overcoming the trust barrier. *Information Management & Computer Security, 11*(3), 130–138. doi:10.1108/09685220310480417

Al-Khatib, J. A., Rawwas, M. Y. A., & Vitell, S. J. (1997). Consumer ethics: a cross-cultural investigation. *European Journal of Marketing, 31*(11–12), 750–767. doi:10.1108/03090569710190514

All India Radio. (2003). Retrieved March 2, 2003, from http://www.air.org.in

Alqatawna, J., Siddiqi, J., Akhgar, B., & Hjouj Btoush, M. (2008). Towards Holistic Approaches to Secure e-Business: A Critical Review. In *Proceedings of EEE'08,* Las Vegas, USA.

Alqatawna, J., Siddiqi, J., Akhgar, B., & Hjouj Btoush, M. (2008). A Holistic Framework for Secure e-Business. In *Proceedings of EEE'08,* Las Vegas, USA.

American Chamber of Commerce in Egypt. (2007 May). *Information Technology in Egypt.*

American Institute of Certified Public Accountants. (AICPA). (1996). Information Technology Competences in the Accounting Profession. AICPA Implementation Strategies for IFAC International Education Guideline No. 11. New York: AICPA.

Amit, R., & Zott, C. (2001). Value Creation in E-Business. *Strategic Management Journal, 22,* 493–520. doi:10.1002/smj.187

Amsden, A. (1989). *Asia's Next Giant: South Korea and Late Industrialization*. New York: Oxford University Press.

Amsden, A. H., & Mourshed, M. (1997). Scientific publications, patents and technological capabilities in late-industrializing countries. *Technology Analysis and Strategic Management, 9*(3), 343–359. doi:10.1080/09537329708524289

Analysys White Paper. (2006). *The Importance of Local Loop Unbundling in Ireland*. Analysys Consulting Limited. Retrieved from http://www.analysys.com/

Ang, J. E. (2002). *Malay and English Language Achievement in Technologically Rich and Non-Technologically Rich Malaysian Schools*. USA: Unpublished EdD, University of Houston.

Angerer, D. J., & Hammerschmid, G. (2005). Public private partnership between euphoria and disillusionment. Recent experiences from Austria and implications for countries in transformation. *Romanian Journal of Political Science, 5*(1), 129–159.

Apthorpe, R. (1999). Development Studies and Policy Studies: In the Short Run We are All Dead. *Journal of International Development, 11*(4). doi:10.1002/(SICI)1099-1328(199906)11:4<535::AID-JID603>3.0.CO;2-U

Arab Human Development Report. (2002). *Creating Opportunities for Future Generations*. United Nations Development Programme and Arab Fund for Economic and Social Development.

Arce, A. (2003). Re-approaching Social Development: A Field of Action between Social Life and Policy Processes. *Journal of International Development, 15*(7). doi:10.1002/jid.1039

Ashraf, M., Swatman, P., & Hanisch, J. (2008). *An extended framework to investigate ICT impact on development at the micro (community) level*. Presented and published in 16th European Conference on Information Systems (ECIS) 2008, (9-11 June 2008), Galway, Ireland.

Asian Development Bank. (2001). *Education and National Development in Asia: Trends, issues, policies and strategies*. Manila, Philippines: Asian Development Bank.

Attewell, P., & Rule, J. (1984). Computing and organizations: What we know and what we don't know. *Communications of the ACM, 27*(12), 1184–1191. doi:10.1145/2135.2136

Avgerou, C. (1998). How can IT Enable Economic Growth in developing Countries? *Journal of Information Technology for Development, 8*(1).

Avgerou, C. (2000). Recognizing Alternative Rationalities in the Deployment of Information Systems. *Electronic Journal of Information Systems in Developing Countries, 3*(7), 1–15.

Avgerou, C. (2002). *Information systems and global diversity*. Oxford, UK: Oxford University Press.

Avgerou, C. (2003). The link between ICT and economic growth in the discourse of development. In Korpela, M., Monetealerge, R., & Poulymenakou, A. (Eds.), *Organizational information systems in the context of globalization* (pp. 373–386). Amsterdam: Kluwer.

Avgerou, C. (2006). *Taking into account Context in IS research and practice*. London: London School of Economics and Political Science. Retrieved May 13, 2006, from http://www.dmst.aueb.gr/gr2/diafora2/Prosopiko2/visitors_ppts/Avgerou-research-pre-Framing.ppt

Awang, H. (2004). Human Capital and Technology Development in Malaysia. *International Education Journal, 5*(2), 239–246.

Ayaz, M. (1991). Radio: A supplement to agricultural development in Pakistan. *Journal of Rural Development and Administration, 23*(4), 12–22.

Baets, W. (1992). Aligning Information Systems with Business Strategy. *The Journal of Strategic Information Systems, 1*(4), 205–213. doi:10.1016/0963-8687(92)90036-V

Bailey, J. E., & Pearson, S. W. (1983). Development of a Tool for Measuring and Analyzing Computer User Satisfaction. *Management Science, 29*(5), 530–545. doi:10.1287/mnsc.29.5.530

Bajunid, I. A. (2008). Towards a grand narrative of Malaysian education. In Bajunid, I. A. (Ed.), *Malaysia - From Traditional to Smart Schools: The Malaysian Educational Odyssey* (pp. 1–34). Kuala Lumpur, Malaysia: Oxford Fajar.

Bakari, J. K. (2005). *Towards a Holistic Approach for Managing ICT Security in Developing Countries: A Case Study of Tanzania.* Retrieved May 15, 2008, from http://dsv.su.se/en/seclab/pages/pdf-files/05-011.pdf

Bakry, S. (2003). Toward the Development of a Standard E-readiness Assessment Policy. *International Journal of Network Management, 13*(2), 129–137. doi:10.1002/nem.466

Bakry, S. H. (2004). Development of e-Government – A STOPE View. *International Journal of Electronic Management, 14*(5), 339–350.

Baldwin, A., Simon, S., & Mont, M. (2002). Trust Services: A Framework for Services-Based Solutions. In *Proceedings of the 26ᵗʰ Annual Computer Software and Applications Conference*, IEEE, UK.

Baliamoune-Lutz, M. (2003). An analysis of the determinants and effects of ICT diffusion in developing countries. *Information Technology for Development, 10*(3), 151–169. doi:10.1002/itdj.1590100303

Ball, D., & McCulloh, W. (1990). International Business (4th ed.). Chicago: Homewood.

Ball, L. D., Dambolena, I. G., & Hennessey, H. D. (1987). Identifying early adopters of large software systems. *Database, 19*(1), 21–27.

Ballantine, J., Levy, M., & Powell, P. (1998). Evaluating information systems in small and medium-sized enterprises: issues and evidence. *European Journal of Information Systems, 7*(4), 241–251. doi:10.1057/palgrave.ejis.3000307

Balutis, A. P. (2001). e-Government 2001 – Part 1: Understanding the Challenge and Evolving Strategies. *The Public Manager*, Spring, 33-37.

Bank Negara Malaysia. (2008). *Bank Negara Malaysia.* Retrieved 10 October, 2008, from http://www.bnm.gov.my

Barrantes, R. (2007). Analysis of ICT demand: What is digital poverty and how to measure it? In *Digital poverty: Latin American and Caribbean perspectives* (pp. 29–54). Warwickshire, UK: Practical Action Publishing.

Barro, R. J., & Lee, J. (2000). *International data on educational attainment: Updates and implications.* CID (Center for International Development Working Paper at Harvard University) Working Paper No. 42. Retrieved December 6, 2006, from http://www2.cid.harvard.edu/cidwp/042.pdf

Bassanini, A. (2002). Growth, Technology Change, and ICT Diffusion: Recent Evidence from OECD Countries. *Oxford Review of Economic Policy, 18*(3), 324–344. doi:10.1093/oxrep/18.3.324

Baudrillard, J. (1994). *Simulacra and Simulation* (Glaser, S. F., Trans.). Ann Arbor, MI: University of Michigan Press.

Bauer, J., Berne, M., & Maitland, C. (2002). Internet access in the European Union and in the United States. *Telematics and Informatics, 19*, 117–137. doi:10.1016/S0736-5853(01)00009-0

Baum, C., & Maio, A. D. (2001). Gartner's Four Phases of e-Government Model. *Gartner Research.* Retrieved May 4, 2006, from http://gartner3.gartnerweb.com/public/static/hotc/00094235.html

Beaumaster, S. (2002). Local Government IT Implementation Issues: A Challenge for Public Administration. In *35ᵗʰ Hawaii International Conference on System Sciences*, Hawaii.

Beaumont, N., & Costa, C. (2002). Information technology outsourcing in Australia. *Information Resources Management Journal, 15*(3), 14–31.

Becker, B., Dawson, P., Devine, K., Hannum, C., Hill, S., Leydens, J., et al. (2005). *Case Studies*. Retrieved from http://writing.colostate.edu/guides/research/casestudy

Bélanger, F., & Carter, L. (2006). The Effects of the Digital Divide on E-government: An Empirical Evaluation. In *Proceedings of the 39th Hawaii International Conference on System Sciences*, IEEE, USA.

Bell, D. (1973). *The Coming of the post-industrial society*. New York: Basic Books.

Bell, D. (1999). *The coming of the post-industrial society* (Anniversary, S., Ed.). New York: Basic Books.

Belleflamme, P. (2001). Oligopolistic competition, IT use for product differentiation and the productivity paradox. *International Journal of Industrial Organization, 19*(1–2), 227–248. doi:10.1016/S0167-7187(99)00017-X

Belson, W. (1982). *The Design and Understanding of Survey Questions*. Aldershot, UK: Gower.

Ben Abd Allah, S., Gueniara El Fatmi, S., & Oudriga, N. B. (2002). Security Issues in e-Government Models: What Governments Should Do. In *IEEE International Conference on Systems, Man, and Cybermatics*, Hammamet, Tunisia.

Bentley, T. (1998). *Information Systems Strategy for Business*. London: CIMA.

Berends, H. (2005). Exploring knowledge sharing: moves, problem solving and justification. *Knowledge Management Research & Practice, 3*(2), 93–105. doi:10.1057/palgrave.kmrp.8500056

Bertelsmann Foundation. (2002). *Balanced e-Government: e-Government – Connecting Efficient Administration and Responsive Democracy*. Retrieved December 7, 2007, from http://www-it.fmi.uni-sofia.bg/eg/res/balancede-gov.pdf

Betz, F. (2002). Strategic Business Models. *Engineering Management Journal, 14*(1), 21–34.

Bhatnagar, S. (2002). E-government: Lessons from Implementation in Developing Countries. *Regional Development Dialogue, United Nations Centre for Regional Development (UNCRD), 24*(Autumn).

Bhatnagar, S. C. (2000). Social Implications of Information and Communication Technology in Developing Countries: Lessons from Asian Success Stories. *Electronic Journal of Information Systems for Developing countries, 1*(4), 1-9.

Bhatnagar, S., & Vyas, N. (2001). Community- Owned Rural Internet Kiosks. *The World Bank*. Retrieved March 12, 2006, from http://www1.worldbank.org

Bhimani, A. (1996). Securing the Commercial Internet. *Communications of the ACM, 39*(6), 29–35. doi:10.1145/228503.228509

Bilbilov, A. (2009). Technology Transfer Program Manager, Macedonia Connects. Interviews with the author, April 29, May 13, 2009.

Bismillah Khatoon bt Abdul Kader. (2008). Malaysia's Experience in Training Teachers to Use ICT. In E. Meleisea (Ed.), *ICT in Teacher Education: Case Studies from the Asia-Pacific Region* (pp. 10-22). Bangkok: UNESCO.

Blakemore, M., & Lloyd, P. (2007). *Trust and Transparency: Pre-Requisites for Effective E-government, Organizational Change for Citizen-Centric E-government*. European Commission.

Blili, S., & Raymond, L. (1993). Information technology: Threats and opportunities for small and medium-sized enterprises. *International Journal of Information Management, 13*(6), 439–448. doi:10.1016/0268-4012(93)90060-H

Blomstrom, M., & Kokko, A. (1998). Foreign Investment as a Vehicle for International Technology Transfer. In Navaretti, G. B. (Eds.), *Creation and Transfer of Knowledge: Institutions and Incentives*.

Boar, B. H. (2001). *The Art of Strategic Planning for Information Technology*. New York: John Wiley & Sons Inc.

Boje, D. (1991). The Storytelling Organization: A Study Of Story Performance In An Office-Supply Firm. *Administrative Science Quarterly, 36,* 106–126. doi:10.2307/2393432

Bollou, F., & Ngwenyama, O. (2008). Are ICT investments paying off in Africa? An analysis of total factor productivity in six West African countries from 1995 to 2002. *Information Technology for Development, 14*(4), 294–307. doi:10.1002/itdj.20089

Boon, O., Hewett, W. G., & Parker, C. M. (2000). Evaluating the adoption of the Internet: A Study of an Australian Experience in Local Government. In *13th International Bled Electronic Commerce Conference*, Bled, Slovenia.

Boris, K., & Schlüter, E. (2007). 'Reconsidered: A Country- and Individual-Level Typology of digital inequality in 26 European Countries. In *Quantitative Methods in the Social Sciences (QMSS)*. Prague: Digital Divide.

Botterman, M., Anderson, R., van Binst, P., et al. (2003). *Enabling the Information Society by Stimulating the Creation of a Broadband*. Rand Europe. Retrieved from http://www.rand.org

Boudriga, N. (2002). Technical Issues in Securing e-Government. In *IEEE International Conference on Systems, Man, and Cybermatics*, Hammamet, Tunisia.

Bowman, B. J., Davis, G. B., & Wetherbe, J. C. (1983). Three Stage Model of MIS Planning. *Information & Management, 6*(1), 11–25. doi:10.1016/0378-7206(83)90016-2

BREAD project. (n.d.). *Broadband in Europe for All: a multi-Disciplinary approach*. Retrieved September 20, 2008 from www.ist-bread.org

BReATH - Broadband e-Services and Access for the Home. (2006 October). *Breath, WP4 Report: Sustainable strategies and service evolution scenarios for broadband access*. Retrieved from http://www.ist-breath.net/

Bridges. (2002). E-readiness as a Tool for ICT Development. *Bridges Organization*. Retrieved February 2, 2006, from http://www.bridges.org

Bridges. (2005). E-readiness Assessment Tools Comparison. *Bridges Organization*. Retrieved May 20, 2006, from http://www.bridges.org

Bridges. (2005). E-readiness Assessment: Who is Doing What and Where. *Bridges Organization*. Retrieved June 22, 2006, from http://www.bridges.org

British Council. (2008). Retrieved from http://www.britishcouncil.org/egypt

Bromley, H. (1998). Introduction: Data-driven democracy? Social assessment of educational computing. In Bromley, H., & Apple, M. (Eds.), *Education, technology, power* (pp. 1–28). Albany, NY: SUNY Press.

Brooks, F. P. Jr. (1987). No silver bullet: essence and accidents of software engineering. *IEEE Computer, 20*(4), 10–19.

Brookshear, J. G. (2003). *Computer science: An overview* (7th ed.). Boston: Addison Wesley.

Brown, C. (2002). G-8 Collaborative Initiatives and the Digital Divide: Readiness for E-government. In *Proceedings of the 35th Annual Hawaii International Conference on System Sciences,* IEEE, USA.

Bruce, B. C. (1993). Innovation and social change. In Bruce, B. C., Peyton, J. K., & Batson, T. (Eds.), *Network-based classrooms* (pp. 9–32). Cambridge, UK: Cambridge University Press.

Brynjolfsson, E., & Hitt, L. (1996). Paradox lost? Firm-level evidence on the returns to information systems spending. *Management Science, 42*(4), 541–558. doi:10.1287/mnsc.42.4.541

Bryson, J. M., & Alston, F. K. (1996). *Creating and Implementing your Strategic Plan: A Workbook for Public and Non-Profit Organizations*. San Francisco, CA: Jossey-Bass Publishers.

Buonanno, G., Faverio, P., Pigni, F., & Ravarini, A. (2005). Factors affecting ERP system adoption: A comparative analysis between SMEs and large companies. *Journal of Enterprise Information Management, 18*(4), 384–426. doi:10.1108/17410390510609572

Burgess, L., & Cooper, J. (1990). A Model for Classification of Business Adoption of Internet Commerce Solutions. In *12ᵗʰ International Bled Electronic Commerce Conference*, Bled, Slovenia.

Burn, J., & Robins, G. (2003). Moving Towards E-government: A Case Study of Organisational Change Process. *International Journal of Logistics Information Management, 16*(1), 25–35. doi:10.1108/09576050310453714

Butt, D., Sreenivasan, R., & Singh, A. (2008). ICT4D in Asia Pacific—An overview of emerging issues. In F. Librero (Ed.), Digital review of Asia Pacific 2007-2008 (3-18). New Delhi, India: Sage Publications and IDRC.

Cairncross, F. (2001). *The Death of Distance.* Cambridge, MA: Harvard Business School Press.

Camfferman, K., & Cooke, T. E. (2002). An analysis of disclosure in the annual reports of UK and Dutch companies. *Journal of International Accounting Research, 1,* 3–30. doi:10.2308/jiar.2002.1.1.3

Camilleri, J. A., & Falk, J. (1992). *The end of sovereignty? The politics of a shrinking and fragmented world.* Aldershot, UK: Edward Elgar.

CAPMAS (Central Agency for Public Mobilization and Statistics). (2009). *Population Statistics in Egypt.* Cairo, Egypt: Central Agency for Public Mobilization and Statistics.

Carter, L., & Belanger, F. (2004). Citizen Adoption of Electronic Government Initiative. In *Proceedings of the 37ᵗʰ Hawaii International Conference on System Sciences*, IEEE, USA.

Caselli, F., & Coleman, W. J. (2001). Cross-country technology diffusion: The case of computers. *The American Economic Review, 91*(2), 328–335.

Castells, M. (2000). *The rise of the network society* (2nd ed.). Oxford: Blackwell Publishers.

Castells, M. (2001). *The Internet galaxy: Reflections on the Internet, business and society.* Oxford, UK: Oxford University Press.

Castells, M. (2004). The Information Age Economy, Society and Culture: *Vol. 1. The Rise of the Network Society.* Oxford, UK: Blackwell.

Cava-Ferreruela, I., & Alabau-Munoz, A. (2006). Broadband policy assessment: A cross-national empirical analysis. *Telecommunications Policy, 30,* 445–463. doi:10.1016/j.telpol.2005.12.002

Cave, M., Prosperetti, L., & Doyle, C. (2006). Where are we going? Technologies, markets and long-range public policy issues in European communications. *Information Economics and Policy, 18,* 242–255. doi:10.1016/j.infoecopol.2006.06.002

Cawley, A., & Preston, P. (2007). Broadband and digital 'content' in the EU-25: Recent trends and challenges. *Telematics and Informatics, 24*(4), 259–271. doi:10.1016/j.tele.2007.01.015

Cecchini, S. (2002). *Can information and communication technology application contribute to poverty reduction? Lessons from rural India.* Retrieved August 13, 2008, from http://www.nijenrodo.nl/download/nice/anrep2000.pdf

Cecchini, S., & Scott, C. (2003). Can information and communications technology applications contribute to poverty reduction? Lessons from rural India. *Information Technology for Development, 10*(2), 73–84. doi:10.1002/itdj.1590100203

Centeno, C. (2004). Adoption of Internet services in the Acceding and Candidate Countries, lessons from the Internet banking case. *Telematics and Informatics, 21*(4), 293–315. doi:10.1016/j.tele.2004.02.001

Central Information Technology Office. (2009). Retrieved March 7, 2009, from http://www.cito.gov.jm

Cerf, V. (1999). *The Internet is for everyone. OnTheInternet.* July-August.

Chanclou, P., Gosselin, S., Fernández Palacios, J., Alvarez, V., & Zouganeli, E. (2006, August). Overview of the Optical Broadband Access Evolution: A Joint Article by Operators in the IST Network of Excellence e-Photon/ONe, Telenor R&D. *IEEE Communications Magazine, 44*(8), 29–35. doi:10.1109/MCOM.2006.1678106

Chandrashekara, P. (2001 January). Mass media in Agricultural extension: Best, yet to come. *Manage Extension Research Review,* 38-44.

Chataway, J. C., Gault, F., Quintas, P., & Wield, D. V. (2003). *Dealing with the knowledge divide.* Geneva: World Summit on the Information Society, United Nations and the International Telecommunications Union.

Chau, P. Y. K., & Jim, C. C. F. (2002). Adoption of Electronic Data Interchange in Small and Medium-Sized Enterprises. *Journal of Global Information Management, 10*(4), 61–85.

Chaudhuri, A., Flamm, K., & Horrigan, J. (2005). An analysis of the determinants of internet access. *Telecommunications Policy, 29,* 731–755. doi:10.1016/j.telpol.2005.07.001

Chen, W., & Wellman, B. (2003). Charting and bridging digital divides: Comparing Socio-Economic, Gender, Life Stage and Rural-Urban Internet Access and Use in Eight Countries. *AMD Global Consumer Advisory Board (GSAB).* Retrieved May 15, 2008, from http://www.amd.com/usen/assets/content_type/DownloadableAssets/FINAL_REPORT_CHARTING_DIGI_DIVIDES.pdf

Chen, Y. C., & Knepper, R. (2005). Digital Government Development Strategies: Lessons for Policy Makers from a Comparative Perspective. In Huang, W., Siau, K., Wei, K. K., & Siau, K. (Eds.), *Electronic Government Strategies and Implementation* (pp. 394–420). Hershey, PA: Idea Group Publishing.

Chesbrough, H. (2006). *Open Business Models.* Cambridge, MA: Harvard Business School Press.

Chiang, J. T. (2000). Institutional frameworks and technological paradigms in Japan: Targeting computers, semiconductors, and software. *Technology in Society, 22*(2), 151–174. doi:10.1016/S0160-791X(00)00002-6

Chitura, T., Mupemhi, S., Dube, T., & Bolongkikit, J. (2008). Barriers to Electronic Commerce Adoption in Small and Medium Enterprises: A Critical Literature Review. *Journal of Internet Banking and Commerce, 13*(2), 1–13.

Chong, S., & Pervan, G. (2007). Factors Influencing the Extent of Deployment of Electronic Commerce for Small- and Medium-sized Enterprises - An Exploratory Study. *Journal of Electronic Commerce in Organizations, 5*(1), 1–29.

Choudrie, J., & Dwivedi, Y. (2004). Towards a conceptual model of broadband diffusion. *Journal of Computing and Information Technology - CIT, 12*(4), 323-338.

Choudrie, J., & Dwivedi, Y. (2005). *A Survey of Citizens' Awareness and Adoption of E-Government Initiatives, the 'Government Gateway': A United Kingdom Perspective.* Paper presented at the E-government workshop, London, UK.

Choudrie, J., & Dwivedi, Y. (2006). *Examining the Socio-economic Determinants of Broadband Adopters and Non-adopters in the United Kingdom.* Paper presented at the Proceedings of the 39th Annual Hawaii International Conference on System Sciences (HICSS'06) Track 4, Hawaii.

Choudrie, J., & Papazafeiropoulou, A. (2007). Assessing the UK policies for broadband adoption. *Information Systems Frontiers, 9*(2-3), 297–308. doi:10.1007/s10796-006-9022-3

Ciborra, C. U. (1993). *Teams markets and systems.* Cambridge, UK: Cambridge University Press.

CIO. (2006). The State of Information Security. *CIO Magazine and PricewaterhouseCoopers.* Retrieved May 15, 2008, from http://www.pwc.com/extweb/pwcpublications.nsf/docid/3929AC0E90BDB001852571ED0071630B

Clark, A. D. (2005). The capability approach: its development, critiques and recent advances. Manchester, UK: Institute for development policy and management, University of Manchester.

Clarke, R. (2000). *Appropriate Research Methods for Electronic Commerce*. Retrieved February 3, 2007, from http://www.anu.edu.au/people/Roger.Clarke/EC/ResMeth.html

Cloke, C., Sabariah Sharif, & Ambotang, A. S. (2006). A qualitative study of pedagogical issues arising from the introduction of the Malaysian Smart School initiative. *Jurnal Pendidik dan Pendidikan, 21*, 129-147.

CM's pat for SHGs. (2003, September 2). *The New Indian Express*, p. 6.

Cohen, S., & Eimicke, W. (2002). The Future of E-government: A project of Potential Trends and Issues. In *Proceedings of the 36ᵗʰ Hawaii International Conference on System Sciences*, IEEE, USA.

Colle, R., & Roman, R. (2003). Challenges in the Telecentre Movement. In Marshall, S., Taylor, W., & Yu, X. (Eds.), *Closing the Digital Divide: Transforming Regional Economics and Communities with Information Technology*. Westport, CT: Praeger.

Comber, C., Watling, R., Lawson, T., Cavendish, S., Mceune, R., & Paterson, F. (2002). *ImpaCT2: Learning at Home and School: Case Studies*. Coventry, UK: BECTA.

Conklin, A., & White, G. B. (2006). e-Government and Cyber Security: The Role of Cyber Security Exercises. In *39ᵗʰ Hawaii International Conference on System Sciences*, Hawaii.

Cook, J. (1995). Training methods and media. *International Agricultural Development, 15*(4), 8–9.

Cooke, T. E. (1998). Regression analysis in accounting disclosure studies. *Accounting and Business Review, 28*(3), 209–224.

Cordis. (2007). *Information & Communication Technologies. Introduction*. Retrieved March 18, 2009, from http://cordis.europa.eu/fp7/ict/programme/home_en.html

Cox, M. J. (1997). *Effects of information technology on students' motivation: final report*. Coventry, UK: NCET.

Cragg, P. B., & King, M. (1993). Small-firm computing: Motivators and inhibitors. *Management Information Systems Quarterly, 17*(1), 47. doi:10.2307/249509

Creswell, J. W. (2002). *Research Design: Qualitative, Quantitative, and Mixed Methods Approaches*. Thousand Oaks, CA: Sage Publications.

Cronin, F. J., Colleran, E. K., Parker, E. B., & Dollery, B. (1993). Telecommunications infrastructure investment and economic development. *Telecommunications Policy, 17*(6), 415–430. doi:10.1016/0308-5961(93)90013-S

Cross, M. (2005, August 4). Ethiopia's digital dream. *Guardian Unlimited*. Retrieved November 20, 2008, from http://technology.guardian.co.uk/online/story/0,3605,1541785,00.html

Croteau, A., Solomon, S., Raymond, L., & Bergeron, F. (2001). Organizational and Technological Infrastructures Alignment. In *34ᵗʰ Hawaii International Conference on System Sciences*, Hawaii.

CSPP. (n.d.). *Readiness Guide for Living in the Networked World*. Retrieved March 20, 2006, from http://www.cspp.org

Cyert, R., & March, J. (1963). *A Behavioral Theory of the Firm*. Englewood Cliffs, NJ: Prentice Hall.

Dahawy, K., & Conovere, T. (2007). Accounting Disclosures in Companies Listed on the Egyptian Stock Exchange. *Middle Eastern Finance and Economics, 1*(1).

Dahawy, K., Merion, B., & Conover, T. (2002). The Conflict between IAS Requirements and the Secretive Culture in Egypt. *Advances in International Accounting, 15*(1).

Dahawy, K., Tooma, E., & Kamel, S. (2005). The Use of IT in Teaching Accounting in Egypt: the Case of BeckerConviser. *Communications of the IIMA, 5*(3).

DAI (Digital Access Index). (2003). Gauging ICT Potential Around the World. *International Telecommunication Union (ITU)*. Retrieved July 23, 2007, from http://www.itu.int/ITU-D/ict/dai/material/DAI_ITUNews_e.pdf

Darwish, A. (2007). *Electronic Government – Egypt*. Retrieved February 3, 2008, from http://www.egypt.gov. eg/english/documents/

Das, S. R., Zahra, S. A., & Warkentin, M. E. (1991). Integrating the Content and Process of Strategic MIS Planning With Competitive Strategy. *Decision Sciences*, *22*(1), 953–984.

Davidow, W., & Malone, M. (1992). *The Virtual Corporation: Structuring and Revitalizing the Corporation for the 21ˢᵗ Century*. New York: HarperBusiness.

Davis, F. D. (1985). *A Technology Acceptance Model for Empirically Testing New End-User Information Systems: Theory and Results*. Doctoral Dissertation, MIT Sloan School of Management, Cambridge, MA.

Davis, F. D. (1989). Perceived Usefulness, Perceived Ease of Use and User Acceptance of Information Technology. *Management Information Systems Quarterly*, *13*(3), 319–339. doi:10.2307/249008

Dawes, S. (2002). The Future of e-Government. *Center for Technology in Government*. Retrieved March 10, 2007, from http://www.ctg.albany.edu/publications/reports/future_of_egov/future_of_egov.pdf

DD seeks funds from Agricultural ministry for its rural bonanza. (2003, August 4). *The New Indian Express*, p. 9.

De Alcantara, C. H. (2001). *The Development Divide in a Digital Age*. Issue Paper, United Nations Research Institute for Social Development, Technology, Business and Society Programme.

De Bijl, P., & Peitz, M. (2005). *Local Loop Unbundling in Europe: Experience, Prospects and Policy Challenges*. Working Paper 29/2005, Bruchsal, February 2005.

De Boer, S. J., & Walbeek, M. M. (1999). Information technology in developing countries: a study to guide policy formulation. *International Journal of Information Management*, *19*(3), 207–218. doi:10.1016/S0268-4012(99)00014-6

De Silva, H., & Zainudeen, A. (2007 March). Teleuse on a Shoestring: Poverty reduction through telecom access at the bottom of the pyramid. *LIRNEasia*. Retrieved August 9, 2007, from http://www.lirneasia.net

DeConti, L. (1998). Planning and Creating a Government Website: Learning from the Experience of US States. *Information Systems for Public Sector Management, Working Paper Series No. 2, Institute for Development Policy and Management*. Retrieved June 3, 2002, from http://www.amn.ac.uk/idpm

Delamaide, D. (1994). *The new super-regions of Europe*. New York: Penguin.

DeLone, W. H., & McLean, E. R. (1992). Information Systems Success: The Quest for the Dependent Variable. *Information Systems Research*, *3*(1), 60–95. doi:10.1287/isre.3.1.60

Delone, W. H., & Mclean, E. R. (2003). The Delone and Mclean model of information systems success: a ten year update. *Journal of Management Information Systems*, *19*(4), 9–30.

Denscombe, M. (1999). *The Good Research Guide for Small Scale Social Research Projects*. Buckingham, UK: Open University Press.

Dewan, S., & Kraemer, K. L. (2000). Information technology and productivity: Preliminary evidence from country-level data. *Management Science*, *46*, 548–562. doi:10.1287/mnsc.46.4.548.12057

DFID. (2005). *Monitoring and evaluating Information and Communication for Development (ICD) programmes: Guidelines. Information and communication for development*. UK: Department for International Development.

Dholakia, R. R., & Kshetri, N. (2004). Factors Impacting the Adoption of the Internet among SMEs. *Small Business Economics*, *23*(4), 311–322. doi:10.1023/B:SBEJ.0000032036.90353.1f

Dielman, T. E. (1996). *Applied Regression Analysis for Business and Economics* (2nd ed.). Belmont, CA: Wadsworth Publishing Company.

Dimova, S. (2003). Teaching and learning English in Macedonia. *English Today, 19*(4), 16–22. doi:10.1017/S0266078403004036

Distaso, W., Lupi, P., & Manenti, F. (2006). Platform competition and broadband uptake: Theory and empirical evidence from the European Union. *Information Economics and Policy, 18*, 87–106. doi:10.1016/j.infoecopol.2005.07.002

Docktor, R. (2004). *Successful Global ICT Initiatives: Measuring Results Through an Analysis of Achieved Goals, Planning and Readiness Efforts, and Stakeholder Involvement*. Presentation to the Council for Excellence in Government.

Doost,. R. (1999). Computers and accounting: where do we go from here? *Managerial Auditing Journal, 14*(9).

Doring, T., & Schnellenbach, J. (2006). What do we know about geographical knowledge spillovers and regional growth? A survey of the literature. *Regional Studies, 40*(3), 375–395. doi:10.1080/00343400600632739

Dossani, R., Misra, D. C., & Jhaveri, R. (2005). *Enabling ICT for Rural India*. Retrieved August 13, 2008, from http://ruralinformatics.nic.in/files/4_12_0_90.pdf

Dowlath, P., & Seepersad, J. (1999). Understanding information sources in the communication process: preparing for the information revolution in extension. In *Proceedings of the 15th Annual Conference of AIEEE*, Republic of Trinidad & Tobago.

Downing, C. E. (1999). System Usage Behavior as a Proxy for User Satisfaction: An Empirical Investigation. *Information & Management, 35*(4), 203–216. doi:10.1016/S0378-7206(98)00090-1

Downing, C. E., Field, J. M., & Ritzman, L. P. (2003). The value of outsourcing: a field study. *Information Systems Management, 20*, 86–91. doi:10.1201/1078/43203.20.1.20031201/40088.11

DRDA. (2006). *District Rural Development Agency of Nagapattinam*. Retrieved August 16, 2006, from http://nagapattinam.nic.in/drda.html#sgsy

Driouchi, A., Azelmad, E. M., & Anders, G. C. (2006). An econometric analysis of the role of knowledge in economic performance. *The Journal of Technology Transfer, 31*, 241–255. doi:10.1007/s10961-005-6109-9

Drori, G. S., & Jang, Y. S. (2003). The Global Digital Divide: A Sociological Assessment of Trends and Causes. *Social Science Computer Review, 21*(2), 144–161. doi:10.1177/0894439303021002002

Duhan, S., Levy, M., & Powell, P. (2001). Information systems strategies in knowledge-based SMEs: the role of core competencies. *European Journal of Information Systems, 10*(1), 25–40. doi:10.1057/palgrave.ejis.3000379

Dutta, A., & Roy, R. (2005). The Mechanics of Internet Growth: A Developing-Country Perspective. *International Journal of Electronic Commerce, 9*, 143–165.

Earl, M. J. (1989). *Management Strategies for Information Technology*. Englewood Cliffs, NJ: Prentice-Hall.

Earl, M. J. (1993). Experiences in strategic information systems planning. *Management Information Systems Quarterly, 17*(1), 1–24. doi:10.2307/249507

Earl, M. J. (1996). *Information Management: The Organizational Dimension*. Oxford, UK: Oxford University Press.

Earle, N., & Keen, P. (2000). *From. Com to. Profit: Inventing Business Models That Deliver Profit And Value*. San Francisco: Jossey-Bass.

eBSN. (2008). *The European e-Business Support Network: What is eBSN?* Retrieved March 18, 2009, from http://ec.europa.eu/enterprise/e-bsn/about/ebsn/index_en.html

Economic Planning Unit. (2001). *Third Outline Perspective Plan, 2001-2010*. Kuala Lumpur, Malaysia: Economic Planning Unit, Government of Malaysia.

Economist. (2007, May 10). To do with the price of fish. *The Economist*. Retrieved October 16, 2007, from http://www.economist.com/finance/displaystory.cfm?story_id=9149142

Edmiston, K. (2003). State and Local e-Government: Prospects and Challenges. *American Review of Public Administration, 33*(1), 20–45. doi:10.1177/0275074002250255

Education Development Center. (2006). *Technology Implementation in Macedonia*. Retrieved June 3, 2008, from http://main.edc.org/newsroom/features/macedonia_technology.asp

Edwards, S. (2002). Information technology and economic growth in developing countries. *Challenge, 45*(3), 19–43.

Eisenhardt, K. M. (1989). Building Theories from Case Study Research. *Academy of Management Review, 14*(4), 532–550. doi:10.2307/258557

EISI-G (Egyptian Information Society Initiative- Government). (2005). *Egyptian Information Society Initiative- Government*. Cairo, Egypt: Ministry of States and Administrative Development.

EISI-Government Team. (2003). EISI-Government: Action Plan and Roadmap. *Ministry of Communications and Information Technology*. Retrieved May 12, 2005, from http://www.egypt.gov.eg/english/documents/

El Sayed, H., & Westrup, C. (2003). Egypt and ICTs: How UCT Bring National Initiatives, Global Organizations and Local Companies Together. *Information Technology & People, 16*(1).

El Sherif, A. (2004). FDI Profile in Egypt. Workshop on Capacity Building for Promoting FDI in Africa: Trends, Data Compilation and Policy Implications. In *United Nations Conference on Trade and Development (UNCTAD) Meeting*, 22-24 November 2004, UNECA, Addis Abba.

Eleftheriadou, D. (2008). Small - and Medium-Sized Enterprises Hold the Key to European Competitiveness: How to Help Them Innovate through ICT and E-business. *The Global Information Technology Report 2007-2008*. World Economic Forum.

El-Halawany, H., & Huwail, E. I. (2008). Malaysian Smart Schools: A Fruitful Case Study for Analysis to Synopsize Lessons Applicable to the Egyptian Context. *International Journal of Education and Development using ICT, 4*(2).

Elliott, S. (Ed.). (2002). *Electronic Commerce B2C Strategies and Models*. Chichester: John Wiley.

Ergazakis, E., Ergazakis, K., Flamos, A., & Charalabidis, Y. (2009). KM in SMEs: a research agenda. *International Journal of Management and Decision Making, 10*(1/2), 91–110. doi:10.1504/IJMDM.2009.023916

Eschenfelder, K. R., Beachboard, J. C., McClure, C. R., & Wyman, S. K. (1997). Assessing US Federal Government Websites. *Government Information Quarterly, 14*(2), 173–189. doi:10.1016/S0740-624X(97)90018-6

Etta, F. (2005). Policy matters: Recommendations for responsible policy making. In Etta, F. E., & Elder, L. (Eds.), *At the crossroads: ICT policy making in East Africa* (pp. 295–297). Nairobi, Kenya: East African Educational Publishers Ltd., & IDRC.

EU. (n.d.). *Financing ICT for development: The EU approach*. Retrieved April 15, 2008, from http://www.dfid.gov.uk/pubs/files/eu-financ-wsis-english.pdf

Eurobarometer: E-communications household survey. (2006 July). European Commission. Retrieved from http://ec.europa.eu/information_society/policy/ecomm/doc/info_centre/studies_ext_consult/ecomm_household_study/eb_jul06_main_report_en.pdf

Europe, R. A. N. D. (2003). *Benchmarking Security and Trust in the Information Society in Europe and the US, Information Society Technologies*. European Commission.

European Commission. (2002). Benchmarking National and Regional E-business Policies for SMEs. Final report of the E-business Policy Group of the European Union, Brussels.

European Commission. (2007). *Sectoral e-Business Policies in Support of SMEs: Innovative approaches, good practices and lessons to be learned*.

European Commission. (2008). *The European e-Business Report 2008*. The impact of ICT and e-business on firms, sectors and the economy. 6th Synthesis Report of the Sectoral e-Business Watch.

European Commission. DG Enterprise and Industry. (2008). *A comprehensive policy to support SMEs*. Retrieved from http://ec.europa.eu/enterprise/entrepreneurship/sme_policy.htm

European Commission. DG Enterprise and Industry. (2008). *Sectoral e-Business Watch*. Retrieved July 19, 2008, from http://www.ebusiness-watch.org/about/sectoral_ebiz.htm

European Commission. DG Information Society and Media (2005). eEurope 2005. *Europe's Information Society Thematic Portal*. Retrieved March 18th 2009 from http://ec.europa.eu/information_society/eeurope/2005/index_en.htm

European Commission. DG Information Society and Media. (2008). *Strategy for an innovative and inclusive European Information Society*. Retrieved April 18, 2009, from http://ec.europa.eu/information_society/doc/factsheets/035-i2010-en.pdf

European Council. (2008). Lisbon Strategy. Slovenian Presidency of the EU. Retrieved April 18th 2009 from http://www.eu2008.si/en/Policy_Areas/European_Council/Lissabon.html

European Network of Living Labs. (2006). *eLivingLab Kranj*. Retrieved April 18, 2009, from http://www.openlivinglabs.eu/slovenia-elivinglab.html

European Parliament. (2000). *Lisbon European Council 23 And 24 March 2000 - Presidency Conclusions*. Retrieved July 19, 2009, from http://www.europarl.europa.eu/summits/lis1_en.htm

E-Japan. (2001). *E-Japan strategy*. Retrieved January 12, 2007, from http://www.kantei.go.jp/foreign/it/network/0122full_e.html

E-Japan. (2001). *E-Japan 2002 program*. Retrieved January 16, 2007, from http://www.kantei.go.jp/foreign/it/network/0626_e.html

E-Japan. (2004). *Basic concept on IT international policy centered on Asia (provisional translation)*. Retrieved January 13, 2007, from http://www.kantei.go.jp/foreign/policy/it/040910concept_e.pdf

E-Japan. (2005). *IT policy package - 2005 - Towards the realization of the world's most advanced IT nation – (provisional translation)*. Retrieved January 3, 2007, from http://www.kantei.go.jp/foreign/policy/it/itpackage2005.pdf

E-Japan. (2006). *New IT reform strategy - Realizing ubiquitous and universal network society where everyone can enjoy the benefits of IT*. Retrieved January 18, 2007, from http://www.kantei.go.jp/foreign/policy/it/ITstrategy2006.pdf

FAO. (1998). Knowledge and information for food security in Africa: From traditional media to the internet. *CAB International Database*. Retrieved December 3, 2001, from http://www.cabsubsets.org/cabsbin/bw_frames_action/

Farquhar, B., Langmann, G., & Balfour, A. (1998). Consumer Needs in Global Electronic Commerce. *Electronic Markets*, 8(2), 9–12. doi:10.1080/10196789800000017

Feagin, J., Orum, A., & Sjoberg, G. (1991). *A case for case study*. Chapel Hill, NC: University of North Carolina Press.

Feigenbaum, E. A., & McCorduck, P. (1983). *The fifth generation: Artificial intelligence and Japan's computer challenge to the world*. Boston, MA: Addison Wesley.

Feinson, S. (2003 June). National Innovation Systems Overview and Country Cases. In Bozeman, B. (Eds.), *Knowledge Flows and Knowledge Collectives: Understanding The Role of Science and Technology Policies in Development. Synthesis Report on the Findings of a Project for the Global Inclusion Program of the Rockefeller Foundation*.

Fernandez, A. P. (2005 March). *Self-Help Affinity Groups: their role in poverty reduction and financial sector development*. Paper presented at the International Conference on Micro-finance in the global strategy for meeting the millennium development goals, Dublin, Ireland.

Field, A. (2003). *Discovering Statistics Using SPSS for Windows: Advanced Techniques for the Beginner.* London: Sage Publications.

Fink, D., & Disterer, G. (2006). International case studies: To what extent is ICT infused into operations of SMEs? *Journal of Enterprise Information Management, 19*(6), 608–625. doi:10.1108/17410390610708490

Finland, E. U. Presidency. Helsinki manifesto Launching Event - European Network of Living Labs: A Step Towards a European Innovation System. Retrieved April 18th 2009 from http://www.tietoyhteiskuntaohjelma.fi/ajankohtaista/events/en_GB/1147340579176

Firth, L., & Mellor, D. (2005). Broadband: Benefits and problems. *Telecommunications Policy, 29*, 223–236. doi:10.1016/j.telpol.2004.11.004

Fishman, C. (2008). *The Wal-Mart Effect.* New York: Penguin Press.

Flay, B. R. (1987). *Seeking the smokeless society: Fifty-six evaluated mass media programs and campaigns worldwide.* Washington, DC: American Public Health Association.

Flecknoe, M. (2001). *The use of virtual classrooms for school improvement.* Paper presented at the BELMAS Annual Conference.

Fletcher, P. D. (1999). Strategic Planning for Information Technology Management in State Government. In Garson, D. (Ed.), *Information Technology and Computer Applications in Public Administration: Issues and Trends* (pp. 81–89). Hershey, PA: Idea Group Publishing.

Fletcher, P. D. (2003). The Realities of the Paper work Reduction Act of 1995: A Government-Wide Strategy for Information Resources Management. In Garson, D. (Ed.), *Public Information Technology: Policy and Management Issues* (pp. 74–93). Hershey, PA: Idea Group Publishing.

Florida, R. (2002). *The Rise of the Creative Class.* New York: Basic Books.

Fogg, B. J. (2002). Stanford Guidelines for Web Credibility. *A Research Summary from the Stanford Persuasive Technology Lab.* Retrieved August 22, 2003, from http://www.webcredibility.org/guidelines

Fogg, B. J., Marable, L., Stanford, J., & Tauber, E. R. (2002). How do People Evaluate a Website's Credibility? Results from a Large Study. *Consumer Webwatch News.* Retrieved October 4, 2006, from http://www.consumerwebwatch.org/news/report3_credibilityresearch/stanfordPTL_TOC.htm

Forman, M. (2002). *e-Government Strategy.* Washington, DC: Executive Office of the President Office of Management and Budget. Retrieved April 7, 2006, from http://www.usa.gov/Topics/Includes/Reference/egov_strategy.pdf

Forno, D. A. (1999). Sustainable development starts with agriculture. In *Sustainable agriculture solutions: The action report of the sustainable agriculture initiative* (pp. 8–11). London: Novello Press Ltd.

Fransman, M. (Ed.). (2006). *Global Broadband Battles – Why the U. S. and Europe Lag While Asia Leads.* Stanford, CA: Stanford University Books.

Frasheri, N. (2002) Critical View of e-Governance Challenges for Developing Countries. *IFIP WG9.4 Work Conference ICT and Development,* May, Bangalore, India

Frieden, R. (2005). Lessons from broadband development in Canada, Japan, Korea and the United States. *Telecommunications Policy, 29*, 595–613. doi:10.1016/j.telpol.2005.06.002

Frooman, J. (1999). Stakeholder Influence Strategies. *Academy of Management Review, 24*(2), 115–191. doi:10.2307/259074

Fukasaku, K., Kawai, M., Plummer, M. G., & Trzeciak-Duval, A. (2005). *Policy Coherence Towards East Asia.* Tokyo, Japan: OECD.

Fukuda-Parr, S., Lopes, C., & Malik, K. (2002). *Capacity for Development: New Solutions to Old Problems.* London: Earthscan Publications.

Galliers, R. D. (1991). Strategic information systems planning: myths, reality and guidelines for successful implementation. *European Journal of Information Systems, 1*(1), 55–64. doi:10.1057/ejis.1991.7

Galperin, H. (2005). Wireless Networks and Rural Development: Opportunities for Latin America. *Information Technologies and International Development, 2*(3), 47–56. doi:10.1162/1544752054782420

Garai, A., & Sahadrach, B. (2006). *Taking ICT to every Indian village: opportunities and challenges.* New Delhi: One World South Asia.

Garner, L. (1986). Critical Success Factors in Social Services Management. *New England Journal of Human Services, 6*(1), 27–30.

Gartner Group. (2002). Majority of E-government Initiatives Fail or Fall Short of Expectations. In *E-government at Gartner Symposium*, San Diego, USA. Retrieved July 9, 2007, from http://symposium.gartner.com/story.php.id.1367.s.5.html

Gasmi, F., Laffont, J. J., & Sharkey, W. W. (2000). Competition, universal service and telecommunications policy in developing countries. *Information Economics and Policy, 12*, 221–248. doi:10.1016/S0167-6245(00)00016-0

Gefen, D., Pavlou, P. A., Warkentin, M., & Rose, G. M. (2002). e-Government Adoption. In *8th Americas Conference on Information systems*, Dallas, TX.

Gefen, D., Warkentin, M., Pavlou, A., & Rose, G. (2002). E-government Adoption. In *Proceedings of the 8th Americas Conference on Information Systems*, USA.

Gelinas, U., Sutton, S., & Hunton, J. (2005). *Accounting Information Systems* (6th ed.). Mason, OH: Thomson Southwestern.

GeoSINC International. (2002). E-readiness Guide: How to Develop and Implement a National E-readiness Action Plan in Developing Countries. In *Information for Development Program (InfoDev)*. Washington, DC: The World Bank.

Gerrard, M. (2001, September). Public-Private Partnerships. *Finance & Development*, 48–51.

Gerring, J. (2004). What is a case study and what is it good for? *The American Political Science Review, 98*(2), 341–354. doi:10.1017/S0003055404001182

Giddens, A. (Ed.). (1974). *Positivism and sociology.* London: Heinemann.

Gigler, B.-S. (2004). Including the Excluded - Can ICTs empower poor communities? In *Proceedings of the 4th International Conference on the Capability Approach*, Italy, 5-7 September, 2004.

Gillet, S., Lehr, W., & Osorio, C. (2004). Local government broadband initiatives. *Telecommunications Policy, 28*, 537–558. doi:10.1016/j.telpol.2004.05.001

Giuliano, R., Luglio, M., & Mazzenga, F. (2008). Interoperability between WiMAX and Broadband Mobile Space Networks. *IEEE Communications Magazine, 46*(3), 50–57. doi:10.1109/MCOM.2008.4463771

Government of Tamil Nadu. (2006). *Rural Development and Panchayati Raj Department, Policy note 2006-07.* Retrieved August 16, 2006, from http://www.tn.gov.in

Government of the Republic of Slovenia, Ministry for Health. (2005). *eHealth 2010 – Strategy of computerising the Slovenian healthcare system 2005–2010.* Retrieved March 18, 2009, from http://www.ris.org/uploadi/editor/1130935067OsnutekeZdravje2010-01.pdf

Government of the Republic of Slovenia, Ministry of Higher Education, Science and Technology. National strategy of e-learning 2006–2010.

Government of the Republic of Slovenia, Ministry of the Economy. (2006a). *Strategy of transition to digital broadcasting.*

Government of the Republic of Slovenia, Ministry of the Economy. (2006b). *Strategy of developing broadband networks in the Republic of Slovenia.* Retrieved March 18, 2009, from http://www.mg.gov.si/fileadmin/mg.gov.si/pageuploads/EKP/Predlogi/V_medresorskem/Z.Unijat_-_Strategija_BB_Rev3_medresorsko.pdf

Government of the Republic of Slovenia. (2007). *Development Strategy for the Information Society in the Republic of Slovenija – si2010*. Retrieved July 19th 2009 from: http://www.mvzt.gov.si/fileadmin/mvzt.gov.si/pageuploads/pdf/informacijska_druzba/61405-EN_Strategija_razvoja_informacijske_druzbe_v_RS_si2010.pdf

Government of the Republic of Slovenia. Ministry of Public administration. (2006). *Strategy of e-government for the period 2006–2010 (SEP-2010)*. Retrieved March 18, 2009, from http://www.mju.gov.si/fileadmin/mju.gov.si/pageuploads/mju_dokumenti/pdf/SEP- 2010.pdf

Grant, G., & Chau, D. (2005). Developing a Generic Framework for e-Government. *Journal of Global Information Management, 13*(1), 1–30.

Greene, K., Lee, B., Springall, E., & Bemrose, R. (2002). Administrative support staff in schools: ways forward. London: DfES.

Gregorio, D. D., Kassicieh, S. K., & De Gouvea Neto, R. (2005). Drivers of E-business activity in developed and emerging markets. *Engineering Management. IEEE Transactions, 52*(2), 155–166.

Gronlund, G., Andersson, A., & Hedstrom, K. (2005). NextStep E-government in Developing Countries. In *The Swedish Program for Information and Communication Technology in Developing Regions*. Sweden: Orebro University.

Grover, V., Cheon, M. J., & Teng, J. T. C. (1996). The effect of service quality and partnership on the outsourcing of information systems functions. *Journal of Management Information Systems, 12*(4), 89–116.

Guillén, M. F., & Suárez, S. L. (2005). Explaining the Global Digital Divide: Economic, Political and Sociological Drivers of Cross-National Internet Use. *The University of North Carolina Press Social Forces, 84*(2), 671–708.

Guillen, M., & Suarez, S. (2001). Developing the Internet: entrepreneurship and public policy in Ireland, Singapore, Argentina, and Spain. *Telecommunications Policy, 25*, 349–371. doi:10.1016/S0308-5961(01)00009-X

Gunasekaran, A., Love, P. E. D., Rahimi, F., & Miele, R. (2001). A model for investment justification in information technology projects. *International Journal of Information Management, 21*(5), 349–364. doi:10.1016/S0268-4012(01)00024-X

Guo, X., & Lu, J. (2005). Effectiveness of e-Government Online Services in Australia. In Huang, W., Siau, K., Wei, K. K., & Siau, K. (Eds.), *Electronic Government Strategies and Implementation* (pp. 214–241). Hershey, PA: Idea Group Publishing.

Gurstein, M. (2000). *Community informatics: Enabling communities with information and communication technologies*. London: Idea Group Publishing.

Haaker, T. E. F., & Bouwman, H. (2006). Balancing Customer and Network Value in Business Models for Mobile Services. *International Journal of Mobile Communications*.

Habermas, J. (1989). *The Structural Transformation of the Public Sphere: An inquiry into a category of Bourgeois Society*. Cambridge, MA: MIT Press.

Hackney, R., & Jones, S. (2002). Towards E-government in the Welsh (UK) Assembly: An Information Systems Evaluation. In *ISOneWorld Conference and Convention*, Nevada, USA.

Hackney, R., Jones, S., & Irani, Z. (2005). E-government Information Systems Evaluation. In *Conceptualising Customer Engagement, E-government Workshop (eGOV05)*. London, UK: Brunel University.

Hackney, R., Xu, H., & Ranchhod, A. (2006). Evaluation Web Services: Towards a framework for emergent contexts. *European Journal of Operational Research, 173*, 1161–1174. doi:10.1016/j.ejor.2005.07.010

Hagmann, C., & McCahon, C. S. (1993). Strategic information systems and competitiveness. *Information & Management, 25*(4), 183–192. doi:10.1016/0378-7206(93)90067-4

Hamilton, S., & Chervany, N. L. (1981). Evaluating Information System Effectiveness: Comparing Evaluation Approaches. *Management Information Systems Quarterly, 5*(3), 55–69. doi:10.2307/249291

Handoussa, H., & Abou Sheif, H. (2003). The Middle East in the Light of Change: Challenges and Opportunities of Globalization. In *Conference on the Future of Globalization: Explorations in the Light of Recent Turbulence Organized by the World Bank and the Yale Center for the Study of Globalization*, October 10-11, 2003.

Hargittai, E. (1999). Weaving the Western Web: explaining differences in Internet connectivity among OECD countries. *Telecommunications Policy, 23*, 701–718. doi:10.1016/S0308-5961(99)00050-6

Harkness, W. L., Kettinger, W. J., & Segars, A. H. (1996). Sustaining Process Improvement and Innovation in the Information Service Function: Lessons Learned from Bose Corporation. *Management Information Systems Quarterly, 20*(3), 349–367. doi:10.2307/249661

Harris, R. (1998). Information Technology – The New Cargo Cult? Information Technology in Developing Countries – *Newsletter of the International Federation and Information Processing (IFIP) Working Group 9.4*, Vol. 8, No. 1, January

Harris, R. W. (2005). Explaining the success of rural Asian telecentres. In Davison, R. M., Harris, R. W., Qureshi, S., Vogel, D. R., & Vreede, G.-Jd. (Eds.), *Information systems in developing countries: theory and practice* (pp. 83–100). Hong Kong: City University of Hong Kong Press.

Harris, R. W., & Bhatarai, M. (2003). *Fact-Finding Review of ICT in Development in a Rural-Urban Setting. UN-HABITAT and Roger Harris Associates. Rural-Urban Partnerships Programme (RUPP) under Support Services Policy and Programme Development*. SPPD.

Harrison, C., Comber, C., Fisher, T., Haw, K., Lewin, C., Lunzer, E., et al. (2002). ImpaCT2: The impact of information and communication technologies on pupil attainment. London: DfES/Becta.

Hashem, S. (1999, July 22). Technology Access Community Centers in Egypt: A Mission for Community Empowerment. In *Proceedings of the Internet Society Conference.*

Hashem, S. (2002). Bridging the Digital Divide in Egypt: Facing the Challenges. In *UNCTAD E-Commerce First Expert Meeting,* 10-12 July 2002.

Hassab El-naby, H., Epps, R., & Said, A. (2003). The Impact of Environmental Factors on Accounting Development: An Egyptian Longitudinal Study. *Critical Perspectives on Accounting, 14*(3).

Hassan, M. (2008). The development of accounting regulations in Egypt: Legitimating the International Accounting Standards. *Managerial Auditing Journal, 23*(5).

Hawkins, R. (1996). Standards for communication technologies: Negotiating institutional biases in network design. In Mansell, R., & Silverstone, R. (Eds.), *Communication by design: The politics of information and communication technologies* (pp. 157–186). New York: Oxford University Press.

Hawkins, R. (2004). Looking Beyond The Dot Com Bubble: Exploring The Form And Function Of Business Models In The Electronic Marketplace. In B. Preisel, H. Bouwman & C. Steinfeld (Eds.), E-Life After The Dot Com Bust. Heidelberg, Germany: Physica-Varlag.

Headrick, D. R. (1981). *The tools of empire: Technology and European imperialism in the nineteenth century.* Oxford: Oxford University Press.

Heeks, R. (1998). Foundation of ICTs in Development: Pushing and Pulling. *Information Technology in Developing Countries Newsletter, 4*(1), 1–2.

Heeks, R. (2001). Building e-Governance for Development: a Framework for National Donor Action. *e-Government Working Paper, No. 12.* University of Manchester, UK: IDPM.

Heeks, R. (2002). i-development not e-development: Special issue on ICTs and development. *Journal of International Development, 14*(1), 1–11. doi:10.1002/jid.861

Heeks, R. (2002). Information Systems and Developing Countries: Failure, Success, and Local Improvisations. *The Information Society, 18*(2), 101–112. doi:10.1080/01972240290075039

Heeks, R. (2003). Most e-Government-for-Development Projects Fail. *iGovernment Working Paper, No. 14*. University of Manchester, UK: IDPM.

Heeks, R. (2003). Most E-government for Development Projects Fail: How Can Risk Reduced. In Institute for Development Policy and Management (IDPM), University of Manchester, UK.

Heeks, R. (2003). E-government for Development: The Impact of E-government Failure. In Institute for Development Policy and Management (IDPM), University of Manchester, UK.

Heeks, R. (2004). E-government for Development: Basic Definitions. In Institute for Development Policy and Management (IDPM), University of Manchester, UK.

Heeks, R. (2005). *ICTs and the MDGs: on the Wrong Track*. Information for Development Magazine.

Heeks, R. (2005). Foundation of ICTs in Development: The information chain. *eDevelopment Briefing, 3*(1), 1-2.

Heeks, R. (2005). *ICTs and the MDGs: On the Wrong Track?* UK: Development Informatics Group, University of Manchester.

Heeks, R. (2008). ICT4D 2.0: The Next Phase of Applying ICT for International Development. *Computer, 41*(6), 26–33. doi:10.1109/MC.2008.192

Heeks, R., & Bailur, S. (2007). Analyzing e-government research: Perspectives, Philosophies, Theories, Methods, and Practice. *Government Information Quarterly, 24*(2), 243–265. doi:10.1016/j.giq.2006.06.005

Heeks, R., & Kenny, C. (2002). *ICTs and development: Convergence or divergence for developing countries?* Paper presented at the Norwegian Association for Development Research Conference, Trondheim, Norway, November 14-15, 2002.

Henderson, J. C., & Sifonis, J. G. (1988). The value of strategic IS planning: understanding consistency, validity and IS markets. *Management Information Systems Quarterly, 12*(2), 187–200. doi:10.2307/248843

Henderson, J. C., & Venkatraman, N. (1993). Strategic Alignment: Leveraging Information Technology for Transforming Organizations. *IBM Systems Journal, 32*(1), 4–16. doi:10.1147/sj.382.0472

Hickman, L. (1990). *John Dewey's pragmatic technology*. Bloomington, IN: Indiana University Press.

Hieo, W. (2001). National Infocomm Strategy and Policy: Singapore's Experience, International Council for Information Technology in Government Administration. *ICA Information, 74*.

Hitt, L., & Tambe, P. (2007). Broadband adoption and content consumption. *Information Economics and Policy, 19*(3-4), 362–378. doi:10.1016/j.infoecopol.2007.04.003

Ho, A. T. K. (2002). Reinventing Local Governments and the e-Government Initiative. *Public Administration Review, 62*(4), 434–444. doi:10.1111/0033-3352.00197

Ho, C. F., & Wu, W. H. (1999). Antecedents of Customer Satisfaction on the Internet: An Empirical Study of On-Line Shopping. In *32nd Hawaii International Conference on System Science*, Hawaii.

Hochstrasser, B., & Griffiths, C. (1991). *Controlling IT Investment, Strategy and Management*. London: Chapman & Hall.

Hoekman, B., & Mattoo, A. (2007). Regulatory cooperation, aid for trade And the GATS. *Pacific Economic Review, 12*(4), 399–418. doi:10.1111/j.1468-0106.2007.00366.x

Hogbin, G., & Thomas, D. V. (1994). *Investing in Information Technology: Managing the Decision-making Process*. Cambridge, MA: McGraw-Hill/IBM Series.

Hoing, S. (1999 May). The Changing Landscape of Computarized Accounting Systems. *The CPA Journal*.

Horngren, C., Foster, G., & Datar, S. (2000). *Cost Accounting: A Managerial Emphasis*. London: Prentice Hall International Inc.

Hosman, L., Fife, E., & Armey, E. (2008). The case for a multi-methodological, cross-disciplinary approach to the analysis of ICT investment in the developing world. *Information Technology for Development*, *14*(4), 308–327. doi:10.1002/itdj.20109

Hossain, L. (2003). Is a formalized structure a necessary prerequisite for implementing national telecommunication plan developing and developed economies? *Technovation*, *23*, 39–49. doi:10.1016/S0166-4972(01)00084-0

HPG. (2001). *Improving budgeting and financing for promising IT initiatives*. Harvard Policy Group on Network-Enabled Services and Government.

Hsiao, F. S. T., & Hsiao, M.-C. W. (2001). Capital flows and exchange rates: recent Korean and Taiwanese experience and challenges. *Journal of Asian Economics*, *12*(3), 353–381. doi:10.1016/S1049-0078(01)00092-6

Hu, Y., Xiao, J., Pang, J., & Xie, K. (2005). *A Research on the Appraisal Framework of e-Government Project Success. In 7th international conference on Electronic commerce*. Xi'an, China.

Huijboom, N., & Hoogwout, M. (2004). Trust in E-government Cooperation. In *Proceedings of the 3rd International Electronic Government Conference*, Zaragoza, Spain.

Hunsberger, K. (2006 June). A country connects. *PM Network*, 46-54.

Iacovou, C. L., Benbasat, I., & Dexter, A. S. (1995). Electronic Data Interchange and Small Organizations: Adoption and Impact of Technology. *Management Information Systems Quarterly*, *19*(4), 465–485. doi:10.2307/249629

IAMAI. (2007). Retrieved August 13, 2008, from http://www.iamai.in/section.php3?secid=16&press_id=813&mon=2

ICT Trust Fund. (2007). Retrieved January 10, 2008, from http://www.ictfund.org.eg

IDRC. (1993). *Measuring the impact of information on development*. Ottawa, Canada: The International Development Research Centre.

Igbaria, M., & Nachman, S. A. (1990). Correlates of User Satisfaction with End User Computing. *Information & Management*, *19*(2), 73–82. doi:10.1016/0378-7206(90)90017-C

IICD. (2007). *IICD supported project: Eastern Corridor Agro-Market Information Centre (ECAMIC)*. Retrieved July 10, 2007, from http://www.iicd.org/projects/articles/Ghana-ECAMIC

Iivari, J., & Ervasi, I. (1994). User Information Satisfaction: IS Implementability and Effectiveness. *Information & Management*, *27*(4), 205–220. doi:10.1016/0378-7206(94)90049-3

Ikiara, G. K., Olewe-Nyunya, J., & Odhiambo, W. (2004). Kenya: Formulation and implementation of strategic trade and industrial policies. In Soludo, C., Ogbu, O., & Chang, H. (Eds.), *The politics of trade and industrial policy in Africa* (pp. 205–224). Ottawa, Canada: IDRC and Africa World Press, Inc.

Indjikian, R., & Siegel, D. S. (2005). The impact of investment in IT on economic performance: implications for developing countries. *World Development*, *33*, 681–700. doi:10.1016/j.worlddev.2005.01.004

InfoDev (Information for Development Program). (2002). *The E-government Handbook for Developing Countries*. InfoDev Program, The World Bank.

Information and Decision Support Center. (2000). *Annual Report on Egypt*.

Information and Decision Support Center. (2005). *Annual Report on Egypt*.

Information and Decision Support Center. (2008). Retrieved June 25, 2008, from http://www.idsc.gov.eg

Information Society Technologies. (2008). *About IST The overall vision*. Retrieved March 18, 2009, from http://cordis.europa.eu/ist/about/vision.htm

Information Society. (2001). *eEurope Go Digital. Getting Europe on-line and doing e-business.* Retrieved March 18, 2009, from http://ec.europa.eu/information_society/topics/ebusiness/godigital/index_en.htm

Intarakumnerd, P. (2004 April). *Thailand's National Innovation System in Transition.* Presented at the First Asialics International Conference on Innovation Systems and Clusters in Asia: Challenges and Regional Integration, National Science and Technology Development Agency, Bangkok, Thailand.

International City/County Management Association (ICMA). (2002). *Electronic Government 2002.* Washington, DC: Author. Retrieved May 13, 2006, from http://bookstore.icma.org/freedocs/e_government_2002.pdf

International Telecommunication Union. (2009, January 25). Retrieved from http://www.itu.int

Irani, Z., Love, P., & Montazemi, A. (2007). E-government: Past, Present and Future. *European Journal of Information Systems, 16*(2), 103–105. doi:10.1057/palgrave.ejis.3000678

Ismail, N., & King, M. (2006). The Alignment of Accounting and Information Systems in SMEs in Malaysia. *Journal of Global Information Technology Management, 9*(3).

ISO. (2005). ISO/IEC 27001. *Information technology - Security techniques - Information security management systems - Requirements.* Retrieved May 25, 2008, from http://www.iso.org/iso/catalogue_detail?csnumber=42103

ITU Internet Report: Digital.Life. International Telecommunications Union, December 2006.

ITU. (1984). *The missing link: Report of the independent commission for worldwide telecommunications development.* Retrieved November 5, 2008, from http://www.itu.int/osg/spu/sfo/missinglink/index.html

ITU. (2003). *World Telecommunication Indicators database.* Retrieved from http://www.itu-t.org

ITU. (2005). *ITU's New Broadband Statistics.* Retrieved from http://www.itu.int/osg/spu/newslog/ITUs+New+Broadband+Statistics+For+1+January+2005.aspx

ITU. (2006). *World Telecommunication/ICT Development Report.* Geneva, Switzerland: International Telecommunication Union.

ITU. (2008). *ICT Statistics Database. International Telecommunication Union.* Retrieved July 9, 2008 from http://www.itu.int/ITU-D/icteye/Indicators/Indicators.aspx#

Jafari, S. M., Osman, M. R., Yusuff, R. M., & Tang, S. H. (2006). ERP Systems Implementation In Malaysia: The Importance Of Critical Success Factors. *International Journal of Engineering and Technology, 3*(1), 125–131.

Jain, R. (1995). MIS in large public programs: the literacy program in India. *Journal of Global Information Management, 3*(1), 18–30.

Jain, S. P., & Goria, S. (2006). *Digital library for Indian farmers (DLIF) using open source software: a strategic planning.* Retrieved January 24, 2009, from http://www.ifla.org/IV/ifla72/index.htm

Jamali, K., Wandschneider, K., & Wunnava, P. V. (2007). The effect of political regimes and technology on economic growth. *Applied Economics, 39*, 1425–1432. doi:10.1080/00036840500447906

James, J. (2003). *Bridging the Global Digital Divide.* Cheltenham, UK: Edward Elgar.

Jerinabi, U., & Arthi, J. (2005). Impact of Information Technology and Globalisation on Women's career, In *Proceedings of the International Conference on Information and Communication Technology of Management,* Melaka, Malaysia.

JIVA. (2007). *TeleDoc: Healthcare to touch everyone.* Retrieved July 10, 2007, from http://www.jiva.com/teledoc/

Johnston, J. (2003). *The Millennium Development Goals and Information and Communications Technology.* Berlin: United Nations Information and Communication Technologies Task Force.

Jomo, K. S. (1997). *Southeast Asia's Misunderstood Miracle: Industrial Policy and Economic Development in Thailand, Malaysia, and Indonesia.* Boulder, CO: Westview.

Jomo, K. S. (2003). Growth and Vulnerability Before and After the Asian Crisis: The Fallacy of the Universal Model. In Andersson, M., & Gunnarsson, C. (Eds.), *Development and structural change in Asia-Pacific: globalising miracles or end of a model?* (pp. 171–197). London: Routledge.

Jordana, J., Fernandez, X., Sancho, D., & Welp, J. (2005). Which Internet Policy? Assessing Regional Initiatives in Spain. *The Information Society, 21*, 341–351. doi:10.1080/01972240500253509

Jutla, D., Bodorik, P., & Dhaliwal, J. (2002). Supporting the e-business readiness of small and medium-sized enterprises: approaches and metrics. *Internet Research: Electronic Networking Applications and Policy, 12*(2), 139–164. doi:10.1108/10662240210422512

Kalakota, R., & Whinston, A. B. (1997). *Electronic commerce: A manager's guide*. Reading, MA: Addison-Wesley.

Kamel, S. (1995) Information Superhighways, a Potential for Socioeconomic and Cultural Development. In M. Khosrow-Pour (Eds.), *Managing Information and Communications in a Changing Global Environment: Proceedings of the 6ᵗʰ Information Resources Management Association International Conference (IRMA)*, Atlanta, Georgia, USA, 21-24 May (pp. 115–124).

Kamel, S. (1997). DSS for Strategic Decision-Making. In Khosrow-Pour, M., & Liebowitz, J. (Eds.), *Information Technology Management in Modern Organizations* (pp. 168–182). Hershey, PA: Idea Group Publishing.

Kamel, S. (2004) Diffusing ICT Usage Through Technology Access Clubs: Closing the Digital Divide. In Z. Irani & S. Kamel (Eds.), *Proceedings of the Information Science, Technology and Management (CISTM) Conference on Improving Business Performance through Knowledge Management*, Alexandria, Egypt, 8-9 July.

Kamel, S. (2005). Assessing the Impacts of Establishing an Internet Cafe in the Context of a Developing Nation. In *Proceedings of the 16ᵗʰ International IRMA Conference on Managing Modern Organizations with Information Technology*, San Diego, California, 15-18 May (pp. 176-181).

Kamel, S. (2005). The Evolution of Information and Communication Technology Infrastructure in Egypt. In G. Hunter & A. Wenn (Eds.), Information Systems in an e-World (pp. 117-135). Washington, DC: The Information Institute, Kamel, S. (1998). Decision Support Systems and Strategic Public Sector Decision Making. In Egypt in Information Systems for Public Sector Management Working Paper Series. Institute for Development Policy and Management, University of Manchester, Paper No. 3

Kamel, S. (2009). The Evolution of the ICT Sector in Egypt – Partnership4Development. In *Proceedings of the 11ᵗʰ International Business Information Management Association (IBIMA) Conference on Innovation and Knowledge Management in Twin Track Economies: Challenges and Opportunities*, Cairo, Egypt, 4-6 January (pp. 841-851).

Kamel, S., & Tooma, E. (2005). *Exchanging Debt for Development: Lessons from the Egyptian Debt-for-Development Swap Experience*. Working Document, World Summit on the Information Society.

Kamel, S., Ghoneim, A., & Ghoneim, S. (2002). The Role of the State in Developing the eCommerce in Egypt. In *Role of the State in a Changing World Conference*, Cairo, Egypt.

Kamel, S., Radwan, S., & El Oraby, N. (2009). The Experience of the Italian-Egyptian Debt Swap Program (2001-2008). Partners for Development, Technical Support Unit, Embassy of Italy (Egypt) and Ministry of International Cooperation (Egypt).

Kamel, T. (2006). *Egypt Reforms: An update from the ICT Sector*.

Kampschror, B. (2006, March 28). From warfare to wireless in Macedonia. *The Christian Science Monitor.*

Kanungo, S. (2004). On the emancipatory role of rural information systems. *Information Technology & People, 17*(4), 407–422. doi:10.1108/09593840410570267

Kaplinsky, R., & Morris, M. (2007). Do Asian drivers undermine export-oriented industrialization in SSA? *World Development, 36*(2), 254–273. doi:10.1016/j.worlddev.2007.06.007

Kara, J., & Quarless, D. (2002). *Guiding Principles for Partnerships for Sustainable Development ('type 2 outcomes') to be Elaborated by Interested Parties in the Context of the World Summit on Sustainable Development (WSSD).* Johannesburg Summit, 7 June 2002.

Kartiwi, M., & MacGregor, R. C. (2007). Electronic Commerce Adoption Barriers in Small to Medium-Sized Enterprises (SMEs) in Developed and Developing Countries: A Cross-Country Comparison. *Journal of Electronic Commerce in Organizations, 5*(3), 35–51.

Katsikas, S. K., Lopez, J., & Pernul, G. (2005). Trust, Privacy and Security in E-business: Requirements and Solutions. In *Proceedings of the 10th Panhellenic Conference on Informatics (PCI'2005)*, Volos, Greece, November 2005 (pp. 548-558).

Kaul, S., Ali, F., Janikiram, S., & Wattenstrom, B. (2008). *Business Models for Sustainable Telecommunications Growth in Developing Countries.* Oxford, UK: Wiley-Blackwell. doi:10.1002/9780470987759

Kaurani, M. D. (1995). *Media support to Agriculture. MANAGE Occasional paper 4.* Hyderabad, India: MANAGE.

Kavajecz, K., & Keim, D. (2003). *Packaging Liquidity: Blind Auctions and Transaction Cost Efficiencies.* Wharton School working paper reprints.

Keen, P. (2004). *A Manifesto for Electronic Commerce.* Presented at Bled Electronic Conference.

Keen, P. (2004). Building New Generation E-Business: Exploiting the Opportunities of Today. In Preisel, B., Bouwman, H., & Steinfeld, C. (Eds.), *E-Life After The Dot Com Bust.* Heidelberg: Physica-Varlag.

Keen, P., & Sol, H. (2005). *Coordination by Design: Escaping the Commodity Trap.*

Keen, P., & Williams, R. (2005). Is Industry Thinking Inhibiting Value Creation? Paper to be presented at ICE2005 conference, Xi'an, China.

Keen, P., & Williams, R. (2008). *The Innovation Path: Connecting Business Model Opportunities with Value-Creating Capabilities.*

Keller, K., Sternhal, B., & Tybout, A. (2002 September). Three Questions You Need To Ask About Your Brand. *Harvard Business Review.*

Kenny, C., Schware, R., & Williams, E. (2007). The impact of reform on telecommunications prices and services in the countries of the OECS. *Information Technology for Development, 13*(4), 411–415. doi:10.1002/itdj.20069

Kerlinger, F. N. (1986). *Foundations of Behavioral Research* (3rd ed.). New York: Harcourt Brace Jovanovich College Publishers.

Kettinger, J. (1994). National Infrastructure Diffusion and US Information Super Highway. *Information & Management, 27*(6), 357–369. doi:10.1016/0378-7206(94)90016-7

Kettinger, W. J., & Grover, V. (1995). Toward a Theory of Business Process Change Management. *Journal of Management Information Systems, 12*(1), 9–30.

Kettinger, W. J., Teng, J. T. C., & Guha, S. (1997). Business Process Change: A study of Methodologies, Techniques, and Tools. *Management Information Systems Quarterly, 21*(1), 55–80. doi:10.2307/249742

Khazanchi, D., & Munkvold, B. E. (2003). On the Rhetoric and Relevance of IS Research Paradigms: A Conceptual Framework and some Propositions. In *36th Hawaii International Conference on System Sciences*, Hawaii.

Kiiski, S., & Pohjola, M. (2002). Cross-country diffusion of the Internet. *Information Economics and Policy, 14*, 297–310. doi:10.1016/S0167-6245(01)00071-3

Kim, S. (2003). Information technology and its impact on economic growth and productivity in Korea. *International Economic Journal*, *17*(3), 55–75. doi:10.1080/10168730300080019

KIMI. (2002). *The evaluation of ICT adoption in SMEs*. Retrieved from www.kimi.or.kr

KIMI. (2003). *Whitepaper of ICT Adoption of SME 2003*. Retrieved from http://www.kimi.or.kr/pds/2003w-paper/sub/header.html

King, N. (1998). Template analysis. In Symon, G., & Cassell, C. (Eds.), *Qualitative methods and analysis in organizational research* (pp. 118–134). London: Sage Publications.

Kirytopoulos, K., Voulgaridou, D., Panopoulos, D., & Leopoulos, V. (2009). Project termination analysis in SMEs: making the right call. *International Journal of Management and Decision Making*, *10*(1/2), 69–90. doi:10.1504/IJMDM.2009.023915

Koehler, M. J., & Mishra, P. (2005). What happens when teachers design educational technology? The development of technological pedagogical content knowledge. *Journal of Educational Computing Research*, *32*(2), 131–152. doi:10.2190/0EW7-01WB-BKHL-QDYV

Koh, C. E., & Prybutok, V. R. (2003). The Three Ring Model and Development of an Instrument for Measuring Dimensions of e-Government Functions. *Journal of Computer Information Systems*, *33*(3), 34–39.

Kossak, F., Essmayr, W., & Winiwarter, W. (2001). Applicability of HCI Research to e-Government Applications. In *9th European Conference on Information Systems*, Bled, Slovenia

Kottemann, J. E., & Boyer-Wright, K. M. (2009). Human resource development, domains of information technology use, and levels of economic prosperity. *Information Technology for Development*, *15*(1), 32–42. doi:10.1002/itdj.20114

Kransberg, M. (1991). IT as Revolution. In Forester, T. (Ed.), *Computers in the Human Context*. Cambridge, MA: MIT Press.

Krishna, S., & Madon, S. (Eds.). (2003). *Digital Challenge: Information Technology in the Development Context*. Aldershot, UK: Ashgate.

Krishna, S., Ojha, A. K., & Barrett, M. (2000). Competitive advantage in the software industry: An analysis of the Indian experience. In Avgerou, C., & Walsham, G. (Eds.), *Information technology in context: Studies from the perspective of developing countries* (pp. 182–197). Aldershot, UK: Ashgate.

Krishnaswamy, G. (2005). eServices in Government: Why We Need Strategies for Capacity Building and Capacity Utilization? In *International Business Information Management Association (IBIMA 2005)*, Cairo, Egypt.

Kumar, R., & Best, M. L. (2006). Social Impact and Diffusion of Telecenter Use: A Study from the Sustainable Access in Rural India Project. *Journal of Community Informatics, 2*(3). Retrieved February 12, 2008, from http://www.ci-journal.net/index.php/ciej/article/view/328

Kuppusamy, M., & Santhapparaj, A. S. (2005). Investment in information and communication technologies (ICT) and its payoff in Malaysia. *Perspectives on Global Development and Technology*, *4*(2), 147–167. doi:10.1163/1569150054739014

Kurland, N., & Bailey, D. (1999). Telework: The Advantages and Challenges of Working Here, There, Anywhere, and Anytime. *Organizational Dynamics*, *28*(2), 53–68. doi:10.1016/S0090-2616(00)80016-9

Kurnia, S., & Johnston, R. B. (2000). The Need of a Processual View of Inter-organizational Systems Adoption. *The Journal of Strategic Information Systems*, *9*(4), 295–319. doi:10.1016/S0963-8687(00)00050-0

Kvasny, L., Payton, F. C., Mbarika, V., & Chong, J. (2006). *Information technology education and employment for women in Kenya*. Paper presented at the SIGMIS-CPR, Claremont, California, USA.

Kwon, T. H. (1990). *A diffusion of innovation approach to MIS diffusion: conceptualization, methodology, and management strategy*. Paper presented at the 11th International Conference on Information Systems, Copenhagen, Denmark.

Lallana, E. C. (2004). *An Overview of ICT Policies and e-Strategies of Select Asian Economies*. Bangkok, Thailand: United Nations Development Programme-Asia Pacific Development Information Programme.

Lance, K., & Bassole, A. (2006). SDI and National Information and Communication Infrastructure (NICI) Integration in Africa. *Information Technology for Development, 12*(4), 333–338. doi:10.1002/itdj.20051

Landauer, T. K. (1995). *The trouble with computers: Usefulness, usability, and productivity*. Cambridge, MA: MIT Press.

Lanvin, B. (2005). E-strategies for development: Efficient e-strategies require strong monitoring and evaluation. In Schware, R. (Ed.), *E-development: From excitement to effectiveness* (pp. 47–63). Washington, DC: The World Bank Group.

Lau, T., Kim, S., & Atkin, D. (2005). An examination of factors contributing to South Korea's global leadership in broadband adoption. *Telematics and Informatics, 22,* 349–359. doi:10.1016/j.tele.2004.11.004

Laudon, K., & Laudon, J. (2003). *Management Information Systems* (8th ed.). Upper Saddle River, NJ: Prentice Hall.

Layne, K., & Lee, J. (2001). Developing Fully Functional e-Government: A Four-Stage Model. *Government Information Quarterly, 18*(2), 122–136. doi:10.1016/S0740-624X(01)00066-1

Lazarsfeld, P., Berelson, B., & Gaudet, H. (1944). *The people's choice*. New York: Duell, Sloan, & Pearce.

Lederer, A. A., & Salmela, H. (1996). Toward a theory of strategic IS planning. *The Journal of Strategic Information Systems, 5*(3), 237–253. doi:10.1016/S0963-8687(96)80005-9

Lederer, A. L., & Sethi, V. (1988). The implementation of strategic information systems planning methodologies. *Management Information Systems Quarterly, 12*(3), 445–461. doi:10.2307/249212

Lee, C., & Chan-Olmsted, S. (2004). Competitive advantage of broadband Internet: a comparative study between South Korea and the United States. *Telecommunications Policy, 28,* 649–677. doi:10.1016/j.telpol.2004.04.002

Lee, J. W. (2001). Education for technology readiness: Prospects for developing countries. *Journal of Human Development, 2*(1), 115–148. doi:10.1080/14649880120050

Lee, S. T., Gholami, R., & Tong, T. Y. (2005). Time series analysis in the assessment of ICT impact at the aggregate level-lessons and implications for the new economy. *Information & Management, 42,* 1009–1022. doi:10.1016/j.im.2004.11.005

Lefebvre, L. A., Lefebvre, E., & Harvey, J. (1996). Intangible assets as determinants of advanced manufacturing technology adoption in SME's: toward an evolutionary model. *IEEE Transactions on Engineering Management, 43*(3), 307–322. doi:10.1109/17.511841

Leong, Y. K. (1997). Lifelong Learning and Vision 2020 in Malaysia. In Hatton, M. J. (Ed.), *Lifelong Learning: Policies, Practices, and Programs* (pp. 129–139). Ontario, Canada: Canadian International Development Agency.

Levenburg, N. M., Schwarz, T. V., & Motwani, J. (2005). Understanding adoption of internet technologies among SMEs. *Journal of Small Business Strategy, 16*(1), 51–69.

Levy, B., & Spiller, P. T. (1994). The Institutional Foundations of Regulatory Commitment: A Comparative Analysis of Telecommunications Regulation *Journal of Law, Economics and Organization.*

Levy, B., & Spiller, P. T. (1996). *Regulations, institutions, and commitment: Comparative studies in telecommunications*. London: Cambridge University Press.

Levy, M., & Powell, P. (2005). *Strategies for Growth in SMEs: The role of information and information systems*. Amsterdam: Elsevier.

Levy, M., Loebbecke, C., & Powell, P. (2003). SMEs, co-opetition and knowledge sharing: the role of information systems. *European Journal of Information Systems, 12*(1), 3–17. doi:10.1057/palgrave.ejis.3000439

Levy, M., Powell, P., & Galliers, R. (1999). Assessing information systems strategy development frameworks in SMEs. *Information & Management, 36*(5), 247–261. doi:10.1016/S0378-7206(99)00020-8

Levy, M., Powell, P., & Worrall, L. (2005). Strategic Intent and E-Business in SMEs: Enablers and Inhibitors. *Information Resources Management Journal, 18*(4), 1–20.

Li, E. Y. (1997). Perceived Importance of Information System Success Factors: A Meta Analysis of Group Differences. *Information & Management, 32*(1), 15–28. doi:10.1016/S0378-7206(97)00005-0

Li, W., Qiang, C. Z.-W., & Xu, L. C. (2005). Regulatory Reforms in the Telecommunications Sector in Developing Countries: The Role of Democracy and Private Interests. *World Development, 33*(8), 1307–1324. doi:10.1016/j.worlddev.2005.03.003

Liikanen, E. (2003). E-government and the European Union. [UPGRADE]. *The European Journal for the Informatics Professional, 4*(2), 7–10.

Lijphart, A. (1971). Comparative politics and the comparative method. *The American Political Science Review, 65*, 682–693. doi:10.2307/1955513

Lim, P. W. (2000 May). Path Dependence in Action: The Rise and Fall of the Korean Model of Economic Development. *Korea Development Institute.*

Lin, W. T. (2008). The business value of information technology as measured by technical efficiency: Evidence from country-level data. *Decision Support Systems, 46*, 865–874. doi:10.1016/j.dss.2008.11.017

Linder, J., & Cantrell, S. (2001). *What Makes a Good Business Model, Anyway?* Madon, S. (2000). The Internet and Socio-economic Development: Exploring the Interaction. *Information Technology & People, 13*(2).

Liu, C., & Arnett, K. P. (2000). Exploring the Factors Associated with Website Success in the Context of Electronic Commerce. *Information & Management, 38*(1), 23–33. doi:10.1016/S0378-7206(00)00049-5

Liu, S. (2001). *An e-Government Readiness Model.* Dissertation Prepared for the Degree of Doctor of Philosophy, University of North Texas, TX.

Locke, S., & Cave, J. (2002). Information Communication Technology in New Zealand SMEs. *Journal of American Academy of Business, 2*(1), 235–240.

Lomerson, W. L., McGrath, L. C., & Schwager, P. H. (2004). An examination of the benefits of e-business to small and medium size businesses. In *Proceedings of the 7th Annual conference of the Southern Association for Information System.* Southern Association for Information System.

London, T., & Hart, S. L. (2004). Reinventing strategies for emerging markets: beyond the transnational model. *Journal of International Business Studies, 35*, 350–370. doi:10.1057/palgrave.jibs.8400099

Longwe, B., & Rulinda, C. (2005). Of gateways and gatekeepers: The history of Internet exchange points in Kenya and Rwanda. In Etta, F. E., & Elder, L. (Eds.), *At the crossroads: ICT policy making in East Africa* (pp. 199–212). Nairobi, Kenya: East African Educational Publishers Ltd., & IDRC.

Lucas, H. C. (1999). *Information technology and the productivity paradox.* New York: Oxford University Press.

Luger, M. I., & Stewart, L. S., & Traxler, J. (2002 July). *Identifying Technology Infrastructure Needs in America's Distressed Communities: A Focus on Information and Communications Technology.* Report for the U.S. Economic Development Administration. Office of Economic Development Kenan Institute for Private Enterprise at the University of North Carolina at Chapel Hill.

Mac Gregor, R., & Vrazalic, L. (2005). The Role of Small Bsuiness Clusters in Prioritising Barriers to E-commerce Adoption: A Study of Swedish Regional SMEs. In CRIC Cluster conference: Beyond Cluster-Current Practicies & Future Strategies, Ballarat, June 30 – July 1, 2005.

Macedonian Information Agency. (2008, May 26). *Gostivar high school obtains 800 PCs within project 'Computer for Every Child.'* Retrieved June 4, 2008, from http://www.mia.com.mk/portal/page?_pageid=113,166290&_dad=portal&_schema=PORTAL&VestID=46388856&prikaz=24&cat=6

Machlup, F. (1962). *The production and distribution of knowledge in the United States.* Princeton, NJ: Princeton University Press.

MacKenzie, D., & Wajcman, J. (1999). *The social shaping of technology* (2nd ed.). Buckingham, UK: Open University Press.

Macome, E. (2002). *The dynamics of the adoption and use of ICT-based initiatives for development: results of a field study in Mozambique.* PhD thesis, Faculty of Engineering, Built Environment and Information Technology, University of Pretoria.

Madden, G., & Simpson, M. (1996). A probit model of household broadband service subscription intentions: A regional analysis. *Information Economics and Policy, 8,* 249–267. doi:10.1016/0167-6245(96)00008-X

Madon, S. (1991). *The impact of computer-based information systems on rural development: A case study in India.* PhD thesis, Imperial College of Science, Technology & Medicine.

Madon, S. (1997). Information-Based Global Economy and Socioeconomic Development: The Case of Bangalore. *The Information Society, 13*(3), 227–244. doi:10.1080/019722497129115

Madon, S. (2000). The Internet and socio-economic development: exploring the interaction. *Information Technology & People, 13*(2), 85–101. doi:10.1108/09593840010339835

Madon, S. (2003). Studying the developmental impact of e-governance initatives. In *Proceedings of the Internationals Federation of Information Processing, IFIP,* Working Group 8.2 and 9.4, Athens, Greece, 15-17 June 2003.

Magretta, J. (2002). *Why Business Models Matter.* Harvard Business Review.

Mahadevan, B. (2000). Business Models for Internet-based E-commerce. *California Management Review, 42*(4), 55–69.

Mahajan, V. (2009). *Africa Rising.* Upper Saddle River, NJ: Wharton Publishing.

Malaysian Communications and Multimedia Commission and Ministry of Energy, Water and Communications. (2006). *The National Broadband Plan: Enabling High Speed Broadband Under MyICMS 886.* Cyberjaya, Malaysia: Malaysian Communications and Multimedia Commission. Retrieved from http://www.mcmc.gov.my

Manawy A. (2006, October 14). For Everything not to be Fine. *Al Ahram Newspaper,* 2006.

Mansell, R., & Wehn, U. (1998). *Knowledge societies: information technology for sustainable development. Published for and on behalf of the United Nations.* New York: Oxford University Press.

Mansell, R., & When, U. (1998). *Knowledge societies: Information technology for sustainable development.* New York: Oxford University Press.

Marchionini, G., Samet, H., & Brandt, L. (2003). Digital Government. *Communications of the ACM, 46*(1), 25–27.

Marcus, S. (2005, April). Broadband adoption in Europe. *IEEE Communications Magazine, 43*(4), 18–20. doi:10.1109/MCOM.2005.1421895

Margetts, H., & Dunleavy, P. (2002). *Cultural Barriers to e-government.* Academic article for the report: Better Public Services Through e-government. Retrieved March 10, 2006, from http://www.governmentontheweb.org

Mariscal, J. (2005). Digital divide in a developing country. *Telecommunications Policy, 29,* 409–428. doi:10.1016/j.telpol.2005.03.004

Márquez-Berber, S. R. (2003). *Computers and agriculture: The Mexico case.* Retrieved August 16, 2003, from http://www.agen.ufl.edu/comconf/6thproc/cahome.html

Marshall, C., & Rossman, G. B. (2006). *Designing Qualitative Research* (4th ed.). London: Sage Publications.

Marshall, M. (2008). NComputing raises $28M to spread cheap computers to poor. *VentureBeat.com*. Retrieved June 29, 2008, from http://venturebeat.com/2008/01/13/ncomputing-raises-28m-to-spread-cheap-computers-to-poor/

Martin, J. (1982). Stories As Scripts In Organizational Settings. In A. Hasdorf & A. Isen (Eds.), Cognitive Social Psychology. New York: Elsevier-North Holland.

Mary, V., & Vasanthakumar, J. (2001). Analysis of farm broadcast and farm telecast with regard to time allotment to different subjects and communication sources of programmes. *Journal of Extension Education, 12*(1), 2995–3003.

Mata, F. J., Fuerst, W. L., & Barney, J. B. (1995). Information technology and sustained competitive advantage: a resource-based analysis. *Management Information Systems Quarterly, 19*(4), 487–505. doi:10.2307/249630

Mbarika, V. W. A., Okoli, C., Byrd, T. A., & Datta, P. (2005). The Neglected Continent of IS Research: A Research Agenda for Sub-Saharan Africa. *Journal of the Association for Information Systems, 6*(5), 130–170.

McCaney, K. (2000). Reverse Auction. *Government Computer News, 19*(13), 1–3.

McCole, P., & Ramsey, E. (2005). A Profile of Adopters and Non-adopters of eCommerce in SME Professional Service Firms. *Australasian Marketing Journal, 13*(1), 36–48.

McConnell International. (2000). Risk E-business: Seizing the Opportunity of Global E-readiness. *McConnell International*. Retrieved March 7, 2005, from http://www.mcconnellinternational.com/ereadiness/ereadinessreport.htm

MCIT (Ministry of Communications and Information Technology). (2005). *Ministry of Communications and Information Technology Indicators, MCIT*, Cairo, Egypt. Retrieved December 1, 2005, from http://www.mcit.gov.eg/indicator

MCIT (Ministry of Communications and Information Technology). (2005). *Egypt's Information Society (Annual Report)*. Cairo, Egypt: Ministry of Communications and Information Technology.

MCIT (Ministry of Communications and Information Technology). (2006). *Ministry of Communications and Information Technology Indicators*. Cairo, Egypt: MCIT. Retrieved November 15, 2006, from http://www.mcit.gov.eg/indicator

MCIT (Ministry of Communications and Information Technology). (2006). *Year Book 2006, Annual Report*. Cairo, Egypt: Ministry of Communications and Information Technology.

MDC. (2004). *Multimedia Super Corridor Impact Survey 2004 - Performance of MSC-status companies in phase I (2003) (Report)*. Malaysia: Cyberjaya.

MDec. (2005). The Smart School Roadmap 2005-2020: An Educational Odyssey - A consultative paper on the expansion of the Smart School initiative to all schools in Malaysia. Kuala Lumpur, Malaysia: MDec.

MDeC. (2007). *Malaysian Smart Schools*. Retrieved 15 August, 2007, from http://www.msc.com.my/smart-school/

MDeC. (2007). *Multimedia Development Corporation of Malaysia*. Retrieved January 10, 2007, from http://www.mdc.com.my

Mehrtens, J., Cragg, P. B., & Mills, A. M. (2001). A model of Internet adoption by SMEs. *Information & Management, 39*(3), 165–176. doi:10.1016/S0378-7206(01)00086-6

Menou, M. J. (1993). *Measuring the impact of information on development*. Ottawa, Canada: IDRC.

Menou, M. J., & Potvin, J. (2007). *Toward A Conceptual Framework For Learning About ICT's And Knowledge In The Process Of Development A GK LEAP Background Document*. Retrieved January 22, 2007, from http://www.cidcm.umd.edu/ICT/research/ICT_and_Conflict/Resources%20About%20Assessments/LEAP_Conceptual_Framework.doc

Merrill Lynch. (2006). Egypt: The Investment, Jewel on the Nile. *Global Securities Research and Economic Group of Merrill Lynch*, June.

Meso, P., Datta, P., & Mbarika, V. (2006). Moderating information and communication technologies' influences on socioeconomic development with good governance: A study of the developing countries. *Journal of the American Society for Information Science and Technology, 57*(2), 186–197. doi:10.1002/asi.20263

Metaxiotis, K. (2009). Editorial to the Special Issue on Decision Support Systems and Knowledge Management in SMEs. *International Journal of Management and Decision Making, 10*(1/2), 1–3.

Mia, L., & Clark, B. (1999). Market Competition, Management Accounting Systems and Business Unit Performance. *Management Accounting Research, 10*(2). doi:10.1006/mare.1998.0097

MIC. (2002). *The planning of development of ICT in SME*. Retrieved from http://www.mic.go.kr

Midgley, J. (1995). *Social Development: The developmental perspective in social welfare* (1st ed.). New Delhi: Sage Pulication.

Midgley, J. (2003). Social Development: The Intellectual heritage. *Journal of International Development, 15*(7). doi:10.1002/jid.1038

Milner, H. (2006). The Digital Divide: The Role of Political Institutions in Technology Diffusion. *Comparative Political Studies, 39*, 176–199. doi:10.1177/0010414005282983

Mindel, J., & Sicker, D. (2006). Leveraging the EU regulatory framework to improve a layered policy model for US telecommunications markets. *Telecommunications Policy, 30*, 136–148. doi:10.1016/j.telpol.2005.11.004

Ministry of Communication and Information Technology (MCIT). (2008). Retrieved December 22, 2008, from http://www.mcit.gov.eg

Ministry of Communications and Information Technology (MCIT). (2005). *Oracle technology platform drives Egypt's comprehensive e-government initiative*. Retrieved from http://www.ameinfo.com/61511.html

Ministry of Communications and Information Technology. (2005). Retrieved from http://www.mcit.gov.eg

Ministry of Communications and Information Technology. (2005) Egypt Information Society Initiative (4th Ed.).

Ministry of Communications and Information Technology. (2005). *Building Digital Bridges: Egypt's Vision of the Information Society.*

Ministry of Communications and Information Technology. (2006). *Building Digital Bridges: Egypt's Vision of the Information Society.* Retrieved from http://www.mcit.gov.eg/brochures/BuildingBridges(all).pdf

Ministry of Communications and Information Technology. (2007). *Egypt's ICT Strategy 2007-2010.* Ministry of Communication and Information Technology May, 2008.

Ministry of Communications and Information Technology. (2007). Retrieved February 10, 2009, from http://www.mcit.gov.eg

Ministry of Communications and Information Technology. (2007). *Egypt's ICT Golden Book.*

Ministry of Communications and Information Technology. (2008). *The Future of the Internet Economy in Egypt: Statistical Profile.* Ministry of Communication and Information Technology May, 2008.

Ministry of Communications and Information Technology. (2008). *Egypt ICT Trust Fund: ICT for Small and Medium Enterprises.* Ministry of Communication and Information Technology. Retrieved from http://www.ictfund.org.eg/ICT4SMEs.html

Ministry of Communications and Information Technology. (2009). *The Future of the Internet Economy in Egypt.* Statistical Profile.

Ministry of Local Development (MOLD). (2008). Retrieved June 18, 2008, from http://www.mold.gov.eg

Mitchell, R. K., Agle, B. R., & Wood, D. J. (1997). Toward a Theory of Stakeholder Identification and Salience: defining the Principle of Who and What Really Counts. *Academy of Management Review, 22*(4), 853:866.

Mitroff, I., & Kilmann, R. (1975, July). Stories Managers Tell: A New Tool For Organizational Problem Solving. *Management Review*, 18–28.

MOEFT. (2002). *Streamlining the Regulatory Procedures for Small and Medium Enterprises (The One-Stop-Shop Model). Workshop report.* Ministry of Economy and Foreign Trade – Egypt.

MOEFT. (2004). *Priority Policy Issues for the Development of the Micro, Small and Medium Enterprises Sector in Egypt. Workshop report.* Ministry of Economy and Foreign Trade – Egypt.

MOEFT. (2005). *Small and medium enterprises policies. MOEFT Newsletter, 5.* Ministry of Economy and Foreign Trade – Egypt.

MOEFT. (2006). *Research Policy Priorities for SME Development. Workshop report.* Ministry of Economy and Foreign Trade – Egypt.

Mohamed, M. (1998). *The Way Forward.* London: Weidenfeld & Nicolson.

MoICT. (2006). *E-Initiative Database.* Ministry of Information and Communications Technology (MoICT). Retrieved April 12, 2008 from http://www.moict.gov.jo/MoICT/MoICT_Initiative.aspx

MOICT. (2006). *The e-Readiness Assessment of the Hashemite Kingdom of Jordan 2006.* Ministry of Information and Communication technology (MoICT).

Moodley, S. (2005). A critical assessment of the state ICT for poverty reduction discourse in South Africa. *Perspectives on Global Development and Technology, 4*(1), 1–26. doi:10.1163/1569150053888254

Moon, J. M. (2002). The Evolution of e-Government Among Municipalities: Rhetoric or Reality? *Public Administration Review, 62*(4), 424–433. doi:10.1111/0033-3352.00196

Moshi, L. (2005, March-April). *African languages in a global age: The case of Kiswahili.* Paper presented at the 36th Conference on African Linguistics, Savannah, GA.

MSAD (Ministry of State for Administrative Development). (2006). *Program of Enhancing the Efficiency of Egypt's Administrative Agencies.* Cairo, Egypt: Ministry of State for Administrative Development.

Mullen, H., & Horner, D. S. (2004). Ethical Problems for e-Government: An Evaluative Framework. *Electronic. Journal of E-Government, 2*(3), 187–196.

Mwangi, W. (2006). The Social Relations of E-government Diffusion in Developing Countries: The Case of Rwanda. In *Proceedings of the International Conference on Digital Government Research,* San Diego, USA.

Myers, M., & Avison, D. (2002). *Qualitative Research in Information Systems: A Reader.* Thousand Oaks, CA: Sage Publications.

MYRADA. (2006). *Characteristics that can describe a sangha as 'good'. MYRADA Rural Management Systems Series Paper No. 15.* Bangalore, India: MYRADA.

Nahon, K. B. (2006). Gaps and Bits: Conceptualizing Measurements for Digital Divide/s. *The Information Society, 22*(5), 269–278. doi:10.1080/01972240600903953

Nairn, G. (2006, March 28). Broadband network is the envy of the West. *Financial Times London.*

Nakamura, Y., & Shibuya, M. (1996). Japan's technology policy - A case study of the R&D of the fifth generation computer systems. *International Journal of Technology Management, 12*(5-6), 509–533.

Nambiar, S. (2006, November). Enhancing Institutions and Improving Regulation: The Malaysian Case. *EABER Working Paper Series Paper No. 4.* Paper prepared for discussion at the Microeconomic Foundations of Economic Performance in East Asia Conference, Manila.

National Sample Survey Organization (NSSO). (1997). *Final population totals excluding J&K. 53rd Round NSSO, December, 1997.* New Delhi, India: NSSO.

National Sample Survey Organization (NSSO). (2005). *Access to modern technology for farmers. 59th round NSSO, December 2003.* New Delhi, India: NSSO.

National Telecommunications and Information Administration (NTIA). (1999). *Falling through the Net: defining the digital divide*. Retrieved May 25, 2008, from http://www.ntia.doc.gov/ntiahome/fttn00/contents00.html

National Telecommunications and Information Administration (NTIA). (2000). *Falling through the Net II: toward digital inclusion*. Retrieved May 25, 2008, from http://www.ntia.doc.gov/ntiahome/fttn00/contents00.html

Navarra, D. D., & Cornford, T. (2003). A Policy Making View of e-Government Innovations in Public Governance. In *9ᵗʰ Americas Conference on Information Systems*, Tampa, Florida.

NCA. (2006). *2006 Informatization White Paper*. Seoul, Korea: Author.

Ndou, V. (2004). E-government for Developing Countries: Opportunities and Challenges. *The Electronic Journal on Information Systems in Developing Countries, 18*(1), 1–24.

NECCC (National Electronic Commerce Coordinating Council). (2001). *Citizen Expectations for Trustworthy Electronic Government*. USA: National Electronic Commerce Coordinating Council.

Neto, I., Kenny, C., Janakiram, S., & Watt, C. (2005). Look before you leap: The bumpy road to e-development. In Schware, R. (Ed.), *E-development: From excitement to effectiveness* (pp. 1–22). Washington, D.C.: The World Bank Group.

Niederman, F., Brancheau, J. C., & Wetherbe, J. C. (1991). Information systems management issues for the 1990s. *Management Information Systems Quarterly, 15*(4), 475–500. doi:10.2307/249452

Nikolovska, Z. (2009). Chief of Party, eSchools Macedonia. Interview with the author, May 16.

Ninan, S. (2002, June 23). Rural revolution. *The Hindu*, p. 3.

Nine states to get internet kiosks with cotton focus. (2003, April 25). *The Hindu Business Line*, p. 6.

Nobes, C. (2001). *Introducing GAAP 2001: A Survey of National Accounting Rules Benchmarked Against International Accounting Standards*. Retrieved from http://kpmg.de/library/pdf/011120_GAAP_2001_en.pdf

Nomura, T. (2007). Contribution of education and educational equality to economic growth. *Applied Economics Letters, 14*, 627–630. doi:10.1080/13504850500425857

Norris, P. (2000). The Global Divide: Information Poverty and Internet Access Worldwide. Internet Conference at the International Political Science World Congress in Quebec City, 1-6 August 2000.

Norton, S. (1992). Transaction costs, telecommunications, and the microeconomics of macroeconomic growth. *Economic Development and Cultural Change, 41*(1), 175–196. doi:10.1086/452002

Nour, M., Abdel Rahman, A., & Fadl Allah, A. (2008). A Context-Based Integrative Framework for e-Government Initiatives. *Government Information Quarterly, 25*(3), 448–461. doi:10.1016/j.giq.2007.02.004

NSW (New South Wales) Audit Office. (2001). eReady, eSteady, e-Government. *State Library of New South Wales Cataloguing-in Publication Data*. Retrieved May 11, 2006, from http://www.audit.nsw.gov.au/publications/better_practice/2001/e_gov_bpg_sept_01.pdf

Nua Internet Surveys. (2001). *The Kelsey Group: US Small Businesses Move Online*. Retrieved from http://www.nua.ie/surveys/?f=VS&art_id=905356432&rel=true

Nunnally, J. (1978). *Psychometric Theory* (2nd ed.). New York: McGraw Hill.

Oberer, B. (2002). International Electronic Government Approaches. In *Proceedings of the 35ᵗʰ Annual Hawaii International Conference on system Sciences*, IEEE, USA.

OECD. (1997). *Globalization and Small and Medium Sized Enterprises (SMEs)*. Paris: Organization for Economic Cooperation and Development.

OECD. (2000). *Small and Medium-sized Enterprises: Local Strength, Global Reach*. Retrieved from http://www.oecd.org

OECD. (2002). *Guidelines for the Security of Information Systems and Networks: Towards a Culture of Security.* Retrieved May 25, 2008, from http://www.oecd.org/dataoecd/16/22/15582260.pdf

OECD. (2003). *Integrating information and communication technologies in development programmes.* Retrieved April 20, 2008, from http://www.oecd.org/dataoecd/2/57/20611917.pdf

OECD. (2003). *OECD Science, Technology and Industry Scoreboard.* Retrieved from http://www1.oecd.org/publications/e-book/92-2003-04-1-7294/PDF/B45.pdf

OECD. (2004). *OECD Broadband Statistics.* Retrieved from http://www.oecd.org/document/60/0,2340,en_2825_495656_2496764_1_1_1_1,00.html

OECD. (2004, February 12). Recommendation of the OECD council on broadband development. Retrieved from http://www.oecd.org/document/36/0,2340,en_21571361_34590630_34238436_1_1_1_1,00.html

OECD. (2005). *Financing ICTs for development – Efforts of DAC members.* Retrieved May 14, 2008, from http://www.oecd.org/dataoecd/41/45/34410597.pdf

OECD. (2005). *Multiple play: pricing and policy trends.* Working Party on Telecommunication and Information Services Policies. Retrieved from http://www.oecd.org/dataoecd/47/32/36546318.pdf

OECD. (2008). *OECD Broadband Portal.* Retrieved from http://www.oecd.org/sti/ict/broadband

Ohmae, K. (1985). *Triad power.* New York: The Free Press.

Ojo, A., Janowski, T., & Estevez, E. (2007). *Determining Progress Towards E-government: What are the Core Indicators?* Japan: Center for Electronic Governance, United Nation University.

Ong, E.-T. (2006, December). *The Malaysian Smart Schools Project: An Innovation to Address Sustainability.* Paper presented at the 10th UNESCO-APEID International Conference on Education Learning Together for Tomorrow: Education for Sustainable Development, Bangkok, Thailand.

Osemy, A., & Prodhan, B. (2001). *The Role of Accounting Information Systems in Rationalizing Investment Decisions in Manufacturing Companies in Egypt.* Research Memorandum. Center for International Accounting and Finance Hull University.

Otto, P. (2003). New Focus in E-government: From Security to Trust. In M. Gupta, (Ed.), *Proceeding of International Conference on E-governance, Promises of E-governance: Management Challenges*, New Delhi, India.

Oxley, J., & Yeung, B. (2001). E-commerce readiness: Institutional environment and international competitiveness. *Journal of International Business Studies, 32*, 705-723. doi:10.1057/palgrave.jibs.8490991

Page, S. (1999). *Regionalism among developing countries.* Basingstoke, UK: Macmillan. doi:10.1057/9780333982686

Palvia, P. C., & Palvia, S. C. (1999). An Examination of the IT Satisfaction of Small-Business Users. *Information & Management, 35*(3), 127–137. doi:10.1016/S0378-7206(98)00086-X

Palvia, P., Midha, V., & Pinjani, P. (2006). Research models in information systems. *Communications of the Association for Information Systems, 17*, 1042–1063.

Papaioannou, S., & Dimelis, S. (2007). Information technology as a factor of economic development: Evidence from developed and developing countries. *Economics of Innovation and New Technology, 16*(3), 179–194. doi:10.1080/10438590600661889

Papantoniou, A., Hattab, E., Kayafas, E., & Loumos, V. (2001). Change Management, a Critical Success Factor for E-government. In *Proceedings of the 12th International Workshop on Database and Expert Systems Applications,* IEEE, Germany.

Paraskevas, A., & Buhalis, D. (2002). Outsourcing IT for small hotels: The opportunities and challenges of using application service providers. *The Cornell Hotel and Restaurant Administration Quarterly, 43*(2), 27–39. doi:10.1016/S0010-8804(02)80029-5

Pardo, T. A., & Scholl, H. J. J. (2002). Walking Atop the Cliffs: Avoiding Failure and Reducing Risks in Large-Scale e-Government Projects. In *35ᵗʰ Hawaii International Conference on System Sciences*, Hawaii.

Parent, M., Vandebeek, C., & Gemino, A. (2004). Building Citizen Trust Through E-government. In *Proceedings of the 37ᵗʰ Hawaii International Conference on System Sciences*, IEEE, USA.

Parker, M., & Benson, R. (1989). Enterprise wide information economics: Latest concepts. *Journal of Information Systems Management*, 6(4), 7–13. doi:10.1080/07399018908960166

Parolini, C. (1999). *The Value Net: A Tool for Competitive Advantage*. New York: John Wiley.

Pau, L. F. (2002). The communications and information economy: issues, tariffs and economics research areas. *Journal of Economic Dynamics & Control*, 26(9-10), 1651–1675. doi:10.1016/S0165-1889(01)00089-6

Peccarelli, B. (2004 June). Technology in Accounting. *Accounting Technology Magazine*.

Perez, M., Sanchez, A., & Carnicer, M. (2002). Benefits and barriers of telework: perception differences of human resources managers according to company's operations strategy. *Technovation*, 22, 775–783. doi:10.1016/S0166-4972(01)00069-4

Perkins, D. N., & Simmons, R. (1998). Patterns of mis-understanding: An integrative model for science, math and programming. *Review of Educational Research*, 5(3), 303–326.

Perry, J., & Sadowsky, G. (1996 November). If you build it, they will connect. *OnTheInternet*.

Petroska-Beska, V., & Najcevska, M. (2004). Macedonia: Understanding history, preventing future conflict. *United States Institute of Peace*, Special Report No. 115.

Pettigrew, A. M. (1990). Longitudinal Field Research on Change: Theory and Practice. *Organization Science*, 1(3), 267–292. doi:10.1287/orsc.1.3.267

Pew Internet. *Digital divisions*. (2005, October 15). Retrieved from http://www.pewInternet.org/

Phillips, C., & Bhatia-Panthaki, S. (2007, August). Enterprise development in Zambia: reflections on the missing middle. *Journal of International Development*, 19(6), 793. doi:10.1002/jid.1402

Pigato, M. (2001). *Information and Communication Technology, Poverty and Development in sub-Saharan Africa and South Asia*. Retrieved April 8, 2003, from http://www.worldbank.org/afr/wps

Pilipovic, J., Ivkovic, M., Domazet, D., & Milutinovic, V. (2002). e-Government, eBusiness and eChallenges. Amsterdam: IOS Press.

Pitt, L. F., Watson, R. T., & Kavan, C. B. (1995). Service Quality: A Measure of Information Systems Effectiveness. *Management Information Systems Quarterly*, 19(2), 173–187. doi:10.2307/249687

Platt, W. (2008). Senior Vice President of Engineering and Support, *NComputing*. Interviews with the author, June 17 & 30, July 23.

Pohjola, M. (2000). Information technology and economic growth: A cross-country analysis. Helsinki, Finland: United Nations University World Institute for Development Economics Research (UNU/WIDER).

Pohjola, M. (2001). Information technology and economic growth: A cross country analysis. In Pohjola, M. (Ed.), *Information Technology and Economic Development*. Oxford, UK: Oxford University Press.

Policy framework for agricultural extension. (2000). Extension division, Dept. of Agriculture & Co-operation, Ministry of Agriculture, Govt. of India

Poon, S., & Strom, J. (1997). *Small Business Use of the Internet: Some Realities*. Paper presented at the Association for Information Systems Americas Conference, Indianapolis, IN.

Porter, M. (1994). From Strategy to Advantage: The Evolving Competitive Paradigm. In Duffy, P. (Ed.), *The Relevance of a Decade*. Cambridge, MA: Harvard Business School Press.

Porter, M. E. (1980). *Competitive Strategy*. New York: The Free Press.

Porter, M., & Millar, V. (1998). How Information Gives You Competitive Advantage: The Information Revolution is Transforming the Nature of Competition. In Matarazzo, J., & Connolly, S. (Eds.), *Knowledge and Special Libraries*. Oxford, UK: Butterworth-Heinemann.

Powell, T. C., & Dent-Micallef, A. (1999). Information Technology as Competitive Advantage: The Role of Human, Business, and Technology Resources. *Strategic Management Journal*, *18*(5), 375–405. doi:10.1002/(SICI)1097-0266(199705)18:5<375::AID-SMJ876>3.0.CO;2-7

Prathap, D. P. (1994). *Participation of farmers in Credit Management Groups organized by an NGO*. Un Pub. M Sc. (Ag.) Thesis. Annamalai nagar: Annamalai University.

Prathap, D. P. (2004). Relative effectiveness of farm communication through mass media including new media: An experimental approach with rural women. *Dissertation Abstracts International, 66*(10). (Publication No. AAT 3193131).

Prathap, D. P., & Ponnusamy, K. A. (2006). Effectiveness of Four Mass Media Channels on the Knowledge Gain of Rural Women. *Journal of International Agricultural and Extension Education, 13*(1), 73–81.

Prattipati, S. (2003). Adoption of E-governance: Differences Between Countries in the Use of Online Government Services. *Journal of American Academy of Business*, *3*(1), 386–391.

Premkumar, G., & Roberts, M. (1999). Adoption of new Information Technologies in rural small businesses. *Omega. The International Journal of Management Science, 27*(4), 467–484.

Press, L. (1999a January). Connecting Villages: The Grameen Bank Success Story. *OnTheInternet*.

Press, L. (1999b October). Developing Countries Networking Symposium. *OnTheInternet*.

Pucihar, A., Bogataj, K., & Lenart, G. (2009). Increasing SMEs' efficiency through the single European electronic market as a new business model. In Paape, B., & Vuk, D. (Eds.), *Synthesized organization* (pp. 347–368). Frankfurt am Main, Deutschland: P. Lang.

Purao, S., & Campbell, B. (1998). *Critical Issues for Small Business Electronic Commerce: Reflections on Interviews of Small Business in Downtown Atlanta*. Paper presented at the Proceedings of the AIS Americas Conference on Information Systems, Baltimore, MD.

Putnam, R. D. (2000). *Bowling alone*. New York: Simon & Schuster.

Qiang, C. Z., Clarke, G. R., & Halewood, N. (2006). The Role of ICT. In *Doing Business Information and Communications for Development—Global Trends and Policies*. Washington, DC: World Bank.

Quinn, R. E., & McGrath, M. R. (1985). The Transformation of Organizational Cultures: A Competing Values Perspective. In Frost, R., Moore, L. F., Louis, M. R., Lundberg, C. C., & Martin, J. (Eds.), *Organizational Culture* (pp. 315–334). Beverley Hills, CA: Sage.

Qureshi, Q., Keen, P., & Kamal, M. (2007). Knowledge Networking for Development: Building Bridges across the Digital Divide. In *Proceedings of the 40th Annual Hawaii International Conference on System Sciences (HICSS-40)*, Waikoloa, Hawaii.

Qureshi, S., & Keen, P. (2005). Activating Knowledge through Electronic Collaboration: Vanquishing the Knowledge Paradox. *IEEE Transactions on Professional Communication, 48*(1). doi:10.1109/TPC.2004.843296

Ragin, C. C. (1987). *The Comparative Method: Moving Beyond Qualitative and Quantitative Strategies*. Berkeley, CA: University of California Press.

Rai, A., Lang, S. S., & Welker, R. B. (2002). Assessing the Validity of IS Success Models: An Empirical Test and Theoretical Analysis. *Information Systems Research, 13*(1), 50–69. doi:10.1287/isre.13.1.50.96

Rajesh, M. (2003). A study of the problems associated with ICT adaptability in developing countries in the context of distance education. *Turkish Online Journal of Distance Education, 4*(2). Retrieved June 30, 2003, from http://tojde.anadolu.edu.tr/tojde/articles.htm

Ramasamy, B., Chakrabarty, A., & Cheah, M. (2002). *Malaysia's leap into the future: an evaluation of the Multimedia Super Corridor* (Research Paper Series No. 08/2002). Nottingham, UK: Centre in Europe Asia Business Research, Nottingham University Business School.

Ramasamy, B., Chakrabarty, A., & Cheah, M. (2004). Malaysia's leap into the future: an evaluation of the multimedia super corridor. *Technovation, 24*, 871–883. doi:10.1016/S0166-4972(03)00049-X

Ramdani, B., & Kawalek, P. (2009). Predicting SMEs' adoption of enterprise systems. *Journal of Enterprise Information Management, 22*(1/2), 10–24. doi:10.1108/17410390910922796

Ramos, S., Feijóo, C., Pérez, J., Castejón, L., González, A., & Rojo, D. (2004). New perspectives on broadband development and public policies. *The Journal of the Communications Network, 3*(1), 28–33.

Ranis, G. (1989, September). The Role of Institutions in Transition Growth: The East Asian Newly Industrializing Countries. *World Development, 17*(9), 1443–1453. doi:10.1016/0305-750X(89)90085-5

Rao, S. S., Metts, G., & Monge, C. A. M. (2003). Electronic commerce development in small and medium-sized enterprises: a stage model and its implications. *Business Process Management Journal, 9*(1), 11–32. doi:10.1108/14637150310461378

Rao, T. P. (2001). *E-Commerce and Digital Divide: Impact on Consumers*. Paper Presented at the Regional Meeting for the Asia-Pacific: New Dimensions of Consumer Protection in the Era of Globalization, Goa, India.

Rappa, M. (n.d.). *Managing the Digital Enterprise, Web site courseware*. Retrieved from http://www/digitalenterprise.organization/models/models.html

Rashid, M. A., & Al-Qirim, N. A. (2001). E-Commerce Technology Adoption Framework by New Zealand Small to Medium Enterprises. *Research Letters Information Mathematical Science, 2*(1), 63–70.

Ray, H. (1978). *The basic village education project: Guatemala*. Washington, DC: Academy for Educational Development.

Raymond, L. (1990). Organisational context and information systems success: a contingency approach. *Journal of Management Information Systems, 6*, 5–20.

RBI. (2006). *Micro credit: A lifeline for the poor*. Retrieved October 4, 2006 from http://www.rbi.org.in/scripts/FAQView.aspx?Id=7

Reffat, R. (2003). *Developing a Successful e-Government*. Working Paper, School of Architecture, Design Science and Planning, University of Sydney, Australia.

Reich, B. H., & Benbasat, I. (2000). Factors that influence the social dimension of alignment between business and information technology objectives. *Management Information Systems Quarterly, 24*(1), 81–113. doi:10.2307/3250980

Reka, A. (2008). The Ohrid Agreement: The travails of inter-ethnic relations in Macedonia. *Human Rights Review, 9*, 55–69. doi:10.1007/s12142-007-0029-z

Republic of Macedonia. (2005). *National Strategy for Information Society Development Action Plan*. Skopje, Macedonia: Author.

Reuters. (2008, June 1). *Macedonia election tainted by violence and fraud*.

Rimmer, J. (2002). *e-Government – Better Government*. Retrieved May 5, 2003, from http://www.noie.gov.au/publications/speeches/Rimmer/Breakfast/egov_sep18.htm

Riquelme, H. (2002). Commercial Internet adoption in China: Comparing the experiences of small, medium and large businesses. *Internet Research: Electronic Networking Applications and Policy, 12*(3), 276–286. doi:10.1108/10662240210430946

RIRDC. (1997). *A framework for developing regional communications initiatives.* Melbourne: Centre for International Research on Communication and Information Technologies.

Roberts, J. (2000). From know-how to show-how? Questioning the role of information and communication technologies in knowledge transfer. *Technology Analysis and Strategic Management, 12*(4), 429–443. doi:10.1080/713698499

Robson, C. (2006 March). It's All About Communication. *Journal of Association of Chartered Certified Accountants.*

Rockart, J. F., & Earl, M. J. (1996). Eight imperatives for the new IT organisation. *Sloan Management Review, 38*(1), 43–56.

Rodriguez-Pose, A., & Crescenzi, R. (2008). Research and development, spillovers, innovation systems, and the genesis of regional growth in Europe. *Regional Studies, 42*(1), 51–67. doi:10.1080/00343400701654186

Rogers, E. M. (1995). *Diffusion of Innovations.* New York: Free Press.

Roller, L., & Waverman, L. (2001). Telecommunications Infrastructure and Economic Development: a simultaneous approach. *The American Economic Review, 91*(4), 909–923.

Röller, L., & Waverman, L. (2001). Telecommunications Infrastructure and Economic Development: A Simultaneous Approach. *The American Economic Review, 91*(4), 909–923.

Roman, R., & Colle, R. D. (2003). Content creation for ICT development projects: Integrating normative approaches and community demand. *Information Technology for Development, 10*(2), 85–94. doi:10.1002/itdj.1590100204

Romer, P. (1998). Innovation: The New Pump of Growth. *Blueprint: Ideas for a New Century.*

Rorty, R. (1991). *Objectivism, Relativism, and Truth: Philosophical Papers (Vol. 1).* Cambridge, UK: Cambridge University Press.

Rudaki, J. (1998). Accounting Education in Developing Countries: Literature Review. *Journal of Social Sciences and Humanities of Shiraz University, 14*(1).

Sabouni, I. (2006). National ICT Strategy for Syria: Methodology, Outcome and Implementation. In *Workshop on ICT Policy Making in ESCWA Member Countries*, 2-4 May, Beirut, Lebanon.

Sachs, J. (2000, June 24). A New Map of the World. *Economist Magazine*, 81-83.

Sahay, S. (1998). Implementing GIS technology in India: Issues of time and space. *Accounting. Management and Information Technologies, 8*(2-3), 147–188. doi:10.1016/S0959-8022(98)00002-2

Salem, F. (2007). Benchmarking the e-Government Bulldozer: Beyond Measuring the Tread Marks. *Measuring Business Excellence, 11*(4), 9–22. doi:10.1108/13683040710837892

Salmela, H., & Spil, T. A. M. (2002). Dynamic and emergent information systems strategy formulation and implementation. *International Journal of Information Management, 22*(6), 441–460. doi:10.1016/S0268-4012(02)00034-8

Salmela, H., Lederer, A. L., & Reponen, T. (2000). Information systems planning in a turbulent environment. *European Journal of Information Systems, 9*(1), 3–15. doi:10.1057/palgrave.ejis.3000339

Samaha, K., & Stapleton, P. (2008). Compliance with international accounting standards in a national context: some empirical evidence from the Cairo and Alexandria stock exchanges. *Afro-Asian Journal of Finance and Accounting, 1*(1), 40–66. doi:10.1504/AAJFA.2008.016890

Samassekou, A. (2003). Towards a Shared Information Society for All, WSIS 2003 Connecting the World. In The World Summit on the Information Society, 10-12 December, Geneva, Switzerland.

Saunders, M. N. K., Lewis, P., & Thornhill, A. (2009). *Research methods for business students. Financial Times* (5th ed.). Upper Saddle River, NJ: Prentice Hall.

Saunders, M., Lewis, P., & Thornhill, A. (2000). *Research Methods for Business Students* (2nd ed.). London: Prentice-Hall.

Savage, S., & Waldman, D. (2005). Broadband Internet Access, Awareness and Use: Analyses of United States Household Data. *Telecommunications Policy, 29,* 615–633. doi:10.1016/j.telpol.2005.06.001

Sawada, M., Cossette, D., Wellar, B., & Kurt, T. (2006). Analysis of the urban/rural broadband divide in Canada: Using GIS in planning terrestrial wireless deployment. *Government Information Quarterly, 23*(3-4), 454–479. doi:10.1016/j.giq.2006.08.003

Sayed, F. (2004). *Innovation in Public Administration: The Case of Egypt. United Nations Department for Economic and Social Affairs.* UNDESA.

SBI plans to make rural areas e-savvy. (2003, April 13). *The New Indian Express,* p. 3.

Schedler, K., & Scharf, M. C. (2001). Exploring the Interrelations between Electronic Government and the New Public Management: A Managerial Framework for Electronic Government. In *Association for Public Policy Analysis & Management Conference (APPAM 2002),* Dallas, TX.

Scholl, H. J. J. (2003). e-Government: A Special Case of ICT-Enabled Business Process Change. In *36th Hawaii International Conference on System Sciences,* Hawaii.

Scholl, H. J. J. (2005). The Dimensions of Business Process Change in Electronic Government. In Huang, W., Siau, K., Wei, K. K., & Siau, K. (Eds.), *Electronic Government Strategies and Implementation* (pp. 44–67). Hershey, PA: Idea Group Publishing.

Schumpeter, J. A. (2002). The economy as a whole: Seventh chapter of The Theory of Economic Development. *Industry and Innovation, 9*(1/2), 93–145.

Schunk, D. H. (2003). *Learning theories: An educational perspective* (4th ed.). Upper Saddle River, NJ: Prentice-Hall.

Schware, R. (2005). Overview: E-Development: From Excitement to Effectiveness. In R. Schware (Ed.), e-development from excitement to effectiveness. Prepared for the World Summit on the Information Society, Tunis, November.

Sciadas, G. (2004). *International benchmarking for the information society.* Presented at ITU-KADO Digital Bridges Symposium, Asia Telecom 2004, Busan, Republic of Korea.

Scupola, A. (2003). The adoption of Internet commerce by SMEs in the south of Italy: An environmental, technological and organizational perspective. *Journal of Global Information Technology Management, 6*(1), 52–71.

Searle, J. R. (1995). *The Construction of Social Reality.* New York: Simon and Schuster.

Seddon, P. (1997). A Respecification and Extension of the DeLone and McLean Model of IS Success. *Information Systems Research, 8*(3), 240–253. doi:10.1287/isre.8.3.240

Seddon, P. B., & Kiew, M. Y. (1996). A Partial Test and Development of DeLone and McLean Model of IS Success. *Australian Journal of Information Systems, 4*(1), 90–109.

Seddon, P. B., Staples, S., Patnayakuni, R., & Bowtell, M. (1999). Dimensions of Information Systems Success. *Communications of the AIS, 1*(20), 1–39.

Sein, M., & Ahmad, I. (2001). A Framework to Study the Impact of Information and Communication Technologies on Developing Countries: The Case of Cellular Phones in Bangladesh. In *Proceedings of the BITWORLD 2001,* Cairo, Egypt.

Sein, M., & Harindranath, G. (2004, January). Conceptualizing the ICT Artifact: Toward Understanding the Role of ICT in National Development. *The Information Society, 20*(1), 15–24. doi:10.1080/01972240490269942

Seliem, A. A. M., Ashour, A. S., Khalil, O. E. M., & Millar, S. J. (2003). The relationship of some organisational factors to information systems effectiveness: a contingency analysis of Egyptian data. *Journal of Global Information Management, 11*(1), 41–70.

Sen, A. (2000). *Development as freedom* (1st ed.). New Delhi: Oxford University Press.

Seo, H. J., & Lee, Y. S. (2005). Contribution of information and communication technology to total factor productivity and externalities effects. *Information Technology for Development, 12*(2), 159–173. doi:10.1002/itdj.20021

Seyal, A. H., Awais, M. M., Shamail, S., & Abbas, A. (2004). Determinants of Electronic Commerce in Pakistan: Preliminary Evidence from Small and Medium Enterprises. *Electronic Markets, 14*(4), 372–387. doi:10.1080/10196780412331311801

Seybold (1998). *Customer.com.* New York: Random House.

Shalhoub, Z. (2006). Trust, Privacy, and Security in Electronic Business: The Case of the GCC countries. *Information Management & Computer Security, 14*(3), 270–283. doi:10.1108/09685220610670413

Shamblin, L. (2005). Giving every Macedonian student a gateway to the world. In Bracey, B., & Culver, T. (Eds.), *Harnessing the Potential of ICT for Education: A Multistakeholder Approach.* New York: United Nations ICT Task Force.

Sharma, R. C. (2002). Interactive radio counselling in distance education. *University News, 40*(10), 8–11.

Sharma, S. (1996). *Applied Multivariate Techniques.* New York: John Wiley & Sons.

Shaxson, N. (2007). *Poisoned wells: the dirty politics of oil in Africa.* London: Palgrave.

Shiva, V. (1991). *Most farmers in India are women.* New Delhi, India: FAO.

Siehl, C., & Martin, J. (1982). *Learning Organizational Culture.* Research Paper 654, Stanford Graduate School of Business.

Sinacore, A. L., Blaisure, K. R., Justin, M., Healy, P., & Brawer, S. (1999). Promoting Reflexivity in the Classroom. *Teaching of Psychology, 26*(4), 267–270. doi:10.1207/S15328023TOP260405

Singer, B. B. (1974). The future-focussed role-image. In Toffler, A. (Ed.), *Learning for Tomorrow* (pp. 19–32). New York: Vintage Books.

Sipior, J. C., & Ward, B. T. (2005). Bridging the Digital Divide for e-Government inclusion: A United States Case Study. *Electronic. Journal of E-Government, 3*(3), 137–146.

Smart School Task Force. (1997). *The Malaysian Smart School - An MSC Flagship Application: A conceptual blueprint.* Kuala Lumpur, Malaysia: Author.

Smith, A. G. (2001). Applying Evaluation Criteria to New Zealand Government Website. *International Journal of Information Management, 21*(2), 137–149. doi:10.1016/S0268-4012(01)00006-8

Snellen, I. (2000). Public Service in an Information Society. In Governance in the 21st Century: Revitalizing the Public Service, Canadian Centre for Management Development, Montreal and Kingston.

Soeftestad, L. T., & Sein, M. K. (2003). ICT and Development: East is East and West is West and the Twain may yet Meet. In Krishna, S., & Madon, S. (Eds.), *Digital Challenge: Information Technology in the Development Context* (pp. 63–83). Aldershot, UK: Ashgate.

Soh, C., Mah, Q. Y., Gan, F. Y., Chew, D., & Reid, E. (1997). The use of the Internet for business: The experience of early adopters in Singapore. *Internet Research: Electronic Networking Applications and Policy, 7*(3), 217–228. doi:10.1108/10662249710171869

Solow, R. (1987, July 12). We'd better watch out. *Book Review No. 36, The New York Times.*

Soper, D., Demirkan, H., Goul, M., & St. Louis, R. (2006). The Impact of ICT Expenditures on Institutionalized Democracy and Foreign Direct Investment in Developing Countries. In *Proceedings of the 39th Annual Hawaii International Conference on System Sciences (HICSS'06)*, Track 4, 2006.

Soumitra, D. (2003). ICT challenges for the Arab world. In *The Global Information Technology Report 2003-2004: Towards an Equitable Information Society (Global Information Technology Report)*. World Economic Forum. Retrieved June 25, 2008, from http://www.mafhoum.com/press7/218T42.pdf

Souter, D. (2004). ICTs and economic growth in developing countries. *The DAC Journal, 5*(4), 7–40.

SPO. (2006). *Information society strategy 2006-2010.* Retrieved May 7, 2008, from http://www.bilgitoplumu.gov.tr/yayin/Information%20Society%20Strategy_Turkey.pdf

SPO. (2006). *Program tanimlama dokumani.* Retrieved May 7, 2008, from http://www.bilgitoplumu.gov.tr/btstrateji/Program%20Tan%FDmlama%20Dokumani_Temmuz%202006%20Nihai.pdf

Sprecher, M. (2000). Racing to e-Government: Using the Internet for Citizen Service Delivery. *Government Finance Review, 16*(5), 21–22.

Srivastava, S., & Teo, T. (2005). Citizen Trust Development for E-government Adoption: Case of Singapore. In *Proceedings of the 9th Asia Pacific Conference on Information Systems,* Bangkok, Thailand.

Stansfield, M., & Grant, K. (2003). An investigation into issues influencing the use of the Internet and electronic commerce among small-medium-sized enterprises. *Journal of electronic commerce research, 4*(1), 15-33.

State Statistical Office. Republic of Macedonia. (2005). Census of Population, Households, and Dwellings in the Republic of Macedonia, 2002, Final Data. Skopje, Macedonia: Author.

Stewart, A., & Gray, T. (2006). The authenticity of 'Type Two' multistakeholder partnerships for water and sanitation in Africa: When is a stakeholder a partner? *Environmental Politics, 15*(3), 362–378. doi:10.1080/09644010600627592

Stowers, G. N. L. (2004). Measuring the Performance of e-Government. *IBM Centre for the Business of e-Government.* Retrieved March 10, 2007, from http://www.businessofgovernment.org/pdfs/8493_Stowers_Report.pdf

Strachan, G. (2007, 2008). Project Director, *Macedonia Connects.* Interviews with the author, October 1, 23, 2007 & June 17, 2008.

Straub, D. W. (1989). Validating Instruments in MIS Research. *Management Information Systems Quarterly, 13*(2), 147–169. doi:10.2307/248922

Straub, D. W., Loch, K. D., & Hill, C. E. (2001). Transfer of information technology to the Arab world: a test of cultural influence modelling. *Journal of Global Information Management, 9*(3), 6–28.

Sulaiman, V. R. (2003). *Innovations in agricultural extension in India.* Retrieved August 16, 2006, from www.fao.org/sd/KN1_en.htm

SURS – Statistični urad RS. (2007). *Uporaba informacijsko-komunikacijske tehnologije v podjetjih z 10 in več zaposlenimi osebami. 1 Četrtletje 2007.* Retrieved March 18, 2009, from http://www.stat.si/novica_prikazi.aspx?id=1284

Suvedi, M., Campo, S., & Lapinski, M. K. (1999). Trends in Michigan farmers' information-seeking behaviors and perspectives on the delivery of information. *Journal of Applied Communications, 83*(3).

Swaminathan, M. S. (2003). Towards hunger free India: Count down to 2007. *Current Science, 84*(10), 1297–1300.

Swanson, E. B. (1986). A Note of Informatics. *Journal of Management Information Systems, 2*(3), 86–91.

Tabachnick, B., & Fidell, L. S. (2001). *Using Multivariate Statistics.* Boston: Allyn and Bacon.

Tallon, P. P., Kraemer, K. L., & Gurbaxani, V. (2000). Executives' Perceptions of the Business Value of Information Technology: A process-Oriented Approach. *Journal of Management Information Systems, 16*(4), 145–173.

Tanburn, J., & Singh, A. D. (2001). *ICTs and Enterprises in Developing Countries: Hype or Opportunity?* Paper No. 17, International Labour Office, Geneva. Retrieved June 5, 2008 from http://www.ilo.org/dyn/empent/docs/F1089912836/WP17-2001.pdf

Tapscott, D. (1995). *Digital Economy: Promise and Peril in the Age of Networked Intelligence.* New York: McGraw-Hill.

Tapscott, D., & Caston, A. (1993). *Paradigm Shift: The New Promise of Information Technology.* Boston: McGraw-Hill Irwin.

Tassabehji, R. (2005). Inclusion in e-Government: A Security Perspective. In e-Government Workshop '05 (eGOV05), Brunel University, London.

Tassabehji, R., & Elliman, T. (2006). Generating Citizen Trust in E-Government Using A Trust Verification Agent. In *Proceedings of the European and Mediterranean Conference on Information Systems (EMCIS)*, Spain.

Telem, M. (2001). Computerization of school administration: impact on the principal's role – a case study. *Computers & Education, 37*, 345–362. doi:10.1016/S0360-1315(01)00058-6

Teng, J., Cheon, M., & Grover, V. (1995). Decisions to outsource information systems functions. Testing a strategy-theoretic discrepancy model. *Decision Sciences, 26*(1), 75–103. doi:10.1111/j.1540-5915.1995.tb00838.x

Tennert, J. R., & Schroeder, A. D. (1999). Stakeholder Analysis. In *60th Annual Meeting of the American Society for Public Administration*, Orlando, FL.

Teo, T. S. H., & Ang, J. S. K. (2001). An examination of major IS planning problems. *International Journal of Information Management, 21*(6), 457–470. doi:10.1016/S0268-4012(01)00036-6

Teo, T. S. H., & King, W. R. (1996). Assessing the impact of integrating business planning and IS planning. *Information & Management, 30*(6), 309–321. doi:10.1016/S0378-7206(96)01076-2

Teo, T. S. H., Ang, J. S. K., & Pavri, F. N. (1997). The state of strategic IS planning practices in Singapore. *Information & Management, 33*(1), 13–23. doi:10.1016/S0378-7206(97)00033-5

The Computer System Policy Project (CSPP). (2000). *Living in the Networked World Readiness Guide.* Retrieved March 10, 2006, from http://www.cspp.org/documents/NW_Readiness_Guide.pdf

Thomas, W. (1998). Maintaining and Restoring Public Trust in Government Agencies and Their Employees. *Administration & Society, 30*(2), 166–193. doi:10.1177/0095399798302003

Thompson, J. L. (2001). Strategic Management (4th Ed.). Pacific Grove, CA: Thompson learning.

Thong, J. Y. L. (1999). An Integrated Model for Information Systems Adoption in Small Businesses. *Journal of Management Information Systems, 15*(4), 187–214.

Thorpe, R., & Little, S. E. (Eds.). (2001). *Global change: The impact of Asia in the 21st Century.* London: Palgrave.

Timmers, P. (1999). *Electronic Commerce Strategies and Models for Business-to-business Trading.* Chichester: John Wiley.

Toffler, A. (1980). *The third wave.* New York: Bantam Books.

Top 20 Countries with highest number of Internet users. (2007). Retrieved November 14, 2008, from http://www.InternetWorldStats.com.

Tornatzky, L. G., & Fleischer, M. (1990). *The Process of Technological Innovation.* Lexington, MA: Rowman & Littlefield, Lexington Books.

Towler, D. (2002). Digital Revolution or Digital Divide. *Journal of Vocational and Technical Education and Training, 2*, 41–45.

Transparency International. (2006). *Transparency International Corruption Perceptions Index,* Germany. Retrieved June 14, 2007, from http://www.transparency.org

Traunmüller, R., & Wimmer, M. (2003). e-Government at a Decisive Moment: Sketching a Roadmap to Excellence. In *2ⁿᵈ International Conference (EGOV 2003)*, Prague, Czech Republic.

Trkman, P., & Turk, T. (2009). A Conceptual Model for the Development of Broadband and E-Government. *Government Information Quarterly*, *26*(2), 416–424. doi:10.1016/j.giq.2008.11.005

Trkman, P., Jerman-Blažič, B., & Turk, T. (2008). Factors of broadband development and the design of a strategic policy framework. *Telecommunications Policy*, *32*(2), 101–115. doi:10.1016/j.telpol.2007.11.001

Tsujii, S. (2004). Paradigm of Information Security as Interdisciplinary Comprehensive Science. In *Third International Conference on Cyberworlds (CW'04)*, 2004 (pp. 9-20).

Tuncalp, S. (1988). The marketing research scene in Saudi Arabia. *European Journal of Marketing*, *22*(5), 15–22. doi:10.1108/EUM0000000005282

Turban, E., King, D., Lee, J., Warkentin, M., & Chung, H. M. (2002). *Electronic Commerce 2002: A Managerial Perspective*. Upper Saddle River, NJ: Prentice-Hall.

Turban, E., Lee, J. K., King, D., & McKay, J. (2008). *Electronic Commerce 2008: A Managerial Perspective* (International Ed.). Upper Saddle River, NJ: Prentice Hall.

Turban, E., Lee, J., King, D., & Chung, H. M. (2000). *Electronic Commerce: A Managerial Perspective*. Upper Saddle River, NJ: Prentice Hall.

Turk, T., Jerman-Blažič, B., & Trkman, P. (2008). Factors and sustainable strategies fostering the adoption of broadband communications in an enlarged European Union. *Technological Forecasting and Social Change*, *75*(7), 933–951. doi:10.1016/j.techfore.2007.08.004

Udo, G. G. (2000). Using analytic hierarchy process to analyze the information technology outsourcing decision. *Industrial Management & Data Systems*, *100*(9), 421–429. doi:10.1108/02635570010358348

Ulrich, P., & Chacko, J. G. (2005). Overview of ICT policies and e-strategies: An assessment on the role of governments. *Information Technology for Development*, *11*(2), 195–197. doi:10.1002/itdj.20011

Umble, E. J., Haft, R. R., & Umble, M. M. (2003). Enterprise resource planning: implementation procedures and critical success factors. *European Journal of Operational Research*, *146*(2), 241–257. doi:10.1016/S0377-2217(02)00547-7

UN. (2004). *Financing ICTD*. Retrieved April 7, 2008, from http://www.itu.int/wsis/tffm/final-report.pdf

UNDESA (United Nations Department for Economic and Social Affairs). (2003). e-Government Readiness Assessment Survey. Division for Public Administration and Development Management (DPADM), NY.

UNDESA (United Nations Department for Economic and Social Affairs). (2004). *Global E-government Readiness Report 2004*. Division for Public Administration and Development Management.

UNDESA (United Nations Department for Economic and Social Affairs). (2005). *Global E-government Readiness Report 2005*. Division for Public Administration and Development Management.

UNDP. (n.d.). *How to build open information societies: A collection of best practices and know-how*. Retrieved April 10, 2008, from http://unpan1.un.org/intradoc/groups/public/documents/UNTC/UNPAN018476.pdf

United Nations Department of Economic and Social Affairs (UNDESA). (2005). Global e-Government Readiness Report 2005: From e-Government to eInclusion. *Division for Public Administration and Development Management (DPADM)*, NY. Retrieved September 10, 2008, from http://unpan1.un.org/intradoc/groups/public/documents/un/unpan021888.pdf

United Nations Department of Economic and Social Affairs (UNDESA). (2008). UN e-Government Survey 2008: From e-Government to Connected Governance. *Division for Public Administration and Development Management (DPADM)*, New York. Retrieved September 10, 2008, from http://unpan1.un.org/intradoc/groups/public/documents/UN/UNPAN028607.pdf

United Nations Economic Commission for Africa. (2003a) *Policies and Plans on the Information Society: Status and Impact.*

United Nations Economic Commission for Africa. (2003b). *E-Strategies*. National, Sectoral and Regional ICT Policies, Plans and Strategies.

United Nations Foundation & World Economic Forum. (2003). *Public Private Partnerships: Meeting in the middle*. Retrieved February 18, 2007, from https://www.weforum.org/pdf/Initiatives/GHI_2003_Meeting_in_the_middle.pdf

van Dijk, J. (2006). Digital divide research, achievements and shortcomings. *Poetics, 34*(4-5), 221–235. doi:10.1016/j.poetic.2006.05.004

Van Grop, A. (2008). *Increasing regulatory capacity: The role of the region in shaping national ICT policy in southern Africa*. Unpublished doctoral dissertation, The Pennsylvania State University.

Vargas, C. M. (2000). Community development and micro-enterprises: fostering sustainable development. *Sustainable Development, 8*(1), 11. doi:10.1002/(SICI)1099-1719(200002)8:1<11::AID-SD119>3.0.CO;2-7

Venkatesh, V., Morris, M., Davis, G., & Davis, F. (2003). User acceptance of information technology: Toward a unified view. *Management Information Systems Quarterly, 27*(3), 425–478.

Venkateshwarlu, K. (2002, October 6). Community Radio has villagers excited. *The Hindu*, p. 12.

VeriSign. (2004). *Internet Security Intelligence Briefing, 2*(2). Retrieved May 28, 2008, from http://www.verisign.com/static/017574.pdf

Vicente Cuervo, M., & Lopez Menendez, A. (2006). A multivariate framework for the analysis of the digital divide: Evidence for the European Union-15. *Information & Management, 43*, 756–766. doi:10.1016/j.im.2006.05.001

Vickery, G. (2002). *E-business Experience in the OECD Countries: Results of a Multi-Country, Multi-Sector Study*. Retrieved from http://www.oecd.org

Victoria, M. (2002). *Putting People at the Centre: Government Innovation Working for Victorians*. Retrieved March 10, 2008, from http://www.mmv.vic.gov.au/egov

Vijapurkar, M. (2002, June 18). Newspaper readership up, says study. *The Hindu*, p. 8.

Vilanilam, J. V. (1993). *Science Communication and Development*. New Delhi, India: Sage Publications.

Vodaphone. (2005). Africa: the impact of mobile phones. *Vodafone Policy Paper Series No. 2*. Retrieved January 13, 2008, from http://www.vodafone.com/assets/files/en/GPP%20SIM%20paper.pdf

von Mises, L. (1998). National Economy: Human Action. Auburn, AL.: Von Mises Institute. (Original manuscript published in 1949).

Wagner, D. A., Day, B., James, T., Kozma, R. B., Miller, J., & Unwin, T. (2005). *Monitoring and Evaluation of ICT in Education Projects: A Handbook for Developing Countries*. Tunis: InfoDev.

Walczuch, R., Braven, G. d., & Lundgren, H. (2000). Internet Adoption Barriers for Small Firms in the Netherlands. *European Management Journal, 18*(5), 561–572. doi:10.1016/S0263-2373(00)00045-1

Wallsten, S. (2002 February). *Does Sequencing Matter? Regulation and Privatization in Telecommunications Reforms*. World Bank Working Paper.

Walsham, G. (1993). *Interpreting Information Systems in Organizations*. Chichester, UK: Wiley.

Walsham, G. (2001). *Making a world of difference: IT in global context*. New York: John Wiley & Sons, Ltd.

Walsham, G., & Sahay, S. (2006). Research on information systems in developing countries: current landscape and future prospects. *Information Technology for Development, 12*(1), 7–24. doi:10.1002/itdj.20020

Wan, H. A. (2000). Opportunities to Enhance a Commercial Website. *Information & Management, 38*(1), 15–21. doi:10.1016/S0378-7206(00)00048-3

Ward, J. (1995). *Principles of Information Systems Management*. London: Routledge.

Ward, J., & Peppard, J. (2002). *Strategic Planning for Information Systems* (3rd ed.). Chichester, UK: Wiley Series.

Warschauer, M. (2002). Reconceptualizing the Digital Divide. *First Monday, 7*(7). Retrieved May 22, 2008, from http://www.firstmonday.dk/issues/issue7_7/warschauer/#author

Warschauer, M. (2003). *Technology and Social Exclusion: Rethinking the Digital Divide*. London: MIT Press.

WASEDA University. (2006). *The 2006 WASEDA University e-Government Ranking*. Retrieved September 12, 2008, from http://egov.sonasi.com/repository/the-2006-waseda-university-e-government-ranking/download

Waverman, L. Meschi, M., & Fuss, M. (2005). *The impact of telecoms on economic growth in developing countries*. Paper presented at 2005 TPRC conference. Retrieved November 6, 2007, from http://web.si.umich.edu/tprc/papers/2005/450/L%20Waverman-%20Telecoms%20Growth%20in%20Dev.%20Countries.pdf

Weerakody, V., Sarikas, O. D., & Patel, R. (2005). Exploring the Process and Information Systems Integration Aspects of e-Government. In e-Government Workshop '05 (eGOV05), Brunel University, London.

Weigel, G., & Waldburger, D. (Eds.). (2004). ICT4D: Connecting People for a Better World. Lessons, Innovations and Perpsectives of Information and Communication Technologies in Development. Berne, Switzerland: Swiss Agency for Development and Cooperation (SDC) and Global Knowledge Partnership (GKP).

Weingast, B. (1995). The Economic Role of Political Institutions: Market-Preserving Federalism and Economic Development. *Journal of Law Economics and Organization, 11*(1), 139–152.

Welsh, A. H., & White, J. F. (1981). A small business is not a little big business. *Harvard Business Review, 59*(4), 18–32.

West, D. (2008). *Improving Technology Utilization in Electronic Government around the World*. Retrieved November 13, 2008, from http://www.brookings.edu/~/media/Files/rc/reports/2008/0817_e-Government_west/0817_e-Government_west.pdf

West, D. M. (2000). *Assessing e-Government: The Internet, Democracy, and Service Delivery by State and Federal Government*. Retrieved June 12, 2002, from http://www.insidepolitics.org/egovtreport00.html

West, D. M. (2006). *Global e-Government, 2006*. Retrieved July 10, 2006, from http://www.InsidePolitics.org

Wheeler, D. (2003). Egypt: building an information society for international development. *Review of African Political Economy, 30*(98). doi:10.1080/07

Wigand, R. T., Picot, A., & Reichwald, R. (1997). *Information, organisation, and management: Expanding markets and corporate boundaries*. New York: Wiley.

Wilford, S. H. (2004). *Information and Communication technologies, Privacy and Policies: An Analysis from the Perspective of the Individual*. Doctoral Dissertation, De Montfort University, Leicester, UK.

Wilkin, C., & Castleman, T. (2003). Development of an Instrument to Evaluate the Quality of Delivered Information Systems. In *36th Hawaii International Conference on System Science*, Hawaii.

Wilkin, C., & Hewett, B. (1999). Quality in a Respecification of DeLone and McLean's IS Success Model. In *1999 IRMA International Conference*, Hershey, PA.

Willcocks, L., & Lester, S. (1991). Information systems investments: evaluation at the feasibility stage of projects. *The International Journal of Technological Innovation and Entepreneurship (Technovation), 11*(5), 283–301.

Willcocks, L., & Lester, S. (1999). *Beyond the IT Productivity Paradox: Assessment Issues.* Chichester, UK: Wiley.

Wilson, E. J. III, & Wong, K. (2003). African information revolution: a balance sheet. *Telecommunications Policy, 27,* 155–177. doi:10.1016/S0308-5961(02)00097-6

Wimmer, M., & Bredow, B. (2002). A Holistic Approach for Providing Security Solutions in E-government. In *Proceedings of the 35th Hawaii International Conference on System Sciences,* IEEE, USA.

Wittgenstein, L. (1958). *The Blue Book.* New York: Harper.

Wong, P.-K. (2002). ICT production and diffusion in Asia: Digital dividends or digital divide? *Information Economics and Policy, 14,* 167–187. doi:10.1016/S0167-6245(01)00065-8

Woodroof, J., & Burg, W. (2003). Satisfaction/Dissatisfaction: Are Users Predisposed? *Information & Management, 40*(4), 317–324. doi:10.1016/S0378-7206(02)00013-7

Working Group on e-Government in the Developing World. (2002). Roadmap for e-Government in the Developing World – 10 Questions e-Government Leaders Should Ask Themselves. *Pacific Council on International Policy.* Retrieved May 10, 2006, from http://www.pacific-council.org/pdfs/e-gov.paper.f.pdf

World Bank. (2002). *Report on the Observance of Standards and Codes.* Egypt: Accounting and Auditing.

World Bank. (2003). *ICT for Development Contributing to the Millennium Development Goals: Lessons Learned from Seventeen InfoDev Projects.* Washington, DC: The World Bank.

World Bank. (2005). *Financing information and communication infrastructure needs in the developing world: Public and private roles – Draft for discussion.* Retrieved January 18, 2007, from http://lnweb18.worldbank.org/ict/resources.nsf/a693f575e01ba5f385256b500062af05/04c3ce1b933921a585256fb60051b8f5/$FILE/financingICT_Draft.pdf

World Bank. (2006). *ICT at a glance.* Retrieved August 4, 2008, from http://devdata.worldbank.org/ind_ict.pdf

World Bank. (2006). *Information and Communication Technology for Development.* Global Trends and Policies.

World Bank. (2006). *Information and Communications for Development (IC4D)—Global Trends and Policies.* Washington, DC: The World Bank.

World Bank. (2006). *World Development Indicators.* Washington, DC: IBRD, World Bank.

World Bank. (2008). *Country Classification: Data and Statistics.* The World Bank. Retrieved November 2, 2008, from http://web.worldbank.org

World Bank. (2008). *Europe and Central Asia. Selected World Development Indicators.* Retrieved November 15, 2008, from http://ddp-ext.worldbank.org

World Bank. (2008). *Little Data Book on ICT.*

World Bank. (2009). *Little Data Book of ICT.*

World Factbook, C. I. A. (2008). *Macedonia.* Retrieved November 15, 2008, from https://www.cia.gov/library/publications/the-world-factbook/geos/mk.html

World Summit on the Information Society. (2009). Retrieved February 10, 2009, from http://www.wsis-online.net

Wynn, M. (2009). Information system strategy development and implementation in SMEs. *Management Research News, 32*(1), 78–90. doi:10.1108/01409170910922041

Xavier, P. (2003). Should broadband be part of universal service obligations? *Info - The journal of policy, regulation and strategy for telecommunications, 5,* 8-25.

Xia, W., & King, W. R. (2002). Determinants of Organizational IT Infrastructure Capabilities. *MIS Research Center Working Papers.* University of Minnesota.

Ya'akob, A., Mohd Nor, N. F., & Azman, H. (2005). Implementation of the Malaysian Smart School: an investigation of teaching-learning practices and teacher-student readiness. *Internet Journal of e-Language Learning and Teaching, 2*(2).

Yang, L., Lu, Y., & Fu, G. (2005). Study on E-government Construction. In *Proceedings of the 7ᵗʰ International Conference on Electronic Commerce (ICEC)*, Zi'an, China.

Yankee Group. (2007). *Asia Mobile Forecast 2007.* Boston, MA: Yankee Group.

Yin, R. K. (1993). *Applications of Case Study Research.* London: Sage Publications.

Yin, R. K. (1994). *Case Study Research: Design and Methods.* Thousand Oaks, CA: Sage Publications.

You cannot carry your television set to the beach. (2002, July 31). *The New Indian Express,* p. 9.

Zahra, S. A., & Covin, J. G. (1993). Business Strategy, Technology Policy and Firm Performance. *Strategic Management Journal, 14*(6), 451–478. doi:10.1002/smj.4250140605

Zaidman, N., Scwartz, D., & Te'eni, D. (2008). Challenges to ICT implementation in multinationals Education. *Business and Society: Contemporary Middle Eastern Issues, 1*(14).

Zain, M. Z. M., Atan, H., & Idrus, R. M. (2004). The impact of information and communication technology (ICT) on the management practices of Malaysian Smart Schools. *International Journal of Educational Development, 24*(2), 201–211. doi:10.1016/j.ijedudev.2003.10.010

Zeleza, P. T. (2005). Postscript: Challenges of the ICT revolution in East Africa. In Etta, F. E., & Elder, L. (Eds.), *At the crossroads: ICT policy making in East Africa* (pp. 283–294). Nairobi, Kenya: East African Educational Publishers Ltd., & IDRC.

Zhao, P., & Grimshaw, D. J. (1991). *A comparative study of the application of IT in China and the West: Culture and stages of growth model (Warwick Business School Research Papers, No. 32).* Coventry, UK: Warwick Business School Research Bureau.

Zhao, Y. (Ed.). (2003). *What teachers should know about technology: Perspectives and practices.* Greenwich, CT: Information Age Publishing.

Zhu, K., Kramer, K., & Xu, S. (2003). Electronic business adoption by European firms. *European Journal of Information Systems, 12,* 251–268. doi:10.1057/palgrave.ejis.3000475

Zmud, R. W., & Boynton, A. C. (1991). Survey Measures and Instruments in MIS: Inventory and Appraisal. *Harvard Business School Research Colloquium, 3,* 149–180.

Zuboff, S. (1988). *In the age of the smart machine: The future of work and power.* New York: Basic Books.

Zupan, G. (2008). Internet usage in enterprises with 10 or more persons employed, Slovenia 1s quarter 2008. Statistical Office of the Republic of Slovenia.

Zupančič, D. (2004). *Cross-border eInvoicing in eRegion – Companies & Chambers of Commerce Perspective.* Merkur day 2004 & 8th Executive Business, Government, and University Meeting On Cross-border eInvoicing in eRegion, Slovenia.

About the Contributors

Sherif H. Kamel is Dean of the School of Business at the American University in Cairo and Professor of Management Information Systems at the Department of Management. Kamel served as Associate Dean for Executive Education (2008-2009). Prior to that, he was Director of the Management Center (2002-2008) and was Director of the Institute of Management Development (2002-2006). Before joining AUC, he was Director of the Regional IT Institute (1992-2001) and he co-established and managed the training department of the Cabinet of Egypt Information and Decision Support Centre (1987-1992). He has accumulated experience in building and managing professional development institutions addressing management development and leadership. He consults to government organizations and corporations adressing professional and executive development, management and IT strategy deployment. Kamel is a co-founding member of the Internet Society of Egypt (1996). His research and teaching interests include management of information technology, information technology transfer to developing nations, electronic business, human resources development, and decision support systems and has published widely in the areas of IS and management. Kamel serves on the editorial and advisory board of a number of IS journals and is the associate editor of the Journal of Cases on Information Technology, Journal of IT for Development and the Electronic Journal of IS in Developing Countries. He is the editor of Electronic Business in Developing Countries: Challenges and Opportunities (2005) and Managing Globally with Information Technology (2003). He holds a PhD from London School of Economics and Political Science (1994), an MBA (1990), and a BA in Business Administration (1987) from The American University in Cairo.

* * *

Ja'far Alqatawna is a PhD research student at Sheffield Hallam University, England. He received his B.Eng degree in Computer Engineering from Mu'tah University, Jordan, followed by MSc. in Information and Communication Systems Security from The Royal Institute of Technology (KTH), Sweden. He was part of research project for investigating XACML as a policy language for distributed networks at Security, Policy and Trust Lab (SOPT) of the Swedish Institute of Computer Science (SICS), Sweden. Alqatawna has also gained practical experience as a System Integrator at FDS, Dubai and deployment of business-critical applications, database administration, security solutions and network management. He has been part of many ITIL projects at multinational companies in the Gulf region. Ja'far is lecturer at King Abdullah II School for Information Technology, University of Jordan from where he obtained a scholarship to pursue his postgraduate studies in UK. He has benefitted from the opportunity to learn from notable scholars in the field of information security such as Prof. Sead Muftic, Prof. Louise

Yngström and currently he is under the supervision of Prof. Jawed Siddiqi who leads the Informatics Research Group at Sheffield Hallam University, UK. His Current research interests are in the field of e-Business Security in which he is trying to adopt a new research approach which goes beyond the technical dimension of e-Business security to develop multi-dimensional framework to integrate security in a way that provides trustworthy e-Business environment that considers the interests of the different stakeholders of e-Business.

Mahfuz Ashraf has a broad scholastic training which encompasses a number of various areas: Marketing, Information Systems (IS) and Information Technology (IT). Dr. Ashraf was awarded a PhD from University of South Australia. Ashraf's PhD training in IT, sponsored by Australian Government International Post Graduate Scholarship (IPRS), gave him a unique opportunity to learn extensive academic research (analytical/report writing) and produce scholarly research papers worldwide within the domain of IT, IS ICTD and Business. Dr. Ashraf is now working as lecturer in Department of Management Information Systems, University of Dhaka, Bangladesh and doing research in Brainstorm Bangladesh. Based on his doctoral research experience and prior education/experiences, Dr. Ashraf brings to his work a nuanced and sophisticated understanding of interpretive research methodologies and theories drawn from a wide range of fields including information systems (understanding social/contextual issues of diffusion-adoption-implementation of IT), and development economics (capability approach). Dr. Ashraf's doctoral study focused on exploring socio-economic impact with an emphasis on understanding human behaviour, attitudes and perceptions towards ICT-led development projects in rural areas of developing countries. Dr. Ashraf's ICTD impact work has recently been recognized at Singapore Internet Research Centre, Singapore and IDRC, Canada [two years (2009-11) research grant]. He is the principal investigator of the project; 'An impact assessment framework to evaluate the effectiveness of Information Communications Technology (ICT)-led development project at micro (community) level in a developing country; Bangladesh'. He is also supervising project (2009) at public sector in Ministry of Planning, Government of Bangladesh.

Nahed Azab is an IT consultant and lecturer. She plays an active role in planning and updating the curriculum, compiling and editing the material and course work, and teaching a number of IT undergraduate and postgraduate courses at the American University in Cairo and the Regional Information Technology Institute. In particular Mrs. Azab focuses on Electronic Commerce, Electronic Marketing and Management Information Systems. She is also at her final stage in her PhD at the School of Engineering and Information Sciences - Middlesex University, London. Mrs. Azab obtained her MSc. In Business Information Technology, School of Computing Sciences - Middlesex University, London (July 2002). She graduated with a BSc. from the faculty of Engineering - Ein shams University, Cairo (1984). Her 25-year career path encompassed software programming, analysis and design, computer center management, software instruction and general IT consultancy work. Mrs. Azab presented a number of academic papers in journals, books, and conferences.

Mohammad Hjouj Btoush was awarded in 1992 a Bachelor Degree of Computer Science (BSc) from Mu'tah University (Jordan). In 2004 he obtained a Master degree in Computer Science (MSc) from the Graduate Studies School at Amman Arab University (Jordan). In 1992 he joined Karak Community College of-Al-Balqa Applied University- Jordan as a lecturer in the Computer Science Department where he taught the following courses: Computer Network Management, Operating Systems, e-Commerce,

Database Management Systems, Management Information Systems, System Analysis Design, and Software Engineering. During that time he also co-authored a book entitled *Computer Skills*. In 2006, he obtained a scholarship to study for a PhD under the supervision of Prof. Jawed Siddiqi who leads the Informatics Research Group at Sheffield Hallam University, UK. His PhD thesis investigated the perception of users and providers of e-services in Jordan. In 2009 he submitted and successfully defended his thesis. His current research interests include: Information systems evaluation, specifically, within the context of electronic Government, operating system, Information security, and software engineering,

Khaled Dahawy is an Associate professor in the Department of Management, at the American University in Cairo (AUC). He received his Ph.D. from the University of North Texas (UNT), MBA from Pennsylvania State University (Penn State), and bachelor from AUC. His research interests include financial accounting, international accounting, auditing, and accounting information systems. He has several papers and cases that are published in academic accounting journals, and presented in academic and practitioners conferences. He teaches financial accounting, international accounting, tax accounting and auditing, and has received the department of management teaching excellence award, in 2004. Dr. Dahawy has considerable connections with accounting students extracurricular activities at AUC and has initiated and acts as the advisor to the Accounting Link, which is the accounting club at AUC that links the academic and practical aspects of accounting. Dr. Dahawy is a certified public accountant (CPA) from the State of Illinois, USA, certified from the Egyptian Society for Accountants and Auditors (ESAA), and is certified by the Egyptian Accounting Syndicate. He has extensive practical experience as an expert in the Capital Market Authority (CMA) and has served as a consultant in many missions with the World Bank, United Nations, and the National Democratic Party (NDP). He is also a member of the board of the Council for financial and Managerial Affairs in the NDP, the head of the youth committee in the Rotary Club of Cairo, and member of the Egyptian Junior Businessmen Association (EJB). In addition, Dr. Dahawy has conducted several training courses and presentations to teach accounting for numerous diverse constituents.

Gerald Goh Guan Gan is a Lecturer in Knowledge Management at the Faculty of Business and Law, Multimedia University, Malaysia. His research interests include investigations into socio-technical issues of knowledge management, mass media and ICT. His current research includes the role of media technology on health decision making and knowledge sharing among school teachers.

Laura Hosman is a Ciriacy-Wantrup Postdoctoral Research Fellow at the University of California, Berkeley. Her work focuses on the role for information and communications technology (ICT) in developing countries, particularly in terms of its potential effects on socio-cultural factors, human development, economic growth, and sustainability. Presently, she studies the role of corporate involvement in bringing technology to the developing world through Public-Private Partnerships. She also focuses on ICT-in-education projects. She received her Ph.D. from the University of Southern California, in Political Economy and Public Policy.

Dan J. Kim (Ph.D. SUNY Buffalo) is an Associate Professor of Computer Information Systems at University of Houston Clear Lake (UHCL). His research interests are in multidisciplinary areas such as electronic commerce, mobile commerce, information security and assurance. Recently he has focused on trust in electronic commerce, wireless and mobile commerce, and information security and assurance. His research work has been published or in forthcoming more than 70 papers in refereed journals and conference proceedings including *Information Systems Research, Journal of Management Information Systems, Communications of ACM, Decision Support Systems, International Journal of Human-Computer Communications of AIS, Interaction, Journal of Organizational and End User Computing, IEEE Transactions on Professional Communication, Electronic Market, IEEE IT Professional, Journal of Global Information Management,* and *International Journal of Mobile Communications,* ICIS, HICSS, AMCIS, INFORMS, ICEC, ICA, and so on. He received the best-paper runner-up award at the International Conference on Information Systems (ICIS) 2003, the best research paper award at Americas Conference on Information Systems (AMCIS) 2005, and the Emerald Literati Network 2009 Outstanding Paper Award.

Melih Kirlidog holds a BSc degree in Civil Enginering from Middle East Technical University, Turkey, an MBA in MIS, and a PhD from University of Wollongong, Australia. He has worked as an ICT analyst and consultant for over twenty years in Turkey and Australia. His current research interests include intercultural ICT development and implementation, ICT in developing countries, decision support systems, and community informatics. Since November 2002 he works as a full time academic in Department of Computer Engineering at Marmara University, Turkey.

Gregor Lenart is a teaching assistant and senior researcher at the Faculty of Organizational Science, University of Maribor. He is also a member of eCenter and head of the eCollaboration Laboratory. His current research includes computer supported collaborative work, group support systems and knowledge management. He is also actively involved in several EU research projects focusing on mobile commerce and e-business.

Khor Yoke Lim is an Associate Professor with the School of Communication, Universiti Sains Malaysia. Her research interests include investigations into health, technology and identity. Among her current research include a study on communication, stigma and HIV persons, as well as information access and usage among cancer patients. She is a fellow of the Women Development Research Center in Universiti Sains Malaysia and is the primary investigator for a research on mainstreaming gender in corporate social responsibility. Some recent publications include a book chapter on "Chinese newspapers, ethnic identity and the state" in *Media and Chinese Diaspora* published by Routledge, London (2006) and co-author on "An exploratory study on the adoption of business-to consumer internet banking among Malaysian professionals" in *International Journal of Management & Entrepreneurship,* (2008, Vol 4:1). She is in the editorial board of a refereed international journal published by Universiti Sains Malaysia called *Kajian Malaysia (Journal of Malaysian Studies).*

Stephen Little is based at the Open University Business School, U.K. and holds visiting positions at the Rotterdam School of Management, the Netherlands and the University of Bolton, U.K. He is Chairman of the Asia Pacific Technology Network (APTN), and a member of the council of the Design Research Society He has held full-time appointments at Manchester Metropolitan University, UK the University of Wollongong NSW and Griffith University Queensland, Australia and has held visiting appointments at The Australian National University, Canberra and the Australian Graduate School of Management, Sydney. He is a member of IFIP Working Group 8.2 and his current research interests include the role of ICTs in supporting the circulation of skilled labour and capacity transfer between regions. As a member of the MODE collaboration he is examining the mechanisms of technology transfer from the ATLAS experiment at CERN to member organisations and stakeholders.

Bushra Tahseen Malik, a researcher specialized in the fields of development economics and market analysis. After completing her graduation in Economics from University of Dhaka, Bangladesh, she joined in Brainstrom Bangladesh as researcher in early 2009. Her research interest concentrates on poverty alleviation, ICT and development and e-Governance. As an early research career, Bushra has published two articles in journals and conference proceedings.

Nicholas C. Maynard is a Policy Researcher at the RAND Corporation where he focuses on information technology, S&T policy, and economic development. His current projects include technology acquisition, economic development policies, and best practices for R&D management. Dr. Maynard has led research teams to develop strategic plans for technology development initiatives as well as performed several national case studies, and developed a plan for cross-border technology centers. Dr. Maynard also led a multi-year effort to benchmark the US national innovation system for European Commission, comparing the US system against its peers in Europe and the Americas. Dr. Maynard received his BA and MA from the University of Chicago in Political Science and he completed a Public Policy PhD at University of North Carolina at Chapel Hill. His dissertation research on national technology strategies was supported through a National Science Foundation grant.

D. Puthira Prathap, Senior Scientist, Sugarcane Breeding Institute (Indian Council of Agricultural Research), Coimbatore , INDIA is a media expert with an extensive academic background. Before joining Sugarcane Breeding Institute, he was an Agricultural Officer with the Government of Tamil Nadu (1996-1998) and Scientist In charge of Extension and Grassland & Fodder Agronomy at the Central Sheep and Wool Research Institute's regional centre at Kodaikanal, Tamil Nadu. His PhD dissertation on mass media fetched him the prestigious *Jawaharlal Nehru Award for Outstanding Postgraduate Research, 2005* of the Indian Council of Agricultural Research (ICAR) and his papers have appeared in several national and international journals. A producer of many radio and television programmes related to Agriculture, Dr. Prathap acts as a reviewer for three international journals besides handling various research projects.

Andreja Pucihar is an Assistant Professor of e-business and management of information systems at the Faculty of Organizational Sciences, University of Maribor. Since 1995, she has been involved in eCenter and its several research and e-commerce activities. She is a head of eMarkets Laboratory and contact person for Living laboratory for research fields of eMarkets, eSMEs and eGovernment. She is involved into several EU projects focusing on e-business and e-government and intensively cooperates with industry. Her current research includes: e-marketplaces, e-business, supply chain management, e-government and new e-business models. She is also a conference chair of annual international conference Bled eConference (http://BledConference.org).

Dina F. Rateb is currently Associate Professor for Management Information Systems in the Department of Management of the School of Business, Economics and Communications (BEC) at The American University in Cairo (AUC) as well as the Director of the Business, Economics, and Communication Computer Center (BECCC). As the Director of BECCC she managed to initiate a good number of academic related technology on campus such as video conferencing. Previously, she was an Instructor for Management Information Systems at the University of Pittsburgh, Pittsburgh, PA. She received her Ph.D. from the Katz Graduate School of Business, University of Pittsburgh back in 1992. Dr. Rateb's research interests focus on Decision Support Systems, Experts Systems, Ecosystems, Accounting and Financial Information Systems, Database Management, as well as End User Development and Support. Dr. Rateb is also the advisor for Volunteers in Action (VIA) and was first and previous advisor of Hand in Hand as well as the acting advisor for Anti Cancer Team (ACT) and AYDC. Additionally, she is in the Student Organization Juricidical and Legislative Board ever since its setup in the year 2007. Through her work with the students she managed to instigate Family Planning for the first time at AUC back in the year 2001. She is heavily involved with student activities and on promoting Philanthropic and Civic Engagement on campus as well as Service Learning.

Khaled Samaha is currently an assistant professor of accounting in the Department of Management at the American University in Cairo (AUC). He received his Ph.D. in accounting form the University of Manchester – UK, M.Sc. from the University of Birmingham - UK. Samaha is a Certified Public Accountant (CPA) from the Egyptian Society for Accountants and Auditors (ESAA), and is certified by the Egyptian Accounting Syndicate. Samaha has extensive practical experience in the application of International Financial Reporting Standards (IFRSs) and has recently published two papers about convergence with IFRS in Egypt. He is currently serving as a member on the editorial board of the Afro Asian Journal of Finance & Accounting that is published by Inderscience. Samaha has served as an audit consultant to several companies listed on the Egyptian Stock Exchange, as well as the Ministry of Transport. He has also served as a consultant in many assignments with the World Bank and the Bi-national Fulbright commission (The commission for educational and cultural exchange between the USA & Egypt). His research interests include harmonization and compliance with International Financial Reporting Standards (IFRS), financial reporting and corporate governance mechanisms, audit procedures and methodologies, financial reporting on the internet and the implementation of accounting information systems in small and medium size enterprises (SMEs).

Jawed Siddiqi has been the Director of the Computing Research Centre, Professor of Software Engineering, Head of the Software Engineering Division and Head of Research in the School of Computing and Management Sciences at Sheffield Hallam University where he currently continues as Professor of Software Engineering. Siddiqi received a BSc in Mathematics from the University of London and an MSc and PhD in Computer Science from the University of Aston in Birmingham. He is a Chartered Engineer, a Fellow of the British Computer Society and the IEEE Computer Society. He was Editor of the British Computer Society Formal Aspects of Computer Science Newsletter (1991-1995) and continues to serve as an elected executive officer. From 1991 to 1993, he was a Visiting Researcher at the Centre for Requirements and Foundation at Oxford University Computing Laboratory where he worked with Professor Joseph Goguen on the British Telecom funded Requirements Engineering project. Professor Siddiqi has an international presence and has served on numerous and continues to serve on several programme committees. He is a founder member of the IEEE International Conference on Requirements Engineering and a permanent member of its steering committee.

Peter Trkman is an assistant professor at the Faculty of Economics of the University of Ljubljana. His research interests encompass technology adoption, e-government and various aspects of the supply chain, business process, information and operations management. He has participated in several national and international projects (both research and consulting) and published over 50 papers/book chapters, including papers in Computers & Operations Research, European Journal of Operational Research, Government Information Quarterly, International Journal of Production Economics, International Journal of Production Research, Journal of Computer Information Systems, Supply Chain Management – An International Journal and Telecommunications Policy.

Tomaž Turk is an associate professor and researcher at the Faculty of Economics of the University of Ljubljana. Currently his research work includes topics from information technology adoption, economics of information technology, communication networks management and Internet society issues. He has participated in several national and international projects and published over 50 papers/book chapters.

Index